MOON

VIETNAM

DANA FILEK-GIBSON

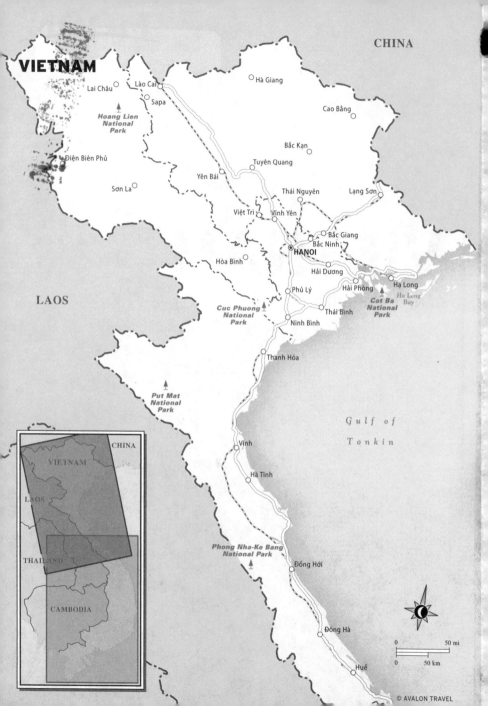

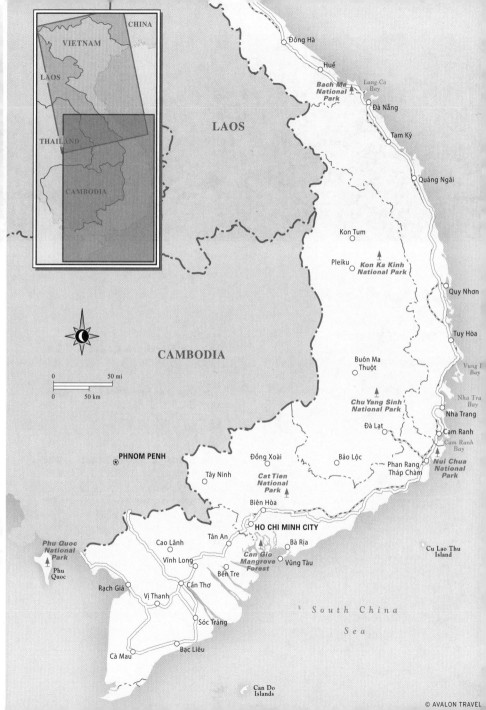

Contents

DISCOVER
Vietnam

ietnam grabs hold of you from the moment you step off the plane. Your senses are assaulted by the blare of bus horns and revving motorbikes, the scent of grilled meat wafting from street carts, and the influx of people, always moving, always with purpose. This is a country on the move.

Forty years after a devastating war, Vietnam is in the midst of a comeback, rising in a cacophonous clash of old and new, modern and traditional. You're just as likely to see a luxury car roll past a rusty one-speed bike as you are to find the upper echelon of society eating from plastic tables on the street. Amid the bustling street stalls and the frenzied markets, the country thrives.

Beyond its cities, another Vietnam awaits. Venture to the countryside or along the coast and find tranquil beaches and sleepy farming towns; never-ending rice paddies and the eerie labyrinth of limestone islands.

Vietnam grasps your full attention. With open arms, an open mind, and a sense of adventure, you'll find yourself embracing it right back.

Clockwise from top left: bicycle in Hoi An's Old Town; paddling through the Mekong Delta; masks at Hanoi's Temple of Literature; fishermen reel in the day's catch; incense; Hue's Temple of Literature.

Planning Your Trip

Where to Go

Hanoi

Regal and refined, Vietnam's thousand-year-old capital offers a hodgepodge of historical sights from across centuries, not to mention top-notch shopping in the vibrant **Old Quarter,** where you'll find plenty of mouthwatering cuisine alongside some of the city's best local color. Circle by **Hoan Kiem Lake,** the elegant, aging **Temple of Literature,** and somber **Ho Chi Minh Mausoleum** for the city's best sights, and get an introduction to Vietnam's array of local culture at the excellent **Museum of Ethnology.**

Ha Long Bay and the Northern Coast

The mysterious, mesmerizing waters of the north coast form a seascape like no other, draped in lush, mist-covered jungle and dotted with

gravity-defying limestone islands. Kick back on an **overnight cruise** around Ha Long, cycle your way across **Cat Ba Island,** climb the jagged cliffs of **Lan Ha Bay,** or admire these labyrinthine landscapes from a **kayak.** Even inland, the karsts of **Ninh Binh** provide the perfect backdrop for a peaceful rowboat ride through rice paddies and beautiful northern countryside.

The Central Provinces

Replete with crumbling imperial tombs, trendy modern shops, sleek contemporary skyscrapers, and the riotous colors of ancient pagodas, the central provinces are a jam-packed juxtaposition of old and new. **Hue,** former capital of the Nguyen dynasty, boasts impressive royal relics, while everything from winding, picturesque **Hai Van Pass** to the jaw-dropping **Phong Nha-Ke**

mosaic mural in Hanoi

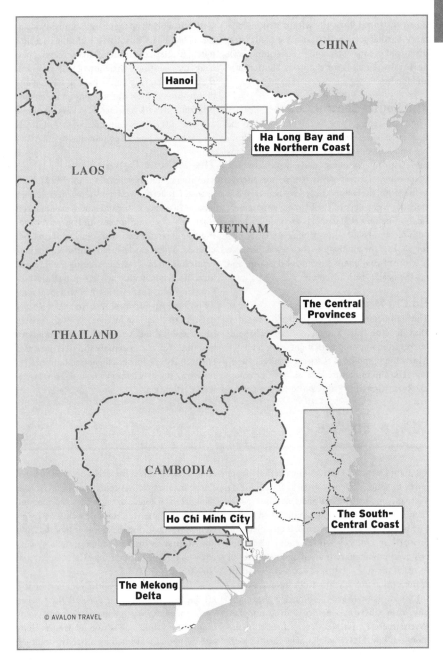

Bang National Park sits within striking distance. Farther south is **Danang,** Vietnam's latest ultra-cool urban center, and the charming town of **Hoi An,** an oasis for shoppers, shutterbugs, and foodies.

The South-Central Coast

The south-central coast has all but cornered the market on beach destinations in Vietnam. From hip and happening **Nha Trang Beach,** brimming with nonstop energy and aquatic activities, to the tranquil shores of **Mui Ne,** a resort enclave to the south, the belly of the "S" is where travelers flock for a few days of R&R between more hectic destinations. Water sports are popular here, with plenty of snorkeling, diving, and kitesurfing. **Dalat,** the anomaly of the region, boasts a mixture of cool mountain air, rural charm, and off-the-beaten-path adventure.

Ho Chi Minh City

The high-octane commercial hub of the country, Ho Chi Minh City (known to locals as Saigon) buzzes from morning until night, caught up in a whirlwind of motorbikes, street vendors, megamarkets, and miniature local shops. The colossal **Reunification Palace** and **Notre Dame** Cathedral break up the chaotic clutter of downtown District 1. **Chinatown** kicks the pace up a notch, its 21st-century residents careening past hazy, incense-filled ancient pagodas and ramshackle houses. Hop on the back of a *xe om* and breeze through local traffic, enjoy an ice-cold *ca phe bet* (sidewalk coffee) in 30-4 Park, or dine at any one of the city's thousands of **street stalls** for the best cuisine the country has to offer.

The Mekong Delta

The nine spidering veins of the mighty Mekong branch out across western Vietnam, creating a bizarre fusion of water and land where markets float, boats become houses, and narrow, winding tributaries wend through lush **fruit orchards.** The area's leisurely, laid-back attitude captivates many a traveler seeking a glimpse of local life. Navigate the early-morning **Cai Rang Floating Market,** overnight with a local family on lush **An Binh Island,** tour the Khmer pagodas of sleepy, seductive **Tra Vinh,** or step into the storybook setting of **Sa Dec.** Angkor-bound travelers can explore the riverine sights of **Chau Doc,** while beachgoers should cast off for **Phu Quoc,** Vietnam's fastest-growing island destination.

When to Go

Vietnam's weather changes considerably from north to south. The best months for exploring Vietnam are **September** and **October,** just as rainy season comes to a close in the south but before winter has settled over northern Vietnam, or **April** and **May,** when the country's northern destinations have thawed and rain has yet to reach the south. **High season** runs outside of both these times, with visitor numbers peaking **November-March.** Things get especially busy over Christmas before sliding into **Tet** (Vietnamese Lunar New Year), the following month. While this is a holiday of fascinating local traditions, it makes for a poor visit, as the entire country shuts down for weeks before and after. Those businesses that remain open often hike their prices to double or triple the usual amount, and transportation is unreliable. While fewer foreigners travel during the summer months, **July** and **August** see droves of domestic holidaymakers, who flock to hot spots like Ha Long Bay and Nha Trang.

If you're sticking to the north, your best months are **September-October** or **April-June,** when you'll encounter warm temperatures and plenty of sunshine, while high season tends to be chilly and perpetually plagued by mist. The light fog that sits atop everything north of Hue can be beautiful, provided you don't arrive expecting sunny days. Down south, cooler temperatures prevail **November-March,** but the build-up to rainy season begins shortly thereafter, bringing temperatures to a balmy 100 degrees with high humidity before the downpours start in mid- to late May. Though travelers have to plan around the afternoon showers, rainfall between May and September is predictable, only becoming a true free-for-all at the end of the season in October.

Before You Go

Passports and Visas

Visitors are required to secure a **tourist visa** prior to arrival in Vietnam. This can be arranged up to six months before your trip. Visas are assigned in one- and three-month increments with both single- and multiple-entry options. Costs run USD$100-180, depending upon the nature of the visa.

Travelers entering Vietnam over land must visit an embassy or consulate to prepare their visa ahead of time. Air travelers have the additional option to apply for pre-approval, a significantly more cost-effective route, though this is only available to those arriving at one of Vietnam's three major airports: **Tan Son Nhat** in Ho Chi Minh City; **Noi Bai** in Hanoi; or **Danang International Airport.** Although pre-approval is not advertised by the Vietnamese government, it is a legitimate option, provided you arrange your documents through a reliable company. International air travelers must have a passport with at least six months' validity at time of travel.

As of 2014, foreign overnight visitors to Phu Quoc are eligible for a 30-day **visa exemption.** Check with the Vietnamese embassy regarding updated policies on this exemption rule. Any travel on the mainland still requires a tourist visa.

A woman works in the terraced rice paddies of Vietnam's northwest.

colorful incense, used at pagodas, temples, and family altars

street near Thien Mu Pagoda, Hue

Vaccinations

While there are **no required vaccinations** for Vietnam, the Centers for Disease Control recommend that travelers vaccinate against **Hepatitis A** and **typhoid** prior to visiting in order to prevent food-borne illness. Additional preventative measures, such as the **rabies vaccine,** are suggested for cyclists and those who may come into contact with animals.

Though **malaria** does exist in Vietnam, its prevalence is low, with only rare incidences in the Mekong Delta. Most travelers opt to use insect repellent and cover up at dawn and dusk.

Transportation

Most travelers arrive at either **Tan Son Nhat International Airport** in Ho Chi Minh City or **Noi Bai International Airport** in Hanoi and set off from there. **Public transportation** is easily accessible, from planes and trains to buses and boats. For shorter journeys, hitting the road is the cheapest option; for long-distance trips—from Hanoi to the central provinces, for example, or the central provinces down to Nha Trang—you're

better off in the air or on the rails. **Budget airlines** like Jetstar and VietJet fly to a number of domestic destinations, while **overnight trains** run the spectrum from cheap hard-seat cars to air-conditioned sleeper berths.

Vietnam often convinces long-term travelers to buy a **motorbike,** driving the length of the country and then selling it at the end of their journey. This is the **most independent** option and affords you the freedom to explore. Outside of major coastal cities you'll be hard-pressed to find any English speakers or Western amenities, so a **phrasebook** and a good **map** will come in handy. **Cars** can be rented here, but, due to driving regulations, it is required that you have a **Vietnamese driver.**

What to Pack

Most Western amenities are available in Vietnam, though some are more affordable and accessible than others. **Sunscreen,** for instance, is available in many coastal destinations, though it can be tricky to find and is always more expensive. It's best to bring your own from home. Other items, like **contact lens solution** and **feminine products,** can be difficult to come by.

Vietnam tends to be **more formal** than the United States. In rural areas and outside of major hubs like Ho Chi Minh City and Hanoi, local women often dress more conservatively than their Western counterparts, opting for long pants and covered shoulders. Many Vietnamese women in the city have adopted a Western approach to fashion. You can get away with shorts, T-shirts, and tank tops in most tourist destinations. When visiting pagodas or sights of national importance, it's important for both men and women to opt for **conservative clothing,** wearing **long pants** and **covering shoulders,** as this is considered a sign of respect.

floating market, Chau Doc

The Best of Vietnam: Down the Dragon's Spine

While Vietnam is, at points, no wider than 30 miles across, the distance from the northern border down to the deep south is on par with a drive from Boston to Miami, and on roads far more congested and far less maintained. This itinerary describes a brisk two-week trip, covering the full length of Vietnam's coast, with a few detours to the interior. For a more relaxed pace, extend your trip to three weeks and linger in the places you like best.

Hanoi

Spend a weekend in the capital city, focusing on the hectic, narrow alleys of the Old Quarter.

DAY 1

Touch down at **Hanoi**'s Noi Bai International Airport and head toward the city. Dive right into the action with a cyclo ride around the **Old Quarter,** taking in its frenetic pace from the safety of your seat. Stroll around the placid **Hoan Kiem Lake** to see where locals hang out and catch a glimpse of **Turtle Tower** and the ornate **Ngoc Son Temple.** You can grab lunch in the Old Quarter or head to the clutch of cafés and restaurants around **St. Joseph's Cathedral** before charting a course south to **Hoa Lo Prison** and the **Vietnamese Women's Museum.**

Wind down the day on the streets of the chic **French Quarter,** either atop the **Press Club** terrace or at the roadside **Tadioto.** In the evening, grab dinner at **Ngon** before catching a **water puppet** or *ca tru* (ancient chamber music) show in the Old Quarter.

DAY 2

Rise early for a morning bowl of pho, Hanoi's favorite breakfast food, before heading off to **Ba**

Hoi An's vibrant Hainan Assembly Hall

Dinh Square to line up for a visit at Ho Chi Minh Mausoleum. Once you've paid your respects, swing by Uncle Ho's famed stilt house or head to the nearby One Pillar Pagoda for a different era of Hanoian history. From there, the Military History Museum, flanked by the Flag Tower and Lenin Park, is just a short walk away.

In keeping with the Communist spirit, stop for coffee at Cong Caphe or head straight down to KOTO for lunch. Spend the afternoon getting to know Hanoi's Temple of Literature before wandering back toward the Old Quarter. Once traffic picks up and rush hour is in full swing, head for some *bia hoi* (freshly brewed light beer) and a night on the town.

Ha Long Bay Cruise

DAYS 3-4

Set off early for Ha Long Bay on a two-day, one-night cruise. It's a four-hour drive to the docks; you'll have a chance to stop for lunch before leaving shore. While itineraries vary from company to company, you can kick back, take in the scenery from your sun deck, and explore a cave or two.

Provided the skies are clear, a sunrise on Ha Long Bay is worth waking up for. Enjoy breakfast on the boat and another day of guided activity, which usually includes a cruise by some of the bay's more famous landscapes, like Incense Burner and Ga Choi, as well as kayaking.

Your boat will dock back at Ha Long City around noon and from there it's a four-hour drive back to Hanoi. After you return, either hop on an overnight train to Danang or fly there via one of the country's budget airlines. Both are roughly the same cost. The train departs in the evening, while flyers have the choice of going straight to the airport or spending another night in Hanoi and heading out first thing the following day.

Alternate Option: North to Mountainous Sapa

If you're not one for the water, leave Hanoi for Sapa, where you can opt to trek through Vietnam's northern mountains, visiting remote villages.

DAYS 3-4

Catch an overnight train from Hanoi and head to Sapa. You'll arrive in Lao Cai in the morning and take a quick minibus ride to the small mountain town. Take the rest of the morning to explore the town, passing by its museum and shopping along Cau May street. In the afternoon, head to Cat Cat village or hire a motorbike to visit the nearby waterfalls and Tram Ton Pass. You'll also want to arrange a trek for the following day, either through a local guide or one of the tour outfits in town.

Rise early and set off with your local guide to one of the nearby minority villages and get a more intimate look at the varied cultures of Vietnam. The trek takes a few hours, including lunch. In the afternoon, return to Sapa for a bit of R&R and any last-minute shopping before heading back to Hanoi via overnight train or bus.

Hoi An

Hoi An draws visitors with its photogenic wooden houses, nearby beaches, and tailor-made clothing. Stop for a long weekend for custom clothing and picturesque landscapes.

DAY 5

Train travelers from Hanoi will arrive in Danang by late morning; those traveling via air will arrive around noon. Hop in a cab bound for Hoi An, your base for the next three days. Spend an easy day exploring the Old Town, from its charming local market to the famous Japanese Covered Bridge and a clutch of Chinese Assembly Halls. Browse the wares of tailors, jewelers, and dressmakers that have set up shop downtown. Dive into mouthwatering local dishes unique to Hoi An, including *cao lau* (local noodles), fried wontons, and white rose dumplings. Around mid-afternoon, visit the *banh beo* (steamed rice flour cake) vendor that sets up shop in front of the Ngu Bang Assembly Hall.

Place your order for custom-made clothes as soon as possible, allowing time for alterations later on. Sip wine on the waterfront at sundown at White Marble Wine Bar.

Best Beaches

Long Beach, Phu Quoc Island

Blessed with miles upon miles of stunning coastline, it's no surprise that Vietnam offers something for everyone in the realm of beach destinations. From mainstays on the tourist trail to remote, near-deserted islands, this country's pristine shores afford a healthy mix of active, fast-paced water sport hubs and easygoing seaside venues.

- **Con Dao:** This island oasis has **dense jungle,** sun-bleached shores, and **soaring seaside cliffs.** It's one of the country's most alluring beaches but also one of the most difficult to reach. Reward yourself with its striking coastlines, turquoise waters, and some of the **best diving** in Vietnam.

- **Mui Ne:** A well-traveled spot on the south-central coast, this ever-expanding **resort town** delivers low-key shores and **Western comforts.** It's also known as the country's **kitesurfing capital.**

- **Nha Trang:** This **bustling beach hotspot** welcomes sunbathers, snorkelers, and divers to explore its shores. After dark, the party moves on land, where **all-night celebrations** last until the wee hours. **Doc Let** to the north offers a quieter, more exclusive shoreline.

- **Ninh Chu:** The sleepy town of **Phan Rang-Thap Cham** offers **local culture** combined with a crescent stretch of sand that is quiet and authentic. Ninh Chu's laid-back atmosphere and relative anonymity help preserve its off-the-beaten-track vibe.

- **Phu Quoc:** Vietnam's go-to resort destination, popular with couples and families, Phu Quoc Island houses several good options. **Long Beach** is lively, happening but not claustrophobic. **Sao Beach** to the south is pristine. **Ganh Dau** and **Bai Dai** to the north are a perfect place to commune with nature and escape the more touristed parts of the island.

DAY 6

For your second day in Hoi An, rent a bicycle and set off, pedaling to the photogenic **Tra Que vegetable village** north of town. Wander through the rows of veggies, then grab a meal on the breezy veranda of **Baby Mustard.**

Carry on north to hit the beach, either peaceful **An Bang** or the more happening **Cua Dai** to the east. Spend the afternoon catching rays before you cycle back to town. Some top-notch dinner spots include **Ba Le Well, Miss Ly's,** and **Morning Glory.** For dessert, swing by the **Cargo Club** for decadent cakes and pastries, then grab a beer at **Dive Bar.**

DAY 7

Your last day in Hoi An can be spent a few different ways. Venture up the coast to the limestone **Marble Mountains** before carrying on to cosmopolitan **Danang** for a visit to the **Museum of Cham Sculpture** or over to nearby Son Tra peninsula, where the statue of Quan Am at **Linh Ung Pagoda** dominates the landscape.

If you'd rather stay put, Hoi An has plenty of tours and courses, including the **Taste of Hoi An** food tour, as well as a slew of **cooking classes** and a **photo tour** for aspiring shutterbugs.

At the end of the day, board a night bus or make your way back to Danang and hop on a train bound for Nha Trang.

Nha Trang

Spend a few days taking in the energy of Nha Trang Vietnam's **beach capital** and nonstop **party hub.**

DAY 8

Roll into **Nha Trang** in the early hours of the morning. From there, you'll have the option to hit the beach or head to the local **mud baths** for a restorative spa day. For some local culture, make for **Long Son Pagoda** and its giant Buddha on a hill, or go over the river to the ancient Hindu **Po Nagar Towers.**

Rest up for the evening, as Nha Trang comes alive after dark, with all-night beach parties at

the steps to Linh Ung Pagoda, Danang's largest Buddhist center of worship

the **Sailing Club** and plenty of cheap drinks and busy dance floors throughout the backpacker neighborhood.

DAY 9

Leave the planning to the professionals on your second day in Nha Trang and book a full-day tour on the water. Travelers can choose from **snorkeling, diving,** or **day-cruise** excursions, exploring **local marine life** or simply kicking back on a sun deck. Upon your return to shore, hop on an overnight train bound for Ho Chi Minh City or head to the airport to fly there.

Ho Chi Minh City

DAY 10

Spend your first morning in Ho Chi Minh City taking it easy with a coffee in the shadow of **Notre Dame Cathedral.** From here, both the **Central Post Office** and the **Reunification Palace** are within walking distance. Wander north toward **Turtle Lake** for lunch and then carry on to the city's **War Remnants Museum** for the afternoon.

Head to the backpacker area later in the day for a happy hour drink or dress up and spring for a cocktail at **Chill Skybar** or the sky-high **Saigon Skydeck** to appreciate the city from a different angle.

For dinner, grab a cab to District 1's Tan Dinh neighborhood, where local favorites like **Banh Xeo 46A** and upmarket eateries like **Cuc Gach Quan** await. For live music, check out **Q4** or **Yoko** in the evening, or hit the dance floor at **Apocalypse Now.**

DAY 11

Today, visit bustling **Chinatown,** where the mammoth **Binh Tay Market** sprawls over several blocks and a tasty array of Chinese meals can be found. Back toward downtown, **Thien Hau Pagoda** is an incense-filled haze of reds and golds, lacquered woodwork, and ornate effigies, with neighboring **Chaozhou Congregation Hall** and **Cho Lon Mosque** adding an extra level of diversity to the mix.

Return to District 1 for some retail therapy at **Ben Thanh Market** and along posh **Le Loi,** passing by the colonial-era **Hotel de Ville** and local **Opera House.** Pop into the historic **Rex Hotel** for a sunset drink on its rooftop bar or head back to the backpacker district for a laid-back evening.

Mekong Delta

This **whirlwind tour** of the delta hits the highlights. To spend more time exploring, follow the itinerary *Touring the Mekong Delta* on page 19.

DAY 12

From Ho Chi Minh City, board a bus to **Can Tho,** the largest city in the **Mekong Delta.** You'll arrive in the late morning, leaving the rest of the day to explore the **riverfront.** Around sundown, turn up at **Ninh Kieu Park,** the liveliest spot in the city after dark, with plenty of shopping and street stalls.

DAY 13

Get up early to visit **Cai Rang Floating Market.** This will take up most of your morning and some of the afternoon.

Get back on the bus to Ho Chi Minh City by mid- to late afternoon. Spend your last night with the city's best jazz musicians at **Sax N Art Jazz Club,** venture out for a classy drink at **Last Call,** or unwind on the rooftop of **Pacharan.**

Touring the Mekong Delta

Down in the far reaches of the south, the Mekong Delta is a more authentic, off-the-beaten-track part of Vietnam. Things move a bit slower, with less infrastructure than other parts of the country and fewer English speakers. Spend as little as a single day from Saigon out to My Tho or Vinh Long, or keep busy for as long as a week, following the Tien River toward the border before hopping over to Chau Doc and onward into Cambodia.

The Delta via Ho Chi Minh City

Bookend a trip to Ho Chi Minh City with a long weekend in the delta. It's an easy bus ride from HCMC to Vinh Long, one of the delta's northern towns.

DAY 1

From downtown Ho Chi Minh City, head to the **Western bus station** and find a vehicle bound for **Vinh Long.** Once you arrive, you'll want to arrange a **homestay,** either by visiting one of the local travel outfits, stopping by the ferry to **An Binh,** where you should be able to recruit a willing local to put you up for the night, or simply heading across to the island on your own and scoping out potential accommodations.

Spend some time with your local family, but don't forget to hop on a **bicycle** and explore the rest of the island, too. You'll find a charming church and plenty of fruit orchards down An Binh's narrow concrete paths. For a locally made gift, give the folks at **Viet Artisans** a ring to put together your own handmade souvenir in its workshop. Make a point of catching sunset over the river, and eat dinner with your host family.

DAY 2

In the morning, travelers have two choices. The first is to enlist the services of your homestay family or an island boat to head out to **Cai Be floating market.** Do this early, as much of the vibrancy of the market is lost by late morning.

statue at a pagoda in the Mekong Delta

produce for sale at Cai Rang's floating market

The second option is to linger a little longer on An Binh, enjoying your breakfast and a final goodbye to your host family before you head to **Can Tho,** where another, larger floating market awaits.

Once you arrive, you'll have the rest of the day to explore the city's charming waterfront, including the colorful **Ong Pagoda,** swing by a **Khmer wat,** or visit the local **museum.** At some point, you'll need to arrange your floating market tour for the following day, either with an independent boat at Ninh Kieu Pier or via a hotel or tour outfit.

In the early evening, grab a seat along the river and take in Can Tho's bustling nighttime activity. If you're interested in local cuisine, you can hit the town with **Open Tour CT,** which runs nightlife tours in addition to its daytime offerings. You'll probably want to get to bed at a reasonable hour, as Can Tho's floating market is an early-morning affair.

DAY 3

Rise before the sun to visit **Cai Rang Floating Market,** the Delta's largest on-the-water trading post. Depending upon your tour, travelers can spend most of the morning and even part of the afternoon plying the waters of the Can Tho River.

Get back to the downtown docks by mid-afternoon at the latest and either spend the rest of the day taking it easy or hop straight on a bus bound for **Tra Vinh.**

DAY 4

Enjoy an early breakfast at one of the shops overlooking the town's main roundabout. From here, you can rent a **bicycle** and set off for **Ba Om Pond, Ang Pagoda,** and the **Khmer Cultural Museum.**

Head back to town for lunch. Spend the afternoon exploring the shaded lanes of Tra Vinh, swinging by **Ong Pagoda** and **Ong Met Pagoda** on the way. If you're up for another Buddhist hall of worship, **Hang Pagoda** is a cycle or taxi ride away, but you can just as easily relax at one of the local cafés in town. Grab dinner at the local market or stop in to **La Trau Xanh** for a fancier meal.

The Delta to the Cambodian Border

This itinerary works well as a bookend to your Vietnam trip, especially if you're continuing onward to Cambodia.

DAY 1

Starting from Ho Chi Minh City, make your way to the delta, specifically Vinh Long. See Day 1 of *The Delta via Ho Chi Minh City* (page 19) for a suggested itinerary for today.

DAY 2

In the morning, take a boat to **Cai Be floating market.** Head there early, as much of its vibrancy is lost by late morning. Relax while your vessel meanders down narrow canals and back up the river to An Binh. From here, catch a ferry back to Vinh Long and take the bus to **Sa Dec.** Perhaps the most photogenic town in the Delta, Sa Dec is worth a visit to see the **house of Huynh Thuy Le,** the richly decorated **Kien An Cung Pagoda,** and Sa Dec's famous **flower gardens.**

Hop on a bus headed for **Cao Lanh** (or hire a car to drive there) and find accommodations for the night. Those pressed for time can also take a direct bus from Vinh Long to Cao Lanh.

DAY 3

Plan for an early start, as you'll want plenty of time to reach **Tram Chim National Park** before late morning for the best bird-watching. Keep an eye out for red-headed sarus cranes, the world's tallest flying bird, along with the 230 other bird species found here. After your tour, head back to Cao Lanh to check out the local **Nguyen Sinh Sac Memorial Park** and **Do Cong Tuong Temple.**

DAY 4

In the morning, depart for **Chau Doc.** You'll arrive around noon, leaving the rest of the day for relaxing and exploring this small border town. Grab lunch near Chau Doc's local market before making the trip out to **Sam Mountain.** Scale the

altar to Lady Xu, protector of Chau Doc's Sam Mountain

many steps to the top by passing through **Tay An Pagoda** or hitch a *xe om* ride to its summit.

On your way back down, swing by **Cave Pagoda** and the **Temple of Lady Xu.** In the afternoon, book a boat trip for the following morning through one of the local hotels. Evenings in Chau Doc are a tame affair, so you'll have plenty of opportunity for rest and relaxation as the sun goes down.

DAY 5

Take a guided ride on the **Bassac River (Hau River),** passing **fish farms** and **floating houses,** as well as Chau Doc's **floating market.** Upon returning to shore, wander around Chau Giang District, home to the town's **Cham community** and the green-and-white minaret of **Mubarak Mosque** or kick back near the waterfront. **Victoria Chau Doc** is a great place to unwind, with a top-notch bar and restaurant, as well as a riverside pool.

DAY 6

For your last day in Vietnam, motor out to **Tra Su Bird Sanctuary,** awash with flooded forests of cajuput trees and feathered residents. Enjoy a peaceful rowboat ride and the views from its soaring watchtower. Avid history buffs and nature enthusiasts can carry on to **Ba Chuc** or explore the surrounding countryside. Enjoy the rest of your afternoon; cross into Cambodia the following day.

Pick Your Park

Vietnam counts 30 national parks to its credit. Several of the parks that welcome foreign visitors stand out from the bunch for their impressive landscapes, diverse wildlife, and unique outdoor adventures.

IF YOU'RE LOOKING FOR...

Active Adventures: Offering the same stunning scenery as Ha Long but with greater access to its lush, jungle-covered karsts and tranquil bay, **Cat Ba National Park** boasts a combination of hiking trails, soaring seaside cliffs, and a handful of caves, all of which serve as an idyllic backdrop for trekking, swimming, climbing, and cycling adventures. Though they're not easily spotted, the island is also home to the Cat Ba langur, one of the world's most endangered primates.

History and Nature Intertwined: Set on an island with dual reputations for its heartbreaking colonial past and unparalleled natural beauty, **Con Dao National Park** is one of the country's least-visited and, therefore, best-preserved green spaces. Devouring nearly all of Con Son, the largest island in the Con Dao archipelago, this park is home to 160 species of land animals as well as over 1,000 varieties of aquatic creatures, making it a worthy spot for hiking, swimming, diving, and snorkeling for travelers who make the time to reach this remote island.

Mountain Hiking: North of Dalat, the rolling slopes of **Lang Biang Mountain** are but one part of the primitive **Bidoup-Nui Ba National Park.** The best hiking trails are on this mountain, as well as beautiful panoramic vistas of Dalat and the Central Highlands. Climb the challenging path up to the summit or take it easy at Rada Lookout below. Local guides lead visitors deeper into the forest for more off-the-beaten-track adventures.

Untouched Caves: Far and away a highlight among Vietnam's already-captivating array of natural sights, **Phong Nha-Ke Bang National Park** boasts a maze of subterranean chambers beneath its soaring limestone karsts. Down rivers

Lan Ha Bay, Cat Ba Island

and buried under mountains, these gargantuan caverns harbor a host of ethereal, mind-bending vistas that remain largely untouched by local tourism—at least for now. While not all adventures in Phong Nha are easy on the wallet—a foray into Son Doong, the largest cave on Earth, costs around USD$3,000—affordable, adventurous caving tours are now accessible to the average traveler, and tourism in the park is set to take off.

Bird-Watching: The waterlogged fields of **Tram Chim National Park** are home to over 230 bird species, including the six-foot-tall sarus crane, the world's tallest flying bird. Navigate its calm waters by motorboat, winding through a series of narrow canals that burrow deep into the park's flooded forests for a glimpse of Vietnam's diverse bird life.

Hanoi

Highlights

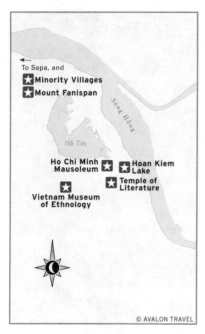

To Sapa, and
★ Minority Villages
★ Mount Fanispan

Sông Hồng

Hồ Tây

Ho Chi Minh Mausoleum ★   ★ Hoan Kiem Lake

★ Temple of Literature

★
Vietnam Museum of Ethnology

© AVALON TRAVEL

★ **Hoan Kiem Lake:** Take in the bustle and noise of downtown Hanoi from the shores of this legendary lake, where history and mythology meet (page 29).

★ **Ho Chi Minh Mausoleum:** Pay a visit to Vietnam's most revered national hero, embalmed and at peace under glass in a blocky, Soviet-style mausoleum (page 37).

★ **Temple of Literature:** A long series of lacquered pavilions and spacious courtyards, lotus ponds, and stone stelae, this Confucian temple marks the site of Vietnam's first university (page 40).

★ **Vietnam Museum of Ethnology:** Learn all there is to know about Vietnam's 54 ethnic groups, from the Kinh of the coast to the H'mong, Thai, Gia Rai, and scores of other lesser-known minorities that populate the country's mountainous interior (page 42).

★ **Minority Villages:** Whether perched on the steep cliffs of the Hoang Lien mountain range or sheltered by lush green river valleys, Sapa's minority villages are a world apart from the rest of the country (page 82).

★ **Mount Fansipan:** Reach the "Roof of Indochina" via a long, action-packed ascent that winds through clouds and over limestone ridges to the summit of Vietnam's highest peak (page 86).

In a thousand-year-old city, you would expect some things to get lost in the mix, obscured by cramped shops and narrow houses or buried under the incessant blare of traffic. But along the busy streets of Hanoi, every era of the city's history

shines, in its gracefully aging cathedral, sturdy Communist architecture, and the vibrant Old Quarter. Whether you're wandering the bustling shopping streets of its older neighborhoods, diving into history at the Temple of Literature, or visiting the embalmed remains of Ho Chi Minh, Vietnam's most respected national hero, there's no denying that the soul of Vietnam lies in Hanoi.

The capital is sleek and sophisticated, playing the wise older sibling to Ho Chi Minh City's freewheeling antics down south. A well-established art scene and strong café culture permeate most of the city, along with a self-assuredness that comes from having survived a millennium of ups and downs. Flashy boutiques and shopping malls are beginning to make an appearance around town, a stark contrast to the narrow, teetering tube houses of the city's downtown districts.

Most travelers to Vietnam pass through the capital, not only for its sights, sounds, and savory cuisine, but also for its status as a hub, connecting popular destinations like Sapa and Ha Long Bay with the rest of Vietnam.

Hanoi is a place to savor rather than sightsee. While its eclectic attractions make for a fascinating, patchwork history, the main draw of the capital is its infectious energy, which permeates every nook and cranny of Hanoi's jam-packed neighborhoods.

HISTORY

The fertile, low-lying Red River Delta has been inhabited since prehistoric times. Well before it became the capital of Vietnam, the region was used as an administrative and political center by the Chinese, who colonized Vietnam for a millennium-long stretch beginning in 208 BC. The city's official history began in AD 1010, when emperor Ly Thai To moved the capital from Hoa Lu north to a bend on the western bank of the Red River.

Previous: Sapa's remote minority villages; downtown Hanoi at rush hour. **Above:** incense urn at the Temple of Literature.

Hanoi

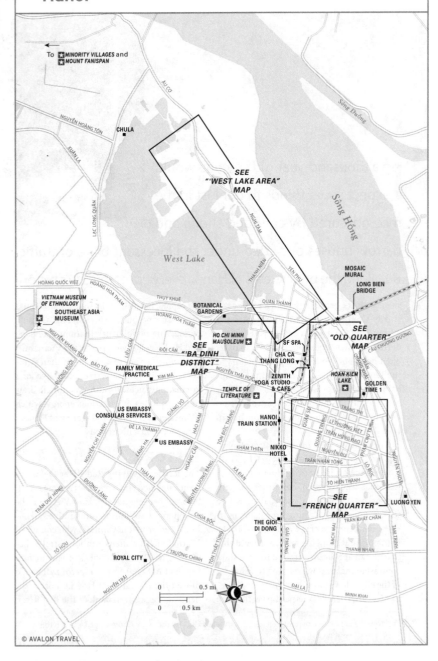

To ✚ MINORITY VILLAGES and
✚ MOUNT FANISPAN

CHULA

SEE "WEST LAKE AREA" MAP

West Lake

Song Hồng

Song Đuống

MOSAIC MURAL

LONG BIEN BRIDGE

VIETNAM MUSEUM OF ETHNOLOGY

SOUTHEAST ASIA MUSEUM

BOTANICAL GARDENS

HO CHI MINH MAUSOLEUM

SF SPA

SEE "BA DINH DISTRICT" MAP

CHA CA THANG LONG

SEE "OLD QUARTER" MAP

FAMILY MEDICAL PRACTICE

ZENITH YOGA STUDIO & CAFÉ

TEMPLE OF LITERATURE

HOÀN KIEM LAKE

GOLDEN TIME 1

US EMBASSY CONSULAR SERVICES

HANOI TRAIN STATION

US EMBASSY

NIKKO HOTEL

SEE "FRENCH QUARTER" MAP

LUONG YEN

THE GIOI DI DONG

ROYAL CITY

0   0.5 mi

0   0.5 km

© AVALON TRAVEL

Originally known as Thang Long ("ascending dragon"), the imperial citadel remained in this spot for centuries.

At the turn of the 19th century, emperor Gia Long, the first of the Nguyen Dynasty, moved his capital to Hue, situated at the center of the country. During much of the Nguyen Dynasty's reign, Hanoi served as a regional capital. It received its current moniker in 1831, courtesy of emperor Minh Mang, Gia Long's son and successor. The city later reclaimed its capital status in 1902, when the colonial French government chose it as the head of French Indochina. It continued to serve as the seat of power after Ho Chi Minh declared Vietnamese independence in 1945. Nine years later, the Geneva Accords of 1954 granted northern Vietnam to the Viet Minh, who carried out their political operations in the grand colonial buildings left behind by the French.

The American War ushered in darker days, with heavy bombing reducing large parts of the city to rubble. Long Bien Bridge saw routine bombardments, while Bach Mai Hospital was almost completely destroyed during the Christmas bombings of 1972. The damage to the city would take years to rebuild. After the war, Hanoi struggled to regain its footing, through Vietnam's 1979 border war with China and the poor economic policies that followed reunification. When the country's *doi moi* reforms were enacted, allowing for greater economic freedom, Vietnam began to blossom into the country that it is today, bringing Hanoi out of its misery and back on the path to prosperity.

PLANNING YOUR TIME

Hanoi is no more than a three-day affair, thanks to its compact size, allowing visitors to cover plenty of ground in a short time. For additional adventures, such as Perfume Pagoda or Tam Coc, set aside an extra day. Trips to Sapa require as few as two days or as many as five, if you have time to spare.

Most museums are closed on Mondays, and many pagodas close for at least two hours for lunch. Sightsee in the mornings, when more of the city's attractions are open.

Weather conditions in Hanoi are different from the tropical temperatures of the lower half of the country. Between November and February, Hanoi gets cold, with a steady mist and temperatures 50-60°F. Conditions become more pleasant around March and stay that way until the end of May, when temperatures start to rise. The heat reaches unbearable, sweltering temps in August, before another brief period of mild weather in September and October.

ORIENTATION

Hanoi is divvied up into 12 districts, 17 communes, and one hamlet, though most travelers stick to the downtown districts and the areas just beyond.

Hoan Kiem District is home to the eponymous Hoan Kien Lake, Hanoi's most famous landmark and a useful point of reference when navigating the city. Hoan Kiem is comprised of the bustling **Old Quarter,** where much of the city's commercial activity takes place, the posh **French Quarter,** and, along its western side, the **Cathedral District.** Along with picturesque St. Joseph's Cathedral, the Cathedral District houses cheap backpacker accommodations and trendy boutiques.

Northwest of Hoan Kiem, **Ba Dinh District** is where many of the capital's 20th-century historical sights are situated.

North of these downtown districts, **Tay Ho (West Lake)** is more upscale, with a residential feel and plenty of high-end shops and restaurants.

Hanoi's streets are tricky to get the hang of, with windy and narrow streets, and street names that change several times over the course of a mile. There are plenty of English-speaking residents downtown who can help to point you in the right direction. The city's public bus system is well-organized, affordable, has wide coverage, and has frequent service downtown and in other tourist-driven areas. *Xe om* and taxis are abundant and businesses are well-marked with street addresses.

Old Quarter

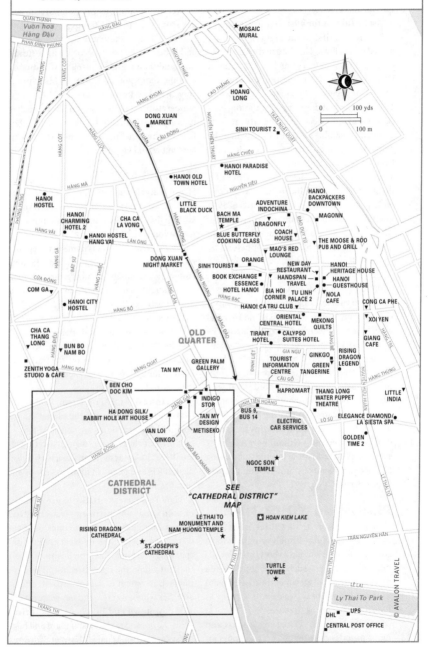

QUÁN THÁNH
Vườn hoa
Hàng Đậu
PHAN ĐÌNH PHÙNG

HÀNG ĐẬU

★ MOSAIC
MURAL

NGUYỄN THIỆP

PHÙNG HƯNG
HÀNG CÓT
HÀNG LƯỢC

CAO THẮNG

■ HOÀNG
LONG

DONG XUAN ■
MARKET

CẦU ĐÔNG

SINH TOURIST 2 ■

HÀNG KHOAI
DONG XUAN

NGUYỄN THIỆN THUẬT

TRÂN NHẬT DUẬT

HÀNG MÃ

HÀNG CHIẾU

● HANOI OLD
TOWN HOTEL

● HANOI PARADISE
HOTEL

NGUYỄN SIÊU

HANOI ■
HOSTEL

HANOI
CHARMING
HOTEL 2

CHA CA
LA VONG

HÀNG VÁI
● HANOI HOSTEL
HANG VAI

LÃN ÔNG

LITTLE
BLACK DUCK

BACH MA
TEMPLE ★

HÀNG ĐƯỜNG

ADVENTURE
INDOCHINA ■

HANOI ●
BACKPACKERS
DOWNTOWN

■ MAGONN

ĐÀO DUY TỪ

DRAGONFLY ■

BLUE BUTTERFLY ■
COOKING CLASS

COACH
HOUSE ■

THE MOOSE & ROO ●
PUB AND GRILL

HÀNG GA

BÁT SỨ

CỬA ĐÔNG

COM GA ▼

DONG XUAN ■
NIGHT MARKET

HÀNG CÂN

HÀNG NGANG

MAO'S RED
LOUNGE

ORANGE ●

NEW DAY ■
RESTAURANT

HANOI
HERITAGE HOUSE ●

SINH TOURIST ■

BOOK EXCHANGE ■
ESSENCE ●
HOTEL HANOI ●

HANDSPAN —
TRAVEL ●

HANOI
GUESTHOUSE

HÀNG BẠC

BIA HOI
CORNER ●

TU LINH
PALACE 2 ▼

NOLA
CAFE ●

HANOI CITY ●
HOSTEL

HÀNG BỒ

HANOI CA TRU CLUB ▼

CONG CA PHE ●

CHA CA
THANG
LONG ▼

HÀNG ĐIẾU

BUN BO ●
NAM BO ▼

HÀNG ĐÀO

OLD
QUARTER

ORIENTAL ●
CENTRAL HOTEL

MEKONG
QUILTS ●

XOI YEN ▼

HÀNG TRE

ZENITH YOGA ■
STUDIO & CAFE

HÀNG NÓN

HÀNG QUẠT

TAN MY ●

GREEN PALM
GALLERY ■

TIRANT ●
HOTEL

● CALYPSO
SUITES HOTEL

GIANG
CAFE ●

ĐINH LIỆT

GIA NGƯ

GINKGO ●

RISING ●
DRAGON
LEGEND

NGUYỄN HỮU HUÂN

HÀNG THÙNG

TOURIST
INFORMATION
CENTRE ●

GREEN
TANGERINE ▼

CẦU GỖ

BEN CHO ▼
DOC KIM

INDIGO ■
STOR

HAPROMART ■

THANG LONG
WATER PUPPET
THEATRE ■

LITTLE ▼
INDIA

HA DONG SILK/ ■
RABBIT HOLE ART HOUSE

TAN MY
DESIGN

ĐINH TIÊN HOÀNG

BUS 9,
BUS 14 ■

ELECTRIC ■
CAR SERVICES

LÒ SŨ

ELEGANCE DIAMOND/ ●
LA SIESTA SPA

VAN LOI ■
GINKGO ■

METISEKO

NGÔ BẢO KHÁNH

GOLDEN ●
TIME 2

HÀNG ĐÔNG

NGOC SON ★
TEMPLE

CATHEDRAL
DISTRICT

SEE
"CATHEDRAL DISTRICT"
MAP

✚ HOAN KIEM LAKE

TRẦN NGUYÊN HÃN

QUANG SỨ

RISING DRAGON ●
CATHEDRAL

★ ST. JOSEPH'S
CATHEDRAL

LE THAI TO
MONUMENT AND
NAM HUONG TEMPLE ★

TURTLE
TOWER
★

ĐINH TIÊN HOÀNG

LÝ THÁI TỔ

LÊ THÁI TỔ

TRÀNG THI

LÊ LAI

Ly Thai To Park

DHL ■ ■ UPS

CENTRAL POST OFFICE ■

© AVALON TRAVEL

0   100 yds
0   100 m

Sights

Hanoi's attractions span the entirety of its illustrious history, covering everything from imperial relics to colonial grandeur, the Communist revolution, and beyond. Scores of age-old pagodas dot the downtown neighborhoods, rubbing shoulders with crumbling art-deco architecture, a pair of legendary lakes, a few blocky Soviet-style buildings, and several museums that showcase the best of Hanoi's art, history, and culture.

This is the kind of place in which the journey rivals the destination. Rather than hop in a cab to the Temple of Literature, enlist the services of a cyclo driver or head for Ba Dinh district on foot. Even if it takes an extra hour and a few wrong turns, exploring the city this way brings its vibrancy to life.

OLD QUARTER

A teeming, tight-knit neighborhood barely contained by the tiny streets north of Hoan Kiem Lake, the historic Old Quarter is bright, chaotic, and fun. Hanoi's most visited commercial district, it has been in business for centuries and holds its own amid the recent crop of shopping malls and high-end stores that have sprung up elsewhere in town. Throngs of shoppers, street vendors, motorbikes, and storefronts crowd the narrow one-way streets and bustling alleys of this dense neighborhood, its cluster of skinny shops and tube houses acting as a large central market.

★ Hoan Kiem Lake

The focal point of the Old Quarter, **Hoan Kiem Lake** (corner of Dinh Tien Hoang and Le Thai To) is tranquility surrounded by chaos, its placid water ringed by traffic. Legend has it that emperor Le Thai To received a magical sword from the heavens, which he used to drive the Ming Chinese out of Vietnam in the early 15th century. After his victory, the king was rowing on the lake when a massive turtle appeared, took the sword from his belt, and sank back into the depths below. Le Thai To realized that the blade had been returned to its original owner, thus the lake became known as Hoan Kiem ("Lake of the Returned Sword"). On a small island near the southern end of the water is **Turtle**

Turtle Tower, Hoan Kiem Lake

A Long Weekend in Hanoi

While the thousand-year-old city holds plenty of history, the most captivating moment in Hanoi is the present. Follow this three-day itinerary to explore the storied past of the capital while experiencing the best of a modern-day Vietnamese metropolis at the same time. Taxis, *xe om*, and public buses are widely available, but it's recommended that you walk unless otherwise specified. Traveling by foot allows travelers to get the real feel of Hanoi's topsy-turvy energy.

DAY 1

Follow the locals and start your day early with breakfast at the hotel or a piping hot bowl of pho on the street. Any good Hanoian adventure begins with a trip to **Hoan Kiem Lake**, the epicenter of town, followed by nearby **Ngoc Son Temple.** From the northern edge of the water, you should be able to enlist the services of a cyclo driver, who will ferry you around the narrow, chaotic streets of the **Old Quarter** in order to witness the city in full swing. If you're up for it, walking is also an option, though the uninitiated will find downtown Hanoi's streets hectic. There are ample opportunities for shopping along **Hang Gai** and around the web of streets north of the lake.

Around lunchtime, you'll want to head toward **St. Joseph's Cathedral** on the western flank of the lake. Swing by the **Le Thai To Monument** and **Nam Huong Temple,** overlooking Hoan Kiem on the way, before cutting in toward the church. If you're feeling peckish, tuck into a savory bowl of *chao suon* (rice porridge), served daily in the alley near the cathedral, or visit the clutch of chic international restaurants sitting in the shadow of its towers. Nearby, **Minh Thuy** is another delicious and affordable option, while the **Hanoi Social Club** offers a tasty, unique alternative. Finish off your midday meal in true Vietnamese form at one of the cafés around St. Joseph's. Several cheap local **street cafés** offer plastic stools and affordable coffee and tea, while the cozy **Hanoi House** provides the same setting with a touch more ambience.

In the afternoon, make your way toward **Hoa Lo Prison** for a bit of history before turning east toward the top-notch **Vietnamese Women's Museum.** As the day winds down, stroll and shop along trendy **Trang Tien** street or pay a visit to the **Opera House** nearby. Enjoy a sunset drink from the terrace bar of the **Press Club** or grab a seat street-side in the artsy front room of **Tadioto.**

Dinner is left up to you, as you'll probably want to hop on a *xe om* or grab a cab to reach one of Hanoi's more authentic local meals. **Ngon** makes a great choice, as do the *cha ca* (pan-fried fish) restaurants a few blocks north of the lake. If you're up for some live entertainment in the evening, the band at **Minh's Jazz Club** puts on a nightly show, as do a rotating list of acts at **Swing.**

Tower, a structure built in 1886 to honor Le Thai Totower. During the French occupation, the tower held a small version of the Statue of Liberty, but it was destroyed when the city was wrested from French rule.

The lake and its surrounding park are a meeting place for locals. If you're lucky, you may spot the lake's sole remaining turtle, considered the offspring of the legendary one.

Ngoc Son Temple

On a small islet near the northern end of Hoan Kiem Lake, the grounds of **Ngoc Son Temple** (Dinh Tien Hoang, 7am-6pm summer, 7:30am-5pm winter, VND20,000, free for children under 15) originally served as a fishing dock for emperor Le Thanh Tong during the 15th century. Though the structure you see wasn't built until 1865, this small patch of land once housed a palace and, later, a pagoda. Ngoc Son Temple combines its Buddhist past with Confucian and Taoist influences.

The temple's front half is dedicated to Quan Cong, a loyal and courageous Chinese general of the Shu Han Dynasty. A flurry of red, black, and gold lacquerwork encircles his three-tiered altar, laden with fruit offerings. Alongside Quan Cong's beloved red horse is La To, a practitioner of traditional medicine and Taoist spirit.

DAY 2

You'll want to get an early jump on your second day, as the sights west of Hoan Kiem Lake require time and patience. In the morning, hop on a bus from the northern edge of the lake to **Ba Dinh Square,** where you can queue up for a visit to **Ho Chi Minh Mausoleum.** Dress respectfully; the rules are strict here. After you've made your way through the procession, you can snap photos of the square or head back toward Uncle Ho's famous **stilt house** and the **One Pillar Pagoda.** From here, those interested in learning more about Vietnam's war-related history should chart a course for the **Military History Museum,** while travelers who'd rather explore a local neighborhood can wander down the maze of alleys that precede **B-52 Lake.** This trip allows you to get a closer look at life in the capital.

Around noon, head south toward the **Temple of Literature.** Just across the street, **KOTO** is a busy lunchtime destination and great spot for a meal. Once you've paid a visit to the temple, you can wander back to the Old Quarter along Nguyen Thai Hoc, shopping as you go, or spend an hour at the **Museum of Fine Arts** nearby. Take the rest of the afternoon to relax and then set off again in the early evening for any one of Hanoi's local *bia hoi* (freshly brewed light beer) shops. The area around *bia hoi* **corner** in the Old Quarter offers a host of affordable street-side dining options as well as a collection of lively dance floors and laid-back hangouts.

DAY 3

Spend the morning at the **Museum of Ethnology** west of downtown. Because it's a trek and the museum itself is extensive, you'll want to allow ample time to explore the grounds, which include several outdoor replicas of traditional minority houses. Head back toward West Lake around noon for a roadside bowl of *bun cha* (grilled meat and rice noodles in fish sauce) on Hang Than street.

After lunch, walk over to **Quan Thanh Temple** before taking a leisurely stroll along **West Lake.** If you're up for it, you can follow the edge of **Truc Bach** lake or simply head straight to **Tran Quoc Pagoda.** It's possible to grab a coffee near here and admire **West Lake** from this vantage point, or to visit the bar at the **Sofitel Plaza Hanoi** for a more upscale environment. Grab dinner at bustling **Xoi Yen** in the Old Quarter before catching a cultural performance in the evening. Both the **water puppet theater** near Hoan Kiem Lake and a pair of *ca tru* (ancient chamber music) troupes hold regular shows throughout the week.

Vietnamese general Tran Hung Dao presides over the latter portion of the temple, tucked behind a high altar. Tran Hung Dao is credited with the defeat of two Mongol invasions, most famously in 1288, when he drove off Kublai Khan and his army after impaling their ships with wooden spikes. He is worshipped as one of the country's collective ancestors.

Ngoc Son houses a small exhibit on the turtles of Hoan Kiem Lake. Just one turtle remains in Hoan Kiem's murky green waters and sightings of the animal are rare.

Leading to Ngoc Son's entrance gate is a bright red footbridge, a popular photo spot.

On the far side of the path, look out for a relief of a tortoise on the left, carrying Le Thai To's famous sword. The area before Ngoc Son boasts nice views of Turtle Tower and the lake.

Hanoi Heritage House

Acting as both a tourist information center and an example of traditional Hanoian architecture, the **Hanoi Heritage House** (87 Ma May, 8:30am-noon and 1:30pm-5pm daily, VND10,000) is a long and narrow building stocked with a variety of Vietnamese handicrafts and helpful English explanations of each item's origin. The house hails from the late 19th century and is punctuated by a small, roofless courtyard, which provided ventilation.

Both levels are stocked with souvenirs, including Dong Ho folk paintings and ceramics, stone carvings, and other traditional wares. While it can feel like a shop, there's no pressure to purchase.

At the front desk are a few books outlining the history of the neighborhood and its many small streets, as well as their former purposes. Curious travelers can ask questions about the city. *Ca tru* (ancient chamber music) performances take place here a few times a week.

Bach Ma Temple

The oldest temple in Hanoi, 11th-century **Bach Ma Temple** (76 Hang Buom, 8am-11am and 2pm-5pm Tues.-Sun., free) may be modest in size but through its humble gates are inner walls drenched in red and gold, lacquered floor to ceiling, and intricate paintings and masterful woodwork. This tranquil hall honors deity Long Do, the chief of Hanoi's first settlement, who lived during the 4th century and is believed to have reappeared several times throughout Vietnamese history, particularly during conflicts with the Chinese, as a protector of the city and its people. Since he would sometimes appear in the form of a white horse, it is fitting that the temple's name translates to white horse. A large statue of a bright white stallion stands at the center of the building, surrounded by offerings and massive, gilded ironwood columns. Overhead, Bach Ma's collection of lintels (large lacquered wooden panels) featuring Chinese inscriptions, bear phrases such as "Thang Long's Guardian to the East" and "Indomitable Spirit of Heaven and Earth."

Temple caretakers typically break for lunch at midday. Visitors who turn up on the 1st or 15th of a lunar month are free to visit from morning to night, as these are special days in Vietnamese culture.

Long Bien Bridge

Long Bien Bridge (east of Tran Nhat Duat), a weathered iron structure, holds a special place in Hanoi's history. Completed in 1902 by French architects, the bridge was originally named after Indochina's governor general, Paul Doumer. It played a key role in both the Franco-Vietnam and American Wars. During the Viet Minh's fight against colonialism, rice and other supplies traveled across Long Bien to the troops at Dien Bien Phu, who defeated their French enemies in 1954. Through the 1960s and '70s the bridge served as a crucial link between Hanoi and the port city of Haiphong. As the only route across the Red River, Long Bien was bombed heavily during the American War and had to be rebuilt in 1973.

Only pedestrians and two-wheeled vehicles are permitted on the bridge. Nearby Chuong Duong Bridge serves as a link for trucks and other large vehicles.

Mosaic Mural

Running beneath Long Bien Bridge along Tran Nhat Duat, Hanoi's **mosaic mural** began as a project to commemorate the city's 1,000-year anniversary. It spans almost 2.5 miles along the western bank of the Red River, making it the longest ceramic wall in the world. Both local and foreign artists took part in the mosaic's creation, combining abstract pieces from international artists with several prominent Vietnamese symbols, such as a mosaic version of a Dong Son drum head and the ever-popular giant turtle of Hoan Kiem Lake carrying a sword on its back.

CATHEDRAL DISTRICT
St. Joseph's Cathedral

An imposing structure amid the narrow houses and one-room shops of downtown Hanoi, **St. Joseph's Cathedral** (40 Nha Chung, tel. 04/3825-4424, 5am-7am and 7pm-9pm daily, free) is one of the city's more recognizable landmarks, its pair of faded Gothic bell towers presiding over a small clearing just west of Hoan Kiem Lake. Originally the site of Bao Thien Pagoda, a Buddhist hall of worship dating as far back as the city itself, the church, built to resemble Paris's Notre

Cathedral District

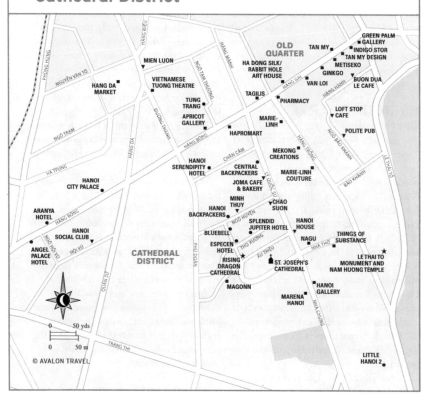

OLD QUARTER

GREEN PALM
GALLERY
TAN MY
INDIGO STOR
TAN MY DESIGN
METISEKO
GINKGO
BUON DUA
LE CAFE
VAN LOI

HANG DIEU
PHONG HUNG
NGUYEN VAN TO
HANG MANH
MIEN LUON
HA DONG SILK/
RABBIT HOLE
ART HOUSE
HANG GAI
NGO TAM THUONG
HANG DA
MARKET
VIETNAMESE
TUONG THEATRE
TAGILIS
PHARMACY
LOFT STOP
CAFE
POLITE PUB
TUNG
TRANG
APRICOT
GALLERY
HAPROMART
MARIE-
LINH
HANG BONG
DUONG THANH
NGO BAO KHANH
HANG TRONG
HA TRUNG
HANG DA
NGO TRAM
CHAN CAM
MEKONG
CREATIONS
BAO KHANH
LE THAI TO
HANOI
SERENDIPITY
HOTEL
CENTRAL
BACKPACKERS
MARIE-LINH
COUTURE
HANOI
CITY PALACE
JOMA CAFE
& BAKERY
HANG BONG
MINH
THUY
ARANYA
HOTEL
CHAO
SUON
HANOI
BACKPACKERS
NGO HUYEN
HANOI
HOUSE
HANOI
SOCIAL CLUB
BLUEBELL
SPLENDID
JUPITER HOTEL
NGO VO VO
HO VU
ESPECEN
HOTEL
NAGU
THINGS OF
SUBSTANCE
ANGEL
PALACE
HOTEL
RISING
DRAGON
CATHEDRAL
PHU DOAN
THO XUONG
AU TRIEU
ST. JOSEPH'S
CATHEDRAL
NHA THO
LE THAI TO
MONUMENT AND
NAM HUONG TEMPLE
CATHEDRAL
DISTRICT
QUAN SU
MAGONN
MARENA
HANOI
NHA CHUNG
HANOI
GALLERY

0   50 yds
0   50 m
TRANG THI
© AVALON TRAVEL

LITTLE
HANOI 2

Dame Cathedral, opened in 1886 to a devout French parish. St. Joseph's remained open until the end of the American War, when the Communist government forbade religious gatherings. The cathedral reopened its doors in the early 1990s.

The modest square before the church, ringed by cafés and boutiques, boasts a statue of Mother Mary and is often busy in the late afternoons with students and locals. Though the front doors are usually closed, there is a side door by which visitors can enter to glimpse the brilliant red, white, and gold interior; most prefer to just take in the building from outside. Visitors can drop by the cathedral's English-language mass on Sundays at 11:30am if they feel so inclined.

Le Thai To Monument and Nam Huong Temple

Overlooking Hoan Kiem Lake, the towering **Le Thai To Monument** (Le Thai To, 8am-5pm daily, free) commemorates Le Thai To, the emperor who played a pivotal role in Vietnam's history and mythology. Also known as Le Loi, this 15th-century king defeated Chinese invaders with the help of a magical sword. Topped by a small statue of the emperor, the 1896 monument is well-preserved and vibrant, bordered by an array of blooms and large shade trees. A sturdy pavilion obscures the base of the memorial where incense and other offerings are laid.

Behind the statue, **Nam Huong Temple** honors the emperor and a handful of other deified citizens. It once served as a popular gathering place for writers, poets, and scholars, moving to its present location at the turn of the 20th century. While the temple is small (the width of the room is about five paces), the emperor's altar holds a riot of colorful offerings, decorative statues, and a few lacquered wooden tablets.

FRENCH QUARTER
Opera House

The capital's grand old Opera House (1 Trang Tien, tel. 04/3933-0113, www.hanoioperahouse.org.vn) is a stately structure overlooking the frenzied August Revolution Square. The theater, a yellow-and-white behemoth built in the colonial style, took a decade to complete, first opening its doors in 1911. Back then, only European performers were invited onto the stage and French colonists made up most of the audience. By 1940, Vietnamese citizens were able to rent out the massive hall, modeled after Paris's own opera house. When politics took center stage in 1945 and Vietnam declared its independence from the French, Hanoi's Opera House served as a meeting venue for gatherings of the new government.

Performances take place year-round. The opulent theater seats 598 spectators over three levels. Though visitors aren't permitted to wander around indoors, the exterior is worth a look while you're in the French Quarter.

National Museum of History and Revolutionary Museum

Housed in the former Louis Finot Museum, Vietnam's National Museum of History (1 Pham Ngu Lao, tel. 04/3824-1384, www.baotanglichsu.vn, 8am-noon and 1:30pm-5pm daily, VND40,000) showcases over 200,000 artifacts, documents, and historic relics. The main building is devoted to ancient civilizations such as the Sa Huynh, Oc Eo, and Champa, along with northern Vietnam's Dong Son, a culture which existed roughly in 1000 BC-AD 100 and whose large bronze drums are a symbol of Vietnam. Scores of artifacts, mostly stone implements, pottery, and jewelry, occupy the downstairs level, while the museum's upper floor packs in several centuries of dynastic rule, from the Dinh and Le eras of the AD 900s to Vietnam's last emperors, the Nguyen dynasty, whose ornate everyday items, from mother-of-pearl inlaid dressers to enamel jars, detailed ceramics, and vibrant lacquerware take up a display to themselves.

Despite a fair amount of English signage throughout the building, a lack of general historical information can leave non-Vietnamese speakers adrift.

Where the National Museum of History leaves off, with the text of Uncle Ho's famous declaration of independence, given at Ba Dinh Square on September 2, 1945, the Revolutionary Museum across the street picks up, with a slightly smaller range of documents, artifacts, and propaganda from the Franco-Vietnam and American Wars.

Entry to both museums is included in the ticket price, and visitors can spread out their visits over more than one day. There is a camera fee (VND15,000) to take photos within the museums. Both museums are closed the first Monday of the month.

Vietnamese Women's Museum

One of Hanoi's better offerings, the Vietnamese Women's Museum (36 Ly Thuong Kiet, tel. 04/3825-9936, www. baotangphunu.org.vn, 8am-5pm daily, VND30,000) takes a comprehensive look at the country's female citizens. Permanent exhibits cover everything from marriage and birth customs to family life, the crucial role of women in Vietnamese history, and the varied traditions practiced by ethnic minorities, all with ample English signage. A handful of temporary displays also pass through the modern, three-story building. The museum's clear organization places the museum a cut above many others in the city.

Hoa Lo Prison

In the heart of the French Quarter is a small

French Quarter

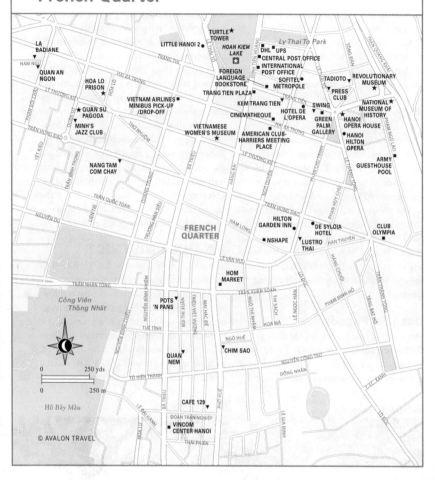

portion of **Hoa Lo Prison** (Hoa Lo and Hai Ba Trung, tel. 04/3824-6358, 8am-5pm daily, VND20,000, free for children under 15), the infamous jail that once housed thousands of Vietnamese revolutionaries during colonialism and, later, American prisoners of war. While most of the original complex has been demolished, the remainder of Hoa Lo serves as a museum, documenting its history and the struggles of its inmates.

Built by the French at the end of the 19th century, the facility then known as the Maison Centrale quickly surpassed its original 450-prisoner capacity, overflowing with nationalist Vietnamese who had rebelled against colonial rule. As many as 2,000 inmates were crammed in at one time, making for dismal conditions on top of the torture doled out by French prison guards. The museum holds ample evidence of these transgressions, including life-sized mannequins of Vietnamese prisoners, lined up and shackled at the feet, as well as a guillotine used by the colonial government during the early 20th century. Following the Franco-Vietnam and American Wars, several of Hoa Lo's inmates went on to serve as high-ranking officials in the Vietnamese Communist Party.

From the 1960s onward, the prison earned a new nickname. Dubbed the "Hanoi Hilton" by American soldiers, the complex was re-purposed by north Vietnamese forces for prisoners of war. Here, the story fractures into two separate accounts: that of its captives—including U.S. Senator John McCain, who spent over five years at Hoa Lo—who recall torture and brutality; and that of the Vietnamese government, which paints a rosy portrait of life on the inside, complete with Christmas dinners and organized sports.

The museum has a small memorial to its Vietnamese prisoners at the back of the complex. Visitors are free to wander the exhibits at their leisure. Skip the information booklets on sale at the ticket booth, as much of their text is featured on signs throughout the museum.

Quan Su Pagoda

Just south of Hoa Lo Prison, the wide yellow **Quan Su Pagoda** (Chua Quan Su, 73 Quan Su, 8am-11am and 1pm-4pm daily, free) is one of Hanoi's most popular centers of worship and is home to the Buddhist Association of Vietnam. Though it's not the city's oldest or even its most decorated pagoda, Quan Su, also known as the Ambassador's Pagoda, began in the 15th century as a guesthouse for visiting emissaries from Buddhist countries and has only grown since then. The current building was constructed in 1942 and features a dimly lit congregation of Buddha effigies on the main altar, a many-armed Quan Am, and a small section dedicated to local martyrs. Despite its downtown location, the pagoda courtyard is a peaceful place most days, though dozens gather here during religious festivals and holidays. For anything and everything Buddhism-related, check out the surrounding shops, where scores of religious books, relics, and other goods are sold.

BA DINH DISTRICT

You could easily pass a day in Ba Dinh District, where many of Hanoi's most prominent historical monuments cluster together south of West Lake. Though these sights focus on Vietnam's 20th-century history, much of it war-related or steeped in Communism, there are a few other worthy attractions in the area, such as the city's Museum of Fine Arts and the centuries-old Temple of Literature.

Ho Chi Minh Mausoleum

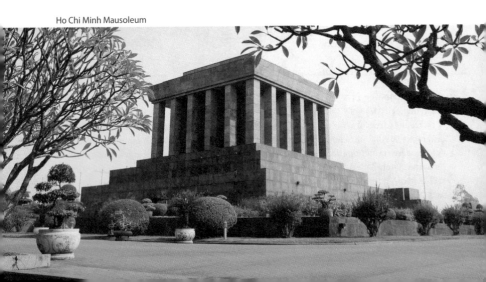

Ba Dinh District

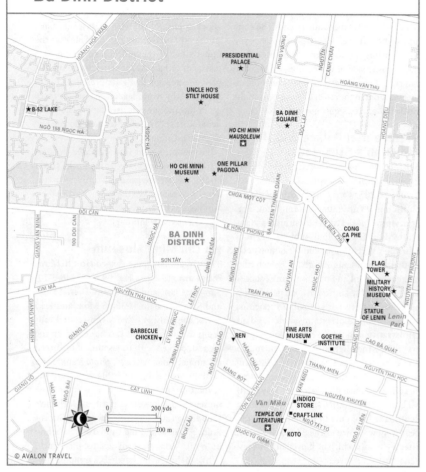

© AVALON TRAVEL

★ Ho Chi Minh Mausoleum

A stark stone cube occupying the western edge of massive Ba Dinh Square, the **Ho Chi Minh Mausoleum** (Ba Dinh Square, tel. 04/3845-5128, www.bqllang.gov.vn, 7:30am-10:30am Tues.-Thurs., 7:30am-11am Sat.-Sun. in summer, 8am-11am Tues.-Thurs., 8am-11:30am Sat.-Sun. in winter, free) bears only the words "President Ho Chi Minh" on its exterior. Guarded day and night by police in crisp white uniforms, this is perhaps one of Hanoi's most bizarre sights. On most mornings, dozens of local visitors line up to catch a glimpse of their leader's embalmed body. The swift, two-line procession moves indoors past one of Uncle Ho's most famous quotations—"Nothing is more precious than independence and freedom"—before gliding in a semi-circle around the body and back outside. Upon his death in 1969, Uncle Ho requested to be cremated and his ashes scattered in three parts throughout the north, south, and central regions of Vietnam, a wish that was obviously ignored.

Respectful dress is a must. Strict silence is observed indoors and no photography or camera equipment is permitted beyond the security checkpoint at the southern end of Ba Dinh Square, nor is the use of cell phones. Once you enter the line, it moves quickly, letting out on the opposite side of the building, where you can collect your electronics and carry on, either back out to the street or to any one of the Uncle Ho-related sights nearby.

Presidential Palace and Ho Chi Minh's Stilt House

Behind Ho Chi Minh's mausoleum, the **Presidential Palace** (1 Bach Thao, tel. 04/0804-4287, www.dutichhochiminhphuchutich.gov.vn, 7:30am-11am Mon.-Fri., 2pm-4pm Tues.-Thurs. in summer, 8am-11am Mon.-Fri., 1:30pm-4pm Tues.-Thurs. in winter, VND25,000) and his famous **stilt house** are remnants of both the French colonial government and its Communist successors. The bright, sunflower-hued palace, once home to the governor general of Indochina, served as both a private residence and administrative building for the colonial powers. Following Vietnam's independence, it was expected that Uncle Ho, as president, would move into the massive house. Instead, he converted the building into a solely political and administrative structure. The president made his home in a smaller structure nearby, now known as the 54 House, named after the year in which he moved in. This residence was short-lived.

At the same time, Ho Chi Minh commissioned a wooden stilt house, built in the style of Vietnam's ethnic minorities, where he lived for most of his remaining days. The modest, two-story building features an open ground floor, used for business, and sparsely furnished living quarters upstairs. The nearby fish pond and mango trees occupied much of the president's down time. A third and equally humble residence sits on the far side of the stilt house, completed in 1967 out of concern for Uncle Ho's well-being, as American bombs began to rain down on Hanoi in greater

numbers. Ho Chi Minh passed away here in September 1969.

Visitors can't access the Presidential Palace, which opens only for visiting heads of state. At the stilt house, you can only observe the upper floor of the building on an adjacent platform. A handful of artifacts are on display, including a few gifts presented to Ho Chi Minh by world leaders, as well as three gleaming antique cars used by the late president for travel, two of which were donated by the Soviet Union.

For more insight into this area, request a free English-speaking guide at the ticket booth. Guides are primarily university students who have taken the job to practice their language skills, so don't be surprised if the tour isn't terribly thorough.

Ho Chi Minh Museum

The gargantuan, lotus-shaped **Ho Chi Minh Museum** (19 Ngoc Ha, tel. 04/3846-3757, 8am-11:30am and 2pm-4pm Tues.-Thurs. and Sat.-Sun, 8am-11:30am Mon. and Fri.) is not the only Ho Chi Minh-related museum in Vietnam, but it is hands-down the biggest, packed with thousands of historical documents and artifacts, photographs, and exhibits on the life and achievements of the revolutionary leader. Over two floors, the museum's displays cover much of Uncle Ho's time abroad and his involvement in politics in France, China, and the United States, before his return to take up arms against the French. While there is heavy-handed Communist glorification and the English signage fails to offer big-picture synopses of Ho Chi Minh's life, it's a worthwhile attraction for history buffs. Before visiting, read even just a few paragraphs about Ho Chi Minh for a better appreciation of the exhibits.

One Pillar Pagoda

The short, squat **One Pillar Pagoda (Chua Mot Cot)** (6am-11am and 2pm-6pm daily, free) is dwarfed by the grand Communist monuments nearby, but it bears an interesting origin story. Standing at 13 feet high, the modest shrine, dedicated to Quan Am, is believed to date back to AD 1049, during the reign of emperor Ly Thai Tong. The legend goes that the inspiration for the pagoda came to the emperor in a dream, but there are conflicting versions of what the vision contained. Some say that the emperor dreamed of Quan Am sitting on a lotus blossom, holding a baby boy in her arms. The emperor, who wished for a son, became a father shortly thereafter and erected the monument as a thank-you to Quan Am. Given that Ly Thai Tong's son was born a few years before he ascended the throne in 1028, it doesn't seem likely that this version is correct.

The second version says that the emperor dreamed of Quan Am bringing him to a lotus lamp. Ly Thai Tong's mandarins worried that it was a bad omen. In an effort to counteract this negativity, the emperor commissioned the pagoda, paying homage to Quan Am.

The pagoda has undergone countless restorations and was rebuilt in 1249 and again in 1954, after the French destroyed it. Opposite the small shrine, **Dien Huu Pagoda** is a newer, more colorful building filled with a collection of statues and shrines that pairs nicely with a stroll up the steps of One Pillar.

The pagoda's proximity to Ho Chi Minh Museum and Ho Chi Minh Mausoleum makes it a frequent stop for visitors in Ba Dinh.

B-52 Lake

B-52 Lake (Ho Huu Tiep) (Ngo 158 Ngoc Ha or Ngo 55 Hoang Hoa Tham) sits amid a sleepy residential neighborhood, all but forgotten. Faded into Hanoi's everyday bustle, its tepid green waters serve as the backdrop for morning commutes, daily garbage collection, and the comings and goings of street vendors. Stretching up from the lake's surface is a stark reminder of the not-so-distant past: the mangled husk of a B-52 fighter jet, shot down during the 1972 Christmas bombings that rocked northern Vietnam. While much of the nearby landscape has changed, the lake remains frozen in time, a modest but powerful visual.

B-52 Lake elicits mixed reactions. For history and war buffs, it's a worthwhile stop paired with a visit to Ho Chi Minh Mausoleum and other surrounding sights. There is a simple plaque that stands at the near end of the water, and the plane's wreckage is surprisingly small.

To reach B-52 Lake you'll have to navigate several small alleys. Keep an eye out for signs that read "Ho B-52" or "Ho Huu Tiep" (the

altar outside of Dien Huu Pagoda

original name of the lake), as there are no English signs.

Military History Museum

The national **Military History Museum** (28A Dien Bien Phu, tel. 04/3823-4264, www. btlsqsvn.org.vn, 8am-11:30am and 1pm-4pm Tues.-Thurs. and Sat.-Sun., VND40,000) gathers various artifacts from Vietnam's two most prominent 20th-century wars, against French and American forces, within a bright white building. The indoor displays feature photos of the destruction that occurred.

The museum's outdoor exhibits provide more intrigue, with a sizable collection of military aircraft and ammunition, including one of the famous tanks that crashed through the gates of Saigon's Independence Palace on April 30, 1975, ending the American War. The museum highlights the cunning and resilience of a nation that, equipped with few resources, took on one of the world's most powerful armies and prevailed.

The grounds of the Military History Museum house Hanoi's red brick **Flag Tower,** a remnant of the imperial era built by emperor Gia Long in 1812. While it is possible to enter the tower and take the steps up to the highest of its platforms, those who pass on the museum can still see the monument from the street, and the photos are just as good, if not better, from here. The museum charges a camera fee (VND30,000), which includes the outdoor exhibits.

★ Temple of Literature

Hanoi's **Temple of Literature** (58 Quoc Tu Giam, tel. 04/3845-2917, 8am-5pm daily winter, 7:30am-5:30pm daily summer, VND20,000) hearkens back to AD 1070, when emperor Ly Thanh Tong ordered the construction of this temple complex. In 1076, emperor Ly Nhan Tong inaugurated Vietnam's first university, Quoc Tu Giam, on the long, rectangular grounds. The professors were court-appointed mandarins, who taught lessons on Confucianism, administration, literature, and poetry.

main gate at the Temple of Literature

While the university no longer stands, its grounds still hold an attractive garden, several lotus ponds, and the temple itself. Outside the main gate, a pair of stone engravings (in traditional Vietnamese characters) commands visitors to dismount from their horses. Through the imposing front door is a pleasant garden, filled with bright red flowers and frangipani trees. Lanterns line the central walkway that leads to the Khue Van pavilion, built in 1805, a tall, ornamental structure topped with bright red lacquered wood.

The temple's most famous attractions rest upon 82 giant stone tortoises, meant to symbolize wisdom and longevity. The 82 stelae honor Quoc Tu Giam's doctoral graduates listing 1,304 names. While you aren't allowed to wander through the rows of stelae, you can see the stone tablets up close.

The courtyard before the Temple of Literature once held altars for 72 of the most respected students to study under Confucius and, later, Chu Van An, a 13th-century scholar considered the father of Vietnamese education. The altar has been replaced with souvenir vendors hawking incense and a few interesting handicrafts.

The temple itself is divided into two sections. Under the first roof, a high altar sits in the open air, flanked by tortoise and crane statues. Everything from the ironwood columns to the gold Chinese inscriptions shines with a heavy lacquer, and incense fills the air. Beyond the high door—used to ensure entrants bow their heads in respect—is a large statue of Confucius and his disciples, dressed in lavish robes. A gold-plated ceramic tortoise sits to the left, while several smaller altars line the outskirts of the room.

Behind the temple are the original university grounds, now known as Thai Hoc courtyard. Completed in 2000, this area is dedicated to three Vietnamese emperors: Ly Thanh Tong, responsible for the original temple's construction, Ly Nhan Tong, founder of the national university, and Le Thanh Tong, the ruler who commissioned the first of the stelae.

While signage within the temple complex is fairly sparse, visitors can hire a guide (VND100,000) at the ticket booth or buy the information booklet (VND8,000). Though nothing beats a knowledgeable and enthusiastic guide, the booklet provides insight and historical background for a fraction of the cost.

WEST LAKE AREA
West Lake

North of the Old Quarter, West Lake (Ho Tay) is Hanoi's largest body of water and is a center for the city's wealthier residents. Ringed with luxury hotels and high-end restaurants, the lake once served as the northern frontier for Thang Long citadel. Of the legends related to the lake's origin, the most popular one goes that the area was once a forest, terrorized by a nine-tailed demon, which Lac Long Quan, original leader of the Vietnamese people, drowned in the waters of West Lake. Another story goes that an 11th-century monk by the name of Khong Lo traveled to China to aid the emperor and, as a reward for his services,

carried home large amounts of bronze. He used that bronze to make a bell with a sound so powerful that it confused a golden calf, who mistook the noise for its mother calling and, in his hurry to find her, created the deep rut that would form West Lake.

A narrow strip of land runs between West Lake and small Truc Bach. Though these two bodies of water were originally one, the southern lake received its own name after the completion of the Co Ngu causeway, upon which Tran Quoc Pagoda now sits. Truc Bach is remembered in Vietnam's war history as the site where, on October 26, 1967, American pilot John McCain parachuted into the water after his plane was shot down. Vietnamese civilians rescued the pilot before turning him in to Hoa Lo, where he spent over five years as a prisoner of war. A plaque near the lakeshore commemorates the event.

A trip to West Lake provides plenty of peace and quiet, and the lake boasts a 10-mile road around its shoreline, making for a scenic stroll or bike ride.

Tran Quoc Pagoda

One of Hanoi's oldest houses of worship, the Tran Quoc Pagoda (Thanh Nien/Co Ngu causeway, 7:30am-11:30am and 1:30pm-6:30pm daily, free) dates back to the 6th century, when its first incarnation was built on the banks of the Red River during the reign of emperor Ly Nam De. Its current home looks out over the gentle waters of West Lake and provides lovely views of the surrounding area.

Through a large yellow gate, the front half of Tran Quoc houses a collection of colorful stupas dwarfed by the 11-tiered tower at their center, which houses a ring of white Buddha statues on all sides. From this courtyard, visitors are able to peek in on the pagoda's ancestral altars, which line the wall of a shallow room off to the right. Farther back, a larger clearing houses a broad, leafy bodhi tree, gifted to the pagoda in 1959 by Indian president Rajendra Prasad. The bodhi tree carries special religious significance, as it was under this type of tree that the Sakyamuni Buddha

West Lake Area

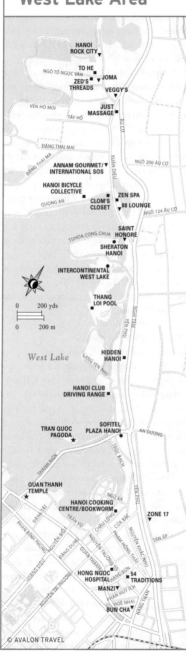

attained enlightenment in India. Another altar sits indoors, dedicated to Buddha and piled high with fruit offerings and lacquered ornamentation.

Quan Thanh Temple

As old as Hanoi itself, **Quan Thanh Temple** (corner of Quan Thanh and Thanh Nien, sunrise-sunset daily, VND10,000) was built in the 11th century under the reign of emperor Ly Thai To. Sitting just below West Lake, the temple honors Huyen Thien Tran Vu, protector of the city's northern gate, one of four directional deities who were believed to guard the Thang Long citadel in Hanoi's earliest days. The existing temple dates back to the 19th century and houses several precious antiques, including a 12-foot, four-ton statue of Tran Vu, cast in 1677, that takes up the back wall, as well as an oddly shaped gong from the 17th or 18th century. Through the temple's high white gate, a pair of stone elephants guard the courtyard leading up to Tran Vu's altar, lined with benches and large shade trees. Inside, lacquered woodwork decorates much of the shrine, while a photocopied map hangs on one of the building's columns, illustrating the parameters of Thang Long citadel and Quan Thanh Temple around 1490.

★ Vietnam Museum of Ethnology

Though it's removed from the rest of Hanoi's attractions, the **Vietnam Museum of Ethnology** (Nguyen Van Huyen, tel. 04/3756-2193, www.vme.org.vn, 8:30am-5:30pm Tues.-Sun., VND40,000) is worth a jaunt out to the western suburbs of the city. Opened in 1997, the large, round building, modeled after a Dong Son bronze drum, features exhibits on all 54 of Vietnam's ethnic communities, from the Kinh, or Vietnamese, who make up roughly 86 percent of the country's population, to dozens of minority groups, including the Cham, H'mong, Muong, Jarai, and Ede, many of whom live in the mountainous regions of northwestern and central Vietnam.

Ample signage guides visitors through the museum's vivid and educational exhibits, which cover customs, traditional dress, religion, architecture, farming techniques, handicrafts, and rituals practiced by each ethnicity. A small section on the 2nd floor organizes interactive activities for younger visitors, including traditional games and crafts.

Behind the building, several examples of traditional architecture are on display, including a stilted Ede longhouse and the soaring pitched roof of a Bahnar communal house, standing at 62 feet tall. **Water puppet performances** (10am, 11:30am, 2:30pm, and 4pm) take place several times a day in the pond nearby.

The museum is home to a small bookshop and souvenir store, as well as a café, run by the Hoa Sua School, an organization that trains disadvantaged Vietnamese youth. Book guided tours (VND100,000) ahead of time by calling the museum. There is also a camera fee (VND50,000) to take photos within the museum grounds.

To the right of the museum entrance is a building that curates a collection of cultural items from across Southeast Asia. Though still very much in its infancy, the Southeast Asian arm of the ethnology museum will feature the same in-depth displays on customs, styles of dress, handicrafts, religions, and other facets of culture within Vietnam and its neighboring nations. It's worth a peek while you're here.

SIGHTSEEING TOURS

In a city as accessible as Hanoi, city tours aren't entirely necessary, as most travelers are able to hit their preferred points of interest alone. There are plenty of standard, generic city tours around town; skip these since they don't enhance your Hanoian experience. A handful of outfits in the capital excel at providing urban excursions with a more personal touch.

Founded in 2006, **Hanoi Kids** (tel. 09/7816-2283, www.hanoikids.org, 9am-5pm daily) is a free, student-run tour service that pairs curious travelers with young Vietnamese hoping to practice their English. All guides participate in regular training sessions before hitting the town with their new foreign friends, and your only costs as a traveler are admission fees and transportation for you and your guide. With equal give and take, these young Hanoians are enthusiastic and outgoing, making the experience feel more like a friendly outing than a run-of-the-mill tour. Due to the popularity of the group, reserving

Chinese characters adorn the entrance of Quan Thanh Temple.

a spot ahead of time is a must. The booking department at Hanoi Kids sometimes needs a reminder. Confirm your tour in advance and, if response seems slow, give the office a call and check in.

A popular and reliable operator for tours both in town and around northern Vietnam, **Adventure Indochina** (1 Hang Buom, tel. 04/6683-5539, www.adventureindochina.com, 8am-8pm daily) arranges trips to Ha Long Bay and Sapa in addition to running city tours of Hanoi, cyclo excursions, a one-day journey focused around the city's pagodas, and a tasty street food tour. Staff are knowledgeable and efficient, and prices tend toward the more affordable end of the spectrum.

Just over two miles north of the Old Quarter, **Hidden Hanoi** (147 Nghi Tam, tel. 09/1225-4045, www.hiddenhanoi.com. vn, 9am-5pm daily Mon.-Sat., VND420,000-945,000) introduces travelers to the finer points of Vietnamese culture through food, language, and walking adventures around the city. Its popular cooking classes take place at the center's charming location on the eastern edge of West Lake, as do a handful of language courses. Several walking tours around the Old and French Quarters take place downtown along with a much-touted street food tour. Prices vary depending upon the activity, but all guides are enthusiastic and knowledgeable, making these tours a worthy investment.

Entertainment and Events

NIGHTLIFE

As the sun sets over the capital, Hanoi's nightlife festivities take place in fast-forward, unraveling in a few short hours between sundown and midnight. By 6pm or 7pm, work has barely let out but locals line the streets, gathering on clusters of low, plastic stools to enjoy fresh beer and *do nhau* (drinking food), as they rehash the day's events. An hour later, nightlife is in full swing, with droves of foreigners and Vietnamese packed onto the makeshift furniture of so many independent beer vendors, noshing on grilled meat or snails, a local favorite, washed down with any one of the country's local brews. The streets of the Old Quarter are especially lively, drawing people from all walks of life.

Across town, the well-heeled pay a visit to swanky cocktail lounges and upmarket watering holes around West Lake and throughout the French Quarter, where top-shelf spirits, terrace seating, and mellow mood music speak to a more refined ambience, while the catch-all bar-and-restaurants near St. Joseph's Cathedral sling cheap beers and other beverages in a casual, laid-back environment. Wherever you are, the night reaches its peak around 9pm, and from there things run on their own steam until midnight, when a fairly strict curfew is enforced and most businesses close their doors for the evening. A handful of bars quietly remain open for another hour or so.

There is hope for late-night revelers. As a city that prides itself very much on traditional values, Hanoi has been resistant to progress on the nightlife front, but several business owners attempted to push the envelope recently. During the second half of 2013, a short-lived but influential neighborhood known as Zone 9, situated a mile south of Hoan Kiem Lake, gave rise to a promising flourish of artistic and cultural venues, but it was promptly and inexplicably shut down by local police only a few months later. While the blow was a setback to Hanoi's after-dark scene, it made an impression on young locals and expats, offering a hopeful glimpse of the city's late-night future.

Bars

Dimly lit and heavily outfitted in red lacquered woodwork, the lovable, laid-back **Mao's Red Lounge** (7 Ta Hien, tel. 04/3926-3104,

Hanoi's Craft Beer Scene

As the workday comes to a close and an army of motorbikes floods the city streets, the place to be in the capital is a small plastic chair by the roadside with an ice-cold glass of *bia hoi* in hand. This light, refreshing lager is a staple of northern nightlife, drawing crowds to the bustling sidewalks of downtown Hanoi on a daily basis. What sets this particular brew apart is its makeup: Local breweries concoct the amber liquid using basic beer ingredients like hops, yeast, and rice. Without any preservatives or additional chemicals, the beer's shelf life becomes especially brief, with most *bia hoi* unfit to drink by the end of the night. Local establishments must plan ahead, ordering just enough to last a single day. In the wee hours of the morning, a representative goes to the brewery to pick up an order of *bia hoi*. From the time

tourists and locals enjoying *bia hoi*

it reaches the premises, shopkeepers work to unload as much of their stock as possible, slinging drinks throughout the day, but the rush comes in the evenings, when Hanoi's sidewalks come alive and a healthy drinking culture helps to push sales along. *Bia hoi* is often enjoyed with street-side snacks, known as *do nhau* in Vietnamese. The brew comes in at roughly four percent alcohol by volume, making it a highly drinkable beverage, if a little watery. Best of all, its price tag runs no higher than VND5,000 in the big city, making it far and away the most affordable beverage around. You can also look for the slightly more expensive *bia tuoi*, a similar recipe with a bit more flavor. Both varieties are commonly translated as "fresh beer."

There are many *bia hoi* shops in downtown Hanoi. The most popular is often referred to as **bia hoi corner** (corner of Ta Hien and Luong Ngoc Quyen, 10am-midnight daily, VND5,000/glass). While not all of the corner shops serve genuine *bia hoi*, you'll find plenty of the brew on the southeast edge of the junction. Beyond this swarm of nighttime activity, a clutch of more locally frequented *bia hoi* are situated around Bat Dan and Duong Thanh near the western side of the Old Quarter, though you won't find any English speakers here. For a more detailed list of the many *bia hoi* watering holes, the Hanoi Bia Hoi's website (www.squeakieice.com/hanoi-bia-hoi) offers a helpful interactive map that covers the most popular *bia hoi* locations in Hanoi's five main districts.

5pm-midnight daily, VND25,000-80,000) is staffed by a friendly crowd and offers reasonable prices on beer, wine, and cocktails. Barside seating, low tables, and a few outdoor spots afford drinkers their pick of atmosphere. The place usually sees at least a steady trickle of visitors in the evenings.

Another laid-back backpacker hangout, **The Coach House** (37 Dao Duy Tu, tel. 09/1204-1416, 4pm-midnight daily, VND20,000-70,000) offers daily drink specials on its range of beer and cocktails. Grab a seat indoors, where contemporary music and walls full of photos give personality to the space, along with its comfy seating and an

array of cobbled-together wooden furniture, or stay outside, enjoying your evening from a low table just beyond the door. The place never gets truly busy, but it has a fun crowd of regulars and an easygoing atmosphere.

True to its name, the **Polite Pub** (5B Bao Khanh, tel. 00/0419-8086, 5pm-midnight daily, VND35,000-150,000) serves as a slightly more upscale watering hole than some of its Old Quarter competition farther north without getting too pretentious. Tucked down a quiet street off Hoan Kiem Lake, the cozy venue serves a list of beer, wine, spirits, and cocktails. Ample seating is available up front, while a pool table occupies the back room.

Lounges

A cozy street-side lounge not far from the Opera House, **Tadioto** (24B Tong Dan, tel. 04/6680-9124, 9am-midnight daily, VND35,000-270,000) exudes a laid-back vibe with plush couches, leather bar stools, and bright red French doors in a prime people-watching neighborhood. Prices are reasonable and a happy hour drink looking out onto Tong Dan is worthwhile. The bar boasts an assortment of beer, wine, and cocktails.

From a rooftop in the French Quarter, Hanoi's chic and sophisticated **Press Club** (59A Ly Thai To and 12 Ly Dao Thanh, tel. 04/3934-0888, www.hanoi-pressclub.com, 7am-10:30pm daily, VND95,000-300,000) affords pleasant views of one of the city's most upscale neighborhoods as well as a range of signature cocktails, top-shelf spirits, wine, and beer. Seating is available indoors at the Press Club's elegant bar or outside on a breezy, palm-fringed terrace. Live music acts occasionally pop up here, while regular drink specials, like the Thursday buy-two-get-one-free deal, run throughout the week.

The swanky and sophisticated **88 Lounge** (88 Xuan Dieu, tel. 04/3718-8029, www.88group.vn, 11am-midnight daily, VND50,000-400,000) overlooks West Lake, with three floors of open-air seating that afford top-notch views of the water from an array of antique upholstered chairs. Pair this with dim lighting, a well-stocked downstairs bar, and an impressive collection of fine wines on display and the place is a hit, functioning as one of the neighborhood's best stand-alone lounges. Prices are steep, but these folks know their wines, not to mention everything else, from whiskey and scotch to soju, sake, and tequila.

Clubs

Loud, lively, and filled with nonstop energy, **Dragonfly** (15 Hang Buom, tel. 09/3699-3557, 7pm-midnight daily, VND40,000-100,000) is a small Hanoian version of a nightclub, slipped between the shops along Hang Buom. Those looking for a spot to let loose on the dance floor will appreciate the up-tempo beats and cheap drinks. For a slightly quieter atmosphere, head to the second floor, though don't expect to leave here without at least a little hearing damage.

When all the other bars have closed and the rest of Hanoi is calling it a night, the fun begins at **Zone 17** (17D Hong Ha, tel. 09/7843-5453, 9pm-6am daily, VND30,000-100,000), a rare after-hours venue in a city where midnight curfew is heavily enforced. Sporting exposed brick walls and bamboo furnishings, the spacious bar holds regular events, including guest DJs and the occasional live music performance. Even on quiet evenings, a cheerful atmosphere and a steady stream of nighttime revelers keep the place busy. Though Zone 17 opens its doors at 9pm, time your visit later in the evening, as the party doesn't really get underway before midnight.

Live Music

Every evening from 9pm, the second floor of the Hotlife Cafe on Quan Su becomes **Minh's Jazz Club** (65 Quan Su, tel. 04/3942-0400, www.minhjazzvietnam.com, 9pm-midnight daily, VND60,000-200,000), a loud and lively lounge that showcases the best of Hanoi's jazz talent. Self-taught saxophonist and accomplished musician Quyen Van Minh, the club's owner, has cultivated an appreciation of jazz in the city, drawing nightly crowds into the intimate café for an impressive live performance. No cover charge is required, though prices double at showtime to accommodate for the musicians.

Bright and eye-catching, the main entrance of **Swing** (21 Trang Tien, tel. 04/3824-5395, www.swinglounge.com.vn, 7am-midnight daily, VND35,000-190,000) is decked out in high-wattage light bulbs, announcing this chic musical venue from a block away. Though it moonlights as an upscale café for the business crowd during the day, the lounge is at its best after dark, when the entire black-and-white space is transformed by nightly performances. The usual beer, wine, and cocktails are on offer, as well as non-alcoholic café beverages, and cozy sofa seating is scattered throughout. Music begins at 9pm and runs until closing time.

Buried down an alley north of West Lake, **Hanoi Rock City** (27/52 To Ngoc Van, tel. 018/8748-7426, www.hanoirockcity.com, 4pm-midnight Sun.-Thurs., 4pm-3am Fri.-Sat., VND50,000-200,000) continues to make its mark on Hanoi's live music scene as one of the premier venues for both local and international artists to showcase their talent. Boasting a spacious interior as well as a sprawling garden area, the funky West Lake venue also hosts the occasional DJ or film screening and keeps a regular list of upcoming acts on its website and Facebook page. Events usually include a cover charge, though it's never more than VND100,000.

THE ARTS

Hanoi boasts a glut of Vietnam's most talented artists, from musicians and photographers to lacquer painters, sculptors, and masters of traditional theater and puppetry. Scores of small, independent galleries and cultural centers exist alongside more formal institutions like the national Museum of Fine Arts and Hanoi's imposing Opera House. Even cafés and a few other small venues have gotten in on the city's arts and culture scene with small film screenings, ongoing exhibitions, artist talks, and other events. For the most up-to-date information, keep an eye on *The Word* (www.wordhanoi.com), whose online and print editions include an events calendar with upcoming shows, concerts, exhibitions, and other performances, as well as **Hanoi Grapevine** (www.hanoigrapevine.com), another reliable event-listing site.

Performing Arts

For everything from ballet to orchestral music, jazz concerts, piano recitals, operas, and traditional Vietnamese theater, Hanoi's historic **Opera House** (1 Trang Tien, tel. 04/3933-0113, www.hanoioperahouse.org.vn, box office: 8am-5pm daily) is the go-to venue.

The talented musicians of the **Hanoi Ca Tru Club** (42-44 Hang Bac, tel. 09/8967-9829, www.catru.vn, 8pm Wed., Fri., and Sun., VND210,000) put on thrice-weekly performances in the heart of the Old Quarter. In a small, intimate space, the 70-minute show celebrates *ca tru*, a centuries-old form of northern Vietnamese poetry set to music, typically featuring one female singer, a male instrumentalist, and a drummer. While the traditional music is well-known throughout the Red River Delta area, *ca tru* is something of a dying art, as most of its musicians are older and the dwindling number of performers have made *ca tru* troupes harder to come by in modern times. Today, accomplished musicians keep the tradition alive through regular shows, usually for foreign visitors. Each performance features a small audience and often requires participation on the part of the attendees. Hanoi Ca Tru Club does a nice job of providing background information on the musical traditions of the north as well as how to join in.

Tickets can be purchased throughout the week, with typical box office hours (8am-5pm), though you'll still be able to snag a seat on the evening of a performance, provided there are spots available. Book your ticket a day in advance. If you can't finagle a seat with the Hanoi Ca Tru Club, you can also try the **Thang Long Ca Tru Club** (87 Ma May, tel. 012/2326-6897, www.catruthanglong.com, 8pm Tues., Thurs., and Sat., VND210,000), another well-known local troupe.

The vivacious characters of **Thang Long Water Puppet Theater** (57B Dinh Tien Hoang, tel. 04/3824-9494, www.thanglongwaterpuppet.org, 1:45pm-9:15pm daily, VND100,000) know how to make a splash, zipping across their watery stage several times a day at Hanoi's best-known *mua roi* (water puppet) venue. As early as the 11th century, rice paddies and other shallow waters in the Red River Delta served as performance spaces for these lacquered wooden puppets and their masters, who maneuver the characters from behind a bamboo screen. Nowadays, the performances, combined with lively voice actors and traditional Vietnamese music are a popular cultural attraction for visitors to the city. Each show runs around 50 minutes, featuring a handful of individual vignettes. While the performance takes place in Vietnamese, the watery antics of these puppets provide enough information that no translation is necessary.

Museums

Spread over three floors, exhibits at the city's **Museum of Fine Arts** (66 Nguyen Thai Hoc, tel. 04/3823-3084, www.vnfam.vn, 8:30am-5pm daily, VND30,000) cover the creative achievements of Vietnamese painters, sculptors, and other craftspeople from the 11th century onward. Beginning with the stone and wood carvings of several of Vietnam's early dynasties, displays proceed chronologically through the country's artistic development, showcasing beautiful functional pieces and religious relics from the earliest days of the empire before carrying on to the 19th- and 20th-century fusion of Western ideas and materials with Vietnamese aesthetics. The resulting artwork, which includes vivid lacquer paintings alongside other mediums, like oil and acrylic, remains straightforward, depicting everyday Vietnamese scenes, portraits, and still life renderings. The most recent paintings hail from the 1980s and '90s. Its sole showroom of conceptual art is a letdown. The museum overall is a rewarding stop on your tour of the city and remains intriguing for both its artwork and the visible evolution of ideas over the years. Visitors are free to explore the many rooms of this 1930s colonial building on their own; a handy map is provided upon arrival that helps guide you through the museum's many numbered exhibits.

One part art space, one part café, the hip and happening **Manzi** (14 Phan Huy Ich, tel. 04/3716-3397, 9am-midnight daily) sits a few blocks beyond the Old Quarter and hosts regular art exhibitions, talks, film screenings, and music and dance performances within its updated French colonial digs. White walls and minimal furniture give the place a gallery feel. Visitors are invited to sit and enjoy the café, either downstairs amid the calm of alley life or upstairs with the art. Both international and Vietnamese artists have been featured in Manzi's two-story space, and its rotating schedule of cultural performances and events is updated regularly on Facebook.

Located just behind the Temple of Literature and a short walk from the Museum of Fine Arts, Hanoi's **Goethe Institute** (56-58 Nguyen Thai Hoc, tel. 04/3734-2251, www.goethe.de, 9am-7pm daily) remains an active part of the local art scene, holding regular exhibits, workshops, and film screenings in its **DOCLAB.** Many of these events are free and open to the public. Check out the institute's website or Facebook page for a list of upcoming exhibitions.

The pristine white walls of **Green Palm Gallery** (15 Trang Tien, tel. 04/3936-4757, www.greenpalmgallery.com, 8am-8pm daily) display some of Hanoi's top contemporary talents, such as Nguyen Thanh Binh, Nguyen The Dung, and Nguyen Manh Hung. With a layout that pays homage to traditional Vietnamese architecture, paintings and sculptures are spread out over three rooms, separated at the center by a small courtyard. Each piece is given its due space, and knowledgeable employees are on hand to answer questions. The gallery also has a second location (39 Hang Gai, tel. 09/1321-8496, 8am-8pm daily) closer to downtown, but the Trang Tien branch offers more peace and quiet.

Rabbit Hole Art House (102 Hang Gai, 2nd Fl., tel. 04/3928-5056, www.rabbitholearthouse.com, 8am-8pm daily) is a modest space where a collective of young, up-and-coming Hanoian artists displays its masterpieces. Crossing a variety of mediums, from sculpture and oil painting to lacquer and ink illustrations, this one-room gallery offers a window into Hanoi's contemporary art scene.

With a laundry list of featured artists, the **Apricot Gallery** (40B Hang Bong, tel. 04/3828-8965, www.apricotgallery.com.vn, 8am-8pm daily) is one of Hanoi's most established showrooms, bringing together a variety of materials and aesthetic styles under one roof. Paintings tend to be oil or acrylic, though there are a few lacquer works here, too, and the long, narrow exhibit space, which extends a few floors up above, offers plenty to admire as you wander from room to room.

Cinema

For a dose of Western culture, the local **CGV** (6th Fl. Vincom Center, 191 Ba Trieu, tel. 04/3974-3333, www.cgv.vn, 8am-midnight daily, VND100,000-115,000) movie theater plays Hollywood blockbusters in English and features all your usual cinematic accoutrements, including a concession stand, 3D glasses, and Dolby digital. Tickets can be purchased at the theater or online.

Buried behind the stocky, square-shaped buildings that run unbroken along Hai Ba Trung, **Cinematheque** (22A Hai Ba Trung, tel. 04/3936-2648, 7pm and 9pm daily, VND60,000) is Hanoi's only art-house cinema. A happy departure from your average trip to the movies, this independent film club hosts daily screenings that run the spectrum from classic films to documentaries, independent shorts, and beyond. Outside the viewing room, a small bar sits in its interior courtyard, removed from the street noise and dotted with plants, while the theater-style seating indoors makes for a genuine cinematic experience without the crowds and noise of a local movie theater. Showings take place at 7pm and 9pm each night; these times can fluctuate, occasionally opting for just one showing at 7pm. Call ahead and inquire about movies and screening times. While Cinematheque is technically a members-only club, first-time visitors are able to join once, provided they pay the mandatory donation fee.

FESTIVALS AND EVENTS

While this celebration sweeps across the whole country, Hanoi's festivities during the **Mid-Autumn Festival** (early-mid Sept.) are especially lively. The holiday, which falls on the 15th day of the eighth lunar month, typically takes place during the first half of September and features scores of colorful decorations. Brightly hued paper lanterns hang from every shop and house in the city, many of them originating from **Hang Ma,** which becomes the city's very own *pho long den* (lantern street) in the weeks leading up to the celebration. Running the gamut from traditional red-and-yellow lanterns to cartoon-shaped paper torches, shops along this narrow Old Quarter road do big business for the holiday, as local families, many of them with young children, partake in the festivities with paper lanterns and moon cake *(banh trung thu),* a round, dense pastry whose reputation is not unlike fruitcake at Christmastime: pretty, ornamental, and not nearly as delicious as it looks.

Shopping

Hanoi's compact and chaotic Old Quarter is a microcosm of dressmakers and tailors, craftspeople, carpenters, souvenir vendors, and galleries. One-stop convenience may elude the city's busy streets, but avid shoppers will appreciate the Hanoian retail experience, stumbling upon small, charming boutiques and modest, out-of-the-way shops, each bringing its own unique personality to the multifaceted neighborhood. Independent designers and skilled artisans display their finest wares, often at a price, while mass-produced items like T-shirts, buttons, and hats fill the narrow crevices between buildings, allowing travelers of all budgets to partake in Hanoi's commercial streets. While most of the city's downtown businesses use price tags, the cost of common souvenirs is negotiable wherever you are.

MARKETS
Dong Xuan Market

The sprawling **Dong Xuan Market** (Dong Xuan and Cau Dong, tel. 04/3828-2170, www.dongxuanmarket.com.vn, 6am-6pm daily), just west of Long Bien Bridge, packs everything under the sun into its two-story shelter. The French-built trading center is a Hanoian institution, famous for its array of products and so popular that it has spilled out onto the streets, turning the road in front of the building into a lively shopping area that becomes the city's night market after dark. Expect to find cheap souvenirs, along with countless bolts of fabric, T-shirts, and many other items.

Hom Market

For fabric shopping, **Hom Market** (Pho Hue, sunrise-sunset daily) just south of Hoan Kiem Lake is the go-to venue, lined with stall upon stall of materials at bargain prices. The usual market items are sold here, from food and household products to shoes, clothing, and other goods, but the real reason to venture into its maze of vendors is the innumerable bolts of fabric. Be sure to haggle, as Hom Market's shrewd businesswomen can drive a hard bargain.

Night Market

Hanoi's regular **night market** (Hang Dao north to Dong Xuan Market, 7pm-midnight Fri.-Sun.) runs from the end of Hang Dao north all the way to Dong Xuan Market, turning the road into a pedestrian-only affair flush with shops selling clothing, dry goods, and souvenirs. Be sure to haggle on this road, as prices tend to start high. Purchasing multiple items can usually get you a discount. While the bazaar only takes place on weekends, many vendors still set up smaller versions of their street stalls on the other days of the week.

SHOPPING DISTRICTS
Trang Tien

Wedged between the southern end of Hoan Kiem Lake and the Red River a few blocks to the east, Trang Tien is Hanoi's luxury shopping neighborhood, replete with high-end fashion, international brands, and familiar designer labels. Ply the narrow streets that spider off August Revolution Square, and you'll discover droves of art galleries, swanky boutiques, and posh cafés.

Running the length of a city block, **Trang Tien Plaza** (corner of Dinh Tien Hoang and Trang Tien, tel. 04/3937-8600, www.

the enormous Dong Xuan Market

The Clothes Make the Traveler

Though much of Hanoi is a retail paradise for women's clothing, it can be hard to know where to start your shopping adventure. The Old Quarter, particularly around Hang Gai and Hang Bong, is chock-full of high-quality brands like **Tan My Design** (61 Hang Gai, tel. 04/3825-1579, www.tanmydesign.com, 8am-8pm daily), **Ha Dong Silk** (102 Hang Gai, tel. 04/3928-5056, hadongsilks@gmail.com, 8am-8pm daily), and **Metiseko** (71 Hang Gai, tel. 04/3935-2645, www.metiseko.com, 8:30am-9pm daily). A handful of standouts in the Cathedral District are worth a visit, such as **Marie-linh** (74 Hang Trong, tel. 04/3928-6304, www.marie-linh.com, 9am-8pm daily) and **Magonn** (19 Ma May, tel. 04/3935-1811, www.magonn.vn, 9am-9pm daily). Much of the clothing on offer is made with Vietnamese sizes in mind. Those who are larger than the average Vietnamese woman may want to check out shops like **Things of Substance** (5 Nha Tho, tel. 04/3828-6965, www.prieure.com.vn, 9am-9pm daily) or the tailors in the Old Quarter or West Lake. For more formal, one-of-a-kind items, a trip to **Chula** (6 Ven Ho Tay, tel. 09/0425-8960, www.chulafashion.com, 9am-6:30pm daily) is highly advised.

For budget shoppers, the long road (known as Hang Dao, Hang Ngang, or Hang Duong at different points) leading from Hoan Kiem Lake to Dong Xuan Market holds a host of clothing and souvenir shops, as does the intersection where Hang Dao and Hang Gai connect. Shops like **Ginkgo** (79 Hang Gai, tel. 04/3938-2265, www.ginkgo-vietnam.com, 8am-10pm daily) and **Orange** (36 Luong Ngoc Quyen, tel. 04/3935-1387, www.orangestyle.vn, 9am-10pm daily) offer affordable T-shirts and bags, while **Tagilis** (12 Hang Bong, tel. 04/3990-7088, www.tagilis.wordpress.com, 9am-9pm daily) is an affordable tailor option. Retail outfits along the Old Quarter's Ma May and Ngo Huyen in the Cathedral District also carry the standard array of souvenirs, T-shirts, casual pants, and sundresses.

The options for men's clothing are fewer and limited to standard shirts and shorts. Keep an eye out for the minimal offerings in local boutiques. The streets south of Hoan Kiem Lake toward Hom Market hold a handful of more exciting men's options, as does **Zed's Threads** (51A To Ngoc Van, tel. 09/4753-6515, www.zedsthreads.com, 10am-6pm daily) in West Lake, though none of these are unique to Vietnam, but are instead a more affordable version of what you might find at home.

---

trangtienplaza.vn, 9:30am-9:30pm Mon.-Fri., 9:30am-10pm Sat.-Sun.) houses several international luxury brands, including Bulgari, Cartier, Estee Lauder, and Lancome, along with designer labels such as Louis Vuitton, Dior, and Versace, over six floors. The center was first built in 1901 to accommodate the city's French colonial shoppers. Its current incarnation opened to the public in 2013 as Hanoi's first luxury shopping center.

The **Foreign Language Bookstore** (64 Trang Tien, tel. 04/3825-7376, 8am-8pm daily), just down the road from Trang Tien Plaza, stocks recent American and European magazines such as *Time, Elle, The Economist* and *Marie-Claire*, along with the usual government-approved collection of English-language classics. The shop's section of Vietnam-related books slowly gives

way to a cache of souvenir items and road and city maps.

Old Quarter

Squeezed into an impossibly small neighborhood north of the lake, Hanoi's historic Old Quarter offers some of the best and most diverse shopping in the city, with stores to fit every budget and taste. From sleek, well-crafted furniture to eye-catching independent boutiques, traditional handicrafts, dime-a-dozen souvenirs, and the odd art gallery, **Hang Gai** and its nearby lanes represent the bulk of the area's offerings. There is also the occasional shop slipped between restaurants and hotels around Ma May, as well as a few of the more affordable souvenir shops buried within the backpacker alley off Ly Quoc Su near the cathedral. Head down sleepy Au

The Streets of the Old Quarter

In centuries past, each narrow road in the Old Quarter carried a specific product. Hang Quat, for instance, sold fans, or *quat*, while Hang Giay made its money from paper, or *giay*. Cha Ca was where you went to buy grilled fish, silver was on Hang Bac, and Hang Duong held much of the city's sugar supply. Today, many of these streets have changed trades. Hang Dau, the former oil street, now specializes in shoes, for instance. But, the traditional names have stuck.

Trieu on either side of St. Joseph's, and the hip clothing stores and independent labels reappear.

For fun, colorful, Vietnam-inspired T-shirts, both **Orange** (36 Luong Ngoc Quyen, tel. 04/3935-1387, www.orangestyle. vn, 9am-10pm daily) and **Ginkgo** (79 Hang Gai, tel. 04/3938-2265, www.ginkgo-viet-nam.com, 8am-10pm daily) offer well-made, affordable men's and women's threads with more originality than the stock souvenir items around town. Ginkgo also has a second location (44 Hang Be, tel. 04/3926-4769, 8am-10pm daily) removed from the frenzy of Hang Gai.

Branding itself as eco-chic women's clothing, **Metiseko** (71 Hang Gai, tel. 04/3935-2645, www.metiseko.com, 8:30am-9pm daily) combines organic cotton, all-natural silk, and other eco-friendly fabrics with bright, solid colors and Vietnamese-inspired prints to create designs with a whimsical feel. All fabrics meet Global Organic Textile standards. The store also features a smaller selection of children's clothing and home goods. Western-level prices apply here, but the thought and quality put into Metiseko's offerings justify their cost.

Pairing the roaring 1920s with vibrant, edgy prints and colors, **Magonn** (19 Ma May, tel. 04/3935-1811, www.magonn.vn, 9am-9pm daily) brings an old-world class to its chic, modern style. The well-stocked hipster boutique features a line of original women's clothing created by a young, Hanoi-based design duo, running the gamut from classy to casual with sleek pencil skirts, flirty A-line frocks, and drop-waist dresses.

The smart, understated clothing at **Indigo Stor** (47 Hang Gai, tel. 04/3938-1859, www. indigo-store.com, 8am-8pm daily) may not jump out at you, but the beauty of these items lies in their simplicity. Using traditional methods, the shop sticks to indigo-dyed clothing for both men and women, using all-natural fabrics and embroidery courtesy of Vietnam's ethnic minorities, whose colorful, intricate needlework jumps out from the plain blue background.

One of a few skilled tailors on the block, **Ha Dong Silk** (102 Hang Gai, tel. 04/3928-5056, hadongsilks@gmail.com, 8am-8pm daily) fashions high-quality custom items. The shop also boasts a range of ready-made women's clothing along with accessories and jewelry. The ground floor of the building houses off-the-rack options; the fabric selection is upstairs.

The two floors of local favorite **Tan My Design** (61 Hang Gai, tel. 04/3825-1579, www.tanmydesign.com, 8am-8pm daily) are a catchall of jewelry, accessories, women's clothing, and housewares, run by three generations of a Hanoian family. From dresses to necklaces, bags, and bedding, Tan My pairs bright, bold colors with a distinctly Vietnamese flair, drawing upon the best of the old and the new. There is a small black-and-white café in the back of the narrow, all-white store. Across the street is Tan My's original location (66 Hang Gai, tel. 04/3825-1579, www.tanmyembroidery.com.vn, 8am-8pm daily), which specializes in beautiful hand-embroidered silks and other fabrics.

Perhaps the most affordable tailor on the block, **Tagilis** (12 Hang Bong, tel.

04/3990-7088, www.tagilis.wordpress.com, 9am-9pm daily) specializes in well-made women's dresses in a range of materials and styles. The cheerful folks who run the shop are willing to copy designs or come up with new ones, and the average knee-length dress should set you back around VND670,000, give or take a few dollars depending upon the cut and fabric. Ready-made items are also available in bright colors and prints.

A long, narrow shop squeezed between the tailors and silk vendors of Hang Gai, **Van Loi** (87 Hang Gai, tel. 04/3828-6758, www.vanloi.com, 8am-7pm daily) does a trade in beautiful wooden furniture, mother-of-pearl dishware, lacquer trays, and other home furnishings. Colorful or traditional, ostentatious or reserved, all items are produced locally and with care. The shop's smaller kitchen items and decorative pieces make easy-to-pack souvenirs.

Cathedral District

A less hectic extension of the Old Quarter, Hanoi's Cathedral District is home to a handful of unique, creative boutiques selling women's clothing, ceramics, and other knick-knacks. Prices are a little more reasonable here, away from the main shopping drag. This area is still well within the bounds of Hanoi's more touristy area, so expect to find plenty of foreign shoppers and souvenirs here.

Hidden amid a street full of European restaurants and dwarfed by the nearby St. Joseph's Cathedral, Japanese brand **Nagu** (20 Nha Tho, tel. 04/3928-8020, www.zantoc.com, 9am-8pm daily) offers a combination of simple, understated women's clothing, accessories, homewares, and kids' toys with a local touch.

The vision of a French-Vietnamese designer, **Marie-linh** (74 Hang Trong, tel. 04/3928-6304, www.marie-linh.com, 9am-8pm daily) creates smart and affordable women's clothing. Combining high-quality fabrics with Eastern and Western influences, the shop's shirts, pants, shorts, and dresses offer casual comfort without sacrificing style.

A more upscale version of Marie-linh is open a few doors down, as is another location (11 Nha Tho, tel. 04/3928-8773, 9am-8pm daily) nearby.

A color-coded boutique that boasts "Western sizes at Vietnamese prices," **Things of Substance** (5 Nha Tho, tel. 04/3828-6965, www.prieure.com.vn, 9am-9pm daily) features women's wear with vibrant tops and flowing cotton and jersey dresses. There are few fitted items here, but the flowy styles are ideal for traveling and work well in the heat. Western-sized pants and a range of funky jewelry round out the shop's offerings.

In the wide, shallow storefront at **Marena Hanoi** (28 Nha Chung, tel. 04/3828-5542, www.marenahanoi.vn, 9am-6pm daily) there is barely enough room to turn around. Its shelves are packed with elegant, well-made ceramics and lacquerware, with much of its stock sticking to traditional themes. Simple blue-and-white designs adorn plates, tea sets, mugs, and small bowls, while lacquer trays and boxes boast brilliant reds or blacks. All items are handmade and prices are reasonable.

Ba Dinh District

Though this district is reserved more for historical sights than retail outlets, the one or two shops you'll find in Ba Dinh District are well worth your time.

54 Traditions (30 Hang Bun, tel. 04/3715-1569, www.54traditions.vn, 8am-6pm daily) celebrates the diverse cultures of Vietnam's 54 ethnicities, particularly its northern minority groups. Founded in 2004, the shop not only sells ancient artifacts, shamanic artwork, textiles, jewelry, and everyday objects of minority people, but also educates its customers on these items. Each purchase comes with at least 1,000 words of information on the object. Some stock dates all the way back to the Dong Son culture, and many items are museum-grade quality. Items range from a few dollars to a few thousand dollars.

Avid readers will be at home among the stacks of **Bookworm** (44 Chau Long, tel. 04/3715-3711, www.bookwormhanoi.com,

Tailor Made

Along Hang Gai and throughout the Old Quarter, tailors are easy to come by but quality and affordability together can be hard to find. A handful of standouts offer reliable service and skill at reasonable prices. Those who wish to have any tailoring done in Hanoi should plan ahead, as tailors in the capital tend to require more time than the speedy seamstresses of Hoi An. The average purchase can take anywhere from a few days to a week to complete, not including extra fittings or alterations. Most Hanoian tailors stock their own fabrics, saving you the trouble of visiting the market, though be prepared to pay a premium for this service. Whether you opt for the materials in-store or choose to purchase your own, it's best to swing by your preferred shop ahead of time to ensure that you buy enough of the required fabric and to get an idea of how much you should be paying for it.

Tagilis (12 Hang Bong, tel. 04/3990-7088, www.tagilis.wordpress.com, 9am-9pm daily) in the Old Quarter is your best bet for reasonably priced women's clothing. For a bit more quality try **Ha Dong Silk** (102 Hang Gai, tel. 04/3928-5056, hadongsilks@gmail.com, 8am-8pm daily), located on the same Old Quarter street, which provides a more upmarket range of fabrics and services. If it's more sophisticated tailoring you seek, West Lake shops like **Clom's Closet** (31A Xuan Dieu, tel. 04/3718-8233, cloclo@suit-ya.com, 9am-8pm daily), which takes orders on anything from men's and women's clothing to kidswear and even home linens, and the high-fashion **Chula** (6 Ven Ho Tay, tel. 09/0425-8960, www.chulafashion.com, 9am-6:30pm daily) come at a price but their quality is unmatched. Finally, men looking for affordable, well-made dress shirts and pants would do well to check out **Zed's Threads** (51A To Ngoc Van, tel. 09/4753-6515, www.zedsthreads.com, 10am-6pm daily), a men's-only tailoring shop also located in West Lake.

9am-7pm daily), an independent English-language bookstore. The shop boasts over 15,000 new and used titles in its two-story collection. A smaller room dedicated to Southeast Asia and Vietnam touches on topics such as history, culture, and local issues.

West Lake

For a calmer shopping experience, the **West Lake** neighborhood is home to more upmarket shopping, falling somewhere in between the Old Quarter and Trang Tien. Though it's less accessible than its southern counterparts, with shops fewer and farther between, the neighborhood includes a unique set of tailors for both men and women, not to mention a greater chance of finding Western sizes than Hanoi's downtown shops.

A small, colorful shop, **To He** (70 To Ngoc Van, tel. 04/3775-4230, www.tohe.vn, 8am-7pm daily) was borne out of a community program aimed at turning disadvantaged Vietnamese children on to their own creativity. The shop runs arts-related activities for kids with disabilities or serious illnesses, as well as those in orphanages, and uses the artwork and inspiration provided by its participants to create lovely printed bags, notebooks, table runners, T-shirts, and other souvenirs, whose proceeds go toward the continuation of the program.

Full of vivid colors and daring designs, the handmade dresses at **Chula** (6 Ven Ho Tay, tel. 09/0425-8960, www.chulafashion.com, 9am-6:30pm daily) are sure to get you noticed. The brainchild of a Spanish duo, this independent design house specializes in formal wear, creating vibrant, original pieces and tailor-made items for women. A wide array of ready-made outfits are available for purchase. You can also commission the skilled Diego to fashion something custom. Prices are similar to American department stores, but the quality is unparalleled.

Stepping into **Clom's Closet** (31A Xuan Dieu, tel. 04/3718-8233, cloclo@suit-ya.com, 9am-8pm daily) feels like entering a very fashionable wardrobe. Tastefully decorated and featuring men's and women's clothing, handbags, and accessories, this upmarket tailor produces truly beautiful formal wear using high-quality materials from around the world. Western prices apply here, but the quality and skill of Clom's tailors is well worth the cost.

While its fashion may not be as bold as other shops, Zed's Threads (51A To Ngoc Van, tel. 09/4753-6515, www.zedsthreads. com, 10am-6pm daily) is one of the only menswear stores in Hanoi that offers strictly men's clothing in sizes that fit Westerners. A range of quality shirts, pants, and suits take up the shop's racks. Made-to-measure services (8am-noon and 1pm-5pm Mon.-Sat.) are available, free of charge, though you'll have to make an appointment beforehand, either by phone or online.

Packed with plush quilts and bright home furnishings, Mekong Creations (58 Hang Trong, tel. 04/3824-4607, www.mekong-creations.org, 9am-9pm daily) offers well-made products for a good cause. Aimed at providing women in southern Vietnam and Cambodia with a sustainable income, this nonprofit organization has been assisting local communities since 2001. An array of quilts, bamboo products, and other housewares feature in this tiny shop, with half of the proceeds from each sale going back to the village from which the product came. For more variety, swing by Mekong Quilts (13 Hang Bac, tel. 04/3926-4831, www.mekong-quilts.org, 9am-9pm daily) nearby.

Sports and Recreation

There are a few activities for recreation once you've exhausted your sightseeing and shopping options. You'll find charming green spaces around the city. Spas are a growing industry, as are cooking classes, for those keen to master the art of Vietnamese cuisine.

PARKS

Scattered throughout Ba Dinh, Hoan Kiem, and Hai Ba Trung districts are Hanoi's array of small but well-loved parks, which serve as exercise tracks for early-risers, meeting spots for midday revelers, and communal areas for friends and family once the workday adjourns. While few of these green spaces could rival the parks you might find at home in terms of size, Hanoi's dozens of miniature clearings are a pleasant break from the madness of its usual hustle and bustle. The ring around Hoan Kiem Lake is the most popular of these areas, drawing hundreds of locals and tourists each day, including a small but devoted collection of young Vietnamese students hoping to strike up a conversation with a passing foreigner to practice their English.

Opposite Hoan Kiem Lake sits Ly Thai To Park (Dinh Tien Hoang between Le Lai and Le Thach), a modest square dominated by its imposing statue of the emperor of the same name. As the founder of Thang Long (what's now known as Hanoi), Ly Thai To features heavily on street signs, businesses, and monuments throughout Hanoi The open concrete square is packed with early-morning exercisers or rollerblading school kids later in the day.

A small wedge of green opposite the Military History Museum, Lenin Park (Dien Bien Phu between Hoang Dieu and Nguyen Tri Phuong) bears a domineering stone statue of its namesake at the far end of the clearing overlooking the city's famous Flag Tower. Trees line the edge of the concrete space, acting as a buffer between the downtown traffic and the relative peace of the square.

For a genuine escape from the Old Quarter chaos, Hanoi's Botanical Garden (Vuon Bach Thao, Hoang Hoa Tham, 7am-10pm daily, VND2,000) offers some much-appreciated silence in a city where noise pollution can wear on a person. In truth, this peaceful green space is pretty average, but thanks to its location and size, the pleasant grounds, equipped with two fish ponds, plenty of seating, and a collection of blocky, abstract sculptures, take the edge off Hanoi's frantic traffic. Animal-lovers would do well to bypass the cage near the entrance, as the birds inside are not par-ticularly well looked after. While the park is a lovely place during the day, it's wise to stay away after dark, as this is a frequent hangout for some of Hanoi's more unsavory characters.

AMUSEMENT PARKS

One of Vincom's two mega malls, **Royal City** (72A Nguyen Trai, tel. 04/6276-7799, www. vincomshoppingmall.com, 9:30am-10pm daily) goes above and beyond your average retail center with an indoor waterfall, movie theater, bowling alley, arcade, water park, and Vietnam's one and only ice skating rink. Entry to the mall is free of charge, but use of the facilities costs money (from VND50,000 for a round of bowling; VND150,000 for ac-cess to the rink; VND170,000 for use of the water park). Vincom offers full-day "tours" of the shopping mall, hitting all of Royal City's major sights.

CYCLING

On the bicycle front, Hanoi has come a long way in recent years, cultivating a healthy crop of both local and expat cyclists who have taken to its streets in style, pedaling every-thing from flashy fixies to sleek, ultra-light road bikes to vintage, basket-toting city ve-hicles. Several small cycling communities exist throughout the city, meeting up for a jaunt down one of the larger roads or around West Lake. The capital has encountered some growing pains recently, as it attempts to make Hanoi a more bicycle-friendly city without altering the breakneck, chaotic traffic that congests its downtown streets. Bicycle rentals are possible and guided tours can be found through the city's best-known foreign cycling community, The Hanoi Bicycle Collective.

For cycling enthusiasts, a visit to **The Hanoi Bicycle Collective** (44 Ngo 31 Xuan Dieu, tel. 04/3718-8246, www.thbc.vn, 9am-6pm Mon.-Fri., 9am-7pm Sat.-Sun.) is a must. Founded in 2009 by Spaniard Guim

Valls Tereul and his Vietnamese wife Thuy Anh Nguyen, the shop has served as a base for Hanoi's foreign cycling community, offering bicycles and cycling gear for sale, city tours for curious travelers, and a regular "bike doc-tor" (Mon.-Sat.) to assist with repairs, as well as a small café (VND50,000-150,000) space. Peruse the upstairs display of goods or kick back on the ground floor with some Spanish tapas. A bulletin board along the café wall boasts a collection of foreign "cyclotourists" who have passed through THBC while travel-ing around the world on two wheels; the shop offers a complimentary maintenance check to those cycling through Hanoi. The shop runs regular tours (VND735,000) of downtown Hanoi and the West Lake area.

SWIMMING

Summertime temperatures in the city can be unforgiving, and one of the better ways to beat the heat is with a trip to the pool. A handful of high-end hotels allow pool access to non-guests, but day passes verge on exorbitant. The venues in this section are a more attractive op-tion for those on a budget.

Overlooking scenic West Lake, the pool at **Thang Loi Resort** (200 Yen Phu, tel. 04/3829-4211 ext. 374, www.thangloihotel.vn, 6am-6pm daily, VND80,000) stays open year-round and offers changing rooms, lounge chairs, and access to the resort's restaurant and bar services. Though the pool is small, its location makes for a pleasant escape from the city's noise and affords nice views of the sur-rounding area. Bring your own towel, as these are not provided. The place gets crowded on weekends, usually in the afternoons, as local families bring their children for a swim.

Hanoi's only saltwater swimming venue, the **Army Guesthouse Pool** (33C Pham Ngu Lao, tel. 04/3825-2896, armyhotel@fpt. vn, 6:30am-9pm daily, VND90,000) escapes much of the downtown chaos, hiding at the end of a quiet, tree-lined avenue behind the Opera House. The lanes are large, and plenty of free space allows serious swimmers the opportunity to get some laps in. This spot is

MASSAGES AND SPAS

While Hanoi boasts its fair share of quality massage parlors, spa services in the capital are more expensive than other destinations in the country. Tipping 15-20 percent is a standard practice in most massage parlors.

Aimed at training disadvantaged local youth for a career in massage therapy, Just Massage (237 Au Co, tel. 04/3718-2737, www.justmassage.org.vn, 9am-9pm daily, VND250,000-700,000) offers everything from Swedish and shiatsu massages to hot stones and aromatherapy treatments. Staff are friendly and speak English, allowing you to communicate with your massage therapist, and prices won't break the bank.

The tranquil SF Spa (30 Cua Dong, tel. 04/3747-5301, www.sfcompany.net, 9am-11:30pm daily, VND250,000-990,000), located on the western edge of the Old Quarter, is among Hanoi's more ambient retreats. Featuring a variety of foot and full-body massages, body treatments, facials, waxing, and all-encompassing spa packages, this charming day spa boasts a chic, simple modern decor along with experienced, English-speaking massage therapists.

Located within the Elegance Diamond Hotel on the eastern edge of the Old Quarter, La Siesta Spa (32 Lo Su, tel. 04/3935-1632, www.hanoielegancehotel.com, 8:30am-9pm daily, VND380,000-1,280,000) is a closer version of its swank home base, Zen Spa (100 Xuan Dieu, tel. 04/3719-1266, www.zenspa.com.vn, 9am-9pm daily, VNDVND380,000-1,280,000), out in West Lake. Boasting the same range of high-quality spa services, massages, facials, and body scrubs, the company's downtown facility provides a tranquil escape from the chaos outdoors, as well as several package treatments inspired by the principle of the five elements: earth, water, fire, metal, and wood.

COOKING CLASSES

Right in the heart of the Old Quarter, the Blue Butterfly (61 Hang Buom, tel. 04/3926-3845, www.bluebutterflyrestaurant.com, 9am and 3pm daily, VND735,000) runs half-day cooking classes every morning and afternoon. Three-hour courses begin with a trip to Dong Xuan Market, where a local chef will explain the finer points of Vietnamese produce before participants head back to the restaurant, don a chef's hat and apron, and begin to cook. Three basic but delicious local dishes feature on the class menu, all of which are included in the recipe book presented at the end of the session. Classes are small with up to 10 or 12 per group. This is a fun and different way for novice chefs to learn about local culture.

Boasting a range of courses designed by Australian chef Tracey Lister, co-author of three books on Vietnamese cuisine, the Hanoi Cooking Center (44 Chau Long, tel. 04/3715-0088, www.hanoicookingcentre.com, 9am-5:30pm daily, VND1,245,000) may offer the most expensive cooking classes in the city, but its experienced staff provide a clean environment, top-of-the-line cookware, and plenty of hands-on instruction about Vietnamese cuisine. Choose from several different themed courses, including a vegan tofu option, a session on barbecue and salads, and a half-day class devoted to spring rolls. Each course runs around four hours, with three in the kitchen and one to enjoy your sumptuous creations, and class sizes average 8-10 people. The center also offers street eats and market tours (Mon.-Sat., VND1,245,000), which take visitors on a four-hour trip around town, enjoying several varieties of local fare. Their Kids Club (VND320,000) allows children to partake in some basic, supervised cooking. Hanoi Cooking Center runs a small café (9am-5:30pm daily, VND70,000-140,000) space on the ground floor, serving mostly Western meals as well as European and Vietnamese coffee.

best avoided on weekends, namely in the afternoons, as families often turn up for downtime at the pool.

Accommodations

The bustling streets and narrow, snaking alleys of Hanoi's downtown districts hold accommodations to fit every budget, from basic dorm beds to palatial five-star suites. Base yourself within reach of Hoan Kiem Lake, as this will ensure a reasonable proximity to most of Hanoi's sights, restaurants, and shopping. With a reputation as one of the country's most walkable metropolises and a surplus of quality budget, mid-range, and high-end accommodations, there is no reason not to stay in the downtown area.

As travelers to the city will quickly learn, the Old Quarter is not a place for light sleepers. While there is no shortage of accommodations in Hanoi, several factors come into play when booking a room, not the least of which is noise level. Those with a tolerance for white noise or, at the very least, a set of earplugs will find no fault in the many rooms north of the lake; those who prefer more quiet may find peace down the web of alleys beside St. Joseph's Cathedral, where many of the cheaper budget accommodations have set up shop. A clutch of luxury hotels populates the French Quarter, many of them bearing unique historical significance in addition to high-end amenities and five-star service.

OLD QUARTER

This small but incredibly dense neighborhood manages to squeeze plenty of top-notch accommodations into a few blocks north of Hoan Kiem Lake, right in the center of the action. Prices run higher here while room sizes can be on the small side. Noise levels are higher than you might find elsewhere in the city.

Under VND210,000

Away from the spirited backpacker haunts, **Hanoi Hostel** (91C Hang Ma, tel. 04/6270-0006, www.vietnam-hostel.com, VND105,000 dorm) offers a peaceful place for weary budget travelers to lay their heads. The mixed and female dorms have clean, comfy beds and en suite bathrooms, personal lockers, daily breakfast, and a free happy-hour beer. The outfit in charge runs a tour service downstairs. While there's not really much of a common area, this hostel's location and laid-back vibe make up for that. There is also a second location (32 Hang Vai, tel. 04/6270-2009) nearby.

Hanoi Backpackers' Downtown (9 Ma May, tel. 04/3935-1890, www.vietnam-backpackerhostels.com, VND158,000 dorm, VND973,000 double) is a good option for those in search of travel buddies, though if it's quiet you seek, then this is not the place to crash. Single mixed dorms, female-only rooms, and double bed dorms are available, all with personal lockers, air-conditioning, Wi-Fi, and communal bathrooms. Breakfast is served in the restaurant each morning. Though a few private rooms are available, you're better off going elsewhere if you'd prefer your own space.

VND210,000-525,000

The **Tu Linh Palace 2** (86 Ma May, tel. 04/3826-9999, www.tulinhpalacehotel.com, VND462,000-588,000, breakfast included) is run by a welcoming and attentive staff and, for the price, offers decent value. Standard amenities such as hot water, air-conditioning, TV, and Wi-Fi access are available. A bar and restaurant on the ground floor round out Tu Linh's offerings.

Rooms at **Hanoi City Hostel** (95B Hang Ga, tel. 04/3828-1379, www.hanoicityhostel.com, VND336,000-378,000, breakfast included) are spacious and a bit worn but right for the price, counting hot water, air-conditioning, TV, Wi-Fi, a fridge, and tea- and coffee-making facilities among its standard amenities. Both front- and back-facing rooms are available, the former boasting large windows and lots of light, the latter offering more quiet away from the traffic noise of the downtown area. The staff can help arrange onward travel and transportation.

VND525,000-1,050,000

Though rooms at the **Rising Dragon Legend** (55 Hang Be, tel. 04/3935-2647, www.risingdragonhotel.com, VND525,000-1,470,000, breakfast included) are decidedly small, this skinny budget venture offers decent value for money, with clean, modern furnishings and comfy beds, hot water, air-conditioning, TV, minibar, in-room safe, Wi-Fi access, and tea- and coffee-making facilities. The hotel staff are a friendly and professional bunch who assist with travel bookings around northern Vietnam.

In a big and hectic city, the **Hanoi Guesthouse** (85 Ma May, tel. 04/3935-2572, www.hanoiguesthouse.com, VND525,000-840,000, breakfast included) truly feels like a homier stay than most, with free refreshments on tap in the lobby and a notably attentive staff. Rooms are a great value, outfitted with TV, Wi-Fi, hot water, air-conditioning, a minibar, an in-room safe, and tea- and coffee-making facilities. Add-ons include airport transfer, travel bookings, laundry, and luggage storage.

Cozy, well-appointed, and right in the heart of the Old Quarter, rooms at the **Hanoi Old Town** (95 Hang Chieu, tel. 04/3929-0783, www.hanoioldtown.com, VND525,000-840,000, breakfast included) feature generously sized beds, hot water, television, air-conditioning, and Wi-Fi access. Facilities are older than other hotels in the area, but staff at the Old Town are a cheerful bunch and assist with travel services and tours around northern Vietnam. For lots of light and a street view, front-facing rooms are a solid choice; but if you prefer peace and quiet, opt for a spot at the back, where noise levels aren't so high.

Rooms at the **Hanoi Paradise Hotel** (53 Hang Chieu, tel. 04/3929-0026, www.hanoiparadisehotel.com, VND735,000-1,680,000)

are smart, cozy, and outfitted with some unusual amenities, including in-room computers that would not be out of place in an antiques museum. Other amenities include air-conditioning, hot water, TV, Wi-Fi, and tea- and coffee-making facilities. Staff are friendly and exceptionally service-minded, taking this mid-range accommodation above and beyond the rest. Both street- and back-facing rooms are available, depending upon your tolerance for city noise levels.

★ **Golden Time Hostel 2** (8 Ly Thai To, tel. 04/3825-9654, www.goldentimehostel.com, VND420,000-945,000, breakfast included) is not a hostel but a budget hotel. Its location east of Hoan Kiem Lake affords travelers the best of both worlds: beyond the bustle and noise of the Old Quarter and yet close to the city center. Rooms are well-kept and come with television, air-conditioning, hot water, Wi-Fi access, and an in-room safe. Some rooms don't have windows. The staff is attentive and assists with transportation and travel bookings. For a slightly cheaper but equally worthy option, **Golden Time 1** (43 Ly Thai To, tel. 04/3935-1091, www.goldentimehostel.com, VND294,000-378,000) is just down the road. While there's less atmosphere here, good service and most of the same amenities apply.

VND1,050,000-2,100,000

Hugging the western edge of the Old Quarter, the **Charming Hotel 2** (31 Hang Ga, tel. 04/3923-4031, www.hanoicharminghotel.com, VND945,000-1,890,000, breakfast included) provides five-star service for a fraction of the price. Rooms are modern and well-appointed, with in-room amenities such as a computer, safe, work desk, TV, and Wi-Fi access, as well as complimentary water and tea- and coffee-making facilities. The hotel offers a handful of different room types, from standard superiors, with and without windows, to spacious executive accommodations.

The 25-room **Oriental Central Hotel** (39 Hang Bac, tel. 04/3935-1117, www.orientalcentralhotel.com, VND945,000-1,575,000, breakfast included) stands out thanks to top-notch staff and a modern look. Well-appointed rooms come with the standard amenities as well as complimentary daily water. The antique-style bronze showerheads and framed photographs of everyday Vietnamese scenes add to the ambience. The superior, deluxe, and suite rooms have varying degrees of natural light. Opt for at least a deluxe, as these afford a better view. Additional services like travel bookings and airport pickup can be arranged.

Calypso Suites Hotel (11E Trung Yen, Dinh Liet, tel. 04/3935-2751, www.calypsosuiteshotel.com, VND840,000-1,575,000, breakfast included), run by the same people as Oriental Central Hotel, bears a similar red, black, and white design scheme and equally conscientious service. Expect standard amenities as well as Wi-Fi, DVD players, and in-room safes. The hotel's alley location minimizes the noise of the Old Quarter.

The **Essence Hanoi Hotel** (22 Ta Hien, tel. 04/3935-2485, www.essencehanoihotel.com, VND1,365,000-2,415,000, breakfast included) provides quality service and posh, mid-range boutique rooms that feature inroom computers, in-room safes, and daily complimentary water on top of the standard amenities. The hotel's restaurant operates throughout the day on an à la carte menu. Services such as laundry, luggage storage, and tour bookings can be arranged at reception. Rooms vary in size and access to natural light; take a step up from the most basic option for a room with a view.

Part of the Elegance chain, **Hanoi Elegance Diamond Hotel** (32 Lo Su, tel. 04/3935-1632, www.hanoielegancehotel.com, VND1,260,000-2,310,000) is one of the company's best properties. Perched on the edge of the Old Quarter, the Diamond houses boutique rooms and the Gourmet Corner, a much-touted top-floor restaurant with pleasant lake views, as well as an outdoor terrace bar. Rooms feature a simple but elegant decor, plush beds, an in-room safe, computer, and complimentary water alongside the usual amenities.

The grand **Tirant Hotel** (36-38 Gia Ngu, tel. 04/6269-8899, www.tiranthotel.com,

VND1,575,000-3,045,000) boasts a larger property than much of its Old Quarter competition, no easy feat in this packed neighborhood. Above the lavish reception area, 63 well-appointed rooms are outfitted in regal furnishings and come with an in-room computer, minibar, and tea- and coffee-making facilities in addition to standard hotel amenities. Breakfast is served in the hotel's downstairs restaurant each morning. A lake-view lounge tops the building, affording pleasant views of Hoan Kiem Lake. You'll find a fitness center and a small swimming pool here, as well as a travel desk, which assists with transportation and tour bookings.

CATHEDRAL DISTRICT

Situated just north of St. Joseph's Cathedral is a tiny backpacker enclave on Ngo Huyen that provides decent rooms at lower prices than in the Old Quarter.

Under VND210,000

The original **Hanoi Backpackers'** (48 Ngo Huyen, tel. 04/3828-5372, www.vietnambackpackerhostels.com, VND158,000 dorm, VND680,000 double, breakfast included) sits about halfway down narrow Ngo Huyen, a stone's throw from the Cathedral and Hoan Kiem Lake. Both mixed and all-female beds are available, with hot water, Wi-Fi, air-conditioning, and personal lockers. While there are a handful of private rooms, it's better to look elsewhere for quiet, because the crowd here likes to party. The staff can help arrange onward travel and transportation.

It's a little less tidy than Hanoi Backpackers', but **Central Backpackers** (16 Ly Quoc Su, tel. 04/3938-1849, www.centralbackpackershostel.com, VND105,000 dorm, VND462,000 double, breakfast included) is an affordable option. Mixed dorms are outfitted with personal lockers, air-conditioning, and Wi-Fi, with hot water in the shared bathrooms. During happy hour, you can enjoy a daily free beer. This is a good backpacker spot. The private rooms are not worthwhile; for peace and quiet, look elsewhere.

VND210,000-525,000

Especen Hotel (28 Tho Xuong, tel. 04/3824-4401, www.especen.vn, VND336,000-525,000) offers clean, spacious rooms in the heart of the Cathedral District. Tucked down an alley, the hotel is a five-minute walk from Hoan Kiem Lake. Rooms offer single- or queen-size beds and come equipped with a television, air-conditioning, Wi-Fi, and hot water. Long-term stays can be arranged for a discounted rate, and the friendly hotel staff can assist with travel plans around the city as well as throughout the north. There are a number of copycats in the area that have duplicated the hotel's sign. Go to this exact address to avoid impostors.

The **Bluebell Hotel** (41 Ngo Huyen, tel. 04/3938-2398, www.hanoibluebellhotel.com, VND420,000-630,000), hidden among the clutch of budget accommodations beside the cathedral, is one of this alley's better options, offering clean and well-priced rooms kitted out with hot water, air-conditioning, tea- and coffee-making facilities, fridge, TV, and Wi-Fi. If you're willing to hike up a few flights of stairs, the higher floors are better, as they tend to minimize the noise. All rooms are well-appointed and the friendly staff can assist with travel bookings and transportation.

In the shadow of St. Joseph's, the **Rising Dragon Cathedral** (38 Au Trieu, tel. 04/3826-8500, www.risingdragonhotel.com, VND462,000-1,575,000, breakfast included) offers great value for the money. Its charming, well-kept accommodations come with not only the standard hotel amenities, from hot water and air-conditioning to television and Wi-Fi access, but also a generous window and private balcony for each room. The balcony is the perfect spot to take in the morning bustle of the neighborhood or wind down after a long day. The unlimited refreshments downstairs are complimentary.

Tucked tightly down an alley off the road circling Hoan Kiem Lake, **Little Hanoi Hostel 2** (32 Le Thai To, tel. 04/3928-9897, www.littlehanoihostel.com, VND462,000 double, breakfast included) is a pleasant surprise. Quaint, quiet, and incredibly close to the water, this mini-hotel's location eliminates much of the noise problem that comes with being downtown. It boasts cozy, well-kept accommodations that count air-conditioning, hot water, Wi-Fi access, TV, and natural light among their amenities. The staff are a cheerful bunch, willing to help with transportation and travel arrangements, as well as city recommendations.

Though it's a little aged, **Tung Trang** (13 Tam Thuong, tel. 04/3828-6267, tungtranghotel@yahoo.com, VND315,000-546,000) stands out for its peaceful location, nestled amid a tangle of alleys just off Hang Bong. Rooms are basic, featuring hot water, air-conditioning, TV, and Wi-Fi access, all complimented nicely by the hospitality of the staff. Front rooms are spacious and include balconies, while smaller, cheaper accommodations are also available.

VND525,000-1,050,000

The most affordable in a chain of well-run, family-owned accommodations, **Splendid Jupiter Hotel** (16 Tho Xuong, tel. 04/3938-1831, www.splendidstarhotel.com, VND525,000-945,000, breakfast included) features bright, comfortable rooms with hot water, air-conditioning, TV, Wi-Fi access, complimentary water, an in-room safe, minibar, tea- and coffee-making facilities, and a DVD player. The staff can help arrange onward travel and transportation.

Decked out in miniature chandeliers, plush carpet, and snakeskin wallpaper, the **Angel Palace Hotel** (173 Hang Bong, tel. 04/6299-8666, www.angelpalacehotel.com.vn, VND945,000-1,470,000, breakfast included) makes a statement with its style as well as its service. All accommodations are modern and well-appointed, counting hot water, air-conditioning, TV, Wi-Fi access, complimentary water, a writing desk, and tea- and coffee-making facilities in the standard list of amenities. Additional services, such as laundry and tour arrangements, can be made with the friendly and professional folks at the front desk.

The smart and service-minded **Aranya Hotel** (128 Hang Bong, tel. 04/3938-2250, www.aranyahotel.com, VND945,000-1,785,000, breakfast included) hovers on the western edge of the Old Quarter. Outfitted with 30 guest rooms, each accommodation features air-conditioning, hot water, television, Wi-Fi access, complimentary water, and tea- and coffee-making facilities. The Aranya also counts a restaurant, spa, and travel services in its offerings.

VND1,050,000-2,100,000

Tried and trusted, the **Hanoi City Palace Hotel** (106 Hang Bong, tel. 04/3938-2333, www.hanoicitypalacehotel.com, VND1,155,000-2,100,000, breakfast included) boasts top-notch service and a chic decor that exceeds the level of most mid-range accommodations. Rooms at this charming boutique hotel feature spacious bathrooms as well as a work desk, minibar, television, in-room safe, tea- and coffee-making facilities, and complimentary water. Suite rooms include a private balcony. Additional touches like a welcome drink and fruit platter highlight the staff's attention to detail. The hotel runs a travel desk, which assists with tours around the city and beyond.

FRENCH QUARTER

The chic French Quarter is home to the city's most historic and high-end hotels. From the world-famous Metropole to elegant modern hotels like Nikko, Hotel de l'Opera, and Hanoi Hilton Opera, this is a neighborhood for the more affluent traveler.

Over VND2,100,000

The spectacular, stately **Sofitel Legend Metropole** (15 Ngo Quyen, tel. 04/3826-6919, www.sofitel.com, VND5,565,000-46,095,000) opened in 1901. Its historic white building, with black shutters and stocky balustrades, earned a reputation as the finest hotel in Indochina, catering to famous visitors and well-to-do residents. The five-star opulence of the Metropole is evident in its plush,

sophisticated rooms, which come with a television and complimentary bottled water. The hotel boasts a pair of luxurious restaurants, a spa, swimming pool, gift shop, sauna, and fitness center.

The five-star **Hanoi Hilton Opera** (1 Le Thanh Tong, tel. 04/3933-0500, www3.hilton. com, VND3,255,000-22,155,000) stands just south of the city's historic theater and exudes class from its regal, vaulted reception hall all the way to the elegant, well-appointed guest rooms. Accommodations feature standard hotel amenities alongside a minibar, in-room safe, Internet access, and tea- and coffee-making facilities. A fitness center, outdoor pool, sports bar, two restaurants, and a swanky café round out the hotel's offerings.

An imposing white building, the plush **Nikko Hotel** (84 Tran Nhan Tong, tel. 04/3822-3535, www.hotelnikkohanoi.com. vn, VND2,310,000-12,495,000, breakfast included) boasts 257 guest rooms, ranging from deluxe rooms to park view and executive lodgings and suites. Outfitted with high-quality amenities such as television, Wi-Fi access, a spacious bathroom, and a small sitting alcove, all rooms are well-appointed and come with use of the hotel swimming pool, whirlpool tub, and fitness center. The Nikko counts a spa, a bar, and three restaurants in its offerings.

A cross between cozy guesthouse and high-end hotel, the **Hilton Garden Inn** (20 Phan Chu Trinh, tel. 04/3944-9396, www.hiltongardeninn3.hilton.com, VND1,995,000-4,200,000) provides a more casual approach to luxury accommodation, with B&B-style lodgings alongside five-star service. Room amenities include television, Wi-Fi access, an in-room safe, desk, refrigerator, and tea- and coffee-making facilities, as well as use of the business center and gym. A bar, restaurant, and 24-hour pantry market round out the inn's additional services.

The **Hotel de l'Opera** (29 Trang Tien, tel. 04/6282-5555, www.mgallery.com, VND3,150,000-6,300,000) is not the first five-star hotel to grace this spot. At the turn of the 20th century, an elegant building known as the Hanoi Hotel served as a popular meeting place for local socialites. That building was eventually torn down in 2004 and rebuilt. Now outfitted with bold decor and first-class facilities, including flat-screen television and Wi-Fi access, the hotel stands out for its unique design, furnished in vivid, eye-catching colors. The chic, ground-floor Cafe Lautrec is a posh and popular French Quarter dining spot.

Tucked between high-rise office buildings and sprawling department stores, the De Syloia (17A Tran Hung Dao, tel. 04/3824-5346, www.desyloia.com, VND2,100,000-2,730,000, breakfast included) is a cozy boutique hotel modeled after a colonial-style villa. Each well-appointed room comes with Wi-Fi access, TV, an in-room safe, minibar, and complimentary water. Guests have access to the hotel's gym and business center. De Syloia's restaurant, Cay Cau, features both Vietnamese cuisine and live traditional music nightly from 7pm.

WEST LAKE

West Lake, with a handful of secluded high-end hotels, is the quietest neighborhood in the capital city. Xuan Dieu, the street bordering the eastern edge of the water, features several nice restaurants and bars, though options are limited.

Over VND2,100,000

Well removed from the chaos of downtown, the Sheraton Hanoi (11 Xuan Dieu, tel. 04/3719-9000, www.sheratonhanoi.com, VND2,310,000-34,965,000) sits just over two miles from the Old Quarter and has a pool, spa, garden, opulent lobby, and several restaurants on its sprawling lake shore property. Guest rooms feature the standard hotel amenities as well as a minibar, fridge, in-room safe, complimentary water, and tea- and coffee-making facilities.

Off the eastern shore of the lake, Intercontinental West Lake (1A Nghi Tam, tel. 04/6270-8888, www.ihg.com, VND2,835,000-34,335,000) boasts over 300 guest rooms, including stunning over-water pavilions connected to the water's edge by a maze of floating walkways. Plush rooms are outfitted with a fusion of traditional Asian-inspired elements and modern decor, and include Wi-Fi access and a private balcony. The hotel's three restaurants serve a range of international and Vietnamese cuisine. The outdoor pool and a state-of-the-art fitness center are free for guests to use.

Nestled between West Lake and Truc Bach, the Sofitel Plaza Hanoi (1 Thanh Nien, tel. 04/3823-8888, www.sofitel.com, VND5,250,000-8,820,000) is blessed with attractive natural surroundings. The Sofitel's location brings travelers closer to the heart of the city while still providing peace and quiet. The five-star hotel boasts 273 guest rooms outfitted with plush modern decor, an in-room safe, Wi-Fi access, and a flat-screen television. A pair of posh restaurants showcase Chinese, Western, and Vietnamese cuisine, while the Summit Lounge overlooks the lake. A swimming pool, spa, and fitness center are part of the Sofitel's offerings.

Food

Holding the distinction of best pho in Vietnam, the capital city collectively enjoys thousands of helpings each morning. Other Hanoian specialties earn equal notoriety for their flavors and textures. The unsung hero is *bun cha,* a delicious northern version of grilled meat and rice noodles doused in *nuoc cham,* a diluted fish sauce that comes with pickled veggies, fresh greens, and the occasional fried spring roll. You'll find this mouthwatering specialty on every street corner and likely smell it from a few blocks away, as the scent of barbecue floats up from street stalls. What Hanoi does, it does well: Mouthwatering, square-shaped seafood spring rolls, also known as *nem cua be,* are a must-eat in the capital. Several *cha ca* (pan-fried fish) restaurants round out the best Vietnamese offerings.

Hanoi's non-Vietnamese fare offers plenty of variety, from Indian and Malaysian meals to Thai, French, and American. Upscale eateries make a greater effort in the service department, opting for a Western approach, and there are more than a few foreign chefs and owners behind some of the city's well-known Western restaurants. The need for reservations is greater here, as the limited space of the Old Quarter means that dining rooms fill up fast.

The streets of Hanoi are a good place to experience roadside dining in Vietnam. Crammed onto already-busy sidewalks and hidden down narrow alleys, chefs serve everything from tasty Vietnamese sandwiches to piping hot soups, rice porridge, barbecue, and local specialties, often at VND40,000 or less per meal.

Safe street food is easy to find, provided you stick to clean outdoor kitchens. When in doubt, look for hot meals, such as soups or grilled meats. High temperatures tend to eliminate some of the risk.

OLD QUARTER
Cafés and Bakeries

Modest and unassuming, Giang Cafe (39 Nguyen Huu Huan, www.giangcafehanoi.com, 7am-10pm daily, VND15,000-30,000), in business since 1946, is hidden from the street by a narrow passageway between two larger storefronts. Try a cup of Hanoi's famous *ca phe trung* (egg coffee). This may not sound appetizing, but the thick, decadent concoction is a treat on a cold day, a combination of egg yolks, condensed milk, and Vietnamese coffee. The modest shop serves regular coffee, tea, and other refreshments at local prices. Its founder, Nguyen Giang, worked as a bartender at the legendary Metropole hotel before opening Giang Cafe.

French-Vietnamese Fusion

One of Hanoi's best-known venues, Green Tangerine (48 Hang Be, tel. 04/3825-1286, www.greentangerinehanoi.com, 11am-11pm daily, VND175,000-600,000) specializes in French and Vietnamese fusion, pairing unlikely ingredients to create unique and memorable dishes. The restaurant's 1928 colonial villa makes a worthy setting for a fancy meal. Prices run high, but the set menus offer decent value, with two-course lunches beginning at VND218,000 and a three-course dinner going for VND499,000. Given its popularity (it has been featured in a handful of high-profile publications, as well as on CNN's Travel website), reservations are a good idea.

Gastropubs

A classy pub and grill, The Moose & Roo (42B Ma May, tel. 04/3200-1289, www.mooseandroo.com, 9:30am-midnight daily, VND120,000-500,000) serves hearty pub dishes, from burgers, steaks, and savory pies to full Western breakfasts. Beer, wine, and cocktails are on offer, including hard-to-find top-shelf scotches and whiskeys. Dining in this cozy narrow space is well worth the price, and it makes for an excellent spot to unwind after a day of shopping and sightseeing.

Indian

The best of Hanoi's clutch of Indian restaurants, **Little India** (23 Hang Tre, tel. 04/3926-1859, www.little-india-hn.com, 10:30am-2:30pm and 6pm-10:30pm daily, VND45,000-115,000) boasts not only an impressive range of Indian cuisine but also a list of Malaysian dishes, including *nasi goreng* and beef *rendang,* as well as a few Chinese meals. Portions are generous, prices are right, and the staff aim to please. As a 100-percent halal establishment, you won't find alcohol here, but you're no more than a few blocks from nightlife venues, should you require a nightcap afterward.

Street Food

A Hanoi institution, **Xoi Yen** (35B Nguyen Huu Huan, tel. 04/3934-1950, 6am-midnight daily, VND15,000-50,000) is always packed with locals. Specializing in savory *xoi* (sticky rice), this restaurant features a menu of assorted toppings, including meats such as *xa xiu,* also known as *char siu* (Chinese-style roast pork), chicken, *cha* (a type of Vietnamese processed meat), or claypot-braised pork, which accompany your choice of sticky rice. Low tables and stools populate both the ground floor and the open-air second story. Visit the one on the corner and not its impostor next door.

Directly opposite Hang Da Market is a small, open-front shop that doles out tasty *mien luon* (87 Hang Dieu, tel. 04/3826-7943, 7am-10:30pm daily, VND20,000-50,000). The bowls of piping hot soup feature glass noodles and fried eel. Order the rice porridge or any of the other eel dishes from a large picture menu mounted on the wall. The metal-and-plastic furniture fit right in with the street-food vibe.

Fresh, flavorful, and good enough for seconds, the ***bun bo nam bo*** (67 Hang Dieu, 7:30am-10:30pm daily, VND55,000/bowl) at the skinny storefront near Hang Da Market is a popular choice among locals. Metal tables line the long, narrow dining area and a dexterous assembly line prepares heaping portions of the tasty rice noodle and beef dish, complete with fresh greens, pickled carrots, peanuts, and sauce.

While there are hundreds of street stalls serving this classic Hanoian dish, the ★ ***bun cha*** (34 Hang Than, tel. 04/3927-0879,

Local institution Xoi Yen stays busy from morning to night.

9am-2pm or until sold out daily, VND35,000/bowl) is the best of its kind. Hearty helpings of grilled pork and ground meat come swimming in *nuoc cham,* a lighter cousin of fish sauce, accompanied by pickled carrots and daikon. Add rice noodles and as many fresh greens as you'd like, stir, and enjoy. This spot only opens for lunch, and its product is well known among locals.

If you're short on time or prefer to stay closer to the Old Quarter, **Bun Cha Dac Kim** (1 Hang Manh, tel. 04/3828-7060, www.bunchahangmanh.vn, 10am-7pm daily, VND60,000/bowl) is another well-known local spot for *bun cha.* The owners overcharge foreigners, sometimes as much as VND90,000 for a meal.

Vietnamese

Even amid scores of backpacker eateries and shops catering to Western tourists, **New Day** (72 Ma May, tel. 04/3828-0315, www.newdayrestaurant.com, 10am-9pm daily, VND30,000-200,000) retains a strong local following. With a well-rounded menu that covers everything from pork, chicken, and beef to frog, duck, oysters, and vegetarian fare, New Day has reasonable prices.

Cha Ca La Vong (14 Cha Ca, tel. 04/3823-9875, 11am-2pm and 5:30pm-9pm daily, VND170,000/person) is the city's oldest restaurant, serving up sizzling pans of *cha ca* (pan-fried fish) since 1871. The modest, two-story spot specializes in only one dish, accompanied by rice noodles and peanuts. The portions are undersized and overpriced, though tasty. The staff is abrupt, but the restaurant is a popular stop. If you'd prefer more service and larger portions, **Cha Ca Thang Long** (21-31 Duong Thanh, tel. 04/3824-5115, www.chacathanglong.com, 10am-10pm daily, VND120,000/person) provides the same dish at a more reasonable price.

At the charming **Little Black Duck** (23 Ngo Gach, tel. 04/6253-5557, www.littleblackduckhanoi.com, 10:30am-10pm daily, VND50,000-380,000), Vietnamese cuisine is the main offering, though dishes like falafel

bun cha, a Hanoian noodle specialty

and fish and chips are on the menu. There are several duck specialties, including a tasty *bun nem vit* (soup with rice noodles, fresh greens, and duck spring rolls). The miniature eatery feels like a café, with only three tables in its ground-floor dining area and the rest occupying a cozy space upstairs. The staff is friendly and eager to please.

Com Ga (1 Cua Dong, tel. 04/3923-3728, comgacafe@gmail.com, 7am-11pm daily, VND55,000-135,000) sits on a busy corner along the western edge of the Old Quarter. The restaurant prides itself on its hearty helpings of the namesake *com ga* (Hoi An-style chicken and rice). The second-floor balcony makes an ideal spot for a drink and late-afternoon people-watching.

CATHEDRAL DISTRICT
Cafés and Bakeries

Seek out the pocket-sized **Hanoi House** (47A Ly Quoc Su, 2nd Fl., tel. 04/2348-9789, 8:30am-11pm daily, VND24,000-87,000) and you'll be rewarded with a cozy, laid-back hideout just far enough from the bustle of the city. All but invisible from the street, this tiny café is down an alley and up a flight of concrete stairs, overlooking St. Joseph's Cathedral. Furnished with low wooden tables and intimate booths, ceramic tea sets, small Chinese ink paintings, and rattan-weaved lanterns, Hanoi House offers the usual coffee and tea options in a pleasantly relaxed space.

A large, comfy, Western-style shop, **Joma Bakery & Cafe** (22 Ly Quoc Su, tel. 04/3747-3388, www.joma.biz, 7am-9pm daily, VND30,000-120,000) offers a taste of home, with delicious breakfasts, sandwiches, bagels, European coffee, and mouthwatering pastries. Relax in the small seating area up front near the main counter, or head out back to the larger café, where cozy couches and quiet tables await. You'll also find another location at **Joma To Ngoc Van** (43 To Ngoc Van, tel. 04/3718-6071, www.joma.biz, 7am-9pm daily, VND30,000-120,000). Both outlets have delivery services. A portion of their sales go to local charitable organizations.

Just off the main drag, the storefront of **Loft Stop Cafe** (11B Bao Khanh, tel. 04/3928-9433, www.loft-stop-cafe.com, 8am-11pm daily, VND25,000-200,000) is lit up by two well-stocked display cases laden with decadent treats. Pastries, cakes, and other goodies attract more than a few visitors. Its cool, quiet, street-side digs offer some respite, and with a range of coffee, tea, and other beverages populating the menu, it's a good place to pop in for dessert or a mid-afternoon snack. The Loft Stop also makes a solid pizza.

International

The **Hanoi Social Club** (6 Hoi Vu, tel. 04/3938-2117, 8am-11pm daily, VND95,000-170,000) dishes out an eclectic array of international fare, including burgers and breakfast foods alongside goulash, roti wraps, mango curry, and Moroccan chicken. Its chefs are able to adjust dishes for vegetarian, vegan, and gluten-free diners. The beverage menu is equally varied, including European coffees and teas as well as a few Vietnamese favorites,

such as egg coffee and *ca phe sua da* (iced coffee with milk). Comfy chairs, whimsical decor, and indie music round out the Social Club's offerings. There is live music on evenings and weekends.

It's hard not to be charmed by the laid-back ambience and breezy second-floor balcony at classy **Buon Dua Le Cafe** (20 Hang Hanh, tel. 04/3825-7388, 6:30am-11pm daily, VND45,000-275,000). Down a quiet side street but close to Hoan Kiem Lake, the place is outfitted with polished wooden furniture and the artwork of local painter Duc Loi. The menu is mainly Vietnamese, with a few Western dishes. The open-air hangout makes a perfect place to start your day or kick back with a happy hour beverage as the sun goes down.

Street Food

One bowl of rice porridge, called *chao suon* (corner of Ly Quoc Su and Ngo Huyen, 7am-7pm daily, VND25,000/bowl), from the small, street-side outfit near St. Joseph's Cathedral and you'll be coming back for seconds. A smooth, stew-like consistency, this particular vendor's porridge is served with savory pork and *quay,* essentially a fried breadstick, on top. On the miniature plastic stools that line the road, sit and enjoy the bustle of the city while tucking into your piping hot *chao.* For extra flavor, toss in some black pepper. Portions are just right, making this a great breakfast or midday snack.

Vietnamese

A top-seven contender on Vietnam's first-ever edition of *MasterChef,* the talented **Minh Thuy** (20 Ngo Huyen, tel. 04/3200-7893, www.minh-thuy.com, 10am-10pm daily, VND40,000-130,000) excels at preparing local dishes as well as her very own European-Asian fusions. Tucked down an alley flush with budget hotels and hungry travelers, the small, one-room restaurant has flourished as both locals and tourists stop in for a bite and a glimpse of the framed *MasterChef* apron. With great food and reasonable prices, this is a go-to spot for lunch and dinner.

FRENCH QUARTER
French

La Badiane (10 Nam Ngu, tel. 04/3942-4509, www.labadiane-hanoi.com, 11:30am-2:30pm and 6:30pm-10:30pm Mon.-Sat., VND230,000-345,000 lunch, VND520,000-1,590,000 dinner) is the city's finest French restaurant. Venture through the restaurant's arching, vine-covered white corridor and you'll find a host of gourmet dishes, from lamb shank and duck breast, tartar and carpaccio to pan-fried foie gras, homemade pasta, and sumptuous desserts. Each meal is a work of art, carefully plated. Chef Benjamin Rascalou, a veteran of the Parisian restaurant circuit, keeps things interesting with a regularly changing menu.

Thai

There is a consensus among locals and expats that **Lustro Thai** (57A Phan Chu Trinh, tel. 04/6278-2628, 9am-11pm daily, VND85,000-265,000) is the best Thai spot in the French Quarter. With generous helpings of authentic fare and a spacious, modern seating area, the restaurant earns its popularity.

Vegetarian

Hidden down an alley, **Nang Tam Com Chay** (79A Tran Hung Dao, tel. 04/3942-4140, 10am-9pm daily, VND25,000-100,000) is a popular Vietnamese vegetarian joint that features scores of meatless dishes, from standard tofu-and-tomato-sauce to mock-meat recreations of traditional local fare. Tasty, filling set lunches go for as little as VND60,000. The small, air-conditioned dining area is usually full of locals at both lunch and dinner.

Vietnamese

Ngon (18 Phan Boi Chau, tel. 04/3942-8162, www.ngonhanoi.com.vn, 6:30am-9:30pm daily, VND45,000-360,000) and its extensive menu provide solid guidance on what to eat and how to eat it. Thanks to the place's market-style setup, diners are able to peruse everything before choosing. Set within a large courtyard, the bustling street food-style eatery is packed during lunch and evenings with tourists and locals. Delve into soups, sautés, spring rolls, and sauces.

BA DINH
Cafés and Bakeries

The folks at **Cong Caphe** (32 Dien Bien Phu, tel. 04/6686-0344, www.congcaphe.com, 7am-11pm daily, VND30,000-50,000) have taken the aesthetics of Vietnamese Communism and applied it to an urban coffee shop, with a decor featuring weathered wood, peeling paint, exposed brick, and stark concrete. The brown-paper menus list coffee, tea, and smoothies alongside coffee-coconut shakes and coffee with yogurt. There are other locations (35A Nguyen Huu Huan, tel. 04/6292-5814, 7am-11pm daily) around town, including a spot on Nguyen Huu Huan. Cong occasionally hosts live music, during which time it serves a few alcoholic beverages.

International

A training restaurant and one of the most popular spots in town, **KOTO** (59 Van Mieu, tel. 04/3747-0337, www.koto.com.au, 7:30am-10pm daily, VND85,000-250,000) has made an impact on the restaurant scene as well as the lives of its many graduates. Started in 1999, KOTO (Know One, Teach One) admits young disadvantaged Vietnamese into its two-year training program, which provides job training in the hospitality industry. The restaurant acts as a training ground for students while serving delicious renditions of both Vietnamese and international favorites. The eatery's location makes it conducive to a lunchtime visit, though things can get hectic around this time. Seating is spread out over four floors.

Many KOTO graduates have gone on to open their own restaurants, the most popular of which is **Pots 'n Pans** (57 Bui Thi Xuan, tel. 04/3944-0204, www.potsnpans.vn, 11:30am-late daily, VND210,000-690,000), an upmarket fusion spot with high-quality service and plenty of ambience. Though it's expensive, the food is truly a work of art; opt for one of the set menus, as these offer the best value.

Street Food

If you are near the Temple of Literature in the afternoon, swing by Ly Van Phuc, where you'll find finger-licking **barbecue chicken** (end of Ly Van Phuc, 4pm-late daily, VND6,000-10,000/piece) starting around 3pm-4pm. Snacks are pay-as-you-go, with varying prices for legs and wings. These tasty treats make the perfect *do nhau* (drinking food) to pair with a beer. Though there are several shops along this street, the ones at the far end are the best.

WEST LAKE AREA
Cafés and Bakeries

Saint Honore (5 Xuan Dieu, tel. 04/332-355, www.sainthonore.com.vn, 6:30am-10pm daily, VND35,000-200,000) is a charming little Parisian-style bistro, replete with flaky, decadent pastries, fresh bread, and a deli counter that wraps around the end of the building. Delicious sandwiches and crepes feature on the menu alongside a range of coffee and tea options; while there are a handful of more sophisticated meals on offer, it's best to stick to simpler fare, as this is where the café excels. Saint Honore also has a second location (31 Thai Phien, tel. 04/3974-9483, 6:30am-10pm daily) closer to downtown.

SELF-CATERING

Hanoian cuisine is as varied as it is delicious. Those with dietary issues, or those who simply prefer more control in the preparation of their meals, will appreciate shops like **Veggy's** (99 Xuan Dieu, tel. 04/3719-4630, 8am-8pm daily), a small but well-stocked grocery store near the northern end of West Lake that's packed with familiar Western brands like Kraft, Campbell's, and Betty Crocker. For even more selection, **Annam Gourmet** (51 Xuan Dieu, tel. 04/3718-4487, www.annamgourmet.com, 7:30am-8:30pm daily), located in the Syrena Shopping Center, offers a range of useful cooking items and canned goods as well as a small bakery and deli counter, where you'll find several different types of cheese and cold cuts. Prices at both of these shops run on the high side, but you'll find many familiar brand names and a much larger selection than local supermarkets.

If you're simply looking for basic groceries and other essentials, the **Hapro Mart** (63 Cau Go, 8:30am-10pm daily) in the Old Quarter sells things like pasta, canned goods, and milk. While it's not very big, the store manages to cover most simple ingredients as well as a few toiletries and other odds and ends. There is also a second location (35 Hang Bong, 8:30am-10pm daily) nearby.

Information and Services

TOURIST INFORMATION

You'll find scores of travel agencies boasting "free tourist information" around the Old Quarter, but this local wisdom extends no further than a brochure of the company's tour packages. Your hotel is usually the best place to seek out unbiased travel tips, not to mention other extras like free maps. If you can't seem to track these down, the **Tourist Information Center** (7 Dinh Tien Hoang, tel. 04/3926-3366, www.ticvietnam.com, 8am-9pm daily) opposite the northern edge of Hoan Kiem Lake provides detailed plans of the city as well as a complimentary Hanoi guide, which lists recommendations on hotels, restaurants, sights, and other attractions in town. While the company operating this office sells its own tours, the free materials on offer make the place a little more helpful than most.

BANKS AND CURRENCY EXCHANGE

You'll find ATMs on nearly every street corner in Hanoi, particularly in the downtown area.

Most hotels and tour agencies offer to exchange currency, as do the majority of banks in the downtown area. Look up the actual exchange rate to ensure that you receive a fair conversion. If you're pressed for time, the bank is your best bet.

Most banks in the capital are open 8am-5pm Monday-Friday. Vietnamese institutions like **Vietcombank** (www.vietcombank.com.vn) and **Sacombank** (www.sacombank.com.vn) tend to take a lunch break during the day, shutting their doors 11:30am-1pm; foreign companies like **HSBC** (www.hsbc.com.vn), **Citibank** (www.citibank.com.vn), and **ANZ** (www.anz.com) stay open all day. Some Vietnamese banks are open on Saturday mornings.

While much of the country remains cash-only, you will find that some places in Hanoi, including high-end hotels and upscale restaurants, are beginning to accept credit cards as a form of payment. This is the exception rather than the rule, so check ahead of time. Many businesses tack on a small additional charge for using plastic over paper money.

INTERNET AND POSTAL SERVICES

Hanoi's **international post office** (6 Dinh Le, tel. 04/3825-4503, www.vnpost.vn, 7am-5pm Mon.-Fri., 8am-5pm Sat.-Sun.) staffs English-speaking employees. For additional services, visit the **central post office** (75 Dinh Tien Hoang, tel. 04/3825-5948, www.vnpost.vn, 7:30am-6:30pm Mon.-Fri., 8:30am-5:30pm Sat.-Sun.) just next door. You are less likely to find an English speaker, but employees will usually point you in the right direction.

When shipping packages, Hanoi offers three options: the local post, often slow and less reliable, though affordable, or **UPS** (10 Le Thach, tel. 04/3824-6483, www.ups.com, 8am-noon and 1:30pm-5pm Mon.-Fri.,

8am-noon Sat.), and **DHL** (Le Thach, tel. 01/800-1530, www.dhl.com, 8am-noon and 1pm-6pm Mon.-Fri.). Both shipping companies have offices on the northern side of the central post office, just around the corner from its front door. Unless absolutely necessary, avoid international shipping, as costs quickly add up.

You'd be hard-pressed to find a hotel in town that does not have a desktop computer in the hotel lobby or, at the very least, a Wi-Fi connection. Indeed, most cafés and restaurants offer free wireless Internet for paying customers.

PHONE SERVICE

Many travelers buy a local cell phone for the trip. SIM cards and basic, reliable Nokia phones are widely available, both new and secondhand, from electronics shops around the Old Quarter as well as at **The Gioi Di Dong** (468-472 Le Duan, tel. 1/800-1060, www.thegioididong.com, 7:30am-10pm daily), with the cheapest options beginning around VND350,000. Once you obtain a phone and SIM card, you'll have to purchase mobile credit, which is found at most local *tap hoa* (convenience stores). The three main cell carriers in Vietnam are Vinaphone, Mobifone, and Viettel, all of whom operate on a pay-as-you-go basis. Credit comes in increments of VND20,000, VND50,000, VND100,000, and VND200,000.

EMERGENCY AND MEDICAL SERVICES

Vietnam employs three separate phone numbers for emergency response services: 113 is meant for police assistance in the event of robberies, traffic accidents, and crime-related incidents; 114 links to the city's firefighters; and 115 covers medical emergencies. None of these hotlines are likely to have an English speaker on the other end and the city's emergency response teams are sluggish at best.

In the event of a medical emergency, the best thing you can do is contact a foreign medical center directly for help. Local facilities like **Hong Ngoc Hospital** (55 Yen Ninh, tel. 04/3927-5568, 8am-5pm daily) are reliable for simple aches and pains. International hospitals such as **Family Medical Practice** (298 Kim Ma, Van Phuc Compound, tel. 04/3843-0748, www.vietnammedicalpractice.com), which staffs experienced English-speaking foreign and Vietnamese doctors, stay open 24 hours and assist with more serious predicaments. **International SOS** (51 Xuan Dieu, tel. 04/3934-0666, www.internationalsos.com) provides a similar level of quality, though its pricing can run high.

PHARMACIES

Scores of pharmacies, also known as *nha thuoc tay,* are scattered throughout the Old Quarter and across town. These facilities stock prescription and over-the-counter remedies, as well as products like tampons and contact lens solution. Most downtown pharmacies also employ at least one English-speaking staff member. The **pharmacy** (119 Hang Gai, tel. 04/3828-6782, 8am-9pm daily) located on Hang Gai is a reliable option, as are the several businesses that run along Phu Doan near the cathedral.

DIPLOMATIC SERVICES

While there is a **U.S. Embassy** (7 Lang Ha, tel. 04/3850-5000, www.vietnam.usembassy.

gov), all inquiries regarding American citizens must be directed to the Rose Garden Building, where **consular services** (Rose Garden Bldg., 170 Ngoc Khanh, 2nd Fl., tel. 04/3850-5000, www.vietnam.usembassy.gov, 8:30am-11:30am and 1pm-3:30pm Mon.-Thurs., by appt. only) are carried out, around the corner from the embassy. Due to the fact that all visitors must have a scheduled appointment on the books, look at the embassy's website ahead of time in order to discern what you'll need before venturing to this area. Appointments can also be made online. For emergencies, American citizens are advised to contact the embassy and consular services (tel. 04/3850-5000) during business hours; outside of these times, contact the embassy's **emergency hotline** (tel. 09/0340-1991) for assistance.

LAUNDRY

The majority of Hanoi's accommodations provide laundry services at an additional cost, and there is usually a markup for going this route. Standard pricing on the street is around VND25,000 per kilo, while you'll pay upwards of VND35,000 for the convenience of going through your hotel. The turnaround is usually about a day's time; in lousy winter weather be prepared to wait a little longer, as dryers are seldom used and the cold, humid winter months tend to leave everything a little damp.

Getting There

AIR

Flights from around the country and across the globe arrive at Hanoi's **Noi Bai International Airport** (HAN, Phu Minh ward, Soc Son district, tel. 04/3886-5047, www.hanoiairportonline.com), 20 miles north of the city. Several budget airlines, including Jetstar, Air Asia, and Viet Jet, pass through here in addition to a host of other international carriers. Customs and immigration procedures move quickly; those completing pre-approved

visa processing should expect to wait in line for a short while before passing through customs inspections. Those traveling domestically from other in-country destinations will be spared this waiting.

Once you've exited the airport, it's about a 45-minute ride into the city by taxi, minibus, or public bus. Many hotels can arrange airport pickup for an additional fee (starting at VND350,000), so long as you contact them in advance.

Taxis from the Airport

The airport is notorious for a host of taxi troubles: drivers quote flat rates that border on extortion or insist that the destination you've presented is closed, full, or for some other reason unavailable in hopes of steering you to another hotel, where they usually receive a kickback. When metered vehicles are available, it is not uncommon for meters to run up the fare at lightning speed. Your best bet is to write down the name and exact address of your hotel before leaving the airport. This way, you have a clear destination to show your driver and, should he or she attempt to take you elsewhere, you are able to politely refuse and point to the place on the paper.

The easiest way to procure a cab from the airport is to walk to the taxi stand (easily visible when leaving the arrivals area), where a flat rate (to downtown) will be posted on the sign out front. Once you have a taxi, confirm again with your driver the exact price as some drivers will still attempt to overcharge. Stick to trusted companies like **Mailinh Airport** (tel. 04/3822-2666). From the airport to the downtown area should cost no more than VND400,000, but sometimes even the most reputable companies are dishonest.

Airport Minibus

An airport **minibus** (7am-7pm daily, VND40,000), courtesy of Vietnam Airlines, leaves from Noi Bai when it has enough passengers to make the journey worthwhile, usually every 30 minutes or so. The minibus drops passengers off in front of the Vietnam Airlines office downtown, one block south of Hoan Kiem Lake. While you may have to wait a few minutes at the airport, this is by far the cheapest and most hassle-free option if you are traveling light. Even if your hotel is not within walking distance of the minibus stop, the combined cost of the minibus fare and a cab from downtown Hanoi to your final destination will be less expensive and reduce the risk of being overcharged by a taxi. The same minibuses also travel the reverse route back to the airport, leaving from the Vietnam

Airlines office (corner of Quang Trung and Hai Ba Trung).

Public Bus from the Airport

A **public bus** (VND5,000) also makes a trip into town from the airport. **Bus number 17** travels via the Chuong Duong Bridge and lets off at Long Bien station, in between Hoan Kiem and West Lake, opposite a stretch of the city's ceramic wall. From here, it's less than a mile to the Old Quarter, making the rest of the journey easily walkable, depending upon your luggage; it's just as easy to catch a cab from here. **Bus number 7** also departs from Noi Bai, traveling to the western suburbs of the city. For more specific directions to your destination, it's possible to double-check your route with Google Maps, as its representation of the Hanoi public bus system is accurate and far easier than attempting to decipher the route listings on the Hanoi Bus website.

TRAIN

Hanoi's mammoth **train station** (120 Le Duan, tel. 04/3942-3697, www.gahanoi.com.vn, 8am-5pm daily) serves southern cities like Danang, Nha Trang, and Saigon, in addition to offering an overnight service north to Sapa. Tickets can be purchased through the station directly as well as from the station's website, and they are offered at travel agencies across town. Ask around when booking through a travel agency, as some outfits charge an excessive commission.

Taxis from the Train Station

The train station attracts plenty of cab drivers eager to catch a fare from an unsuspecting or weary traveler, often at several times the actual price. Opt for one of the **Mailinh** (tel. 04/3833-3333) cabs waiting out front. If you can't find a Mailinh cab, find a driver who will agree upon a fixed price, as rapid-fire taxi meters can turn a few dollars into 10 or 20 before you know it. Expect to pay around VND50,000 for a trip from the train station to Hoan Kiem Lake (10-minute ride). If you can't find someone willing to take a flat rate, walk a block or two away from the station and you'll find that drivers become increasingly more reasonable.

BUS

Hanoi has four separate bus stations scattered around the outskirts of the city. **Giap Bat** (Giai Phong, tel. 04/3864-1467, 5am-6pm daily) handles all routes heading south to destinations such as Ninh Binh and Hue, while vehicles at **Luong Yen** (Nguyen Khoai, tel. 04/3972-0477, 6am-11pm daily) and **Gia Lam** (9 Ngo Gia Kham, tel. 04/3827-1529, 5am-5pm daily) depart for Ha Long and Haiphong on a regular basis. To the west, **My Dinh** (20 Pham Hung, tel. 04/3768-5549, 4:30am-11pm daily) offers the occasional fare to Lao Cai and other northwestern towns, too.

You can eliminate the hassle of getting out to the station and navigating Vietnamese bus timetables and fare collectors by taking one of the comfy, air-conditioned coach buses that leave from the offices of **Sinh Tourist** (52 Luong Ngoc Quyen, tel. 04/3926-1568, www.thesinh-tourist.vn, 6:30am-10pm daily) as well as several other local companies, all of which are located in the downtown area. Sinh Tourist has only the Luong Ngoc Quyen location and another on Tran Nhat Duat (64 Tran Nhat Duat, tel. 04/3929-0394, 6:30am-10pm daily). All other signs advertising "Sinh Cafe," "The Sinh Cafe," or "Sinh Cafe Tourist" are impostors. Go to the correct address and look for the blue-and-white logo.

Hoang Long (28 Tran Nhat Duat, tel. 04/3928-2828, www.hoanglongasia.com, 7am-7pm daily) also offers good value tickets. The company has satellite offices at the Luong Yen, Giap Bat, and My Dinh bus stations as well as its Old Quarter office.

Taxis from the Bus Station

If taxis from the airport come with a bad reputation, the cabs loitering outside of bus stations across the city are in an equally poor standing. Before you even step off the bus, there will be a swarm of drivers crowding the vehicle's entrance, just waiting for a tired, confused, or unsuspecting tourist to wander their way. The best thing you can do when stepping off a bus is grab your luggage and beeline for the exit. Ignore the touts, cab drivers, *xe om*, and anyone else who insists upon giving you a ride and walk to the street. From there, you needn't head more than a block before you find that cab drivers have backed off the hard sell, and it's much easier to pick out a reputable vehicle, insist upon a reasonable metered cab, and set off.

MOTORBIKE

As it rolls into the capital, Vietnam's famous Highway 1 goes by a few different names before splitting in two directions to avoid the city altogether; from here, Ngoc Hoi transitions into Giai Phong and eventually Le Duan, landing you squarely in the heart of town just a few miles from Hoan Kiem Lake. For those arriving from the east, a pair of equally hectic national roads, Highway 14 and Highway 1, come together eight miles outside of the city and head across the Chuong Duong Bridge into town. Travelers from the west will follow Highway 6 directly to the city center, while those coming from the north have a few options. Thang Long Boulevard reaches Hanoi from the northwest, heading in toward Hoan Kiem Lake; there is also an airport road that passes by West Lake before approaching the city from the north. Being an obvious center of activity, no one highway is less crowded than the others. If possible, arrive before or after the evening rush hour.

Getting Around

TAXIS

Taxis in the capital have a less-than-stellar reputation for overcharging tourists, either through hyperactive meters or by making a few extra turns to run up the fare. Companies like Mailinh (tel. 04/3833-3333) and the red-and-blue Taxi Group (tel. 04/3857-5757) are reputable. When hailing a cab downtown, move away from the heavily touristed areas like Ma May or Ly Quoc Su and hop in a taxi near the main road instead, as this will decrease your chances of encountering an opportunist cabbie. Taxis should always be metered; while some drivers attempt to quote a flat rate, these are almost never in your favor and so it's best to stick to the machine. If possible, try to pay with exact change or something close to it, as cab drivers often insist that they don't have small bills in hopes of gleaning a few extra thousand dong from you. Should you find yourself in a situation where you feel as though you're being taken advantage of—the meter is running too high, for example—stop the cab where you are, pay whatever you believe to be fair, and exit the vehicle. Protesting or waiting to negotiate a price may result in more trouble.

XE OM

Walking around the Old Quarter, you will soon become accustomed to the waving hands and calls of "Hello! Motorbike!" that follow travelers around the city. Xe om drivers perch on most corners in the downtown area and can be relentless in their sales pitch. Agree upon a fare before hopping on board. From the Old Quarter to most tourist destinations in the area (barring faraway sights like the Museum of Ethnology and West Lake), your fare should not exceed VND40,000. If a particular driver is not willing to budge on the price, find another driver.

The folks that work Hanoi's xe om are daredevils, weaving through a hectic web of traffic that hurtles haphazardly down the narrow streets of downtown Hanoi. For safety's sake, insist upon wearing a helmet. Even if most Vietnamese helmets are not up to Western standards, better to have a little protection in the event of an accident than none at all.

CYCLOS

Slow-moving and seemingly less dangerous than their motorized compatriots, cyclos are the vehicle of choice for many travelers, as they give you the opportunity to sit back as you ply the streets of downtown Hanoi without fear of being run over by a motorbike or moving so quickly that your only thoughts are of safely making it to a particular destination. These sluggish, human-powered trikes ferry tourists all over the Old Quarter with occasional jaunts out to the French Quarter or Ba Dinh Square and beyond, depending on the passenger's needs. A standard cyclo trip lasts about an hour, weaving through the narrow downtown streets and allowing you to get a genuine feel of the city without the anxiety of tackling Hanoian traffic on your own. You'll have to bargain for your fare; most hour-long journeys begin around VND100,000. Your driver will be cycling you around with his own two legs, and so you should expect to pay more than you would for a motorized trip.

PUBLIC TRANSPORTATION
Bus

Hanoi's public bus (tel. 04/3747-0403, www.hanoibus.com.vn, 5am-9pm daily, VND5,000-7,000) lines run all over town and are the most cost-effective way to navigate its narrow streets. While maps of the entire system are not readily available, Google Maps accurately plots the city's bus routes, which makes finding the right bus line as easy as plugging your start and end destinations into the website. On the street, all stops are clearly marked with a blue sign bearing the bus number and its route, and fares are posted on the outside of each vehicle. Most rides around the city cost VND5,000. From the northern edge of Hoan Kiem Lake, buses 9 and 14 are especially useful, as these stop either directly in front of or not far from several popular sights, including Ho Chi Minh Mausoleum, the Temple of Literature, the Hanoi Flag Tower, and the Museum of Ethnology. While many of the more common downtown bus routes stop service at 9pm, some stop earlier, around 8pm. Both Google Maps and the Hanoi Bus website have accurate information regarding bus run times.

Electric Car

Dong Xuan Market runs an **electric car service** (north side of Hoan Kiem Lake, tel. 04/3929-0509, dongxuantours@gmail.com, 8am-10pm daily, VND150,000/car/35 min., VND250,000/car/hour) that ferries passengers around Hoan Kiem Lake and the Old Quarter area. A handful of standard routes are available, stopping at some of the city's more noteworthy landmarks and shopping areas. Electric cars seat a maximum of seven people and, while it is possible to travel with less than seven to a car, you'll have to cover the cost for the entire vehicle regardless of how few or how many individuals are on board.

VEHICLES FOR HIRE

Motorbike rentals are widely available in the downtown area, especially around Ngo Huyen near St. Joseph's Cathedral and along Dinh Liet to the north of Hoan Kiem Lake. Some of the foreign-owned rental outfits attempt to charge as much as VND210,000 per day, but you can just as easily rent a bike of reasonable quality for VND100,000 from one of the Vietnamese shops nearby. There are a handful of outfits on Dinh Liet that rent out vehicles at reasonable prices. Depending upon the business, some shops may request collateral for the vehicle, in the form of either an ID or a cash deposit. Do a lap around the block and check for any issues before setting off for the day and insist upon a helmet for the trip. Though you'll see plenty of locals flaunting this rule, Vietnamese law requires that all drivers wear a helmet when driving and you are eligible to be pulled over if you fail to do so.

Hanoi's traffic is hectic. Much of the Old Quarter lacks streetlights or stop signs. Narrow roads combined with fast-paced driving can easily result in accidents. Only confident, experienced drivers should brave Hanoian traffic. Many streets in downtown Hanoi are one way, and turning right on red is forbidden in the capital city. Not all rules of the road are closely followed by locals, but you should be aware of the rules.

Vicinity of Hanoi

Beyond the city limits, Hanoi's suburbs and surrounding countryside offer a few easygoing day trips. At the heart of the Red River Delta, a pair of booming traditional handicraft villages complement the urban chaos, while a serene pagoda complex southwest of the city affords an altogether different view of northern Vietnam. Jaunts to Tam Coc and Hoa Lu, Ninh Binh's main attractions, are possible, with plenty of tour providers offering day trips to the area.

PERFUME PAGODA

One of over 30 pagodas dotting the mountains of Ha Tay province, the beautifully austere **Perfume Pagoda (Chua Huong)** (tel. 04/3384-9849, www.lehoichuahuong.vn, 8am-5pm daily, VND50,000 plus boat fare) is Hanoi's most popular day trip destination. Perfume Pagoda, named for the clouds of incense permeating the cave's interior, is located inside a cave at the top of a mountain. Forty miles west of the capital, the pagoda complex

Vicinity of Hanoi

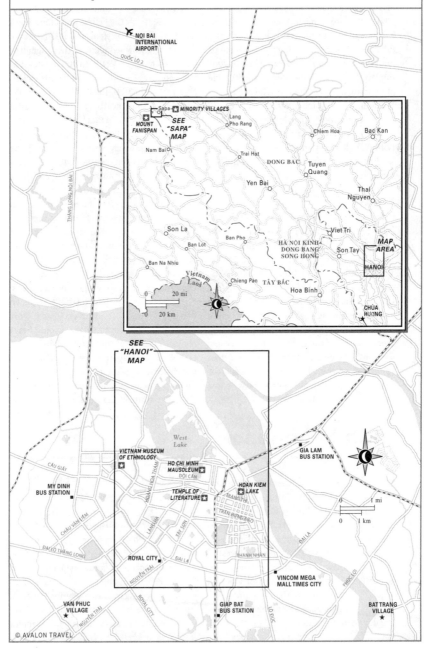

✈ NOI BAI INTERNATIONAL AIRPORT

QUỐC LỘ 2

THĂNG LONG NỘI BÀI

Sapa ⊞ MINORITY VILLAGES

SEE "SAPA" MAP

✚ MOUNT FANISPAN

Lang
Pho Rang

Chiem Hoa   Bac Kan

Nam Bai

Trai Hut

DONG BAC   Tuyen Quang

Yen Bai

Thai Nguyen

Son La

Ban Lot   Ban Pho

Viet Tri

HÀ NỘI KINH
ĐỒNG BẰNG
SÔNG HỒNG   Son Tay   MAP AREA

HANOI

Ban Na Nhiu

Vietnam
Laos   Chieng Pan   TÂY BẮC   Hoa Binh

CHÙA HƯƠNG

0   20 mi
0   20 km

SEE "HANOI" MAP

West Lake

VIETNAM MUSEUM OF ETHNOLOGY ✚

GIA LAM BUS STATION

CẦU GIẤY

MY DINH BUS STATION

HOÀNG HOA THÁM

HO CHI MINH MAUSOLEUM ✚
ĐỘI CẤN

HOAN KIEM LAKE ✚

TRẦN THỦ

CHÂU VĂN LIÊM

LÁNG HẠ   TÂY SƠN

TRẦN HƯNG ĐẠO

ĐẠI LA

0   1 mi
0   1 km

ĐẠI CỒ THĂNG LONG

ROYAL CITY

ĐẠI LA

THANH NHÀN

NGUYỄN TRÃI

VINCOM MEGA MALL TIMES CITY

PHÚC LỢI

VAN PHUC VILLAGE

NGUYỄN TRÃI

ROYAL CITY

GIAP BAT BUS STATION

LÒ ĐÚC

BAT TRANG VILLAGE

© AVALON TRAVEL

sprawls across a series of hills overlooking the Yen River and is considered northern Vietnam's most important Buddhist center of worship. Though it's become increasingly more commercial, with the usual roving vendors and boat drivers, the scenery and famous incense-filled grotto are worth a visit for those looking to escape the city.

Most trips to Perfume Pagoda are done via all-inclusive tour. Tour outfitters transport passengers to Yen Vy, a boat station in the town of Huong Son. From here, travelers board a small wooden **rowboat** (VND40,000/person). The boat glides on a small river past craggy limestone mountains and dense forest, taking about an hour from end to end. When your vessel reaches the pagoda complex, venture through the impressive three-door gate, a stark, towering structure whose black Chinese characters stand out against a bright white background. Past the gates, the temple Chua Thien Tru, also known as Heaven's Kitchen, houses a statue of Quan Am. It's one of the more atmospheric pagodas in the north.

The highlight of the pagoda complex is Huong Tich Cave, which is 164 feet above the water's edge atop a mountain. Though you have the option of reaching Huong Tich on foot, following a winding path up the mountain, most visitors prefer to jump in a bright yellow cable car (VND90,000 one-way, VND140,000 round-trip) to the mouth of the cave, where a set of stone steps descends into the darkened grotto. The cave interior is filled with small altars, obscured by an incense haze, and lacquer effigies. Once you've wandered through, walk back down toward the river. The steps become treacherous in foul weather; you can also hop on the cable car for the return trip. Respectful dress is a must at the complex.

While it's possible to reach the complex on your own via motorbike, the hassle of urban traffic is not really worth the few dollars you might save. Moreover, the journey to Perfume Pagoda is not nearly as picturesque as the sight itself. Dozens of tour companies in Hanoi offer full-day excursions that include transportation, entry fees, lunch, and a guide for as little as VND530,000.

HANDICRAFT VILLAGES

Across Vietnam, dozens of villages lay claim to culinary specialties or unique traditional crafts. These small, tight-knit communities have produced marble statues, fine silk, traditional Vietnamese lacquerware, or handmade pottery for centuries. Just outside of Hanoi, Bat Trang to the south and Van Phuc to the west each boast a long tradition of producing top-quality items and are known throughout Vietnam for their skilled craftspeople.

Bat Trang

Ten miles south and across the Red River, the small village of **Bat Trang** has been making high-quality ceramics since the 15th century and is a popular stop for shoppers in search of ceramics. Today, its pottery is nationally famous and exported around the world, with modern-day potters crafting both the traditional blue-and-white ceramics of the past as well as more colorful contemporary designs. Price tags in some of the larger outlets tend not to vary much from those in the city, but you'll find that there is more room for bargaining here and seemingly endless variety.

Most shops (which are also people's houses) are open around 7am-5pm or 6pm daily, and vendors sell similar objects. Visiting Bat Trang is like perusing a large pottery market.

Often, shops will have someone working on pottery, giving a glimpse of the pottery-making process. Ask permission before taking photos, though most shops will likely give permission. If a vendor invites you to try out the pottery wheel or help you make something, there will almost always be an expectation that you buy something in return.

Travelers can reach Bat Trang independently by taxi, bus, or hired vehicle. Bus 47 departs every half-hour from the large bus stop near Long Bien Bridge just north of the Old Quarter off Hang Dau street. Cyclists and motorbikes can reach the area by way of

Provincial Road 195 on the eastern bank of the river. When crossing, cyclists should use Long Bien Bridge, while other vehicles should use Chuong Duong Bridge directly south.

Van Phuc

West out of town en route to Perfume Pagoda, the whirring looms of **Van Phuc** silk village draw droves of curious shoppers exploring the countryside for the day. As early as the 9th century, local residents raised mulberry trees and silkworms here, spinning their fragile cocoons into fabric for sale both in the village and across the country. During the days of the Nguyen dynasty, Van Phuc was required to produce bolts of silk to clothe the royal family. Today, the village houses over a thousand looms and its goods are often exported beyond Vietnam's borders. While shoppers will find the cost of raw material about the same as in the city, ready-made items like scarves, ties, and shirts are notably less expensive here.

Shops generally open at 8am or 9am and close at 5pm daily. Most of the shops in Van Phuc are also workshops. The silk is made there, so you can watch as local proprietors weave different fabrics with a loom. Shop owners are often happy to let you try out the loom, but you will be strongly encouraged to buy something in return.

While most visitors to Van Phuc get here by way of a day tour to Perfume Pagoda, it is also possible to reach Van Phuc independently. Buses 1 and 2 travel out to the village by way of Highway 6, departing from the French Quarter and the lower part of Hoan Kiem district near the train station. Drivers can access Van Phuc via the same route.

Sapa

Perched high above Muong Hoa Valley, the sleepy little town of Sapa is a world apart from its urban contemporaries, quiet and compact amid the vast open space of Vietnam's remote northwest. Now the go-to destination of the region, its rolling hills and verdant, many-tiered rice terraces are the main attraction, coupled with an array of fascinating minority cultures, whose traditional dress, rituals, religious ceremonies, and ways of life continue to exist in much the same fashion as they have for centuries.

Though its tourism industry has seen a boom in recent years, this hilltop town has long captivated visitors, attracting French attention in the early 20th century. Some ethnic Vietnamese moved into the area in the 1960s, but it wasn't until well after the war's end in the 1990s that Sapa saw any major growth spurt.

The fresh air, ample hiking trails, and opportunity for cultural exchange with some of Vietnam's lesser-known communities draw luxury travelers and adventure seekers with the prospect of striking out for minority villages or scaling the colossal Mount Fansipan, Vietnam's tallest peak.

Inclement weather can ruin a visit to Sapa. The best months are September and October, just before the rice harvests take away much of its visual appeal, or at the start of spring, for better views of the valley. From November to February, temperatures plummet, earning Sapa a reputation as the only town in Vietnam that sees snow. In winter, heavy fog makes for poor visibility, spoiling much of the point of a visit to Sapa.

SIGHTS

Sapa town is a peaceful, charming little place, meandering across hillsides and dotted with modest green spaces amid its ever-growing town center. All of its sights are easily accessed on foot, though you'll get a workout traipsing up and down some of the nearby inclines. In the town center, a small park dominated by a monument to Ho Chi Minh leads onto the large local square, a popular gathering place in the mornings and evenings. Farther north near the main highway, **Sapa Lake** makes for a pleasant stroll, surrounded by manicured gardens and plenty of park benches.

Sapa Market

Nestled in the hillside just below Sapa's main square, the **central market** (between Fansipan and Cau May streets, 6am-6pm daily) is in full swing from dawn to dusk, alive with vendors hawking bulk items like tea and dried fruit along with fresh produce, meat, and hot meals. A handful of souvenirs and other knickknacks make an appearance, but the stalls set up beneath this market's tented covering stick to the bright and colorful necessities of locals. Even if you're not interested in shopping, it's a pleasant place to wander, as you'll find several items, from greens to tea to certain fruits, which are unique to northwestern Vietnam.

Sapa Museum

Located in a traditional wooden stilt house behind the Tourist Information Center, **Sapa Museum** (2 Fansipan, tel. 02/0387-1975, 7:30am-11:30am and 1:30pm-5pm daily, free) gives a solid introduction to the town and the area, telling the story of Sapa's history under

the French and its growth as a town during the 20th century. While a handful of the traditions and customs of Sapa's ethnic minorities are touched upon, there's far less background on the H'mong, Dao, Tay, Phu La, and Giay people who inhabit the region. For this, link up with a local guide to learn more about life in the village.

Our Lady of Rosary Church

The diminutive stone **Our Lady of Rosary Church** (Sapa Town Square, tel. 02/0387-3014, www.sapachurch.org) was first built in 1926 to accommodate Sapa's European parishioners. It is a pretty landmark in town, its gray exterior rounding out the eastern edge of the town square. While the doors are closed outside of mass hours, its steps are often used as a gathering place along with the square nearby.

Cat Cat Village

Cat Cat Village (6am-9pm daily, VND40,000) is home to the Black H'mong. The trip to the village is one of the more accessible walks in the Sapa area. This particular jaunt falls somewhere between a hike and a trek (just over three miles round-trip), with paved, well-trodden paths winding through what is now more of a tourist attraction than

Sapa Lake

Sapa

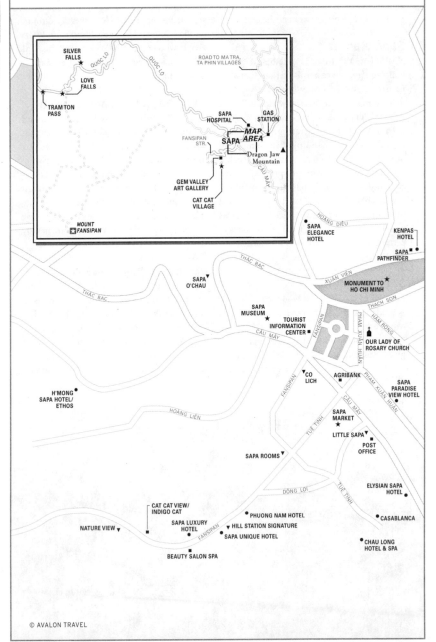

SILVER FALLS

QUỐC LỘ

QUỐC LỘ

ROAD TO MA TRA, TA PHIN VILLAGES

LOVE FALLS

TRAM TON PASS

SAPA HOSPITAL

GAS STATION

FANSIPAN STR.

SAPA

MAP AREA

Dragon Jaw Mountain

GEM VALLEY ART GALLERY

CAT CAT VILLAGE

MOUNT FANSIPAN

HOÀNG DIỆU

SAPA ELEGANCE HOTEL

KENPAS HOTEL

SAPA PATHFINDER

THÁC BẮC

SAPA O'CHAU

XUÂN VIÊN

MONUMENT TO HO CHI MINH

THÁC BẮC

THACH SON

HÀM RÔNG

SAPA MUSEUM

TOURIST INFORMATION CENTER

CẦU MÂY

FANSIPAN

PHẠM XUÂN HUÂN

OUR LADY OF ROSARY CHURCH

H'MONG SAPA HOTEL/ ETHOS

HOÀNG LIÊN

FANSIPAN

CO LICH

AGRIBANK

PHẠM XUÂN HUÂN

SAPA PARADISE VIEW HOTEL

CẦU MÂY

SAPA MARKET

TUÊ TĨNH

LITTLE SAPA

POST OFFICE

SAPA ROOMS

ĐỒNG LỢI

TUÊ TĨNH

ELYSIAN SAPA HOTEL

CASABLANCA

CAT CAT VIEW/ INDIGO CAT

NATURE VIEW

SAPA LUXURY HOTEL

FANSIPAN

PHUONG NAM HOTEL

HILL STATION SIGNATURE

SAPA UNIQUE HOTEL

CHAU LONG HOTEL & SPA

BEAUTY SALON SPA

© AVALON TRAVEL

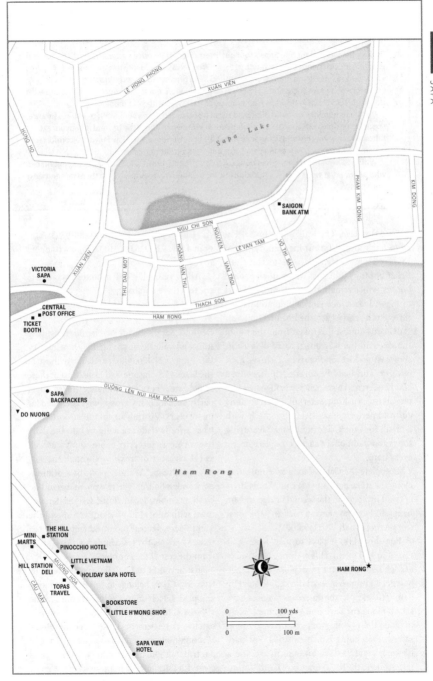

Sapa Lake

SAIGON
BANK ATM

VICTORIA
SAPA

CENTRAL
POST OFFICE

TICKET
BOOTH

LE HONG PHONG

XUÂN VIÊN

PHAM KIM DONG

KIM DONG

NGU CHI SON

NGUYEN

LE VAN TÂM

VO THI SAU

XUÂN VIÊN

THU DÂU MOT

HOÀNG VAN THU

VAN TRÔI

VAN TRÔI

HÙNG HO

THACH SON

HÀM RONG

DUÔNG LÊN NÚI HÀM RÔNG

SAPA
BACKPACKERS

DO NUONG

Ham Rong

THE HILL
STATION

MINI
MARTS

PINOCCHIO HOTEL

LITTLE VIETNAM

HILL STATION
DELI

HOLIDAY SAPA HOTEL

TOPAS
TRAVEL

MUÔNG HOA

CÂU MÂY

BOOKSTORE

LITTLE H'MONG SHOP

HAM RONG

SAPA VIEW
HOTEL

0   100 yds
0   100 m

Finding a Guide in Sapa

Budget travelers might find Sapa's tour outfitters out of their price range. The next-best option is to hire an independent local guide in town. While this is decidedly less expensive, it requires extra work, as you'll find many women around Sapa offering to act as guides though few, if any, are certified. On many occasions, a trek with an independent guide turns into a shopping trip, with dozens of handicraft vendors persuading you to part ways with your money.

Recommendations for good local guides can be obtained from your hotel. For extra assurance, spend some time with your guide beforehand. Ask for details about the trip and make your expectations clear—whether you'd prefer an easy hike or a strenuous one, how far you're comfortable walking, whether you're looking to shop or not—prior to setting off.

While it's a greater gamble than booking through a tour outfit, there are independent guides who are great at what they do. Additionally, their entire fee goes directly to them rather than a third party.

an actual village. The walk down to Cat Cat from Sapa affords stunning panoramas of Muong Hoa Valley. En route to Cat Cat's ticket booth, you'll pass by small clapboard houses, which remain the most authentic part of the village. Once you've paid and passed through the entry gate, the line of handicraft stalls runs almost unbroken from the top of the steps all the way down to Tien Sa Falls, showcasing skirts and scarves, T-shirts, hats, jewelry, and heavily detailed indigo-dyed blankets. Across a suspension bridge that teeters above a rushing waterfall, Black H'mong cultural performances (9am-4pm daily with a break for lunch, additional fee), featuring songs and traditional dances, take place nearly every hour.

Complete the Cat Cat loop by continuing along the stone path and back up. *Xe om* drivers wait just beyond the second bridge and are happy to ferry passengers back to Sapa town (for no more than VND40,000).

For shoppers, it pays to visit when Cat Cat is in full swing (10am-2pm), but travelers who simply want to explore the village and get a glimpse of local life should start by 9am. This early in the day, fewer vendors have set up along the path and you're more likely to elude the roving groups of Black H'mong saleswomen along Fansipan Road. For particularly good views, a bit of local art, and a refreshment, the back veranda of **Gem Valley**

Art Gallery (Cat Cat, tel. 09/1284-9753, 7am-6pm daily, VND25,000-100,000) is a fine spot to rest your legs.

Allow yourself 45-60 minutes to complete the trip there and back.

★ Minority Villages

Beyond Sapa's borders, the surrounding hills and valleys are studded with **minority villages** (VND20,000), particularly those of the Black H'mong and Red Dao. Most of these remote areas bear a resemblance to each other, partly because many groups have coexisted for many years. Visiting any of the minority villages affords visitors a window into the daily lives of Sapa's minority communities, as well as the pleasure of trekking through the verdant landscape. Wander past rows of modest wooden houses, where women dye indigo cloth or embroider intricate designs. Share a meal with a local family, or even spend the night. Here, several thousand feet above sea level, Sapa's nearby residents are a world apart from the rest of the country.

Just beyond Cat Cat, the next-nearest village, **Sin Chai,** belongs to the Black H'mong and prides itself on its traditional music. The villages of **Ma Tra** and **Ta Phin** to the north, patchwork settlements of Red Dao and Black H'mong households, make equally popular day trips (although locals may be more aggressive with sales pitches in these spots).

Farther south, **Ta Van** is home to a Giay community not far from **Lao Chai** village, another Black H'mong settlement, both of which are popular options and can be visited in a single day. Just beyond these two villages is a Red Dao community, **Giang Ta Chai,** which can also be tacked onto a trek if you're up for the walk. To the east, **Hau Thao, Sa Seng,** and **Hang Da,** all Black H'mong villages, are another worthy option for trekkers.

You'll find useful maps of Sapa's vicinity at the **local tourism office** (2 Fansipan, tel. 02/0387-1975, www.sapa-tourism.com, 8am-5pm daily), which can help you to get the lay of the land.

Hiring a guide (VND200,000-300,000) is a must for these excursions, as you're far more likely to get off the beaten path with a local on hand, and these individuals will have answers for your questions regarding the ins and outs of Sapa's minority cultures. Depending on where you go, a good guide can also help to dissuade villagers from pummeling you with sales pitches. Companies like **ETHOS** (tel. 09/1679-5330, www.ethosspirit.com) and **Sapa O'Chau** (8 Thac Bac, tel. 02/0377-1166, www.sapaochau.org, 7:30am-6:30pm daily) run regular tours to several minority villages. On a tour, travelers hike out to the villages and are bused back to Sapa. The walking distance varies based on which villages are visited, ranging 2.5-10 miles. Tours cover no more than three villages in a day, with most going to only one or two (allowing travelers more time in each village).

Many villages can also be accessed by *xe om,* but this takes most of the fun out of the experience, as Sapa's more secluded landscapes are best explored on foot. All villages in the area charge a VND20,000 entry fee for visitors. Homestays and overnight excursions covering several nearby communities can be arranged (with a tour outfitter or freelance guide).

Silver Falls and Love Falls

Just over six miles out of town, a pair of waterfalls line the highway up to Tram Ton Pass. The nearest and most popular is **Silver Falls (Thac Bac)** (6am-6pm daily, VND10,000), a charming natural sight. It's not worth the walk up to the top, as you can get the gist from the ground. The walk up is a steep set of stairs, but the going is easy.

Farther up the road, **Love Falls (Thac Tinh Yeu)** (6am-6pm daily, VND30,000) makes more of an impression. Though it's hidden off the highway about a half-mile into the forest, the trek to the falls makes a nice nature walk, strolling through the trees beside Golden Stream (Suoi Vang). You'll need a good pair of shoes and reasonable mobility to reach the end; the stone walkway later deteriorates into a dirt track in some spots, and a few downed trees have crossed the path. The finale, a pretty, moss-covered cascade more than 300 feet tall, makes the journey worthwhile.

Tram Ton Pass

The towering **Tram Ton Pass,** also known as O Quy Ho, is the highest road in Vietnam, coming in at 1.25 miles above sea level. This never-ending maze of switchbacks teeters on the edge of the Hoang Lien mountains, winding its way from Tam Duong, a small town about 30 miles west of Sapa, up along a narrow, cliff-hugging road before plunging back down to Sapa and, later, Lao Cai. While its highest point, perpetually obscured by dense forest, does not afford the kind of awe-inspiring views you might expect, with time and a motorbike (or, for the very fit, a bicycle) you can venture down the serpentine highway, admiring the view from some of its lower sections. Stop at established pullouts to admire the view and take photos. Drivers on this particular road should exercise great caution, as conditions are risky even in good weather and downright treacherous in foul weather. Take extra care when rounding corners and keep a safe distance from the outside shoulder of the road, as it's a straight drop down.

Dragon Jaw Mountain

Rising above Sapa in the southeast, **Dragon**

Jaw Mountain (Ham Rong, 7am-7pm daily, VND70,000) affords some pleasant views of town as well as your standard helping of Vietnamese kitsch. The most developed peak in the area, Dragon Jaw bears a spidery network of paths crisscrossing its northern side that look out over the sleepy settlement below as well as toward Fansipan. While it's not exactly a genuine commune with nature, the stone steps that ramble up to the **Cloud Yard,** the platform with the best views of Sapa, are a nice way to pass time on your first day or as you wander around town. Thanks to its paths, solid footwear is not so essential here. You'll want to allow an hour or so to fully explore the winding routes up top. Visitors receive a map of the mountain from the ticket booth; this does little to orient you once you've started on the long stairway up. Regardless, you'll find yourself passing by a restaurant, a rather tired orchid garden, several covered lookouts, a park dotted with statues of the 12 Vietnamese zodiac animals, and, inexplicably, Mickey Mouse.

SIGHTSEEING TOURS

In order to get the most out of exploring Sapa, many travelers sign up for a guided tour to one of the nearby villages, to a bustling local market, or simply deep into the mountains for a homestay. Because so much of Sapa's tourism relies upon connecting with other cultures, it is particularly important to be discerning when choosing a tour company, as you want your experience to be authentic and worthwhile not only on your part but also for the local minorities with whom you interact. There are a handful of trekking and tour outfits in town that focus heavily upon ensuring that the benefits of this region's tourism go directly back to its local residents. If trekking to a nearby minority village is on your itinerary, have a local guide bring you along, as that person will be able to explain the ins and outs of his or her culture better than anyone else.

More than just a trekking outfit, the incredible **Sapa O'Chau** (8 Thac Bac, tel. 02/0377-1166, www.sapaochau.org, 7:30am-6:30pm daily) does as much for the local community as it does for its customers, providing authentic, adventurous treks off the beaten path as well as changing the lives of Sapa's young ethnic minorities. In a region where many minority children do not attend school beyond adolescence, Shu Tan, a young H'mong woman, has made it her mission to afford local students the skills, education, and opportunities that have long eluded this part

view of Sapa from Dragon Jaw Mountain

of the country. Beginning in 2009 as a single homestay in Lao Chai, the Sapa O'Chau outfit operates a school for local students as well as its tour outfit. Training programs assist aspiring tour guides in gaining experience in the field. Sapa O'Chau is a two-way cultural exchange, in which both travelers and community members benefit. The outfit arranges single-day treks (VND252,000-735,000) and multi-day treks (VND840,000-2,625,000) to various villages in the surrounding area, as well as homestays, market visits, and other adventures. The outfit runs a popular café (VND20,000-120,000), which makes some mean fish and chips.

ETHOS (H'mong Sapa Hotel, tel. 09/1679-5330, www.ethosspirit.com, VND525,000-1,680,000) goes to great lengths to ensure that its tours are not only authentic and far-removed for the tourist crowds but that each of its excursions benefits the local community. From treks into the nearby hillside and village visits that don't appear on any other tour company's itinerary, ETHOS focuses on genuine human interactions with activities like sharing a meal or visiting someone's home that lend themselves more to one-on-one interaction. The tour agency operates out of H'mong Sapa Hotel (and thus doesn't have official office hours) and assists with train bookings and longer trips, including a guided tour of the Northwest Loop.

SHOPPING

As the only major tourist town in the northwest, shopping is a popular activity in Sapa, particularly when the fog rolls in to obscure its panoramic views. The main handicraft of the H'mong and Red Dao is textiles; both groups are equally skilled in colorful and detailed embroidery, which often features on skirts, jackets, blankets, bags, and other accessories. Silver jewelry and indigo-dyed items are another specialty of the H'mong. Along Cau May and Muong Hoa streets, plenty of retailers hawk knockoff North Face items for the Fansipan-bound, while handicrafts are virtually everywhere, including on the arms of roving vendors, whose sales pitches range from friendly to downright aggressive.

Hidden beneath the Cat Cat View Hotel, Indigo Cat (46 Fansipan, tel. 09/8240-3647, www.indigocat.dznly.com, 9am-7pm Sun.-Fri.) is a small shop that specializes in Fair Trade products made by H'mong women, namely bracelets, bags, skirts, jewelry, and a few other odds and ends. Look out for the small handouts scattered throughout the store, which explain the significance of many of the intricate patterns you see swirled and looped and stitched across the clothing of local minority women. Indigo Cat also sells pre-packaged DIY sewing kits so that you can make your own H'mong-style bracelet using traditional embroidery patterns. Swing by in the afternoons and one of the shop's owners, a H'mong woman, will help to get you started on the craft with an impromptu sewing class.

The town's only bookstore (Muong Hoa, 8am-7pm daily) hides a short walk down Muong Hoa on the left-hand side. Stocked with photocopied paperbacks and a few genuine books, the shop's titles include old and new English-language favorites. Prices aren't listed, so feel free to haggle, particularly if you purchase more than one item.

SPORTS AND RECREATION

With plenty of green space, rolling hills, and incredible scenery, Sapa is an active destination. Sapa is the home base for trekking day trips to surrounding villages and overnight homestays with local families. These journeys range from leisurely to challenging, with Mount Fansipan being the mother of all treks, but there's also room for cycling and, when the weather takes a turn, a hard-earned massage.

Trekking

With dozens of small communities peppering the mountains and valleys of northwestern Vietnam, gaining access to the more authentic, untouched villages of the area requires at least some travel on foot up the steep inclines of the surrounding hills and along the muddy dirt paths that lead to Sapa's more remote residences. In town, easier walks to **Cat Cat Village** and around **Dragon Jaw Mountain** are blessed with paved roads and stone steps. Once you leave town the highway branches off into smaller, rockier trails that bring you away from the buzz of Sapa's tourist center and out to peaceful paddies and stunning mountain vistas. For standard day-long treks and one-night homestays, bring along water and a sturdy pair of shoes. For longer excursions, especially to Fansipan, you'll need to stock up on proper trekking gear. Scores of shops in the area sell North Face goods, most of them knockoffs but some genuine, as well as a host of hiking boots, first-aid essentials, and the like.

Two companies that provide guided treks are **Sapa O'Chau** (8 Thac Bac, tel. 02/0377-1166, www.sapaochau.org, 7:30am-6:30pm daily) and **ETHOS** (tel. 09/1679-5330, www.ethosspirit.com).

H'mong children in Cat Cat village

★ MOUNT FANSIPAN

Towering above its surroundings, Mount Fansipan is often referred to as the "Roof of Indochina," standing well above any other peak in neighboring Laos or Cambodia. Looming over the opposite flank of the Muong Hoa Valley, its silhouette can be seen from the town's hillside windows on a clear day and has begun to attract a growing number of ambitious travelers hoping to reach the summit. Though its trails are a little worse for wear, cluttered with rubbish and beginning to get too well-worn for some, the enigmatic mountain remains a point of interest among many adventure-seeking tourists.

Guided excursions to the top can be attempted in as little as a day or as long as 3-5 days, depending upon your level of fitness and your willingness to sleep in the rather damp and dingy camps that hover around 7,000 and 9,000 feet. One-day treks up to the summit are not for the faint of heart: It's a 10-hour hike at best and the gently rolling trails at the start of the journey soon give way to steeper climbs and a final push up to the summit.

Instead, reasonably fit travelers may want to opt for a two-day trip, while those who'd prefer to take their time can venture out into the wild for longer. Shrouded in a bluish haze, the view from 10,311 feet can be fickle even during the summer months, as wind, rain, and other elements have a mind of their own up here. Standing next to the pyramidal marker that signals the end of your uphill climb is well worth the wet shoes and chilly temperatures.

Climbers who sign up for a trip to the top should invest in a sturdy pair of hiking boots and some warm clothes. A decent jacket is still recommended in summer, as the air cools down significantly at this height. Most guided tours begin around VND1,050,000 per person for a single-day excursion, including transportation, entry fees, a guide, and, for overnight trips, a porter or two. When booking your Fansipan trek, it's important to be clear about what's included in the tour, as you'll want to know whether things like water and snacks are provided or you should be packing your own.

Exploring the Northwest Loop

Venture into Vietnam's far north and you'll discover another world altogether, awash with rich green rice paddies and wide, flowing rivers that wind around the region's many oversized land-scapes. Those who strike out on Vietnam's **Northwest Loop** will be handsomely rewarded with soaring mountains, plunging valleys, isolated villages, and unfathomable vistas. This is an independent adventure on which you'll find few to no English speakers, no high-end hotels, and not a Western meal to speak of. The views from the northwest's serpentine roads make it well worth the journey.

Starting from Hanoi, this 720-mile circuit runs west toward Dien Bien Phu, the city where Vietnam defeated its French enemies once and for all, turning north past Muong Lay and Lai Chau, before scaling the death-defying cliffs of Tram Ton Pass, rolling into Sapa town, and coasting back down to the capital.

Most travelers make the trip on a motorbike in about a week; cyclists can complete the Northwest Loop in two weeks. Invest in a quality vehicle for the journey, as there aren't many repair shops in the area. What shops do exist have far more experience with motorbikes than multi-speed bicycles. Cyclists should stock up on tools, tubes, and other necessities before leaving Hanoi. Before you set off, commit the Vietnamese words for hotel (*khách sạn,* pronounced "cack san"), guesthouse (*nhà nghi,* pronounced "nyah ngee"), and restaurant (*nhà hang,* pronounced "nyah hang") to memory, as these will be essential when you're looking for a place to stop.

Road conditions throughout this region are good, with smooth, sleek asphalt most of the way (with the exception of a treacherous stretch near Muong Lay north of Dien Bien Phu). Opt for heavy-duty tires on both bicycles and motorbikes. Guardrails and barriers are nonexistent. Even though there's little traffic on the roads of the northwest, serious accidents can happen and adequate medical care is a long way away.

A handful of tour outfits in Sapa arrange guided, Easy Rider-style motorbike tours that follow this route, though the cost will be astronomically greater than doing it on your own. You can usually arrange these tours in Hanoi or Sapa and expect to take at least six days to complete the full circuit.

It's highly advised that you pay for the necessary guide for this trek. Going it alone is not only forbidden, but could easily become dangerous, as there is little to direct you once you set out for the summit and, particularly in foul weather, the trail becomes a treacherous, rain-soaked path.

Cycling

There are a small number of local companies that arrange cycling tours or rent mountain bikes to individuals. These excursions are expensive, a fact justified by the quality of the equipment, but then take all the challenge out of the trip by driving travelers uphill before allowing them to roll down to the bottom.

Explore the options from outfitters ahead of time, as some companies offer customized tours.

To combine cycling with a bit of sightseeing, it's possible to rent a mountain bike and blaze your own trail up to Silver Falls and Tram Ton Pass. For more in-depth excursions, book a tour, as the area is remote and finding your way can be difficult without someone to guide you.

Two companies providing bike tours of the area are **Sapa Pathfinder** (13 Xuan Vien, tel. 02/0387-3468, www.sapapathfinder. com, 6:30am-6:30pm daily) and **ETHOS** (tel. 09/1679-5330, www.ethosspirit.com). Sapa Pathfinder rents out well-maintained Trek mountain bikes (VND200,000/day).

Massages and Spas

When the fog rolls into Sapa and a heavy mist obscures its picture-perfect views, a popular activity among weary travelers is a trip to the spa. While there are several outfits in town that advertise spa services, including a traditional Red Dao herbal bath, these are hit or miss. For assured quality at a higher price, the spas at both **Victoria Sapa** (Xuan Vien, tel. 02/0387-1522, www.victoriahotels.asia, 8am-10pm daily, VND630,000-1,260,000) and the **Chau Long Hotel** (24 Dong Loi, tel. 02/0387-1245, www.chaulonghotel.com, 2pm-10:30pm daily, VND400,000-900,000) provide massage services and other treatments. Non-guests are welcome to visit Victoria's sauna or pool (VND210,000 pp). For a more affordable option, the **Beauty Salon Spa** (43 Fansipan, tel. 09/7789-3566, 9am-10pm daily, VND120,000-300,000) opposite Sapa Luxury Hotel does a decent job, with quality spa services.

ACCOMMODATIONS

You'll find plenty of excellent mid-range and luxury accommodations lining the two main tourist streets of town, Cau May and Fansipan, not to mention a scattering of other hotels that ramble up the nearby hillside, affording incredible views of Muong Hoa Valley. Thanks to some fierce competition in the area, travelers can look forward to well-appointed rooms, plush furnishings, and a higher level of service in most hotels above the VND525,000 mark. Solo travelers and those on a shoestring are not spoiled for choice. A handful of quality budget hotels offer well-kept rooms at good prices; dorm beds are few and far between, especially if your requirements include clean bedding and bathrooms. A small number of dorm accommodations exist, namely in the budget hotels along Fansipan street.

Under VND210,000

Dorm beds at the **Phuong Nam Hotel** (33 Fansipan, tel. 02/0350-2633, VND84,000 dorm, VND500,000 double) are some of the most generous in Vietnam, offering a queen-size mattress to weary travelers, along with bright and spacious rooms. En suite bathrooms are small but clean and the back door leads onto a tiny ledge with stunning views of the valley. Hot water and air-conditioning are included in these shared rooms as well as in the hotel's private doubles. If it's privacy you seek, search elsewhere, as the dorm beds represent good value but the private rooms are not up to snuff.

VND210,000-525,000

Amid the jumble of shops and restaurants along Cau May, **Elysian Sapa Hotel** (38 Cau May, tel. 02/0387-1238, www.elysiansapahotel.com, VND357,000-735,000) represents a solid budget option, with cozy beds, hot water, air-conditioning, TV, Wi-Fi, and tea- and coffee-making facilities in each room. Electric blankets and other accoutrements are available during the winter months. Downstairs, the hotel runs a restaurant as well as a travel desk and assists with tour arrangements.

Looking out over the local park, **Kenpas Hotel** (11 Xuan Vien, tel. 02/0387-2692, www.kenpas.com, VND252,000-315,000, breakfast included) offers exceptionally good value for money, with large, well-kept guest rooms that come either with or without a window, the former affording decent views of town. Modern amenities like TV, Wi-Fi access, hot water, fans, and heaters are included in each room, as is plush bedding and a clean, spacious bathroom. Downstairs, the hotel runs a tour outfit as well as a shop specializing in high-quality trekking gear. The staff are a friendly, easygoing crowd.

The friendly folks at **Casablanca** (26 Dong Loi, tel. 09/7441-8111, www.casablancasapahotel.com, VND336,000-630,000) offer decent guest rooms with standard amenities such as air-conditioning, hot water, TV, Wi-Fi, and tea- and coffee-making facilities. The staff is especially cheerful and service-minded, and the location, wedged between the larger tourist streets of Cau May and Fansipan, provides a break from the shops and activity nearby. Breakfast is included in the room rate, but it is possible to book accommodations without the additional cost.

VND525,000-1,050,000

Amid the droves of accommodations

Sapa Luxury Hotel

(46 Fansipan, tel. 02/0387-1946, www.cat-cathotel.com, VND630,000-1,260,000, breakfast included) is in its name. Rising above the smaller buildings across the street, this hotel boasts some incredible views of the valley and, while its rooms are basic, you'll find hot water, air-conditioning, TV, and Wi-Fi among the hotel's amenities, along with electric blankets for the winter months and additional services, such as DVD players and space heaters, available for rent. Discounts are sometimes available for multi-night stays.

While the **Sapa Unique Hotel** (39 Fansipan, tel. 02/0387-2008, www.sapauniquehotel.com, VND735,000-1,155,000) is as good as any on the block, its staff set the place apart with top-notch service and a genuine effort to ensure that travelers enjoy their stay. Rooms are cozy and well-appointed, featuring hot water, air-conditioning, Wi-Fi, television, and modern furnishings. The attached travel outfit, Viet Sapa, is notably reliable.

Tucked off the town's main square, **Sapa Elegance Hotel** (3 Hoang Dieu, tel. 02/0388-8668, www.sapaelegancehotel.com, VND735,000-840,000, breakfast included) earns top marks for its location, overlooking the valley but just far enough removed to lie beyond the reach of Sapa's touristy streets. Outfitted in cozy, modern furnishings, each guest room features hot water, Wi-Fi access, television, a dual air-conditioning and heating system, minibar, in-room safe, and tea- and coffee-making facilities. The hotel's pleasant staff assist with tours and travel arrangements.

VND1,050,000-2,100,000

A breathtaking view of the valley and mountains rolling off into the distance win **H'mong Sapa Hotel** (10 Thac Bac, tel. 02/0377-2228, www.hmongsapahotel.com, VND1,050,000-2,310,000, breakfast included) huge points, complemented nicely by the friendly service, restaurant, mountain view terrace, and excellent tour outfit. Superior accommodations are well-furnished with hot water, TV, Wi-Fi, and an air-conditioning system that blows hot

overlooking the valley, ★ **Sapa Luxury Hotel** (36 Fansipan, tel. 02/0387-2771, www.sapaluxuryhotel.com, VND588,000-1,890,000, breakfast included) stands out for its exceptional hospitality. This family-owned boutique hotel is just a stone's throw from several of the town's main attractions, including Cat Cat Village, the local market, and Cau May shopping street. All rooms are clean and spacious, featuring walk-in showers and twin- or queen-size beds. Rooms are equipped with a mini-bar, television, computer, and Wi-Fi. A complimentary Vietnamese or Western breakfast is served each morning. Depending on the season, it's best to book early, as there are only 10 rooms. The hotel offers pickup service from the train station in Lao Cai for those who call ahead. For budget travelers, small but tidy rooms are available in the back without a mountain view, but for the full experience book a room in the front, where the balcony offers breathtaking panoramas of the valley and Mount Fansipan.

The reason for the success of **Cat Cat View**

Learn to Cook the Sapa Way

The Hill Station Signature restaurant (37 Fansipan, tel. 02/0388-7111, www.thehillstation.com) runs a **H'mong cooking class** (VND580,000) for culinary-minded travelers. During the class, you'll visit a local market to pick out ingredients, work with an English-speaking chef, and learn how to create a menu of five H'mong dishes. Students also visit a farm in nearby Hau Thao village, run by a local family, where the restaurant gets all of its ingredients.

and cold. For a private balcony, upgrade to a deluxe room. Booking directly with the hotel tends to get you a discount.

Perched on the hillside above Cau May, the **Sapa Paradise View** (18 Pham Xuan Huan, tel. 02/0387-2684, www.sapaparadiseviewhotel.com, VND900,000-1,720,000, breakfast included) wins top points for service. Rooms are comfortable and well-appointed, with an in-room safe, television, Wi-Fi access, hot water, and an in-room computer. The upper floors afford pleasant views, while certain rooms also include a private balcony. The hotel assists with booking tours and other travel arrangements. Its ground-floor restaurant is a popular choice, with delicious barbecue and hotpot gracing the menu.

Over VND2,100,000

A beautiful, well-hidden resort overlooking this sleepy town, **Victoria Sapa** (Xuan Vien, tel. 02/0387-1522, www.victoriahotels.asia, VND4,000,000-6,000,000) boasts 77 rooms, a private terrace, and stunning views of the surrounding area thanks to its hillside perch. Spacious accommodations include TV, Wi-Fi access, air-conditioning, hot water, and tea- and coffee-making facilities. Superior, deluxe, and suite rooms are available, some of which come with private balconies. The resort counts a top-notch restaurant, bar, spa, fitness center, kids club, tennis court, and indoor heated pool in its offerings.

FOOD

You won't find too many regional dishes in this foggy northern town, but local favorites include miniature barbecue skewers, which

make for an excellent afternoon snack, as well as roast suckling pig, which you'll find on a spit in front of a few eateries in town. Though it's not native to the area, trout has become a popular local commodity. Sapa's minority groups also have some dishes of their own. Most restaurants in town seem to hold to the notion that Western travelers would prefer Western food, and so it can be tricky to find more authentic Vietnamese fare, though one or two restaurants in Sapa town excel at providing genuine homegrown meals. For cheaper options, stick to the market stalls, as Sapa's eateries, almost all of which cater to foreign tourists, come at a price.

Clustered around the foot of Dragon Jaw Mountain beneath a maze of tarpaulins are several *do nuong* (barbecue) vendors (mid-morning-late afternoon daily, VND5,000-10,000/skewer). These tiny stalls are no more than a single miniature grill and a few tables. The colorful displays of skewers, packed with everything from pork and veggies to chicken wings, dumplings, and tofu, are enticing after a long walk up the mountain. Often accompanied by bamboo tubes of sticky rice, these tasty morsels are enjoyed as a snack or alongside a few drinks and hit the spot during cold, rainy weather.

A local restaurant, **Co Lich** (1 Fansipan, tel. 09/1282-8260, 7:30am-midnight daily, VND60,000-300,000), at the top of Fansipan street, does a tasty suckling pig, which appears on the rotating spit out front. Beyond pork, you'll find a slew of Vietnamese meat and vegetable dishes on its extensive menu, all at reasonable prices.

Though it's nearly invisible from outside,

tucked soundly beneath the Sapa Paradise View Hotel is its restaurant, **Paradise View Restaurant** (Sapa Paradise View Hotel, 18 Pham Xuan Huan, tel. 02/0387-2683, www.sapaparadiseviewhotel.com, 6:30am-9pm daily, VND250,000-365,000), a cozy little spot that prides itself on serving only top-notch barbecue and hotpot dishes. Diners in the mood for authentic local fare will appreciate the restaurant's select offerings, namely the mouthwatering salmon hotpot, whose ingredients are picked fresh from a tank at the back of the restaurant, not to mention the cheerful and conscientious staff.

The charming **Little Sapa** (18 Cau May, tel. 02/0387-1222, 8am-9pm daily, VND45,000-135,000) may well be one of the most affordable eateries in a town of tourist-heavy restaurants. Its well-rounded menu of Vietnamese dishes showcase a more genuine version of Vietnamese cuisine and, while Little Sapa's clientele is largely foreign, the prices and tastes are more local than its competition. Indoors, embroidered tablecloths and plenty of festive lighting add some cheer, and the staff are an industrious and friendly bunch.

Little Vietnam (33 Muong Hoa, 8:30am-last customer daily, VND45,000-190,000) operates out of a tiny, cozy wooden storefront along Muong Hoa just opposite the Bamboo Sapa Hotel. Vietnamese cuisine takes up most of the menu, offering more than just your standard backpacker fare, with a few burgers and sandwiches rounding out the list. Staff are friendly, and most prices manage to come in under VND100,000, making this one of the more affordable spots in the tourist area.

Perched on the hillside overlooking Muong Hoa Valley, **Nature View** (51 Fansipan, tel. 02/0387-1438, 8am-10pm daily, VND60,000-125,000) boasts some of the best views in town, not to mention an extensive list of Vietnamese fare, including chicken, beef, pork, fish, duck, deer, and wild boar. An especially tasty vegetarian set menu is also on offer for lunch and dinner. Regardless of whether you come for a full-blown meal or just an afternoon drink, the breathtaking panoramas from Nature View's dining room are what set the place apart, with large windows and an open-air rooftop affording a clear sight to the valley below.

The chic and omnipresent **Hill Station** (7 Muong Hoa, tel. 02/0388-7111, www.thehillstation.com, 8am-10pm daily, VND75,000-275,000) is clearly doing well for itself, as the trendy eatery now counts a deli, boutique, and signature Vietnamese restaurant in its offerings around town. At its main venue, an exposed brick building just near the foot of Cau May, you'll find deli-style sandwiches, pastries, cheese, and charcuterie on the menu, while the small black-and-white boutique down the road stocks jars of Sapa honey, tea, genuine H'mong jewelry, and other souvenirs.

For an upscale and authentic meal, the ★ **Hill Station Signature** (37 Fansipan, tel. 02/0388-7111, www.thehillstation.com, 8am-10pm daily, VND70,000-145,000) showcases a host of dishes unique to Sapa's minority cultures, from banana flower salad to fried chicken with wild ginger and smoked pork belly. Vegetarian options are available, taking advantage of several mountain greens you won't find elsewhere in Vietnam, along with homemade tofu. Throw in a bit of rustic chic, with low tables and mounds of hemp as seat cushions, simple porcelain, and a killer view of the valley, and Hill Station Signature is easily one of the best eateries in town. Higher tables are also available.

Chefs at the cozy, corner-side **Sapa Rooms** (18 Fansipan, tel. 02/0650-5228, www.tet-lifestyle-collection.com, 6am-7pm daily, VND40,000-80,000) excel in the art of breakfast, serving up thick, golden-brown slices of French toast, sweet corn fritters, lemon souffle pancakes, and wholesome homemade muffins not only in the morning but throughout the day. You'll find top-notch European coffee here, as well as an array of oddly shaped furniture, H'mong-patterned decorations, and other contemporary art. Prices are reasonable, though portions run on the small side.

INFORMATION AND SERVICES

Sapa's **Tourist Information Center** (2 Fansipan, tel. 02/0387-1975, www.sapa-tourism.com, 8am-5pm daily) is one of the more helpful of its kind, dispensing free advice and maps with a smile. Tours can be arranged without the hard sell you might find elsewhere.

The only bank located in the more touristy part of town is an **Agribank** (Cau May, tel. 02/0387-1107, www.agribank.com.vn, 7:30am-11:30am and 1:30pm-5pm Mon.-Fri.) on Cau May, which also has an ATM next door. Should you run into any trouble with this machine, you can find a **Saigon Bank ATM** (corner of Ngu Chi Son and Vo Thi Sau) farther into town, near the lake outside the Riverside II Hotel.

Sapa's **post office** (20 Cau May, tel. 02/0387-1247, 8am-5pm and 6pm-8pm daily) runs a small branch near the market that can handle mail and postal services for travelers. For more in-depth queries, swing by the **central post office** (6 Thach Son, tel. 02/0387-1298, 7am-9pm daily).

The local **hospital** (Dien Bien Phu, tel. 02/0387-1237) sits on the northern edge of town. But, medical care in the remote northern mountains is well below par compared to Vietnamese cities. In the event of an emergency and for any serious issues, head back to Hanoi.

GETTING THERE
By Bus

Buses to Sapa can be tricky to find. **Hung Thanh** (162B Tran Quang Khai, tel. 04/3633-7575, www.hungthanhtravel.vn, 8am-7pm daily, VND300,000) is a reliable company that runs overnight sleeper buses from Hanoi to Sapa and vice versa. Buses leave in the early evening and arrive in the wee hours of the morning right beside Sapa Lake. For the return trip to Hanoi, book your seat through the **ticket booth** (6 Thach Son, tel. 09/1486-4126, 7am-9pm daily) outside Sapa's central post office. There's just one ticket vendor, who may be out when you're there. Phone for someone to sell you the ticket if that happens.

While a handful of bus companies operate buses back to Hanoi, you'll want to be discerning in which one you choose, as the mountain road leading to Sapa is winding and narrow; safe, experienced drivers are an absolute must. Hung Thanh is your best bet above the others.

By Train
When heading to Sapa, the preferred method

Hill Station Signature

of travel is by sleeper train. Bare-bones hard sleeper cabins feature a single thin palette accompanied by a worn blanket and pillow. For more comfort, a number of private companies run plush, soft sleepers equipped with airconditioning, comfier mattresses, and cleaner bedding. A lower berth ticket allows you to be closer to your belongings, which will inevitably be slid underneath the bottom bunk; while it's not especially common, theft does occur on sleeper trains.

Ticket prices among Hanoian travel agents vary drastically based on the agent's fee; ask around before settling on an agency. For the best possible fare, buy your ticket from the train station. Lines and organization are not a major focus at the ticketing counter, but there are one or two agents who speak English and can help to arrange your trip. The journey from Sapa to Hanoi is easier to sort out, with the **ticket booth** (6 Thach Son, tel. 09/1486-4126, 7am-9pm daily) outside the central post office quoting some of the better rates in town. The route back to Hanoi is mysteriously more expensive: where you can find a hard sleeper from Hanoi to Sapa at about VND450,000, you'll be paying at least VND600,000 for the same trip in the opposite direction. The commission attached to train tickets in Sapa runs VND40,000-100,000.

The final stop for northbound trains is not Sapa (which does not have a train station), but the **Lao Cai train station,** roughly 23 miles northeast of town near the Chinese border. From Lao Cai, get to Sapa by taking a minibus. The standard fare for a trip from Lao Cai to Sapa city center is VND50,000.

There are enough minibuses around that you can walk away from anyone who attempts to overcharge. Before paying, get confirmation that the tout leading you to a particular minibus is affiliated with that vehicle—with so many people around, it's easy to pay your fare up-front, only to find that the tout involved is in no way affiliated with that minibus. Wait until you reach town before handing over the fare.

GETTING AROUND
Taxis and *Xe Om*

Plenty of *xe om* drivers hang out near the town square, waiting to offer a ride or rent a motorbike to you. For larger vehicles, call a **Fansipan** (tel. 02/0362-6262) taxi. Keep in mind, most everything in Sapa is within walking distance and there are few scenarios in which you'd need to take a cab, with the exception of Silver Falls.

Vehicles for Hire

Walking around downtown Sapa, you'll see tons of hotels and independent enterprises renting motorbikes to travelers. Semiautomatic vehicles run around VND80,000 per day, while an automatic will set you back VND100,000 a day. Check the brakes and all other functions of the bike before taking off, as roads are steep and medical attention is far away. While traffic may move slower on the uphills, many a truck or motorbike will come racing down an incline at top speed, not always on the appropriate side of the road, and locals often walk along the shoulder of the highway.

Ha Long Bay and the Northern Coast

Boasting wild, uncharted jungles and karst-studded seas, Vietnam's northern coast captivates travelers with its breathtaking scenery. Whether on water or land, the otherworldly landscapes of the region provide a stunning backdrop for adventure.

Ha Long Bay (literally, Bay of the Descending Dragon) is the country's most famous attraction, entrancing millions of visitors each year to tour its islands and caves. The placid waters of the bay are awash with luxury cruise liners and modest wooden junk boats that spill over into Ha Long's smaller and less crowded neighbors, Lan Ha Bay and Bai Tu Long Bay. Jagged, rocky islands pepper the seascape, along with hundreds of weather-worn grottoes, making this one of the most photogenic places in Vietnam.

Blanketed in dense green jungle and razor-sharp limestone peaks, the majority of Cat Ba, Ha Long's largest island, remains untouched, rounding out the western edge of the bay. Here you can lounge on a quiet beach or trek through the jungle in a national park, looking out for the island's varied wildlife.

Where Ha Long is often overrun with tourist junk boats and foreign travelers, the smaller, quieter Lan Ha Bay, located off Cat Ba Island's eastern shores, remains wonderfully unencumbered. The area's trademark limestone karsts rise dramatically out of the sea in sharp, striking ridges and rippled rock faces, their bases worn away by erosion. Lush jungle foliage sprouts from the porous rocks, seemingly growing out of nothing, and if you're lucky you may catch a monkey or two swinging between the trees.

Farther south near Ninh Binh are the mesmerizing karsts of Tam Coc and Trang An, affectionately nicknamed "Ha Long Bay on Land." This region is growing more popular with tourists, and functions as a great base from which to explore northern Vietnam.

HISTORY

For thousands of years, the waters of the north coast played a crucial role in ancient Vietnamese history, with several significant military victories taking place on the Bach Dang River just west of Ha Long Bay. In

---

Previous: Cuc Phuong National Park; Ha Long Bay. **Above:** rocky island in Lan Ha Bay.

Highlights

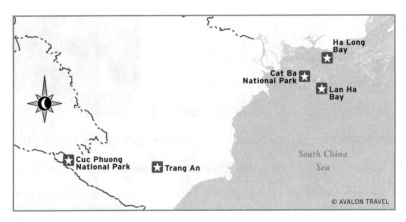

★ **Ha Long Bay:** Relax amid the placid waters and craggy, mist-drenched islands of Vietnam's most storied natural wonder (page 99).

★ **Cat Ba National Park:** Kayak, climb, and hike through the tangle of dense green jungle, still wild and untouched, that extends across the island's northern half and into the bay beyond (page 106).

★ **Lan Ha Bay:** Take in stunning, mist-covered views among the limestone giants of this bay, a captivating miniature version of Ha Long (page 110).

★ **Trang An:** Explore limestone karsts, water-logged paddy fields, ancient temples, and tunnel-like caves in what's called "Ha Long Bay on Land" (page 131).

★ **Cuc Phuong National Park:** With a handful of independent hikes and a top-notch primate conservation center, this park brings adventure and an up-close look at endangered Cat Ba and Delacour's langurs (page 137).

Ha Long Bay and the Northern Coast

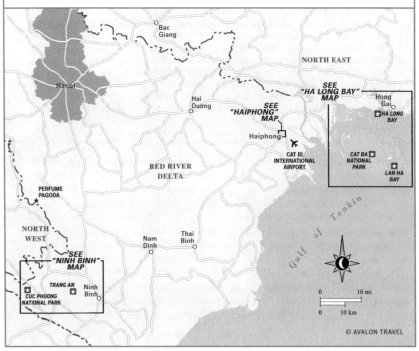

AD 938, emperor Ngo Quyen famously defeated the Chinese in this very place by planting sharpened ironwood spikes beneath the water, which rendered his enemy's vessels immobile when the tide went out. This victory allowed Ngo Quyen to begin the first major Vietnamese dynasty.

By the 12th century, Ha Long Bay was a successful international trading port, drawing in merchants from near and far, though it was still occasionally used for military purposes. Vietnamese revolutionaries used the caves nestled deep within the bay's limestone karsts during the Franco-Vietnam and American Wars. Hospitals and meeting halls were set up inside the dank confines of these underground chambers, many of which remained undetected by enemy forces.

Today, the bay has traded its duties as a military and commercial port for a starring role in the region's tourism, with dozens of white junk boats gliding across the water. Few of Vietnam's attractions have achieved the level of international recognition bestowed upon Ha Long Bay, where even the off season teems with domestic and foreign travelers.

PLANNING YOUR TIME

A visit to Ha Long Bay can take as little as two days or as long as four, depending upon your enthusiasm for on-the-water adventure. Most travelers—particularly those on a shorter schedule—opt for Ha Long Bay or Ninh Binh, as Ninh Binh also goes by the nickname "Ha Long Bay on Land."

In Ha Long Bay, how you travel plays a role in the amount of time you'll need. For a day cruise on the bay, devote two days of travel to arrive in Ha Long city, book a cruise, go on the cruise, and return to Hanoi. For an overnight

The Legend of Ha Long Bay

The name Ha Long Bay, also known as the "Bay of the Descending Dragon," has been around for centuries. The story goes that, in the early days of Vietnam, attacks by sea were a constant threat for the people of the north coast. Seeing their plight, the Jade Emperor, a god-like figure, dispatched Mother Dragon and her children to protect the Vietnamese people. As enemy ships sailed into the bay, preparing for attack, the dragons swooped down, spitting jade pearls into the water, which instantly turned to stone. The treacherous maze of limestone islands caught the enemy ships off guard and they crashed into the rocks. Once the invaders had been defeated, Mother Dragon chose to stay on earth, settling down in Ha Long Bay, while her children made their home nearby in Bai Tu Long.

cruise, set aside 2-3 days, depending on the cruise. For a stay on Cat Ba Island, give yourself a minimum of three days.

A visit to Ninh Binh requires just one or two nights, with an extra day if you're keen to see the langurs at Cuc Phuong National Park. Cuc Phuong can also be reached as a day trip from Hanoi.

The hottest months, between June and August, are an absolute madhouse, as domestic holidaymakers flock here in droves and prices skyrocket. From September to December, things quiet down considerably, while the weather holds steady. Traveling from late December to late February promises a slightly more peaceful atmosphere, though hundreds of Chinese tourists still skip over the border for a quick visit and weekenders arrive from Hanoi. During this time, inclement weather can often sideline boat cruises in Ha Long. Your best bet is to visit between September and early December, when the crowds are thinning out and the weather is calm enough to allow boats onto the bay.

Ha Long Bay and Vicinity

An enigmatic maze of blue-green waters and jagged limestone karsts, Ha Long Bay is the most well-known attraction in the country. Millions of years in the making, this aquatic enclave off the northern coast boasts a staggering 1,969 islands, countless caves, and over 2,000 different species of plant and animal life. Particularly in the colder months, when a dreary mist hangs heavy over the craggy islands and creaking wooden boats of the bay, it's hard not to be drawn in by the mystery of Ha Long.

Beyond its worldwide reputation for captivating scenery—it was voted one of the New 7 Wonders of Nature in 2011—the bay holds great historical significance. Scholars believe Ha Long housed no less than three prehistoric cultures, stretching its history several thousand years into the past. During the 10th and 13th centuries, monumental battles were fought here, including revered general Tran Hung Dao's defeat of Mongol forces in 1288 and the demise of the Han Chinese under Ngo Quyen in 938.

While much of Ha Long's beauty remains, tourism has impacted the area. Many tourist boats are packed onto the same handful of sightseeing routes, and there's more than a little trash floating in the placid water. Local residents have borne the brunt of the bay's popularity as well. Ha Long maintains a few small fishing communities, whose floating houses populate the quieter corners of the bay. These families will soon be forced to move as the government attempts to clear the area for increased tourism.

Ha Long Bay and Vicinity

Bai Chay

Hong Gai

★ HA LONG BAY

Dao Tuan Chau

SEE "HA LONG CITY" MAP

Ha Long Bay

Bai Tu Long Bay

★ CAT BA NATIONAL PARK

Lan Ha Bay

SEE "CAT BA ISLAND" MAP

★ LAN HA BAY

Gulf of Tonkin

© AVALON TRAVEL

★ HA LONG BAY

Ha Long Bay is home to caves, islands, a few small beaches, and sleepy fishing villages. Between the leisurely pace of the bay's cruise boats (a result of the high volume of traffic) and the sheer number of islands in the area, it's impossible to reach all of Ha Long's attractions on a single trip. Most overnight cruises do a nice job of hitting the more noteworthy spots. Because the bay is accessible only by boat tour, you'll have little to no control of which sights you see once you've booked your trip. Check cruise company itineraries for particular attractions before booking. The entry fee for each cave (VND50,000) is usually included in the price of the cruise.

Thien Cung Cave

Thien Cung Cave (8am-5pm daily), or Heaven Palace, sees droves of tourists each day shuffling along its 623-foot path, which winds around towering, distorted stalagmites and beneath spiky, ridged formations that dangle from above. Now one of the most popular attractions in the bay, not to mention the closest to shore, Thien Cung has lost a bit of its natural luster as a network of neon fluorescent lights and the constant flashbulbs of cameras illuminate the interior, but it's still an impressive sight. Its 32,292-square-foot interior consists of two floors, both of which were formed 7,000- 11,000 years ago. (Visitors are only permitted to wander the top level.) The sheer number of people packed into Thien Cung can feel like cattle being herded through the line.

Dau Go Cave

Dau Go Cave (8am-5pm daily) remains obscure, often overlooked on boat tours. Where visitors step off the narrow path leading out of Thien Cung and back to the boating docks, hang a right into Dau Go, about 100 meters away from Thien Cung; you will find it far less crowded and devoid of artificial additions. Its wide entrance opens onto the first chamber, a bright and cavernous room. A narrow pathway passes over limestone and under slender, bizarre stalactites, traveling the perimeter of the cave's three chambers before looping back out to the front, where you'll find a small stele engraved with the words of emperor Khai Dinh, who visited Dau Go in 1918.

Dau Go, known in English as the Cave of the Wooden Stakes, gets its name from a famous historical event. It was in this chamber that legendary Vietnamese general Tran Hung Dao prepared the ironwood stakes that he and his men would use to defeat the last Mongol invasion on the Bach Dang River in 1288. The general and his men sharpened the massive spikes and planted them in the nearby river, just deep enough to be invisible during high tide. When the Mongol ships sailed down the Bach Dang and the tide ebbed, they became trapped, propped up on a bed of spikes, and easily defeated by Vietnamese forces.

Sung Sot Cave

Also known as Surprise Cave or Amazing Cave, **Sung Sot Cave** (8:30am-4:45pm daily) is a regular stop on overnight cruises. From its large opening, several steps and 82 feet above sea level, to the picturesque landing just outside the exit, Sung Sot's vaulted chamber houses a variety of formations. One formation resembles the Buddha, while another, beside the cavern's entrance, resembles a horse with a sword. According to local legend, this is where Thanh Giong, a Vietnamese folk hero, came to rest after defeating his enemies. The legend goes that when he died, Thanh Giong left behind his horse and sword at the mouth of Sung Sot in order to protect the cavern against demons. This cave's expanse is impressive, though it can get crowded, and artificial lighting takes away from the natural appeal.

Other Caves

A few other spots feature on some tour itineraries and are equally as interesting, though not

Ha Long Bay

Choosing a Ha Long Bay Tour

Not every cruise ship or tourist boat plying Ha Long Bay is worth the cost. Here are some tips for booking your overnight stay in the bay.

Expect to spend more money for a quality tour. The extra money spent on a cruise with a reputable company can make a monumental difference in the safety, quality, and value of your experience. Any cruise company that offers a rate at or below VND2,100,000 is probably using an aged fleet.

The brochures are too good to be true. Every booking office and travel agency in Hanoi (where most Ha Long trips are arranged) will show you glossy photos of beautiful wooden junk boats and plush beds sprinkled with rose petals. While mid-range and luxury cruise boats tend to match their promotional materials, don't be fooled: More than a few of the budget cruise brochures are either outdated or false. A clue: All boats in Ha Long Bay are painted white.

Choose safety first. A handful of sinkings have occurred in the last decade, most recently in 2011, when 11 foreign tourists and a Vietnamese guide drowned due to poor boat maintenance. Though accidents and fatalities are rare, cheaper cruises tend to use poorly maintained boats, so there is a risk inherent in choosing a lower-priced option.

Know the cancellation policies. Make sure the tour provider clearly outlines its policies regarding weather-related cancellations. Authorities will sometimes shut down the bay (particularly November-January), ordering all boats off the water due to inclement weather. Ask exactly which costs are reimbursed and how the situation will be handled to avoid any further complications.

as popular as the most-visited caves. One of these is **Golden Tortoise Cave (Dong Kim Quy),** teeming with stalactites. According to local legends, this cave is the final resting place of Hoan Kiem Lake's tortoise, a petrified stone formation deep inside the cave.

In the early 15th century, Vietnamese emperor Le Thai To used a magical sword to defeat Chinese invaders. Following his victory, the emperor was rowing on Hanoi's Hoan Kiem Lake when a giant tortoise swam up to his boat, took the sword in its mouth, and disappeared beneath the surface. (This event earned Hoan Kiem Lake its name, which translates to Lake of the Returned Sword.) The tortoise took the blade back to Ha Long Bay where it encountered evil spirits and was forced to defend itself. Though it defeated the assailants, the tortoise was so exhausted that it found a cave in which to rest and soon after turned to stone. Today, visitors rub its back for good luck.

Follow the path through the stalactite and stalagmite formations, and you'll pass the tortoise toward the end of the path.

Another storied set of caves are **Virgin Cave (Dong Trinh Nu)** and the adjacent **Drum Cave (Dong Trong),** named after a pair of unrequited lovers. The tale goes that there was a beautiful woman who loved a young fisherman. The couple hoped to marry, and so one day the young man set off to sea in order to catch fish for their wedding day. While the young man was away, the girl's family, who was very poor, sent their daughter to live with a rich man. Devastated, the young woman refused to go, and her wealthy suitor exiled her to a small island in the bay, where she turned to stone. When the young man heard that she was in danger, he began searching for his lover. From his boat, he shouted as loud as possible but could not make himself heard over the weather, which had turned into a terrible storm. Wet and exhausted, he too turned to stone. In Virgin Cave, the formation is of a young woman lying down with her hair falling over her head, looking toward the sea. In Drum Cave, the formation is of a young man with his face turned toward Virgin Cave, as if calling to the woman. Cruise boats (including Gray Line boats) often stop outside the caves, as guides relate the story of the lovers. Tours don't usually let passengers disembark to explore these caves.

The small **Me Cung Cave** occasionally makes it onto tour itineraries. Its contents offer fascinating insight into the ancient history of the bay, with several fossilized animal remains inside the narrow chamber. Tour guides can point out where the fossils are.

Farther afield on Dau Be Island, **Ho Ba Ham,** or Three-Tunnel Lake, is another seldom-visited spot that is sometimes included on tours stopping at Cat Ba. As the name suggests, its peaceful, walled-in lagoons are accessed by a series of tunnels, usually in wooden boats at low tide.

Titov Island

Named after Soviet cosmonaut Gherman Titov, the second man to orbit the Earth, **Titov Island (Dao Ti Top)** (8:30am-5pm daily) was christened after a 1962 visit by the man himself, in which Titov and his host, Ho Chi Minh, admired Ha Long's scenery from this island's very shores. The island's small stretch of white-sand beach, a rarity in the bay, is slightly grubby but manages to attract a fair number of visitors. The volleyball net and beach chairs for rent—not to mention the view—help, and swimming is a popular activity during the warmer months. Titov's best asset is its hilltop lookout, the reward at the end of a zigzagging maze of 427 stone steps. While you may have to catch your breath once or twice en route to the summit, views at the top are the best in the bay and many a photo op takes place here, making it a highlight of Ha Long's more frequented attractions.

Other Sights

Stippled with miniature islands and solitary rock formations, some teetering upon no more than a few feet of limestone at their base, Ha Long has a host of iconic locales. The **Incense Burner** is a miniature karst standing just off the western side of Dau Go Island. It resembles the incense urns that appear outside local pagodas. It's also featured on Vietnam's VND200,000 note. Farther along, **Dog Rock** and **Ga Choi,** also known as Fighting Cock Island, are equally notable landmarks. These formations are large enough to see from the boat, making for good photos. They are only pointed out in passing, so you'll need to pay attention to catch sight of them.

Cruises

Most travelers prefer to visit Ha Long Bay by two- or three-day cruise. These excursions can be regimented, packing many sights and activities into a short time. Spending a night on the water not only affords you more time to explore the bay but also makes the experience memorable. These all-inclusive cruises eliminate much of the hassle involved in traveling to Ha Long, arranging a boat, and setting fees with a local provider. Accommodations run the gamut from dilapidated wooden junks to lavish luxury cruise liners.

Negotiating with budget tour providers is a must. Overnights on the lower end of the spectrum begin at VND1,680,000 per person for a two-day, one-night cruise. These are often disappointing, and anything lower than that price is likely downright dangerous, as not all boats are properly maintained or inspected on a regular basis. The companies listed in this section have solid reputations for providing safe, affordable, and enjoyable cruises, but there are also dozens of other well-known operators in the area. All listed prices are quoted per person for a double-occupancy cabin; if you're traveling solo, you will likely be required to pay an additional single supplement.

While everything from entrance fees to meals and accommodation is included in the package price, you will, in most instances, be expected to pay for your own beverages, which are usually marked up to a few times the going rate on land. It has become a recent trend to sneak beverages onto boats in an attempt to avoid these fees, but the boat crew does not take kindly to this practice.

Some higher-end companies provide day

trips to the bay, but with a four-hour drive to and from Hanoi, it's hardly worth the effort.

BUDGET

One of the more reliable budget providers, **Halong Fantasea Cruises** (office 71B6 Hang Trong, Hanoi, tel. 04/3938-0529, www.halongfantaseacruise.com, 7:30am-8pm daily, VND903,000/one-day, VND1,995,000-2,205,000/two-day, VND3,255,000-3,465,000/three-day) executes well-run excursions to the bay that save money and are safe and organized. Both deluxe and superior rooms are available, though deluxe offerings tend to be closer to the engine and therefore more prone to noise and a scent of gasoline. A handful of complimentary drinks are included on the trip, though others come with a marked-up price tag. All of Ha Long's most popular sights make the itinerary, including Titov Island and Sung Sot Cave. Daily swimming opportunities and scheduled kayak outings are offered. The three-day tours also stop on Cat Ba Island. Dietary exceptions can be made for vegetarians and those with other restrictions, provided you inform the company ahead of time. The company's booking agents tend to be more straightforward than some of their counterparts, offering honest information on the state of the boat, rooms, and other necessary details.

MID-RANGE

Glory Cruises (office 5/33B Pham Ngu Lao, Hanoi, tel. 04/3927-5797, www.halongglorycruise.com, 9am-5pm Mon.-Fri., 9am-3pm Sat.-Sun., VND2,625,000/one-day, VND3,360,000-3,990,000/two-day, VND5,565,000-6,195,000/three-day) provides a pleasant combination of friendly staff, knowledgeable tour guides, and staterooms for single- and multi-day cruises of the bay. Visit Sung Sot Cave, less-frequented spots like Soi Sim Beach and Lan Ha Bay, and a few fishing villages. Activities like swimming, kayaking, and squid fishing are available, as is evening entertainment like board games and playing cards.

The chic and well-appointed **Pelican Cruises** (office 96 Hang Bac, Hanoi, tel. 04/3933-6222, www.halongpelicancruise.com, 7:30am-5:30pm daily, VND1,785,000/one-day, VND3,465,000-4,830,000/two-day, VND5,628,000-8,715,000/three-day) operates a small fleet of plush high-end junk boats that ferry travelers to some of Ha Long's more famous attractions as well as a few less-frequented ones. Pelican's cabins are

Vietnam's northern bays are serene.

exceptionally well-kept, with modern bathrooms, enclosed showers, and large, comfy beds. Three-day excursions make it out to Lan Ha Bay and its more peaceful surroundings, and activities like swimming and kayaking are included in several itineraries. Ground transportation is not part of the price, with the exception of the one-day trip, though a shuttle bus (VND525,000 round-trip) is available.

The local arm of a century-old American brand, Gray Line Cruises (office 125 Hong Ha Bldg., Hanoi, tel. 04/3717-3229, www. graylinehalong.com, 8am-5:30pm daily, VND945,000/one-day, VND3,885,000-5,145,000/two-day, VND6,510,000-8,610,000/three-day) has been cruising Ha Long since 2013, with modern boats and experienced local guides. The outfit offers one-, two-, and three-day cruises to some of Ha Long's more famous sights as well as Lan Ha Bay, Cat Ba, and the outer edge of Bai Tu Long. Activities like kayaking, swimming, cycling on Cat Ba, and squid fishing are included in some itineraries, and additional snorkeling and diving excursions can be purchased upon request. Transportation to and from Hanoi is not included in the price, though you can hop on the company shuttle bus for a price.

LUXURY

As the only cruise provider fully authorized to venture from Ha Long into neighboring Bai Tu Long Bay, Indochina Junk (office 58 Au Trieu, Hanoi, tel. 04/3926-4085, www.indochina-junk.com, 8am-6pm daily, VND3,510,000/two-day, VND5,670,000/three-day) escapes the well-traveled routes of Ha Long. A series of two- and three-day tours ply the waters east of Vung Vieng floating village, trading the heavy traffic of Ha Long's caves for a quieter cruise to the equally stunning karsts of Bai Tu Long. Better still are the company's efforts to conserve the bay's natural beauty, spearheading a program known as "For a Green Ha Long Bay," which aims to spread the benefits of tourism to local fishermen and communities, organizes clean-up efforts in the bay, and raises awareness about environmental protection within Ha Long's busy waters. All of Indochina Junk's boats are built as traditional Chinese-style junks and include beautiful, well-appointed rooms with air-conditioning, making this a luxury option at mid-range prices.

One of the bay's more well-known operators, Bhaya Cruises (office 47 Phan Chu Trinh, Hanoi, tel. 04/3944-6777, www.bhayacruises.com, 9am-6pm daily, VND3,150,000/one-day, VND3,969,000-7,665,000/two-day, VND7,665,000-15,120,000/three-day) runs a three-vessel fleet of high-end boats that are replicas of emperor Khai Dinh's famous wooden ship. Multi-day cruises ply the waters between Ha Long, Cat Ba Island, and the outer edge of Bai Tu Long, with stops at a combination of much-visited and off-the-beaten-path attractions. Swimming and kayaking at Vung Ha Beach and guided cycling tours of Cat Ba feature on some itineraries. Transportation to and from Hanoi (shuttle VND630,000/group, private car VND4,515,000/group) is not included in the cost.

Also operated by Bhaya, Au Co Cruises (office 47 Phan Chu Trinh, Hanoi, tel. 04/3933-4545, www.aucocruises.com, 9:30am-6pm daily, VND4,179,000/one-day, VND8,295,000/two-day, VND11,760,000-20,200,000/three-day) is the more luxurious offshoot of its parent company. Their vessel, The Au Co, has swanky cabins, with bamboo and sliding glass doors, enclosed showers, and chic design accents. They have a high-end restaurant onboard, making for a posh environment. The one-day cruises are not as worthwhile as the three-day outings, which tour Ha Long, Bai Tu Long, and Cat Ba, and include leisurely activities, such as kayaking at Vung Ha Beach and cycling tours at Cat Ba.

Transportation

The majority of overnight tours include transportation to and from Hanoi in their price. For those making their own way to Ha Long City, booking agents and travel outfits in Hanoi can arrange minibus transport to the city for around VND130,000 per person. The trip takes around four hours and usually includes a stop at an overpriced souvenir outlet somewhere along the way.

Many cruise operators provide a shuttle bus or private car option, but these are far more expensive, with shuttle buses running VND525,000-630,000 per group and private cars costing at least VND4,000,000 per group.

Local buses travel from **Luong Yen bus station** (3 Nguyen Khoai, tel. 04/3927-0477) in Hanoi to **Bai Chay bus station** (near corner of Le Huu Trac and QL18, tel. 03/3364-9230) in Ha Long City. At VND100,000 a head, you're better off arranging tourist transport, as this saves you the additional cost of getting to and from these bus stations, not to mention navigating the bus system.

Most vessels cast off from **Bai Chay Pier** (Ha Long, tel. 03/3384-6592, www.benxe-bentauquangninh.vn, 6:30am-4:30pm daily), Ha Long City's tourist hub. High-end cruises usually depart farther west from **Tuan Chau Island** (Tuan Chau Island, tel. 03/3655-0009, www.tuanchau-halong.com.vn), about seven miles west of Bai Chay Pier. A select few leave from **Hon Gai Pier** (6A Le Thanh Tong), closer to Ha Long City's center. Even those who travel independently to Ha Long City should be in contact with the tour provider to get detailed directions to the correct pier.

BAI TU LONG BAY

Legend puts the home of Mother Dragon in Ha Long Bay; her children are just next door in Bai Tu Long, a cloudy aquamarine expanse dotted with the same limestone karsts, mysterious caves, and lush greenery. Separated by an invisible border a few miles east of the city, this nearby, smaller bay has long played second fiddle to its more famous neighbor but is fast gaining favor among foreign visitors for its less-crowded waters away from the heavy traffic of Ha Long. Local residents live amid its gravity-defying islands and larger-than-life landscapes.

While it is possible to reach the bay's Quan Lan Island on your own, tours of Bai Tu Long are only available through one outfitter, Indochina Junk.

Vung Vieng Fishing Village

Easily Bai Tu Long's most-visited sight, **Vung Vieng** is one of the bay's fishing communities, comprised of a modest collection of floating houses. Residents live 15 miles offshore, in the shadow of soaring limestone karsts, taking shelter in small, buoyant dwellings that are clustered together on Bai Tu Long's placid waters. Local fishers row visitors to village sights, like the schoolhouse and a few residents' homes, for a taste of daily life in Vung Vieng.

Thien Canh Son Cave

Thien Canh Son Cave is the most impressive of Bai Tu Long's caverns, a vast chamber of sparkling stalactites and unusual formations that is lit by just a few standard light bulbs, retaining the cave's natural atmosphere and beauty. It takes 30-45 minutes to tour the expansive interior.

In the evenings, this eerie cavern occasionally becomes a dining room thanks to Indochina Junk, which runs a three-day, two-night tour in which guests can enjoy a meal within the hollows.

Quan Lan Island

Once an 11th-century trading port, **Quan Lan Island** is among a handful of islands in Bai Tu Long inhabited by locals that is now slowly beginning to reap the benefits of tourism. This long, narrow stretch of rock sits on the southern border of the bay, facing away from the mainland toward the stunning Gulf of Tonkin, an hour-long ferry ride from shore, and boasts some of the most secluded beaches in Vietnam. Once you've reached the island, there isn't much to do beyond admire the scenery. Its sleepy village and unbeatable views are enough to attract at least a few visitors and to get local authorities to seriously consider how best to develop the area for foreign visitors.

Transportation

TOURS

Thanks to a fair amount of guidebook hype and growing tourist interest, more than a few tour providers list the bay in their travel programs. **Indochina Junk** (58 Au Trieu, tel. 04/3926-4085, www.indochina-junk.com, 8am-6pm daily, VND3,510,000/two-day, VND5,670,000/three-day) is the only outfitter approved by local authorities to enter Bai Tu Long's waters. Indochina Junk's tours go all the way to Thien Canh Son Cave, Cap La Island, and the bay's Cong Dam area. All other agencies that include a trip to Bai Tu Long simply touch upon the border of the two bays, stopping over at Vung Vieng fishing village.

FERRIES TO QUAN LAN ISLAND

Independent travelers can overnight on largely undeveloped Quan Lan Island. Daily **high-speed ferries** (tel. 03/3247-3536, 7:30am and 2pm daily, VND120,000) depart from Cai Rong Port, just over 30 miles east of Ha Long City, returning to the mainland at 2:30pm. Local buses from Hanoi make the trip to Cua Ong Market, not far from the port, and from there tourists hop on a boat to Quan Lan.

Once you arrive, there is little to do on the island other than wander and enjoy the view. A handful of guesthouses in the main town offer overnight accommodations. Expect little to no English and limited dining options. Nicer hotels run VND500,000-700,000 per night, with cheaper guesthouses costing around VND150,000-200,000 per night. Amenities will be no more than running water and a fan at the cheaper places, and perhaps an air-conditioner in the nicer hotels, with the potential for hot water. Book ahead of time to ensure there's a room available, though you may need to enlist a Vietnamese speaker, or book through a local travel agency.

CAT BA ISLAND

You would never know how popular Ha Long Bay is from a visit to Cat Ba National Park, surrounded by nothing but nature, or while plying the placid waters of nearby Lan Ha Bay. From Cat Ba Island, you'll enjoy a quieter and more independent version of Ha Long, escaping the heavy traffic of the larger bay's tourist boats. Cat Ba's main town is an unattractive jumble of cookie-cutter hotels and travel agencies, but beyond the main drag is plenty of hiking, cycling, kayaking, and climbing amid the incredible coastline of northern Vietnam.

Cat Ba's wild and wonderful national park is a real must-see, and includes hiking and trekking. Equally appealing are the waters of Lan Ha Bay, a smaller, quieter version of its northern cousin, Ha Long. Lan Ha can be enjoyed on a basic boat tour, scaling the limestone karsts of the bay on a rock-climbing outing, or kayaking through eroded tunnels to one of the bay's 100-plus beaches.

Though it can be gloomy in the off season, particularly as the north's signature mist drifts in and obscures the island's beautiful views, Cat Ba has something to offer even in poor weather. The eerie winter fog is pleasant company compared to the droves of visitors the island receives June-August, when Vietnamese tourists are on holiday.

Getting to Cat Ba requires extra effort, but the rewards are more than worth the work. A growing number of tour companies include stopovers on Cat Ba during their three-day itineraries, but these will only give you an overnight (at most) on the island.

With the exception of Hospital Cave, Cannon Fort, and the Cat Co beaches, most sights in Cat Ba require a guide in order to visit. Much of the island is remote and is most safely enjoyed with a knowledgeable local.

★ Cat Ba National Park

Legend has it that the rugged limestone mountains and winding underground caverns of **Cat Ba National Park (Vuon Quoc Gia Cat Ba)** (tel. 03/1368-8981, www.vuonquocgi-acatba.com.vn, 7am-4pm daily, VND15,000-35,000) came about after a dragon tumbled into the sea, denting the island's terrain with

Cat Ba Island

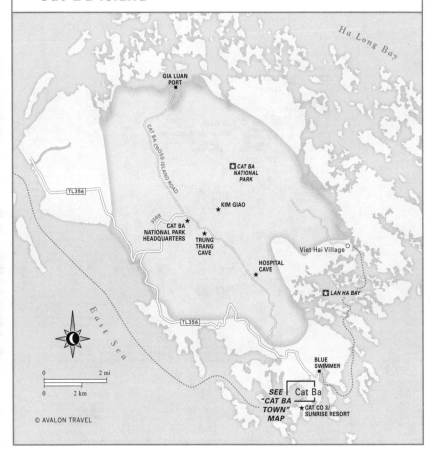

its tail. These rolling hills and rutted formations on the northeastern part of the island provide a habitat for civets, leopards, giant squirrels, dozens of stunning bird species, and over 1,500 varieties of plants, as well as the Cat Ba langur, among the most endangered primates in the world.

A handful of relatively untouched trails wind through the heart of Cat Ba. Most trails range from moderate to strenuous and meander deep into the jungle. On the bay, activities like rock-climbing are available on a few islands, as is swimming, kayaking, and boating.

On most adventures, a guide is necessary to show you the ropes.

TRUNG TRANG CAVE

One of the park's highlights is **Trung Trang Cave** (VND15,000, plus VND70,000/guide), an underground passageway that lies just up the road from Hospital Cave before the park's head office. Discovered in 1938, this cavern winds 984 feet through the base of a limestone karst and was used in the early 1960s as a hideout for members of the Vietnamese navy. Inside the cave, the small, meandering

Cat Ba Town

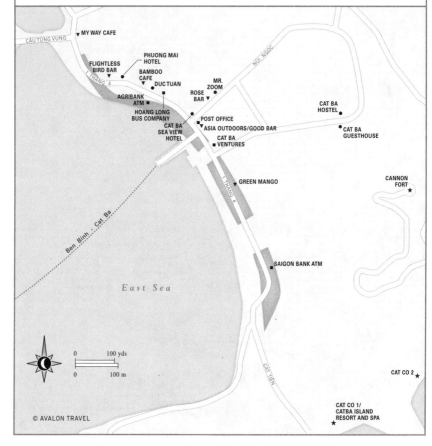

CAU TÙNG VUNG

MY WAY CAFE

PHUONG MAI HOTEL

FLIGHTLESS BIRD BAR

1 THANG 4

BAMBOO CAFE

DUC TUAN

MR. ZOOM

NUI NGOC

AGRIBANK ATM

ROSE BAR

HOANG LONG BUS COMPANY

CAT BA HOSTEL

CAT BA SEA VIEW HOTEL

POST OFFICE

ASIA OUTDOORS/GOOD BAR

CAT BA VENTURES

CAT BA GUESTHOUSE

Ben Binh - Cat Ba

GREEN MANGO

1 THANG 4

CANNON FORT

SAIGON BANK ATM

East Sea

0   100 yds

0   100 m

CAT TIEN

CAT CO 2

CAT CO 1/ CATBA ISLAND RESORT AND SPA

© AVALON TRAVEL

tunnel transitions from smooth, polished walls to spindly stalactites to barnacle-like growths wallpapered against its interior, which is home to scores of tiny bats who nap overhead.

Guides don't speak much English, but they'll point out several formations, some of which resemble elephants, birds, or Buddhas; one or two of these require some imagination. Be prepared to crouch down, as the cavern has low ceilings in some places. Before entering Trung Trang, head past the cave to the national park headquarters to buy an entry ticket and link up with one of the required guides.

KIM GIAO WATCHTOWER

On a clear day, the **Kim Giao Watchtower** (VND15,000) boasts some of the best views on the island. To get there, it's a moderate hike up to the mountain's summit. The two-hour out-and-back journey (just over a half-mile each way) begins at the park's headquarters on a paved route that turns into a well-trodden dirt path, which then becomes stone steps on the ascent. The path zigzags up to a small lookout, where you can take in a panoramic view of the park.

Guides (VND100,000) can be arranged either directly from the park or through one of the tour operators in town as a half-day excursion.

TREK TO VIET HAI VILLAGE

The most challenging trek in the park is to **Viet Hai Village** (VND35,000, plus VND500,000/guide), a nine-mile, four- to five-hour journey. The hike rambles up massive limestone boulders and over five different jungle peaks before sliding into a peaceful farming village on the eastern side of the island. This is one of the best excursions Cat Ba has to offer. If you're lucky, you might catch a rare glimpse of wild macaques and even the Cat Ba langur.

Though the route begins as a tame, paved road from the national park headquarters, it soon deteriorates into limestone boulders to scramble over and, later, a narrow dirt path that winds its way through some of the island's most untouched areas. Two or three miles in, the hike passes by Frog Lake, which is no more than an oversized puddle. Upon reaching Viet Hai Village, you will have an easy seaside walk to the port, where a slow boat floats you back to town.

Substantial footwear is a must, as are long pants. Mosquito protection is not a bad idea, and you'll probably want to bring a backpack or something that keeps your hands free, as the latter part of the descent into Viet Hai Village has you scrambling over rocks.

Tours still run on rainy days and can be just as fun, though the wetter the trail gets the more treacherous it becomes. Most guides are highly experienced and do a good job of keeping you safe, but some of the more challenging passes can still be dangerous for less-confident hikers. This is a difficult hike on a normal day; it's very difficult on a rainy day.

While the national park provides travelers with all the tools required to do this trek, it's more cost-effective to hop on a tour from town. To do the trek independently, it costs VND35,000 for the park entry, VND500,000 for the required guide, and an additional VND500,000 to hire a boat from Viet Hai back to Cat Ba Town. For a full-day excursion

through one of the local tour providers, the going rate is around VND380,000 per person and includes both lunch and transportation to and from Cat Ba.

Hospital Cave

A popular stop en route to Cat Ba National Park, **Hospital Cave (Hang Quan Y)** (8am-5pm daily, VND15,000) was used as a medical facility, shelter, and strategy base for north Vietnamese forces during the American War. Alongside their Chinese allies, Communist soldiers constructed a three-story complex inside the massive cave from 1963 to 1965 with 17 rooms, including patient beds, an operating theater, a meeting hall, a cinema, and several other facilities. The first floor, made entirely of concrete, was where most operations took place and boasts incredible acoustics—one person's voice will reverberate throughout the entire floor. The second-floor space, where films were sometimes played, provides more natural surroundings, with vaulted limestone ceilings. The cave could house 200 people at any given time during the war. Though bombs were dropped around this site, nothing inside the cavern was ever damaged by American attacks, as this particular cave remained undetected throughout the war.

When visiting Hospital Cave, your only option is to park across the street at a small roadside café, where entry tickets are sold. It's not required, but you're better off hiring the sole on-site **guide** (VND30,000), an outgoing man by the name of Mr. Cuong who is knowledgeable and well versed in the history of the place, bringing to life the war within these bare concrete rooms. Afterward, the café across the street is a nice spot for a drink and the owners are a friendly crowd.

Cannon Fort

On a clear day, the view from **Cannon Fort** (Phao Dai Than Cong, tel. 03/1388-8686, 7am-5pm daily, VND50,000) is one of the best on the island. Built by the French in 1942, this 20th-century military lookout was used to protect the city of Haiphong from attack during the Franco-Vietnam War, and later used during the Japanese occupation and the American conflict. Three sides of the island are visible from the top of this 580-foot hill, including some stunning views of the fishing port and the bay, and you'll be able to catch a glimpse of the two hilltop cannons for which the place is named. There is a small exhibition room located in one of the bunkers, though it lacks signage. In all, the main reason for a visit here is the view, so make this trip only on a clear day.

The road leading to Cannon Fort begins in Cat Ba Town. There is a sign at the bottom of the hill directing visitors to the fort.

Cat Co Beaches

A short walk from Cat Ba town, the trio of **Cat Co beaches,** snuggled into many coves on the southeastern tip of the island, are worth a visit during warm weather. There are resorts located right on the water, which regulate access to the beaches, particularly Cat Co 2 and 3. In order to spend time on the beach, you're expected to purchase a drink or meal from the resort, but you don't need to be staying at a resort.

Cat Co 1 is a more local affair and the most easily accessible of the beaches. It's where **Cat Ba Island Resort and Spa** (Cat Co 1, tel. 03/1368-8686, www.catbaislandresort-spa.com) has set up a **water park** (6am-6pm daily, VND200,000) along the shore that is popular with Vietnamese tourists during the summer. The park is virtually a ghost town in the off season. During November and December, it's often possible to access Cat Co 1 for free.

From the main road, hang a left and you'll come to the **Cat Ba Beach Resort** (Cat Co 2, tel. 03/1388-8686, www.catbabeachresort. com, 6am-10pm daily) on Cat Co 2.

A pretty cliffside path from Cat Co 1 leads around to the **Cat Ba Sunrise Resort** (Cat Co 3, tel. 03/1388-7360, www.catbasunriseresort.com, 7am-8pm daily) on Cat Co 3, a quieter stretch of sand where resort guests and outside visitors can come and soak up the sun. Of the three resorts, this is the only one worth staying at overnight.

★ Lan Ha Bay

In the small, quiet **Lan Ha Bay,** located off Cat Ba's eastern shores, trademark limestone karsts rise sharply out of the sea. Dotted with roughly 400 islands, over 100 miniature white-sand beaches, and a secluded fishing village here and there, the bay is a popular

Kayaks are a popular way to explore Lan Ha Bay.

Good Bar

(Ben Beo, tel. 03/1368-8237, www.blueswimmersailing.com, 8am-10pm daily) also offers kayaking tours.

Tours

Nearly every hotel, restaurant, and guesthouse on 1 Thang 4 offers standard excursions to the national park and the island's surrounding bays.

Half- and full-day guided jungle treks to the national park are available for as little as VND350,000 per person. For the best value, shop around along the harborfront. The folks at **Cat Ba Ventures** (223 1 Thang 4, tel. 09/1246-7016, www.catbaventures.com, 7:30am-8pm daily) are a good choice for both trekking and boat tours, though they only seem eager to offer a helping hand after you've forked over your cash.

Nightlife

Cat Ba doesn't offer much in the way of nightlife, but you'll find a few casual hangouts stretched along the harborfront. Most places close up shop by around 10pm, though there are one or two bars that will stay open until the last customer leaves.

Outfitted with retro polka dot couches and a whole host of Kiwi paraphernalia, the **Flightless Bird Bar** (189 1 Thang 4, tel. 03/1388-8517, 10am-last customer daily, VND20,000-80,000) serves drinks only and is a pleasant spot for a late afternoon beverage or some sound travel advice. The cozy indoor room plays a selection of Western music and the bar is stocked with beer and both Vietnamese and Western spirits as well as the occasional bottle of wine. This is also, inexplicably, the place to go for a foot or head massage, or a manicure, as these services are cheap (most under VND60,000) and can be combined with your happy hour.

The liveliest nighttime hangout in Cat Ba town, **Good Bar** (Noble House, 222 1 Thang 4, tel. 03/1388-8363, 7am-10:30pm downstairs, 2am upstairs daily, VND20,000-100,000) slings cold beers, cocktails, spirits, and some pretty average Western food downstairs in its

venue for kayaking, sailing, and deep-water soloing excursions, in addition to standard boat cruises. Lan Ha gets busy in the summer months, when domestic tourists hit the island, but with so many travelers opting for a trip to nearby Ha Long over the bay, this is a far more serene and authentic option.

Lan Ha is experienced via boat tour from Cat Ba Island. Prices for boat tours begin around VND550,000 for a full-day outing to Lan Ha Bay with a brief stop at one or two of Ha Long's most famous sights. These are a popular option, though read the itinerary before signing up; some outings are advertised as day tours of Ha Long when, in reality, boats tend to stick to Lan Ha and only make a quick jaunt into the larger bay.

One boat tour outfitter is **Cat Ba Ventures** (223 1 Thang 4, tel. 09/1246-7016, www.catbaventures.com, 7:30am-8pm daily). Another, **Asia Outdoors** (Noble House, 2nd Fl., 222 1 Thang 4, tel. 03/1368-8450, www.asiaoutdoors.com.vn, 8am-8pm daily), offers rock-climbing and kayaking trips. **Blue Swimmer** ground-floor restaurant and two stories up, past the Asia Outdoors office, where the setting is reminiscent of a bar, complete with pool and foosball tables, a wide balcony overlooking the harbor, and a good music selection. Happy hour specials and regular drink deals are offered, though most only apply to the upper level and not the downstairs restaurant-style seating area. Confirm with your server to avoid surprises on the bill.

The hole-in-the-wall **Rose Bar** (15 Nui Ngoc, tel. 03/1388-8472, catbarosebar@gmail.com, 5pm-late daily, VND15,000-115,000) just off the main drag is a slightly cramped and heavily graffitied bar room that boasts a dart board, pool table, foosball, and other games. The menu matches that of most similar businesses in town, with beer, cocktails, and spirits on offer at good prices, and draws a fair number of thirsty patrons throughout the night. If you're dying to hear your own playlist, patrons are allowed to hook their own iPods into the bar's sound system for a people's choice music selection.

Sports and Recreation

With the incredible outdoors so close to town, the wild and wonderful Cat Ba has fast developed into Vietnam's best-known adventure tourism hub. Activities like cycling, climbing, trekking, and kayaking are popular here and can be arranged through most tour companies in town. Sand flies are present at the beaches; repellent can be a big help with this. Most tour outfits have their own repellent for guest use, but check beforehand.

CYCLING

The only place to offer quality mountain bikes for exploring the island is **Blue Swimmer** (Ben Beo, tel. 03/1368-8237, www.blueswimmersailing.com, 8am-10pm daily, VND315,000/day), located beside the harbor in Lan Ha Bay about five minutes from town. All bikes are imported Treks, which helps to justify the high price, and they can be brought to your hotel if requested. Guided day trips are available for an additional fee, and the

company has a few sample itineraries listed on its website for those interested in blazing their own trails.

ROCK CLIMBING

Easily the best location for rock climbing in Vietnam, Cat Ba and its infinite limestone mountains are a perfect place to get started as a beginner or flex your climbing muscles as a seasoned pro. Whether on a beach in Lan Ha Bay or deep within Butterfly Valley, the island offers more than enough opportunity to scale its many rock faces. For experienced climbers, deep-water soloing is an option, affording those keen on seeing the bay with a more challenging way to climb. **Asia Outdoors** (Noble House, 2nd Fl., 222 1 Thang 4, tel. 03/1368-8450, www.asiaoutdoors.com.vn, 8am-8pm daily), Cat Ba's first and only certified climbing outfit, runs daily trips (VND1,722,000 per person) to its beachfront climbing space in Lan Ha Bay combined with a bit of kayaking. They can also tailor trips to a traveler's individual requests. Staff are fun, friendly, and knowledgeable in both climbing and the area. For more information, stop by the office and chat with the staff or pick up a copy of Asia Outdoors' climbing guidebook for Vietnam.

KAYAKING

Lan Ha's soaring cliffs and peaceful waters are best explored by kayak. Paddle your way across open channels and into small, secluded lagoons; sidle up beside a towering rock face; or float your way through the eroded arches that sit beneath the bay's gravity-defying islands. Dozens of travel outfits in Cat Ba town offer kayaking excursions around Lan Ha at varying rates. When booking, clarify whether or not you'll have a guide paddling along with you and exactly how much time you'll have to explore. The folks at **Blue Swimmer** (Ben Beo, tel. 03/1368-8237, www.blueswimmersailing.com, 8am-10pm daily, VND315,000/day) offer daily rentals as well as a test paddle if you're not sure but want to give it a try.

Saving Cat Ba's Langurs

It's rare to spot a Cat Ba langur, one of the world's most endangered primates, swinging through the trees of the island's national park. These small, golden-headed creatures are native only to Cat Ba Island, and decades of poaching have reduced their numbers from approximately 2,500 in the 1960s to somewhere between 60 and 70 today. Hunted almost exclusively as an ingredient in traditional Chinese medicine, the langur's population reached rock-bottom in 2000, with only 53 animals remaining in the wild.

Thanks to the efforts of a number of German conservation groups, including the Muenster Zoo and the Frankfurt Zoological Society, the fate of the langur is looking up. The Cat Ba Langur Conservation Project (www.catbalangur.org) helps monitor preservation efforts, which protect the natural habitat of seven small sub-populations within Cat Ba National Park who use caves for shelter and survive mostly on flowers, shoots, and leaves. Only three of the seven groups are able to reproduce, further challenging the future of the species. Local communities have become involved in the protection endeavors and Cat Ba's langur is now considered a symbol of the island. For more information, check the Conservation Project's website.

TREKKING

With the vast majority of Cat Ba covered in dense jungle, trekking opportunities abound here, both in and around the national park. For a venture farther off the beaten track, excursions in Butterfly Valley and around Lien Minh, one of the oldest villages on the island, offer more scrambling over rocks and up hills. Guides are required on all trips and can be hired via the national park or booked through a tour in town. To hike to Viet Hai via Frog Lake in Cat Ba National Park, jump on a tour from town to save some money. Tour operators also do this same journey, including a hike up to Kim Giao watchtower, but **Asia Outdoors** (Noble House, 2nd Fl., 222 1 Thang 4, tel. 03/1368-8450, www.asiaoutdoors.com.vn, 8am-8pm daily) is really the only one to venture into Butterfly Valley.

Accommodations

Hotels on Cat Ba are multiplying at a breakneck pace, with a new construction job starting every other day. You'll find tons of hotels along 1 Thang 4, with rooms that offer excellent views of the harbor at slightly higher but still-reasonable prices. The hostels and guesthouses tucked down Nui Ngoc and farther from the water go for much less. In the off season, private beds can be had for as little as VND60,000 a night, though many hoteliers also work as tour guides or travel agents and so these accommodations are usually accompanied by a big push for tours and additional services. Few hotels on the island offer an included breakfast that is actually worth the price tag. Don't expect too much out of your hotel's wireless connection, as there is usually a single router placed on the ground floor that is weak at best. Hoteliers on the island have taken to keeping the "on" switch for the water heater downstairs at reception, so expect to ask for your hot shower beforehand.

The summer months are especially hectic on Cat Ba. If you're dying to grab a waterfront spot or have a particular hotel in mind, make your reservation 1-2 weeks ahead of time. During the rest of the year, hotels have many vacancies, so you can book a room the day of. Listed rates are based on the high season for foreign tourists (Nov.-Dec.), rather than the Vietnamese high season (June-Aug.), when the island is at its busiest and prices are highest. Verify rates beforehand if you plan to visit June-August.

UNDER VND210,000

At the top of Nui Ngoc away from the harbor, **Cat Ba Hostel** (160 Nui Ngoc, tel. 09/7789-4883, www.catbahostel.com, VND60,000 dorm, VND160,000 double) is a worthy choice for budget travelers, with unbeatable prices and clean, well-kept accommodations to match. Hot water, air-conditioning, TV, and Wi-Fi are featured in all rooms, and you'll find personal lockers in the dorms, as well as en suite bathrooms. Downstairs, the hostel runs a travel outfit and can offer advice on the surrounding area.

Directly opposite Cat Ba Hostel, **Cat Ba Guesthouse** (227 Nui Ngoc, tel. 09/0600-0227, VND60,000 dorm, VND120,000 double) may not have the same additional services to offer, but its accommodations are just as good as the competition, with hot water, air-conditioning, TV, and Wi-Fi access throughout the building. Five-bed dorms include a communal balcony and en suite bathroom, while doubles are a little older but still great for the price.

Dirt-cheap and clean, **Mr. Zoom Backpacker Hostel** (25 Nui Ngoc, tel. 03/1369-6230, VND80,000-210,000) is tucked just off the harbor-front road and offers no-frills accommodations for the backpacker crowd. Rooms include hot water, air-conditioning, and semi-hard beds. The owner speaks English well and can arrange tours and various excursions around the island. Note, there is a karaoke bar nearby that gets active during the evenings, though it never stays open too late.

Right in the middle of 1 Thang 4 street, the **Cat Ba Sea View** (220 1 Thang 4, tel. 03/1388-8201, www.catbaseaviewhotel. com, VND160,000-250,000) is the nicest of the island's harbor-front accommodations and boasts a notably friendly staff to go with its tidy, well-kept rooms. Amenities include television and Wi-Fi access, hot water, air-conditioning, plush duvet covers, and a fridge. Beautiful views of the harbor are available on the street-facing side of the hotel, while rooms at the back provide equally good value accommodations without the window. There is a small restaurant and café downstairs.

VND210,000-525,000

Right in the center of town, rooms at the **Phuong Mai** (193 1 Thang 4, tel. 09/1461-8308, VND210,000-250,000) are on par with most other accommodations along this street. The amiable owner, Mr. Khanh, and his family go a long way to make the experience unique. Mr. Khanh can help with advice on the island. Rooms come with hot water, Wi-Fi access, air-conditioning, and TV, not to mention some nice views of the harbor. The first two stories of the building serve as a hair salon.

The **Duc Tuan Hotel** (210 1 Thang 4, tel. 03/1388-8783, www.ductuancatbahotel.com, VND210,000-315,000) offers clean, well-appointed rooms, many of which come with a nice harbor-front view. Amenities include air-conditioning, hot water, touch-and-go Wi-Fi access, TV, a minibar, an in-room safe, and tea- and coffee-making facilities. Mattresses are a little hard but not the worst on the island. Downstairs, you'll find that the hotel operates a restaurant and a tour-booking agency out of the ground floor, in addition to renting out motorbikes and bicycles. Breakfast is included in the room rate, but it is also possible to opt out of this, if preferred. Prices dip as low as VND210,000 in winter.

VND1,050,000-2,100,000

The finest of the lot on Cat Ba, **Sunrise Resort** (Cat Co 3, tel. 03/1388-7360, www. catbasunriseresort.com, VND1,800,000-4,600,000) is nestled away in the peaceful cove of Cat Co 3 beach, far enough removed from town to avoid the tourist trail but still well within walking distance. As the only property on the beach, its spacious, modern rooms feature the height of local luxury, including television, Wi-Fi access, a minibar, hot water, air-conditioning, tea- and coffee-making facilities, an in-room safety box, and the best sea views on the island. More posh accommodations also throw in a balcony, and all guests are free to enjoy a complimentary breakfast, as well as use of the beach out front. Restaurant and massage services are available on site, though additional services tend to be overpriced.

Food

Most of the fare on the island is bland, with every harbor-front hotel offering a similar menu of standard but overpriced backpacker grub. For cheaper options, head inland up Nui Ngoc. Wherever you eat, don't expect to be wowed: this is not the place to revel in the tastes of Vietnamese cuisine. For snacks and other necessities, you can also swing by the cache of convenience stores off the main road on Nui Ngoc south of the main harbor.

Completely outfitted in its namesake, the **Bamboo Cafe** (1 Thang 4, tel. 03/1388-7552, 7am-9:30pm daily, VND40,000-145,000) offers a decent mix of Western and Vietnamese dishes at reasonable prices, not to mention some of the better service in town. Owned by a former tour guide, the restaurant serves average meals in addition to offering useful travel advice. The rest of the family, who staff the eatery, are equally amiable and willing to help.

For your European caffeine fix, **My Way Cafe** (164C 1 Thang 4, 7am-10pm daily, VND15,000-70,000) makes the best lattes, cappuccinos, and coffee-related beverages on the island and also offers happy hour specials on its alcoholic drinks, most of which are less than VND110,000. Solid Vietnamese offerings are served, though service can be slow at times.

You'll find the best dining on Cat Ba at **Green Mango** (1 Thang 4, tel. 03/1388-7151, www.greenmango.vn, 7am-7pm daily, VND80,000-470,000), a white-tablecloth place that is well-priced for its offerings, which include Western breakfasts, pizzas, and other dishes. Both indoor and outdoor seating is available, with the latter facing the harbor. The restaurant has inconsistent hours during the low season.

Information and Services
TOURIST INFORMATION

With so many travel and tour agencies attached to hotels, it can be difficult to come across independent information on Cat Ba, as most of these booking offices are not interested in assisting travelers unless they can earn a cut in the process. **Asia Outdoors** (Noble House, 2nd Fl., 222 1 Thang 4, tel. 03/1368-8450, www.asiaoutdoors.com.vn, 8am-8pm daily) has plenty of useful information on its website and is more than willing to help in person, as are the friendly folks at **Flightless Bird Bar** (189 1 Thang 4, tel. 03/1388-8517, 10am-last customer daily). You can also ask your hotel for a map, which most hotels are willing to at least loan out to travelers.

BANKS

There is an **Agribank ATM** (1 Thang 4) located right on the main drag of Cat Ba town as well as a **Saigon Bank ATM** (1 Thang 4) down the farther end of the harbor. These are the only two ATMs on the island, so bring enough currency. Some hotels may be able to change currency, but make sure the rate isn't too high. If possible, change your money before arriving on the island.

INTERNET AND POSTAL SERVICES

The island's **post office** (corner of 1 Thang 4 and Nui Ngoc, tel. 03/1388-8569, 8am-noon and 2pm-6pm daily) is often closed during the winter months but sports a letter box outside the building, which is allegedly emptied twice a day. It's probably better to save your mail for your next destination to ensure that it arrives. Most wireless connections on the island are dismal; if Internet is a must, your best bet is to ask your hotel.

MEDICAL SERVICES

There are no real medical facilities on Cat Ba with the exception of the island's sole hospital, a small and often-empty clinic that lies about a mile out of town and is poorly equipped.

For anything that a first-aid kit can't fix, head back to the mainland.

Getting There
FROM HA LONG CITY

A rusted, open-air local **ferry** (Tuan Chau Island, 7:30am, 11:30am, and 3pm daily, VND50,000) runs to Cat Ba Island from the city of Ha Long each day, arriving on the northern side of the island at Gia Luan port. The ferry ride is 35-45 minutes. This point of entry often makes a bad first impression, so it is strongly recommended that you reach the island via Haiphong rather than Ha Long.

As you disembark at Gia Luan port, the usual group of touts will appear, demanding exorbitant rates (VND200,000-800,000) for motorbikes and taxis into Cat Ba town. While such harassment is a common occurrence in Vietnam, this is where things really get ugly. There is a **green local bus** (VND20,000), which runs directly into Cat Ba town. In some cases, the touts turn on the bus drivers when tourists attempt to board the bus, shouting and intimidating them into denying tourists entry or overcharging them.

Some bus drivers lie and attempt to convince tourists that theirs is the local bus, though the correct vehicles are green in color and have a sign saying Cat Ba on the front. If you wait for the correct bus or walk on and ignore the touts and the impostor buses, you will be stalked by touts, now on motorbikes, as they know that you have no other option when heading the 14 miles into town.

All this can make for an unpleasant experience. There are two solutions to this. The first is to simply pay the inflated fare and avoid any confrontation (though this encourages such behavior to continue). Your next best bet is to board the local bus anyway, even if touts are bullying the bus driver into overcharging you. Negotiate the price with the bus fee collector when the touts are out of earshot. It's still possible to be slightly overcharged—VND50,000, for example, instead of VND20,000. The tickets show the fare printed directly on the paper, so you can attempt to contest any overcharging. The bus ride into town is 15-20 minutes.

FROM HAIPHONG

The fastest and most hassle-free way to reach Cat Ba is from Haiphong. Daily **hydrofoil boats** (45-min. ride, VND200,000) depart as early as 7am and run until 3pm, dropping passengers directly in the heart of Cat Ba town. These aging vessels are operated by **Cat Ba Island Resort and Spa** (Cat Co 1, tel. 03/1358-8999, www.catbaislandresort-spa.com). Tickets are sold at the Haiphong dock (4 Ben Binh) and should be purchased ahead of time during summer. The rest of the year, tickets can be purchased at the time of departure. Ticket vendors roam the pier in Haiphong, but not all are honest. Check the resort's website for full details and the correct price, or pop into the (often unstaffed) ticket office, where prices are listed on the wall. There are some independent vendors who sell legitimate tickets, but check that the price is printed on them before purchasing. The boats also run in the opposite direction, with boats departing from the **Fish Harbor** (Cang Ca) opposite 1 Thang 4 street in Cat Ba town at 8am, 10am, 2pm, and 4pm daily.

Bus-boat-bus tickets (VND150,000-200,000) can be purchased from both Haiphong (3.5 hours) and Hanoi. The bus hops on a series of ferries via Cat Hai Island before arriving on Cat Ba and bringing passengers directly into town. When booking your bus ticket, confirm where it lets off. To get back to Haiphong from Cat Ba, the most reliable bus provider on the island is **Hoang Long** (217 1 Thang 4, tel. 03/1388-7224, www.hoanglongasia.com, 7am-5pm daily).

Getting Around
BUSES

If you're not comfortable on a motorbike, the cheapest and easiest way to get to Cat Ba National Park and its many sights is by **local bus** (VND20,000). Minibuses depart from the town center at 8am and follow the road out to the park's headquarters, passing by Hospital Cave. For the return trip, it's just as easy to flag down a minibus heading in the opposite direction in order to get back to town.

TAXIS AND *XE OM*

Motorbike drivers are easily found on the harbor-front street. Should you venture anywhere else (the national park, for example), arrange transportation back ahead of time. Larger vehicles can be hired through your hotel. Taxis are few and far between here.

VEHICLES FOR HIRE

Most hotels and guesthouses around town rent out motorbikes to travelers, starting around VND80,000 for the day. Bicycles are also available, though it's recommended that you opt for the more expensive, high-quality rental if you're planning a cycling day, as the island's hills are not easily tackled on a basic bike. Check the quality of your vehicle before setting off: Cat Ba's less-than-stellar roads can be challenging enough even on a well-maintained vehicle.

HA LONG CITY

Despite the bay's majestic waters and jungle-clad karsts, Ha Long City is a rather underwhelming place. It's best used as a home base from which to do a day cruise of Ha Long Bay, as a substitute for the pricey overnight cruises. Few people stray beyond the droves of hotels and clutch of restaurants lining the main drag, where Bai Chay, Ha Long Bay's most active pier, welcomes countless visitors each day.

Bai Chay

To kill some time in town, take a stroll along **Bai Chay Beach,** a small beach east of the pier of the same name. There are decent views of the bay's jagged peaks from here, like a mismatched set of teeth spread out along the horizon. Several cafés along this stretch face the water, inviting travelers to come in and relax. Neither the beach nor the water are particularly clean, making this a sightseeing-only spot.

Accommodations

Few travelers stay more than a night or two in Ha Long City. Budget visitors are best off staying close to Bai Chay Pier, where boats depart for Ha Long Bay every morning. Here, a string of cheap and cheerful mini-hotels line the left side of Vuon Dao street, just off the main road.

A few mid-range options dot the main road, but if you're looking to unwind in style, there are posh hotels gathered around Tuan Chau Pier, seven miles west of Bai Chay. The majority of luxury cruise boats depart from Tuan Chau. The only upmarket hotel near Bai Chay is the Novotel.

It's easiest to wait to book a bay tour until you reach Ha Long City. From here, every hotel has its own travel service and it's all but assumed that you'll be using your hotel's tour outfitter for your bay tour. If you book with a different company from your hotel, expect your hotelier to be (at best) a little gruff. It's a good idea to consider the tour offerings and the hotel behind the tour as one unit.

June through August, room rates are highest, and reservations are imperative, as local tourists arrive in droves to visit the bay. Costs can be higher on weekends for the same reason.

VND210,000-525,000

The bright, spotless rooms at ★ **Viet Hoa Hotel** (35 Vuon Dao, tel. 03/3384-6035, VND210,000-315,000) are part of a string of budget hotels along Vuon Dao, but this one stands out due to its owners, who go out of their way to be helpful and are one of the only tour providers on the block that do not overcharge travelers to an alarming rate. Hot water, air-conditioning, television, Wi-Fi, and a minibar are included in the hotel's amenities, along with private balconies for street-facing rooms. Mattresses at Viet Hoa—and, indeed, most accommodations in this vicinity—are not exactly plush, so don't bother if you can't handle a solid bed.

In possession of the most impeccably clean bathrooms in Ha Long City, **New Century Hotel (The Ky Moi)** (27 Vuon Dao, tel.

Ha Long City

TUAN CHAU

Tuan Chau Island

FERRY TO/FROM CAT BA ISLAND

TUAN CHAU PIER

HOANG QUOC VIET

18

BAI CHAY BUS STATION

VIETCOMBANK

NOVOTEL

LY QUOC SUR

BAI CHAY

HA LONG

HONG HANH 3

TOURIST INFORMATION CENTER

BAMBOO BAR

LINH DAN

GRAND HA LONG HOTEL

VINACE

BAI CHAY BEACH

EMERAUDE CAFÉ

THONG NHAT 2

HA LONG EDEN

POST OFFICE

VIET HOA

NEW CENTURY HOTEL

BAI CHAY PIER

BMC, HAI AU

HA LONG

SEE DETAIL

HA LONG

CAU BAI CHAY

Ha Long Bay

Chu Luc Bay

HON GAI BUS STATION

HON GAI PIER

QUANG NINH GENERAL HOSPITAL

Vung Oan Island

Hang Dinh Island

Hang Ma Island

Gieng Goi Island

Do Island

Met Island

0   25 km
0   25 mi

© AVALON TRAVEL

Seeing the Bay in One Day

It's possible to access some of Ha Long's more popular sights in a single day. Four-, six-, and eight-hour cruises are available through Ha Long City's hotels and the city's ticketing office at Bai Chay Pier. These tours stop at Dau Go and Thien Cung Caves, a floating fishing village, Titov Island, and Sung Sot Cave, depending upon the length of the outing. The six- and eight-hour excursions are a pleasant way to pass a day.

For the most inexpensive tours, public boats at **Bai Chay Pier** (Ha Long, tel. 03/3384-6592, www.benxebentauquangninh.vn, 6:30am-4:30pm daily, VND100,000 pp) cast off every day at 8am, visiting Thien Cung and Dau Go Caves as well as a few of the bay's more famous landmarks. Factor in additional costs for the bay's **entry fee** (VND120,000) as well as VND50,000 for each of the sights visited. Bai Chay only offers four-hour excursions.

For longer trips, private boats can also be hired at the pier. With costs beginning at VND400,000-500,000 per hour, you may prefer to arrange through a hotel or booking agency, where you can find six- and eight-hour excursions that tack on activities like swimming and kayaking as well as a few more of the bay's sights.

The hotel or booking agent will almost certainly charge a commission, though the amount can vary drastically depending upon the company. A six-hour tour of the bay, including lunch and all entry fees, should come to around VND600,000 per person. Some agencies will quote VND1,000,000 or more. Ask for a breakdown of the included costs so that you can see just how much goes to the hotel or booking agency. Day tours from high-end cruise providers begin around VND1,000,000, so booking at or above this price through a local hotel or booking agency is probably not worth your money. To avoid some of this hassle, pay a visit to the folks at **Viet Hoa Hotel** (35 Vuon Dao, tel. 03/3384-6035), who are a trustworthy group and tend to charge more reasonable prices.

Once you have booked your tour, request that the booking agent write down all included sights, activities, and amenities on your receipt. Because the booking agency and the tour operator are often different companies, miscommunications can arise. With many of the boat guides speaking limited English, a record of your itinerary can help to resolve any issues.

It is also possible to arrange a daylong outing with higher-end cruise companies, though most of these tours originate in Hanoi. This requires a four-hour drive to and from the city (from VND1,155,000). With only a fraction of the day spent on the water, it's far more worthwhile to organize an overnight excursion if you plan to enter this price range.

03/3384-4314, VND252,000-315,000) makes for a solid budget option. Rooms are basic but spacious and count Wi-Fi access, a television, hot water, air-conditioning, and a fridge in their amenities, though beds are hard. Cheap boat trips can be arranged from here, as well as motorbike rentals, transportation, and a whole host of other add-ons.

Hidden in the shadow of Muong Thanh across the street, **Ha Long Eden** (Ha Long, tel. 03/3384-6145, VND480,000-900,000) may not be a five-star affair, but its rooms represent good value for money. Clean, well-appointed accommodations come with comfy beds, hot water, air-conditioning, television, and Wi-Fi access. Some rooms include pleasant views of the bay, and the staff are an amiable bunch. Prices can go up as much as 15 percent on weekends, as this is when more local tourists visit. During the off-season, this isn't an issue.

Beside Ha Long Eden, **Thong Nhat 2** (Ha Long, tel. 09/1716-8999, VND400,000-900,000) is a slightly older hotel whose view is somewhat obscured by its next-door neighbor. Nonetheless, rooms are well-kept, featuring Wi-Fi access, television, air-conditioning, and hot water. Rooms at the back offer partial views of the bay. Should you find that Thong Nhat 2 is full, check out the other Thong Nhats (1, 3, and 4) on either side.

A short uphill jaunt from the main drag,

the rooms at Linh Dan (104 Bai Chay, tel. 03/3652-2696, www.linhdanhalong.com, VND300,000) are spacious and clean, featuring large windows, Wi-Fi access, television, hot water, air-conditioning, and a fridge. Bathrooms are on the small side, but the hotel's location offers more peace and quiet than some of the other accommodations closer to the bay.

OVER VND2,100,000

While it's not a four-star accommodation as advertised, the Grand Ha Long (Ha Long, tel. 03/3384-4042, www.grandhalonghotel.com.vn, VND1,900,000-5,300,000, breakfast included) is a worthy option for this price range. Rooms are well-appointed, featuring standard amenities as well as Wi-Fi access. Though the furniture is slightly undersized, beds are comfortable. Use of the swimming pool is included in the room rate. Some rooms offer a nice view of the bay overlooking Bai Chay Beach. Downstairs, the hotel operates a restaurant and bar within its retro lobby.

★ Novotel Ha Long Bay (Ha Long, tel. 03/3384-8108, www.novotelhalong.com.vn, VND3,230,000-5,220,000) is the sole standout in the high-end price range. Of the four different room types, the bay-facing rooms are best, affording incredible views and large bathtubs, cozy beds, and a balcony. Downstairs are a swanky restaurant, café, and an outdoor seating area that overlooks the bay. Spa services and a fitness center are available to guests, as are cooking classes, kayaking, city tours, and bay cruises. Breakfast can be included for a few extra dollars.

Food

The strip along Bai Chay Beach offers enough culinary variety for a day or two. The city's one specialty is its seafood, which comes from the bay and is particularly fresh.

Come dinner time, the Hong Hanh 3 (Ha Long, tel. 03/3381-2345, 6am-10pm daily, VND95,000-200,000) is often busy, doling out excellent local seafood in both its cozy interior and on the patio next door. Dishes are prepared family-style and therefore more expensive. Service is quick and the place is popular with locals, too.

A good lunch or dinner spot, the hotel restaurant at Linh Dan (104 Bai Chay, tel. 03/3384-6025, www.linhdanhalong.com, 8am-8pm daily, VND70,000-200,000) does a tasty turn in seafood, from shrimp and squid to snails and fish, as well as a handful of beef and chicken offerings. Seats are available indoors and out. The prices are right for these delicious meals.

A bright orange building opposite Bai Chay Pier, BMC - Hai Au (Ha Long, tel. 03/3384-5065, www.haiaujunk.com, 7am-10pm daily, VND20,000-150,000) is more café than restaurant with a longer list of drinks—coffee, tea, beer, wine, and cocktails—than food. Portions are generous and make for a filling breakfast or lunch.

The small, windowed dining room at Vinace (Ha Long, tel. 03/3351-1538, 8am-midnight daily, VND115,000-230,000) serves pizza, pasta, risotto, and seafood dishes that, while not exactly authentic Italian cuisine, are a delicious and worthy Western option. Its wine list and European coffee, plus desserts like tiramisu, round out the menu. Look for the bright red "Italian" sign flashing just opposite Emeraude Cafe.

Among the many boxy buildings lining the road behind Bai Chay Beach, Bamboo Bar (Ha Long, tel. 03/3364-0899, baranhphong@vnn.vn, 7am-2am daily, VND50,000-150,000) is a cheerful spot outfitted in bamboo and offering burgers, pasta, pizza, and a few Vietnamese options, as well as beer, wine, and cocktails. Western food prices are more reasonable than other nearby restaurants and the staff are a friendly bunch.

One of the swankier outlets on the strip, Emeraude Cafe (Ha Long, tel. 03/3384-9266, www.emeraude-cruises.com, 8am-9pm daily, VND80,000-355,000) does a reasonable take on Western food like burgers, steak, and pizza, though portions run small. European coffee is available. The servers are attentive and friendly. The building, a pretty white bungalow with arched windows, features wireless Internet and a bank of computers for customer use, as well as plenty of magazines and newspapers to while away the hours.

Information and Services

TOURIST INFORMATION

Ha Long's local tourist information center (Ha Long, tel. 03/3362-8862, www.halong-tourism.com.vn, 8:30am-5pm daily) does a great job of cluing travelers in on all of the sights both in the bay and beyond, provided you ask the right questions. Look to the giant wall map inside the office for a bit of guidance and feel free to inquire about the office's complimentary info booklet, a small paperback printed by the bay's management department that details the history of the area as well as giving a round-up of its most famous attractions. Maps of the bay are available free of charge.

Ha Long is one of the few cities in Vietnam that has an active tourist hotline (tel. 03/3384-7347). While there's no guarantee that your complaint will be addressed, any issues you might have regarding tourism in the city or the bay can be lodged here.

BANKS

ATMs are all over Ha Long road. For currency exchange, the local Vietcombank (Ha Long, tel. 03/3381-1808, www.vietcombank.com.vn, 7:30am-11:30am and 1pm-4:30pm Mon.-Fri.) near Bai Chay Pier can help.

INTERNET AND POSTAL SERVICES

A large post office (To 1, Khu 2, Ha Long, tel. 03/3384-6203, 7:30am-11:30am and 1pm-5pm Mon.-Sat., 8:30am-10:30am and 2:30pm-4pm Sun.) sits on the corner of Ha Long and Vuon Dao streets and provides mail services.

For Internet access, most hotel rooms come with Wi-Fi access. If you're in need of a computer, the tourist information center (Ha Long, tel. 03/3362-8862, www.halongtourism.com.vn, 8:30am-5pm daily) offers 30 minutes of free Internet use at the desktop computers in its office. You can also grab a drink at the

Emeraude Cafe (Ha Long, tel. 03/3384-9266, www.emeraude-cruises.com, 8am-9pm daily), where a bank of computers with Internet access is available to customers.

MEDICAL SERVICES

Quang Ninh General Hospital (Tue Tinh, tel. 03/3382-5489, www.benhviendktin-hquangninh.vn) is the best medical facility in the area. For any serious conditions, head to Hanoi.

Getting There

BUS

From Hanoi (4 hours, VND200,000), mini-buses most often drop off passengers along Vuon Dao or the main strip. The majority of budget and mid-range cruise outfitters include bus transportation from Hanoi in the cost. If you don't have a tour booked in advance, any travel agent or hotel in Hanoi can arrange a minibus to transport you to Ha Long City. This costs more than taking a local bus from Hanoi (VND80,000-100,000), but the tourist bus will pick you up from your hotel.

The Bai Chay bus station (near corner of Le Huu Trac and QL18, tel. 03/3364-9230) sits just over three miles from the Bai Chay Pier. From here, daily buses depart for Hanoi.

BOAT

From Gia Luan port on the northern side of Cat Ba Island, a local ferry (VND50,000) runs at 9am, 1pm, and 4pm every day (confirm ahead of time during the off-season). The ride across the bay takes about 1.5 hours. It lands seven miles from Bai Chay at the southern end of Tuan Chau Island (Tuan Chau Island, tel. 03/3655-0009, www.tuanchau-ha-long.com.vn).

Make the trip back from Cat Ba into Ha Long City, or book a bus-boat-bus ticket (wherein the bus boards a ferry) from Cat Ba directly to your next destination. Those who arrive in Ha Long City via Tuan Chau Island will have to either snap up one of the few *xe om* drivers loitering around the ferry dock or opt for a taxi into town. A *xe om* ride costs around VND80,000, while a cab ride is about VND130,000.

Getting Around

The *xe om* drivers of Ha Long are particularly eager to help you find your way: Expect to receive more than a few honks, shouts, and catcalls walking down the main road. For taxis, the local **Mailinh** (tel. 03/3362-8628) cabs are one of a few companies in town.

Many of the hotels along Vuon Dao rent out motorbikes or bicycles to travelers. Those that provide this service tend to advertise it on the front door, so you shouldn't have too much trouble finding a vehicle.

HAIPHONG

The third-largest city in Vietnam, Haiphong is a hectic northern port seldom visited by foreign travelers but for a few who use the town as a transit point en route to Cat Ba Island. Haiphong's bustling streets function as a significant economic and political center up north as well as an important transportation hub for imports and exports within the country. You will find a few traces of colonial architecture in town, leftover from the days of the French, who aided in developing Haiphong's port during the 1870s, as well as a monument to revered local and national hero Le Chan, a gutsy female general who led the charge against Chinese colonists in the third century.

Given the fact that Haiphong's major draw is its daily hydrofoils to Cat Ba Island, a stopover in the city needn't last more than one night. In the downtown area, and specifically along Dien Bien Phu, there are plenty of hotels, restaurants, and other necessities to tide you over until your boat comes. A stroll along the former Bonnal Canal or a quick visit to one of the local pagodas can keep you entertained.

Sights

There are a handful of sights around Haiphong that can be explored in an afternoon, most of them on foot. When visiting Haiphong's pagodas and temples, dress respectfully, as the local reception of foreign tourists is sometimes stony and any revealing clothes will likely not be well-received.

HAIPHONG MUSEUM

The **Haiphong Museum** (66 Dien Bien Phu, tel. 03/1382-3451, 8am-11am Tues., 8am-11am and 7:30pm-9:30pm Wed.-Sun., VND5,000) is a Gothic behemoth situated right in the center of town. Covering a hectare of land, the large colonial-style building was completed in 1919 and houses a nice collection of ancient ceramics and wood carvings from the Le and Tran dynasties, vintage photographs from the days of French colonialism, and a few other odds and ends, including a coin collection, an old-school Mobylette bike, and a rickshaw. The standard exhibit on Vietnamese sovereignty in the Paracel and Spratly islands is also on display. English signage is available, but translations are only sometimes comprehensible. This is not a bad spot to pass the time if you're wandering around town.

HAIPHONG PARK

A sliver of land winding from Dien Bien Phu around to the Tam Bac River, Haiphong's local **park** lies in the center of town and boasts a charming esplanade, complete with flower stalls and manicured gardens. Once the Bonnal Canal during colonial days, parts of this waterway have been filled in, but a small stretch remains, complementing some of Haiphong's other architectural sights, including the Opera House and a generous **statue of Le Chan** (intersection of Me Linh and Nguyen Duc Canh), local heroine and revered Vietnamese historical figure. The statues are over 24 feet tall and weighs 19 tons.

OPERA HOUSE

If you're strolling along the parkway downtown, chances are you'll pass Haiphong's **Opera House** (65 Dinh Tien Hoang, tel. 03/1382-3084), a grand, pale yellow colonial hall completed in 1904. Built by the French, this 400-seat theater is shuttered on most

Haiphong

days, but its architecture complements the waterfront scene and the large open square before it.

NGHE TEMPLE

From the outside, **Nghe Temple (Den Nghe)** (sunrise-sunset daily) appears to be nothing special, its stark gray walls rubbing shoulders with a local schoolyard. But, through the three-door entrance gate is a lavish homage to local hero Le Chan, a female general who aided in the 2nd century uprising of the Trung sisters.

Born in An Bien, a small village northwest of Haiphong, Le Chan was from a well-to-do family. But, at the time, Chinese colonization meant that even the upper echelons of Vietnamese society were subject to oppression. When To Dinh, the leader of what was then known as Giao Chi, a Chinese territory, attempted to make Le Chan his wife, she refused, an act of dissent that caused To Dinh to harm her parents. For 10 years, Le Chan bided her time until, in the spring of AD 40, the Trung sisters launched a rebellion against the Chinese occupation, driving To Dinh and his army out of Vietnam. Le Chan and her forces were instrumental in this takeover. Two years later, the Chinese returned in greater numbers, rekindling the battle. The Trung sisters, who had ruled Vietnam in the interim, committed suicide rather than risk capture by the Han Chinese. Upon their death, Le Chan continued to fight for another year, falling back to fiercely defend the village of Lat Son until, in AD 43, when defeat was inevitable, she threw herself off Giat Dau mountain. Vietnam's remaining generals buried her in secret and she has been a revered hero ever since.

The original temple on this site was no more than a modest shrine. Today's two main halls, built in 1919 and renovated several times over the years, are ornate and intricate. Several stone animals, including elephants, horses, and lions, populate the courtyard, while Le Chan's altar is off to the right. Beautiful floral arrangements surround the legendary woman's statue, and lacquered woodwork hangs overhead.

Nghe Temple

Entertainment and Events
NIGHTLIFE

Nightlife in Haiphong is fairly tame, with most locals gathering for a cup of coffee after work or an evening glass of wine. All of the city's bars and cafés shut their doors by midnight.

The narrow, dimly lit **Julie's Bar** (22C Minh Khai, tel. 03/1352-1198, www.juliesbarhaiphong.vn, 5pm-last customer daily, VND20,000-120,000) gets livelier later in the evening, starting around 8pm, and a friendly staff serves beer and cocktails. A good music selection plays in the background, making this an inviting spot for a nighttime drink.

The cozy little café at **Phono Box** (79 Dien Bien Phu, tel. 03/1382-3333, 9am-midnight daily, VND25,000-160,000) makes a nice setting for a mellow evening drink, with exposed brick walls, leather chairs, and a collection of throwback records on repeat. Beer and cocktails are served alongside a lengthy wine selection, and you'll also find full Western meals (from VND90,000).

With cushy retro sofa chairs and saxophone music in the background, **Maxim** (51 Dien Bien Phu, tel. 03/1382-2934, 6:30am-11pm daily, VND20,000-90,000) gives off a laid-back jazz-lounge vibe. Though it's most popular during the evenings, this corner property in downtown Haiphong gets regular visitors throughout the day, when it functions as a café. Occasional live music and a mellow atmosphere really get things rolling after dark. Reasonably priced food (from VND40,000) is also served.

FESTIVALS AND EVENTS

Toward the start of September each year, the annual **Do Son Buffalo Fighting Festival,** a long-held tradition, takes place 12 miles south of the city center. Shortly after the Lunar New Year, local participants begin their search for a prize buffalo. Once a trainer has settled upon a chosen animal, he or she prepares the buffalo to fight. Training can last up to eight months.

The preliminary stages of the competition take place around late June or early July, with the first showdown held on the eighth day of the sixth lunar month. These contests continue up until the ninth day of the eighth lunar month (early September), when the final competition is attended by scores of Vietnamese from near and far.

During the competition, buffaloes do not harm one another; rather, the animals lock horns to assert their strength. The loser usually flees, chased by the winner, signaling the end of a fight. After the festival, all the buffaloes are slaughtered. Their blood is offered to the Jade Emperor, while the meat is sold at the market and its consumption is believed to be good luck.

Accommodations

Accommodation costs tend to be higher in Haiphong than other Vietnamese cities. The best value options run no less than VND250,000 in most places. Conditions in the city's cheaper hotels are pretty abysmal and make it worth shelling out the extra couple bucks for a comfier bed and a room that's been properly cleaned. On the more expensive end, you can find plenty of well-appointed mid-range and top-tier accommodations thanks to Haiphong's regular business visitors.

VND210,000-525,000

One of the better mid-range options, **Kim Thanh Hotel** (67 Dien Bien Phu, tel. 03/1374-5264, www.kimthanhhotel.com.vn, VND395,000-550,000) is clean and well kept, though its beds are of the more solid variety. TV, air-conditioning, hot water, and Wi-Fi are in each room, and the staff assists with general queries regarding Haiphong.

The well-kept ★ **Maxims Hotel** (3K Ly Tu Trong, tel. 03/1374-6540, www.maximshotel.vn, VND420,000-890,000) is your best bet when it comes to mid-range accommodations in Haiphong. Rooms are clean and feature modern furnishings with comfy beds, air-conditioning, TV, and Wi-Fi access. The downstairs restaurant serves food throughout the day and staff can assist with travel-related queries. Due to the limited number of mid-range options in town, this hotel is often full; check availability before arriving.

Though it's fairly basic, **Bao Anh Hotel** (20B Minh Khai, tel. 03/1382-3406, www.hotelbaoanh.com, VND400,000-1,000,000) boasts one of the better locations in town, alongside a street full of restaurants and close to the city center. Accommodations are clean, modern, and equipped with TV, Wi-Fi,

Maxims Hotel

a minibar, hot water, and air-conditioning. Breakfast is included in the room rate, though you're better off skipping the rather limited selection and venturing out on your own.

VND525,000-1,050,00

A clear step above the less-expensive mid-range options in Haiphong, **Monaco Hotel** (103 Dien Bien Phu, tel. 03/1374-6468, www. haiphongmonacohotel.com, VND600,000-800,000) boasts a spacious reception area decked out in European decor and, inexplicably, a pair of sphinxes guarding the main staircase. The staff are hit-or-miss here. Rooms are plush as far as mid-range accommodations go, featuring television, Wi-Fi access, hot water, air-conditioning, a minibar, and modern furnishings. Breakfast is included in the room rate.

VND1,050,000-2,100,00

The palatial reception hall at **Classic Hoang Long Hotel** (25 Tran Quang Khai, tel. 03/1328-2666, www.classic-hoanglonghotel. com, VND1,460,000-3,160,000) is chock full of mismatched decorations, from Greek statues to Buddhist figurines, a replica of an ancient Vietnamese brass drum, and a grand, wraparound staircase. While rooms upstairs don't necessarily live up to this same eclectic style, the accommodations at Classic Hoang Long are well-appointed, featuring hot water, air-conditioning, TV, Wi-Fi access, and, in the case of VIP rooms, retro furniture, tea- and coffee-making facilities, and an in-room computer. Breakfast is included in the room rate.

OVER VND2,100,00

The rather posh **Nam Cuong Hotel** (47 Lach Tray, tel. 03/1382-8555, www.namcuonghaiphonghotel.com.vn, VND1,800,000-3,900,000) sits a short way south of the park and boasts four varieties of high-end accommodations, all of which are outfitted with a host of amenities, including Wi-Fi access and daily, fresh fruit and water. Guests are also invited to a welcome drink and can enjoy the daily complimentary buffet breakfast in the hotel restaurant. Use of the sauna, whirlpool tub, and swimming pool are all free of charge.

Overlooking the water, **AVANI Harbor View** (12 Tran Phu, tel. 03/1382-7827, www. avanihotels.com, VND2,730,000-3,675,000) is Haiphong's best accommodation. An updated grand colonial-style building, complete with arched windows and balustrades, this four-star hotel houses 122 guest rooms, two restaurants, two bars, a swimming pool, spa, and fitness center. Rooms come in varying levels of luxury, but each bright and well-appointed room features television, Wi-Fi access, a minibar, tea- and coffee-making facilities, a spacious sitting area, work desk, and in-room safe. Hotel eateries serve a range of Asian and Western cuisines, and additional activities like tai chi and cooking classes are available.

Food

At **Hoa Dai** (39 Le Dai Hanh, tel. 03/1382-2098, 7am-11pm daily, VND40,000-80,000), the laminated page upon which the restaurant lists its menu selection is entirely in Vietnamese. Thankfully, the owner speaks a few words of English and there are some handy ClipArt illustrations to guide you. You'll find beef, pork, and fish among the offerings. Prices are not written on the menu, so ask beforehand.

Though its faded white exterior could use a renovation, the lively **Van Tue** (1A Hoang Dieu, tel. 03/1374-6338, www.vantue.com.vn, 9am-9pm daily, VND45,000-350,000) is a popular local restaurant that serves all manner of Vietnamese cuisine, including scores of beef, chicken, pork, and vegetarian dishes, including more adventurous fare like frog and eel. Staff speak some English and the price tag makes Van Tue not only one of the more active spots in town but also one of the more affordable.

An extension of the establishment of the same name on Minh Khai, **Julie's Bar** (24A Le Dai Hanh, 9am-midnight daily, VND60,000-120,000) is a cheap and cheerful Indian food joint that offers both quiet indoor seating and a pleasant upstairs patio from which to watch the street below. Its selection is limited to a few curries and one or two vegetarian dishes. The staff are friendly, and you'll find beer, cocktails, coffee, and other refreshments.

The chic and sophisticated BKK (22A Minh Khai, tel. 03/1382-3994, bkk_haiphong@hotmail.com, 10am-10pm daily, VND75,000-225,000) serves delicious Thai and pan-Asian cuisine, including coconut curries and spicy salads, in a posh colonial building just off the main drag. Its extensive wine collection, sleek wooden furniture, and collection of black-and-white vintage photographs add to the experience. Dine inside or al fresco on the equally classy front patio. Prices are more expensive but fit the style and service of the place.

Down a street of international restaurants, Texas BBQ (22H Minh Khai, tel. 03/1365-3450, www.texasbbq.com.vn, 8am-10pm daily, VND85,000-500,000) is the only spot in town to offer Tex-Mex cuisine, including quesadillas, tacos, and enchiladas, as well as pizza, burgers, and steak, making for a hearty departure from local cuisine. Delivery service is available, but the bright, narrow dining room is equally inviting.

While there are droves of small local cafés in Haiphong, Central View Coffee Lounge (Central Tower, 43 Quang Trung, 4th Fl., tel. 03/1626-0808, 7:30am-11pm daily, VND25,000-90,000) is a swankier version, perched above a few floors of offices in the downtown Central Tower, which overlooks the city's main park, offering a breezy, pleasant view of the bustle below. Both Vietnamese and European coffee is served, as well as fruit shakes, tea, and alcohol in the evenings.

Information and Services

Haiphong Tourist (65 Hoang Van Thu, tel. 03/1356-9600, www.haiphongtourism.gov.vn, 7am-11:30am and 2pm-5pm daily) has a small tourist information kiosk that can supply you with free city maps, helpful advice, and a handy guide booklet with plenty of hotel and restaurant recommendations as well as some background on the city's sights.

You should have no trouble locating an ATM downtown. The local Sacombank (119-121 Dinh Tien Hoang, tel. 03/1356-9113, www.sacombank.com.vn, 7:30am-11:30am and 1pm-4:30pm Mon.-Fri., 7:30am-11:30am Sat.) exchanges currency.

The city's central post office (3 Nguyen Tri Phuong, tel. 03/1382-3004, 7am-8pm daily) assists with all mail-related queries.

The largest and best-equipped local hospital is the Vietnam-Czech Friendship Hospital (Benh Vien Viet-Tiep) (1 Nha Thuong, tel. 03/1383-2721), though any serious illnesses or injuries should be brought to Hanoi.

Getting There

BOAT

Speedboats make daily trips to Haiphong from Cat Ba Island. Slightly tired but functional vessels are operated by Cat Ba Island Resort and Spa (4 Ben Binh, tel. 03/1358-8999, www.catbaislandresort-spa.com, VND200,000), with departures at 8am, 10am, 2pm, and 4pm. The trip takes about 45 minutes. Boats depart from the town's main pier, just opposite 1 Thang 4 street. Other speedboat options are available for the same cost, but the boats are smaller and the travel time longer.

BUS

Shuttles depart every 10 minutes daily from Hanoi's Luong Yen and Gia Lam bus stations (two hours, VND80,000) for Haiphong, arriving at Tam Bac bus station (corner of Tam Bac and Quang Trung, tel. 03/1385-8067, 4:30am-9pm daily).

From southern destinations like Ninh Binh (2.5 hours, VND160,000), buses stop at Niem Nghia bus station (Tran Nguyen Han), about two miles from the city center; the same station should be used to travel south from Haiphong.

Hoang Long (45 Le Thanh Tong, tel. 03/1355-2866, www.hoanglongasia.com,

8am-5pm daily, VND110,000) receives two daily buses from Cat Ba via the bus-boat-bus route. Buses depart from Cat Ba's town center each afternoon.

TRAIN

Though it's not wired into the general north-south Reunification Line, Haiphong's **train station** (75 Luong Khanh Thien, tel. 03/1392-1333, 7am-5pm daily) is connected to Hanoi. Trains from Hanoi (2.5 hours, VND60,000) make daily runs to Haiphong. Expect to pay more for soft seats.

AIR

Flying is the least popular and most expensive way of getting to Haiphong, but it's possible. **Cat Bi International Airport** (HPH, Le Hong Phong, tel. 03/1397-6408) sits five miles southeast of downtown Haiphong and welcomes multiple daily flights from Danang and Saigon (2 hours, VND900,000-1,500,000). **Vietnam Airlines** (ticketing office 166 Hoang Van Thu, Haiphong, tel. 03/1381-0890, www.vietnamairlines.com), **VietJet** (ticketing office 7 Tran Nguyen Han, Haiphong, tel. 03/1363-0032, www.vietjetair.com) and **Jetstar** (ticketing office 36 Hoang Van Thu, Haiphong, tel. 03/1355-9550, www.jetstar. com) serve Cat Bi airport and have ticketing offices in town.

Getting Around

For four-wheeled vehicles, try a local **Mailinh** (tel. 03/1383-3833) or **Hai Phong** (tel. 03/1373-7373) taxi. As usual, *xe om* are present on street corners across town.

Hired vehicles can be arranged through several hotels. As a less-touristed destination, you won't find many affordable motorbike rentals, so be prepared to jump on a *xe om* if necessary, or stick to exploring on foot. If you prefer a bicycle, most accommodations don't advertise the option but it is possible to procure a bike from some hotel receptionists.

Ninh Binh

Sixty miles south of Hanoi, the small, provincial town of Ninh Binh may not come off as a worthy tourist destination, but venture out west and you'll be greeted by the sharp and mysterious limestone peaks of Tam Coc and Trang An. Known as "Ha Long Bay on Land," Ninh Binh's serene flooded fields stand in stark contrast to its scores of karst formations, casually rising out of the pancake-flat landscape and shrouded in lush jungle greenery. Throw in a handful of ancient temples and one of the earliest capitals in Vietnamese civilization, all of which fit nicely into the romantic, mist-obscured countryside, and you've got reason enough to spend at least a day in Ninh Binh.

Several Hanoian tour companies make day trips to the area, hitting Tam Coc, Bich Dong Pagoda, and the nearby rice paddies, but it's just as easy to do the trip on your own. Given the modest costs of accommodation and food, Ninh Binh is an excellent spot from which to explore northern Vietnam's stunning scenery, especially in the cold and misty winter. Summer brings plenty of sun and better visibility. Tam Coc is best enjoyed during April and May, before the rice harvest takes away its signature paddy fields. Trang An is at its best around October, when water levels are low and the area's caves are more accessible.

Trang An and Tam Coc are a short drive or cycle away from Ninh Binh. Blue-and-white road signs are posted here and there to help direct you. Most hotels and guesthouses can either arrange a tour for you on the spot or point you in the direction of one. Most sights around Ninh Binh will require a boat,

Ninh Binh

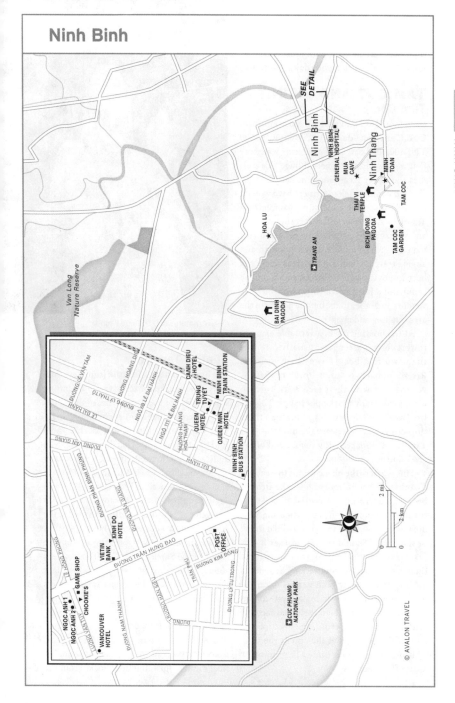

© AVALON TRAVEL

as the best views in the area are from the water. Rowboat rides tend to take more time than the average sight, with most trips lasting 2-3 hours, so plan your day accordingly.

TAM COC AND VICINITY
Tam Coc

Long touted as Ninh Binh's main event, **Tam Coc** (7am-5pm daily, VND80,000 entry, VND100,000 boat) is a meandering waterway that weaves through emerald-hued rice paddies and under great limestone karsts. In the flooded country fields, farmers have worked around the soaring mountains that interrupt Tam Coc's otherwise-flat terrain, creating an eye-catching array of greenery and rutted cliffs. Now an increasingly popular stop among travelers, some of the area's luster has been lost to concrete embankments along the canal and a healthy contingent of souvenir vendors and other touts, but the beauty of the area remains undeniable.

At the boating dock, a veritable army of rowers ferry passengers, usually no more than two to a boat, down the Ngo Dong River and back, often reclining to maneuver the oars with their feet, a trick which features in many tourist photo ops. The entire two-hour trip brings you through three tunnel-like caves beneath the mountains of Tam Coc before reaching the far end of the river journey.

This is where the magic begins to wear off: Thanks to the number of visitors, the area has become something of a tourist trap. At the turnaround point, a group of floating vendors lie in wait, eager to sell you a cold drink or some fruit. Should you refuse, they'll suggest that you buy a drink for your boat driver, though these are later sold back to the vendors at half-price, cutting both parties in on the profit. Some drivers even make a pit stop on the return trip to haul out their own cache of souvenirs for you to peruse. Tips are expected and freely requested at the end of the ride. This pressure to tip is higher than in other areas of Vietnam.

Quan Am statue at Bich Dong Pagoda

Thai Vi Temple

The humble **Thai Vi Temple** (sunrise-sunset daily, free) hearkens back to the 13th century, when rulers of the Tran dynasty thrice defeated Yuan-Mongol armies attempting to invade Vietnam. Within the small shrine, you'll find an effigy of Tran Thai Tong, a king who abdicated the throne to live as a monk after the Yuan-Mongol's first unsuccessful invasion in 1258, as well as Tran Quang Khai and Tran Hung Dao, Vietnam's most famous military general, who drove the invaders out of the country on two occasions. The countryside setting makes Thai Vi a nice tangent from the bustling main area of Tam Coc. The temple is about a half-mile from Tam Coc. Take a right just before the ticket booth on a small, narrow road, which leads out to Thai Vi.

Bich Dong Pagoda

A three-tiered mountainside masterpiece, **Bich Dong Pagoda** (sunrise-sunset daily, free) rambles up a limestone rock. From the bottom, a long, souvenir-lined walkway leads you across a small stone bridge to the pagoda's entrance, where the first shrine, Chua Ha, pays homage to the ancestors. Farther uphill, Chua Trung is a larger building, housing statues of the Buddha. Beyond the middle altar, a small cave winds around in an S shape, leading up to the final structure, Chua Thuong, where Quan Am has a shrine to herself. There is a beautiful (though small) white stone statue of the goddess looking out over the cliff. The views are pleasant from here. If you're keen to get all the way to the top, follow the path beyond the pagoda up to the very peak, where you can take in the surrounding fields in all their glory. It's a fairly easy walk up to the top with stairs (but not too many). The pagoda is one mile past Tam Coc, along the main road.

Mua Cave

While the actual **Mua Cave** (tel. 03/0361-8754, www.hangmuaninhbinh.com, 7am-5pm daily, VND50,000)—a small cavern at the base of a limestone karst—may not be worth your time, the view from the top of the nearby mountain earns this sight a place among Ninh Binh's other wondrous natural landscapes. Now part of a slightly gaudy, oversized tourism complex, the karsts bordering its far end are made accessible by a maze of 486 stone steps and zigzagging white battlements that give the place a medieval feel. Pause at each clearing and look back at the expanse of low-lying, water-logged rice paddies below. On a clear day, the views from the top, beside Mua Cave's Quan Am statue, are stunning. In the fog, its series of Buddhist spires and misty, jungle-clad hills paint an eerie, mysterious portrait of the area.

The front gate may be closed on weekdays and during the off-season. It is still possible to get inside if a caretaker is nearby. Follow the dirt track around the perimeter of the complex, where it dead-ends into the caretaker's house. Pay the entry fee and the caretaker will grant you access.

The cave is just under four miles from Ninh Binh. Ask for directions in Tam Coc.

★ Trang An

Winding through a maze of jungle-covered limestone karsts and picturesque countryside scenery, a ride in one of the modest wooden rowboats at **Trang An** (5am-5pm daily, VND150,000) is time well spent. Far less frequented by foreign tourists than the waters of Tam Coc, this stunning river landscape, dotted with temples devoted to local heroes and meandering tunnels that burrow beneath the area's rustic cliffs, is hugely popular with the Vietnamese. Business is booming at Trang An, helped by the addition of a larger, updated tourism complex and its status as a UNESCO World Heritage Site. It's the first World Heritage Site in Vietnam to receive dual distinctions, for natural and cultural properties.

It's hard to miss the brand-new boating docks, thanks to a massive billboard and the string of brightly colored flags swaying outside the main entrance. With a ticket, visitors can board one of the rowboats, which seat 4-6, and be on their way. Local boat operators are well versed in the 9.5-mile route, sometimes even rowing with their feet. It's impressive to see a single person navigate the labyrinthine passageways that snake beneath these limestone mountains with such ease. Keep an eye out for stalactites as you pass through each of Trang An's nine caves, as well as a host of other strange and otherworldly formations, from odd, concrete-like ridges to a glimpse or two of sparkly stone. One cave in particular houses a well, roughly 42 feet deep, whose water was once used for distilling rice wine; nowadays, you can see a tasteful display of ceramic jars meant to symbolize the process. There are three temple stops throughout the three-hour ride, each featuring a shrine to a different local hero connected to Ninh Binh's ancient history. It's best to arrive early in the morning to avoid the crowds, and steer clear on weekends, as Hanoians sometimes make day trips down to Ninh Binh, further adding to the madness. While you may be spared the request for a tip, it's possible that your boat driver will insist upon gratuity. You are not obligated to provide one; tip only where you feel inclined to do so.

If you're pressed for time or on a budget, you can also swing by the **smaller version** (6:30am-5:30pm daily, VND45,000) of Trang An farther down the road en route to Hoa Lu. This ride isn't as impressive and only lasts two hours. It's also referred to as Trang An, but the difference between the two complexes is obvious from their size.

TRINH TEMPLE

The first stop along the Trang An route, **Trinh Temple** is dedicated to two of King Dinh Tien Hoang's generals, Ta Thanh Tru and Huu Thanh Tru, who are credited with rescuing the king's youngest son, Dinh Toan. After the king and his two older sons were assassinated, the two generals carried the young boy into hiding. Boats stop here for 15-20 minutes to give tourists time to look around.

TRAN TEMPLE

Up and over a high limestone karst, **Tran Temple** lies at the end of a rambling stone staircase that reaches the peak of the mountain. The temple is a small stone structure with dragons carved into the roof. Hemmed in by thick foliage, it offers little in the way of scenic vistas. Follow the stairs down the other side of the mountain and you'll discover a modest shrine to Quy Minh Dai Vuong, a general of the 18th King Hung, the last in a line of rulers who are believed to be the founding fathers of the Vietnamese people.

The original temple was constructed during the 10th century under Dinh Tien Hoang. It was rebuilt in 1258 by emperor Tran Thai Tong, who came to Trang An and lived as a monk for a time. The altar out front is from the days of the Nguyen dynasty and is often busy with locals paying their respects. Boats stop at a dock on the far side of a karst from the temple; from there, a steep walk (about 10 minutes each way) is required to see the temple. It's possible to go inside the temple,

but the more decorative aspects are seen from the outside.

PHU KHONG

The largest of the temple areas at Trang An, **Phu Khong** has a few low stone buildings, decorated with yin yang tiles and dragon carvings. The most important structure is a shrine that houses eight figures. These represent a group of mandarins loyal to King Dinh Tien Hoang who, upon the assassination of their beloved leader, committed suicide in order to follow the emperor into the afterlife. Near the mandarins' temple is a Buddhist pagoda, built in the same style as its neighbors. Boats stop at Phu Khong to give visitors time to explore.

Hoa Lu

For the latter half of the 10th century, the ancient citadel at **Hoa Lu** (6am-6pm daily summer, 6:30am-6:30pm daily winter, VND10,000) served as the political, cultural, and economic center of the Dai Co Viet, predecessors to modern-day Vietnamese. A pair of 17th-century temples in honor of the Dinh and Tien Le dynasties stand on the grounds of the former city.

Hoa Lu was originally founded in 968 by King Dinh Tien Hoang, who was later assassinated alongside two of his sons. Le Hoan, a high-ranking military official, ascended the throne to become Le Dai Hanh, first ruler of the Tien Le dynasty.

Today, the remaining Dinh and Le temples are almost identical, with large wooden effigies of each emperor in his respective building. Dinh Tien Hoang is flanked by the two sons who died with him and his temple faces Ma Yen, the mountain atop which he was buried. In Le Dai Hanh's domain, his son sits to his right, while a memorial for his wife stands at his left. Both structures feature traditional Vietnamese architecture, including an entrance partitioned into three doors and high door frames, which force visitors to look down when entering the temple, thus showing respect to the deities inside. A stop at the Dinh and Le temples is really only worthwhile if combined with a visit to Trang An. Hoa Lu is seven miles from downtown Ninh Binh and about two miles north of the main gate at Trang An. If you're already visiting Trang An, continue on the main road to find the main entrance of Hoa Lu.

Bai Dinh Pagoda

The largest Buddhist complex in the country, **Bai Dinh Pagoda** (5am-5pm daily) began construction in 2004, and was completed in 2015. This massive center of worship has set several records, including the longest pagoda corridors in Asia, which trail on for over a mile from the entrance all the way up to the main hall. At the far end of a long stone bridge, a three-door front gate ushers visitors inside, where two towering guardians supervise the comings and goings at the pagoda. From here, Bai Dinh's endless covered walkways begin, rambling up the hillside accompanied by a collection of 500 stone arhat statues, each weighing five tons and standing over eight feet tall.

While there are several shrines dedicated to different statues of the Buddha and other prominent Buddhist figures, such as Quan Am, the centerpiece of this opus is the grand main hall, where a trio of enormous 50-ton, floor-to-ceiling gold-plated Buddhas sit in a row, representing the past, present, and future. Surrounded by 2,000 smaller sparkling Amitabha Buddhas set in alcoves in the walls, the sheer size of the room and its contents are enough to inspire awe in visitors. A wander around to the rest of the shrines, including a larger-than-life thousand-arms-and-eyes sculpture of Quan Am, confirm that the rest of the sprawling complex is, indeed, just as lavish.

While Bai Dinh's volume does make for an interesting spectacle, the newness of the complex detracts from its wow factor. Visitors to the pagoda usually pull up to an **electric car station** (VND30,000 per person one-way) just over a mile from the main entrance. You're free to walk in on your own, though it's easier to just take the ride, as you'll be doing plenty of walking once you reach the pagoda grounds.

TOWARD CUC PHUONG NATIONAL PARK

Van Long Nature Reserve

About 20 miles northwest of Ninh Binh, the **Van Long Nature Reserve** (Gia Van, tel. 03/0386-8798, 7am-5pm daily, VND75,000)

pond at the colossal Bai Dinh Pagoda

is a protected wetland home to hundreds of plant and animal species, including 72 varieties of birds and the largest wild population of Delacour's langurs, one of the most endangered primate species in the world. Limestone karsts dot the marsh, which is only accessible by rowboat.

If possible, it's best to time your visit during the summer, as this is when your chances of seeing wildlife are highest. Your driver will likely request a tip at the end; provide a tip at your discretion. At least half of the entrance fee goes to the nature reserve, so without a tip, the boat drivers take home only about VND35,000 for 2-3 hours' work.

TOURS

Single-day tours to Ninh Binh's main attractions can be arranged either from Ninh Binh or from Hanoi. Tours leaving from Ninh Binh tend to be more motorbike taxi services than guided excursions. While there are a few travel outfits based in the town, your best option when booking a tour in Ninh Binh is to talk to your hotel. Most accommodations can arrange a trip that includes Tam Coc, Bich Dong Pagoda, and a few other surrounding sights, though you can also pick and choose your own itinerary. You'll find a lot more variety and service in the day trips offered from Hanoi, but these excursions are more expensive, as they require transportation to and from town.

Hanoi Exposed Tours (tel. 09/4834-6026, www.hanoiexposedtours.com, VND735,000-1,785,000), the company behind local outfit Chookie's, runs tours to Tam Coc, Hoa Lu, and Bai Dinh. **Asiana Travel Mate** (7 Dinh Tien Hoang, tel. 04/3926-3366, www.ticvietnam.com, 8am-9pm daily) does day trips to Tam Coc.

ACCOMMODATIONS

Ninh Binh doesn't yet have droves of quality accommodations, but there are a few well-priced guesthouses and smaller, family-run hotels that do the trick. These are fairly spread out over the city's modest downtown area.

Some of the budget options surround the local train station. You can also find a string of hotels and guesthouses outside of town around the Tam Coc boat station: the upside to this location is its easy access to nearby sights. But, with Tam Coc well on the tourist trail, it's also a little exhausting to stick around here for any longer than a few minutes, as vendors and restaurant owners are quick with sales pitches.

Under VND210,000

Queen Mini Hotel (21 Hoang Hoa Tham, tel. 03/0387-1874, VND63,000 dorm, VND126,000-315,000 double) sits on a cozy corner opposite the larger Queen Hotel and not far from another similarly named accommodation. This is the most affordable of the lot and provides budget backpackers with unbelievably cheap dorm beds or private rooms that come with air-conditioning and hot showers. The staff are amiable, though expect a hard sell on things like bus tickets, vehicle rentals, and tours. Tour information is readily available and there are a handful of affordable eateries in the area.

VND210,000-525,000

Ngoc Anh Hotel (36 Luong Van Tuy, tel. 03/0388-3768, www.ngocanh-hotel.com, VND315,000-483,000, breakfast included) takes the prize for best-kept rooms in the city, with spotless tile bathrooms, comfy beds, and all the usual amenities. Three different types of rooms are available. The cheapest options run small but are perfectly adequate, while middle- and top-tier choices are virtually the same, though the more expensive rooms come with more light. The staff is cheerful, informative, and will set you up with vehicle rentals and affordable tours of the area. You can also check out **Ngoc Anh 2** (26 Luong Van Tuy, tel. 03/0388-3768, www.ngocanh-hotel.com, VND315,000-483,000), just down the road if you find that the original is full.

Canh Dieu Hotel (74 Nguyen Van Cu, tel. 03/0388-8278, www.canhdieuhotel.com.vn, VND350,000-450,000) is one of the nicer budget accommodations near the train station, with both standard and slightly larger superior rooms on offer. Hot water, air-conditioning, TV, and Wi-Fi access are all provided, along with complimentary breakfast. Additional services like laundry, tour bookings, and transportation are available.

The smartest accommodation on the block, **Queen Hotel** (20 Hoang Hoa Tham, tel. 03/0389-3000, www.queenhotel.vn, VND420,000-630,000) is well furnished and clean, with generous beds and enormous bathrooms. All rooms feature hot water, airconditioning, TV, and Wi-Fi access, as well as a minibar and complimentary breakfast included in the rate. Three types of accommodations are available, from good value standard rooms to spacious deluxe beds, which also come with a balcony and bathtub. Downstairs, the hotel arranges tours and transportation to nearby sights.

VND525,000-1,050,00

The charming, family-run **Vancouver Hotel** (1/75 Luong Van Tuy, tel. 03/0389-3270, www.thevancouverhotel.com, VND735,000-1,365,000) sits down a quiet alley just off Luong Van Tuy and provides a rare mid-range option among mostly budget guesthouses. Its chic rooms feature Wi-Fi, television, an in-room safe, tea- and coffee-making facilities, hot water, air-conditioning, and some heavenly mattresses, alongside more space and ambience than you'll find in most of Ninh Binh's other accommodations. Breakfast is included in the room rate.

Over VND2,100,000

A tranquil boutique resort set amid rice fields, **Tam Coc Garden** (Hai Nham Hamlet, tel. 03/0324-9118, www.tamcocgarden.com, VND2,205,000-2,940,000) consists of 16 rustic countryside rooms. The retreat is close enough to Tam Coc to provide easy access to nearby sights, while maintaining some distance from the tourist melee. Each room offers minimalist decor and modern amenities, with plush low beds, handcrafted wooden furniture, and the famous pottery of Bat Trang

village. Wi-fi is not provided in all rooms. The bamboo-outfitted restaurant offers pleasant views of the surrounding rice paddies. Bicycle rentals are free. The friendly staff can offer local recommendations.

FOOD

Don't expect to find much variety in Ninh Binh, as most eateries remain humble, front-of-the-house set-ups with a few plastic chairs and a selection of Vietnamese dishes. The town itself is known for its goat meat, which is often served in a hotpot or with *com cháy*, another local specialty made from rice that is sun-dried and later fried. This is usually served in the same way as steamed rice, with an accompanying meat or tofu dish. Vegetarians take care, as the name of the dish can be misleading: You'll see signs all over town for *com cháy*, the Ninh Binh specialty. Vegetarian food, or *com chay*, is spelled almost exactly the same.

One of a few modest, open-front shops clustered around the train station, **Trung Tuyet** (14 Hoang Hoa Tham, tel. 03/0387-4510, 7am-10pm daily, VND30,000-140,000) seems to be the friendliest and best-equipped of the bunch, with welcoming owners and a host of good, cheap meals. Standard Vietnamese meals and a few backpacker favorites, including banana pancakes, appear on the menu. It's also possible to order your food in different portion sizes, depending upon your level of hunger, and you'll likely get an orange slice or two at the end of the meal as a goodwill offering.

The covered courtyard of the **Kinh Do Hotel** (18 Phan Dinh Phung, tel. 03/0389-9152, kinhdonb@yahoo.com, 6am-11pm daily, VND20,000-120,000) doubles as a café and restaurant during the day, serving a neat selection of Vietnamese fare, including beef, pork, chicken, and tofu dishes, as well as the local specialty, goat. Breakfast is available, and the attached hotel and tour outfit can be of use if you have travel questions.

A brand-new business near the bank of hotels on Luong Van Tuy, **Chookie's** (17 Luong

Van Tuy, tel. 09/4834-6026, 11am-10pm daily, VND50,000-100,000) serves as both a restaurant and the local headquarters of Hanoi Exposed Tours (hanoiexposedtours.com). Now proudly boasting the only European coffee machine in town, this bright spot is decked out in vibrant artwork and run by a friendly, English-speaking staff, which includes the knowledgeable Van, a Ninh Binh local and tour guide. The menu includes a few Vietnamese options but also offers some of the only Western food in Ninh Binh, with items like tuna melts and burgers featured on the menu. This is a great spot to visit for sound travel advice, as the staff are well-versed in Ninh Binh's tourism attractions and more than willing to help you navigate your way around town.

Just before the Tam Coc boat station, the cheerful folks at **Minh Toan Restaurant** (Tam Coc, tel. 09/4844-3268, 8am-8pm daily, VND30,000-180,000) offer your usual Vietnamese fare, including pork, chicken, beef, and tofu in addition to snails, goat, and *com chay*. Both indoor and outdoor tables are available and the family that runs the place is a little less pushy than some of the other local restaurants along the strip. This is a worthy lunch stop for those touring the Tam Coc area.

INFORMATION AND SERVICES
Tourist Information

Hotel owners are your best bet for things like maps, restaurant recommendations, and general advice. While you're not likely to find a detailed plan of Ninh Binh anywhere, the rudimentary maps offered at most accommodations do the trick, and receptionists are willing to share their knowledge with passing travelers. For additional info, you can swing by **Chookie's** (17 Luong Van Tuy, tel. 09/4834-6026, 11am-10pm daily), a newly opened arm of the Hanoi-based agency, Hanoi Exposed Tours.

Banks

You'll find ATMs handy along Tran Hung Dao and near many of Ninh Binh's hotels. The local **Vietin Bank** (951 Tran Hung Dao, tel. 03/0387-2614, www.vietinbank.vn, 7:30am-11:30am and 1:30pm-5pm Mon.-Fri., 7:30am-11am Sat.) can assist with currency exchange and has an ATM out front.

Internet and Postal Services

The **central post office** (1 Tran Hung Dao, tel. 03/0387-1104, 7:30am-11:30am and 1pm-6pm Mon.-Sat., 7:30am-11:30am and 1:30pm-5pm Sun.) is located near Lim Bridge. For Internet, try the **game shop** (1 Luong Van Tuy, 6am-11pm daily, VND4,000/hour) near Chookie's just off the main road.

Medical Services

The colossal **Ninh Binh General Hospital (Benh Vien Da Khoa Ninh Binh)** (Tue Tinh, tel. 03/0387-1030, www.benhvienninhbinh.vn) lies south of Lim Bridge and can deal with minor ailments, though don't expect to find an English-speaking doctor here.

TRANSPORTATION

Local buses to Ninh Binh come in from Hanoi (1.5 hours, VND160,000) and the surrounding area on a daily basis and arrive at the **bus station** (207 Le Dai Hanh, tel. 03/0387-1069) just opposite Lim Bridge.

The **Ninh Binh train station** (Hoang Hoa Tham, tel. 03/0367-3619, 7am-5pm daily) has daily runs north and south, with regular arrivals from Hanoi (2.5 hours, VND80,000 and up) and a slew of southern destinations.

Xe om can be found outside of bus stations and on street corners around town. For larger vehicles, try **Mailinh** (tel. 03/0363-6363) or **Hoa Lu** (tel. 03/0388-7888) taxis.

Most hotels and guesthouses in Ninh Binh rent out motorbikes (from VND100,000 a day) and bicycles (around VND30,000). Around the backpacker enclave at Tam Coc, prices go up, sometimes as much as double.

★ CUC PHUONG NATIONAL PARK

The oldest national park in Vietnam, **Cuc Phuong National Park (Vuon Quoc Gia Cuc Phuong)** (tel. 03/0384-8006, www.cucphuongtourism.com, 7am-5pm daily, VND40,000) has been protected land since 1962. It's home to several species of langurs, a fast-disappearing monkey found throughout the Asian continent. Its most famous resident, the black-and-white Delacour's langur, is among the most critically endangered primates in the world, with an estimated 200 remaining in Vietnam. Thanks to the park's conservation efforts, at least some of their diminishing numbers are protected, as are a host of other primates and turtles. Beyond these creatures, the 22,200-hectare park is also home to 336 species of birds, 76 species of reptiles, and a host of other insects, amphibians, and fish.

Cuc Phuong offers many do-it-yourself hikes throughout the park. Visit a prehistoric cave dwelling or trek through the dense jungle to see a great, towering thousand-year-old tree. Local guides can bring you on bird-watching and wildlife-spotting tours, organize homestays with the park's minority Muong population, or arrange a camping excursion in the woods. While nature hikes can be a fun way to pass the day at any time of year, Cuc Phuong is at its best March-June, when the rain recedes and more of the park's animals are out and about. Cuc Phuong is an easy and accessible trip from either Ninh Binh or Hanoi, as either a daylong or overnight excursion.

Sights

Most day visitors to Cuc Phuong get away with hitting the major highlights of the park on their own. Just before the main entrance, the visitors center provides useful maps and information. For daylong explorations of Cuc Phuong, **bicycle rentals** (VND100,000) make for a fun and active way to explore the park and get around to its major attractions. Visitors to the primate and turtle conservation centers are required to hire a **guide** (VND50,000) to introduce the animals within each complex; while it's a little unnecessary, these people manage to provide interesting information on the various endangered species within each center. Farther along, it's possible to make an independent visit to Mac Lake, a pretty little spot just inside the entrance gate, as well as the prehistoric cave and ancient tree. Park guides can be hired for lengthier

monkeys at Cuc Phuong's Endangered Primate Rescue Center

excursions into Cuc Phuong's grounds, including a trek into the jungle in search of ancient fossils, a stroll around the botanical garden, and a multi-day camping trip through the best of Cuc Phuong's foliage. All of these things can be arranged at the park's headquarters upon arrival.

Bring insect repellent, as Cuc Phuong's smallest residents can be pesky in the thick of the jungle, and substantial footwear is advised, particularly during rainy times, as the park's limestone rocks can become pretty treacherous when wet.

ENDANGERED PRIMATE RESCUE CENTER

Founded in 1993 by the Frankfurt Zoological Society, Cuc Phuong's **Endangered Primate Rescue Center** (9:30am-11:30am and 1:30pm-4pm daily, guide required, no separate admission) rehabilitates primates that were once a part of the illegal wildlife trade, a black-market industry fueled by demand for traditional Chinese remedies, many of which contain animal parts. Specializing in endemic species like Cuc Phuong's signature Delacour's langur and the nearby Cat Ba langur, both of which are among the most endangered primates in the world, this center cares for and studies newly rescued creatures before releasing the rehabilitated animals into a seven-hectare, semi-wild enclosure. From there, the monkeys learn to fend for themselves in the wild again before returning to their natural environment. Visitors to the center are given a tour of the animals and a brief introduction into its rescue operation. Guides take visitors to the animals' cages, where some of the more curious monkeys will approach for a closer look.

After you've paid your park entry fee at the visitors center, your guide will escort you to the rescue center.

TURTLE CONSERVATION CENTER

The **Turtle Conservation Center** (8am-11:30am and 1:30pm-4:30pm daily, guide required) sits opposite the Endangered Primate Rescue Center and focuses on rescuing and protecting turtles from the illegal wildlife trade, in which these creatures are used for food or traditional medicine. Visitors are able to roam the grounds, where a host of different species live in small ponds and wooded areas. An informative display explains some of the challenges and problems that stem from this ever-growing illicit industry as well as the work of the center. The turtles wander the center freely, with only low barriers separating their living spaces from the center's footpaths. Visitors are required to have guides, to protect the safety of the animals. Guides can talk more in depth about the different species.

PREHISTORIC CAVE

Discovered in 1966, the **Prehistoric Cave (Dong Nguoi Xua)** at Cuc Phuong National Park is believed to date back as far as 7,500 years ago. When it was first unearthed, locals came across stone implements and other ancient tools inside the cave, as well as a few tombs, suggesting that its residents were not simply cave dwellers but also practiced their own customs and traditions.

From the road, rent a **flashlight** (VND10,000) or bring your own to explore the darkened recesses of the cavern. It's a 300-meter walk from the road up a few flights of stone steps to the entrance, where the wide, round space is filled with miniature shrines and small incense urns. This is a nice pit stop on the way to the thousand-year-old tree and the larger Palace Cave.

The cave is about three or four miles along the park road. There will be a sign and a parking guard present on the roadside, making the cave easy to find.

PALACE CAVE AND THE THOUSAND-YEAR-OLD TREE

From the park's interior outpost (different from the office at the park entrance), it's about 30 minutes on the paved walkway to **Palace Cave.** Hemmed in by dense jungle on either side, this path winds through lush, canopied grounds where you may be able to spot a few creatures en route. Palace Cave is a long tunnel that's virtually untouched (so bring a flashlight).

After exploring the cave, continue on the path for about 10 minutes to the park's **thousand-year-old tree.** While this sight doesn't warrant the trip on its own, the cave is impressive and the moderate one-mile stroll through the jungle is a pleasant excursion. To make things more interesting, you can complete the full loop from the park's outpost along the paved trail to the ancient tree and then back around the long way, following a 4.3-mile dirt track back to the outpost, though be aware that this is a more challenging route. The path on this side of the loop is not maintained and is harder to follow.

Tours

Independent day tours from both Ninh Binh and Hanoi are available. Your best option is to hire a park-authorized guide, who will be able to lead you on anything from a daylong hike to a longer overnight excursion. For multiday trips, get in touch with the park beforehand, either via phone or email, to confirm a guide's availability. Cuc Phuong's website (www.cucphuongtourism.com) is a useful resource in planning your visit.

Accommodations

Cuc Phuong National Park runs a barebones **guesthouse** (VND105,000/person, VND420,000/double) with two different room options. The cheaper accommodations include an outdoor bathroom and shower but lack most basic amenities, such as hot water and air-conditioning. For a few extra dollars, you can have a standard double with indoor bathroom, as well as hot water and air-conditioning. Neither option is particularly posh, but they do the job for a short stay.

To book a room at the guesthouse, get in touch with the park's tourism office (tel. 03/0384-8006, www.cucphuongtourism. com). Availability depends upon the day. Vietnamese tourists travel in large groups, so if a Vietnamese group comes through,

the guesthouse could easily fill up in one go. Otherwise, you shouldn't have a problem arranging a room at the guesthouse, but book ahead.

Food

There are two **restaurants** (7am-8pm daily, VND20,000-150,000) within the park, one at the main headquarters and another at the park's outpost near Palace Cave and the thousand-year-old tree. The menu features plenty of grilled meats and Vietnamese dishes, as well as a limited number of vegetarian choices, at reasonable prices. There is also a snack shop just outside the visitors center.

Transportation

Cuc Phuong National Park lies roughly 35 miles from Ninh Binh and 80 miles from Hanoi. Both single- and multi-day trips to the park can be arranged from either destination.

FROM NINH BINH

Travelers departing from Ninh Binh will have to arrange transportation to the park, either by hired car, taxi, or hired motorbike. While cars run on the expensive side, particularly for individual travelers, this is a good option for groups. Make your return arrangement with the same driver, as there are no cars to hire in the park area.

Travelers who feel comfortable at the helm of a motorbike can navigate the back roads of Ninh Binh on their own, though signage is limited and English speakers are nonexistent. Depending on the weather, roads leading out to the park can become treacherous, as certain sections are more dirt track than paved highway.

From Ninh Binh, head south along 30 Thang 6 street, which turns into Highway 1 as you exit the city. The road will curve west and change names to Quang Trung. Turn right onto Dong Giao street and keep straight. It will take 24 miles to reach Cuc Phuong. Jot down the name of the national park in case you need directions. Most locals will know the park and can point you in the right direction.

FROM HANOI

From Hanoi, the same hired vehicle options apply, though travelers hoping to make the trek solo are far better to depart from Ninh Binh, as an 80-mile journey on a motorbike will eat up more of your day than the actual visit. Instead, you're better off taking the **Cuc Phuong bus** (VND150,000) from Hanoi's Giap Bat station at 9am and catching the return vehicle back from the park at 3pm to save yourself time and hassle. It may be wise to overnight here if you opt for the bus, as the three-hour drive leaves you little time to enjoy the park in a single day.

VEHICLES FOR HIRE

Bicycles (VND100,000/day) can be rented from Cuc Phuong's visitors center by the day to explore the park grounds.

The Central Provinces

Look for ★ to find recommended
sights, activities, dining, and lodging.

Highlights

© AVALON TRAVEL

★ **Imperial City:** Step into the bygone world of mighty emperors and opulent palaces in Hue's Imperial City, former capital of the Nguyen dynasty (page 146).

★ **Phong Nha-Ke Bang National Park:** Explore a mind-blowing maze of ethereal subterranean chambers, never-ending rice paddies, and dense green jungle (page 170).

★ **Linh Ung Pagoda:** Stand beside the towering white figure of Quan Am, Danang's 30-story-tall protector, while admiring panoramas of the sophisticated metropolis from Son Tra peninsula (page 181).

★ **Hai Van Pass:** Take a ride on Vietnam's most breathtaking coastal road, complete with lush emerald mountains and picture-perfect panoramas of the East Sea (page 192).

★ **Hoi An's Old Town:** Eat like a king, shop 'til you drop, and discover the laid-back charm of Hoi An's vibrant meeting halls and centuries-old traditional houses (page 198).

With the stunning curves of a mountainous coastline and the heartbreaking scars of war, Vietnam's central provinces are a microcosm of captivating destinations. The region boasts top-notch cuisine and natural, cultural, and historical attractions, catering to both adventurous backpackers and luxury travelers. The central provinces are home to an imperial citadel, a sun-soaked port town, and an ultra-modern city. Explore Hoi An, a shopper's paradise, where master tailors can put together a dress, a shirt, or a pair of pants in less than a day. Take to the shores of Danang, the central region's coolest contemporary city, powered by a fusion of hip cosmopolitan culture and Vietnam's laid-back local scene. Dive into the fascinating history of Hue, Vietnam's last imperial capital.

Beyond its urban hot spots, central Vietnam holds a host of wild landscapes, replete with jungles, rice paddies, and gargantuan limestone formations. Phong Nha-Ke Bang National Park and its jaw-dropping subterranean chambers, hollowed out by several million years of erosion, are a must-see. The eerie, overgrown ruins of My Son, former Cham holy land, and several crumbling relics of the American War, including the dividing line between north and south Vietnam, add to the awe and mystery of the region.

HISTORY

If Vietnamese culture hails from its northern region and the country's southern territory helped to shape its more recent history, then Vietnam's central provinces were instrumental through many of the events in between. As early as 1,000 BC, the region was home to the Sa Huynh culture, an ancient people whose tenure overlapped with the Dong Son in the north.

The Sa Huynh culture was a precursor to the Hindu nation of Champa, responsible for three settlements that stretched from the port of Hoi An west to the temples of My Son around the 4th century AD. After several decades of conflict with the Vietnamese, at the end of the 10th century, the Cham were driven down the coast and out of the central region.

Previous: Phong Nha-Ke Bang National Park; dragon mosaic in Hue's Imperial City. **Above:** bowl of *com hen* (steamed baby clams and rice).

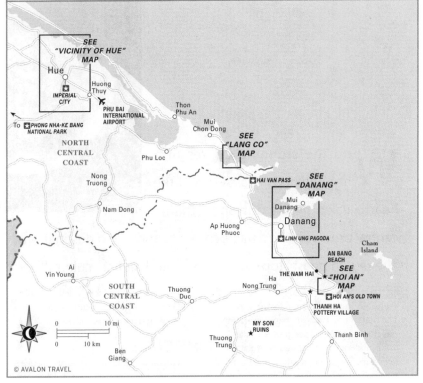

The Central Provinces

SEE "VICINITY OF HUE" MAP

Hue

IMPERIAL CITY

Huong Thuy

PHU BAI INTERNATIONAL AIRPORT

To PHONG NHA-KE BANG NATIONAL PARK

NORTH CENTRAL COAST

Nong Truong

Nam Dong

Phu Loc

Thon Phu An

Mui Chon Dong

SEE "LANG CO" MAP

HAI VAN PASS

SEE "DANANG" MAP

Mui Danang

Danang

LINH UNG PAGODA

Ap Huong Phuoc

Cham Island

AN BANG BEACH

THE NAM HAI

SEE "HOI AN" MAP

HOI AN'S OLD TOWN

THANH HA POTTERY VILLAGE

Ai Yin Young

SOUTH CENTRAL COAST

Thuong Duc

Ha Nong Trung

MY SON RUINS

Thuong Trung

Thanh Binh

Ben Giang

0   10 mi
0   10 km

© AVALON TRAVEL

At that time, international trade had been a longstanding business in Hoi An. The thriving port welcomed ships from as near as Thailand and India and as far as France, Portugal, and England. In the 16th century, scores of Chinese and Japanese traders began setting up shop in what was then known as Faifo. The town was the most prosperous economic center in central Vietnam until the 19th century, when the waters of the Thu Bon River became too shallow for ships to dock at the port.

Beginning in 1802, when the newly crowned emperor Gia Long moved Vietnam's capital to Hue, the region began to play an influential role on the national level. The emperor was first in a 13-generation line of rulers that would make up Vietnam's last imperial dynasty. Moving the capital south afforded

him influence over the northern and southern halves of the country, and ushered in an age of cultural fanfare in Hue that attracted poets, painters, scholars, and mandarins from across the country.

The French stormed Danang's port in 1859, imposing colonial rule. By the 20th century, growing dissent among the general population had many calling for an end to French colonialism. As World War II approached, public opinion, influenced by the ideals of the Viet Minh, favored a new form of political authority, headed by the Communist Party. Emperor Bao Dai, the final ruler of the Nguyen dynasty, turned over power to the Viet Minh in 1945, just days before Ho Chi Minh gave his independence speech at Ba Dinh Square.

Though this ended Hue's tenure as capital

of Vietnam, the central region was not finished shaping national history. Several provinces became instrumental in conflicts throughout the American War. Home to the Ben Hai River, which served as the boundary between north and south Vietnam, Quang Tri, an area about 50 miles north of Hue, saw some of the heaviest fighting and bore thousands of tons of bombs, Agent Orange, and other dioxins. Now-infamous places like Khe Sanh, Hamburger Hill, and the Rockpile dot the countryside in Quang Tri and its southern neighbor, Thua Thien-Hue, a stark reminder of Vietnam's recent military struggles.

PLANNING YOUR TIME

Hue and Hoi An are the main highlights of the region. On a cross-country road trip, allocate one week to cover the region. From each of these cities, shorter, day-long excursions to nearby sights like My Son and the DMZ area are possible for visitors with a more relaxed schedule.

If you have more time, take a day to travel from Hue to Hoi An (or vice versa) and stop along the way to enjoy the beach at Lang Co or Danang's stunning Hai Van Pass. Remote Phong Nha-Ke Bang National Park, easily the country's best up-and-coming destination, is worth a visit, but requires more time and money than a visit to most coastal towns. It's a full day of travel to get there and back, and you should spend at least two days there, so budget 4-5 days.

The main route between Hue and Hoi An is Highway 1, which runs through Danang. This is the most popular route and is easy to navigate.

The central provinces are home to some of the country's most extreme weather. Its location on the belly of the "S" makes it more prone to storms. This area is rocked by flash floods, monsoon rains, and other storms every year, often sweeping away houses and affecting local crops. Hoi An is notorious for its November deluge in particular, when locals get around by canoe. While plying these temporary canals makes for a memorable shopping experience, the weather in central Vietnam is more of a hindrance than a novelty. Time your visit outside of September-January, when rainfall is highest. August is a brutally hot month in the region. February-May are the best months in central Vietnam, with temperatures on the rise but not yet unbearable.

Hue

Boasting an intricate patchwork of imperial legacy and wartime history, French colonialism and ancient civilization, Hue is a city with an exceptional past. For 13 generations, this charming riverside town served as the Nguyen dynasty's political, cultural, and intellectual center, housing an impressive royal citadel along the northern bank of the Perfume River, not to mention scores of historical relics still scattered across town and throughout the southern countryside, evidence of Vietnam's last imperial rulers. As a result of its unique past and grand architecture, Hue's imperial sights were granted UNESCO status in 1993 and have since become a major tourism draw for the city. Travelers keen on delving into the nation's earlier history will appreciate the storied Imperial City complex as well as Hue's surrounding royal tombs, each paying homage to the life and achievements of a different Vietnamese king. Foodies can dig into a plethora of bite-sized local specialties, as this city boasts a well-deserved reputation as one of the country's top culinary destinations.

Beyond imperial history, food, and culture, many of Hue's riverine streets provide a picturesque setting for an afternoon cycle, passing by the many-tiered bell tower at Thien Mu Pagoda or the sleepy streets bordering the smaller An Cuu River. Outside of town, Hue's surroundings are an attractive sea of verdant rice paddies and pretty coastal landscapes, but they also served as the backdrop for some of the American War's most brutal battles. Regular trips to the demilitarized zone north of the city and along the coastal route south toward Danang add to Hue's appeal. The city experiences its best weather between March and June, when temperatures climb and the mist dissipates; during January and February, however, it's constant rain. While you could easily pass four days in the former capital, most travelers prefer to stick around for two or three and still manage to visit the Imperial City, one or two royal tombs, and a few other countryside attractions.

SIGHTS

The Imperial City, Hue's main attraction, lies directly at the center of town and is easily accessible from the backpacker area. You'll have to rely on a bicycle or motorbike to make it to sights like the royal tombs or Thanh Toan bridge. Bicycle rentals are an inexpensive and popular way to get around town, and you could easily pass an afternoon exploring Hue's riverside roads on two wheels. Dragon boats can ferry you to and from sights like Thien

Mu Pagoda, the Imperial City, and Hue Nam Shrine.

The sheer number of historical sights in Hue can make it hard to decide which places to visit. Even though the high price can be discouraging, make a point to see the Imperial City and one or two of the royal tombs. There is a package ticket (VND280,000) that includes access to the Imperial City, the Royal Antiquities Museum, and the royal tombs of Khai Dinh and Minh Mang, as well as one that adds the tomb of Tu Doc (VND360,000). Though the offer isn't openly advertised, you can request these tickets at Ngo Mon Gate, the main entrance into the Imperial City, and use them over multiple days, allowing you to give due diligence to each sight without breaking the bank. There's no official limit to how long the ticket is good for.

★ Imperial City

From the early 19th century through the end of the Vietnamese monarchy in 1945, Hue's **Imperial City** (23 Thang 8, 7am-5:30pm daily, VND150,000) housed an impressive cache of temples, palaces, and administrative buildings belonging to the 13 kings of the Nguyen dynasty. On the northern side of

Imperial City gate

the Perfume River, the walled Citadel complex reached a total of 148 buildings during its prime, most of which were constructed between 1802 and 1832. Today 20 remain, making for a captivating sight. Wide, opulent palaces and dimly lit temples pepper the now-overgrown grounds, boasting a mix of traditional Vietnamese architecture, vibrant lacquered woodwork, and ornate rooftops, not to mention 143 years' worth of imperial history.

Avoid heat and crowds by turning up in the early morning. Allot at least 1.5 hours to explore this sight at your own pace; there is a fair bit of ground to cover and you'll likely want to stop and take photos or rest at some point. Electric car services are available, as are **tour guides** (VND100,000). English-speaking guides are in high demand, so call the **Hue Monuments Conservation Center** (23 Tong Duy Tan, tel. 05/4351-3818, www.hueworldheritage.org.vn, 7am-5:30pm Mon.-Fri.) ahead of time to reserve a guide. Guides hired at the Imperial City tend to lead only a "greatest hits" tour, skipping the mostly destroyed Forbidden Purple City and the Thai Binh Reading Pavilion to swing by the Mieu Temple Complex, and can sometimes push hard for a tip. Hiring a guide is not a bad option for someone who has time constraints and a limited budget, but if you're looking to get the whole story then you're better off arranging a private guide or hopping on a public tour with a more knowledgeable leader.

NGO MON GATE AND THE SALUTATION COURT

Before you pass through the enormous **Ngo Mon Gate** (Noon Gate), take a moment to look toward the equally huge **flag tower** flying Vietnam's colors on the opposite side of the road. This tower is Hue's most recognizable icon. The massive three-tiered stone structure has been around since 1807 and is as much a symbol of the city and central Vietnam as anything else within the Citadel complex.

To enter the Imperial City, visitors cross over a small moat and go through one of the five doors at Ngo Mon Gate. In addition to providing access to the administrative buildings and living quarters of the royal family, the top of this structure was once reserved for the king during special ceremonies and Lunar New Year celebrations. In the days of the monarchy, the pavilion was reserved strictly for men; no women were permitted to ascend its stone steps until the tail-end of the Nguyen dynasty, when emperor Bao Dai invited his queen to stand beside him. Below, each of the gate's five doors granted access to a different group of individuals, with the central opening kept strictly for royalty, the two beside for civil and military mandarins, and the far doors used for elephants.

On the other side of Ngo Mon is the **Salutation Court,** a large open space often used for royal celebrations, such as birthdays, as well as the twice-monthly Grand Audience, an event in which the king and all high-ranking mandarins gathered within the Imperial City. Beyond a rectangular fishpond, the clearing's three levels were used to organize civil and military mandarins into their respective ranks, lining up single-file beside the miniature stelae bordering either side of the courtyard today. Lesser members of the royal family, relatives of the Queen Mother, for example, were relegated to the back, near the entrance; soldiers, horses, and elephants took up the pair of green lawns beside the stone courtyard.

THAI HOA PALACE AND THE RIGHT AND LEFT HOUSES

At the far end of the Salutation Court is **Thai Hoa Palace,** the Imperial City's largest and best-preserved structure. Wide and rectangular, this double-roofed building holds the original throne of the Nguyen dynasty. Its exterior, decorated with yin-yang tiles and vivid mosaic facades, captures the spirit of the Imperial City's heyday. Inside, the palace's pair of roofs are bolstered by 80 solid ironwood columns lacquered in red and gold. Up above, decoration alternates between a series

Hue

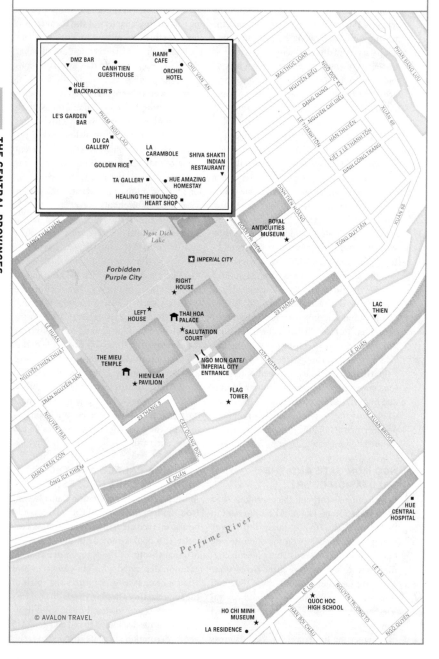

DMZ BAR

HANH CAFE

CANH TIEN GUESTHOUSE

ORCHID HOTEL

HUE BACKPACKER'S

LE'S GARDEN BAR

DU CA GALLERY

LA CARAMBOLE

SHIVA SHAKTI INDIAN RESTAURANT

GOLDEN RICE

TA GALLERY

HUE AMAZING HOMESTAY

HEALING THE WOUNDED HEART SHOP

MAI THUC LOAN

NGUYEN BIEU

NGO DUC KE

DANG DUNG

NGUYEN CHI DIEU

LE THANH TON

HAN THUYEN

KIET 3 LE THANH TON

XUAN 68

DINH CONG TRANG

XUAN 68

CHU VAN AN

Ngoc Dich Lake

IMPERIAL CITY

DINH TIEN HOANG

ROYAL ANTIQUITIES MUSEUM

TONG DUY TAN

Forbidden Purple City

RIGHT HOUSE

LEFT HOUSE

THAI HOA PALACE

SALUTATION COURT

23 THANG 8

DOAN THI DIEM

CUA NGAN

LE DUAN

LAC THIEN

THE MIEU TEMPLE

HIEN LAM PAVILION

NGO MON GATE/ IMPERIAL CITY ENTRANCE

FLAG TOWER

DANG THAI THAN

LE CHUAN

NGUYEN THIEN THUAT

PHAN NGUYEN HAN

NGUYEN TRAI

DANG TRAN CON

ONG ICH KHIEM

23 THANG 8

CAU QUANG DUC

LE DUAN

CUA QUANG DUC

PHU XUAN BRIDGE

PHAN DANG LUU

HUE CENTRAL HOSPITAL

Perfume River

LE LOI

LE LAI

QUOC HOC HIGH SCHOOL

HO CHI MINH MUSEUM

LA RESIDENCE

LE LOI

NGUYEN TRUONG TO

PHAN BOI CHAU

NGO QUYEN

© AVALON TRAVEL

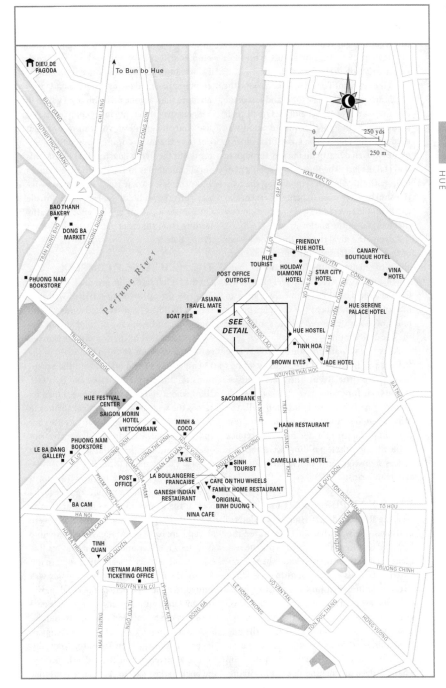

DIEU DE PAGODA

To Bun bo Hue

BACH DANG

CHI LANG

TRINH CONG SON

HUYNH THUC KHANG

BAO THANH BAKERY

DONG BA MARKET

CHUONG DUONG

TRAN HUNG DAO

PHUONG NAM BOOKSTORE

Perfume River

HAN MAC TU

DAP DA

LE LOI

FRIENDLY HUE HOTEL

CANARY BOUTIQUE HOTEL

HUE TOURIST

HOLIDAY DIAMOND HOTEL

STAR CITY HOTEL

NGUYEN CONG TRU

VINA HOTEL

POST OFFICE OUTPOST

NGUYEN THI MINH

VO THI SAU

ASIANA TRAVEL MATE

BOAT PIER

PHAM NGU LAO

SEE DETAIL

HUE HOSTEL

TINH HOA

NGUYEN CONG TRU

KIET 15

HUE SERENE PALACE HOTEL

TRUONG TIEN BRIDGE

BROWN EYES

JADE HOTEL

NGUYEN THAI HOC

BA TRIEU

SACOMBANK

BEN NGHE

TRAN QUANG KHAI

HANH RESTAURANT

HUE FESTIVAL CENTER

SAIGON MORIN HOTEL

VIETCOMBANK

MINH & COCO

LE BA DANG GALLERY

PHUONG NAM BOOKSTORE

LE LOI

TRUONG DINH

HOANG HOA THAM

LUONG THE VINH

HUNG VUONG

TRAN CAO VAN

TA-KE

NGUYEN TRI PHUONG

SINH TOURIST

CAMELLIA HUE HOTEL

LE QUY DON

TON DUC THANG

TO HUU

POST OFFICE

LA BOULANGERIE FRANCAISE

CAFE ON THU WHEELS

FAMILY HOME RESTAURANT

GANESH INDIAN RESTAURANT

ORIGINAL BINH DUONG 1

BA CAM

HA NOI

TRAN CAO VAN

NINA CAFE

NGUYEN HUE

PHAM HONG THAI

TINH QUAN

HAI BA TRUNG

NGO QUYEN

TRUONG CHINH

VIETNAM AIRLINES TICKETING OFFICE

NGUYEN VAN CU

NGO GIA TU

LY THUONG KIET

DONG DA

LE HONG PHONG

VO VAN TAN

TON DUC THANG

HUNG VUONG

0   250 yds

0   250 m

of poems and picture characters just below the ceiling. The building, completed in 1805, has undergone major renovations twice, in 1833 and again in 1923, and now stands as the most intact structure in the complex.

At the center of Thai Hoa's main room, the royal throne might not be the grand seat of the empire you might expect, but this small chair made of red-and-gold lacquered wood was used from the reign of Gia Long, first emperor of the Nguyen dynasty, all the way through to Bao Dai, its last. The throne sits upon a platform with three levels, symbolizing the relationship between human beings, heaven, and earth, and is covered by a decorative canopy that hangs over the platform.

Beyond the royal throne, the second room of the palace offers an informational video about the history of the Imperial City that's worth a watch, as well as a model of what the Citadel looked like in its prime. This gives an idea of the grandeur of the complex before much of it was destroyed by the conflicts of the late 20th century.

After you've wandered through Thai Hoa Palace, you'll exit onto the sunny grounds bordered by the Right and Left Houses. While their functions have changed considerably—one is now an exhibition hall, the other a photo studio where guests can dress up in imperial garb for portraits on a replica of the throne—these buildings were once the offices of the Nguyen dynasty's civil and military mandarins.

FORBIDDEN PURPLE CITY

Past the Right and Left Houses is a deteriorating stone wall that once separated the Imperial City from the emperor's private residence. This structure is in good shape compared to the rest of the **Forbidden Purple City,** most of which now exists as an open field, its few ruins buried under a tangle of grass. During the height of the Nguyen dynasty, Can Chanh Palace served as the administrative building in which the emperor conducted his daily business, while Can Thanh Palace just behind housed his living quarters. Today, you would never know the two even existed but for a small plaque in the middle of the open space. Though its skeleton is still recognizable, the Kien Trung Palace, built in 1827 and once home to the empress, has met a similar fate, as it is now no more than a stone platform from which to look out over the empty inner complex. If you use your imagination, you can reconstruct not only the homes of the emperor and empress but the living quarters that housed his royal concubines to the left and the princes and princesses to the right. A covered walkway runs the width of the Forbidden Purple City, as do a pair of newly renovated paths leading from the front gate through to Kien Trung Palace.

THE MIEU TEMPLE COMPLEX

On the far left side of the grounds, **The Mieu Temple Complex** holds a trio of well-preserved buildings constructed under Minh Mang, second emperor of the Nguyen dynasty. Dedicated to the worship of Nguyen royalty, **The Mieu Temple** honors 10 of the 13 emperors in the dynasty, with the exceptions of Duc Duc, Hiep Hoa, and Bao Dai, all of whom abdicated the throne. Lined up across the wide hall are identical shrines to the emperors, beginning with an incense altar and photograph at the front, followed by fruit offerings and each king's lacquered wooden tablet at the far end of the hall.

Opposite The Mieu is the **Hien Lam Pavilion,** an open-air structure that looks back at the temple and the nine bronze urns that stand between them. These, too, were placed here by Minh Mang, who chose nine as a lucky number and believed that his lineage would produce at least nine kings. In the days of the empire, The Mieu Complex was limited to male members of the royal family and civil and military service; even the empress was not permitted to enter. Around the back of the complex, women honored emperors past at **Phung Tien Temple,** especially on the anniversary of their death. Today, the pockmarked gate to the temple is all that remains. The nearby **Chuong Duc Gate** is an impressive and colorful sight.

THAI BINH READING PAVILION

On the other side of Thai Hoa Palace and the Forbidden Purple City, the **Thai Binh Reading Pavilion,** built under Thieu Tri, remains intact, though it can only be viewed from outside.

Not far from here is the slightly dusty **Royal Theater,** another explosion of red and gold, where twice-daily musical performances (10am and 2:30pm daily, VND100,000) are held. Farther back, the crumbling, moss-covered walls of **Ngoc Dich Lake** add to the scenery. From here, use the walkway heading east to reach the exit at Hien Nhon Gate, where electric shuttles make the short trip from the Imperial City to the Royal Antiquities Museum for free.

Royal Antiquities Museum

Gain free admission to the **Royal Antiquities Museum** (3 Le Truc, 7am-5:30pm daily, VND40,000), a short walk from the Imperial City, by bringing along your Imperial City ticket. Housed inside Long An Palace, the collection features an array of artifacts from eras past, including carved wooden furniture inlaid with mother-of-pearl, dishware from the reign of several emperors, vivid enamel trinkets, and massive porcelain vases, not to mention items used in the sacrificial ceremonies held at Nam Giao. A few replicas of traditional royal dress are on display at the back; the garden outside is peppered with stone mandarin statues and antique cannons; and there is a small side room with a display on Ham Nghi, a Nguyen emperor and noted revolutionary.

Dieu De Pagoda

On the northeastern bank of the narrow Dong Ba River, **Dieu De Pagoda** (100B Bach Dang, sunrise-sunset daily, free) is on the site of emperor Thieu Tri's birth. First constructed in 1844, the long grounds of this pagoda are filled with drooping palms and well-tended flowers. The main hall is watched over by four guardians on either side, while indoors is the requisite Buddha statue as well as a few others nearby.

The Royal Tombs

Dotting the hillsides south of town are an impressive collection of tombs that belong to the deceased emperors of the Nguyen dynasty. These larger-than-life memorials, sometimes

The Mieu Temple

designed and even lived in by an emperor prior to his death, come in all shapes and sizes, showing off the individual personality of each ruler. In every complex, you'll find a handful of common elements, including a Salutation Court, where concrete statues of mandarins and horses usher the emperor into the afterlife, as well as a lengthy inscription detailing that particular ruler's biography and accomplishments. There are also areas for worship and for the grave itself.

The tombs vary in size and style, depending upon both the ruler and the time period in which he lived. Minh Mang, for instance, was one of the earlier Nguyen emperors and a staunch nationalist, living in the first half of the 19th century and refusing any and all connections with Europe and the outside world. His tomb is stark, employing traditional Vietnamese architecture. Khai Dinh, second-to-last emperor to occupy the throne, spent much of his life working alongside the colonial government and was something of a Francophile, evidenced by the ostentatious mosaics and life-sized bronze statue within his tomb. The tombs of Gia Long, Dong Khanh, and Thieu Tri are close by but less interesting (and not as worthy of the time and money needed to view them).

TOMB OF TU DUC

The closest of Hue's imperial burial sites is the **tomb of Tu Duc** (7am-5:30pm daily, VND100,000), just over four miles from town. A sprawling complex of romantic landscapes and crumbling, moss-covered stone, the tomb was built in 1864. Tu Duc, the longest-reigning emperor of the Nguyen dynasty, did not pass away until 1883, giving him over a decade to enjoy the peace and serenity of his own grave.

Luu Khiem Lake, surrounded by wistful greenery and a fading stone border, is to the right of the main entrance. To the left on a raised platform is Chi Khiem Temple, which honors both Tu Duc and his empress Le Thien Anh, who died in 1902.

The tomb complex is occupied by

structures that mimic the Imperial City, with mandarin houses, a palace, and other buildings. During the 16 years between the completion of the tomb and Tu Duc's death, these buildings functioned as a workspace for the emperor and his mandarins. The first structure, **Hoa Khiem Temple,** mirrors Thai Hoa Palace in many ways and once served as an administrative building, though after the emperor's death it was converted into a temple honoring the royal couple. Today, you can see lacquered wooden tablets dedicated to the emperor and empress on an altar at the end of the hall.

Behind Hoa Khiem is **Luong Khiem Temple,** originally Tu Duc's secondary residence, which has functioned as a temple for Tu Du, the Queen Mother, since her death in 1901. On both sides of these buildings are rooms known as On Khiem and Minh Khiem, which acted as royal theaters, used for performances by the king's concubines. On the left beside this group of palaces are the former residences of Tu Duc's concubines, whose numbers were believed to be over 100. Now buried under a tangle of grass and wildflowers, the area remains an attractive sight.

Three royal tombs lie beyond the worship area. Tu Duc's is the largest, preceded by a Salutation Court and a gargantuan structure housing the stele on which the emperor's autobiography was engraved. While it was typical in the Nguyen era for the son of each emperor to write his father's funereal stele, Tu Duc did not have any children and so penned his own life story.

Past the stele is a pond and a towering wall, which keeps the actual tomb from view. An ornamental entrance gate opens to a view of the understated concrete tomb, with a single tiny incense urn upon it. To the right, Queen Le Thien Anh's modest tomb is enshrouded by a high stone wall (in traditional temples, this wall is often lacquered wood). Just beside the queen is a small grave for emperor Kien Phuc, adoptive son of Tu Duc, who served as emperor for a mere eight months before dying in 1884 at age 15.

To get to the tomb, follow Huyen Tran Cong Chua south from Hue for four miles. The entrance to the tomb is on Doan Nhu Hai, a small side street.

TOMB OF KHAI DINH

A departure from the more traditional elements of his predecessors' mausoleums, the **tomb of Khai Dinh** (7am-5:30pm daily, VND100,000) rambles up a hillside in three separate sections, about five miles south of Hue. The 12th emperor of the Nguyen dynasty, Khai Dinh ruled Vietnam for only nine years, from 1916 to his death in 1925. Construction of his intricate memorial lasted until 1931. Vietnam's second-to-last monarch, Khai Dinh became fond of European culture, as evidenced by the style and decoration of his tomb.

From the roadside, a soaring wrought-iron three-door gate opens onto the first set of stone steps. These lead up to a pair of ceremonial right and left houses honoring the civil and military mandarins who served under Khai Dinh. Nowadays, the buildings function as a souvenir shop and a place to hire tour guides. (The guides are seldom present, despite the sign posted out front.) More stone steps lead to the second level and the stelae of Khai Dinh, which easily surpass 10 feet in height. The stelae are housed in a black stone pavilion, surrounded by rows of mandarin statues as well as a pair of towering stupas, which represent the power of the Nguyen dynasty. From both this level and the one above, rolling green hills come into view.

On the top tier, decked out in all white, the exterior of Thien Dinh Palace contradicts the dour ambience of the lower levels. Its main hall explodes into a riot of green, blue, gold, and red. Inside the building is a small foyer featuring an informational video, a photo exhibit and a bronze statue of the emperor, and a modest collection of Khai Dinh's French porcelain. In the central room, a mind-blowing mosaic covers every inch of the walls and ceiling with wide-eye dragons and sparkling patterns. An incense altar bears the emperor's photograph and is flanked by two tortoise and crane statues. Deeper into the tomb is a life-sized bronze statue of Khai Dinh, cast in France in 1920, seated upon a replica of the throne, complete with three-tiered platform and a massive cement canopy. Flashy orange glass rises from the back of the platform, forming sun rays behind the emperor. At the back of the room

Detailed carvings surround the entrance to the tomb of Khai Dinh.

are another altar and lacquered wooden tablets belonging to Khai Dinh and his empress.

TOMB OF MINH MANG

Set upon a sweeping natural landscape, the **tomb of Minh Mang** (7am-5:30pm daily, VND100,000) is a tribute to traditional Vietnamese architecture and bears a strong resemblance to buildings in the Imperial City. Completed in 1843, two years after emperor Minh Mang's death, this 28-hectare complex is one of the more lavish mausoleums from the Nguyen era. Minh Mang spent over a decade searching for the perfect place to position his tomb. The emperor left behind 142 children—78 princes and 64 princesses—and had an estimated 500 concubines.

The entrance to the walled complex is on the left side of the main gate. At the center of the vast green landscape is the Salutation Court, where a small number of stone mandarin statues and elephants line the path up to the Stele House, guarding the emperor in the afterlife. Inside the stele house, a 10-foot tall stone tablet is etched with 2,500 characters describing the life and accomplishments of Minh Mang, as written by his son and successor, Thieu Tri.

Farther along, Hien Duc Gate leads the way to the tomb's worshipping area, where a pair of structures, called right and left houses, honor the civil and military mandarins who served under Minh Mang. The altar dedicated to the emperor and his first wife, Ta Thien Nhan Ho Thi Hoa, sits at the center of Sung An Temple, a barren building. Behind this, another set of houses served as the living quarters for Minh Mang's royal eunuchs and concubines after his death.

Just past these buildings is a section of Trung Minh Lake that breaks up the long path toward the tomb. Beyond a trio of side-by-side bridges, the two-story Pavilion of Light, the tallest building in the complex, was built in 1841. It symbolizes the emperor's passing from one world to the next, as well as his contributions to his people. Across the pavilion, lush gardens and another lake, Tan Nguyet, lie

long walkway at the tomb of Minh Mang

before Minh Mang's actual tomb. While there is nothing to see at the end of this walkway, as the tomb has been sealed and does not open except for the anniversary of the emperor's death, it's worth the short walk if only to look back at the sight of the pavilion surrounded by natural beauty.

Nam Giao Esplanade

At first glance, **Nam Giao Esplanade** (Le Ngo Cat and Dien Bien Phu, sunrise-sunset daily, VND20,000) may appear to be nothing more than a park, but its three-tiered terrace is the site where, from as early as 1806, emperors of the Nguyen dynasty came to offer sacrifices to a higher power. Because monarchs were considered to be the descendants of God, only an emperor could rightfully pay respects to his "parents," heaven and earth. Each spring, an annual tribute was offered by the emperor. The central platform represents the relationship between man at the lowest level, earth in the middle, and, within the circular terrace at the top, heaven. The ceremony would begin at

2am and last several hours, with offerings and burning incense. The emperor would arrive at Nam Giao a few days before to prepare. High-ranking mandarins and the emperor himself were responsible for tending to the pines surrounding the ceremonial area. The last offering ceremony was held in 1945 by emperor Bao Dai. The esplanade is just under two miles south of Hue.

Tu Hieu Pagoda

Surrounded by nature, **Tu Hieu Pagoda** (Le Ngo Cat, tel. 05/4388-6991, sunrise-sunset daily, free) began as a small hut in 1843, built by a local monk. It grew into something larger a few years later, when the royal eunuchs of the Nguyen dynasty contributed to its renovation and Tu Hieu became a full-fledged pagoda. Tucked at the end of a narrow, winding road off Le Ngo Cat, this secluded building sits amid a tangle of greenery, fronted by a half-moon pond that holds a collection of large fish as well as turtles. Within the main hall, altars to Buddha and the pagoda's monks can be found, as can a shrine for the royal eunuchs who backed the project. A few of the crumbling, moss-covered tombs scattered around the pagoda belong to these individuals. The pagoda is about two miles south of Hue.

Ho Quyen Royal Arena

Though it's a little tricky to find, the **Ho Quyen Royal Arena** (Kiet 373 Bui Thi Xuan, sunrise-6pm daily) is worth a visit if you're en route to the royal tombs. From the mid-1800s to the turn of the 20th century, this large, circular clearing was used for elephant fights, which the king and his fellow spectators enjoyed from atop the solid stone border of the arena. Though it's no longer possible to scale the crumbling walls, the arena's caretaker can unlock the gates and let you inside for a different perspective. To the right of the arena is a large pond surrounded by trees and vines, where the elephants were raised. A small temple opposite the pond honors the creatures and their caretakers. Ho Quyen is

particularly appealing for its lack of tourists and the peaceful, friendly neighborhood in which it now resides. For shutterbugs, this is a great spot to explore and get a taste of Hue's past history and local life today.

Getting to Ho Quyen can be tricky. The arena is located down an alley off Bui Thi Xuan, not far beyond the turnoff for the royal tombs, but the blue-and-white sign signaling the turnoff is small and only in Vietnamese. If you keep an eye out for "Ho Quyen," you'll find the signpost on your left opposite a roadside market.

Hue Nam Shrine

Though it bears many of the same traces of Hue's bygone imperial era, the **Hue Nam Shrine** (end of Huyen Tran Cong Chua, 7am-5:30pm daily, VND40,000) is an unusual departure from much of the rest of the city's history. The current structure, built under Minh Mang, is a shallow wooden temple devoted to the goddess Thien Y A Na, a motherly deity who watches over Vietnam and its people. As far back as the 13th century, the Cham empire, a medieval kingdom that ruled large parts of central Vietnam and the south-central coast, used this land to worship Lady Po Nagar, their protector and most revered goddess. Her story served as the origin for her Vietnamese counterpart, Thien Y A Na.

Beyond the temple, which was last renovated in the late 1880s, a handful of shrines dot the nearby riverbank, including altars dedicated to the goddesses of the five elements (water, earth, fire, wood, and metal) and to the famous red and white horses of Chinese general Quan Cong. On the lower level leading up to Hue Nam Shrine, still another shelter houses an altar for the general. The view of the Perfume River from Hue Nam's vantage point is worth admiring.

To get to Hue Nam, follow Huyen Tran Cong Chua, the road leading out to most of the royal tombs, all the way to its end. Bearing right, you'll come to a dead end at the riverbank, where a boatman waits for passengers to ferry across. Bidding starts as high

155 HUE THE CENTRAL PROVINCES

as VND50,000 a person, but with some persuasion you should be able to get this price down. Once you're let off at the other side, chances are the ferry will leave you while it runs back to look for other passengers; stand at the docking area when you're ready to leave and he'll swing back around. Hue Nam isn't necessarily a must-see attraction, but the atmosphere and the pleasant ride through the countryside bolster its appeal.

Thien Mu Pagoda

Thien Mu Pagoda (Kim Long, sunrise-sunset daily, free), perched on a hill overlooking the Perfume River, is one of Hue's most famous religious buildings. Since its inception in 1601, the long and narrow grounds of the complex have acquired a few add-ons to make it the sight it is today. From the stone steps out front, the first thing to greet you is Phuoc Dien, the iconic, aging, seven-tiered tower, which was actually last to arrive at Thien Mu in 1844. Before that, the four small structures surrounding Phuoc Dien were built to house various artifacts, including a trio of stone stelae, the largest of which rests atop a massive white tortoise, meant to symbolize wisdom and longevity, which appeared in 1715. One of the houses also stores a massive bell, cast in 1710. You'll get the best views of the river from this area, as Kim Long street wraps around a curve in the riverbank.

Farther back, the guardians of the pagoda usher you through a three-door entrance gate, their glowering faces watching over each of the passageways that leads onto the main hall, where several golden Buddhas await. Around back, another piece of Vietnamese history sits parked to the left of the pagoda: a pale blue car in which the Venerable Thich Quang Duc, senior monk at Ho Chi Minh City's Xa Loi Pagoda, rode to the intersection of Cach Mang Thang Tam and Nguyen Dinh Chieu on the morning of June 11, 1963 before setting himself on fire in protest of the religious oppression of the southern government. As the first monk to do so, Thich Quang Duc's death generated a massive international outcry and an increasingly negative image of southern president Ngo Dinh Diem's administration. The monk's heart, which had failed to burn during the process, was preserved and regarded as a religious relic. Today, the car at Thien Mu is accompanied by a photograph of Thich Quang Duc's heart and the Pulitzer Prize-winning photograph by Malcolm Browne that captured his self-immolation on camera. At the end of the pagoda grounds, you'll pass the monks' quarters and a collection of decorative bonsai trees before reaching a small clearing with a gray stone stupa.

The pagoda is just over three miles west of Hue, on the north side of Perfume River.

Van Mieu

West of Thien Mu Pagoda, on the same street, Hue's very own Confucian **Van Mieu** (Kim Long, 7am-5:30pm daily, free), or Temple of Literature, was established in 1808 in order to properly train mandarins for civil service. Though there's not much left of the original site, this is where the stelae etched with the names of Hue's doctorate recipients are kept beneath a pair of covered pavilions. Between 1830 and 1919, 33 stone tablets were placed here. The site sees few tourists; visitors are free to wander through the entrance gates and around the grassy area nearby. Out front, opposite the main gate just beside the river is another three-door archway made of stone with colorful enamel panels across the top, renovated thanks to Polish funds. Van Mieu's riverfront views and history make the temple a pleasant add-on for visitors of Thien Mu Pagoda.

Ho Chi Minh Museum

Hue's **Ho Chi Minh Museum** (7 Le Loi, tel. 05/4382-2152, www.baotanghochiminh.vn, 7am-11am and 1:30pm-4:30pm Tues.-Sun., VND10,000) offers an interesting look into the life of Vietnam's most famous patriot, who lived in Hue twice in his younger days. An upstairs exhibition room features a sizable collection of old photographs, which capture places like Dong Ba Market and the Citadel area during the early 20th century. Clunky English signage and revolutionary artifacts are on display alongside photos of Ho Chi Minh himself, charting his decades-long transformation from Nguyen Tat Thanh, a boy from Nghe An province, to young revolutionary Nguyen Ai Quoc, to the man with the trademark beard that went on to become president.

Quoc Hoc High School

Hue's **Quoc Hoc High School** (10 Le Loi) is the alma mater of many of Vietnam's most famous political figures from both the north and south. Lining the Perfume River, its dark red buildings were originally the site of a royal navy headquarters from the early 1800s. They were transformed into the country's National College in 1896. Students from the upper echelons of Vietnamese society were trained for government service under the emperor. A host of national leaders, from southern president Ngo Dinh Diem to heavy-hitting northern generals and politicians like Vo Nguyen Giap, Le Duan, and even Ho Chi Minh attended the school. Uncle Ho was later expelled for participating in demonstrations against the French government. Today, Quoc Hoc High School remains one of the most prestigious institutions in the country. It's possible to go inside (5pm-6:30pm daily) by getting the permission of the onsite security guard, but you can get the gist from just passing by.

An Dinh Palace and Tu Cung Residence

If the Citadel showcases the heyday of the Nguyen dynasty, a pair of buildings on Phan Dinh Phung mark its demise. Not far from An Cuu Market, the regal yellow **An Dinh Palace** (97 Phan Dinh Phung, VND20,000) remains in good condition, though it is now used as an administrative building and visitors are not permitted inside. Still, from the street beside An Cuu River you can catch a glimpse of what was once the private residence of Prince Buu Dao, who later became emperor Khai Dinh, and his son, emperor Bao Dai. Though Bao

Dai's first stint at An Dinh was as a crown prince, his second stay here was much less pleasant: after abdicating the throne and handing over the imperial sword and seal to the Communist government in 1945, Bao Dai and his family were forced to move out of the Citadel, returning to An Dinh for a short time before they left the country for France, where the last of Vietnam's royal family lived out their days.

The only person to stay behind was Bao Dai's mother, Tu Cung, who remained in An Dinh until 1954, when southern president Ngo Dinh Diem took the property and the Queen Mother was forced to move down the road to **Tu Cung Residence** (145 Phan Dinh Phung), a smaller colonial house in which she stayed until her death in 1980. While neither of these buildings is regularly open to visitors, they are worth a peek if you're exploring the area around An Cuu River, whose beautiful stone embankments make a good backdrop for an afternoon cycle around town. Visitors are rarely invited inside the house, but, if you're lucky, there may be a caretaker present at Tu Cung to let you see the interior. The mostly barren house has some interesting old photos of the royal family and an altar to the Queen Mother.

Thanh Toan Covered Bridge

A little over four miles east of town, the **Thanh Toan Covered Bridge** (Thuy Thanh District) is a smaller version of Hoi An's Japanese covered bridge, bedecked with glazed yin-yang tiles and a colorful roof. The wooden structure was built in 1776 thanks to the financial contributions of Tran Thi Dao, a wealthy local woman and wife of a high-ranking mandarin. The bridge's frame is made of seven compartments, with the middle one housing an altar dedicated to the bridge's benefactor.

The bridge is only one part of the area's appeal: While it can be tough to find, the ride to Thanh Toan takes you into the countryside, surrounded by miles of green paddy fields and a surprising number of large, decorative temples amid the humble houses of rice farmers. With few signs to guide you, expect to get lost at least once or twice on the short trip to Thanh Toan. Follow Truong Chinh out of town until it turns into Hoang Quoc Viet and as you get farther into the fields, a couple of aging kilometer stones will be there to guide you; look for "Thanh Toan." There are usually farmers in the rice paddies who can help direct you. With a growing number of guided tours heading out to Thanh Toan, they'll probably be able to guess what you're looking for.

Once you get on the final stretch toward Thanh Toan, keep an eye on the buildings to your left: Between ramshackle wooden houses and concrete bungalows are jaw-dropping temples and pagodas, covered top to bottom in mosaics and vibrant murals. One of the last ones before you reach Thanh Toan is the **Tran Family Temple** (sunrise-sunset daily, free), where several generations of Ms. Tran Thi Dao's ancestors are worshipped alongside the patron herself, who has a small shrine in the courtyard. You'll recognize this particular building by the small sign posted out front. If you're lucky, the caretakers will be around and more than willing to let you in for a look.

TOURS

You'll find dozens of cheap city tours around the Pham Ngu Lao area; these trips tend to provide varying levels of information, exclude entrance fees, and often act as more of a bus service. Visit sights like the Imperial City and the royal tombs on your own and save that extra cash for tours farther beyond the city limits to places like Thanh Toan bridge, some of the less-visited tombs, or the DMZ area. Plenty of Easy Rider-style motorbike excursions are available around the countryside and onward to other destinations, as are more traditional trips to these same places.

If you're keen on learning about royal history, more in-depth tours of the imperial sights are available from outfits like **Asiana Travel Mate** (47 Le Loi, tel. 05/4394-1133, www.deluxegrouptours.com, 8am-9pm daily),

Thanh Toan Covered Bridge

which does half- and full-day tours of the city's most famous attractions with smaller group sizes and more experienced guides.

The friendly folks at **Cafe on Thu Wheels** (3/34 Nguyen Tri Phuong, tel. 05/4383-2241, minhthuhue@yahoo.com, 7am-10pm daily) run local tours to the Imperial City, the royal tombs, and several nearby sights, as well as out to the DMZ area and farther afield. Both group and private tours are available, and custom arrangements can be made. The office runs a small café with cheap local food and drinks.

Hue to Go Tours (tel. 09/7357-1166, www. huetogotours.com, VND315,000-1,008,000) arranges a variety of motorbike excursions in and around the city. You can choose from single- or multi-day trips to places like Phong Nha, Bach Ma National Park, the DMZ area and a whole host of sights in town, as well as adventures to Hoi An and farther afield. Guides are English-speaking and attentive. Hopping on the back of an Easy Rider motorbike is a more expensive option than the average backpacker choices, but it's worth the money if you're interested in getting off the beaten path and combining your transportation with sightseeing. Though the outfit doesn't have a physical office, you can arrange tours or ask questions by contacting Hue To Go via phone or email.

Boat Tours

If you're interested in plying the waters of the Perfume River, dragon boat tours are an option. The cheapest of these are available at the **boat pier** (51 Le Loi), where a gaggle of boat touts will be more than happy to take you along the river to several famous sights, such as the Citadel, Thien Mu Pagoda, Hue Nam Shrine, and a royal tomb or two. These trips begin around VND150,000 a head, excluding entrance fees to the sights. A typical river outing takes most of the day, starting around 8am and wrapping up at about 3pm. If you're keen to catch a ride on the river, this can be a nice way to see the sights, though the trip is less of a guided tour and more of a water taxi service. Dragon boats generally include a driver in the fee rather than a certified guide. Similar trips booked through more reputable tour outfits will be able to supply an English-speaking guide to properly introduce the places you visit.

ENTERTAINMENT AND EVENTS
Nightlife

Though it's not nearly as active as Hanoi or Ho Chi Minh City, Hue is probably the liveliest spot in central Vietnam, with several bars open late around the backpacker area. There is plenty of outdoor seating for happy hour, and several late-night watering holes offer regular drink specials, pool tables, and dance floors. Most of this is focused on Pham Ngu Lao and Chu Van An streets.

A regular fixture of Hue's nightlife scene, **DMZ Bar** (60 Le Loi, tel. 05/4382-3414, 7am-late daily, VND20,000-185,000) serves beer and cocktails both outside on their corner patio, a great spot for people-watching on a warm night, and inside next to the pool table and bar. Though there isn't a dedicated dance floor, loud music and a few drinks usually get people moving. Happy hour specials are often available and the staff are a pleasant bunch.

The best place to start your evening is at **Hue Backpacker's** (10 Pham Ngu Lao, tel. 05/4382-6567, www.vietnambackpackerhostels.com, 8am-late daily, VND25,000-120,000). A cast of lively characters get the party going around happy hour and keep the masses entertained 'til the early morning with games like the "duck egg challenge" (in which one consumes a full fertilized duck egg, along with a shot of rice wine and a local beer), beer pong, and a host of other alcohol-related activities. Regular drink specials are offered throughout the night as well as several local beers and every manner of cocktail imaginable. The place also makes its own infused vodkas, which range from strawberry to garlic to Fisherman's Friend. Plenty of seating is scattered throughout the open downstairs bar as well as along the sidewalk.

Both the laid-back garden seating and lively indoor areas at **Brown Eyes** (56 Chu Van An, tel. 05/4382-7494, browneyesbarcafe@yahoo.com, 5pm-late daily, VND30,000-260,000) are open until the wee hours of the morning, mixing affordable cocktails and strong bucket drinks. Lighter beverages like beer and wine are also available, and you'll find a pool table in the dark interior alongside a cartoonish rendition of Michael Jackson in full "Thriller" regalia. Later in the evening, the back corner of Brown Eyes often doubles as an impromptu dance floor.

A newer fixture on the Hue nightlife scene, **Le's Garden Bar** (14 Pham Ngu Lao, tel. 09/4449-1468, 8am-12:30am daily, VND25,000-80,000) offers beer, cocktails, and just about every manner of drink imaginable. The indoor bar is equipped with a TV and pool table, while the veranda out front has plenty of tables to sit and watch the world go by. Food is available, though it's best to stick to drinks here.

Festivals and Events

Taking place over seven days in April, the **Hue Festival** (www.huefestival.com, mid- to late April) has been a huge draw for the city since its inception in 2000, running every other year on the even numbers. Showcasing the traditional arts and culture of Vietnam through song, dance, and other performances, the festival brings in an international element, inviting musicians and dance troupes from Europe, Africa, South America, Australia, and elsewhere in Asia to share in its cultural exchange. The event ushers in large crowds with its activities, including fashion shows and banquet dinners. Tickets can be purchased on-site for individual events, with most prices VND100,000-300,000, depending upon the venue. As you might expect, travelers visiting Hue during this time will want to book ahead for accommodations.

SHOPPING

While Hue isn't necessarily a retail hot spot, it's possible to pick up many of the standard Vietnamese souvenirs you see throughout the country. If you're willing to bargain, Dong Ba Market is not a bad place to start; you can also visit a few shops scattered around Pham Ngu Lao street and the rest of the backpacker area that specialize in original artwork and locally made handicrafts.

Markets

The city's busiest trading center is **Dong Ba Market** (Tran Hung Dao, sunrise-sunset daily), which remains a flurry of activity from sunup to well after sundown. Just east of the Citadel, this market is frequented by both locals and foreign travelers; you'll find a plethora of household items alongside clothing, bags, shoes, souvenirs, and food products, from the grayish-purple *mam tom* (fermented shrimp paste) to local treats like peanut candies. Be sure to haggle as prices start off steep. If all else fails, remember that there are often other market stalls offering the same product.

Art Galleries

Showcasing the work of both established and up-and-coming local artists, the **Ta Gallery** (44 Pham Ngu Lao, tel. 05/4382-4894, www.tagallery.com, 8am-10:30pm daily) stocks mostly lacquer paintings but also dabbles in oil on canvas and other mediums. Beyond artwork, a handful of authentic handicrafts can be purchased here, including traditional Phuoc Tich ceramics, which are a dark red hue and follow age-old production methods. A small selection of women's clothing is on sale at the back of the shop as well.

Run by local artist Pham Trinh, the **Du Ca Art Gallery** (22 Pham Ngu Lao, tel. 05/4382-5287, www.phamtrinhart.com, 10am-10pm daily) blends some of Vietnam's most traditional images—women in *ao dai* (traditional Vietnamese garment), for instance, or conical hats and bamboo poles—with a more modern, abstract flare. Working mostly in lacquer but also dabbling in oil and acrylic paints, the artist has had scores of exhibitions in Vietnam as well as several abroad in Japan, Switzerland, China, Germany, and Poland; you'll find his work on display inside this small shop in the middle of the backpacker area. For more artwork, head to the **New Space Gallery** (24 Pham Ngu Lao, tel. 05/4384-9353, 9am-11:30am and 2pm-6pm daily) next door.

Housed in a grand, white colonial building overlooking the river, the **Le Ba Dang Gallery** (15 Le Loi, tel. 05/4383-7411, lebadangarthue@gmail.com, 7:30am-11:30am and 1:30pm-5pm daily, VND20,000) displays the work of Le Ba Dang, a prolific artist born in Quang Tri province in 1921. The collection, which spans several rooms over two floors, is a fascinating range of mediums, with everything from wood and paper cutouts to oil and acrylic paintings, 3-D mixed media pieces, silk, and a variety of unusual topographical paper creations. Vivid black, white, and red paintings mimic traditional Chinese calligraphy, while colorful graphic prints and detailed abstract paintings line the walls of other small rooms. At the back, a small souvenir shop sells postcards and some of the artist's smaller paintings.

Gifts and Souvenirs

The modest **Tinh Hoa** (6B Vo Thi Sau, tel. 05/4361-6992, tinhhoaart@gmail.com, 4pm-10pm daily) shop sells a variety of locally made souvenirs, including Hue handicrafts like *phap lam* (enamel on metal), a once-popular art in the royal capital that fell into disuse and has recently been revived among local artisans. Decorative kites, paper lotus flowers, and an array of woven bamboo creations line the shop's walls, as does the dark red pottery of Phuoc Tich, a nearby village with a few hundred years of experience making their signature handicraft.

Made entirely from recycled materials, the souvenirs at **Healing the Wounded Heart** (23 Vo Thi Sau, tel. 05/4381-7643, www.hwhshop.com, 8am-noon and 2pm-10pm daily) are for two worthy causes: creating eco-friendly products from materials that would otherwise be thrown away and providing housing, a steady income, and employment to residents with disabilities in Hue. The shop, which works in conjunction with California-based SPIRAL Foundation and the Hue College of Medicine and Pharmacy, began in 2009 and has since improved the lives of its artisans as well as funded over a dozen heart surgeries for young Vietnamese patients in need. Traditional baskets made from strips of aluminum instead of bamboo are sold here, along with bags fashioned out of colorful rice sacks and a variety of crafty creations using recycled telephone wires. Interested travelers can visit the artisans at HWH's nearby **workshop** (69 Ba Trieu, tel. 05/4381-7643, 8am-noon and 2pm-10pm daily).

Bookstores

For reading material, the riverfront **Phuong Nam Bookstore** (15 Le Loi, tel. 05/4394-6766, langnghehue@pnc.com.vn, 8am-8pm daily) has a small selection of English-language paperbacks, including the classics, current best sellers, and an extensive collection of Haruki Murakami novels. The shop sells a few souvenirs in addition to running a café at the back (which turns into a karaoke joint at night). There's also a gargantuan **Phuong Nam** (131-133 Tran Hung Dao, tel. 05/4352-2000, www.pnc.com.vn, 8am-8pm daily) across the water at the end of Truong Tien Bridge that offers a bit more variety.

ACCOMMODATIONS

The majority of accommodations cluster around the area southeast of Truong Tien Bridge, where a small backpacker enclave caters to the foreign crowd. The surrounding shops, restaurants, and travel agencies are set up with tourists in mind. For a slightly quieter option away from the hustle and bustle, look to alley 34 of Nguyen Tri Phuong, where a handful of budget options and cheap and cheerful restaurants are tucked off the main road.

Standard amenities for budget spots are hot water, air-conditioning, and Wi-Fi. Those amenities plus a fridge, minibar, and a coffeemaker are standard in mid-range hotels. At the budget hotels, the advertised hot water and Wi-Fi are likely to be unreliable.

Under VND210,000

The city's most famous budget spot, ★ **Hue Backpackers** (10 Pham Ngu Lao, tel. 05/4382-6567, www.vietnambackpackerhostels.com, VND150,000-220,000 dorm, breakfast included) occupies some of the best real estate on Pham Ngu Lao. The mixed and all-female dorms come with air-conditioning, Wi-Fi, lockers, and a shared bathroom with hot water. Queen-size dorm beds are available for a few extra bucks. The upstairs verandas are great for relaxing. The lobby functions as a café and bar. Hue Backpackers is very social, so it is noisier than the average.

In the heart of town, the **Hue Amazing Homestay** (21 Pham Ngu Lao, tel. 09/1263-0219, www.hueamazinghomestay.com, VND105,000 dorm, breakfast included) is a cross between a hostel and a homestay. Run by friendly Mr. Duyen, facilities are basic but include hot water, Wi-Fi, air-conditioning, and a free beer. Valuables can be stored safely at reception. Quality tours are organized through this hostel. This is a good spot to link up with other backpackers. Rooms are comfortable but separated by only a small partition.

Walk by **Hue Hostel** (40 Chu Van An, tel. 012/1662-0015, www.huehostel.com, VND105,000 dorm, VND168,000 double, breakfast VND20,000 extra) too fast and you might miss it. It's a worthy place, with comfortable beds and clean bathrooms, small personal lockers, hot water, Wi-Fi, and air-conditioning or a fan. A communal area has a computer with Internet access and a kitchenette, and the staff is helpful and sociable. A few private rooms are offered at good prices, but they're nothing special, and the bathroom is shared with dorm guests.

Original Binh Duong 1 (17/34 Nguyen Tri Phuong, tel. 05/4382-9990, www.binhduonghotel.com, VND84,000 dorm, VND168,000-252,000 double) is an updated budget hotel offering great value. Private rooms are basic but modern, and feature air-conditioning, hot water, television, fridge, and big, comfy beds. Dorm beds are the cheapest rate in town, though they don't include personal lockers and, with three beds to a small room, you'll be sleeping within arm's reach of your neighbor. Spend a few extra dollars for the private rooms and you'll get more space.

VND210,000-525,000

Down an alley chock full of budget options not far from Pham Ngu Lao, **Canh Tien Guesthouse** (9/66 Le Loi, tel. 05/4382-2772, www.chez.tiscali.fr, VND210,000-315,000) is a large, family-run accommodation with friendly owners and spacious rooms with basic furnishings. Amenities include hot water, air-conditioning, and Wi-Fi access, and the guesthouse's location off the main road helps to keep it quiet at night.

Rooms at the **Star City Hotel** (2/36 Vo Thi Sau, tel. 05/4383-1358, www.starcityhotelhue.com, VND315,000-598,000, breakfast

included) are a steal and well appointed with newer decor, plenty of light, and ample space. Air-conditioning, Wi-Fi, television, and hot water are among each room's amenities, along with some space-age showerheads in certain rooms. The staff are a welcoming bunch.

A short walk from the riverside, the **Canary Boutique Hotel** (8/43 Nguyen Cong Tru, tel. 05/4393-6447, VND378,000-630,000, breakfast included) is down a small alley off the main road. It offers great value for its well-appointed rooms. Modern furnishings, comfy beds, and standard mid-range amenities are provided. The pleasant staff add to its value. There is a Canary Hotel on the main stretch of Nguyen Cong Tru not far away, so make sure you're at the right place.

For a good value mid-range spot, the **Friendly Hue Hotel** (10 Nguyen Cong Tru, tel. 05/4383-4666, www.thanthienhotel.com.vn, VND440,000-1,070,000, breakfast included) does the job, pairing comfortable rooms with modern furnishings and a hotel staff to match its name. Amenities include TV, hot water, air-conditioning, Wi-Fi, and a fridge. Assistance with transportation and travel can be arranged, and there is a restaurant downstairs.

A bright white building on the corner of Chu Van An, **Jade Hotel** (17 Nguyen Thai Hoc, tel. 05/4393-8849, www.jadehotelhue.com, VND315,000-525,000, breakfast included) is owned by the same people responsible for the Holiday Diamond and provides decent rooms and friendly service at a reasonable price. Three options are available, with increasingly more space and better views. Amenities include the usual hot water, Wi-Fi, air-conditioning, and television.

VND525,000-1,050,000

Hidden down at the end of Hue's hotel street, rooms at the **Vina Hotel** (57/3 Nguyen Cong Tru, tel. 05/4625-2114, www.vinahotel.com.vn, VND525,000-840,000, breakfast included) are well-priced considering its many accoutrements, from the minibar and in-room safe to TV, Wi-Fi, air-conditioning, hot water, and tea- and coffee-making facilities. A restaurant, bar and spa are also part of Vina, and staff help to arrange onward transportation and tours around the city.

The charming, purple ★ **Orchid Hotel** (30A Chu Van An, tel. 05/4383-1177, www. orchidhotel.com.vn, VND735,000-1,155,000, buffet breakfast included) stands out for its top-notch staff, who are especially service-minded. Its rooms also exceed mid-range standards, with modern decor and furnishings, standard amenities, a minibar, television, tea- and coffee-making facilities, and an in-room computer. The hotel is close to both the riverfront and the backpacker area.

Down a popular alley off Nguyen Cong Tru, the **Holiday Diamond Hotel** (6/14 Nguyen Cong Tru, tel. 05/4381-9845, www. hueholidaydiamondhotel.com, VND504,000-756,000, breakfast included) offers superior, deluxe, and city view rooms close to both the river and Hue's backpacker area. The decor is a little uninspired, but each room comes with high-quality amenities, including hot water, air-conditioning, Wi-Fi, television, DVD player, minibar, tea- and coffee-making facilities, and, in some cases, an in-room computer.

Despite the dusty alleyway leading to it, the **Serene Palace Hotel** (21/42 Nguyen Cong Tru, tel. 05/4394-8585, www.serenepalace-hotel.com, VND630,000-1,050,000) is modern, well appointed, and a short walk from the backpacker area. The usual mid-range amenities apply. The decor is splashy, with a busy wooden cutout framing the wall-mounted TV, and showers are especially good. Service-minded hotel staff assist with travel information, tours, and transportation.

VND1,050,000-2,100,000

The cozy **Camellia Hue Hotel** (57-59 Ben Nghe, tel. 05/4394-3943, www.camellia-hotels.com.vn, VND840,000-2,520,000) is on the fancier end of mid-range options but its modern, well-appointed rooms represent good value and are centrally located. Amenities include air-conditioning, hot water, television, Wi-Fi, minibar, tea- and coffee-making facilities, an in-room safe, and a personal laptop with Internet connection. Some rooms offer nice balcony views, and the swimming pool and fitness center are free for hotel guests.

Over VND2,100,000

The historic **Hotel Saigon Morin** (30 Le Loi, tel. 05/4382-3526, www.morinhotel. com.vn, VND2,100,000-6,300,000, breakfast included) is one of the oldest hotels in the city. Famous guests like Andre Malraux and Charlie Chaplin have spent the night here, and the restaurant and bar was popular with French colonials during the early 1900s. Rooms are chic and well appointed, combining old world charm with modern amenities, such as cable TV, generous bathtubs, work desks, and an in-room safe. Guests have full access to the on-site swimming pool and fitness center. There is also a spa and souvenir shops.

Chic and sophisticated, ★ **La Residence** (5 Le Loi, tel. 05/4383-7475, www.la-residence-hue.com, VND3,150,000-11,550,000) sits at the far end of Le Loi, a sprawling white building overlooking the river. With art deco influences, rooms are furnished in tasteful, modern elegance, featuring bold colors against white walls. Amenities include hot water, air-conditioning, TV, Wi-Fi, an in-room safe, coffeemaker, and, in some rooms, a private balcony. The hotel counts an upscale restaurant, ritzy bar, fitness center, spa, saltwater pool, and tennis court in its offerings, not to mention complimentary bike rentals and a travel desk.

FOOD

Considered one of Vietnam's most famous culinary cities, Hue has no shortage of sumptuous dishes unique to the region. You'll find an abundance of street food on every corner, as well as outside the bustling Dong Ba Market, where you can sample all manner of local fare. A few international options are available, featuring mostly standard backpacker meals like cheeseburgers and pancakes. With so many delectable local options, you should have no problem finding something to suit your palate.

Cafés and Bakeries

The brightly lit display of decadent cakes and flaky pastries should be enough to get you in the door of **La Boulangerie Francaise** (46 Nguyen Tri Phuong, tel. 05/4383-7437, www.laboulangeriefrancaise.org, 7am-8:30pm daily, VND15,000-80,000), but its charitable cause is another good reason to stop in for coffee and a bite to eat. In addition to providing excellent Western-style baked goods, the shop runs a training school for disadvantaged young Vietnamese, teaching them to become pastry chefs and bakers. Trainees work as café staff and often go on to work at high-end hotels. All proceeds from the shop go toward funding a local orphanage.

Opposite Dong Ba Market is the bustling **Bao Thanh Bakery** (265 Tran Hung Dao, tel. 05/4352-4160, 5:30am-9:30pm daily, VND5,000-20,000), complete with flashing neon lights and neatly arranged rows of Asian baked goods, both savory and sweet.

International

Hue offers an interesting handful of non-Vietnamese options, though it's nowhere near as varied as other cities. More than a few local restaurants are geared toward foreigners with even those specializing in Vietnamese cuisine offering Western backpacker favorites like banana pancakes and hamburgers. Beyond the places listed here, you're better off sticking to local meals, as foreign cuisine is not Hue's strongest suit. For reasonably priced Western dishes, check out **Hue Backpacker's** (10 Pham Ngu Lao, tel. 05/4382-6567, www.vietnambackpackerhostels.com).

The menu at **La Carambole** (19 Pham Ngu Lao, tel. 05/4381-0491, la_carambole@hotmail.com, 7am-11pm daily, VND80,000-280,000) is a blend of French and Vietnamese, featuring Hue specialties alongside duck l'orange and steak frites. Its bistro ambience adds luxury, with cozy indoor tables and a nice al fresco section. The cheese platter and wine are particularly exciting for travelers who have been away from home for a while. La Carambole is often full; it is possible to make a reservation or, if you'd rather wing it, turn up earlier or later to escape the rush.

For a break from local fare, you can visit either **Shiva Shakti** (27 Vo Thi Sau, tel. 05/4393-5627, 10am-11pm daily, VND65,000-175,000) or **Ganesh** (34 Nguyen Tri Phuong, tel. 05/4382-1616, 10am-10pm daily, VND65,000-175,000). These two Indian places are pretty much identical, down to the menu, which is exactly the same, though staff seem to be more cheerful at Shiva Shakti. Prices are reasonable and portions are a decent size.

With a minimalist approach to decor and a fake cherry blossoms peppering the restaurant, **Ta-ke** (34 Tran Cao Van, tel. 05/4384-8262, www.dongkinhtourhue.com, 10am-10:30pm daily, VND35,000-220,000) attempts to evoke Japanese culture while preparing its menu of sushi and other Japanese fare. Both à la carte items and large meals are available. It's a short walk from the main backpacker neighborhood.

Street Food

To eat like a local, the central market is always a good place to start, but you can also venture down to the far end of Truong Dinh, where there are plenty of tasty street-side dining options, as well as a few backpacker-friendly joints closer to the center of town along Vo Thi Sau.

Deep within the maze of the bustling **Dong Ba Market** (Tran Hung Dao, sunrise-sunset daily) you'll find several food stalls surrounded by low tables and plastic stools. Not all of these spots are the cleanest; peruse your options first and check for posted prices. Dishes include the signature *bun bo Hue* (soup with beef and rice noodles) and *bun thit nuong* (rice noodles and grilled pork). You can also find a few street vendors in front of the market, where things are a little cleaner and street-side dining is available.

Hue's Cuisine

Known nationwide, Hue cuisine is a point of pride among the Vietnamese, thanks to its varied and flavorful dishes. For an introduction into the city's food scene, sample some of the following bite-sized snack foods:

- *Banh beo:* Often served in a porcelain dish, these miniature steamed rice cakes are usually topped with dried shrimp and pork crackling. For best results, add liberal amounts of fish sauce to the mix and enjoy.

- *Banh loc:* Slightly different from other Hue snack foods, *banh loc* uses tapioca starch to make a small steamed dumpling with a whole prawn at the center alongside a hint of pork fat.

- *Banh nam:* Another variety steamed rice cake, *banh nam* comes wrapped in banana leaves and features a center of minced pork and shrimp. These, too, are best eaten with ample amounts of fish sauce.

- *Banh ram it:* Another version of a steamed dumpling, *banh ram it* pairs a steamed sticky rice dumpling with a crunchy, fried base. You'll find pork and shrimp at the center, and fish sauce is the recommended condiment.

Beyond mini-meals, you can also look out for these heartier local dishes:

- *Bun bo Hue:* One of the city's most popular meals, this rice-noodle-and-beef soup features an orange-hued broth with a bit of a kick. Add-ons like ham hock and congealed duck blood are also sometimes included, as well as the standard helping of fresh greens.

- *Banh khoai:* A local version of *banh xeo,* this savory pancake includes the usual bean sprouts, pork and shrimp, though in a crunchier shell. Servings are usually individual and, while the meal includes fresh greens, the entire spread is often enjoyed with chopsticks rather than wrapped inside a whole salad leaf, meaning an equally delicious meal with a little less mess.

- *Com hen* and *bun hen:* Whether with rice or rice noodles, Hue's *hen,* or baby clams, are a local favorite that often come topped with fresh veggies and a bit of broth on the side.

There is a general consensus among the people of Hue that the city's best *com hen* (baby clams with rice) comes from **Ba Cam** (2 Truong Dinh, tel. 05/4625-0003, 6am-2pm daily, VND20,000/bowl). This small, street-side eatery dishes out medium-sized portions of *hen* (baby clams) with your choice of rice or noodles, a few veggies, and some broth on the side. Breakfast starts early and is usually finished by late morning, so make sure you get here before the pot is empty.

The humble front yard of a bungalow house in Phu Cat District serves some of the best ★ *bun bo Hue* (5 Nguyen Du, 3pm-7pm daily, VND25,000) around. This particular collection of low plastic tables is a popular choice among local residents and offers a nice opportunity to explore a less-visited part of town.

Vegetarian

For vegetarian fare, you'll find that there are plenty of meat-free restaurants around town, though several spots have taken to offering an English menu for foreigners that lists all the same dishes at two or three times the price. This is less true at some of the vegetarian rice stalls gathered around the corner of Vo Thi Sau and Nguyen Cong Tru, though cleanliness is not the main priority here. Thanks to the influx of foreign tourists in the area, many restaurants, including more local eateries, have begun offering at least a few meatless options for diners.

Located on the ground floor of the Parkview Hotel, **Tinh Quan** (9 Ngo Quyen, tel. 05/4383-7382, tinhquan@parkviewhotelhue.com, 6:30am-9pm daily, VND15,000-50,000) boasts a large indoor dining area and dozens of well-priced vegetarian dishes. If possible, stick to the tofu and heartier plates, as some of the meatless versions of local specialties don't cut it. On the 1st and 15th of each lunar month, this restaurant is packed with local diners honoring the special Buddhist days.

Vietnamese

Not far from the backpacker area, **Hanh Restaurant** (11 Pho Duc Chinh, tel. 05/4383-3552, 9:30am-5:30pm daily, VND25,000-60,000) sees enough foreign visitors to have an English menu but stays true to its Vietnamese tastes, offering a selection of Hue specialties, including *banh beo* (steamed rice cakes) and *banh khoai* (the local version of a savory pancake), as well as rice noodles with grilled pork and a few other tasty dishes. Prices are reasonable and dining is more authentic than at some of the eateries in the area that cater specifically to tourists.

Just outside the Citadel walls, **Lac Thien** (6 Dinh Tien Hoang, tel. 05/4352-7348, 8am-10pm daily, VND25,000-85,000) is a small, cheerful, family-run business that does tasty local food at local prices. Dishes include *bun thit nuong* (rice noodles and grilled pork), *banh beo* (steamed rice cakes), and several

other Hue specialties. Their signature plate is *banh khoai* (a local version of the Vietnamese savory pancake).

A lovely spot on the main backpacker drag, **Golden Rice** (40 Pham Ngu Lao, tel. 05/4362-6938, giangthinh.goldenrice@gmail.com, 9am-10pm or until last customer daily, VND40,000-200,000) may cater to a tourist crowd but it does so with excellent Vietnamese dishes, ranging from chicken, beef, seafood, and pork to vegetarian offerings and local specialties. Meals are well-priced and there is a room upstairs for overflow. This is a popular spot in the evenings; if possible, plan on an early or late dinner to avoid the crowds.

The cheap and cheerful **Nina Cafe** (16/34 Nguyen Tri Phuong, tel. 05/4383-8636, www.ninascafe.jimdo.com, 7:30am-10:30pm daily, VND35,000-95,000) is hidden from sight down the budget alley 34 off Nguyen Tri Phuong. It has covered outdoor seating and lanterns and faux greenery to add to its decor. The welcoming folks at Nina expertly prepare the usual tome of Vietnamese dishes, all served with a smile.

While it's located in a tourist area and caters mostly to Western visitors, the few staff at **Family Home Restaurant** (11/34 Nguyen Tri Phuong, tel. 05/4382-0668, 8am-10pm

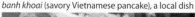

banh khoai (savory Vietnamese pancake), a local dish

daily, VND40,000-90,000) go out of their way to make you feel welcome and serve tasty renditions of several local meals, including signature Hue specialties. Pork, chicken, and beef appear on the menu, as do a few vegetarian options, and the exceptionally pleasant owners make this a place worth visiting. Breakfast is also available, as are a few backpacker favorites, like banana pancakes.

INFORMATION AND SERVICES
Tourist Information

There is a tourist information kiosk or travel agent on just about every corner in downtown Hue, though many are more interested in selling their own services than assisting travelers. **Hue Tourist** (120 Le Loi, tel. 05/4381-6263, www.tourconduongdisan.com, 8am-5:30pm Mon.-Sat.) does a nice job of providing helpful travel tips to visitors without the pressure to book a tour and also provides the best of the city's free maps. For more in-depth information on some of Hue's World Heritage sites, swing by the **Hue Festival center** (17 Le Loi, tel. 05/4385-8858, www.huefestival.com, 7:30am-10pm daily), a one-room outfit just opposite the Hotel Saigon Morin, where an array of free pamphlets offer historical background on the most-visited of the royal tombs as well as the Imperial City.

Banks and Currency Exchange

You'll find dozens of ATMs in and around the backpacker area, including a set of them on either side of the Century Riverside Hotel on Le Loi. For currency exchange or a proper bank, stop by the **Vietcombank** (2A Hung Vuong, tel. 05/4382-7337, www.vietcombank.com.vn, 8am-11am and 1:45pm-4:30pm Mon.-Fri., 7:45am-10am Sat.) just behind the Saigon Morin Hotel. There is also a **Sacombank** (2 Ben Nghe, tel. 05/4383-9002, www.sacombank.com.vn, 7:30am-11:30am and 1:30pm-5pm Mon.-Fri., 7:30am-11:30am Sat.) nearby.

Internet and Postal Services

The most accessible post office is a small outpost (44 Le Loi, tel. 05/4383-2072, 8am-11am and 2:30pm-5pm daily) located just beside the Century Riverside Hotel. For Internet you can head to the central **post office** (8 Hoang Hoa Tham, tel. 05/4382-3496, 7am-8pm daily) or pop into any one of the small Internet shops around town.

Medical Services

For illnesses and injuries, the **Hue Central Hospital** (16 Le Loi, tel. 05/4382-2325, www.bvtwhue.com.vn) is just past the Phu Xuan Bridge.

GETTING THERE
Air

Just over nine miles from town, **Phu Bai International Airport** (HUI, 9 miles southeast of Hue off Highway 1) receives daily flights from Ho Chi Minh City and Hanoi. **Vietnam Airlines** (23 Nguyen Van Cu, tel. 05/4382-4709, www.vietnamairlines.com, 7:30am-11:30am and 1:30pm-4:45pm daily) flies to these destinations and has a ticketing office in the city. There is a **VietJet** (Phu Bai International Airport, www.vietjetair.com) counter inside the airport.

Flights from Hanoi to Hue are just over an hour and cost VND650,000-1,100,000. There are about four flights each day. Flights from HCMC to Hue are 1.5 hours long and cost VND299,000-650,000. There are about four flights per day.

Bus

Hue has two bus stations on either side of the city. All local buses arriving from Hanoi to the north pull in to the **northern bus station** (132B Ly Thai To, tel. 05/4352-2716). The ride to Hue from Hanoi on a sleeper bus is 10-12 hours and costs VND280,000. Buses from southern destinations like Danang and Hoi An arrive at the **southern station** (97 An Duong Vuong, tel. 05/4382-5070). From Danang or Hoi An, buses leave twice daily (morning and afternoon). The ride to Hue is about three hours and costs VND100,000. The northern station is four miles from the center of Hue, while the southern station is three miles away. Hail a cab to get to your hotel from either station.

Both **Sinh Tourist** (48 Nguyen Tri Phuong, tel. 05/4384-8626, www.thesinhtourist.vn, 6:30am-10pm daily) and **Hanh Cafe** (28 Chu Van An, tel. 05/4383-7279, 7am-7:30pm daily) have offices in downtown Hue and modern, air-conditioned buses.

Train

The **Hue train station** (2 Phan Chu Trinh, tel. 05/4382-2175, 7am-5pm daily) sits about a mile from the backpacker area at the end of Le Loi. Both slow and express trains arrive from all over the country, and daily departures bound for both northern and southern destinations are available. It's possible to walk to your hotel from the station, provided you're willing to carry your luggage.

From Danang, the train ride is about 2.5 hours and costs VND336,000-420,000.

There are four daily departures (two in the early morning and two in the early afternoon).

From Hanoi, the ride is about 12 hours and costs VND735,000-1,302,000. There are six daily departures (two in the morning, four in the evening).

GETTING AROUND

Mailinh (tel. 05/4389-8989) taxis are all over town, as are droves of *xe om* drivers.

One of the more popular ways to get around town is by bicycle. Most hotels and guest-houses rent out city bikes at about VND30,000 per day. You can also stop by an independent rental outfit, of which there are many around the backpacker area. For reliable bikes, try **Minh & Coco** (1 Hung Vuong, tel. 05/4382-1822, 6:30am-11pm daily, VND30,000/bicycle, VND80,000-100,000/motorbike). Expect to put down some collateral in exchange for the vehicle.

Vicinity of Hue

DMZ TOURS

A popular option for history buffs and those traveling between Hue and Phong Nha-Ke Bang National Park, **DMZ tours** showcase some of the most significant sites of the American War. Both single- and multi-day trips around this region focus on central Quang Tri province, where the 17th parallel sliced northern and southern Vietnam in half for roughly two decades. Now filled with rice paddies and small villages once more, this is where some of the war's most brutal battles took place.

After the 1954 Geneva Accords ensured Vietnamese independence from the French, it was agreed that a temporary boundary along the banks of Quang Tri's Ben Hai River would divide the north and south until general elections were held to unify the country. Over the next decade, this area became a barren wasteland, rutted with bomb craters and leftover

weapons. From the time the Americans arrived on the scene until the end of the conflict, thousands of tons of bombs and heavy napalm use plagued the province. In addition to suffering the constant threat of violence back in the 1960s and '70s, the area today is also notably affected by things like Agent Orange and unexploded ordnance, carrying on the terrible legacy of war.

Most DMZ tours cover the highlights in a single day. It's a long journey, so it's possible to expand the tour over two or three days. Hop on an Easy Rider-style motorbike excursion, which guarantees one guide per person, or opt for the less-expensive (albeit less personal) bus tour. The **Phong Nha Farmstay** (1 km east of Ho Chi Minh Hwy. E., tel. 05/2367-5135, www.phong-nha-cave.com, VND500,000) offers day trips from Hue to Phong Nha or vice versa, stopping along the way to check out the Vinh Moc Tunnels, the Hien Luong

Vicinity of Hue

NORTHERN BUS STATION

TL10

To Tam Giang Lagoon

TL10

BUN BO HUE

DIEU DE PAGODA

SEE "HUE" MAP

IMPERIAL CITY

THANH TOAN COVERED BRIDGE

TL3

AN DINH PALACE

TL3

THIEN MU PAGODA

VAN MIEU

HUE TRAIN STATION

TU CUNG RESIDENCE

SOUTHERN BUS STATION

HO QUYEN ROYAL ARENA

TL3

TU HIEU PAGODA

NAM GIAO ESPLANADE

TOMB OF TU DUC

To PHONG NHA-KE BANG NATIONAL PARK

HUE NAM SHRINE

FERRY TO HUE NAM SHRINE

QL49

QL1A

TOMB OF KHAI DINH

AH1

QL1

TOMB OF MINH MANG

QL49

0   1 mi

0   1 km

© AVALON TRAVEL

Bridge, Ben Hai River, and DMZ monument. Minibuses leave Phong Nha at 6:30am and arrive in Hue around 12:30pm.

Two other outfitters that offer DMZ tours are **Cafe on Thu Wheels** (3/34 Nguyen Tri Phuong, tel. 05/4383-2241, minhthuhue@yahoo.com, 7am-10pm daily, VND378,000/group) and **Hue to Go Tours** (tel. 09/7357-1166, www.huetogotours.com, VND1,008,000).

While each tour is different, most visit a handful of noteworthy spots within Quang Tri.

Vinh Moc Tunnels

Not far from the 17th parallel, the quiet village of Vinh Linh was hit by 7,000 tons of bombs between 1965 and 1972. Instead of fleeing, the residents of Vinh Linh, most of whom were poor farmers, chose to tunnel beneath a group of seaside hills, creating the **Vinh Moc Tunnels.** Where the Cu Chi tunnels near Ho Chi Minh City were used expressly for fighting, the wider underground passageways of Vinh Moc became a subterranean village complete with a hospital, school, meeting hall, and plenty of residential housing (a narrow cubicle that could fit a family of five). The tunnels, completed in 1968, were made up of three levels: one at 39 feet, one at 49 feet and one at 75 feet below ground. The deepest tunnels were used for weapon storage and bomb shelters, while the middle section provided accommodation for roughly 300 villagers at a time. At its height, Vinh Moc was home to around 600 people. The success of the Vinh Moc Tunnels also came from their secrecy, as American officials knew nothing of this underground village during the war.

17th Parallel

From 1954 until the end of the American War, the Ben Hai River separated north and south Vietnam at the **17th parallel,** with only the modest wooden **Hien Luong Bridge** serving as a connector. On the southern side, not far from the riverbank, was Doc Mieu, a large American base that housed planes and was often used to survey the northern side. The bridge still stands, leading across the river to a large statue of a woman and child, both of whom are looking north, waiting for their husbands and fathers to return. A massive flag tower, now decorated in colorful murals, marks the official DMZ line, and the exhibition hall across the road is filled with plenty of shrapnel, artifacts, and photographs, which give a chilling visual of the now-flat rice paddies surrounding Ben Hai, once pocked and cratered by bombs.

Truong Son Soldiers' Cemetery

Though soldiers' cemeteries are spread throughout the country, and even the smallest towns and villages are outfitted with their own cemeteries for fallen soldiers, the largest of Vietnam's military cemeteries is **Truong Son Soldiers' Cemetery.** It is located 60 miles north of Hue almost directly on the 17th parallel, where seemingly endless rows of headstones bear testament to the human cost of the war. Instead of the large cemetery, some tours pass by **Gio Linh Cemetery,** a smaller but no less heartbreaking memorial near the Ben Hai River, where the vast majority of graves are emblazoned with the words *"chua biet ten"* ("name unknown").

Long Hung Church

The site of a major 1972 battle that lasted 81 days and became one of the bloodiest in the entire war, **Long Hung Church** sits inconspicuously along Highway 1. Today, it stands completely gutted, with only the shell of the building still in place, its frame rife with bullet holes. In a country that has largely moved on and rebuilt, this site provides a very real visual of the scope of the destruction that took place during the U.S. Army's 1972 Easter Offensive. Look above the doorframe for the tattered, faded star and banner of the north Vietnamese army.

★ PHONG NHA-KE BANG NATIONAL PARK

A labyrinth of subterranean tunnels and jaw-dropping, otherworldly landscapes, **Phong Nha-Ke Bang National Park** (TL20, Son Trach village, tel. 05/2367-7323, www. phongnhatourism.com.vn, 7am-5pm daily, entry fees charged per cave) may be off the beaten path for now, but its anonymity is fading fast. Ever since a team of British cavers turned up in 2009 to explore the vast interior of Son Doong, the world's largest cave, at 5.5 miles long and tall enough to comfortably house a high-rise, tourism to the area has taken off.

Just over 130 miles north of Hue, Phong Nha's major draw is its three sprawling cave systems, Phong Nha, Vom, and Nuoc Mooc, which combine to roughly 90 miles of darkened passageways and have earned the area World Heritage status. Decked out in eerie, alien rock formations and spindly stalactites, these tunnels are estimated at around 3-5 million years old and, according to researchers, may be a mere handful of the caves in existence between here and the Laotian border.

It's possible to visit the park without a tour group, but you'll be limited to certain caves. For many of the more impressive caves, visitors must be a part of a tour group. Phong Nha offers cave tours only through certified companies and limits the number of annual visitors to Son Doong, which can be explored for a cool USD$3,000 a head.

Day trips from Hue are cheap, though these

The World's Largest Cave

You could fit a jumbo jet or a city block inside **Son Doong** and still have room left over. This massive grotto stretches about three miles into the earth, with a range of landscapes you'd seldom imagine inside a darkened cave. A river roars through Son Doong, tumbling over cliffs and around corners. Clouds pass through its many chambers each day. Thanks to a pair of large skylights, Son Doong is also home to a jungle, complete with monkeys, snakes, flying foxes, and birds, not to mention a few new species discovered within its massive boundaries.

The discovery of this jaw-dropping subterranean world belongs to Ho Khanh, a local farmer who happened upon the entrance one day in 1991. At the time, the find was of little consequence, and so the man carried on but filed its location away in the back of his mind. Not until 2009 would Howard Limbert and the British Cave Research Association enlist Ho Khanh's assistance in tracking down the cavern once more. The team of cavers was able to measure the size and length of Son Doong, and the results turned out to be far greater than Malaysia's Deer Cave, the previous record holder. There is still plenty to be learned about Son Doong and the surrounding area—many believe there are even bigger underground chambers nearby.

An expert team of caving professionals at **Oxalis** (Son Trach village, tel. 05/2367-7678, www.oxalis.com.vn) have begun running six-day excursions into Son Doong at USD$3,000 a head. The outrageous cost makes at least some sense when you consider the number of porters required, not to mention the fact that you have to rappel down a cliff and trek through the jungle just to reach Son Doong's entrance. In order to preserve the wildlife and landscapes of the cave, only 220 permits were issued in 2014. Oxalis is the only outfit with permission to enter the cave.

are hardly worth the effort, as the long drive to and from the park eats up most of your time. Staying closer to the park offers you the chance to experience Phong Nha in greater depth. On longer excursions, you may find yourself wading into a subterranean river, rappelling down a rock face, or camping out in a cave. While these adventures are a little more expensive than most, the quality of the park's conservation efforts and the expertise of local caving companies more than justify the price tag.

Visit Phong Nha between February and September, when the weather allows for full access to its underground attractions. Rainy season, particularly the months of October and November, can be restrictive, as rivers rise and the area's rainfall renders some of the more adventurous options unavailable. Phong Nha is a budding tourism destination, so don't expect to find five-star hotels or fine dining. Travel to and from the area can require more time and money due to its remoteness, but those who do so will find this destination one of the most memorable in Vietnam.

Sights

This area is teeming with caves, both within the national park and beyond to the Laotian border. The most famous and accessible of these is Phong Nha Cave, which, along with nearby Paradise Cave and the Nuoc Mooc Eco-Trail, are affordable and do not require a guide to visit. These are good options for those short on both money and time.

Single- and multi-day guided excursions can be arranged to Hang En, known for its resident swallows, and the Tu Lan cave system, a series of subterranean passages outside of the park.

PHONG NHA CAVE

Though it's no longer the king of the park's underground attractions, **Phong Nha Cave** (6:30am-5:30pm daily, VND80,000 plus boat fee) remains the most visited spot in the area. Accessible only by boat, the echoing chambers of this cavern have been common knowledge for centuries. As early as the late 1800s, a missionary by the name of Leopold Cadiere ventured into the low opening just beyond Son

Trach village with nothing more than a small wooden boat and a light. The Frenchman made it just over a quarter-mile into the darkness before turning back; while inside, he discovered a set of ancient Cham etchings, suggesting that the cave had been in use well before Cadiere's discovery. It wasn't until 1924 that another adventurer, an English astronomer, ventured almost a full mile into its recesses and back.

Tourism to the site began in the colonial era, when a handful of wealthy French came to behold Phong Nha, but this, too, met an abrupt end during the Franco-Vietnam and American wars, when the cave was re-purposed as a weapons cache and hideout for Viet Minh and north Vietnamese troops. The next expedition into Phong Nha didn't occur until 1990, when Howard Limbert and the British Cave Research Association wandered the full length of the cave.

Phong Nha reaches 272 feet from the riverbed to the ceiling. To get to the cave, hop on a boat from the dock near the **park ticket office** (tel. 05/2367-7323, www.phongnhatourism.com.vn, 7am-5pm daily), where you'll buy your ticket to the cave and pay for the boat ride. These small wooden vessels travel down a little river, going just over a quarter-mile into the cave before stopping on a sandy embankment inside. From here, wander through a maze of artificially lit and oddly shaped stalactites, stalagmites, and other formations. Hop back onto the boat to return to Son Trach village from here. Between the boat docks and the mouth of the cave, you can also swing by **Tien Son Cave** (VND40,000), a smaller grotto discovered in 1935 and newly outfitted with a wooden boardwalk and an extensive lighting system, though Phong Nha is the more worthwhile of the two attractions. Let your boat driver know if you'll be visiting Tien Son so you're not left behind at the caves. Signing up for a discovery tour through the national park lets visitors head over a mile inside in the cavern, with options to travel by either kayak or wooden boat.

Boats cost VND320,000 for the entire 14-seat vessel; the more people ride, the lower the price per person. Link up with fellow travelers outside the ticket office in order to minimize costs. Try to visit either mid-morning or later in the afternoon, around 2pm or 3pm, as large tour groups come through just after lunch.

PARADISE CAVE

Thirteen miles from the park's visitors center, **Paradise Cave (Dong Thien Duong)** (7am-5pm daily, VND120,000) is one of five entrances into the Vom cave system and an increasingly popular spot for travelers in the area, as it lacks the over-the-top lighting that takes away from some of Phong Nha's natural appeal. Though it was originally discovered in 1992 by members of the British Cave Research Association, researchers failed to map the cave entrance and later lost its location. Thankfully, locals were able to pinpoint the entrance once more in 2005 and, after further research, experts explored the entire subterranean chamber, which spans two miles.

Paradise Cave is one of the few sights in the park that can be visited independently. From Phong Nha village, take the Ho Chi Minh West highway, stopping at the ticket booth before carrying on to the entrance. A sign bears the cave's Vietnamese name where the road veers off onto a smaller concrete path. Past the entrance gate, there's a 15- to 20-minute walk before you reach the cave itself, following a paved route through the forest and up a mountainside; electric car services are also available along this road (VND60,000 pp), but the vehicles only go as far as the foot of the hill.

The effort is rewarded by the initial descent into Paradise Cave: from the very top, a long, winding wooden staircase, dimly lit by solitary, glowing bulbs, ferries you deeper and deeper into the cavern, whose soaring ceilings dwarf the large viewing platform below. While you'll be forced to take extra care on your way down, as the steps are often damp and slippery, this affords you plenty of time to get a glimpse of the eerie, ridged formations and towering stalagmites that line the wooden walkway. Regular visitors can wade just over a half-mile into the cave, while the national park's tours bring you all the way to its end. Once you've reached the far end of the path, make the return trip back up to the entrance before shuffling down a total of 518 steps back to the jungle path. Thanks to its rapidly growing popularity, trips to Paradise Cave are best timed during the week and either earlier or later in the day, avoiding lunch time, as this is when most tour groups come through.

NUOC MOOC ECO-TRAIL

The **Nuoc Mooc Eco-Trail** (7am-5pm daily, VND50,000 adults, VND30,000 children, plus kayak hire) may offer a little less wow factor than some of Phong Nha's other sights, but it's believed that the rushing waters of its natural spring may signal an even bigger cave in the area, dwarfing the mammoth chambers of Son Doong. If experts are correct, this waterway could lead through a subterranean cavern that winds all the way to Laos. For the time being, Nuoc Mooc is a good spot to enjoy a leisurely walk among the trees. Visitors are allowed to swim in the blue waters of the spring. If you're keen to paddle around, kayaks (VND100,000 per hour) can be rented from the park. The trail is en route to Paradise Cave, just off the main road.

DARK CAVE

Branching off of the Chay River, **Dark Cave** (7am-5pm daily, VND80,000 plus VND300,000 boat hire) is, as you might imagine, without the lighting system of its sister caves at Phong Nha and Paradise, making for a more authentic experience as you wade into the pitch-black cavern's large underground lake. Visitors float along a modest waterway to reach the mouth of the passage, hopping out to wander through its soaring 262-foot chamber, which carries on for nearly 1.5 miles in the darkness. While it is possible to go it alone, the cave can be tricky to find and most people prefer to hop on a guided tour, either through the national park headquarters or on Phong Nha Farmstay's caving day trip.

HANG EN

A new attraction in the park, **Hang En** was first explored in May 2011 and opened to visitors only a few months later. The mile-long cavern is home to scores of swallows, which nest in the far reaches of the subterranean chamber, and leads onto the river valley that holds the mouth of Son Doong. Its entrance,

Paradise Cave

a staggering 459 feet across, and the sheer size of Hang En's interior make it among the largest caverns in the world. Hang En can only be reached by guided tour, but those who do will have the opportunity to trek through thick, untouched jungle, stop by some of the most remote villages in Vietnam, spend the night inside a cave, and reach the river valley that leads onto Son Doong. Both the national park and Oxalis (Son Trach village, tel. 05/2367-7678, www.oxalis.com.vn, 7:30am-11:30am and 1:30pm-5:30pm Mon.-Fri., VND1,785,000-8,925,000) run two-day excursions to Hang En.

TU LAN CAVE SYSTEM

The Tu Lan cave system is a 200-hectare karst center just outside of Phong Nha-Ke Bang National Park near the Laotian border. Discovered in 2009 by a group of fishermen, recent expeditions into the caves have led to the discovery of several underground chambers over the last few years, expanding the system even farther. Tu Lan gained worldwide attention when National Geographic photographer Carsten Peter captured a prize-winning shot of Hang Ken, one of Tu Lan's caverns, on film for the magazine. Oxalis (Son Trach village, tel. 05/2367-7678, www.oxalis.com.vn, 7:30am-11:30am and 1:30pm-5:30pm Mon.-Fri., VND1,785,000-8,925,000) exclusively runs one- to four-day trips to Tu Lan, which offer trekking, overnights in the jungle, and plenty of time to explore the caves as well as a host of other impressive aboveground sights.

Tours

Only three outfits operate tours to the area's caves. The most affordable of these options are the Phong Nha-Ke Bang National Park tours (Son Trach village, tel. 05/2367-7323, www.phongnhatourism.com.vn, 7am-5pm daily, VND720,000-7,499,000). The folks at Phong Nha Farmstay (1 km east of Ho Chi Minh Hwy. E., tel. 05/2367-5135, www.phong-nha-cave.com, 7am-8pm daily, VND600,000-4,600,000) arrange slightly pricier one- and two-day trips that are well worth the extra cash, including the service of guides with stronger English skills.

For the crème de la crème of cave tours, book with Oxalis (Son Trach village, tel. 05/2367-7678, www.oxalis.com.vn, 7:30am-11:30am and 1:30pm-5:30pm Mon.-Fri., VND1,785,000-8,925,000), the specialized caving and trekking outfit that has exclusive rights to both Son Doong and the Tu Lan cave system. Though these excursions are expensive, the company spares no cost on expert guides, safety equipment, and transportation.

Accommodations

Most accommodations in Son Trach village are basic but do the job. Rooms are limited, as overnights are becoming the preferred way to visit Phong Nha and the number of hotels hasn't caught up with the demand. Book a bed in advance, particularly during high season.

A handful of small local hotels are clustered along the road not far from the Phong Nha-Ke Bang visitors center offering private rooms on the cheap; more social hostel beds are also available, both in town and at a few nearby homestays. Because this area is on the verge of a tourism boom, accommodation options within the area are rapidly changing and new homestays are opening all the time.

A five-minute walk from the Phong Nha-Ke Bang visitors center, Easy Tiger (TL20, tel. 05/2367-7844, easytigerphongnha@gmail.com, VND160,000 dorm) provides clean, cozy, four-bed dorms outfitted with mosquito nets and personal lockers as well as an en suite bathroom with hot water. Downstairs, the lively common area makes a good place to unwind on the patio, grab a beer at the bar, or play a game of pool. Occasional live music and regular happy hour specials take place at night. The hostel rents out bicycles (at exorbitant rates) and books quality tours from its reception desk. Staff can help when arranging onward travel to northern and southern destinations.

One of the first places in the area to cater to foreign travelers, Phong Nha Farmstay

(1 km east of Ho Chi Minh Hwy. E., tel. 05/2367-5135, www.phong-nha-cave.com, VND170,000 dorm, VND600,000-800,000 double) opened in 2010 and has since grown into the area's best-known accommodation. In addition to its 10-bed dorm and private double rooms, the French colonial-inspired building boasts breezy verandas overlooking the surrounding rice paddies, a garden, a swimming pool, a restaurant, and a top-notch travel outfit. Rooms include mosquito nets, air-conditioning, and hot showers.

While the **Van Anh Hotel** (Son Trach village, tel. 05/2367-7260, VND150,000) may not offer the same range of services as its Western-owned counterparts, backpackers looking for a cheap private room can save money by opting for a local hotel like this one or a few of the others also located on this same stretch of road. Rooms offer basic, no-frills accommodation with hot water, air-conditioning, and hard beds. The owners are a friendly local couple and the hotel sits well within striking distance of the national park's visitors center near Easy Tiger, where you'll find Western meals and cold beers readily available.

Food

There is little in the way of dining variety in Phong Nha. Those who opt for a homestay or accommodation farther from the main road upon which the park's visitors center is located will likely be bound to that same place for meals. If you stay closer to town, there are one or two independent options available. **Easy Tiger** (TL20, tel. 05/2367-7844, easytigerphongnha@gmail.com, morning-midnight daily, VND100,000-150,000) is a popular spot for reasonably priced Western food, cold beers and making new travel buddies; the nearby **Cavern Bar** (Son Trach village, cavernbar@gmail.com, 8am-last customer daily, VND15,000-65,000) offers average local meals as well as coffee, tea, and beer.

Information and Services

For local travel information, the **Phong Nha-Ke Bang National Park visitors center/ticket office** (tel. 05/2367-7323, www.phongnhatourism.com.vn, 7am-5pm daily) displays a list of the most affordably priced caving tours and assists with booking its own tours, though English speakers are harder to come by at this office. For more in-depth information, make a stop at **Easy Tiger** (TL20, tel. 05/2367-7844, easytiger-phongnha@gmail.com), whose staff can introduce you to a number of tour options as well as one or two free activities.

The only **ATM** in town is located opposite the national park visitors center and can be temperamental. Bring enough currency to cover all your expenses before arriving in Phong Nha to prevent any problems. If you're interested in taking a caving tour, look into the expected costs beforehand, as these add up quickly.

You'll find Internet access at most hotels, but other basics like mail service will have to wait for a larger destination.

There is no reliable medical service available in Phong Nha. Instead, the closest hospital of any quality lies in Dong Hoi, 40 miles away. For minor injuries, some of the town's accommodations will likely have a first-aid kit and be able to assist; any serious illness or injury will require a 30-minute car trip to the coast.

Getting There

Transportation to and from Phong Nha requires extra planning and cash. Book your bus or train tickets ahead of time. Most vehicles arrive in Dong Hoi, the nearest major city, about 40 miles from the actual park. From there, you can attempt to flag down a taxi or *xe om* driver who is willing to make the trip to Phong Nha (45 minutes, VND600,000), or hop on the once-daily local bus from Dong Hoi station. It is also possible to arrange a place on the shuttle car organized by **Easy Tiger** (TL20, tel. 05/2367-7844, easytigerphongnha@gmail.com, VND120,000-500,000) so long as you book ahead of time. The cost varies depending upon the number of passengers.

BUS

The cheapest way to get to Phong Nha-Ke Bang from Hue is by bus. The least-confusing route is to get to **Dong Hoi station (Ben Xe Dong Hoi)** (corner of Nguyen Huu Canh and Tran Hung Dao, tel. 05/2382-2150, 4am-9pm daily), where you can hop on the **local bus** (up to an hour, VND40,000) to Phong Nha, which leaves once a day at 2pm.

Travelers coming from Hue can arrange transportation straight to the park by hopping on one of the **day tour minibuses** bound for Phong Nha and getting off in town. Most travel agencies in Hue can organize this for you, and the cost usually runs VND220,000-250,000; clarify that you'd like a ride only and not the full day tour. **Hue Hostel** (40 Chu Van An, tel. 012/1662-0015, www.huehostel.com, VND150,000) offers this service at their tour desk. The ride is 3.5-4 hours, leaving from the hostel.

Another great option combines your trip with sightseeing en route: the **Phong Nha Farmstay** (tel. 05/2367-5135, www.phong-nha-cave.com, 7am-8pm daily) offers a **minibus** (VND500,000) to and from Hue that visits a handful of major sights in the DMZ area, allowing you to see the Vinh Moc tunnels and the Ben Hai River, former site of the country's north-south border, on your way to or from Hue. This is the best and most cost-effective option for exploring both Phong Nha and the DMZ, as these sights lie conveniently between the two destinations. The cost covers transportation and a guided tour to some of the less-accessible sights in the area. Minibuses leave Phong Nha at 6:30am daily and arrive in Hue around 12:30pm, making the return trip from Hue at 1pm and getting to Phong Nha by 6:30pm.

TRAIN

The nearest **train station** (Thuan Ly, tel. 05/2383-6789, 24 hours daily) to Phong Nha-Ke Bang National Park is in Dong Hoi. Trains from Hue (three hours, VND399,000-505,000) run a few times daily. From the train station, take the local bus or a taxi to the park.

Getting Around

Son Trach village is about a 10-minute walk from end to end, but for exploring, you'll need a bicycle or motorbike. Bicycles can be rented from some local hotels. With limited options in the area, prices for a daily rental are exponentially greater than in other destinations, with the going rate around VND20,000 per hour or VND120,000 per day. Motorbikes, too, are overpriced. They're available from Van Anh Hotel (Son Trach village, tel. 05/2367-7260) for VND200,000 per day. For longer excursions, hire a car.

BACH MA NATIONAL PARK

With fickle weather patterns and a slow pace of development, **Bach Ma National Park** (tel. 05/4387-1330, www.bachmapark.com.vn, 7am-5:30pm daily, VND40,000) sees fewer visitors than some of its more famous counterparts, but the views from atop Bach Ma mountain, overlooking Lang Co and the sparkling East Sea, are worth the extra effort for birders and nature enthusiasts. Fourteen miles from the coast, the park sits between Danang and Hue, crisscrossed with a half-dozen hiking trails through its heavily forested lowlands and up to the summit of Bach Ma, 4,750 feet above sea level. Though it didn't become an official member of Vietnam's national parks until 1991, the 22,000-hectare park has welcomed visitors since the early 1930s, when the French built a hill station (mountain retreat town) halfway up its namesake mountain, complete with a resort, swimming pool, and tennis courts. Vietnam's tumultuous struggle for independence cut short the holiday in the mid-1940s, and Bach Ma spent the next few decades as a strategic military outpost, working for both U.S. and Vietnamese forces before the end of the American War in 1975.

Today, Bach Ma's flora and fauna serve a small but growing number of avid ornithologists and wildlife watchers. Nearly 250 bird species nest in the park's forests, several endemic species among them, including the Annam partridge and the Edwards' pheasant, previously thought to be extinct until its rediscovery just outside the park boundaries in 1996. Bach Ma also qualifies as an area of great importance for plant life, with well over a thousand different species of flora packed into its diverse landscapes, which range from coastal lagoons to mountainous forests dotted with a series of rushing waterfalls. A few dozen mammals and other creatures roam the area, namely several varieties of monkey.

While most travelers prefer to visit the park from Hue, 42 miles north, there's no reason you can't make Danang your point of departure, as it's equidistant from Bach Ma's headquarters. The best time to visit is March-September, before the leeches come out. Being in one of the wettest regions of the country, rain is a year-round affair here, so it's best to keep a close eye on the weather, as the forecast can change at the drop of a hat. Warm clothes and water-resistant garments are always a wise choice. Birders will appreciate the park's overnight facilities since you'll have to rise early to make the most out of your wildlife-watching time here.

Sights and Recreation

The main activity on most trips to Bach Ma is hiking. A collection of six short footpaths spider off the main road up to the summit, taking adventurers deep into the forest, where dozens of streams and waterfalls add to the secluded beauty of the park. The most popular of these routes is **Rhododendron Trail,** a mile-long path that leads to the rushing Do Quyen Waterfall. Visitors are free to admire the view from above or brave the 689 steps down to the bottom of the 984-foot drop, though you will have to climb back up. Other pathways, such as the **Five Lakes Trail,** meander past a series of freshwater pools where visitors are free to jump in and have a swim, while the route up to Hai Vong Dai summit affords stunning views of the coast on a clear day. Not far from the peak, you'll find the deserted remains of Bach Ma's modest hill station, including a now-empty post office and several rundown villas, as well as a small network of tunnels

used by the north Vietnamese army from 1973 until the war's end.

While none of these hikes require a guide, it's wise to use one, as getting lost is easy in the dense forest. You'll also want to stay on the marked trails since this park is still in the early stages of its development and, with a past that includes heavy military involvement, unexploded ordnance may still be around. The **visitors center** (7am-5:30pm daily) at the park entrance arranges English-speaking guides for travelers, provided you call ahead of time; they also stock a few English-language brochures and other helpful handouts.

Accommodations

Visitors who wish to overnight in the park and get an early start on the following day are free to do so. Bach Ma offers a more conventional campsite along with two bare-bones **guesthouses** (VND300,000-500,000 double), one at the base of the mountain near the visitors center and another near the summit. Rooms are damp, given the constant rainfall in the area, but they come with hot water. Advanced bookings are a good idea, and it's easiest to book through a tour company in Hue for language purposes.

Food

Bach Ma's sole on-site restaurant, near the visitors center, prepares just about any Vietnamese dish you request, catering to vegetarians and other dietary restrictions, though you'll have to order your meals in advance (through your tour guide). With a limited number of patrons, the kitchen only opens upon request, and often shuts down for the day by 7pm.

Getting There

Bach Ma National Park can easily be visited from Hue in a single day, whether by bus, car, motorbike, or guided tour. Finding the park entrance is straightforward, with no more than a single turn off Highway 1. Motorbikes and other vehicles are forbidden from driving up the steep road to Bach Ma's summit.

Arrange transportation to the top from the visitors center (via a park-approved vehicle) or make your way on foot.

BUS

While it's possible to reach the park via local bus, this option requires more time and patience. Travelers can hop on a bus from either Hue (30 miles) or Danang (50 miles), disembarking in Phu Loc town. From there, you'll have to commission a *xe om* driver for the remaining two-mile drive to the park (around VND40,000-50,000).

HIRED VEHICLES

For private transportation, travelers can hire both cars and motorbikes in Hue. From the city it's a straight shot down Highway 1 before turning off the main road in Phu Loc town (20-30 minutes). It's another two miles to the park from here. Bring a map as you'll likely need to ask for directions. You'll see signs for the park on the side of the highway. A day's rental costs around VND600,000.

It's also possible to hire a *xe om* driver directly from Hue, though the fare is steep (starting at VND400,000), and you'll have to negotiate a rate for the driver to wait while you're in the park.

TOURS

The simplest option, particularly for solo travelers, is to hire a guide directly from Hue and sign up for a day tour. Due to the relative anonymity of Bach Ma, only private tours are offered. Reliable companies like **Hue To Go** (tel. 09/7357-1166, www.huetogotours.com, VND987,000) provide motorbike transportation and amiable, experienced guides to ferry you to and from the site. Most other independent companies also arrange private excursions upon request.

Danang

While it's often overlooked by travelers zipping from Hue to Hoi An or vice versa, Danang's sleek, sky-high towers and cosmopolitan riverfront offer an optimistic glimpse into the country's future. Surrounded by rolling mountains and a pristine coastline, this sophisticated city retains the telltale markers of urban Vietnamese life—street food stalls and bustling markets, droves of motorbikes, and modest, family-run shops alongside trendy new buildings—but trades the frenzy of Hanoi's narrow streets and Saigon's overcrowded neighborhoods for a more organized and efficient version of chaos.

The Danang Museum and the Museum of Cham Sculpture can fill an afternoon, while nearby My Khe Beach and the haunting white figure of Quan Am across the sea at Linh Ung Pagoda provide a stunning shoreline upon which to relax. The city may not boast dozens of historical sights or the array of local cuisine found in neighboring cities, but its casual atmosphere and natural landscapes make mellow Danang an easy place to love, worth at least a day of your time.

Western Danang boasts the majority of the city's museums, dining, and nightlife. While this neighborhood is farther from the beach, its central location offers more services and amenities. Far quieter and more spread out, the eastern side of the city sits directly on the beach and offers accommodations that live up to the prices, unlike some of the city's downtown hotels. Stick to the area south of Pham Van Dong for a more concentrated area where you won't need to walk so much in order to find restaurants or other services.

While some prefer to just make a day trip into town from Hoi An, travelers can also stay a night or two to fully appreciate the nearby beach. Danang experiences heavy rainfall and severe storms in September-December. The city is at its best in February-May, when temperatures are reasonably warm and skies

Danang and Vicinity

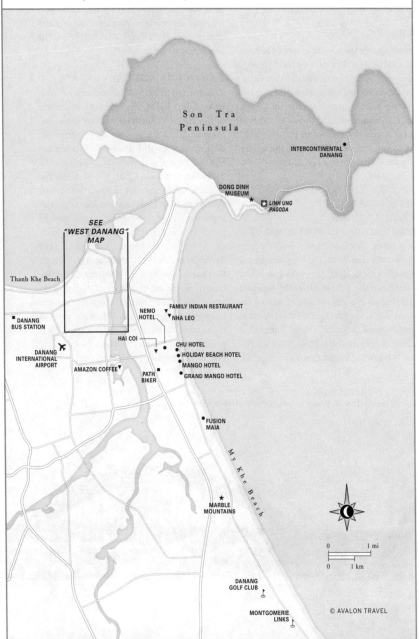

Son Tra Peninsula

INTERCONTINENTAL
DANANG

DONG DINH
MUSEUM
LINH UNG
PAGODA

SEE
"WEST DANANG"
MAP

Thanh Khe Beach

FAMILY INDIAN RESTAURANT

NEMO
HOTEL   NHA LEO

DANANG
BUS STATION

HAI COI   CHU HOTEL
DANANG   HOLIDAY BEACH HOTEL
INTERNATIONAL   MANGO HOTEL
AIRPORT   AMAZON COFFEE   GRAND MANGO HOTEL
          PATH
          BIKER

FUSION
MAIA

My Khe Beach

MARBLE
MOUNTAINS

0   1 mi

0   1 km

DANANG
GOLF CLUB

MONTGOMERIE
LINKS   © AVALON TRAVEL

are clear. The summer months are filled with good weather, though it really heats up around July and August.

SIGHTS

Spread out over the downtown area, the coast, and nearby Son Tra peninsula, Danang's sights are mostly ornamental, providing pleasant photo ops alongside a bit of history. Centrally located attractions like the Dragon Bridge, the museum, and the local cathedral are easily reached on foot in the downtown area. If you stay near the beach, you will require the assistance of a taxi or motorbike to get into town.

West Danang
DRAGON BRIDGE

The 2013-built **Dragon Bridge** (Vo Van Kiet and Nguyen Van Linh) spans nearly a half-mile over the Han River. The long, slender yellow body of the bridge's namesake dragon arcs up and down along the length of the structure, providing an eye-catching sight during the day. At night, the real spectacle takes place, as the dragon's 15,000 LED lights come to life, turning an array of colors throughout the evening. Weekend visitors can see a pyrotechnic display every Saturday and Sunday night around 9pm, when the creature's sea-facing head spits out fireballs, followed by powerful water cannons spraying from the dragon's mouth. Look for the crowd that gathers at the bridge to watch the show.

DANANG CATHEDRAL

Constructed in 1923 and designed by French priest Louis Vallet, the pale pink bell tower of the **Danang Cathedral** (156 Tran Phu, mass in Vietnamese 5am and 5pm weekdays, mass in English 10am Sun.) stands 229 feet tall, topped with a rooster, earning it the nickname "Chicken Church" among locals. Its grand Gothic exterior matches that of most European-built cathedrals in Vietnam, rising above a large courtyard that separates the building from Tran Phu street while, out back, an alcove dedicated to the Virgin Mary sits hidden at the corner of the property. Though the church is not actually open outside of mass hours, you can get the gist by admiring its exterior architecture, or catch a glimpse of the indoors during a service. While the gates at the front of the building are often closed, it is possible to enter from the office of the Danang Diocese next door.

Danang's famous Dragon Bridge slithers across the Han River.

statue of Quan Am at Linh Ung Pagoda

DANANG MUSEUM

In every province, there is a government-run museum that offers a brief flash of the region's past, present, and future. The large and modern **Danang Museum** (24 Tran Phu, tel. 0511/388-6236, btdn@danang.gov.vn, 8am-11:30am and 2pm-4:30pm Tues.-Sun., free) is truly a cut above the rest. With three floors of informative exhibits and ample English signage, this museum is one of the city's more interesting sights. The first floor features everything from Sa Huynh jewelry and ceramics dating back a thousand years or more to displays on fishing practices and local burial rituals associated with whales, while the second and third levels showcase a collection of artifacts from the French and American wars that is more extensive and informative than others in the region. Customs and traditions of the area's ethnic minorities are included, providing insight into some of Vietnam's lesser-known cultures.

The museum is the historical site of Dien Hai Rampart, a military fort originally constructed in 1813 near the Danang port, which was moved 10 years later to its current location. The building itself is a modern construction, but you can still see the stone walls that once bordered the original rampart encircling the museum grounds.

MUSEUM OF CHAM SCULPTURE

Danang's **Museum of Cham Sculpture** (2 2 Thang 9, tel. 0511/347-0114, www.cham-museum.danang.vn, 7am-5:30pm daily, VND40,000) is the most complete and well-preserved collection of Cham artifacts in the country. Founded in 1919 by French archaeologist Henri Parmentier, the museum showcases dozens of sculptures, friezes, and other engravings from as far back as the 7th century alongside valuable information on Cham history and Hinduism. The sprawling ground-floor displays are separated into geographic sections, grouping each collection by the site at which it was discovered. The museum does an impressive job of organizing the sculptures, blending columns and pieces of sandstone and terra cotta frieze into the building itself. Particularly for those who plan to visit the Cham ruins at My Son or along the south-central coast, this is a must-see, as it helps patrons to appreciate just how detailed and impressive the towering structures were during the height of the Cham empire.

East Danang
★ LINH UNG PAGODA

Visible from Danang's My Khe Beach, the awe-inspiring figure of Quan Am, a Buddhist bodhisattva and the most important female figure in Buddhism, at **Linh Ung Pagoda** (Hoang Sa, sunrise-sunset daily, free) is enough to make you do a double-take as you lounge on shore. Rising up from the lush greenery of Son Tra peninsula, this imposing statue, the tallest of its kind in Vietnam, looks out over the gentle curve of My Khe and is believed to protect the coast and its fishermen from harm. At 30 stories tall, this version forms a trio of Quan Am statues together with two statues at two other Linh Ung Pagodas (on Marble Mountain and atop Ba Na Hill) outside of Danang. The trio is thought to act as protectors of the region.

Though you'll pass the large and colorful main entrance to Linh Ung first, visitors enter the pagoda complex through a side road just past the gate. From here, a set of stone steps leads up to the main hall of worship, a vibrant and decorative building flanked by nine statues on either side. But the main event is Quan Am herself, standing at the far end of a massive clearing. This area is packed on holidays and weekends with droves of visitors, both foreign and local, who come to pay their respects to the bodhisattva and to take in stunning views of the My Khe shoreline and downtown Danang.

Make your visit to the pagoda in the early morning or late afternoon to avoid the worst of the heat. Dress respectfully—this is one of Danang's more revered religious sites.

BEACHES
My Khe Beach
Danang's most accessible stretch of sand, **My Khe Beach** (Pham Van Dong and Vo Nguyen Giap) is hardly out of town, with only a short distance separating it from the city center, but its four miles of unbroken coast provide a pleasant escape from the urban landscapes farther inland. Bordered by the East Sea Park, a small, shadeless patch of concrete and trees, My Khe is notably clean for a city beach and boasts plenty of room to sunbathe. There are beach chairs for rent (VND20,000-30,000), though you should bargain, as they are sometimes overpriced. Several restaurants and bars are also set up around the shoreline to accommodate hungry and thirsty beach-goers.

You'll spot a few "no swimming" flags in the area: these do not prohibit you from wading into the ocean a short way, but local lifeguards will call you back should you venture too far out. My Khe and the surrounding coast experience strong undertows and can, at times, be dangerous.

Thanh Khe Beach
Hugging the bay just north of the city, **Thanh Khe Beach** (Nguyen Tat Thanh) is a much quieter area than its counterpart on the other side of Son Tra peninsula, with only a few fishermen reeling in the day's catch; but, it is more frequented by Vietnamese tourists during the summertime. Its shores are notably clean and a sea wall separates the area from Nguyen Tat Thanh's racing traffic. Thanks to the peninsula and its protection, Thanh Khe sees calmer waters for swimming and wading than My Khe. There are few amenities available here—just a few restaurants across the road.

ENTERTAINMENT AND EVENTS
Nightlife
Danang's riverfront lights up after dark, making it the go-to spot for locals and foreigners, with plenty of bars and cafés overlooking the water. On the weekends, festivities can run into the early hours of the morning, but most venues wrap up around midnight. Out toward the beach, a more laid-back atmosphere exists, with a few casual hangouts scattered among the local hotels and restaurants.

Equal parts Italian restaurant and hipster garage bar, **Luna Pub** (9A Tran Phu, tel. 0511/389-8939, www.lunadautunno.vn, 11am-1am daily, VND25,000-270,000) offers an endless, pricey list of foreign and domestic beers along with serious cocktails. Occasional live music events take place, as well as some DJ-ing from the hollowed-out truck parked at the back of the restaurant.

Just north of the Han Bridge, **Golden Pine Pub** (52 Bach Dang, tel. 09/3521-0113, goldenpine@gmail.com, 9am-midnight daily, VND25,000-100,000) is a hangout with graffitied wooden furniture, a pool table, cheap beers, and a rotating selection of Western tunes. Its prices and location make it a good

West Danang

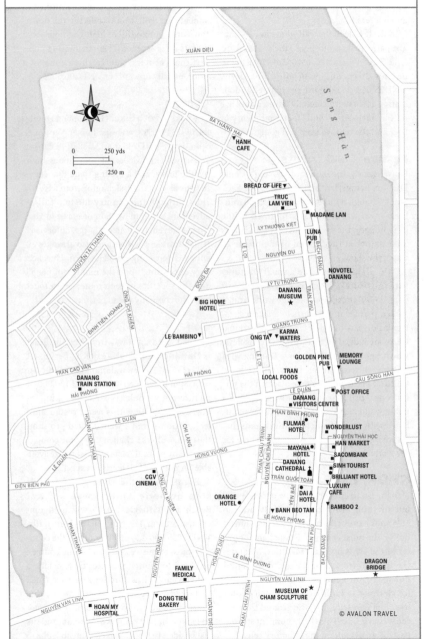

XUÂN DIỆU

Sông Hàn

BA THÁNG HAI

▼ HANH
CAFE

0   250 yds
0   250 m

BREAD OF LIFE ▼

TRUC
LAM VIEN ■

■ MADAME LAN

LÝ THƯỜNG KIỆT

LUNA
PUB
▼

LÊ LỢI

BẠCH ĐẰNG

NGUYỄN DU

● NOVOTEL
DANANG

LÝ TỰ TRỌNG

ĐỐNG ĐA

DANANG
MUSEUM
★

TRẦN PHÚ

● BIG HOME
HOTEL

NGUYỄN TẤT THÀNH

ĐINH TIÊN HOÀNG

ÔNG ÍCH KHIÊM

QUANG TRUNG

LE BAMBINO ▼

ONG TA ▼

KARMA
WATERS

GOLDEN PINE
PUB
▼

MEMORY
LOUNGE
▼

TRẦN CAO VÂN

LÊ LỢI

CẦU SÔNG HÀN

DANANG
TRAIN STATION
■

HẢI PHÒNG

TRAN
LOCAL FOODS
▼

HẢI PHÒNG

LÊ DUẨN

■ POST OFFICE

DANANG
VISITORS CENTER ■

LÊ DUẨN

PHAN ĐÌNH PHÙNG

HOÀNG HOA THÁM

CHI LĂNG

FULMAR
HOTEL ●

WONDERLUST ●

NGUYỄN THÁI HỌC

LÊ DUẨN

HÙNG VƯƠNG

PHAN CHÂU TRINH

NGUYỄN CHÍ THANH

MAYANA ●
HOTEL

HAN MARKET ■

■ SACOMBANK

DANANG
CATHEDRAL ✝

SINH TOURIST ■

● CGV
CINEMA

ÔNG ÍCH KHIÊM

TRẦN QUỐC TOẢN

BRILLIANT HOTEL ▼

ĐIỆN BIÊN PHỦ

LÊ DUẨN

YÊN BÁI

DAI A ●
HOTEL

LUXURY
CAFE ▼

ORANGE
HOTEL ●

▼ BANH BEO TAM

BAMBOO 2 ▼

PHAN THANH

NGUYỄN HOÀNG

HOÀNG DIỆU

LÊ HỒNG PHONG

TRẦN PHÚ

BẠCH ĐẰNG

LÊ ĐÌNH DƯƠNG

DRAGON
BRIDGE
★

FAMILY
MEDICAL ●

NGUYỄN VĂN LINH

NGUYỄN VĂN LINH

■ HOAN MY
HOSPITAL

▼ DONG TIEN
BAKERY

PHAN CHÂU TRINH

HOÀNG DIỆU

MUSEUM OF
CHAM SCULPTURE ★

© AVALON TRAVEL

spot to unwind along the riverfront. The staff are friendly. Happy hour specials are usually on offer as well as a few snacks, sandwiches, and burgers.

A lively hole in the wall whose low ceilings are patterned in old beer labels, **Bamboo 2** (2 Thai Phien, tel. 09/0554-4769, www. bamboo2bar.com, 9am-midnight daily, VND25,000-85,000) offers cramped indoor seating downstairs, sidewalk tables, a pool bar on the open-air second floor, and plenty of beer and cocktails to keep you going.

Festivals and Events

On weekends, the mouth of Danang's iconic Dragon Bridge **breathes fire** (9pm Sat.-Sun.). Though it's a short display (15-20 minutes)—two sets of fireballs, followed by the dragon spraying water—locals and visitors alike gather at the far end of the bridge to watch the show.

Two nights a year, the annual **Danang International Fireworks Competition** (Apr. 29-30) brings together the world's most skilled pyrotechnic experts to create a spectacular display over the Han River. National teams are judged on their respective displays, which light up the skies above Danang with an array of reds, greens, blues, and yellows. Cultural performances take place on the waterfront. April 30 is also Reunification Day, a public holiday in Vietnam, and this fact combined with the firework festivities means that it's wise to book ahead if you plan to come for the festival.

SHOPPING

Danang isn't a city for shopping or souvenirs, but anything of interest will likely turn up at **Han Market** (Bach Dang, sunrise-sunset daily), the most centrally located and popular of the city's open-air facilities. Meander the stalls of fresh produce and dried squid downstairs or head up to the second floor for clothing and other goods. Watch out for the *mam tom* section of the ground floor on the western side: This thick, pungent shrimp paste is an assault on the olfactory senses.

SPORTS AND RECREATION

Recreational activities are mostly limited to sunbathing, golf, and wandering the downtown area. A handful of high-end hotels and resorts offer access to their swimming pools or fitness centers, though these come at a price, usually upwards of VND200,000.

Cycling

The folks at **Path Biker** (141 Chuong Duong, tel. 09/1349-0718, www.pathbiker.com, 7am-5pm daily, VND735,000-2,520,000) can set you up with knowledgeable tour guides, high-quality bikes, and a cycling route that caters to your level of fitness, ranging from leisurely rides through the countryside to a full-on adventure south to My Son or north to Hue. Chan Nguyen, the man in charge, tailors each trip to travelers' wishes and also arranges excursions departing from Hoi An or Hue. Fees vary depending upon the number of people and the specifics of each route; get in touch with the company ahead of time.

Golf

Perched just a short way from My Khe Beach is **Danang Golf Club** (My Khe Beach, tel. 0511/395-8111, www.dananggolfclub.com, 6am-8pm daily, VND1,375,000-3,120,000), a picturesque 18-hole course overlooking the ocean. Complete with several restaurants, locker rooms, and a well-stocked pro shop, the course offers a challenging game complemented by natural scenery. Lessons are available for golfers of all levels of experience.

Right beside the Danang Golf Club, **Montgomerie Links** (near My Khe Beach, tel. 0510/394-1942, www.montgomerielinks.com, tee times 6am-3pm daily, VND1,035,000-1,725,000) is one of the country's most exclusive and challenging courses, boasting top-notch facilities that include a clubhouse as well as a driving range. Designed by famed golfer Colin Montgomerie, this course regularly makes the number one spot on lists of the best courses in Vietnam and sits just beside My Khe Beach en route to Hoi An.

You may want to steer clear on weekends, as it gets crowded.

ACCOMMODATIONS

Visitors who prefer to take advantage of the beach are better off finding a spot on the eastern side of the river closest to the water, while foodies and city slickers may want to stick to downtown Danang in the west. Wherever you stay, both sides of the Han River are easily reached; without a motorbike, you may find yourself hopping into cabs or onto the back of a *xe om* fairly often, as there are a few miles between the downtown area and the beach.

West Danang
VND210,000-525,000

In a decidedly mid-range city, **Fulmar Hotel** (11 Yen Bai, tel. 0511/381-0808, www.fulmarhotel.com, VND300,000-400,000) is one of the most affordable accommodations on the western side of town. While the rooms are well-kept and stocked with the usual amenities—air-conditioning, hot water, television, and fridge—they are also closet-like in size. If all you're planning to do in your hotel is sleep, this shouldn't be an issue; but if you require more space, look elsewhere.

The charming **Mayana Hotel** (40 Nguyen Thai Hoc, tel. 0511/386-6777, www.mayanahotel.com, VND420,000-567,000, breakfast included) sits just west of the riverfront and provides cozy, well-appointed rooms with ambience. From the gilded handles on the front door to the ornate tiled floors and plush beds, Mayana's decor adds to its character. Amenities include hot water, air-conditioning, TV, a minibar, coffee- and tea-making facilities, and a work desk.

Dai A Hotel (51 Yen Bai, tel. 0511/382-7532, www.daiahotel.com.vn, VND483,000-700,000, breakfast included), a large and inviting property near Danang Cathedral, offers spacious rooms with uninspired decor, but the hotel staff are friendly and the accommodations clean. All accommodations feature air-conditioning, hot water, TV, and a minibar.

VND525,000-1,050,00

Rooms at the **Big Home Hotel** (191 Dong Da, tel. 0511/387-3555, www.bighomehotel.com, VND600,000-1,000,000), with slightly faded accommodations, are clean, tidy, and well-equipped. Amenities include hot water, air-conditioning, TV, a fridge, and Wi-Fi access. Breakfast is served downstairs each morning, among an interesting collection of antique bicycles and Mobylettes.

VND1,050,000-2,100,000

Tucked away in a skinny building just off Thai Phien, the exceptionally welcoming staff and bright corridors of **Orange Hotel** (29 Hoang Dieu, tel. 0511/356-6176, www.danangorangehotel.com, VND1,155,000-1,365,000, breakfast included) are a pleasant introduction to this boutique accommodation. Rooms offer more space than other lodgings in the area and feature hot water, air-conditioning, a minibar, and TV.

Luxurious and elegant, the **Brilliant Hotel** (162 Bach Dang, tel. 0511/322-2999, www.brillianthotel.vn, VND1,670,000-2,110,000, breakfast included) lives up to its name. With unobstructed views of Dragon Bridge and the Han River, each beautifully furnished room includes plush beds and floor-to-ceiling windows, hot water, air-conditioning, a minibar, television, and access to the hotel's swimming pool and fitness center. A spa and several restaurants are attached to this four-star accommodation.

OVER VND2,100,000

An emblem of the city's fast-paced development and growing business community, every room in the **Novotel Danang Premier** (36 Bach Dang, tel. 0511/392-9999, www.novotel-danang-premier.com, VND3,192,000-4,893,000) offers beautiful views of the Han River from its waterfront location. Rooms are outfitted with large, plush beds, hot water, air-conditioning, TV, wifi access, tea- and coffee-making facilities, a balcony, and a minibar. Additional gadgets like in-room espresso machines and iPod docking stations are included in the more upscale offerings. The Novotel runs several bars and restaurants, including a panoramic bar on the building's 35th floor, as well as a swimming pool for guests.

East Danang

VND210,000-525,000

Named after a beloved Pixar character, **Nemo Hotel** (100/2 Nguyen Van Thoai, tel. 0511/395-1951, levy@danangnemohotel.com, VND350,000-500,000) features modern accommodations with large windows and plenty of light. Each room's separate all-glass toilet and shower cubicles make for an odd bathroom configuration, but lodgings are clean and well-kept and you'll find the usual amenities here: air-conditioning, hot water, TV, Wi-Fi access, and comfy duvets. The hotel is a short walk from the beach, and its location off the main road minimizes traffic noise.

Located amid a street of popular budget and mid-range accommodations, **Mango Hotel** (50 An Thuong 1, tel. 0511/395-4345, mangohoteldanang@gmail.com, VND400,000-750,000, breakfast included) provides friendly service at a more affordable price than most in the neighborhood. TV, hot water, Wi-Fi access, and air-conditioning are included in the room rate. While not as lavish as its sister hotel on the corner, Mango's excellent location near the beach makes this a worthy spot for budget travelers.

VND525,000-1,050,00

Perched at the end of a string of near-beach-front accommodations, ★ **Grand Mango Hotel** (60 An Thuong, tel. 0511/398-5888, www.grandmangohotel.com, VND750,000-1,000,000) offers well-appointed rooms and friendly service at one of the best prices around. Its rooms run the gamut from comfortable, city-facing standard accommodations to bright, ocean-view digs. Television, Wi-Fi, hot water, air-conditioning, and coffee- and tea-making facilities are included in each room, and the hotel can assist with other services, including transportation and travel. **Chu Hotel** (2-4 An Thuong 1, tel. 0511/395-5123, www.chuhotel.com, VND900,000-1,200,000, breakfast included) sits just behind the mammoth Holiday Beach Hotel and pulls off well-appointed accommodations and a pleasant eatery all in one, with the shaded outdoor patio acting as a café and restaurant while the upper floors house comfortable modern rooms with an antique feel, featuring brass accents and dark, polished wood furniture. Your choice of standard, superior, and deluxe rooms are available, and the usual amenities apply: air-conditioning, Wi-Fi, hot water, television, and a minibar.

OVER VND2,100,000

The opulent **Holiday Beach Hotel** (Vo Nguyen Giap, tel. 0511/396-7777, www.holidaybeachdanang.com, VND2,065,000-12,426,000) is a smaller, more central version of the resorts down the road. From the sparkling, high-ceilinged reception area to plush guest rooms, which feature marble bathrooms, Japanese-imported bathtubs, and NASA-certified mattresses (in addition to the standard amenities), Holiday Beach lives up to its price tag, with extras like complimentary spa services. The hotel boasts several bars and restaurants, a fitness center, daily shuttles to Hoi An, and a large, ground-floor swimming pool as well as a smaller rooftop version.

Son Tra's five-star **Intercontinental Danang** (Son Tra Peninsula, tel. 0511/393-8888, www.danang.intercontinental.com, VND6,048,000-25,200,000) is the peak of luxury. The views are reason enough to spend your time here—the property rolls gently down the side of Son Tra Mountain and onto the beach. It features spacious rooms and lavish suites, along with a spa, fitness center, two swimming pools, several restaurants, and activity centers for kids and teens. Rooms come with a balcony, rainforest shower, vanity sinks, flat-screen TV, iPod docking station, and the standard amenities. Top-tier lodgings include butler service and afternoon tea. Additional activities such as trekking, snorkeling, yoga, tai chi, and kayaking can be arranged.

FOOD

Danang boasts an interesting combination of local and international cuisine. Homegrown dishes like *mi quang* (rice noodle soup with shrimp and pork) and *bun cha ca* (rice noodle soups with fish cakes) make up the city's best local offerings, while one or two European eateries provide sumptuous and authentic fare from across the world.

Cafés and Bakeries

For some excellent Asian-style pastries, try the **Dong Tien Bakery** (93 Nguyen Van Linh, tel. 0511/368-9986, www.dongtienbakery.com.vn, 5am-10:30pm daily, VND5,000-20,000). These tasty treats are more than worth the trek from the riverfront, particularly the mung bean pastries. Dong Tien has another location (15 Dong Da, tel. 0511/389-9191, www.dongtienbakery.com.vn, 5am-10:30pm daily, VND5,000-20,000) near the town center, as well as several farther from the downtown area.

The chic black-and-white storefront of **Wonderlust** (101 Tran Phu, tel. 0511/399-0123, 7:30am-10pm daily, VND15,000-35,000) would not be out of place in North America, with its windowed facade and bright, minimalist interior. Serving both Vietnamese and Western coffee as well as pastries and cupcakes, the café offers just enough space downstairs for a quick cup of joe. There's plenty of room upstairs to spread out and while away an afternoon.

Luxury Cafe (182 Bach Dang, tel. 0511/384-9776, 6am-2am daily, VND20,000-50,000) sits on one of the best corners in town, with a perfect view of Dragon Bridge and the waterfront, plenty of shade, and a nice breeze passing through. Coffee, fruit juices, and other drinks are on the expensive side, but it's the location you pay for. Vietnamese breakfast is served here, and at night the café transforms into a bar until the wee hours of the morning.

Italian and Pizza

Luna Pub (9A Tran Phu, tel. 0511/389-8939, www.lunadautunno.vn, 11am-1am daily, VND110,000-400,000) comes off like an upscale mechanic's garage, though far more chic. With exposed brick and copper piping, a hollowed-out truck-turned-DJ-station, and waitstaff in blue coveralls, this Italian joint serves mouthwatering classics with a quirky bent, such as beef tenderloin with gorgonzola sauce, Nordic pizza, and green lasagna. Homemade pastas, pizza, and hearty fish and meat entrées come out of the large open kitchen. The pub's lengthy menu includes a host of foreign and local beers as well as delectable desserts. A top-notch selection of Italian gelato takes up space on the blackboards behind the bar.

A visit to **Nha Leo** (11 Ha Chuong, tel. 09/3501-9443, 5pm-10pm Tues.-Sun., VND100,000-230,000) feels like discovering a secret, as this modest pizzeria is hidden down an out-of-the-way street and easy to miss. Inside, there is a warm dining room. The food speaks for itself, with an array of heavenly pies, including four-cheese, Moroccan, Camembert, and even banana bacon toppings available. Save room for dessert, as there are usually equally sumptuous cakes on display.

International

Helping to improve the lives of deaf Vietnamese for nearly 10 years, **Bread of Life** (4 Dong Da, tel. 0511/356-5185, www.breadoflifedanang.com, 8:30am-9:30pm Mon.-Sat., VND40,000-200,000) is popular not only for its do-good reputation but for the top-notch pastries, Western breakfasts, vegetarian meals, and Mexican fare to come out of its kitchen. Founded in 2005 by Bob and Kathleen Huff, an expat couple with a long history in Vietnam, the organization has provided hearing-impaired locals with sign language and vocational training as well as English classes, housing, and other services.

Indian

The tasty **Family Indian Restaurant** (231 Ho Nghinh, tel. 09/1400-1984, Familyres.dn@gmail.com, 10am-10:30pm daily, VND55,000-150,000) rounds out the end of a string of budget hotels with delicious Indian fare and friendly service. The menu features a nice range of dishes, including vegetarian cuisine as well as traditional Indian desserts and drinks. The chef prepares each dish with your preferred level of spice, from mild to moderate to flaming hot. Both indoor and outdoor seating is available. A handful of Vietnamese dishes make it onto the menu, though Indian cuisine is the main event here.

French

A genuine French eatery hidden down one of the city's alleys, **Le Bambino** (122/11 Quang Trung, tel. 0511/389-6386, www.lebambino. com, 5pm-10pm daily, VND120,000-475,000) has a menu that lists sumptuous European fare, like lamb shank and foie gras, not to mention a long list of wines. The cozy dining room looks into a small, open courtyard at the center.

Street Food

You'll find plenty of street food along **Nguyen Chi Thanh.** Down the southern end are a few nice *banh cuon* shops, which serve steamed rice-flour crepes with mushroom, Vietnamese cold cuts, fish sauce, and fresh greens. Farther north you'll find some of the city's best *bun cha ca* (rice noodle soup with fish and fish cake).

The humble storefront of **Ong Ta** (113 Nguyen Chi Thanh, tel. 0511/389-8700, 5am-10pm daily, VND25,000) is a well-known vendor of Danang's signature version of *bun cha ca*, featuring assorted greens, and, in this city, tomato and even pumpkin. Portions are generous, so bring your appetite. This particular street is lined with a range of good options in case your meal doesn't fill you up.

The dining room at **Hai Coi** (2 Nguyen Van Thoai, tel. 09/0208-7612, 3pm-1am daily, VND10,000/wing) is nothing more than a collection of low plastic chairs and metal tables, but this lends itself well to a beer-and-chicken restaurant. Sizzling, open-flame barbecues line the sidewalk out front, where you watch your Hanoian-style chicken wings are grilled to perfection, and cases of beer are readily on hand. These finger-licking wings are too good to pass up. With dirt-cheap prices and a lively crowd in the evenings, this is an excellent spot to take in the local atmosphere.

Vegetarian

A proudly vegan establishment, **Karma Waters** (113/10 Nguyen Chi Thanh, tel. 0511/384-9790, 6am-9pm daily, VND20,000-150,000) whips up both Vietnamese and international meatless cuisine with a twist, offering options beyond the usual local vegetarian fare. Items like tofu and tumeric, Indian curries, and tofu-mushroom hamburgers feature on the menu as well as a particularly good vegan coffee and a few gluten-free baked goods. Diners can watch the staff prepare their meal from the open kitchen at the back, or sit up front and take in the laid-back alley life that takes place just outside.

Vietnamese

With both garden and indoor seating, the popular **Tran Local Foods** (4 Le Duan, tel. 0511/375-2779, 7am-10pm daily, VND16,000-99,000) dishes out a variety of Danang specialties in an atmosphere with sufficient levels of kitsch and more lime green than your eyes can handle. From do-it-yourself pork spring rolls, the restaurant's bestselling item, to *mi quang* (rice noodle soup with shrimp and pork), *banh beo* (a steamed rice flour cake), and the incredibly strong *bun mam* (Vietnamese seafood gumbo), Tran's is a popular spot for many Danang residents.

A local favorite, **Truc Lam Vien** (8-10 Tran Quy Cap, tel. 0511/358-2428, www.truclam-vien.com.vn, 6am-10pm daily, VND80,000-250,000) pairs Vietnamese cuisine with a peaceful garden setting, its open-air pavilions modeled in traditional Hue-style architecture. A range of chicken, beef, seafood, and vegetable dishes are served, as well as a few cheaper breakfast options and the usual list of refreshments. Truc Lam Vien is most active at night but also functions as a café during the day and is open for breakfast and lunch.

An inviting yellow building at the end of

Bach Dang, **Madame Lan** (4 Bach Dang, tel. 0511/361-6226, www.madamelan.vn, 6am-10pm daily, VND40,000-330,000) serves an extensive list of local dishes, including *mi quang* (rice noodle soup with shrimp and pork), and plenty of fresh seafood, with an English menu to boot. Its simple wooden furniture and open-air seating are an upmarket take on local street-dining.

INFORMATION AND SERVICES
Tourist Information

For a friendly chat and a wealth of useful information, stop by the **Danang Visitor Center** (32A Phan Dinh Phung, tel. 0511/355-0111, www.danangtourism.gov.vn, 7:30am-11:30am and 1:30pm-5:30pm Mon.-Fri.), whose receptionists are more than happy to chime in with their personal recommendations on restaurants, sights, and the rest. Free maps featuring the city's bus routes and a host of important phone numbers are available. You can also hop on Danang's citywide complimentary Wi-Fi and visit sites like **indanang.com** for more helpful tips.

Danang runs an **assistance hotline** (tel. 0511/355-0111) for foreign visitors that fields anything from general questions to complaints of overcharging and other unbecoming behavior that might tarnish the city's image. This feedback is usually taken seriously, so report any issues.

Banks and Currency Exchange

As one of the country's larger cities, you'll find no shortage of banks in the downtown Danang area. Many financial institutions staff English-speaking employees. For currency exchange and an ATM, visit the local **Sacombank** (130-132 Bach Dang, tel. 0511/358-2612, www.sacombank.com.vn, 7:30am-11:30am and 1:30pm-5pm Mon.-Fri., 7:30am-11:30am Sat.) or other nearby facilities.

Internet and Postal Services

You'll find a **post office** (66 Bach Dang, tel. 0511/384-5054, 6:30am-7pm daily) on the riverfront that can assist with your needs. Danang is one of the only cities in Vietnam to provide complimentary Wi-Fi throughout town.

Medical Services

Danang's medical facilities are notably better than most in the area. **Family Medical Practice Danang** (50-52 Nguyen Van Linh, tel. 0511/358-2699, www.vietnammedical-practice.com, 24 hours daily) staffs Western doctors and receives patients at its clinic in addition to running a 24-hour emergency hotline. **Hoan My Hospital** (161 Nguyen Van Linh, tel. 0511/365-0676, www.hoanmydanang.com) is the only Vietnamese hospital of any quality that doesn't overcharge foreigners for its medical services.

GETTING THERE
Air

The present-day **Danang International Airport** (DAD, www.danangairportonline.com) is one of the country's nicer facilities (ironically, it is also one of the most contaminated Agent Orange sites in Vietnam), receiving both domestic and international flights daily from **Jetstar** (tel. 0511/364-6646, www.jetstar.com, 9am-5pm daily), **VietJet** (tel. 0511/361-4795, www.vietjetair.com, 8am-5pm daily), and **Vietnam Airlines** (tel. 0511/365-5089, www.vietnamairlines.com, 6:30am-10pm daily).

Flights from Ho Chi Minh City to Danang (a little over an hour, VND480,000-700,000) depart every two hours or so.

Flights from Hanoi to Danang (a little over an hour, VND380,000-700,000) leave with the same frequency as flights from HCMC.

Bus

Local buses from Hoi An and Hue arrive at the gargantuan **Danang Bus Station** (159 Ton Duc Thang, tel. 0511/376-7679), where there are connections to the rest of the country at any hour of the day or night.

From Hoi An, hop off downtown rather

THE CENTRAL PROVINCES
DANANG

than at the bus station. Public vehicles travel the length of Bach Dang, the riverfront street, before turning and heading to the station, which is actually four miles away from the city center. Buses from Hoi An (30 minutes, VND18,000) run 5:30am-6:30pm. Check the fare on the side of the bus to avoid being overcharged.

From Hue (2.5 hours, VND100,000), it's a 60-mile trip.

Private bus companies **Sinh Tourist** (154 Bach Dang, tel. 0511/384-3258, www.thesinh-tourist.vn, 7am-9:30pm daily) and **Hanh Cafe** (105 3 Thang 2, tel. 0511/352-5052, www.hanhcafe.vn, 7:30am-6pm daily) have offices in Danang. Buses let off at their respective office locations. Both outfits book onward transportation to Hue and other cities. There is also a **Mailinh Express** (tel. 0511/379-2929, www.mailinhexpress.vn, 6am-8pm daily) counter at the bus station that does daily runs to less-visited interior cities like Buon Ma Thuot, Kon Tum, and Quy Nhon. **Phuong Trang** (tel. 0511/378-6786, www.futabuslines.com.vn, 6am-9pm daily) also does trips down to Quy Nhon and Nha Trang.

Train

The major stop for the central region on the country's Reunification Line, Danang's **train station** (200 Hai Phong, tel. 0511/382-3810, 7am-5pm daily) links the city with the rest of the coast. There is no train service connecting Danang with Hoi An, making Danang a popular transit hub for train travelers.

There are four daily trains from Hue to Danang (2.5 hours, VND336,000-420,000), two in the morning and two in the evening.

The ride from Nha Trang to Danang (10 hours, VND714,000-1,050,000) is a long one, so consider buying a higher-priced ticket for a more comfortable seat. There are five daily departures.

GETTING AROUND
Taxis and *Xe Om*

You'll find *xe om* drivers near the local market and on every other street corner. For taxis,

you can flag down a cab from **Mailinh** (tel. 0511/356-5656), **Hoang Long** (tel. 0511/327-2727), or **Vinasun** (tel. 0511/368-6868).

Buses

Danang's **public bus system** has five separate routes that crisscross the city and its surroundings. A shuttle to My Son runs 5:30am-5pm daily. Bring along the exact fare, as you are not likely to receive change from the fee collector. Look out for the posted price on the side or back of the bus. When traveling around the city, fares run around VND5,000. While the city's central bus station is far from the downtown area, you'll find that most buses pass by the riverfront, so you may want to catch a bus from there rather than making the trek to the station.

Vehicles for Hire

Renting a motorbike in Danang is easily done, but not always at a reasonable price. Many rental outfits charge upwards of VND120,000 per day, and not all vehicles come in great shape. Your best bet is to head to **Mama's Motos** (4 Dong Da, tel. 0511/356-5185, www.breadoflifedanang.com, 8:30am-9:30pm Mon.-Sat., VND80,000-140,000), operated out of the Bread of Life restaurant, where the owner Kathleen can set you up with a safe and reliable motorbike. You'll need a photocopy of your passport and visa in order to get a vehicle.

MARBLE MOUNTAINS

A collection of limestone karsts sprouting up from amid the modest houses and rice paddies beyond Non Nuoc Beach, the famous **Marble Mountains** (7 miles southeast of Danang, 7am-5:30pm daily, VND15,000) are each named after an element—earth, water, fire, metal, and wood—and house a popular array of religious sites. Thuy Son (Water Mountain) is the largest of the five and offers the most impressive assortment of Buddhist relics.

From the foot of Thuy Son, visitors scale a set of stone steps up to **Linh Ung Pagoda,** one of the oldest religious venues in Danang.

Built sometime in the 15th century, this colorful, mosaic-clad structure was rebuilt in 1825 by emperor Minh Mang, a staunch Buddhist who spent several prayer stints in these mountains during his reign.

Around the back of the pagoda is a set of caves, which house several statues of the Buddha in different positions, as well as the mountain's oldest relic, a 7th-century Cham Hindu altar, complete with sandstone gate and a small *linga-yoni* statue. Off to the right is a clearing known as Chess Cave, where the emperor used to play board games during his free time in the mountains.

Up another level of stairs, you'll come to the seven-tiered Xa Loi tower, which houses yet another altar as well as affording some pleasant views of the surrounding area. This is where the elevator (VND15,000) lets off if you prefer not to walk up the first half of the stone staircase. From here, follow the path past the tower to Van Thong Cave, a larger grotto from which you can access the mountain's highest point. Though the path is treacherous—its smooth stones make for limited traction when climbing up the dark passageway to the top, and there are plenty of low-hanging outcroppings on which to hit your head—clamber through the passageway and you'll be

rewarded with Marble Mountains' best views of Non Nuoc Beach and the beautiful landscapes of the coast.

The way back down from Van Thong is more forgiving, with a proper staircase built into the mountainside that leads to the last and largest of the caves, a vaulted room in the heart of the mountain decorated with altars to Buddha and Quan Am, and populated by unusual natural rock formations. During the American War, this grotto served as a hospital and administrative office for the north Vietnamese army.

Opposite the grotto is Linh Ung's counterpart, Tam Thai Pagoda, an equally intricate structure, as well as a west-facing lookout from which to see the nearby town and the remaining Marble Mountains.

Time your visit for the early morning or late afternoon to avoid the heat of the day. As a popular place for both foreign and local visitors, the mountains are busier on weekends and holidays, in part because of their religious significance but also thanks to the booming trade in marble statues that takes place at the base of the mountain. Once a humble, stone-sculpting village, the area around Water Mountain is now teeming with vendors selling genuine marble statues and cheaper versions.

view from the Marble Mountains

You may face some aggressive sales pitches, but the scenery and the countless caves make up for the unwanted attention. For more in-depth information, English-speaking guides (VND100,000) can be hired at the ticket office (beside the steps leading up to the mountain). The Marble Mountains are between Hoi An and Danang and can be reached by taxi, *xe om,* or public bus.

★ HAI VAN PASS

Rising above the pristine white-sand beaches north of Danang, Hai Van Pass is one of cen-tral Vietnam's most touted natural attractions. Over 13 miles, this stunning cliffside road traces the edge of the Truong Son Mountains, overlooking verdant, sloping hills that sink into the turquoise waters of Lang Co Bay. Up top, the pass is nothing special, though a few old military bunkers are leftover from Vietnamese, French, and American forces. The drive itself and the unbelievable scenery are what make Hai Van Pass a must-see.

Visitors can visit the pass by hiring a *xe om* in Danang. It's also possible to do the drive yourself by motorbike, but with the narrow roads and the beautiful scenery, it's much more enjoyable to let an experienced driver take the wheel. The drive to the top takes about an hour and costs more than the average *xe om* ride (around VND500,000 for the round-trip from Danang). Easy Rider-style guides can be hired to take travelers on the drive.

The same things that account for Hai Van's incredible scenery also make the road a dan-gerous one. A small guardrail lines the far side of the asphalt; beyond lies a sheer drop. Caution and focus are a must on this road, as the occasional bus or motorbike can come around a corner at breakneck speed. It's best to stop for photos only on stretches where the shoulder has been widened to accommodate vehicles. You can always walk back to your desired photo spot, if necessary. Factoring in photo stops, budget around three hours to get to the pass, do the drive, and return to Danang.

BA NA HILL STATION

Twenty-three miles west of Danang and 4,878 feet above sea level, Ba Na Hill Station (23 miles west of Danang, tel. 0511/379-1999, www.banahills.com.vn, 7:30am-9pm daily, VND500,000/cable car, VND800,000/day tour) is the central provinces' answer to Dalat. Since the early 1900s, this French-established resort has served as a rustic getaway for the well-to-do of Danang and Hue, complete with beautiful mountain vistas and a much cooler climate than the coast. In its heyday, Ba Na was on the verge of becoming a proper town, outfitted with schools, post offices, hotels, and restaurants. While its long-term residents have dwindled to almost zero, this mountain-top retreat remains a popular domestic tour-ist destination best known for its scenic cable car ascent, one of the world's longest (and a Guinness World Record holder), as well as Linh Ung Pagoda, one of a trio of Buddhist worship halls of the same name in the region.

Cable cars hold 10 people at a time, and travels 4,500 feet to the top of Ba Na at about 20 feet per second. Once at the summit, the principal attraction is the scenery. There are some amusement rides, a wine cave, and a re-sort for overnight guests, but day trips are rec-ommended, as the actual hill station does not provide much in the way of activities.

If you've got your own set of wheels, it's possible to drive to the Ba Na cable car, though it can be tricky to find. Those who don't have their own transportation may want to opt for the day tour (VND800,000); the base of the cable car is roughly 17 miles west of town and a taxi is not worth the cost. Tickets can be pur-chased in both Danang and Hoi An. The Ba Na tour company (72 Nguyen Chi Thanh, Danang tel. 09/0576-6777, www.banahills. com.vn, 7:30am-5pm daily) can assist with queries.

LANG CO

Wedged between a freshwater lagoon on one side and the East Sea on the other, Lang Co is a sleepy fishing village built around a six-mile stretch of Highway 1 and hidden from view by the Truong Son Mountains. Its beautiful combination of saltwater and freshwater, lush green hills, and sandy beaches make this an increasingly popular spot for budget travelers and resort-goers alike to enjoy a more unassuming destination, where things are still quiet and the main attraction is the beach. Most visitors stick around just for the day or overnight, long enough to get in some sunbathing before continuing on to other destinations like the tourist-heavy Hoi An or bustling Hue.

Thanks to its proximity to Danang, a visit to Lang Co can be done as a day trip. The drive to and from the city is just over an hour. With the awe-inspiring Hai Van Pass in between, the journey itself is part of the fun. If possible, try to time your visit in March-August, the warmer, drier months. Rainy season, September-February, can be cold and gray, with temperatures slipping as low as the mid-60s and high winds sweeping through town. July and August see sweltering temperatures.

Beaches

The one and only reason travelers stop in Lang Co is for its beach. While the shores of this small fishing village are not unlike those of My Khe in Danang, Lang Co offers a cheaper, more local option that some prefer over its busier southern neighbors. The six miles of sand along the eastern edge of **Lang Co Beach** are pleasantly deserted, though not without some rubbish here and there. A handful of restaurants are accessible from the beach. From the main road, it's easy to find Lang Co Beach.

Accommodations

For the most part, lodgings in Lang Co are significantly less expensive than Danang. Be prepared for a little less luxury than you might find in a larger place. Budget accommodations are basic and acceptable for a day or two while you're out enjoying the sun. Not all hotels and guesthouses come with English-speaking staff.

UNDER VND210,000

Just opposite Lang Co Beach Resort, **Chi Na Guesthouse** (Loan Ly, Lac Long Quan, tel. 05/4387-4597, VND160,000-200,000) is run by an inviting family and offers decent rooms close to both the lagoon and the beach. The accommodations, with basic furnishings, hot water, air-conditioning, and TV, are right for the price. The proprietors are more than

Lang Co

Lang Co

© AVALON TRAVEL

willing to help with onward bus transportation and local recommendations.

A few doors down from the mammoth Thanh Tam Resort is **Minh Nguyet Guesthouse** (Lac Long Quan, tel. 09/8511-5690, VND200,000), another basic accommodation with friendly owners and a clean bathroom, comfortable beds, hot water, air-conditioning, and a TV. Beach access is about 100 meters from the front steps and, depending upon the season and the length of your stay, you may be able to talk down the price; though even at VND200,000, the rooms are agreeable.

VND210,000-525,000

The **Quynh Lien Hotel** (Loan Ly, Lac Long Quan, tel. 05/4387-3429, www.quynhlienhotel.com, VND300,000-500,000) may be flashier than the droves of guesthouses along Lac Long Quan, but its proprietors are slightly less inviting. Rooms are spacious and feature air-conditioning, hot water, and a television. While some lodgings are without windows, the reception area has great views of the nearby lagoon and the beach is within walking distance of the hotel.

VND1,050,000-2,100,000

A collection of nice, semi-detached villa accommodations, the **Lang Co Beach Resort** (463 Lac Long Quan, tel. 05/4387-3555, langco@dng.vnn.vn, VND1,050,000-1,680,000, breakfast included) sits directly on the beach and features spacious rooms with floor-to-ceiling windows, air-conditioning, hot water, television, mosquito nets, and an in-room safe. Accommodations vary in price depending upon your proximity to the ocean, with both garden and beach views available. The resort also counts a restaurant and a swimming pool for guests in its offerings.

Food

Beyond the eateries attached to various beach resorts, a slew of cookie-cutter rice and noodle stalls line either side of Lac Long Quan, along with a few local truck-stop restaurants. To enjoy the view, take a stroll down the road lining the lagoon, where you'll find several small coffee stands from which to admire the lagoon and the surrounding mountains. Dig in to some local grub at one of the many street stalls lining the main road.

A collection of stalls along the town's main road sell **rice and noodle dishes** (Lac Long Quan between Minh Nguyet Guesthouse and Lang Co Beach Resort, VND15,000-40,000), from the spicy *bun bo Hue* (soup with beef and rice noodles) to *bun thit nuong* (a dry noodle dish accompanied by grilled pork and the occasional fried spring roll) to your standard pick-and-point rice offerings. These are the most inexpensive options, and you're free to shop around at a variety of stalls before settling upon your preferred dish. These stalls usually open and close earlier than proper restaurants.

The walls of **Sao Bien 1 Be Ly** (184 Lac Long Quan, tel. 05/4387-4417, www.saobien1bely.com, 7am-7pm daily, VND55,000-150,000) clue diners into the fact that this place belongs to Ms. Ly, whose portraits take up a majority of the wall space. Sit out near the lagoon, where the scenery is far better and the noise level quieter than at the tables facing the road. Dishes feature mostly seafood, and you'll know it's fresh because most of the dinner offerings are still alive and on display out front. There are other restaurants along the highway offering a similar selection, but these folks are particularly friendly and speak some English.

Information and Services

The small community of Lang Co takes up no more than a few miles along the coast, so ATMs are less common. Bring enough cash to last you through your next destination rather than fuss with money machines in this area, though there are a handful of machines along the highway.

While several places in town advertise Wi-Fi Internet, connections are weak at best. Be prepared to have technical difficulties getting online. Your hotel may be able to help, but if you require a connection, your best bet is to head into town near the southern end of the isthmus.

There are no medical care facilities equipped to deal with even minor illnesses or injuries. For any emergencies, the nearest hospital is in Danang.

Getting There

Lang Co may be a short distance from Danang, but the two places are separated by the steep and spiraling Hai Van Pass. Travelers can scale the winding road and incorporate this stunning section of the coast into their trip, or opt for a ride through the Hai Van Tunnel. Buses and other large vehicles will always take the tunnel; the pass, while beautiful, is decidedly less safe for large vehicles. If you're on a motorbike, you should take Hai Van Pass, as this is one of the most beautiful coastal roads in Vietnam.

Driving through the tunnel via motorbike is technically not allowed, due to its size. Instead, drivers must buy a **motorbike ticket** (VND30,000) and a **bus ticket** (VND8,000), which ensures the passage of both you and your vehicle through to the other side. Vehicles are strapped onto a truck

that makes the journey through the narrow passageway, while you hop on a bus to get to the other side.

If you're not up for driving on your own, it is possible to hire one of the Easy Rider-style *xe om* drivers from the city to take you over the pass. It costs more than your average ride (around VND500,000 from Danang) since the distance is greater and requires trickier driving.

BUS

From the Danang bus station (159 Ton Duc Thang, tel. 0511/376-7679), local buses to Hue depart regularly (5:30am-5pm, every 15 min.). Jump on one of these buses and notify the fee collector that you'd like to get off at **Lang Co** (20-30 minutes, VND50,000-60,000). The collector will alert you when you arrive at Lang Co's main strip. Check the fare board at the Danang bus station to verify the cost.

TRAIN

Lang Co's **train station** (south of Lang Co Bridge, tel. 05/4387-4423, 7am-5pm daily) is about a mile from the beach and only a few stops from the Danang station (200 Hai Phong, tel. 0511/382-3810, 7am-5pm daily). Its route around Hai Van is especially beautiful, hugging the base of the mountain as it brushes the shore. Trips to and from Danang run about 1.5-2 hours and cost VND31,000. There's just one train to Lang Co each morning at 8am.

Getting Around

Most accommodations are within walking distance of the beach, and you'll find restaurants and other services along Lac Long Quan, the main road, or at your resort. If you're heading somewhere farther afield, your only real option is to jump in a **Lang Co Taxi** (tel. 05/4369-6969). It's doubtful that you'll catch *xe om* drivers loitering on this route; if you pop into a restaurant or shop and ask, they may be able to connect you with a driver. There are no official rental shops in Lang Co. Ask your hotel if they have bicycles or motorbikes to rent out.

Hoi An

Crisscrossing the riverfront and drenched in a vibrant saffron yellow, Hoi An is easily the most photogenic town in the country. Now a major stop on the tourist trail, its charming wooden houses and colorful lanterns remain a few centuries in the past, stuck in Hoi An's heyday as a famous trading port. While business has changed—the town makes its living off a thriving tourism industry and an army of skilled tailors, who can turn around a silk dress or three-piece suit in a matter of hours—locals hold steadfastly to their traditions and there is a great sense of pride in the cultural preservation of Hoi An. For visitors, the picturesque old town, a nearby beach, and the best shopping in the country are often the major draws.

The area's first inhabitants, the Sa Huynh, existed a couple thousand years ago. They were followed by the Champa kingdom, a powerful empire that set up religious, political, and economic centers in and around Hoi An. From the 2nd century up through the 14th, the Thu Bon River was used to facilitate trade with nearby kingdoms. In the early 1300s, a Cham king married a Vietnamese princess, gifting the province of Quang Nam to the Vietnamese. Shortly thereafter, the king died and his successor refused to honor the arrangement, angering the Dai Viet, who promptly entered into a war with their southern neighbors that continued for much of the next century.

By the time the 16th century rolled around, trading in Hoi An was back in full swing, with Chinese and Japanese merchants setting up shop on the shores of what was then known as Faifo. This golden age lasted until the 19th century, when the Thu Bon River became too shallow for large trading ships to enter the port. Throughout the next few centuries, Hoi An's original buildings endured, later serving as an administrative center for the French during colonial rule.

Officially recognized as a UNESCO World Heritage site, downtown Hoi An sees over a million tourists each year, sending its modest population through the roof during high season (mid-Nov.-Feb.). While the best time to visit is March-June, when the rains have dried up, this town sees a constant stream of visitors year-round, even in August, its hottest month, and during a feisty rainy season, when typhoons and flooding are not uncommon. In November especially, you'll find parts of the old town underwater and locals in rain ponchos plying the roads in wooden canoes.

Once you've had your fill of the colorful old town and sufficiently emptied your wallet into the hands of Hoi An's tailors, there is a host of attractions waiting beyond downtown Hoi An. From the crumbling temples of My Son to the sunny shores of Cua Dai, the nearby countryside is full of things to do. Many travelers rent bicycles and blaze their own trails, getting lost down countryside alleys and amid stunning rice fields. Danang lies only 18 miles north of Hoi An, making all of the attractions between these two destinations easily reached on a day trip from town.

SIGHTS

The majority of Hoi An's most famous sights are packed into a few blocks north of the riverfront, making this one of the most walkable destinations in the country. From Bach Dang to Tran Phu, this neighborhood can easily be covered in an afternoon, and thanks to a local traffic ordinance, these streets are **pedestrian-only** (8am-11am, 2pm-4:30pm, and 6:30pm-9pm daily) several times throughout the day. Outside of these hours, drivers race kamikaze-style through the narrow roads, which are often still filled with pedestrians.

In the old town area, respectful dress is a must, as Hoi An is big on tradition. Local temples and pagodas enforce this requirement

Hoi An

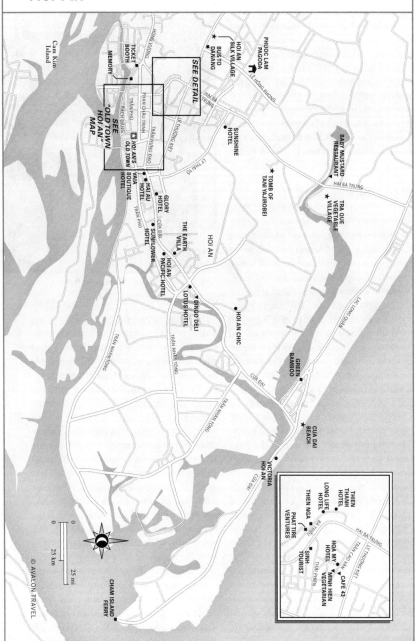

Cam Kim Island

MEMORY

TICKET BOOTH

BUS TO DANANG

HOI AN SILK VILLAGE

PHUOC LAM PAGODA

SEE DETAIL

HUNG VUONG

LE HONG PHONG

HAI BA TRUNG

PHAN CHAU TRINH

TRAN PHU

BACH DANG

SEE "OLD TOWN" HOI AN MAP

HOI AN'S OLD TOWN

TRAN HUNG DAO

LY THUONG KIET

LY THAI TO

SUNSHINE HOTEL

TOMB OF TANI YAJIROBEI

BABY MUSTARD RESTAURANT

HAI BA TRUNG

TRA QUE VEGETABLE VILLAGE

HOI AN

DAI A HOTEL

HAI AU HOTEL

GLORY HOTEL

CUA DAI

THE EARTH VILLA

SUNFLOWER HOTEL

HOI AN PACIFIC HOTEL

LOTUS HOTEL

DINGO DELI

HOI AN CHIC

TRAN PHU

TRAN NHAN TONG

THAI BOUTIQUE HOTEL

GREEN BAMBOO

CUA DAI

LAC LONG QUAN

TRAN NHAN TONG

THAN NHAT TONG

CUA DAI BEACH

VICTORIA HOI AN

CUA DAI

CHAM ISLAND FERRY

© AVALON TRAVEL

0
25 km
0
25 mi

THIEN NGA

LONG LIFE HOTEL

THIEN THANH HOTEL

PHAT TIRE VENTURES

LE PHIEU

HAI BA TRUNG

TRAN CAO VAN

THAI PHIEN

LY THUONG KIET

SINH TOURIST

HOA MY HOTEL

MINH HIEN VEGETARIAN

CAFE 43

more than most. No matter the temperature, stick to long pants and covered shoulders when exploring the town's sights.

As you reach the outskirts of the old town area, you'll notice that the barriers that prohibit motor vehicles from entering often read "ticket requested area." You may be stopped and required to produce a ticket even just to walk within the old town neighborhood. Expect to show one when visiting one of the museums, meeting halls, or other sights included in the UNESCO ticket scheme. Your ticket is good for the entirety of your visit to Hoi An.

★ Old Town

The small riverfront **old town** (Bach Dang north to Tran Phu) remains frozen in its heyday, lined with vivid, centuries-old wooden houses, zigzagging Chinese lanterns, and a menagerie of decorative animals perched atop the roofs of local pagodas and meeting halls.

Several common architectural traits appear in most houses and traditional buildings. Above the front door of a building, you'll often find a pair of intricately carved wooden dials: These are the eyes of the house, meant to watch over its residents and protect the building from evil. Along the ceiling, particularly at the front of a structure, five vertical wooden beams are meant to signify the elements: earth, water, fire, metal, and wood. These intersect with another trio of beams that run horizontally and mirror the three lines in the palm of your hand, which stand for heaven, earth, and human beings. Each building is long and narrow, extending from the reception area back into an open-roofed central courtyard, which is instrumental in cooling the house during Hoi An's sweltering summer months. Still deeper, the living quarters of the family sit at the back of the building, sheltered by a small, second-floor storage space, which gets put to good use in October and November, when floods swallow the ground floor of houses along the riverfront and all of the family's possessions are moved upstairs.

detailed roof of the Hainan Assembly Hall

While locals are accustomed to the rising waters, occasionally the wear and tear necessitates renovations, which can be an ordeal when your home is 200 years old. In order to maintain the identity of the neighborhood, old town houses must be repaired using the same 18th-century materials and construction methods by which they were built. In some cases, the wooden framework within a house is completely disassembled in order to repair just one column. Finding skilled craftspeople and traditional materials can be a tough and costly chore, but this is precisely what your ticket fee goes to. Families in need of building renovation are expected to front a percentage of the costs, usually about half, while the rest is funded by the local government and profits from ticket sales.

Nearly all of the historical monuments within Hoi An's old town run on a **UNESCO ticket** (VND120,000) scheme, whose proceeds go to the preservation and maintenance of the neighborhood's sights. Travelers can purchase an entry ticket, which grants them access to a total of five monuments within the neighborhood, at any of the ticket booths around the old town. Visitors create their own itinerary. In order to get the gist of what old town has to offer, swing by the Japanese Covered Bridge, (Hoi An's most famous landmark), one of the Chinese congregation halls, a traditional house, a museum, and one other monument of your choosing. If you're looking to get the full story on each of Hoi An's sights, enthusiastic and knowledgeable **guides** (VND70,000) can be hired from the ticket booths. Guides provide additional recommendations and other informational tidbits about the area. Tickets can be purchased at any one of the **UNESCO offices** (7am-6pm daily), located at 12 Phan Chu Trinh, 78 Le Loi, 37 Tran Phu, 19 Hai Ba Trung, and 52 Nguyen Thi Minh Khai. Unless stated otherwise, the listings in this section require a UNESCO ticket and are open the same hours as the ticket booth (7am-6pm daily).

HAINAN ASSEMBLY HALL

The only assembly hall in old town to grant free entry, **Hainan Assembly Hall** (Hai Nam, 10 Tran Phu, sunrise-sunset daily, free) is open to all and can be visited without a UNESCO ticket. Though it's not as big or ornamental as some of its old town counterparts, the building comes with an interesting story. Constructed by members of the local Hainan community, the altar at this assembly hall honors 108 Chinese sailors who suffered at the hands of sea captain Ton That Thieu. On July 16, 1851, Captain Thieu's naval ship happened upon three merchant vessels off the coast of Quang Ngai province; the trio of boats belonged to local Hainan immigrants. The captain attacked, firing shots and later boarding the vessels to loot and kill. Though it would eventually become clear that the sailors were innocent, Captain Ton That Thieu ordered his men to kill them all; only one of the 108 survived. In order to cover up his actions, the captain painted the fishing boats black and reported to Emperor Tu Duc that

he had found and captured a group of pirate ships. The emperor later uncovered the truth, and the families of the Hainan sailors received reparations and permission to construct the hall, which now houses a set of large lacquered wooden tablets in honor of the deceased.

The front of the property has been converted into a miniature souvenir shop. The building's architecture, from its brightly hued wooden columns to the intricate rooftop designs, is worth a peek.

BA LE WELL

The locally famous **Ba Le Well** (down the alley opposite 35 Phan Chau Trinh) is an important part of Hoi An's culinary history: This ancient water source—dug by the Cham in the 10th century—provides the key ingredient in *cao lau,* a local specialty. Only *cao lau* noodles made with this particular water are considered the real deal, and local residents take their *cao lau* recipes very seriously. Water collectors gather here during the day, throwing down and retrieving plastic buckets full of Ba Le water to sell to restaurants and other businesses. To find the modest well, nothing more than a stone opening behind a house, head down the narrow alley opposite 35 Phan Chau Trinh, past Ba Le Well restaurant, a popular street food spot, and make a right. It's easy to miss, as the well is pretty unassuming, but you should be able to spot the water collectors first.

JAPANESE COVERED BRIDGE

Hoi An's most famous landmark, the iconic **Japanese Covered Bridge** (Nguyen Thi Minh Khai) is among the oldest structures in town, dating back to the early 17th century, when the Chinese and Japanese quarters of Hoi An's thriving port were separated by a narrow inlet. Its beautiful exterior and age have made this wooden footbridge a popular photo spot for tourists. Shutterbugs vie for a good vantage point on the street just south of the bridge.

Inside, you'll be greeted on the eastern

Old Town Hoi An

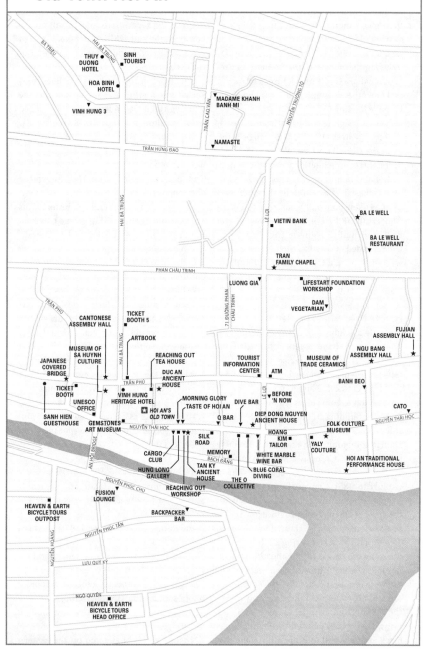

BA TRIỆU

HAI BÀ TRƯNG

THUY DUONG HOTEL

SINH TOURIST

HOA BINH HOTEL

VINH HUNG 3

TRẦN CAO VÂN

MADAME KHANH BANH MI

NGUYỄN TRƯỜNG TỘ

NAMASTE

TRẦN HƯNG ĐẠO

HAI BÀ TRƯNG

LÊ LỢI

VIETIN BANK

BA LE WELL

BA LE WELL RESTAURANT

TRAN FAMILY CHAPEL

PHAN CHÂU TRINH

LUONG GIA

LIFESTART FOUNDATION WORKSHOP

DAM VEGETARIAN

TRẦN PHÚ

CANTONESE ASSEMBLY HALL

TICKET BOOTH 5

71 ĐƯỜNG PHAN CHÂU TRINH

FUJIAN ASSEMBLY HALL

ARTBOOK

MUSEUM OF SA HUYNH CULTURE

REACHING OUT TEA HOUSE

TOURIST INFORMATION CENTER

MUSEUM OF TRADE CERAMICS

NGU BANG ASSEMBLY HALL

HAI BÀ TRƯNG

JAPANESE COVERED BRIDGE

DUC AN ANCIENT HOUSE

ATM

BANH BEO

TICKET BOOTH

TRẦN PHÚ

VINH HUNG HERITAGE HOTEL

LÊ LỢI

BEFORE 'N NOW

CATO

UNESCO OFFICE

MORNING GLORY TASTE OF HOI AN

DIVE BAR

DIEP DONG NGUYEN ANCIENT HOUSE

NGUYỄN THÁI HỌC

SANH HIEN GUESTHOUSE

HOI AN'S OLD TOWN

Q BAR

FOLK CULTURE MUSEUM

GEMSTONES ART MUSEUM

NGUYỄN THÁI HỌC

HOANG KIM TAILOR

YALY COUTURE

AN HỘI BRIDGE

CARGO CLUB

SILK ROAD

MEMORY

WHITE MARBLE WINE BAR

HOI AN TRADITIONAL PERFORMANCE HOUSE

BẠCH ĐẰNG

HUNG LONG GALLERY

TAN KY ANCIENT HOUSE

BLUE CORAL DIVING

REACHING OUT WORKSHOP

THE O COLLECTIVE

NGUYỄN PHÚC CHU

FUSION LOUNGE

HEAVEN & EARTH BICYCLE TOURS OUTPOST

NGUYỄN PHÚC TẦN

BACKPACKER BAR

NGUYỄN HOÀNG

LƯU QUÝ KỲ

NGÔ QUYỀN

HEAVEN & EARTH BICYCLE TOURS HEAD OFFICE

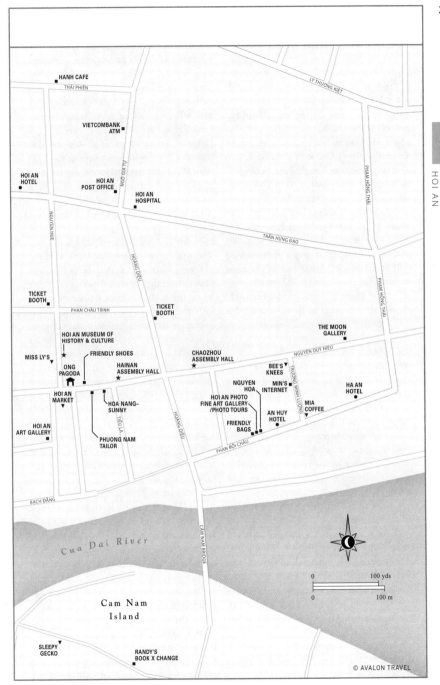

LY THUONG KIET

THÁI PHIÊN

HANH CAFE

VIETCOMBANK ATM

HOI AN HOTEL

HOI AN POST OFFICE

HOI AN HOSPITAL

PHAM HONG THÁI

TRÀN HÙNG ĐAO

NGUYÊN HUÊ

HOÀNG DIÊU

TICKET BOOTH

PHAN CHÂU TRINH

TICKET BOOTH

HOI AN MUSEUM OF HISTORY & CULTURE

THE MOON GALLERY

NGUYÊN DUY HIÊU

MISS LY'S

FRIENDLY SHOES

ONG PAGODA

HAINAN ASSEMBLY HALL

CHAOZHOU ASSEMBLY HALL

BEE'S KNEES

PHAM HONG THÁI

HOI AN MARKET

HOA NANG-SUNNY

NGUYÊN HOA

MIN'S INTERNET

TRUONG MINH LUONG

HOI AN ART GALLERY

TIÊU LA

HOI AN PHOTO FINE ART GALLERY /PHOTO TOURS

AN HUY HOTEL

MIA COFFEE

HA AN HOTEL

FRIENDLY BAGS

PHUONG NAM TAILOR

HOÀNG DIÊU

PHAN BÔI CHÂU

BACH ĐÀNG

Cua Dai River

CAM NAM BRIDGE

Cam Nam Island

0   100 yds
0   100 m

SLEEPY GECKO

RANDY'S BOOK X CHANGE

© AVALON TRAVEL

end by a pair of dog statues guarding the entrance. These statues, along with the monkey statues watching over the western side of the bridge, are historical markers: Construction began in the year of the monkey and ended in the year of the dog. From the open side of the bridge, visitors can look out over the Thu Bon River and the western edge of Hoi An's old town. On the other side, you'll find a later addition by the Chinese community. Known as Chua Cau in Vietnamese, this modest, one-room temple pays homage to the Emperor of the North, Tran Vo Bac De, who controls the weather and is thus a popular figure among sailors and fisherfolk. The bridge itself is short and a quick glimpse into the temple reveals much of its ornamentation. Those hoping to snap a photo should visit early; this bridge is one of the most documented corners of the old town and everyone from camera-toting tourists to avid photographers makes an appearance on this corner during the day.

ONG PAGODA

While there are dozens of other buildings in Vietnam—and throughout Asia—dedicated to the famed Chinese general Quan Cong, Hoi An's **Ong Pagoda** (24 Tran Phu), directly opposite the central market, is a remarkably ornate version that still welcomes regular local visitors. Hoi An residents often stop in to pray to the red-faced, bearded general, who is known for his courage and strong moral character. The pagoda's exterior, built in 1653, boasts a vivid splash of yellow and pink.

The main altar holds a massive statue of Quan Cong, his long beard trailing down past his waist. On either side of Quan Cong is Quan Binh, his adoptive son, and Chau Thuong, one of Quan Cong's loyal mandarins. His horses, one red and one white, flank the three men, making for a crowded and colorful scene.

Visitors can access the Hoi An Museum of History and Culture by walking out the back of the pagoda.

HOI AN MUSEUM OF HISTORY AND CULTURE

Tucked behind Ong Pagoda, the **Hoi An Museum of History and Culture** (through Ong Pagoda) gives a general rundown of the town's beginnings, from ancient Sa Huynh culture through the Cham era and up to its pinnacle as a trading port. Its exhibits include several artifacts from the region's ancient cultures as well as old photographs and plenty of English signage to orient you. Like most other buildings in Hoi An, the museum itself is a historical structure: built in 1653, the former Quan Yin Pagoda honored Quan Am, a prominent female figure in Buddhism.

HOI AN'S ANCIENT HOUSES

The long-and-narrow yellow-hued buildings of the old town exist as they did in centuries past, despite the occasional motorbike flying by out front. Thanks to local preservation efforts and the town's UNESCO status, these houses are required to maintain their original architecture, which accounts in large part for the neighborhood's charm. While visitors can see the telltale signs of 18th- and 19th-century architecture in every tailor and souvenir shop around the old town, a handful of its more storied ancient residences are open for UNESCO ticket-holders to explore. These family-owned houses have been maintained by generations of Hoi An residents and carry a great deal of history alongside their traditional design and building methods.

With over 90 percent of its original structure still intact, **Tan Ky House** (101 Nguyen Thai Hoc) is a prime example of traditional Hoi An architecture. Thick, wooden columns and sun-baked tile floors appear throughout the house, punctuated by its central courtyard, a natural ventilator and a feature of the house's feng shui. Up front, the seventh-generation owners greet their daily visitors with a cup of tea and a brief rundown of the house's history. Beyond the courtyard, walk to the far end of the 98-foot-long house to the place where Tan Ky opens onto the river, once allowing for easy transportation of the former merchant family's goods. When floods overtake much of the old town during October and November, everything goes upstairs by way of a pulley system, hidden in the attic. Along the far wall you can see where the family has documented the level of these floodwaters in years past.

Another relic of centuries past, the most recent incarnation of **Duc An House** (129 Tran Phu) was built in 1850. The land on which it stands has been in the family for roughly 400 years. Once a well-known bookstore in Hoi An, the former shop stocked a host of Vietnamese and Chinese books and served as an important base for Communist activity during the French resistance, in which former resident Cao Hong Lanh was an important local player. Another revolutionary great, Phan Chau Trinh, also regularly dropped by the house. Duc An was later converted into a Chinese pharmacy in the 20th century.

With a blend of Japanese, Chinese, and Vietnamese influences, the **Diep Dong Nguyen House** (80 Nguyen Thai Hoc) sits a block north of the river and houses a generous collection of coins and ceramics, some of which date back generations. The building, constructed in the late 19th century, once served as a pharmacy for traditional medicine and is easy to spot for the large Buddha emblazoned on the front facade.

TRAN FAMILY CHAPEL

Unlike Hoi An's other traditional houses, none of the residents at the **Tran Family Chapel** (21 Le Loi) are among the living. Rather, this small, dimly lit structure honors several generations of a wealthy local family, whose 19th-century relative commissioned the building over 200 years ago. From the entrance gate, a sparse garden takes up the first half of the property, lined with a few ornamental trees and other greenery. The front of the house bears a Chinese-style trio of doors with one large central entryway flanked by two smaller ones. According to custom, the left door is meant for men, the right for women, and the middle for spirits. The middle

door is only opened for the Lunar New Year and the death anniversaries of relatives, during which time the ancestors are able to pass in and out of the building.

Inside, you'll be invited to sit in the reception area, where a 10th-generation family member gives you a quick tour of the building and its many features. The reception room boasts the most noteworthy architecture, with Chinese, Japanese, and Vietnamese influences present in the wooden beams running along the ceiling and the house's front facade. Throughout the building, great emphasis is placed upon yin and yang. Beyond the front room lies the familial altar, a large high table bearing a series of simple painted wooden boxes. These contain the ashes of generations of the Tran family. Because Vietnamese culture celebrates a person's date of death, the boxes are opened on each ancestor's death anniversary for prayers and offerings. To the right of the altar, you'll find still more members of the Tran family in the photographs that line the wall, as well as the family tree book, penned in Chinese script, on a table in the corner. Keep an eye out for the yin-yang coins as well, which sit in a bowl near the ancestral shrine.

CHINESE ASSEMBLY HALLS

Spread throughout the old town are Hoi An's five bright and colorful assembly halls, each built by a different community of Chinese settlers. Hailing from Fujian, Canton, Hainan, and Guangdong provinces in China, each individual group has its own dialect and local traditions, all of which were preserved during Hoi An's heyday through regular gatherings at these ornate halls, where trade and business arrangements were often discussed within the community and deities from each respective province were worshipped. In addition to these four provincial assembly halls, a fifth building held gatherings for all Chinese residents, whose numbers swelled in the 17th century as refugees from southern China fled the country's civil war, settling in Vietnam by the thousands.

Separated from the street by a generous walkway, the **Fujian Assembly Hall (Hoi Quan Phuoc Kien)** (46 Tran Phu) is a swirl of vivid colors, mosaic animals, lavish altars, and grand facades. Originally built in 1697 as the Vietnamese Kim Son Pagoda, its current incarnation was completed in 1757 and, while no longer used as a meeting hall, continues to attract plenty of visitors thanks to its design. Inside, three main altars take up the far end of the building, the middle of which features a group of six Fujianese mandarins who were loyal to the Ming dynasty. As civil war broke out in China in the mid-17th century, these men attempted to avenge the fall of their beloved emperor but failed; they are now honored on the 16th day of the second lunar month each year. To the left, you'll find the god of prosperity, a popular fixture in most Chinese halls, and on your right are the three goddesses of fertility and 12 midwives, all of whom are visited by couples hoping to conceive. Behind each of the three altars is a mosaic animal: the phoenix for female beauty, the unicorn for male strength, and the dragon for royal power. A large wooden replica of a merchant boat is featured in the building, which sailors and fishermen often visited before heading out to sea.

Not far from the Japanese bridge, Hoi An's **Cantonese Assembly Hall (Hoi Quan Quang Trieu)** (176 Tran Phu) is a riot of color packed into a small space. From its busy rooftop decorations to the vivid murals along its wall or the enormous, slow-burn incense coils winding down from the ceiling, this is one of the old town's most eye-catching assembly halls. Built in 1885, the main altars pay homage to Chinese general Quan Cong, flanked by a pair of horses, as well as Thien Hau, goddess of the sea.

Ngu Bang Assembly Hall (64 Tran Phu) once united all of the local Chinese communities under one intricate, brightly hued roof. Built in 1741, the hall worships Thien Hau, goddess of the sea and a vital deity for those who do business on the water. Ngu Bang features ample decoration as well as several smaller altars to Confucius, Chinese revolutionary Sun Yat-Sen, and a group of Chinese soldiers killed by the Japanese during WWII conflicts in Vietnam.

MUSEUM OF FOLK CULTURE
Housed in the largest wooden building in the old town, Hoi An's **Museum of Folk Culture** (33 Nguyen Thai Hoc) runs a full 187 feet from Nguyen Thai Hoc to the waterfront Bach Dang and displays the artifacts and everyday items of the town's traditional occupations as well as its vibrant performing arts scene.

MUSEUM OF SA HUYNH CULTURE
Essentially a one-room exhibition, the **Museum of Sa Huynh Culture** (149 Tran Phu) provides interesting insight into central Vietnam's first documented culture. Displays include ancient pottery, burial jars, primitive tools, and jewelry, most of which dates back to the Iron Age. There's not a great deal of signage to orient visitors.

MUSEUM OF TRADE CERAMICS
The **Museum of Trade Ceramics** (80 Tran Phu) revisits Hoi An's glory days as a successful port by displaying the array of pottery and ceramics that passed through the town during its busiest years. Artifacts date back as early as the 13th century and hail from all over Asia, including Thailand, China, and Japan. Each exhibit includes information on the pieces displayed and visitors are free to wander through the spacious old building.

Beyond Old Town
PHUOC LAM PAGODA
Anyone armed with a bicycle and some spare time will appreciate a wander around **Phuoc Lam Pagoda** (Thon 2, Cam Ha, sunrise-sunset daily, free). Now a few centuries old, this elaborate building, all colorful mosaics and detailed paintings, enjoys relative obscurity, with most tourists sticking to the old town rather than venturing farther

afield. Locals, too, seem to have forgotten the place, as Phuoc Lam sees few visitors, but that doesn't take away from its impressive decoration and aging beauty. Nestled among the foliage of Phuoc Lam are a collection of gravestones—some old, some new—bearing the names of former monks. The interior of the pagoda is not often open, but the few monks who still live here are a welcoming bunch. Dress respectfully, as this is a more traditional pagoda than most.

CAM KIM ISLAND

When you tire of the heckling and persistent cries of street vendors around Hoi An's old town, the large and beautiful **Cam Kim Island** is a perfect escape from the tourist trail. Just a short ferry ride away (15 min.), this peaceful farming community welcomes you instantly into the countryside, trading the bustle of the old town for verdant rice paddies and gracefully aging pagodas. The best thing to do on Cam Kim is bring a bicycle and get lost down the many narrow concrete roads of the island. The locals are an inviting bunch and quick to offer a "hello" or a smile, and some of the younger residents speak English well. With pretty scenery and a pleasant atmosphere, this is a great place for a morning cycle or a late afternoon wander.

To get to the island, hop on a **ferry** (near corner of Bach Dang and Hoang Van Thu, sunrise-sunset daily, VND10,000) from the riverfront. There is no fixed fee for a ride across the Thu Bon, but stand firm and pay no more than VND10,000. Many boats attempt to charge up to VND20,000 per person, but, at VND10,000, you're already paying several times the local price, so haggle for your fare. The best thing you can do is ask the fee before boarding and, should your driver attempt to overcharge you, politely state the price you're willing to pay. If this price is met with any resistance, keep your cool, appear disinterested and say you'll wait. In most cases, the boat drivers fold quickly. Once you've agreed upon a fee, jump on board with your bicycle and enjoy the ride.

Traditional Villages

A traditional village is a small community that has a long history of trading in one particular skill or handicraft. There are traditional villages all over Vietnam, some of which date back centuries. Typically, traditional villages focus on handicrafts like lacquer, silk, and ceramics but there are occasionally outliers like Tra Que, which is known for its fresh produce.

TRA QUE VEGETABLE VILLAGE

A long-time farming community, the sleepy **Tra Que vegetable village** (2.5 mi north of Hoi An on Hai Ba Trung, 8am-5pm daily, VND20,000) has been cultivating its fresh green produce for the better part of a century. Organized into neat plots of lettuce and basil, cabbage and coriander, Tra Que's gardens use a special kind of algae found in the nearby river, which fertilizes the soil and, according to locals, accounts for the area's superior vegetables. Nowadays, in addition to moving heaps of green goods at the market, the farmers of Tra Que have taken advantage of their photogenic fields and famed veggies by inviting outsiders in for a visit. Tour groups regularly make the trip, often by bicycle, to wander the narrow brick lanes that run through Tra Que's fields and enjoy a meal.

Veering off Hai Ba Trung, the entrance into Tra Que is populated by a few local restaurants. But, the best of the bunch is **Baby Mustard (Nha Hang Cai Con)** (Tra Que, tel. 09/3572-5740, babymustard.restaurant@gmail.com, 10am-9:30pm daily, VND35,000-99,000), located on the other side of Hai Ba Trung. With a four-person staff and a modest set of bamboo tables and chairs, this tiny spot cooks up stellar local food, namely its mouthwatering *banh xeo* (savory Vietnamese pancakes). A variety of fish and shrimp dishes make it onto the small menu, along with some vegetarian options. The friendly proprietor is happy to recommend a dish or explain its ingredients. The greens come straight from the fields surrounding the restaurant, and a nice breeze moves through its open-air seating area, making this the perfect spot to sit and enjoy a local lunch or an afternoon drink. Tailor-made **cooking classes** (VND420,000-462,000) are also offered.

Most travelers prefer to take the scenic route to Tra Que, opting for a leisurely cycle along Hai Ba Trung past rice paddies and lazy rivers, an easy ride to do without the aid of a guide. On this road is the **tomb of Tani Yajirobei,** a Japanese merchant who lived in Hoi An during the 17th century and allegedly took a Vietnamese lover. Though it's easy to miss, look for a small stone marker on the roadside that directs you to the gravesite in the middle of a vast, low-lying paddy field. The tomb is an interesting piece of local history and offers some particularly nice views of the surrounding area.

Taxis and *xe om* can also easily make the trip to Tra Que for VND60,000 and VND40,000, respectively. You should be able to find transportation back into town, so there's no need to ask the driver to wait for you.

The village charges a VND20,000 entry fee via the ticket booth just before the village's small roads.

THANH HA POTTERY VILLAGE

A centuries-old vocational community, the expert craftspeople of **Thanh Ha pottery village** (3 mi west of Hoi An, 8am-5pm daily, VND25,000) continue to fashion many of the same pots, jars, and dishes as they did in the days of the Nguyen dynasty, along with a few updated items, like piggy banks, whistles, and other small trinkets. With no more than a pottery wheel and a bit of clay, local potters can produce up to 300 jars in a single day, which then sit in the sun to dry before being placed in front of a wood fire. These items are shelved and sold within the village or shipped outside to other locations throughout Vietnam.

The best way to visit Thanh Ha is by bicycle, as you get to enjoy the countryside landscapes en route, and it's easiest to navigate the narrow brick lanes of the area either on two wheels or on foot. Before you reach the end of the road leading to Thanh Ha, you'll pass a small ticket booth out front. Depending on when you arrive, you may not find anyone on duty and may not be able to pay the ticket price. (If this happens, go ahead and enter, but be sure to buy something from one of the vendors during your visit.) If you continue past the booth, this wider asphalt road turns into a concrete alley. Hang a left when you spot a brick lane, otherwise you'll pass the village entirely and wind up next to a nearby river.

Inside, visitors are free to roam around,

Tra Que vegetable village

peeking in on the small workshops of Thanh Ha. Some of the potters speak a bit of English, though don't expect a lengthy conversation. You may also get a chance to try your hand at the pottery wheel for free; when this happens you are usually expected to buy something from that shop.

HOI AN SILK VILLAGE

While this isn't technically a village so much as a tourist attraction, the **Hoi An silk village** (28 Nguyen Tat Thanh, tel. 0510/392-1144, www.hoiansilkvillage.com, 8am-8pm daily, VND100,000 short tour, VND400,000 long tour) continues to preserve the region's traditional methods of silk-making for posterity. For a fee, you can have a guide steer you through the complex's many buildings, where you'll learn about the silk-making process from start to finish, meet a few dozen silkworms, check out the 100-year-old collection of *ao dai* (traditional garment of Vietnam) on display, witness the dizzying speed of a Vietnamese loom, and learn how to tell genuine silk from its impostors.

The short tour runs around 45 minutes. The longer version takes over an hour, including lunch and the opportunity to try your hand at feeding the silkworms and, later, spinning their cocoons into thread.

At the end, you'll have an opportunity to peruse the silk shop, which features handmade items using traditional silk-making methods. This is a fun opportunity to learn about garment-making and Hoi An history.

Tours

While only the original half-day trip offered by **Hoi An Free Tours** (tel. 09/7958-7744, www.hoianfreetour.com) is, indeed, free of charge, this outfit provides pleasant half- and full-day excursions at better rates than most. Guided by local university students, tourists can visit nearby Tra Que village, participate in a walking tour (USD$2) around Hoi An's old town, or, for a higher fee, dig in to some of the city's best street food. The original, free-of-charge excursion to Cam Kim Island

takes place on Thursdays and Sundays only and participants are expected to cover their own bicycle rental and ferry fare across the river. This group does not have a booking office; make reservations through the website.

Whether you're an avid shutterbug or an iPhone amateur, the **Hoi An Photo Tour** (42 Phan Boi Chau, tel. 09/0567-1898, www.hoianphototour.com, VND735,000) combines stunning countryside scenery and the Thu Bon River with helpful tips and tricks straight from a professional photographer. Founded by French photographer Etienne Bossot, a long-time Hoi An resident, these early morning or late afternoon excursions take travelers to a photogenic fishing village, where the local harbor makes for a frenzied but beautiful scene, or into verdant rice paddies just before sunset. The tour caters to all levels of experience, as well as varying levels of equipment, from a simple point-and-shoot camera to the souped-up, high-quality machines used by the pros. Once you're done for the day, you can swing by Bossot's **Hoi An Photo Gallery** (42 Phan Boi Chau, tel. 09/0567-1898), where beautiful prints of Hoi An and the nearby countryside are on display.

In a place blessed with a cuisine as rich and varied as its history, the **Taste of Hoi An** (Family Restaurant, 108 Nguyen Thai Hoc, tel. 09/0538-2783, www.tasteofhoian.com, VND1,250,000) street food tour provides a solid rundown of all the town's best culinary offerings. This five-hour morning excursion begins with a walking tour of the old town and a trip to the market and several local street food stalls before guests turn back to Family Restaurant, where you'll sit and enjoy your purchases in a quiet and comfortable setting.

BEACHES

Just down the road from Hoi An is **Cua Dai Beach** (end of Cua Dai road). All sun, sand, and wooden lounge chairs, this lazy stretch of coast presents a completely different side of Hoi An, shaking off the old-world ambience that decorates the downtown area in exchange for good old-fashioned beach time. You'll find a cluster of no-frills restaurants lining the waterfront as well as plenty of wide open space. Dozens of eateries also span the length of Cua Dai road, which connects the shoreline to Hoi An proper.

Travelers can easily reach the beach on their own by bicycle, taxi, or *xe om*. Plenty of parking is available near the waterfront. Since competition is steep, one or two of these parking services have chosen to use whistles and batons in order to attract customers. If you find yourself being flagged down by someone without a uniform, feel free to ride on: This is simply a marketing ploy.

Farther up the coast at the end of Hai Ba Trung you'll find **An Bang Beach,** a quieter version of its popular neighbor, Cua Dai. While the two are essentially the same, fewer tourists laze about on this stretch of sand, though there are still plenty of shops and restaurants.

ENTERTAINMENT AND EVENTS
Nightlife

Nightlife isn't especially raucous in Hoi An, though there are a few places across the river that are beginning to resemble the wilder establishments of other Vietnamese towns. Most places shut down by 10pm or 11pm, but a few spots stay open around the old town as well as over the bridge on Nguyen Phuc Chu. Many restaurants and cafés offer happy hour specials, making sundown the best time for a laid-back drink on the river.

Despite the name, **Dive Bar** (88 Nguyen Thai Hoc, tel. 0510/391-0782, www.vietnamscubadiving.com, 10am-1am daily, VND25,000-110,000) is anything but. This cool, casual bar in the middle of the old town would not be out of place on the beach, as its laid-back vibe and accompanying reggae tunes help to create a mellow atmosphere. Colorful cushions and bamboo furniture litter the deceptively large building, which extends all the way back to a small, open-roof courtyard, passing a pool table and plenty of comfy couches on the way. In addition to beer,

wine, and cocktails, the bar serves a variety of Vietnamese food and a few Western snacks (VND50,000-150,000). The bar is so named for its dive outfit, which does trips to nearby Cham Island.

Calm, cool, and in possession of a great soundtrack, the rock- and soul-infused **Before 'N Now** (51 Le Loi, tel. 0510/391-0599, www.beforennow.com, 8am-2am daily, VND30,000-80,000) is a lively spot in the old town where happy hour specials run throughout the evening and well into the night. Contemporary artwork and an easygoing, grown-up atmosphere attract all manner of travelers, both young and old, for a nighttime drink.

Standing among a string of late-night establishments that line the riverfront opposite the old town, **Backpacker Bar** (11 Nguyen Phuc Chu, 1pm-late daily, VND20,000-80,000) is a popular spot for young travelers and the light-of-wallet. Cheap cocktails and regular happy hour deals draw in a lively crowd, as do the dance music, pool table, and patio seating. Shisha (hookah) is available and you'll find plenty of outgoing, like-minded adventurers here.

Across the river on Cam Nam Island, **Sleepy Gecko** (5 Thon Xuyen Trung, tel. 09/0842-6349, www.sleepygeckohoian.com, 10am-late daily, VND25,000-100,000) boasts a nice view of the old town, a pool table, reasonable prices, and far more quiet than you'll experience on the main drag. For a cold beer in a casual setting, the wicker chairs at Sleepy Gecko are the place to be, and Steve, the owner, is a wealth of useful local information. In addition to serving beer and cocktails, the bar has a selection of Western and Vietnamese dishes.

Q Bar (94 Nguyen Thai Hoc, tel. 0510/391-1964, 10:30am-midnight daily, VND45,000-140,000) is Hoi An's resident swanky cocktail lounge hidden among the shops along Nguyen Thai Hoc. Mood music, plush couches, dim lighting, and a massive dye-cut wooden screen create a trendy, ambient vibe that extends all the way from its open storefront back to the intimate seating beyond the bar. In addition to beer, wine, and cocktails, Q Bar offers food after 6pm, including a tapas menu (from VND60,000) and several full meals (VND100,000-180,000).

White Marble Wine Bar (98 Le Loi, tel. 0510/391-1862, www.visithoian.com, 11am-11pm daily, VND100,000-130,000) transforms one of the neighborhood's many heritage buildings into the self-proclaimed first and only wine bar in Hoi An. Featuring a long list of reds, whites, and rosés alongside sumptuous Vietnamese cuisine, this beautiful corner building makes for a perfect place to enjoy a drink at sunset or a nice meal, though prices on its food menu are steep. Wines are imported from all over the world and the downstairs seating area is a prime people-watching location.

Festivals and Events

Every night, as the sun sets over Hoi An, the scores of brightly hued lanterns floating overhead get put to good use, acting as street lights throughout the old town. Head down to the riverfront where young girls in traditional dress sell **lanterns** (from sunset) to passing travelers; the lanterns are then placed upon the water. Though it takes a few hours, as more and more lanterns are set free, the effect of so many tiny lights flickering along Thu Bon River is an impressive sight.

SHOPPING

Famed for its tailors, Hoi An is an easy place for travelers to fill their suitcases and lighten their wallets. Hundreds of shops hawk shoes, clothing, souvenirs, handicrafts, and other knickknacks. Thanks to its history of silk production and a handful of traditional handicraft villages nearby, you'll find almost every storefront downtown packed with Vietnam's best shopping. While the sales pitches can wear over time, this is the best destination for custom-made clothes.

Prices in Hoi An tend to be higher than elsewhere, but you're also more likely to find original, handmade items here. Bargaining is a necessity: Many stores around the old town do not put price tags on their goods, and where one vendor might ask for VND100,000, another could go as high as VND500,000. Shop around first, peruse all your options—and ask for prices—before deciding upon a particular shop. Remember that patience in these negotiations makes a vendor more likely to agree on your asking price. If all else fails, the item you want is probably available in another shop around town.

Souvenirs

The unique, handcrafted ceramics, jewelry, and accessories at **Reaching Out** (103 Nguyen Thai Hoc, tel. 0510/391-0168, www.reachingoutvietnam.com, 8:30am-9pm Mon.-Fri., 9:30am-8pm Sat.-Sun.) are worth a look. Founded in 2000 by resident Le Nguyen Binh, this nonprofit enterprise trains, employs, and supports Vietnamese citizens with disabilities, with the aim of providing opportunities for and raising local awareness about other-abled individuals. In-house craftspeople, most of whom have physical impairments, create greeting cards, handbags, home wares, and other knickknacks in the workshop out back, where visitors are invited to say hello and meet the people behind the products. The innovative take on traditional Vietnamese items like tea sets and lanterns makes it hard to leave without a purchase. Reaching Out also runs a peaceful tea shop on Tran Phu staffed entirely by employees with hearing impairments.

Another socially conscious business, the **Lifestart Foundation Workshop** (77 Phan Chau Trinh, tel. 016/7355-9447, www.lifestartfoundation.org.au, 7am-8pm daily) sells a range of handicrafts and other souvenirs, including jewelry, home wares, and handbags, along with offering a traditional Vietnamese painting course as well as a lantern-making workshop for visitors. The center, founded by Australian Karen Leonard, trains and employs locals with disabilities (many of whom would otherwise be unable to work), in addition to providing disadvantaged youth with educational scholarships. Courses run on a

Tips for Buying Custom Clothing

Packed into the old town and running wild along the surrounding streets, the tailors and shoe-makers of Hoi An offer custom shoes, bags, and clothing with a quick turn-around (usually no more than a day) and at a fraction of what tailor-made items cost in the States. This is the best destination for high-quality custom-made clothing, but the hundreds of options can make it hard to distinguish between good value and too good to be true. When ordering tailored clothes, here are a few things to keep in mind:

Allow yourself enough time. While every tailor in town will claim to make your items in 24 hours or less, you'll want to budget in time for alterations. Tackle your shopping as soon as you arrive in town, so you can allow your tailor plenty of time to perfect your items.

Agree on a price beforehand...and then pay later. With so many tourists milling around town, it's understandable that a shop would require some sort of deposit when taking an order, and it's not uncommon for customers to put down half of the agreed-upon cost up front (always in exchange for a receipt). Unless you've chosen one of the few shops that offers a money-back guarantee, do not pay the full amount for your purchases before they have been made. While there are plenty of good tailors in Hoi An, there are some who produce lower-quality items. If you've paid your entire bill beforehand, you have no negotiating power in alterations or improvements. Prices at most tailors are negotiable, and customers who order multiple garments from a shop can usually arrange a discount.

Pay attention to detail. Once you've chosen a tailor, discussed your options, and placed an order, you'll return the following day for a fitting, at which time you have the opportunity to request adjustments or voice any dissatisfaction you might have. Due to the high volume of orders most tailors receive, not every item comes out perfect, but the mark of a good tailor is in his or her willingness to correct a mistake. Scrutinize each of your purchases and, if something displeases you, speak up before settling up.

daily basis. Both the lantern-making workshop and the painting class are VND525,000 and participants keep their creations at the end.

A more trendy and colorful take on local souvenirs, **The O Collective** (85 Nguyen Thai Hoc, tel. 012/8327-6993, the.o.collective@gmail.com, 9am-9pm daily) houses the work of several different Vietnamese brands that produce everything from fun, modern women's clothing to home wares, accessories, and other odds and ends, including a monster-making workshop for kids. While prices can be steep on some of the larger items, particularly the clothing, this unique array of souvenirs is worth a peek for passing shoppers.

Tailors

One of the most affordable tailors in town, **Hoa Nang—Sunny** (9 Tran Phu, tel. 012/9765-6275, duongchungmy@hotmail.com, 9am-9pm daily) churns out loads of pleasing dresses and suits in a variety of different styles. Off-the-rack clothing is available for purchase, or you can peruse the dozens of dresses around the shop for ideas on your tailored items. Prices are notably cheaper than most places in town, though the quality of the fabric may not live up to other tailors. The skilled Sunny knows her way around a sewing machine and completes one-day orders with quality and ease.

Run by second-generation tailor Thu Thao, **Phuong Nam** (15 Tran Phu, tel. 0510/386-1475, www.hoian-tailors-phuongnam.vn, 9am-8:30pm daily) boasts quality and efficiency while being easier on the wallet than some of Hoi An's other tailors. The small shop offers tasteful ready-made clothing in addition to filling custom orders. Its fabric selection hints at a slightly more male clientele. Phuong Nam has women's dresses off-the-rack. Items are well-made and well-priced.

Though **Silk Road** (91 Nguyen Thai Hoc,

tel. 0510/391-1058, www.silkroadtailor.com, 9am-9pm daily) is only a small shop opposite Hai Cafe, don't let its size fool you. Backed by a team of knowledgeable tailors and an array of fabric options, the tiny shop produces men's and women's clothing and offers helpful tips and recommendations to those who wish to tailor an item but haven't yet decided exactly what they want. Prices are reasonable and reflect the quality of both the fabric and the craftsmanship.

One of the old town's most reputable tailors, **Hoang Kim** (57 Nguyen Thai Hoc, tel. 0510/386-2794, 9am-9pm daily) boasts an endless array of fabrics and a team of skilled craftspeople who can turn around a suit and tie in only a day or two. Salespeople are helpful and attentive. You should have an idea of what you'd like beforehand, as there are less options on-hand, but Hoang Kim's tailors are masters at copying a garment. Prices are reasonable for the quality and the shop's impeccable attention to detail is part of the reason behind its popularity.

A bit of an assembly line rather than a family-run tailor, **Yaly Couture** (47 Nguyen Thai Hoc, tel. 0510/221-2474, www.yalycouture.com, 8:30am-9:30pm daily) is a successful local business that boasts two shops in town (second location: 358 Nguyen Duy Hieu). From the moment you step in the door, an army of sales associates and tailors assist shoppers in selecting designs, picking out a fabric, and taking down measurements. Though it all feels a bit more cookie-cutter than in other shops, there is an obvious reason for Yaly's success. The group's fabrics, skill, and range account for the extra cost.

Accessories

With two shops in the old town area, **Memory** (26 Nguyen Thi Minh Khai, tel. 0510/393-9495, memoryvietnam@gmail.com, 8:30am-9pm daily) produces beautiful, if pricey, original jewelry in a variety of different colors, styles, and materials. While both stores are prolific and cover most of the brand's offerings, its larger building is the most impressive, housed in a whimsical old building full of fun and creative items, though the smaller second shop (96A Bach Dang, tel. 0510/391-1483) is equally lovely.

The small display room at the **Gemstones Art Museum** (130 Nguyen Thai Hoc, tel. 0510/393-8468, www.gam-hoian.com, 9am-10:30pm daily) is well worth a visit for its bizarre but beautiful raw materials, a collection of sparkling gemstones mined from throughout Vietnam. Founded by the talented Vietnamese designer behind the adjoining **Duong shop** (www.duongprecious.com), the cool and unusual exhibition shows shoppers how these precious stones go from raw material to beautiful, original jewelry. The finished products are available for purchase and, given the quality and design, their higher prices are understandable.

An offshoot of the well-known shoemaker Friendly Shoes, **Friendly Bags** (44 Phan Boi Chau, tel. 09/3521-1382, www.friendly-baghoian.com, 9am-9pm daily) is fast gaining ground among those in the market for handmade leather goods. Tucked down a quiet street east of the market, this mini-factory produces high-quality bags in a range of designs with a friendly, professional staff to boot. The owner places a strong emphasis on attention to detail, and a full refund is provided to customers who are not satisfied with their order.

Shoes

With a jam-packed front room, **Nguyen Hoa** (40 Phan Boi Chau, tel. 09/0531-9650, 8:30am-8pm daily) boasts a dizzying variety of shoes, from men's loafers to sneakers, sandals, ladies' flats, wedges, and heels. Pick your own color, pattern, and style and have a cobbler put together your perfect pair. Shoes are well-priced and of decent quality. Check your items before leaving to ensure quality, and don't forget to haggle, as prices are flexible.

One of the most popular shoemakers in town, **Friendly Shoes** (18 Tran Phu, tel. 09/3521-1382, www.friendlyshophoian.com, 8:30am-8:30pm daily) has a reputation for quick, professional service and well-made men's and women's footwear in a variety of materials. Whether it's loafers, heels, flats, sandals, or sneakers, the shop can complete a pair of tailor-made shoes in less than a day and offers a full refund to those not completely satisfied with their order. Peruse the hundreds of shoes that line the store walls in addition to a catalog of previous designs. The expert shoemakers can also copy items from the Internet.

Art and Handicrafts

Hoi An and its surrounding localities are well-known for their lanterns and pottery. You'll find these in shops throughout the old town. For pottery, it's also possible to go straight to the source and pay a visit to nearby Thanh Ha village, where you can watch your souvenirs being made and pick up a few items at a much lower cost. For original artwork, you'll find a few galleries around town with oil and lacquer paintings on display, many of which are concentrated along Nguyen Thi Minh Khai past the Japanese bridge.

Inside a small storefront east of the old town, **The Moon Photo Gallery** (348 Nguyen Duy Hieu, tel. 09/7502-3344, www.

hoianphotogallery.com, 9:30am-9pm daily) displays the work of local photographer Mai Thanh Cuong, who deals in both color and black-and-white images. Countryside scenes and daily life in Hoi An feature heavily in Cuong's work, which has received several awards both internationally and within Vietnam. Prints come in a range of sizes and are reasonably priced.

Located in the heart of the old town, **Hung Long Gallery** (105 Nguyen Thai Hoc, tel. 09/0359-1168, www.hunglong-gallery.com, 9am-6pm daily) showcases the paintings of local artist Nguyen Trung Viet. Often featuring women in *ao dai* (traditional Vietnamese dress), Viet's work has been exhibited in several different countries, from Australia and Spain to the United States, Switzerland, and France, in addition to receiving high recognition from arts organizations within Vietnam.

Right beside the local market, **Hoi An Art Gallery** (6 Nguyen Thai Hoc, tel. 09/0591-1428, www.hoianartgallery.com, 8am-5pm daily) showcases the artwork of local painters within the serene, vibrant setting of Hy Hoa Temple. A variety of oil and silk paintings, lacquer work, and even a few handicrafts are on hand for visitors to peruse.

traditional lanterns in old town Hoi An

Books

For all things Vietnam, **Artbook** (166 Tran Phu, tel. 09/0361-8995, www.artbook.com.vn, 9:30am-9:30pm daily) sells a variety of reading materials dedicated to local history, art, cuisine, and culture as well as plenty of souvenirs, which range from propaganda art postcards to eye-catching notebooks and other knickknacks.

Though you'll find several book exchanges and small shops slinging photocopied paperbacks, **Randy's Book X Change** (Cam Nam, tel. 09/3608-9483, www.bookshoian.com, 9am-7pm daily) on Cam Nam Island is the best. Boasting two rooms packed to the bursting point with English books, not to mention a foreign language section downstairs, you could spend all day perusing the titles in this place. Despite being over a bridge, the shop remains close to the old town. Visitors who make the journey will be rewarded with useful travel advice, including Randy's very own Hoi An "cheat sheet."

SPORTS AND RECREATION

Hoi An is an R&R destination. Aside from shopping—which, in this town, could be categorized as an Olympic event—you won't find too much in the way of active options, but there are plenty of cooking classes and a few cycling opportunities to keep you entertained.

Diving

With the sun-soaked Cham Island nearby, Hoi An has a small but active diving scene, with two major outfits touring the waters nearby. A variety of options are available for certified and non-certified divers as well as a few snorkeling trips. Visibility is best in the area between July and September, but divers still get in underwater exploration as early as February. Hoi An isn't the diving capital of Vietnam, but those who have left Nha Trang or Phu Quoc out of their plans should consider this as their next best bet.

Operating out of Dive Bar, the **Cham Island Diving Center** (88 Nguyen Thai Hoc,

tel. 0510/391-0782, www.chamislanddiving.com, 8am-5pm daily, VND840,000-1,890,000) has been in town for over a decade and offers one-day and multi-day trips with experienced dive masters. PADI courses are available, as is a wealth of free information regarding the islands, the beach, and the town in general. While the diving center is only open until 5pm, feel free to stop by later in the day and ask a few questions, as Dive Bar stays open late.

The combined efforts of an English expat and a Hoi An native, **Blue Coral Diving** (77 Nguyen Thai Hoc, tel. 0510/627-9297, www.divehoian.com, 9am-9pm daily, VND840,000-1,827,000) employs a team of experienced, PADI-certified dive masters alongside a local crew with vast knowledge of the seas around Cham Island. Trips for both certified and non-certified divers are available, as is a snorkeling package and a few PADI courses.

Cycling

Flyers advertising **Heaven and Earth Bicycle Tours** (57 Ngo Quyen, tel. 0510/386-4362, www.vietnam-bicycle.com, 7:30am-10pm daily, VND126,000-1,869,000) can be found on almost every bulletin board and reception desk across town, and with good reason. Hoi An's most popular cycling tour provider, this locally run outfit takes travelers on a leisurely ride out of town and into the nearby countryside, opting for a more off-the-beaten-path experience. Both half- and full-day excursions are available, including trips to Tra Que Vegetable Village and My Son as well as the group's original countryside tour, where you can watch local artisans crafting bricks, straw mats, and wooden ships, among other things. Multi-day homestay trips can be arranged, where travelers will have more opportunity to gain one-on-one contact with locals. To book a tour, visit the main office on An Hoi Island or head to the **outpost** (corner of Nguyen Hoang and La Hoi) closer to the bridge.

The Hoi An arm of popular Dalat-based adventure outfit **Phat Tire Ventures** (62 Ba

Trieu, tel. 0510/391-7839, www.ptv-vietnam. com, 8am-8:30pm daily, VND1,008,000-1,260,000) offers half- and full-day cycles to places like Tra Que Vegetable Village and Cam Kim Island as well as the My Son ruins. High-quality equipment and experienced guides take visitors into Hoi An's surrounding countryside for a day of leisurely cycling. For thrill-seekers, the company provides rock climbing and abseiling adventures at nearby Marble Mountain.

Cooking Classes

It seems every restaurant in town has set up a cooking class for visitors to try their hand at local fare. You'll find half-day courses as cheap as VND315,000, most of which cut right to the chase and roll out a host of prepared ingredients for you to combine as instructed. Others include a market visit, while still more courses go a step beyond and offer hands-on preparation, taking students from start to finish with several local dishes. The classes at **Baby Mustard (Nha Hang Cai Con)** (Tra Que, tel. 09/3572-5740, babymustard.restaurant@gmail.com), a modest little spot near Tra Que Vegetable village, are a solid option.

Combine your cooking with a little sightseeing on the half-day **Thuan Tinh Island Cooking Tour** (Thon 1, Cam Thanh, tel. 09/0647-7770, www.cooking-tour. com, 8:30am-5:30pm daily, VND630,000). Guests visit the local market, exploring the many ingredients that go into Vietnamese cooking before taking a 30-minute boat ride to the picturesque Thuan Tinh Island. From there, you'll prepare a set menu of four tried-and-true local dishes, including beef pho and fresh spring rolls. Each participant leaves with a recipe booklet of some of Vietnam's most popular dishes. The booking fee includes both pickup and dropoff, and vegetarian options are available.

A stone's throw from Cua Dai Beach, **Green Bamboo Cooking School** (21 Truong Minh Hung, tel. 09/0581-5600, www. greenbamboo-hoian.com, 8am-3pm daily, VND735,000) is run by the patient and experienced Ms. Van, a top-notch chef and teacher who provides day-long cooking classes with thorough instruction from start to finish. A market visit is included in the day's outing, and each student is tasked with making one dish. Both carnivorous and vegetarian options are available, and Ms. Van caps her class at 10 students, allowing each participant to gain some hands-on experience. All levels are

Learn how to cook like a local at Baby Mustard's cooking classes.

welcome and the course fee includes a recipe book as well as complimentary pickup and dropoff from your hotel.

ACCOMMODATIONS

There are a few accommodations between the shops and restaurants of the old town, and droves of hotels north of the old town and along the road leading out to Cua Dai Beach. Budget options tend to be concentrated around Hai Ba Trung and Ba Trieu streets, along with a few dorm beds scattered across town. Standard budget amenities include hot water, air-conditioning, and Wi-Fi.

Most places in Hoi An are mid-range, with the majority of hotels charging upwards of VND525,000. Depending on where you stay, this price can still represent great value, as the add-ons (hot water, air-conditioning, Wi-Fi, fridge, minibar, and coffeemaker) included in these accommodations are often much more than what you'd find in a VND210,000 hotel room.

Staying closer to the old town affords easy access to Hoi An's sights, restaurants, and ample shopping. Beach-goers will be fine hanging out near Cua Dai, where there are plenty of restaurants and a place to lay out a towel. As Hoi An's already-astronomical tourism numbers soar, more than a few homestays have opened up. These are not authentic homestays, in which travelers shack up with a local family for the night, but more like a bed-and-breakfast. Many of these smaller, family-owned places are excellent options and provide a more personal experience.

Old Town

VND210,000-525,000

The **Sanh Hien Guesthouse** (7 Nguyen Thi Minh Khai, tel. 0510/386-3631, VND300,000) is more of a homestay, with three small rooms taking up the ground floor of this heritage building. Facilities are basic, with only a bed, a fan, and a small nightstand in each room, plus a shared bathroom out back with hot water. Sanh Hien's location—just three doors down from the Japanese bridge—sets it apart as the only budget accommodation within the old town. There is no Wi-Fi.

VND525,000-1,050,000

An attractive traditional wooden house, the **An Huy Hotel** (30 Phan Boi Chau, tel. 0510/386-2116, VND630,000-850,000, breakfast included) offers a central location at a reasonable price. Rooms are nice and well-kept, and include TVs in addition to the standard amenities. The staff can be hit-or-miss.

VND1,050,000-2,100,000

Ha An Hotel (6-8 Phan Boi Chau, tel. 0510/386-3126, www.haanhotel.com, VND1,155,000-2,185,000, breakfast included) is a charming boutique hotel separated from the road by a lush courtyard garden. Rooms are bright white and well-appointed. The hotel's adjoining restaurant and café serves a range of Vietnamese and Western dishes throughout the day. Ha An operates its own tour outfit, which runs city tours and excursions beyond the old town.

Once the house of a Chinese merchant, the 200-year-old **Vinh Hung Heritage Hotel** (143 Tran Phu, tel. 0510/386-1621, www.vinhhungheritagehotel.com, VND1,785,000-2,205,000) oozes character from its sturdy columns and traditional carved wooden furniture. It's in the heart of the old town. Several high-profile guests have patronized the hotel, including foreign diplomats and Sir Michael Caine. The six updated rooms include standard amenities as well as an in-room safe and a television. The suite rooms have a charming balcony overlooking the street. Breakfast is served at the Vinh Hung Restaurant next door.

OVER VND2,100,000

The rather grand **Hoi An Hotel** (10 Tran Hung Dao, tel. 0510/386-1445, www.hoianhotel.com.vn, VND2,550,000-10,500,000) is a beautiful, sprawling building with a lush interior garden and charming, well-appointed rooms. A modern, sleek reception area gives way to the green courtyard and swimming pool. Guest rooms vary from comfortable deluxe accommodations to posh suites, all of which include basic amenities as well as a private balcony, tea- and coffee-making facilities, and a minibar. A fitness center, spa, and tennis court are on site.

North of Old Town
VND210,000-525,000

Hidden on the narrow part of Tran Cao Van, rooms at the **Hoa My Hotel** (44 Tran Cao Van, tel. 09/0551-8569, www.hoamyhotelhoian.com.vn, VND350,000-400,000, breakfast included) are average but clean and right for the price. Amenities include TV, Wi-Fi access, air-conditioning, and hot water, as well as a hotel pool. The staff are pleasant and this is one of the better value options. Rooms can get a little noisy in the mornings and at night as Tran Cao Van sees a lot of action.

On a street packed with budget options, rooms at the **Hoa Binh Hotel** (696 Hai Ba Trung, tel. 0510/391-6838, www.hoabinhhotelhoian.com, VND189,000 dorm, VND420,000-462,000 double, breakfast included) are fitting for the price, providing clean beds and standard amenities like hot water, air-conditioning, Wi-Fi, television, a fridge, and use of the downstairs pool. Plenty of backpackers turn up for the hotel's dorm beds, which come with personal lockers. A small travel outfit is on-site, and a café serves light meals throughout the day. This is a good spot for the budget crowd.

VND525,000-1,050,000

Sporting a chic red-and-black interior, **Thien Thanh Hotel** (16 Ba Trieu, tel. 0510/391-6545, www.hoianthienthanhhotel.com, VND945,000-1,260,000, breakfast included) comes in a step above the budget offerings on the block, providing more atmosphere as well as complimentary water and standard amenities. Decorative wall hangings made by Vietnam's highland minorities, pottery knick-knacks collected from Thanh Ha village, and throw pillows and lampshades emblazoned with the Chinese symbol for happiness add

to the hotel's charm. Several rooms feature balconies, and the garden patio offers lovely views. Use of the outdoor pool is included in the rate.

North of the old town, **Long Life Hotel** (30 Ba Trieu, tel. 0510/391-6696, www.longlifehotels.com, VND808,500-1,102,500, breakfast included) is a pleasant mid-range option, featuring big, comfy beds and a green-and-white decor. Bathrooms are a generous size and come with large whirlpool tubs. In addition to the standard amenities, there is Wi-Fi, mosquito nets, and daily bottled water. City-view rooms are less expensive and come with a private balcony but are noisier at night. For a few dollars more, garden-view rooms face away from the road. Free bicycle rentals are available, as is use of the pool.

Though it's a little removed from town, the **Sunshine Hotel** (2 Phan Dinh Phung, tel. 0510/393-7899, www.sunshinehoian.com, VND525,000-882,000) makes up for its location with bright, well-appointed rooms, free bicycle rental, and a friendly staff. Three types of rooms are available, standard, deluxe, and superior, each with a private balcony. All feature modern decor and standard amenities, such as hot water, air-conditioning, Wi-Fi access, TV, minibar, an in-room safe, coffee-and tea-making facilities, and complimentary toiletries. A buffet breakfast is served downstairs each morning, and the outdoor swimming pool is open to all guests.

A mid-range option, **Vinh Hung 3** (96 Ba Trieu, tel. 0510/391-6277, www.vinhhung3hotel.com, VND680,000-1,365,000, breakfast included) features a stylish interior and top-notch service. Even its smaller rooms, though windowless, feature a painted bamboo screen, comfy bed, and the standard amenities, including use of the hotel pool. Deluxe and superior options are available.

Trim and tidy, **Thien Nga** (52 Ba Trieu, tel. 0510/391-6330, thienngahoianhotel@gmail.com, VND630,000-735,000, breakfast included) is a small mid-range spot offering both street- and garden-view rooms with hot water, air-conditioning, TV, a fridge, and

Wi-Fi access. The rooms are pleasant, the location is nice, and the staff are friendly.

Cua Dai Beach Road

Accommodations on the road to Cua Dai Beach run the gamut from budget to high-end, with several five-star resorts perched on the edge of the East Sea and a host of mid-range options in between. Some provide daily shuttles both into town and out to the beach. You can also hop on a bicycle and access either area in a matter of minutes.

UNDER VND210,000

Hoi An's backpacker hot spot, **Sunflower Hotel** (397 Cua Dai, tel. 0510/393-9838, sunflowerhoian@gmail.com, VND168,000 dorm, VND462,000-525,000 double, breakfast included) sits a short way out of central Hoi An. Featuring clean, basic rooms with air-conditioning, Wi-Fi access, TV, and hot water, this spot is popular with the budget crowd, particularly its dorms, which offer lockers and en suite bathrooms. Use of the swimming pool is included in the room rate. Additional services, such as laundry, bicycle rentals, tours, and transportation, can be arranged. Thanks to its growing popularity, it's best to book ahead.

VND525,000-1,050,000

Under a mile from the old town, **Hai Au Hotel** (576 Cua Dai, tel. 0510/391-4577, www.haiauhotels.com, VND630,000-882,000, breakfast included) is one of the most popular accommodations along the Cua Dai strip, in large part thanks to its excellent value for money and amiable staff. Rooms are clean, well-kept, and decorated in an eclectic array of colors and patterns. Both the swimming pool downstairs and the restaurant out front are open to guests, and amenities include hot water, air-conditioning, Wi-Fi access, TV, minibar, an in-room safe, and daily bottled water.

Just opposite the Hai Au, **Vaia Boutique Hotel** (489 Cua Dai, tel. 0510/391-6499, www.vaiahotel.com, VND735,000-1,050,000, breakfast included) is a trendy, sleek spot that offers well-appointed rooms with modern Asian elegance. Standard and deluxe options are available, with the former running on the small side, but the plush, generously sized beds make up for this. The usual amenities apply here, from air-conditioning and hot water, TV, minibar, Wi-Fi access, and an in-room safe. Bicycle rentals are free, and guests enjoy complimentary all-day coffee and tea as well as happy hour cocktails.

VND1,050,000-2,100,000

Between Cua Dai Beach and the old town, **Hoi An Pacific** (321 Cua Dai, tel. 0510/392-3777, www.hoianpacific.com, VND1,113,000-1,575,000, breakfast included) is a little rough around the edges but its rooms are tidy and nicely appointed, counting hot water, air-conditioning, TV, Wi-Fi, and coffee- and tea-making facilities among its many amenities. Rooms come in superior, deluxe, and villa, each including pool access. Bathrooms are large and some rooms include a balcony. The villas are particularly nice, with a cozy rattan sitting area and close to the pool. Hourly shuttle buses ferry guests to and from the beach and the old town. The cheerful staff can assist with other travel- and transportation-related services.

Though it appears a little stodgy from the outside, **Glory Hotel Hoi An** (538 Cua Dai, tel. 0510/391-4444, www.gloryhotelhoian.com, VND1,050,000-2,100,000, breakfast included) boasts over 90 guest rooms, all of which feature air-conditioning, hot water, Wi-Fi access, TV, minibar, an in-room safe, a balcony, and a writing desk. Use of the courtyard swimming pool is included in the room rate. Rooms are often discounted February-November. Glory Hotel represents good value for money.

The Earth Villa (380 Cua Dai, tel. 0510/392-6777, www.theearthvilla.com, VND1,050,000-1,470,000, breakfast included), a beautiful set of garden-facing buildings with cozy, well-appointed rooms, lies one mile from Hoi An's old town and boasts a swimming pool and on-site restaurant.

Rooms feature tea- and coffee-making facilities, a television, fridge, Wi-Fi access, hot water, and air-conditioning along with tasteful decor and a generous bathroom.

Bright, cozy, and well-appointed, rooms at the **Lotus Hotel** (330 Cua Dai, tel. 0510/392-3357, www.hoianlotushotel.com, VND1,300,000-2,520,000) are a reasonable size and are set in a traditional-style building that blends seamlessly into its surroundings. Each room comes with a balcony, as well as the usual amenities, including hot water, air-conditioning, Wi-Fi access, TV, a fridge, and tea- and coffee-making facilities. Breakfast is served downstairs, where you'll find pleasant views of the nearby fields. The hotel offers regular shuttles into town for guests and, slightly set back from the street, offers a quieter atmosphere than most.

OVER VND2,100,000

Billing itself as a "green retreat," secluded **Hoi An Chic** (Nguyen Trai, tel. 0510/392-6999, www.hoianchic.com, VND2,940,000-3,990,000) is a mile from the city center. Its beautiful location amid verdant rice paddies makes for a genuine, peaceful countryside experience. The simple, sleek rooms are well-furnished with bright colors. Bathrooms include both an indoor shower and outdoor stone bathtubs. A charming outdoor patio allows guests to enjoy the scenery. Breakfast is served in the breezy, open-air restaurant, and guests are free to laze around the rooftop infinity pool. Free bicycle rentals and shuttles into the old town are available.

The **Victoria Hoi An** (Cua Dai Beach, tel. 0510/392-7040, www.victoriahotels.asia, VND3,392,000-6,572,000) pairs old-world opulence and a beachfront setting. This massive seaside resort offers river- and garden views in its 100-plus rooms, as well as lodgings directly on the beach. All feature tasteful Japanese, French, or traditional Vietnamese decor, as well as a balcony, sitting area, and the standard amenities. A generous ocean-facing pool sits at the center of the complex, complete with rows of comfy deck chairs. The resort

houses a spa, fitness center, restaurant, several bars, and a library. Buffet breakfast is served daily and Victoria's on-site travel outfit can assist in planning excursions around town.

Vietnam's best seaside resort, ★ **The Nam Hai** (Hamlet 1, Dien Duong Village, tel. 0510/394-0000, www.ghmhotels.com, VND13,650,000-21,000,000) consistently rates among the top beach resorts in Southeast Asia. Sprawled across a manicured 35-hectare plot, the resort boasts 60 stunning villas that feature silk-lined beds, plush sofas, lacquered eggshell bathtubs, private gardens, and outdoor rain showers. The smallest lodgings are 860 square feet. Guests have a choice of additional upgrades, such as a beachfront location or private pool. The Nam Hai features two restaurants, a bar, a spa, fitness center, library, private beach, three-tiered infinity pool, and kids' activity villa. Yoga, basketball, table tennis, and badminton are available to guests, as are regular shuttles to and from Hoi An.

FOOD

Hoi An is a foodie's paradise, blessed with an incredible set of local specialties, most of which cannot be found elsewhere in Vietnam. The tastes and traditions of this town's unique cuisine are a must-try. From hearty *cao lau* (a local noodle specialty) to the dim sum-style "white rose" (steamed shrimp dumplings), there are plenty of local meals to keep your taste buds interested. Hoi An's masterful chefs boast the skills to execute not only excellent Vietnamese meals but also a range of sumptuous Western creations. Peruse the menus of several old town eateries and you'll find fusion cuisine, sesame-crusted tuna, and Moroccan couscous, though these are in more upmarket spots.

Cafés and Bakeries

Staffed by employees with hearing impairments, the **Reaching Out Tea House** (131 Tran Phu, tel. 0510/391-0168, www.reachingoutvn.com, 9am-8:30pm daily, VND45,000-110,000) is an extension of the nonprofit shop Reaching Out. Emphasizing local coffees

Specialties of Hoi An

Hoi An is one place where you don't want to miss out on local cuisine. Boasting an array of dishes unique to the area, Hoi An's chefs take great pride in their creations. The most noteworthy of local meals is **cao lau,** a meat and noodle dish sold on every street corner and in every restaurant in the old town and beyond. Topped with fresh greens, fried wontons, and as much—or as little—spice as you'd like, this particular meal is special because of its noodles, which are flat and much denser than average rice noodles, and can only be made with the water from Ba Le Well, the town's ancient Cham water source. While the uninitiated may not know the difference, Hoi An locals insist that they can tell the genuine article from its impostors.

Beyond *cao lau,* Hoi An's other culinary masterpieces include **white rose** *(banh vac).* Not unlike Chinese dim sum, these small, steamed shrimp dumplings are shaped like flowers, hence the name, and served with fish sauce. The town also boasts its own version of **banh xeo** (savory Vietnamese pancakes), which are smaller than their southern counterparts, though just as tasty. Last but not least are **fried wontons,** an item borrowed from the Chinese that, at first glance, resemble tortillas and are packed with pork, egg, or shrimp and topped with vegetables.

and teas, the menu includes a variety of Fair Trade beverages (which can also be enjoyed in a sampler of three), small biscuits, and other goodies. Large wooden easy chairs and communal spaces make for a comfortable environment. Traditional tea sets and small bonsai trees are on display around the shop. Guests communicate with the staff by way of an order form, notepads, and small blocks with phrases like "water," "bill," and "thank you" printed on the front. With no music and no Wi-Fi, this shop is a charming and atmospheric spot.

Run by a coffee connoisseur, **Mia Coffee** (20 Phan Boi Chau, tel. 09/0555-2061, 7:30am-6pm daily, VND20,000-40,000) sits on a sunny corner at the eastern end of the old town. Small tables line the outer edge of the building, while a massive bean roaster keeps the interior smelling of coffee. The owner roasts and packages all his own beans, which are grown in the Central Highlands, and is an expert on caffeinated beverages. Swing by in the morning and you'll find plenty of early-risers getting their caffeine fix for the day.

International

One of Hoi An's best, the long-running ★ **Cargo Club** (107-109 Nguyen Thai Hoc, tel. 0510/391-1227, www.cargo-hoian.com, 8am-11am daily, VND80,000-325,000) is a pretty colonial building with large, shuttered windows and a cozy setup. Its exemplary baked goods run the gamut from croissants and crispy French breads to a mouthwatering array of cakes. The dinner menu is just as noteworthy, featuring couscous, sesame crusted tuna, and lamb shank in its offerings. With a mellow atmosphere and plenty of comfy chairs, Cargo is a prime spot for coffee and cake or a full meal.

Across the river from the old town, **Fusion Lounge** (35 Nguyen Phuc Chu, tel. 0510/393-0333, hoian-lounge@fusion-resorts.com, 8am-10:30pm daily, VND55,000-145,000), an extension of Danang's Fusion Maia Resort, represents new-school Hoi An in its sleek modern setup and unique menu. Boasting items like watermelon-feta salad, surf 'n turf burgers and artisanal European and Asian teas, this forward-thinking eatery makes a splash with good food, good service, and a good riverfront location. The restaurant offers beer, wine, and cocktails, making this a nice spot for a sunset drink on the river.

Just beyond the eastern edge of the old town, decked out in yellow and black, the **Bee's Knees Cafe** (313 Nguyen Duy Hieu, tel. 0510/392-9796, www.beeskneescafe.com, 9am-10:30pm daily, VND70,000-150,000) lives up to its name. The menu boasts a long list of burgers, pasta, and pizza alongside several Vietnamese mains and vegetarian options, and a solid ice cream selection. Staff are friendly and attentive, and the prices are right.

Halfway between Cua Dai Beach and the old town, **Dingo Deli** (277 Cua Dai, tel. 0510/653-5459, www.dingodelihoian.com, 8am-9:30pm daily, VND75,000-140,000) is a jack-of-all-trades, dishing out tasty Western food as well as imported groceries and sound travel advice. Staff are friendly and attentive. Outdoor patio seating and an air-conditioned indoor dining room are available. Burgers, pasta, sandwiches, and meat pies are on the menu, as are hearty Western breakfasts and regular daily specials.

The friendly folks at Hoi An's Indian restaurant, **Namaste** (40 Tran Hung Dao, tel. 09/3498-8674, www.namaste-hoian.com, noon-10pm daily, VND75,000-155,000), go above and beyond, serving a host of mouthwatering Indian meals, from chicken and lamb to fish and vegetarian fare. The inviting indoor dining room is decked out in white tablecloths and warm lighting. Namaste's fare offers a pleasant departure from local cuisine.

Street Food

There are a few street stalls in the old town. But, head a block or two outside the UNESCO zone and there are plenty of roadside eats along Phan Chau Trinh and beyond. Backpackers staying in the Ba Trieu area can take a stroll down Thai Phien to find cheap and tasty local fare.

For all the town's culinary specialties in one centrally located place, the food stalls within the **Hoi An Market** (Tran Phu and Nguyen Hue, sunrise-sunset, VND20,000-50,000) whip up a whole host of tasty local dishes, from *cao lau* (the local noodle specialty) and *mi quang* (rice noodle soup with shrimp and pork) to several other Vietnamese favorites. This is a good spot to survey all the options first. Check with your respective food vendor regarding the price beforehand, even if the amount appears to be posted, as these signs are sometimes ignored.

At the southern end of Tran Cao Van, **Madame Khanh the Banh Mi Queen** (115 Tran Cao Van, 6am-8pm daily, VND20,000) has been selling mouthwatering Vietnamese sandwiches for over 30 years. It's possible to pick and choose your ingredients, but Madame Khanh has her product down to an art, and tucking into a sandwich with all the

cao lau, a specialty noodle dish native to Hoi An

fixings is your best bet. Prices run on the high side for a *banh mi* (Vietnamese sandwich), but the resulting meal is worth every dong. Vegetarians should steer clear, as sandwiches feature several kinds of lunch meat. It's important to remain patient as you wait for your sandwich; service can be slow.

With the colorful Ngu Bang Assembly Hall serving as a backdrop, Hoi An's best ★ *banh beo* (near corner of Tran Phu and Hoang Van Thu, from 2pm daily, VND5,000/piece) vendor sets up shop every afternoon just south of Tran Phu and slings a couple hundred of these heavenly snacks. Each steamed rice cake comes in a miniature porcelain bowl, known as a *chen,* and is topped with a dollop of shrimp paste, some minced pork, and a few deep-fried *cao lau* noodles. Liberal amounts of fish sauce bring an added flavor. The low street-side seating is the perfect place to people-watch. For something truly unique, a "sweet" version of the rice cakes is available; it includes all the same savory toppings as the original.

Not far from its namesake, **Ba Le Well** (45/51 Tran Hung Dao, tel. 0510/386-4443, 9am-10pm daily, VND110,000/person) sits between the alley entrance off Phan Chau Trinh and Hoi An's famous water source. With conventional metal tables and plastic stools, this outdoor eatery offers a variety of local cuisine with a set menu of specialties that includes white rose dumplings, *cao lau* noodles and *banh xeo* (savory Vietnamese pancakes), as well as fruit for dessert. Since it's designed with foreign visitors in mind, the restaurant does a nice job of covering all the bases and saves you the hassle of poring over a menu.

Vegetarian

While meat-free restaurants are trickier to find, most of Hoi An's restaurants offer a vegetarian selection on their menu.

Dam Vegetarian's (alley between 69 and 71 Phan Chau Trinh, 7am-8pm daily, VND15,000-25,000) excellent rendition of the local noodle delicacy, *cao lau,* makes the small shop well worth a visit. You'll find nothing

special in terms of decor, but meals are tasty and affordable. Dam's massive metal street cart offers a nice selection of tofu and veggie dishes as well.

The meatless answer to Cafe 43 across the street, **Minh Hien** (50 Tran Cao Van, tel. 09/3240-3905, 8am-10pm daily, VND25,000-80,000) sticks strictly to tofu and veggies, offering the same laid-back outdoor seating and pleasant service surrounded by an impressive floor-to-ceiling collection of Vietnamese and Japanese comic books. Portions are on the small side, but at prices like these, you can order two mains apiece and still save money.

Vietnamese

A short walk from the old town brings you to **Cafe 43** (43 Tran Cao Van, tel. 0510/386-2587, www.cafe43hoian.com, 8am-10pm daily, VND25,000-140,000), where the shaded open-air dining area is often packed with foreigners and you'll find tasty Vietnamese food at a fraction of the downtown price. This quiet, friendly spot sees a regular crowd of hungry backpackers throughout the day, and its fresh beer keeps the place open well into the night.

Miss Ly's (22 Nguyen Hue, tel. 0510/386-1603, lycafe22@yahoo.com, 10am-10pm daily, VND50,000-150,000) cozy, welcoming little restaurant sits a short walk north of the central market and has been serving customers for decades. Hoi An specialties like *cao lau* and Chinese-style wonton soup are on the menu, as are plenty of other hearty, home-cooked Vietnamese meals. Paintings line the wall and each sturdy wooden table is set with a single rose. Large windows open onto the street, affording diners a pleasant vantage point from which to take in the passing scene. Miss Ly has expanded to a second venue next door.

Along the main old town drag, **Cato** (22 Nguyen Thai Hoc, tel. 0510/391-0171, 10am-8:30pm daily, VND45,000-110,000) offers a host of tasty Vietnamese dishes, including a sampler plate of local specialties, as well as a range of mains, noodles, and soups. Prices are more affordable than most downtown eateries and the staff are a cheerful bunch. Thick central columns and beautiful wooden latticework run the length of this traditional house, making for a pleasant atmosphere.

One of the old town's most popular restaurants, **Morning Glory** (106 Nguyen Thai Hoc, tel. 0510/224-1555, www.restaurant-hoian.com, 8:30am-10pm daily, VND55,000-165,000) is owned by the industrious Ms. Vy, also the mastermind behind Cargo Club and the large, buffet-style Market Restaurant across the river. Its menu showcases a range of home-cooked Vietnamese meals, all of which are prepared in the open kitchen at the center of the restaurant. Diners watch as chefs put together dishes like grilled king prawns and an endless array of clay pot meats. Though portions run small, these delicious renditions of Vietnamese soul food keep customers coming back time and again. The restaurant also runs **cooking classes** (VND672,000-1,155,000), which are taught by Ms. Vy, a third-generation chef.

Though the bakery display case at the front of **Luong Gia** (34 Le Loi, tel. 0510/391-1899, 8am-11pm daily, VND35,000-145,000) is usually enough to convince pedestrians to come inside, the restaurant's meals are equally satisfying. The menu lists a range of Vietnamese dishes, including the usual pork, beef, chicken, and veggies, plus a few Italian options for variety. The friendly owners and casual atmosphere make this place a worthy choice for lunch or coffee and dessert.

INFORMATION AND SERVICES

Hoi An's official **tourist information center** (78 Le Loi, tel. 0510/391-5454, www.hoianancienttown.vn, 7am-9pm daily) doubles as a ticket vendor for the old town sights. It doesn't offer much in the way of free information. With so many independent operators in Hoi An and plenty of helpful hotel receptionists, you should be able to find solid travel advice by asking around. If you're in the neighborhood, **Randy's Book X Change** (Cam Nam, tel. 09/3608-9483, www.

bookshoian.com, 9am-7pm daily) has a small "Hoi An cheat sheet" that visitors are welcome to peruse.

You'll find a **Vietin Bank** (9 Le Loi, tel. 0510/221-2604, www.vietinbank.vn, 7:30am-11:30am and 1:30pm-5pm Mon.-Fri., 7am-11am Sat.), just north of the old town, that can assist with exchanges. ATMs are widely available on the streets lining the outskirts of the old town.

Hoi An's central **post office** (6 Tran Hung Dao, tel. 0510/386-1480, www.hoianpost.com, 6:30am-9pm daily) handles all packages and post. For Internet, several shops just outside the old town area offer access to a computer, including **Min's Internet** (2 Truong Minh Luong, 7am-10pm daily, VND20,000/hour), though its prices, along with most in the area, border on exorbitant.

For minor bumps and bruises, the **Hoi An Hospital** (4 Tran Hung Dao, tel. 0510/391-4660) can fix you up, but anything major is best treated in Danang, about 30 minutes away.

GETTING THERE
Air
Visitors flying to Hoi An from Hanoi or HCMC will land at the **Danang International Airport** (DAD, www.danangairportonline.com), a 30-minute drive from town. Travelers should have no problem hailing a cab or *xe om* driver for the ride to town. Both cost around VND400,000.

Bus
Depending upon your point of departure, buses to Hoi An arrive at various points around the city. From Nha Trang, the ride costs VND249,000. From Hue to Hoi An is VND89,000, and from Danang, it's VND18,000.

While the town has its own long-distance bus station, local vehicles are aging and you'll find better, more comfortable services through **Hanh Cafe** (2 Thai Phien, tel. 0510/386-4609, www.hanhcafe.vn, 6:30am-9pm daily) or **Sinh Tourist** (587 Hai Ba Trung, tel. 0510/386-3948, www.thesinhtourist.vn, 6am-10pm daily), both of which offer routes throughout central Vietnam and beyond.

Local buses from Danang (20-30 minutes, VND18,000) drop riders off at the **public bus station** (corner of Le Hong Phong and Nguyen Tat Thanh, 5:30am-5:30pm daily) hourly.

If you're traveling to Danang from Hoi An, the fee collectors on these buses overcharge foreign patrons. Look at the sign posted beside the bus door (often covered by a jacket) in order to check the correct fare, and have exact change available. Anything you hand the fee collector will be pocketed and no change offered in return.

Train

While Hoi An does not have a train station, more than a few travelers make the train trip up to Danang (from Hue, Hanoi, HCMC, or Nha Trang), then hop in a taxi or on the back of a *xe om* for the remainder of the journey, a 30-minute drive (VND400,000). Cabs and *xe om* drivers will be awaiting fares when the train arrives at the station.

GETTING AROUND

More than most Vietnamese destinations, Hoi An is a very walkable town. The old quarter, where the majority of travelers spend their time, can be covered on foot in an afternoon. There's really no need to bother with additional transportation, though renting a bicycle for the day and wheeling your way around is not a bad idea, either.

Taxis and *Xe Om*

You'll find *xe om* drivers camped out on street corners across town. During the daytime ban on motor vehicles in the old town area, you will have to walk a few blocks north to catch a motorbike ride. The same goes for taxis, but you'll find plenty of **Mailinh** (tel. 0510/392-9292) cabs hovering around the outskirts of the old town.

Hired Vehicles

Bicycles, the preferred method of travel in this town, are readily available at most hotels and guesthouses, as well as through rental shops in the area. Rates usually start around VND30,000-40,000 per day and are a great way to wander around the old town and a little farther afield. For longer trips, you can find motorbike rentals around Hoi An, which run VND120,000-200,000 per day.

CHAM ISLAND

Boasting plenty of sunny, white-sand coast and a pagoda or two, **Cham Island** is often visited by snorkeling and scuba diving outfits, thanks to its attractive underwater landscapes. While these tours tend to be more expensive than the locally run sightseeing-and-snorkeling combos, you're better off paying the extra cash for the fancier excursion, as these usually offer more bang for your buck.

Tours are the most popular way to explore the islands. Most hotel travel outfits offer day trips to the island, but it's more enjoyable to go on your own and spend the night on the island.

If you're pressed for time but determined to see the island, the once-daily **ferry** (Song Hoi Tourist, Au Co, tel. 0510/386-1332, www.songhoitourism.com, VND150,000) leaves Cua Dai Harbor at 8:15am and returns from the island at 1:30pm, giving you just a few hours to explore the island on your own. The ride is 30 minutes long. It's a good idea to have a Vietnamese speaker call ahead and ensure that the boat is running.

Travelers with more time can look into island homestays, which are reasonably priced and help support the local community. Facilities are basic—a Western toilet, a cold shower, and a bed with mosquito net—and electricity doesn't run most of the day. For those looking to escape the mainland hustle, accommodations on Cham Island are a worthy option. For more information on homestays, check out the website for **Homestay Bai Huong** (www.homestaybaihuong.com), which coordinates homestays (VND120,000/person) with local island residents and travelers. Bring enough cash for your trip, as there are no ATMs on Cham Island.

MY SON RUINS

Buried deep within the mountains west of Hoi An, the **My Son Ruins** (Duy Phu, Duy Xuyen, tel. 0510/373-1309, www.mysonsanctuary.com.vn, 6am-5pm daily, VND100,000) are a complex of Angkorian-age Hindu temples that have partially withstood the test of time, existing today as moss-covered, mystical stone structures. Before it was a tourist hot spot, a UNESCO site, or a thriving 18th-century port town, Hoi An belonged to the kings of Champa, a powerful matriarchal kingdom that worshipped several Hindu gods, most commonly Shiva, and began building temples in the My Son valley as early as the 4th century. Subsequent rulers added to the site's collection of religious structures, resulting in several eras of Cham architecture comprising the ruins.

By the time French explorers stumbled upon the temples in 1885, My Son was an overgrown, forgotten place. In the following decades, teams of French and Vietnamese architects studied and spruced up the site, occasionally removing sculptures and other important pieces for posterity. Thirteen temple groups were discovered, with the original count numbering over 70 structures.

Scholars continued to study the area until WWII and the onset of the Franco-Vietnam War. As the country gained independence and Vietnam slid into another armed conflict, American bombs destroyed significant portions of the My Son complex, toppling a 92-foot tower, one of the site's most important structures. Thanks to the efforts of Polish architect Kazimierz Kwiatkowski (who was instrumental in helping Hoi An achieve its UNESCO status) and a Vietnamese colleague, Hoang Dao Kinh, My Son received a second facelift in the 1980s before gaining UNESCO recognition in 1999.

Today, visitors to the site often make the 25-mile journey by way of a day tour, many of which are offered at travel outfits in Hoi An. These trips range in price, but all provide the added benefit of a local guide, as the site itself does not offer much in the way of historical

intricate carvings at My Son Ruins

information. For independent travelers, the road to My Son is fairly agreeable, and large, hard-to-miss signs direct you most of the way.

Once you arrive, you'll be required to purchase a ticket at the entry gate, where a pair of exhibition rooms display artifacts from the temples as well as a collection of historical images related to the temples' restoration. This is a must for independent travelers, as it helps you appreciate the history and architecture of the site. From here, drive another mile up to the complex, where tour buses park and Cham cultural performances take place thrice daily at 9:30am, 10:30am, and 2:30pm.

A small footpath leads to the largest and most significant temple groups, B, C, and D, which are clustered together in a clearing. These structures date between the 7th and 13th centuries and feature some of the most intact temples at My Son. Two of the D temples now serve as miniature exhibits, showcasing well-preserved statues and other relics. These structures suffered under

American ammunition: Look for a large, perfectly round bomb crater sitting on one edge of the complex.

To the northeast, group A hails from the 9th century and used to house the complex's tallest temple, though you wouldn't know it from the modest structures in existence today. Farther on, group G bears the only written record of construction at My Son, its looping Sanskrit letters carved into a tablet to the left of the main temple.

Groups E and F stand together at the edge of the grounds. Some of the oldest temples still in existence, these 8th-century structures bore the most damage from Vietnam's wars, with one or two now at risk of collapsing.

Most tours arrive at My Son around mid-morning. If you have your own set of wheels, it's best to visit before or after this time, as the crowds detract from My Son's appeal.

Extensive de-mining efforts have helped to remove most of the unexploded ordnance threat from the My Son area, but stick to the well-worn paths and Cham towers, as the lush jungle around the site may still hold more than trees and temples.

The South-Central Coast

A vibrant, sun-soaked shoreline runs unbroken from the tumultuous cliffs of Quy Nhon down to Mui Ne's bizarre tropical sand dunes. The bulk of Vietnam's most-visited mainland beaches belong to this region. Rounding out the

belly of the "S," this gently curving stretch of coast is a feast of greens and blues, with lush jungle green palms and azure waters, providing a picture-perfect backdrop for the region's sleepy fishing villages and bustling city thoroughfares. Whether you're an adventure junkie plying the surf of Mui Ne, a party animal living it up on the sands of Nha Trang, or just a traveler in search of some good old-fashioned rest and relaxation on the quieter shores of Phan Rang or Quy Nhon, there are plenty of places to lay your towel here.

Beyond the beach, the south-central coast boasts an equally colorful history as the former kingdom of Champa, an ancient Hindu civilization whose red-brick ruins still dot the shoreline today, and as a thriving part of the nation's fishing industry, awash with brightly hued wooden boats and miles of wispy white fishing net. Farther inland, 80 miles from shore, the highlands town of Dalat provides an excellent contrast to its coastal cousins, with adventure travel written all over the undulating mountains and dense forests.

The major stopover on the south-central coast is Nha Trang, the largest and flashiest of the region's cities, where sunny beach days give way to all-night parties. Some may venture away from the sand and on to Dalat, gateway to Vietnam's interior and home to mountainous adventure. Those seeking a more anonymous beach destination will be rewarded at Phan Rang or Quy Nhon, whose peaceful shores can be a much-needed escape from the buzz and chaos of Vietnam's larger cities without having to take a step off the beaten track.

While parts of this coast enjoy clear skies year-round thanks to a semi-arid climate, south-central Vietnam is at its best from February to April, when the temperature has risen but the rain has yet to arrive. Sunshine prevails through the summer months until August, though the heat during the latter part

Previous: Nha Trang Beach; Fairy Spring. **Above:** Po Nagar Towers.

Look for ★ to find recommended
sights, activities, dining, and lodging.

Highlights

★ **Po Nagar Towers:** These rust-hued Hindu temples date back as early as the 8th century and honor the ancient Cham goddess Po Nagar, Lady of the Kingdom (page 240).

★ **Nha Trang Beach:** Nha Trang's brilliant white shores and turquoise waters are the highlight of this sun-drenched southern hub (page 245).

★ **Nha Trang's Mud Baths and Hot Springs:** Get down and dirty in the thermal mud baths of Nha Trang (page 250).

★ **Xuan Huong Lake:** The crown jewel of Dalat, this picturesque lake makes it into many a photo of Vietnam's rustic highland resort town (page 271).

★ **Hang Nga Crazy House:** With its odd angles and warped facades, this unique building is a departure from architectural convention (page 272).

★ **Mui Ne's White Dunes:** A bizarre windswept landscape of sparkling white sands overlooks the ocean (page 291).

of this period can get oppressive. The fall is reserved for the rainy season, when winds pick up along the southern part of the coast and cooler weather settles over Nha Trang and Quy Nhon.

HISTORY

For over a thousand years, from the beginning of the 2nd century to the mid-1600s, Vietnam's south-central coast belonged to the powerful kingdom of Champa. Divided into four separate states, this matriarchal Hindu empire made its living off maritime trade, dealing in luxury goods like eaglewood and silk, in addition to constructing hundreds of soaring red-brick religious towers. The kingdom's original capital, situated just west of Hoi An, housed its major religious, political, and economic centers at the height of the Champa reign during the 9th century. This tenure was short-lived: the empire was often embroiled in military conflicts with the Khmer, their neighbors to the west, as well as the northern Dai Viet, ancestors of today's Vietnamese.

As outside forces began to overtake their land, the Cham were forced to flee south, their territory growing smaller and smaller until, in the 15th century, the Dai Viet dealt a fatal blow to the kingdom, destroying the Champa capital in what is now Binh Dinh province. Many escaped to Cambodia, scattering the Cham community across two countries, while the kingdom in Vietnam was reduced to a tiny portion of what is now Ninh Thuan and Binh Thuan provinces. As the Vietnamese and, later, the French took over, this once-great empire was reduced to a handful of often-marginalized groups along the south-central coast and hidden away in the Mekong Delta.

Nowadays, the largely Vietnamese population makes its living offshore, with thousands of brightly colored wooden fishing boats plying the bountiful waters of the East Sea. Like the rest of the country, the south-central coast experienced hardships under French colonialism in the mid-1800s and later fought the battles of the Franco-Vietnam and American Wars. While this region saw less violence

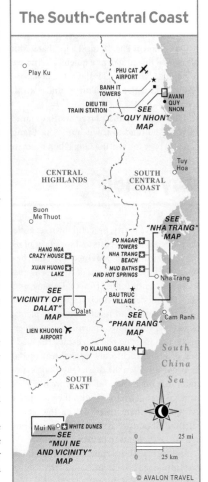

than some others in the country, there are still places, particularly around Phan Thiet and Mui Ne, where landmines and other evidence of Vietnam's troubled past remain. Nonetheless, this coast continues to support a strong fishing industry in addition to boasting a growing tourism industry and some of the country's best fish sauce.

PLANNING YOUR TIME

Most travelers can hit all the highlights of this region in a little over a week, though you may need more time if you veer off the coast to Dalat. Spend 3-4 days in Nha Trang. If you crave beach time beyond that, spend 2-3 days in Quy Nhon or Phan Rang-Thap Cham. Mui Ne can be substituted as a quieter alternative to popular Nha Trang. Dalat is the polar opposite of the region's coast towns, and is worth a stay of 2-4 days.

This region spans a large swath of land, so travelers tend to town-hop. Nha Trang can be a base for visiting Quy Nhon or Phan Rang-Thap Cham. Culture vultures and history buffs will breeze through the area fairly quickly, making short stops in each destination to glimpse the pagodas and historical sites scattered along the shore, while beach bums are sure to stick around longer, as this is Vietnam's prime spot for sun and sand.

Highway 1, the largest national road, is the major route for traveling between the region's cities.

Quy Nhon

Quy Nhon is a pretty, peaceful town set amid the plunging seaside cliffs and soaring mountains of Binh Dinh province. Halfway between the hustle and bustle of Nha Trang and Vietnam's central cities, Hoi An, Danang, and Hue, this modest provincial capital is blessed with brilliant, sun-kissed shores and plenty of genuine small-town charm, both of which make it an inviting place to escape the madness of larger beachfront cities or break up the long journey down the coast. Quy Nhon's surroundings offer room for adventure in a less-trodden part of Vietnam, with the province's ever-present Cham towers dotting the nearby hills and vibrant green rice paddies spread out across the flatlands in between.

Summer is a busy time with affluent domestic tourists vacationing north of Nha Trang. Quy Nhon doesn't see much traffic the rest of the year, as temperatures drop and it rains November-February.

The town's quiet is sure to be short-lived. Construction work is ongoing on a waterfront cable car, which will connect the beach to Phuong Mai Peninsula. Most travelers passing through Quy Nhon stick around for a few days at most before carrying on, as the only real attraction is the beach.

SIGHTS

Beyond the beach, Quy Nhon does not offer much in the way of sights, though its nearby Cham towers make for an interesting and scenic adventure outside the city limits. Most travelers get around town just fine on foot.

Long Khanh Pagoda

Over 300 years old, **Long Khanh Pagoda** (141 Tran Cao Van, tel. 05/6374-9388, www.todinhlongkhanh.com, sunrise-sunset daily) is Quy Nhon's most famous Buddhist building and worth a peek if you're wandering around town. Its entrance gate, just around the corner from the local football stadium, opens onto a soaring nine-tiered tower flanked by stone dragons and guarded by a statue of Quan Am. This building is the largest and newest on the premises, and has the least character. Inside the complex is a 55-foot blue-green Buddha standing at the center of the pagoda's bonsai garden. Caretakers and monks often hang out here during the day; you may have to ask one of them to let you into the often-locked main hall, a squat but beautiful bungalow with aging roof tiles. Inside, Long Khanh boasts two separate altars, each with a trio of statues lined up before a larger Buddha. The main hall is in reasonably good shape, considering its most recent construction was in the early 18th century. The caretakers are friendly and happy to give tours of the place.

Binh Dinh Museum

In a courtyard surrounded by cannons and

Quy Nhon

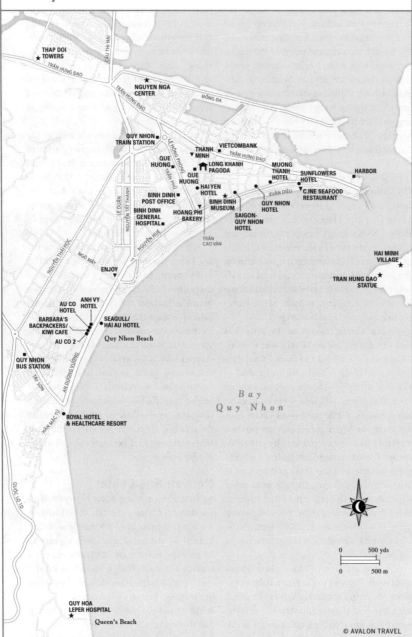

THAP DOI
TOWERS

TRẦN HƯNG ĐẠO

NGUYEN NGA
CENTER

ĐỐNG ĐA

TRẦN HƯNG ĐẠO

QUY NHON
TRAIN STATION

THANH
MINH

VIETCOMBANK

TRẦN HƯNG ĐẠO

QUE
HUONG

LONG KHANH
PAGODA

MUONG
THANH
HOTEL

SUNFLOWERS
HOTEL

HARBOR

QUE
HUONG

XUÂN DIỆU

HAI YEN
HOTEL

C.INE SEAFOOD
RESTAURANT

BINH DINH
POST OFFICE

HOANG PHI
BAKERY

BINH DINH
MUSEUM

QUY NHON
HOTEL

BINH DINH
GENERAL
HOSPITAL

SAIGON-
QUY NHON
HOTEL

TRẦN
CAO VÂN

HAI MINH
VILLAGE

ENJOY

TRAN HUNG DAO
STATUE

ANH VY
HOTEL

AU CO
HOTEL

BARBARA'S
BACKPACKERS/
KIWI CAFE

SEAGULL/
HAI AU HOTEL

AU CO 2

Quy Nhon Beach

QUY NHON
BUS STATION

B a y
Q u y   N h o n

ROYAL HOTEL
& HEALTHCARE RESORT

| 0 | 500 yds |
| 0 | 500 m |

QUY HOA
LEPER HOSPITAL

Queen's Beach

© AVALON TRAVEL

LÊ HỒNG PHONG
TRẦN PHÚ
LÊ DUẨN
NGUYỄN TẤT THÀNH
NGÔ MÂY
NGUYỄN HUỆ
NGUYỄN THÁI HỌC
AN DƯƠNG VƯƠNG
TÂY SƠN
HÀN MẶC TỬ
QUỐC LỘ 1D
CẦU THỊ NẠI

old military vehicles, the oddly shaped **Binh Dinh Museum** (26 Nguyen Hue, tel. 05/6382-6997, 7am-11am and 2pm-5pm Mon.-Fri.) houses the same exhibits you'd expect to find in a provincial museum, featuring sections on the history, industry, and people of the region, peppered with a few English signs to orient foreign visitors. Displays on the ethnic minorities of Binh Dinh and the Cham sculpture section at the back are particularly interesting, as is the revolutionary history exhibit on the right. The entire second level is reserved for photographs of Ho Chi Minh.

Thap Doi Towers

On a street corner heading northwest out of town, the **Thap Doi Towers** (corner of Tran Hung Dao and Thap Doi, 6:30am-10:30pm daily, VND8,000) are a piece of 12th-century history surrounded by the present-day bustle of Quy Nhon. Sporting vegetation on the roof, the 59- and 65-foot towers have held up well over time, with the larger of the two still home to a massive stone *linga* and *yoni* (statue representing male and female energies).

So few Cham remain in the area that this site doesn't see many religious visitors. The local government has turned Thap Doi into a small park of sorts, with a handful of benches set up around the well-manicured lawn, and several tall, willowy palm trees on the premises. While most other Cham towers along the Vietnamese coast are perched atop rocky hills or surrounded by arid landscapes, these two stand out against a vibrant green backdrop. Thap Doi's architecture is also original, differing slightly from other Cham designs. Instead of the usual reliefs of Shiva that top most of these red-brick towers, Thap Doi's multi-tiered rooftop features the bird Garuda, a prominent creature in Hindu mythology.

Visitors are free to roam the park on their own. It doesn't take much time to explore the entire grounds. Across the street are a handful of cafés and street food stalls where you can stop for a quick coffee break or a snack.

Tran Hung Dao Statue

The mammoth **Tran Hung Dao statue** (Hai Minh village, sunrise-sunset daily), built in 1972, leans off the edge of Phuong Mai Peninsula facing the Quy Nhon shoreline and can only be accessed by boat. Tran Hung Dao, a 13th-century war hero and one of Vietnam's most famous military leaders, is credited with twice defeating the Mongol army led by Kublai Khan, first emperor of China's Yuan dynasty.

To get to the statue catch a boat at the **harbor** (Ham Tu) on the eastern edge of town. Some polite but stern haggling should bring the price down as low as VND20,000 or VND30,000 one-way for an individual traveler. This is also a good time to arrange return transport, as boats to and from the village do not follow a regular schedule.

When you've made it safely across the sea, follow the shoreline to the right past Hai Minh's buildings to the rocky, forested edge of the peninsula. Hidden between the overgrown brambles and debris is a small, semi-paved path up toward the statue, which will be visible from the moment you land. Of course, the statue itself is worth a look, but the real showstopper here is the view of Quy Nhon from this vantage point, as you can see its coastline decorated with circular fishing boats and bright, colorful wooden vessels. With more time, you can also do some wandering around the area to catch partial glimpses of the other side of Phuong Mai Peninsula as well as the nearby lighthouse.

Nguyen Nga Center

At first glance, the modest **Nguyen Nga Center** (91A Dong Da, tel. 05/6381-8272, www.nguyennga.org, 7:30am-7pm daily) hidden on the far side of town appears to be nothing more than a souvenir shop: its shelves are stocked with knickknacks and jewelry, handbags, artwork, and a few items of clothing. The story behind this narrow building and the people in it is an inspiring tale that makes the trip out here all the more worthwhile. Founded by the inimitable Ms.

fishing boats moored near Quy Nhon Beach

stick to Quy Nhon's local beaches. Sand flies occasionally make an appearance here.

Quy Nhon Beach

Quy Nhon Beach (An Duong Vuong) is peaceful, accessible, and clean, making it a large part of the town's appeal. Stretching past the local university and alongside Children's Park, Quy Nhon's yellow sands remain uncluttered, affording easy public access to visitors and shores free from roving vendors or additional fees. On the northern end, fishing boats pull into the harbor, making this a less desirable place for swimming, but there are a few nice cafés and plenty of seafood restaurants nearby.

Around the middle of Xuan Dieu heading toward An Duong Vuong, a set of volleyball nets and a lifeguard's tower hint at the action Quy Nhon gets during high season; there are some nice views here. The best place to lay out and catch some rays is past the large roundabout where Xuan Dieu ends and An Duong Vuong begins. Fishing vessels are less common here and this stretch of sand sees considerably less foot traffic during the day.

Quy Hoa Beach and Leper Hospital

Quy Hoa Beach, home to **Quy Hoa Leper Hospital** (south of Quy Nhon, tel. 05/6374-7999, www.quyhoandh.org.vn, 6am-5pm daily, VND5,000), is the last place in town you'd think to visit. The beach is a blustery, deserted shoreline where dramatic waves crash onto the white sand, and a few benches and other oddly shaped structures, including a guitar-shaped lookout, dot the coast.

Hidden between the mountains just off a coastal stretch of Highway 1, Quy Hoa began as a leper colony in 1929, with about 30 patients in the care of French Catholic priest Paul Maheure. Over the years, nuns were sent to help and additional buildings were constructed as the number of patients grew, housing a few famous Vietnamese figures with the disease, including poet Han Mac Tu. Nowadays, the center is a crucial part of local

Nguyen Nga, this versatile facility functions as a training school and nonprofit organization for residents with physical disabilities across Binh Dinh province, teaching them a variety of skills, from sewing, tailoring, and music to English and computer classes. The center sells handicrafts and other products made by the students. Nguyen Nga also provides scholarships and employment opportunities to graduates, as well as offering micro-financing loans to locals with disabilities hoping to start their own business. Visitors, shoppers, and volunteers are always welcome to stop by for a chat with employees and residents.

BEACHES

There are two main beaches in Quy Nhon. Quy Nhon Beach is a very accessible main city beach. Quy Hoa Beach is just a few miles south of town between two mountains. Still farther south, you'll find a handful of resorts and guesthouses that offer access to other parts of the coast, but day-trippers generally health care, serving the Central Highlands population, which often has little to no access to adequate health care.

Once you've paid the entrance fee, head left toward the beach and you'll pass the grave of Han Mac Tu. The celebrity park, a garden of statues near the water, is also decorated with busts of prominent doctors and scientists, both foreign and Vietnamese, who made notable contributions to leprosy research.

Quy Hoa is best reached by motorbike, whether on your own or with a hired *xe om*, as its narrow village roads tend to be too tight for larger vehicles. Follow An Duong Vuong south from Quy Nhon, bearing left up the hill when the road splits into several smaller lanes. A small pass brings you to the top of the mountain, where you'll keep an eye out for blue-and-white signs reading "Quy Hoa"; take another left down into the village and on to the hospital gates.

ACCOMMODATIONS

Thanks to Quy Nhon's popularity among domestic tourists, hotels are readily available along the beachfront, which is likely where you'll want to stay during the summer months when the weather is best. A handful of good budget and mid-range options are found toward the center of town. Off-season travelers will find room rates heavily discounted.

Under VND210,000

Barbara's Backpackers (12 An Duong Vuong, tel. 05/6389-2921, VND80,000 dorm, VND200,000 d) offers bare-bones dorm beds at an unbeatable price. Mosquito nets and hot water are provided. No lockers are available, but valuables can be left at reception. A temperamental Wi-Fi connection exists in the open-air Kiwi Cafe out front, which serves Western and Vietnamese dishes and also boasts an up-to-date Quy Nhon city guide. Public access to the nice part of the beach is just across the road. English-speaking staff can help arrange guided tours, motorbike rentals, and bus and train tickets.

VND210,000-525,000

Opposite the four-star Seagull Hotel, **Au Co** (8 An Duong Vuong, tel. 05/6374-7699, VND252,000-315,000) is an oddly shaped corner building with generous rooms. Arched ceilings and stone columns add character to the place, not to mention its sturdy wooden beds. Large bay windows, hot water, air-conditioning, Wi-Fi access, and television are available in each room, and most offerings also have a balcony. You can also find a **second location** (24 An Duong Vuong) just a few steps down the road.

The charming **Anh Vy Hotel** (8 An Duong Vuong, tel. 05/6384-7763, www.anhvyhotel. com, VND220,000-260,000) is one-third of a trio of budget spots near the beach. Long, narrow rooms include air-conditioning, hot water, Wi-Fi access, a television, and a minibar. Rates are reasonable and its shared balconies offer pleasant sea views. The staff doesn't speak much English, but the receptionists are friendly and a small shop downstairs sells snacks and essentials for travelers.

The green-and-white interior of **Hai Yen Hotel** (104 Hai Ba Trung, tel. 05/6382-2480, VND200,000-250,000) feels far more like a home than a hotel, with welcoming owners and bright, cozy rooms. Hot water, air-conditioning, Wi-Fi, and television come standard, and guests have the option of taking either a private balcony or a larger bathroom along with their accommodation. In truth, the beds are a little hard, but the friendly folks who run the place make it well worth the stay.

A pale-yellow art deco building overlooking the beach, the **Quy Nhon Hotel** (8 Nguyen Hue, tel. 05/6389-2401, www.quynhonhotel.com.vn, VND400,000-550,000) manages to provide a reasonable amount of ambience in its mid-range rooms. This government-run property offers several varieties of accommodation, each featuring air-conditioning, Wi-Fi access, hot water, and a television, not to mention complimentary breakfast in the hotel's restaurant. There is also a café on-site boasting wireless Internet. The staff can assist in travel arrangements and tours around Quy Nhon as well as the rest of the province.

Along with good value and location, the amiable folks at **Sunflowers Hotel** (13-17 Nguyen Hue, tel. 05/6389-1277, www.sunflowershotel.com, VND490,000-590,000) make this a worthy mid-range spot, particularly on the upper floors where sea views are best. While the hotel is not splashy, each room is tidy and well-kept, featuring hot water and air-conditioning, Wi-Fi access, a television, and complimentary breakfast. Many rooms come with a balcony, though these are cramped. This is also one of the few places where you'll find affordable front-facing sea views.

VND525,000-1,050,000

Complete with uniformed bellhops and a grand, cavernous entrance hall, the regal **Muong Thanh Hotel** (2 Nguyen Hue, tel. 05/6389-2666, www.quynhon.muongthanh.vn, VND700,000-1,800,000) goes above and beyond the average mid-range accommodation. Well-appointed modern rooms come with large flat-screen TVs, air-conditioning, hot water, and an in-room safe, as well as a view of the coast. Breakfast is included in the room rate, as is use of the hotel swimming pool. You'll also find a whirlpool tub and tennis courts on the premises, making this the best value hotel near the beach.

VND1,050,000-2,100,000

The **Saigon-Quy Nhon Hotel** (24 Nguyen Hue, tel. 05/6382-9922, www.saigonquynhonhotel.com.vn, VND1,400,000-2,800,000) is a stately place, if a little stuffy, and features a host of add-ons, from massage services to a swimming pool, travel assistance, a fitness center, and a restaurant. Rooms come with hot water, Wi-Fi access, television, air-conditioning, tea- and coffee-making facilities, and an in-room safe. A complimentary buffet breakfast is also provided downstairs. While the hotel lacks character, its level of service is a cut above the rest. Like its other beachfront

competition, sea views are equally stunning here.

You'll find well-appointed rooms at the **Seagull Hotel** (Hai Au Hotel, 489 An Duong Vuong, tel. 05/6384-6926, www.seagullhotel.com.vn, VND840,000-6,300,000), just opposite Quy Nhon University and about as close to the ocean as you can get. Amenities include TV, air-conditioning, Wi-Fi, hot water, tea- and coffee-making facilities, a minibar, and complimentary breakfast. The balconies offer as good a sea view as any in town, and there are several restaurants onsite, not to mention a bar, massage center, and travel outfit attached. While the hotel itself isn't particularly full of character, it is easily the best seaside option down this end of the beach.

The **Royal Hotel & Healthcare Resort** (1 Han Mac Tu, tel. 05/6374-7100, www.royalquynhon.com, VND1,155,000-2,835,000), also known as Hoang Gia, is a four-star retreat overlooking Quy Nhon Beach. Its well-appointed rooms feature TV, Wi-Fi, a sitting area, and a balcony. While both ocean and city views are available, opt for a seaside room, as street-facing rooms are noisier and less atmospheric. Breakfast is complimentary and amenities include a spa, a swimming pool and tennis courts.

Over VND2,100,000

Ten miles south of town, **AVANI Quy Nhon** (Bai Dai Beach, Ghenh Rang, tel. 05/6384-0132, www.avanihotels.com, VND2,310,000-3,150,000) features beachside lodgings along with a garden spa, an outdoor swimming pool, and a restaurant and bar. Combining Cham architecture and Vietnamese decor, accommodations are built into the hillside, with both deluxe room and junior suite options available. All spacious lodgings include a television, hot water, Wi-Fi access, and air-conditioning, as well as complimentary breakfast. A private beach bound by a pair of rocky escarpments is just steps away. The on-site spa also provides massage, facial, and body treatments.

FOOD

Attached to Barbara's Backpackers, **Kiwi Cafe** (12 An Duong Vuong, tel. 05/6389-2921, 7am-9pm daily, VND40,000-100,000), serves both Western eats and tasty Vietnamese, as well as an ever-changing list of daily specials. While most backpacker-friendly places offer a selection of watered-down local dishes, meals at Kiwi Cafe have pizzazz, deviating from what you might expect in a delightfully appetizing way. Cheap beer and other cold beverages are also available, as is free travel information—ask about Barbara's Quy Nhon guide—and a book exchange.

A humble corner restaurant, **Que Huong** (125 Tang Bat Ho, tel. 05/6382-1123, 10am-8:30pm daily, VND50,000-170,000) is a good place to take a break from the coast's over-abundance of seafood. This pleasant, two-story local eatery serves tasty chicken, beef, and pork dishes along with a few veggies and fish, offering plenty of selection at reasonable prices. There is also a second location (185 Le Hong Phong, tel. 05/6382-9395, 10am-8:30pm daily, VND50,000-170,000) just around the corner on Le Hong Phong.

Dead-center on the main drag, **C.ine Seafood Restaurant** (94 Xuan Dieu, tel. 05/6651-2675, 9am-10pm daily, VND70,000-250,000) is one of several seafood eateries overlooking the beach and an obvious vendor of Heineken beer, as evidenced by the green-and-red advertisements plastered everywhere. Shrimp, squid, crab, fish, and hotpot dishes are listed on the menu, which comes in English as well as Vietnamese, though you'll likely have to point out your order for the staff, as few of them speak English.

One of Quy Nhon's two Western restaurants, **Enjoy** (334 Dien Hong, tel. 05/6352-3315, 10:30am-11:45pm daily, VND80,000-170,000) features a menu of pizzas and pastas as well as a few Asian-inspired dishes and plenty of seafood entrées. German beer, wine, and milkshakes also make the list. Its brand-new air-conditioned dining area gives a level of ambience to the place and, while the Western dishes are nothing out of this world, this isn't a bad spot to try if you're craving something other than local fare.

For vegetarians, the small, easy-to-miss **Thanh Minh** (151 Phan Boi Chau, tel. 05/6382-1749, 6am-8pm daily, VND15,000-35,000) is a narrow storefront complete with a street cart that serves tasty rice dishes with an array of sautéed vegetables and tofu. Thanh Minh makes a great spot for breakfast or lunch; arrive early, as food gets cold around 1:30pm-2pm.

A walk-up storefront not far from Le Hong Phong, **Hoang Phi Bakery** (74 Nguyen Hue, tel. 05/6381-2430, 8am-8pm daily, VND5,000-15,000) displays a lovely collection of Asian-style pastries and other sweet treats that work well as a snack or a compliment to your morning coffee.

INFORMATION AND SERVICES
Tourist Information

For free maps and a wealth of local information, **Barbara's** (12 An Duong Vuong, tel. 05/6389-2921, 7am-9pm daily) boasts its very own Quy Nhon guide for guests to peruse at their leisure. Recommendations cover restaurants, hotels, and sights, in addition to practical tidbits regarding Internet, banks, and postal services. This is a great spot for independent travelers seeking information on do-it-yourself trips in the city and around. You can also visit **Seagull Travel** (489 An Duong Vuong, tel. 05/6374-7747, www.seagulltravel.com.vn, 7:30am-11:30am and 1:30pm-5pm daily), attached to the Seagull Hotel, which hires out English guides (VND735,000 per day) and provides other travel- and transportation-related services.

Banks

The **Vietcombank** (148 Le Loi, tel. 05/6382-1497, www.vietcombank.com.vn, 7am-11am and 1:30pm-4:30pm Mon.-Fri., 7am-11am Sat.), downtown, assists with currency exchange and has an ATM out front. There are plenty of ATMs situated near the university and outside of Seagull Hotel on the southern end of the beach.

Internet and Postal Services

The **Binh Dinh post office** (127 Hai Ba Trung, tel. 05/6382-1025, 8am-11am and 2:30pm-6:30pm daily) takes all mail and packages. For Internet access, head to one of the dozens of Internet shops in town.

Medical Services

The rundown **Binh Dinh General Hospital** (106 Nguyen Hue, tel. 05/6382-4300) is the closest you'll find to the beach, but facilities are dismal and English speakers will likely not be found here. If possible, head to Nha Trang or, better yet, Saigon.

GETTING THERE
Bus

Quy Nhon's **central bus station (Ben Xe Khach Quy Nhon)** (71 Tay Son, tel. 05/6384-6246, 5am-6pm daily) receives daily arrivals from as far as Saigon to the south and Danang to the north. The most comfortable option from Saigon (once daily, VND280,000) is **Phuong Trang** (Quy Nhon bus station, tel. 05/6224-2424), which has an office in the station. **Mailinh Express** (Quy Nhon bus station, tel. 0563/939-3939) also offers buses to and from Danang (VND155,000).

Local minibuses serve the same routes, but they're often overcrowded and drivers tend to overcharge foreigners.

Train

Trains arrive daily at the **Dieu Tri station** (Nguyen Dinh Thu, tel. 05/6383-3255, 7am-5pm daily), six miles west of Quy Nhon, from northern destinations, such as Danang (VND399,000-672,000) and Hanoi (VND1,029,000-1,575,000), as well as Nha Trang (VND336,000) and Saigon (VND777,000-1,092,000) to the south.

From the train station, it costs VND80,000-100,000 for a taxi ride into town.

Air

Though not many travelers opt to fly to Quy Nhon, it's possible to get here from Saigon and Hanoi. The **Phu Cat Airport (San Bay Phu Cat)** (UIH) lies 20 miles north of downtown Quy Nhon and is served by Vietnam Airlines and budget carrier VietJet.

Taxis can transport you to and from town (VND350,000-400,000), but you may be able to arrange pick-up through your hotel in advance (VND350,000 per vehicle).

GETTING AROUND
Taxis and Xe Om

Xe om drivers camp out at intersections across town, particularly along Xuan Dieu. For taxis, you can call **Mailinh Express** (tel. 0563/838-3838) or simply flag one of their cabs down.

Vehicles for Hire

While there are no official places from which to rent motorbikes or bicycles, **Barbara's** (12 An Duong Vuong, tel. 05/6389-2921, 7am-9pm daily, VND150,000-200,000), at the top end of An Duong Vuong, has both available, though they're overpriced. You can ask your hotel or guesthouse, as they may have motorbikes or bicycles available to rent out.

VICINITY OF QUY NHON

The undulating mountains and sun-bleached coastlines surrounding Quy Nhon are ripe with opportunities to get even more off the beaten path. Anyone with a motorbike can hop on the main road out of town and discover a slew of centuries-old Cham relics, as well as a few other less-frequented sights. Adventuresome travelers hanging around Quy Nhon for an extra day or two can hop on a bike and ramble across the Binh Dinh countryside.

Banh It Towers

The **Banh It Towers** (12 miles north of Quy Nhon on Highway 1, 7am-11am and 1pm-5pm daily, VND7,000), another relic of the Cham kingdom, are a 12-mile drive from town heading north. Overlooking lush rice paddies and rolling mountains, these four hilltop structures date to the turn of the 12th century. While construction of a full-fledged tourism area is underway around the tower gates, the place remains quiet, with only a few visitors passing through. The first tower is midway up a hill, a small building dwarfed by the trio of structures above. The remaining towers each bear their own unique architectural traits. The tallest houses a large altar as well as a many-armed statue of Shiva. The repository boasts a boat-shaped roof, pointed at either end, and the smallest of the main structures, a short distance from the hilltop, resembles the gate tower down below.

If you aren't asked to pay at the main entrance, chances are you'll be approached by someone to collect the visitor's fee as you walk up the hill. Though the temple caretaker doesn't look very official, there is a sign listing the correct price out front. Parking costs an additional VND5,000.

Nha Trang

With sparkling blue waters and sun-bleached shores, frenetic traffic, and all-night parties, Nha Trang is the beach hub of mainland Vietnam. Set amid a vibrant, tropical landscape, this bustling metropolis plays the part of sunny seaside escape along the coast but maintains its local flavor farther inland, throughout the crowded markets and chaotic street stalls of the city.

Long a favorite of beach-going travelers, Nha Trang's coastline is well equipped to entertain, with dozens of dive outfits, snorkeling excursions, and boat trips around the bay. A cluster of small islands near the southern edge of town harbor a host of marine life, while Hon Tre Island, easily spotted from shore, boasts the country's only island amusement park. On land, cultural attractions like the Po Nagar Towers, a prime example of ancient Cham architecture, and Long Son Pagoda, home to a 78-foot statue of the Buddha, do their part to occupy visitors, along with plenty of shopping, top-notch international cuisine, and a buzzing nightlife.

Nha Trang continues to expand beyond the borders of its small downtown backpacker district, sprouting new hotels and restaurants all along the coast. The city's electric energy quickly seduces many visitors into a few extra days on the beach. Those seeking a quiet seaside oasis would do well to look elsewhere.

The best time to visit Nha Trang is from March to September, as rain and wind take over the area from October to December, making the waters rougher and the temperature a few degrees cooler. Whenever you go, three or four days in town is plenty of time to spend a day on the water, laze around on the beach, venture outside of town, and pay a visit to the local mud baths (a must-do in Nha Trang).

SIGHTS

Nha Trang's attractions stretch across the city and into the nearby countryside. Most sights within town are easily reached on foot, as is the main beach, while a handful of places north and south of downtown will likely require a taxi or xe om. The Po Nagar Towers to the north of town go well with a trip to the local hot springs or a visit to Bai Duong, while a southern jaunt to the Bao Dai Villas and the Oceanography Museum can be paired with Vinpearl or, farther south, Bai Dai.

Downtown
LONG SON PAGODA
Backing onto nearby Trai Thuy Hill, **Long Son Pagoda** (20 23 Thang 10, tel. 05/8382-2558, sunrise-sunset daily) is home to a blindingly white 78-foot statue of the Buddha. Though it once stood at the top of the hill, the pagoda, originally built in 1886, was moved to safer ground after a storm in 1900 caused

the building to collapse. The front entrance is adorned with interesting mosaics. Inside, the pagoda's muted tones give way to a riot of color, with bright religious flags and gilded woodwork lining the main hall. A lavish, many-armed Buddha sits at the front altar, backed by hundreds of tiny hands.

Ascend Trai Thuy Hill by walking past the right of the building up a set of stone steps. En route, you'll be greeted by a large, reclining gray stone Buddha, which rests just behind the main building, and the pagoda's large bell, which weighs over 3,300 pounds. For a small donation, tourists can sit inside the bell while a local monk performs a Buddhist chant.

At the top of the hill is another set of stairs, flanked by a pair of concrete dragons; the stairs bring you up to the largest statue. Towering above its surroundings, the pristine, white Buddha sits on a lotus flower, eyes closed and smiling. Around its base are a series of reliefs commemorating the monks who protested Vietnam's southern government by lighting themselves on fire. Before the main incense urn at the very front of the statue is Thich Quang Duc, the first monk to self-immolate in 1963. You can also head around to the back of the giant hollow Buddha, where there is a small altar inside the statue's base.

NHA TRANG CATHEDRAL

The bell tower of the imposing **Nha Trang Cathedral (Nha Tho Nui)** (7am-11am and 2pm-5pm Mon.-Sat., 7am-11am and 2pm-7:45pm Sun.) soars 90 feet above the city, making this one of Nha Trang's more visible landmarks. The cathedral's gray faux-stone exterior, high arches, and ridged battlements give off the appearance of a Gothic castle, along with the vibrant stained-glass reliefs occupying the front of the church.

The cathedral sits atop a hill, at the base of which is Ave Maria Square, a concrete clearing beside the city's six-way roundabout. There, a sculpture of Maria herself presides over a few palm trees and a semicircle of park benches. The steps on the right of the statue lead uphill, where you'll pass a wall of placards honoring the deceased. At the top of the staircase, a statue of Jesus is sheltered by a cave-like shrine, while statues of saints stand sentinel around the cathedral gate. Along the far side of the building are still more placards, cemented along the walkway descending back onto Nguyen Trai.

ALEXANDRE YERSIN MUSEUM

Tucked at the southern end of Nha Trang's Pasteur Institute, the **Alexandre Yersin**

statue of a reclining Buddha on a hillside above Long Son Pagoda

Vicinity of Nha Trang

DOC LET RESORT

WHITE SAND DOC LET RESORT

0   5 mi

0   5 km

★ BA HO STREAM

SEE "NHA TRANG NORTH" MAP

★ PO NAGAR TOWERS

Bai Duong

MUD BATHS AND HOT SPRINGS

NHAT PHONG 3

SOUTHERN BUS STATION

NHA TRANG BEACH

LONG SON PAGODA

EVASON ANA MANDARA

VINPEARL LAND

SEE "NHA TRANG SOUTH" MAP

Bach Dang Park

BAO DAI VILLAS

★ OCEANOGRAPHY MUSEUM

VINPEARL GOLF CLUB

CAU DA HARBOR

DIAMOND BAY GOLF

ENTRANCE TO BAI DAI

THE SHACK

LONG BEACH SURF CLUB

Bai Dai

CAM RANH AIRPORT

© AVALON TRAVEL

Museum (8-10 Tran Phu, tel. 05/8382-2406, www.pasteur-nhatrang.org.vn, 7:30am-11am and 2pm-4:30pm Mon.-Fri., VND26,000) may not seem like much, but its exhibits manage to pack a great deal of information and scores of artifacts from the famed Swiss doctor's life into a few small rooms. Antique gadgets, from microscopes to old-school medical tools and test tubes from Yersin's study, are on display around the museum, as are dozens of letters, which he wrote to his mother and sister while living in Vietnam. Those keen on history and science will enjoy learning about one of the most influential Europeans of Vietnam's colonial era. All signage is in English, French, and Vietnamese.

LONG THANH GALLERY

A photographer since age 13, the man behind **Long Thanh Gallery** (126 Hoang Van Thu, tel. 05/8382-4875, www.longthanhart.com, 8am-5pm daily) began his career as an apprentice in his uncle's camera shop and has been snapping photos ever since. Using only analog machinery, Long Thanh's simple, evocative, black-and-white portraits and countryside scenes have garnered him international acclaim as well as overseas exhibits in Europe, the United States, and Australia. Long Thanh keeps to his gallery, down a quiet street north of the Nha Trang Cathedral, where the doors are open throughout the day and visitors can drop in for a look at some of his best work. Long Thanh and his wife are usually around the shop, and the friendly pair are always up for a chat. Call ahead to arrange a private showing outside of gallery hours.

North of Nha Trang
★ PO NAGAR TOWERS

One mile north of town, the **Po Nagar Towers** (2 Thang 4, 6am-6pm daily, VND21,000) bear not one but two histories. From the 8th to the 13th centuries, the Cham empire built these Hindu temples to honor Po Nagar, their most significant female deity.

When the Vietnamese arrived in 1635, ending Cham authority, they adopted the towers and Po Nagar became Thien Y A Na, a young girl taken in by an elderly, childless couple who taught her people to farm rice.

Inside the entrance gates are 22 columns (once 24). Here, the Cham would prepare offerings before hiking up the steep steps at the far end of the clearing. The tallest of the four towers is dedicated to Po Nagar and houses a black stone statue of the deity, which dates back to AD 1050.

Beside the main tower, a slightly smaller structure belongs to Shiva (in the Cham version) or Thien Y A Na's husband (for the Vietnamese). Inside is the largest *linga* and *yoni* statue (symbols representing male and female energies) on-site.

The remaining two towers are more humble, each housing a smaller *linga* and *yoni* statue. The one beside the two large structures honors Skanda, first-born son of Shiva, as well as the adoptive parents of Thien Y A Na. Behind Po Nagar's main tower, the smallest structure is dedicated to Ganesh, second-born son of Shiva, and the children of Thien Y A Na, Princess Quy and Prince Tri.

Peek inside the exhibition room at the back, where replicas of the towers' statues are on display. Near the steps, Po Nagar also offers nice views of the Cai River.

Many tour groups and independent travelers pass through the towers. Respectful dress is a must inside the temples. Guests can use the gray robes located near the main tower, free of charge, if they are not dressed appropriately.

HON CHONG

Overlooking the sea, the rocky promontory of **Hon Chong** (Pham Van Dong, tel. 05/8628-9137, 6am-6pm daily, VND21,000) extends out from the southern end of Bai Duong Beach in a series of smooth, tan, stone formations. By the ticket booth, three traditional Vietnamese houses display local specialties and handicrafts, plus an array of musical instruments used by the region's ethnic minorities. Musical demonstrations occur when visitors arrive in large numbers.

Down a set of stairs, you'll clamber over a jumble of sandy rocks as you head toward the sea. Passing under the formation known as Heaven's Gate, in which a substantial rock hangs precariously between two larger stones, can be a nerve-racking experience. The formation has been this way for centuries without incident.

THE SOUTH-CENTRAL COAST

NHA TRANG

red brick towers at Po Nagar

Downtown Nha Trang

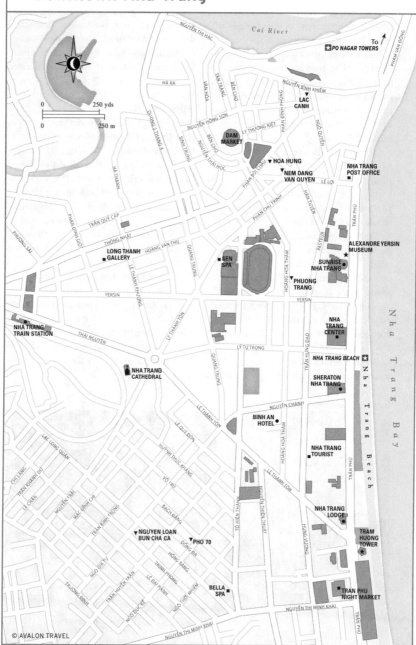

Cai River

To PO NAGAR TOWERS

250 yds

250 m

NGUYEN THI HAC

PHAM VAN DONG

HÀ RA

NGUYEN BINH KHIEM

LAC CANH

NGUYEN HONG SON

DAM MARKET

LY THUONG KIET

HOA HUNG

NEM DANG VAN QUYEN

NHA TRANG POST OFFICE

LE LOI

DUONG 2 THANG 4

BEN CHO

NGUYEN THAI HOC

PHAN BOI CHAU

PHAN DINH PHUNG

NGO QUYEN

HÀ THANH

PHAN CHU TRINH

HAN TUYEN

PASTEUR

TRAN PHU

PHAM DINH GIOT

TRAN QUY CAP

THONG NHAT

ALEXANDRE YERSIN MUSEUM

PHUONG SAI

LONG THANH GALLERY

HOANG VAN THU

QUANG TRUNG

SEN SPA

SUNRISE NHA TRANG

PHUONG TRANG

HOANG HOA THAM

YERSIN

LE THANH PHUONG

YERSIN

NHA TRANG CENTER

NHA TRANG TRAIN STATION

THAI NGUYEN

LY THANH TON

LY TU TRONG

TRAN HUNG DAO

NHA TRANG BEACH

QUANG TRUNG

NHA TRANG CATHEDRAL

SHERATON NHA TRANG

LE THANH TON

NGUYEN CHANH

LAC LONG QUAN

LE QUY DON

HUYNH THUC KHANG

BINH AN HOTEL

HOANG HOA THAM

NHA TRANG TOURIST

CHI LANG

TRAN KHANH DU

LE CHAN

NGUYEN TRAI

MAC DINH CHI

VO TRI

BACH DANG

TO HIEN THANH

NGUYEN THIEN THUAT

LE THANH TON

NHA TRANG LODGE

TRAN BINH TRONG

NGUYEN LOAN BUN CHA CA

PHO 70

DONG DA

HONG BANG

HONG VUONG

TRAM HUONG TOWER

NGO GIA TU

TRUONG BINH

TRAN HUYEN TRAN

THANH PHONG

LE DAI HANH

NGO HOA NHIEM

BELLA SPA

TRAN PHU NIGHT MARKET

NGO DUC KE

NGUYEN THI MINH KHAI

NGUYEN THI MINH KHAI

TRAN PHU

Nha Trang Bay

Nha Trang Beach

© AVALON TRAVEL

Towering above the rest, at the far end of the promontory, is Hon Chong, the stone after which the place is named. Legend has it that fairies used to bathe in the waters near Hon Chong. One day, while spying upon these bathing beauties, a rather inebriated giant stumbled and nearly slipped off the rocks. The massive gouge in Hon Chong that resembles a handprint is where the giant caught himself and managed not to fall in. As you face the ocean, to your right is Hon Do, or Red Island, a small piece of land that houses a Buddhist pagoda and is so named for the color it turns at sunrise.

While it is possible to hire an English-speaking guide (VND50,000) from the ticket booth, this is not really necessary, as the major draw of the place is its scenery. Most visitors simply wander around on the rocks, snap some photos, and then enjoy a coffee at the adjoining café, which overlooks Hon Chong and Bai Duong Beach.

South of Nha Trang
OCEANOGRAPHY MUSEUM

The city's **Oceanography Museum (Bao Tang Hai Duong Hoc)** (1 Cau Da, tel. 05/8359-0036, www.vnio.org.vn, 6am-6pm daily, VND30,000) features several different exhibits, some more interesting than others, covering the roughly 20,000 wildlife and plant specimens collected from Vietnamese waters by the research arm of the institute. A miniature aquarium is the highlight of the place, with large, open pools home to dozens of saltwater creatures, including jet-black stingrays, massive sea turtles, a pair of seals, rope-like moray eels, colorful reef fish, and small sharks.

Farther on, a cavernous, tiled room catalogues the region's species with row upon row of creatures and plant life. English signage is available in most exhibits, though information can be sparse at times. You'll also find the 18-meter-long skeleton of a whale on display as well as the bones of the endemic dugong, a distant underwater relative to the elephant.

BAO DAI VILLAS

Visited for its breezy beach, seaside views, and history museums, the **Bao Dai Villas** (Cau Da, tel. 05/8359-0147, baodai@dng.vnn.vn, 8am-5pm daily, VND15,000) is a collection of five charming colonial buildings that once served as a vacation estate for Vietnam's last emperor, Bao Dai. Before they became home to royalty, these lemon-hued buildings briefly functioned as part of the Indochinese Institute of Oceanography. In 1926, the emperor was gifted two of the villas.

Nghinh Phong, one of the buildings, serves as a museum. It's perched on the edge of a seaside cliff amid ample greenery. While the exhibits within the villa are uninspired—no more than a few family photographs and a handful of the emperor's possessions—the history of Nghinh Phong's residents is rather interesting and the panoramic views make the trip worthwhile, particularly for shutterbugs hoping to capture Nha Trang Bay and nearby Hon Tre Island from a different angle. The villa complex also houses two restaurants and the Queen's Beach, a small cove hidden from the wind where daytime visitors come to relax. The remaining four villas are currently rented out as hotel accommodations.

TOURS

With scores of local travel companies and plenty to do both in the water and on land, Nha Trang offers many day-long tours. The only way to access the nearby islands is via boat tour. These generic trips receive mixed reviews, with most boat tours taking you around to a local fishing village, the Tri Nguyen Aquarium on Mieu Islet, one or two snorkeling locations, and a beach, all while providing copious amounts of local alcohol. In most cases, prices are dirt cheap, with additional fees to enter the aquarium or to use the island beaches. Red, white, and blue fliers for the **Nha Trang Boat Trip** (1/24 Tran Quang Khai, tel. 05/8352-4471, www.nhatrangtour.com.vn, 8:30am-4:45pm daily, VND200,000) are all over town and there's no doubt you'll track one down during your stay

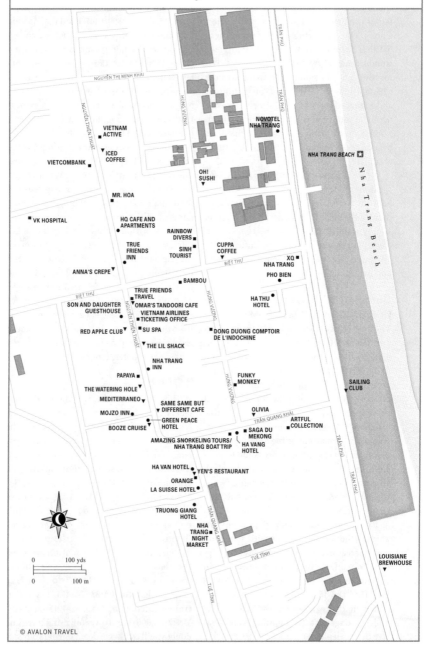

Southern Nha Trang

NGUYEN THI MINH KHAI

TRAN PHU

HÙNG VƯƠNG

NGUYEN THIEN THUAT

NOVOTEL NHA TRANG

NHA TRANG BEACH ✪

Nha Trang Beach

VIETNAM ACTIVE

ICED COFFEE

VIETCOMBANK

OH! SUSHI

MR. HOA

HQ CAFE AND APARTMENTS

VK HOSPITAL

RAINBOW DIVERS

TRUE FRIENDS INN

SINH TOURIST

CUPPA COFFEE

BIỆT THỰ

XQ NHA TRANG

PHO BIEN

ANNA'S CREPE

BAMBOU

BIỆT THỰ

TRUE FRIENDS TRAVEL

SON AND DAUGHTER GUESTHOUSE

OMAR'S TANDOORI CAFE

VIETNAM AIRLINES TICKETING OFFICE

HA THU HOTEL

RED APPLE CLUB

SU SPA

DONG DUONG COMPTOIR DE L'INDOCHINE

THE LIL SHACK

HÙNG VƯƠNG

NHA TRANG INN

PAPAYA

FUNKY MONKEY

THE WATERING HOLE

MEDITERRANEO

MOJZO INN

SAME SAME BUT DIFFERENT CAFE

OLIVIA

TRẦN QUANG KHẢI

ARTFUL COLLECTION

SAILING CLUB

GREEN PEACE HOTEL

BOOZE CRUISE

AMAZING SNORKELING TOURS/ NHA TRANG BOAT TRIP

SAGA DU MEKONG

HA VANG HOTEL

HÙNG VƯƠNG

TRẦN PHÚ

TRẦN PHÚ

HA VAN HOTEL

YEN'S RESTAURANT

ORANGE

LA SUISSE HOTEL

TRUONG GIANG HOTEL

NHA TRANG NIGHT MARKET

TRẦN QUANG KHẢI

TUỆ TĨNH

LOUISIANE BREWHOUSE

0   100 yds

0   100 m

TUỆ TĨNH

© AVALON TRAVEL

the boat's top deck when you get tired of the underwater sights.

Beyond the sea, **Vietnam Active** (47 Nguyen Thien Thuat, tel. 09/0362-6061, www. vietnamactive.com, 8am-noon and 2pm-9pm daily, VND945,000-4,200,000) offers unique on-land trips, pairing cycling with sightseeing to visit Nha Trang's major points of interest as well as parts of the surrounding countryside. Though it's expensive, enthusiastic guides and high-quality equipment are provided, as are a range of activity options that run from easy to moderate. The company also offers city bicycle and mountain bike rentals by the day.

Dozens of Easy Rider outfits have set up shop in Nha Trang offering tailor-made single- and multi-day motorbike tours. While these trips tend to be expensive, they are worth the price tag, as experienced local guides take you off the beaten path and deep into the Vietnamese countryside. This is one of the best ways to explore Vietnam. Easy Rider companies like **True Friends Travel** (89 Nguyen Thien Thuat, tel. 09/0642-4266, www.nhatrangeasyridertours.com, VND1,155,000-1,575,000/day) and **Easy Rider Motorcycle Trips VN** (7G/4 Hung Vuong, tel. 09/0538-4406, easyridertrips.com, VND1,260,000-1,365,000/day) offer single- and multi-day trips throughout Vietnam's interior, from Nha Trang to Dalat and onward through the Central Highlands to Hoi An or south along the coast to Mui Ne. Some outfits even venture so far as Saigon and the Mekong Delta. Most operators are willing to tailor their trips to your specific requests.

BEACHES
★ Nha Trang Beach

The main event in this seaside city, **Nha Trang Beach** (Tran Phu) is occupied morning, noon, and night by locals getting in an early swim or foreign tourists sunning on the coarse yellow sand. Clean and well maintained, this stretch of coast runs parallel to bustling Tran Phu but is, thankfully, separated by a long and narrow park, complete

Nha Trang Beach

here. **Funky Monkey** (75A Hung Vuong, tel. 05/8352-2426, www.funkymonkeytour.com, 7am-10pm daily, VND200,000) runs its own version of the same day out.

Those who prefer to have a vessel to themselves can hire private boats from the **Cau Da Tourist Harbor** (7 Tran Phu, tel. 05/8359-0479, 7am-4:30pm daily, slow boats VND300,000-800,000, high-speed boats from VND800,000), where both slower boats and high-speed canoes take passengers out to the bay's four islands, essentially following the same route as the public tour groups.

Another option for seafaring travelers is to pair your time on the water with an activity, such as snorkeling or diving. These tours cater to all levels of experience. The **Amazing Snorkeling Tour** (1/24 Tran Quang Khai, tel. 05/8352-4471, www.vietnamsnorkeling.com, 9am-3:30pm daily, VND320,000) provides you with reasonably good snorkeling equipment and a hearty lunch on the boat, as well as the freedom to simply swim or lie out on with patches of grass and a series of abstract statues.

From shore, you can take in pleasant views of the nearby islands, including a clear line of sight toward the Hollywood-esque sign at Vinpearl Land, as well as the incredibly blue Nha Trang Bay. Beach chairs are available for rent from independent vendors, or you can opt to visit one of the many beachfront cafés and restaurants, where paying customers are given free reign of the sun beds by the water. Traveling vendors—some friendly, some a little persistent—also make the rounds, offering food and drinks as well as souvenirs and other knickknacks. Keep an eye on your belongings, as theft on the beach is not unheard of.

Bach Dang Park

The sands of **Bach Dang Park** (Tran Phu near the Vinpearl ferry terminal) are a modest stretch of beach past the swanky Ana Mandara Resort. You'll find relative peace and quiet here compared to the crowded coastline farther north. While there isn't much in the way of services this far south, the park is only about a mile and a half from the main part of Tran Phu and the spot is pleasantly devoid of traveling vendors.

North of Nha Trang
BAI DUONG

On the other side of the small Hon Chong promontory, **Bai Duong** (Pham Van Dong) is barely a stone's throw from the downtown area but manages to avoid some of the chaos that characterizes the city's main beach. While many are happy to sit and sun alongside the masses, those who prefer more peace and quiet but lack the time to make a trip out to Bai Dai will appreciate Bai Duong. The beach is still very much in the city, with a major thoroughfare zipping by at the back, but a low barrier and a few feet of sand put at least some distance between you and the traffic. Sun chairs are available for rent, and there are plenty of cafés and restaurants in the surrounding area. Though, unlike the main beach, you'll likely have to get up from your seat in order to be served.

South of Nha Trang
BAI DAI

Half an hour south of Nha Trang, **Bai Dai** (Khu Du Lich Bai Dai) may not be as clean or well maintained as the city's main strip, but its wide, empty beach and white-capped waters are ideal for novice surfers or those looking to spend an afternoon away from town. The shoreline is unpopulated, leaving travelers free to stretch out on their own.

At the top of the beach, stilted bamboo huts crouch together, slinging drinks, snacks, and seafood. **The Shack** (Bai Dai town, tel. 012/6441-4102, www.shackvietnam.com, 9:30am-late daily, VND40,000-200,000), a modest little hangout, hides inside the mix of makeshift eateries, offering Mexican food, surfing lessons, board rentals, and beach chairs.

Bai Dai lies roughly 13 miles from town, so it's worth at least a half-day trip. Taxis will be able to take you out for about VND250,000-300,000 one-way, but the drive can be easily done on your own via motorbike. Keep an eye out for the sign that reads "Khu Du Lich Bai Dai" as you pass Mia Resort, about seven miles from the airport, where the road turns into a barren four-lane highway. Hang a left here and follow the dirt path in toward the beach.

ENTERTAINMENT AND EVENTS
Nightlife

Nightlife is a thriving part of Nha Trang's backpacker culture. While destinations like Phu Quoc or Mui Ne tend to draw a quieter crowd, visitors in this fast-paced seaside city are ready to party, and the foreign enclave carved out beside Nha Trang Beach does not disappoint. Packed into a few short city blocks you'll find thumping dance music and laid-back sports bars, classy cocktails, dirt-cheap street-side beers, and Nha Trang's version of the infamous 'bucket,' a mixed drink or three

Staying Safe After Dark

With dozens of tourists letting loose on the beaches, dance floors, and rooftops of Nha Trang, there are bound to be a few unsavory characters wandering the streets after dark. Pickpocketing, theft, and spiked drinks are common occurrences around Nha Trang's backpacker area and along the beachfront. When heading out for the night it's a wise idea to bring only the bare essentials and take care not to walk around alone.

One especially popular form of pickpocketing targets men. After a late night, guys leaving local bars will be approached by one or more friendly women, who proposition the victim before suddenly leaving. By the time the man realizes what's happened, the women are long gone with the full contents of his pockets. *Xe om* drivers, too, can pose a danger after dark. If you're planning to use local transportation to return to your hotel, it's best to use a taxi.

The most worrisome danger of Nha Trang's nightlife is drink-spiking. While the perpetrators tend to work independently, sometimes even local bartenders in a few of the city's less-reputable establishments get in on fixing a traveler's drink. More than a few backpackers have lost a night and woken up missing a phone or some cash. Avoid the area both in and around Why Not Bar after dark as acts of drink-spiking, theft, and violence are not uncommon here. While the Sailing Club is always a fun beachfront party, theft often occurs on the sidewalks in front of this establishment. If you're heading home from here late at night, walk with a buddy or, better yet, grab a cab.

In the event that you or a friend feel as if you've been drugged, seek medical attention immediately. The **VK Hospital** (34/4 Nguyen Thien Thuat, tel. 05/8352-8866), near the heart of the backpacker neighborhood, staffs English-speaking doctors and offers around-the-clock emergency services.

in a plastic jar. With so many places open late, travelers are free to stay out and party all night long, but it's important to stay safe.

BARS

Starting around 9pm, a lively crowd begins to gather both in and around the **Red Apple Club** (54G Nguyen Thien Thuat, tel. 05/8352-4500, 6pm-midnight daily, VND30,000-70,000). With cheap drinks and a coveted street-side spot next to several backpacker hostels, this longstanding bar is outfitted with a pool table, a small dance floor, and ample seating in the alley outside. Bucket drinks and the odd happy hour special also help to make this a popular spot, as well as an easy place to meet travel buddies.

While the name doesn't necessarily ooze class, **Booze Cruise** (110 Nguyen Thien Thuat, tel. 05/8352-1105, www.boozecruise-barandgrill.com, 8am-3am daily, VND15,000-100,000) is one of Nha Trang's finer casual hangouts, with friendly staff, a variety of sports channels on offer, and a dance floor. Its spacious storefront and nearly all-afternoon happy hour convince most passing travelers to stop in at this blue-and-orange behemoth at least once for a cheap drink and some eats from the bar's Western menu. Booze Cruise also runs (surprise!) a regular booze cruise (from VND380,000) around the nearby islands with unlimited cocktails and food.

Though still in the heart of the backpacker area, **The Watering Hole** (72 Nguyen Thien Thuat, tel. 09/3560-0230, 9:30am-midnight daily, VND20,000-130,000) boasts a much more laid-back vibe than most of its counterparts. Cocktails run around VND85,000-95,000 apiece and there is also draught beer available, as well as all the European sports channels you can handle. Both bar and table seating are provided, and there is a classier atmosphere than most other backpacker bars.

NIGHTCLUBS

The best party on the beach, **Sailing Club** (72-74 Tran Phu, tel. 05/8352-4628, www.sailingclubnhatrang.com,

7am-late, VND60,000-150,000, cover charge VND100,000-200,000) turns the sands of Nha Trang into a loud and lively outdoor gathering every night, complete with DJs, cocktails, and plenty of room to dance. Drink prices are notably more expensive than most backpacker spots and there is often a cover charge here, depending upon the event. Given the ambience and the beachfront location, the entry fee makes sense.

Long after the sun sets, the breezy veranda at **Louisiane Brewhouse** (29 Tran Phu, tel. 05/8352-1948, www.louisianebrewhouse.com.vn, 7am-late, VND30,000-130,000) stays open late, offering drink specials and occasionally live music by the sea. While this place doesn't get as wild as the nearby Sailing Club, Louisiane offers a more relaxed atmosphere, perfect for a couple of end-of-day beers on the beach. Keep an eye out for drink deals and special events.

Festivals and Events

Traditionally a Cham celebration, the annual **Thap Ba Festival** takes place from the 20th to the 23rd of the third lunar month, usually sometime in April by the Gregorian calendar. Over three days, hundreds of revelers visit the four Po Nagar towers just north of town, where a celebration is held in honor of the temple's namesake, Lady Po Nagar, a goddess credited with teaching the Cham people how to farm and earn a living. On the first day of the festival, a nearly 1,000-year-old statue located within the complex's main tower is undressed, bathed, and then dressed again in a new costume and crown for the coming year. Traditional dances and other cultural performances take place over the three days. On the final day, a more solemn worship rounds out the end of the celebration, as devotees from near and far pay their respects to the goddess and pray for protection and good fortune. The festival usually attracts a crowd of ethnic Cham as well as local Vietnamese residents, though anyone is welcome to stop by the Po Nagar Towers and observe the festivities.

An Unusual Souvenir

Rare, fragile *yen sao* **(edible bird's nests)** are a hot item among Asian customers, as their consumption is said to have medical benefits. Made from the saliva of wild swiftlets, these nests can go for as much as USD$2,000 per kilogram. They are difficult to come by, as the tiny creatures make their homes in hard-to-reach seaside caves along the south-central coast. They are sold in a few shops in Nha Trang and are usually dissolved into a soup before being eaten. The *yen sao* found in many local convenience stores is a bland, watered-down version. Shops that sell the actual nests will have signs emblazoned with *yen sao* out front.

SHOPPING

There are plenty of places in Nha Trang where you can part ways with your money, however most of these retail outfits offer the same items you'll find in several other cities along the coast. Nha Trang is a popular spot for accessories made from ostrich and crocodile, such as purses, handbags, and belts. Those in search of beach essentials like sunscreen, swimwear, and other gear will find them scattered along Nguyen Thien Thuat and on Tran Phu near the Sailing Club. This main backpacker area around the beach features plenty of shopping for foreigners, from souvenirs and knickknacks to swimsuits and other essentials.

Markets and Shopping Malls

A sprawling, constant bustle of activity, the narrow streets surrounding **Dam Market** (Ben Cho, sunrise-sunset daily) are chock-full of produce and snack vendors, while the stalls within its circular inner quarters boast row upon row of clothing, souvenirs, and a variety of other odds and ends. If you wander long enough, you may even find one or two food stalls hidden within the maze of tented outdoor shops. Bargain for any purchases made here.

Designed with tourists in mind, the local **night market** (alley 3 Tran Quang Khai, 5pm-10pm daily) gets going around sundown and hawks all manner of souvenirs, from clothing and jewelry to bags, notebooks, household items, and other knickknacks. Most of the goods on offer are pretty standard Vietnam souvenirs, but the market atmosphere gives you the opportunity to bargain like a proper local rather than shelling out the same amount you might pay in a fixed-price shop.

Nha Trang Center (20 Tran Phu, tel. 05/8625-9222, www.nhatrangcenter.com, 9am-10pm daily) is a sleek, air-conditioned shopping mall featuring major international brands such as Nike, L'Occitane, and Tag Heuer, as well as local labels like Saga du Mekong and Vinasilk. Over three separate floors, open-plan shops run the gamut from affordable to expensive. There is also a food court upstairs, featuring a range of international cuisine, as well as a cinema and arcade. You can also catch some impressive views of Nha Trang Bay from the white wicker chairs of **Cool Cafe** (3pm-11pm daily, VND25,000-60,000), the center's rooftop coffee lounge, which overlooks Tran Phu and the beach.

Across the street from Tram Huong Tower along the city's main drag, the **Tran Phu Night Market** (Tran Phu beside Khanh Hoa Cultural Center, 5:30pm-11pm daily) runs throughout the evening and offers plenty of souvenirs, clothing, and even some dining options for hungry shoppers.

Gifts and Souvenirs

Expat and photographer Thiery Beyne is behind **Artful Collection** (1 Tran Quang Khai, tel. 012/6376-1020, www.artfulgallery. fr, 9am-10pm daily), a gallery that showcases the Frenchman's work with stunning, vivid images of life in Vietnam, from lush, flat rice paddies to the soaring mountains of Sapa. In addition to standard prints, Artful Collection also spices up items such as bags, clocks,

mugs, notebooks, and computer cases with Beyne's images. Wander in during the evening and you may meet the photographer himself.

In case you missed the showrooms in Saigon and Dalat, the Nha Trang arm of the XQ empire, **XQ Nha Trang** (64 Tran Phu, tel. 05/8352-6579, www.xqhandembroidery.com, 8am-10pm daily), sits at the very top of Biet Thu and boasts a sizable collection of impressive hand-embroidered still lifes and portraits. A small souvenir shop on the far end of the complex also sells neat gifts, albeit expensive, with mugs, postcards, notebooks, and other items for sale. The hand embroidery, too, is available for purchase, but most images cost several hundred dollars.

A narrow storefront easily missed among the many small shops packed along Hung Vuong, **Dong Duong Comptoir de L'Indochine** (3L Hung Vuong, tel. 05/8352-3233, dongduongstore@gmail.com, 8am-10pm daily) is unique in its range of carved stone jewelry boxes and other souvenirs, not to mention a host of propaganda posters and propaganda-style recreations of famous movie posters. Prices are reasonable and the items inside offer something different than your standard Vietnam souvenirs.

Clothing

There are plenty of clothing shops in the backpacker area, particularly those offering beachwear for travelers. You'll find local outposts of popular Vietnamese brands like **Papaya** (60 Nguyen Thien Thuat, www.papaya-tshirt.com, 8am-10pm daily), **Orange** (3/3 Tran Quang Khai, 9am-9pm daily), and **Bambou** (15 Biet Thu, tel. 05/8352-3616, www.bambou-company.com, 8am-10:30pm daily), as well as a few worthy originals.

Take a walk around the backpacker area and you'll find more than one storefront bearing the name **Saga du Mekong** (1/21 Tran Quang Khai, tel. 09/0357-3602, www.sagadu-mekong.com, 8am-10:30pm daily). Founded by a French expat, this fast-growing brand uses high-quality cotton, linen, and bamboo fiber to create simple, well-made clothing and has become so popular in recent years that several offshoots of the original, including Saga Konnexion and Saga Etnik, have sprouted up in local stores and shopping malls across town.

Books

In addition to the mobile book vendors slinging photocopied paperbacks, a handful of stationary **book exchanges** are scattered throughout the backpacker area on both Nguyen Thien Thuat and Biet Thu streets. If you're wandering the neighborhood, there is a reliable vendor just outside **19 Biet Thu** (8am-9pm daily). Bargain hard for your reading material.

SPORTS AND RECREATION

Nha Trang plays just as hard in the daylight as it does after dark. Underwater adventures come by the dozen in this town, with scores of snorkeling and diving outfits catering to all levels of experience. Beyond the sea, a handful of onshore activities can keep you entertained, including a fast-growing massage and spa industry. A few other odds and ends also exist here, like the odd yoga session or cooking class.

★ Mud Baths and Hot Springs

Nestled in the hills north of town, Nha Trang's spa-like hot springs and mud baths offer a unique way to spend an afternoon. Soak in private tubs of warm mud or hot mineral water before lounging around in the communal swimming pools with other guests. Spa and massage services can also be purchased at an extra cost. The experience is a relaxing escape from town and a must-do in Nha Trang.

There are two reputable hot springs in town. **Thap Ba** (15 Ngoc Son, tel. 05/8383-5335, www.thapahotspring.com.vn, 7am-7pm daily, VND120,000-650,000 per person) is the older of the two, and less expensive, so it attracts a higher percentage of Vietnamese holidaymakers and backpackers. If you don't mind spending the extra cash, the newer **i-Resort** (19 Xuan Ngoc, tel. 05/8383-8838, www.i-resort.vn, 8am-6pm daily, VND300,000-450,000 per person) has posh facilities and better scenery as well as a few add-ons, including a restaurant and some nice private facilities. The best views are from the VIP rooms, which cost more. Fees vary depending upon the package you choose. Each venue requires at least a few hours to go through the entire process. Both resorts are expansive, with a dozen or so baths built into

freshwater pool at i-Resort

the hillside overlooking Nha Trang. Since Nha Trang's mud baths are a big attraction, both resorts are always busy, but i-Resort gives more space and quiet to its customers.

Ask your hotel about transportation out to the hot springs, as many places offer a shuttle, or hop on the public bus. Each of the hot springs also offers their own electric car service, but these aren't really worth the price. You're better off catching a taxi if you prefer to go on your own. Don't forget to bring your swimsuit.

Vinpearl Land Amuseument Park

Plastered across the western side of Hon Tre Island are the bright white, blocky letters of Vinpearl Land (Hon Tre Island, tel. 05/8359-0611, www.vinpearlland.com, 8am-9pm daily, VND500,000), Vietnam's very own amusement park. Featuring an aquarium, several roller coasters, a water park, a beach, and arcade games, the island is a popular attraction for families with young kids as well as action-seekers. The island is reached by the world's longest sea-crossing cable car, which affords impressive views of the beach, the city, and the water. Tickets for the park cover both your cable car ride and access to Vinpearl's facilities. Most visitors make a day of the outing in order to get the most for their money.

Diving

Though it's not the most scenic underwater location in Vietnam, diving in Nha Trang is popular for its prices. Dozens of diving outfits are open in the backpacker area, providing travelers with everything from fun dives to PADI certification, however not all companies come with certified instructors or high-quality equipment. Both Rainbow Divers (90A Hung Vuong, tel. 09/0878-1756, www.divevietnam.com, 6am-9:30pm daily) and Sailing Club Divers (72-74 Tran Phu, tel. 05/8352-2788, www.divenhatrang.com, 7:30am-8pm daily) are well-known and reliable outfits that offer a range of services to beginner and experienced divers.

Snorkeling

An all-day adventure with fun, sun, and plenty of underwater sights, the Amazing Snorkeling Tour (1/24 Tran Quang Khai, tel. 05/8352-4471, www.vietnamsnorkeling.com, 9am-3:30pm daily, VND320,000) lives up to its name as one of the better budget tours available in town. Prices include a full day of snorkeling plus equipment, fruit, and a generous Vietnamese lunch on the boat. The tour guides are a cheerful and eclectic cast of characters with a great sense of humor. The boat makes several different stops near the local islands. Even if you're not much of a snorkeling enthusiast, this is still a nice way to spend your day while on a budget.

Parasailing

Though it's not an officially advertised activity in most travel agencies around the city, there are a couple boats on the beach that offer parasailing rides. You'll be rewarded with high-flying views of the aquamarine Nha Trang Bay as well as the city's ever-changing skyline. Most rides go up and down the main coast, stopping at least once to let you float back down to earth before picking up again and sending you back into the air. Most parasailing boats are freelance enterprises, which means there's ample opportunity for you to bargain, however costs are still steep. The 15- to 20-minute ride costs around VND300,000.

Surfing

While Nha Trang's main beach isn't ideal on account of its crowded waters, Bai Dai is a nice spot for novice surfers, as the waves are strong enough for newbies to practice without getting in over their heads. The surf is at its best from November to March, after which time the water starts to get a little too quiet to catch a wave. At present you'll find two outfits on the beach who are willing to teach newcomers the tricks of the trade. In addition to food, Jet ski rentals, kayaks, and stand-up paddleboards, the folks at The Shack (Bai Dai town, tel. 012/6441-4102, www.shackvietnam.com, 9:30am-late daily, board rental VND180,000 per hour, surf lessons VND600,000 per hour) provide board rentals and surf lessons, while the Aussie surfers at **Long Beach Surf Club** (Bai Dai town, tel. 012/2858-1230, www.longbeachboardriders.com, 9am-late daily) offer a similar range of services farther down the way.

Golf

Nestled in the hills of Hon Tre Island, the **Vinpearl Golf Club** (Hon Tre Island, tel. 05/8359-0919, www.vinpearlgolf.com, 6:30am-6pm Tues.-Sun., VND945,000-2,100,000) is an 18-hole island course that looks out over Nha Trang Bay. Situated on the far side of Hon Tre, the course and its clubhouse offer impressive, uninhibited panoramas of the ocean as well as a moderately challenging course for both beginner and experienced golfers. A driving range and pro shop are also on the premises.

Taking advantage of the breathtaking coastline south of town, **Diamond Bay Golf** (Phuoc Ha Hamlet, Phuoc Dong Commune, tel. 05/8371-1722, www.diamondbaygolf.com, 6:30am-3pm daily) is an 18-hole course surrounded by natural marshes and palm trees. The facility boasts a driving range, pro shop, restaurant, clubhouse, and villa accommodations.

Massages and Spas

New spas open up every day in the city, particularly around the backpacker area. Prices at even the most affordable spots are not as competitive as other coastal destinations in Vietnam. Tipping is expected at these facilities. The most professional businesses will either ask that the customer fill out a tip collection form, or won't ask at all. Either way, being solicited for tips without a form is not considered acceptable. If you find yourself being pestered for a gratuity after your trip to the spa, you have the right to politely decline.

A short walk from the buzz of the backpacker area, **Bella Spa** (76A Dong Da, tel. 05/8351-2089, 10am-11pm daily, VND60,000-350,000) is one of the more affordable massage options in town. Though it may not be as serene as some of Nha Trang's other spas—the masseuses tend to get chatty—the service is good and the staff are experienced. A variety of body scrubs, facials, and different massages are available in addition to a sauna and steam room. Tips will be formally requested at the end of your service, so be prepared to contribute something extra.

A tall-and-narrow shop not far from Nha Trang Cathedral, **Sen Spa** (1A Ly Thanh Ton, tel. 05/8350-6565, www.senspanhatrang.com, 8am-8pm daily, VND100,000-450,000) offers reasonably priced massage and spa services with professional staff. Masks, facials, body scrubs, and massages are all on the spa menu, and the owners are an outgoing couple who do their best to ensure each customer's satisfaction. This is easily one of the best mid-range choices in town.

Su Spa (93AB Nguyen Thien Thuat, tel. 05/8352-3242, www.suspa.com.vn, 9am-11pm daily, spa treatments VND336,000-1,575,000, spa packages VND1,575,000-4,998,000) may charge Western prices, but this tranquil spa, smack-dab in the middle of the backpacker district, does a good job of providing quality massages, manicures, and other spa treatments, alongside a higher level of service.

ACCOMMODATIONS

Most travelers prefer to camp out close to the beach for easy access. Whatever your price range, this city has the accommodations to match: in the low season, you'll find dorm beds for as little as VND63,000, while high-season prices at any one of Nha Trang's luxury hotels have the potential to make a serious dent in your wallet. With so many options available, there are a handful of budget places that feature less-than-glowing reputations.

Under VND210,000

Hidden beside Green Apple Restaurant in a wide alley enclave off the main road, **Son and Daughter** (54A Nguyen Thien Thuat, tel. 05/8352-1709, www.son-daughter.com, VND100,000 dorm, VND200,000-380,000

d) boasts spotless rooms, a friendly staff, and an excellent location. Both basic private rooms and dorm beds are available, with six-bed co-ed accommodations with an en suite bathroom and personal lockers. In the low season, dorm beds are dirt cheap: around VND63,000 a night.

The pleasant and accommodating folks at **True Friends Inn** (79/1 Nguyen Thien Thuat, tel. 05/8352-8399, VND126,000-168,000 dorm) offer standard dorm beds complete with lockers, air-conditioning, Wi-Fi access, shared bathrooms, and complimentary breakfast. Four-, six-, and eight-person rooms are available. While this is a great place to meet fellow travelers, True Friends is not for light sleepers, as the walls are paper-thin and the Beer Pong bar next door stays open late. The company also runs a travel outfit down the road that offers boat and city tours around Nha Trang as well as Easy Rider adventures.

Tucked along Nguyen Thien Thuat, **HQ Cafe and Apartments** (55/8 Nguyen Thien Thuat, tel. 05/8625-2520, www.hqcafevn.com, VND126,000 dorm, VND315,000-420,000 d, breakfast included) offers modern, well-appointed rooms close to the beach but far enough from the city's nightlife to escape some of the noise pollution. Dorm-style and private rooms are available with air-conditioning, hot water, TV, and Wi-Fi access. Common rooms and sitting areas include a television and large refrigerator, as well as an en suite bathroom and lockers for each eight-person dorm. HQ also arranges tours and can assist travelers with laundry and transportation.

The welcome greeting at ★ **Mojzo Inn** (120/36 Nguyen Thien Thuat, tel. 05/8625-5568, www.mojzo-inn.com, VND168,000 dorm, VND378,000-462,000 d) is reason enough to shack up at this chic, well-appointed boutique hostel. From the moment you enter the building, Ly and her staff remember you by name and treat each guest as part of the family. Modern rooms feature air-conditioning, hot water, and television. There is unlimited free water and fruit in the cozy common area. Private rooms run small, but the dorms are a neat, six-person set-up, including lockers and en suite bathrooms, with plenty of space for budget travelers. A notably tasty breakfast is served each morning on the hotel rooftop and Wi-Fi is available throughout the building.

Pho Bien (64/1 Tran Phu, tel. 05/8352-5115, phobienhotelint@yahoo.com, VND147,000 dorm, VND357,000-630,000 d)

Mojzo Inn

stands out for a few reasons. From its unbeatable location directly opposite the beach to its clean, tidy rooms and exceptionally personable staff, this budget hotel does a great job of providing value as well as helpful travel advice. Rooms come with hot water, air-conditioning, Wi-Fi access, a minibar, and TV. Thanks to a recent renovation, the lodgings are nicer than ever.

VND210,000-525,000

Tucked down an alley off the main road, **Truong Giang Hotel** (3/8 Tran Quang Khai, tel. 05/8352-2125, www.truonggianghotel.hostel.com, VND252,000-378,000) features basic, no-frills beds at excellent prices. Each modest room comes with air-conditioning, hot water, TV, a minibar, and Wi-Fi access. Guests have the option of accommodations with or without a window. Rooms on the higher floors are cheaper, as the hotel does not have an elevator.

Hidden behind Vietnam Xua restaurant in a quiet courtyard off the street, **Nha Trang Inn** (103 Nguyen Thien Thuat, tel. 09/0533-1591, VND252,000-336,000) is a bare-bones guesthouse, but its location is spot-on and Minh, the proprietor, is a welcoming guy. All accommodations come with air-conditioning, hot water, Wi-Fi access, and a television, as well as a quieter atmosphere than most other accommodations on the block. With affordable prices and an excellent location, this is one of the better options on Nguyen Thien Thuat for budget backpackers.

Removed from the backpacker area, **Binh An Hotel** (28H Hoang Hoa Tham, tel. 05/8352-3181, www.binhanhotel.com, VND252,000-294,000) is a steal for the price. This charming little hotel boasts comfortable lodgings with plush beds, Wi-Fi access, and a television. Rooms are a decent size and feature modern furnishings as well as the option of a balcony overlooking Hoang Hoa Tham. The owners are a cheerful, elderly couple who greet their guests with individual signs and warm hellos. The hotel is a short walk from the beach and close to the center of town.

In the same beach-side alley as Pho Bien, **Ha Thu Hotel** (64/2 Tran Phu, tel. 05/8352-2800, VND210,000-252,000) is an equally worthy spot, with basic but adequate rooms including hot water, Wi-Fi access, air-conditioning, and TV. Beds are a little hard, but balcony options are available overlooking the small alley out front, and many rooms have a sea view, though this is slightly obscured by the buildings across the street.

VND525,000-1,050,00

Though it's a little older than some of its competition, rooms at the **Ha Vang Hotel** (22-23 Tran Quang Khai, tel. 05/8352-6662, www.goldensummerhotel.com.vn, VND630,000-840,000) are clean, spacious, and well-kept with modern amenities, including hot water, television, a minibar, air-conditioning, and complimentary breakfast. The upper floors offer decent views of the ocean, though this may change as more high-rise buildings go up in the area.

At the **Green Peace Hotel** (102 Nguyen Thien Thuat, tel. 05/8352-2835, www.greenpeacehotel.com.vn, VND600,000-800,000, breakfast included), the staff and location make this a worthy place to stay. At the western end of Nguyen Thien Thuat, Green Peace counts hot water, air-conditioning, Wi-Fi access, a fridge, and television among the amenities in its well-appointed rooms. The standard room is cramped, so upgrade to a superior (VND100,000 extra). The nicest rooms also include a balcony.

Decked out in a chic pink decor, the **Ha Van Hotel** (3/2 Tran Quang Khai, tel. 05/8352-5454, www.in2vietnam.com, VND546,000-735,000) gives off something of a Parisian feel in its rooms, which feature a sitting area complete with plush upholstered chairs and an elegant bed and generous bathroom. A full-service accommodation, Ha Van boasts air-conditioning, hot water, Wi-Fi access, television, and a minibar in its rooms, as well as add-ons such as laundry service. The pastry shop downstairs serves tasty cakes all day long and the staff are friendly and inviting from the moment you step inside. A rooftop bar rounds out the hotel's offerings.

Rooms at the family-run **La Suisse Hotel** (34 Tran Quang Khai, tel. 05/8352-4353, www.lasuissehotel.com, VND567,000-630,000) may be a little aged but remain adequate and offer the added benefit of distance between your room and Tran Quang Khai's noisy main drag. In-room safety boxes, a minibar, air-conditioning, hot water, and TV are all standard amenities, and the hotel also offers complimentary breakfast to all its guests, as well as free afternoon tea, coffee, and cake.

VND1,050,000-2,100,000

Hands-down the best value on Tran Phu, the **Nha Trang Lodge** (42 Tran Phu, tel. 05/8352-1500, www.nhatranglodge.com, VND1,600,000-5,500,000) may be a little outdated but its location can't be beat and, compared to the cost of other beachfront accommodations, rooms are a steal. All floors are blessed with superb views of the ocean, and you'll find air-conditioning, hot water, Wi-Fi access, a minibar, tea- and coffee-making facilities, and a television in each room. Breakfast is included in the room rate, as is access to the hotel's pool. Additional travel and spa services are also available.

Over VND2,100,000

Blessed with one of the nicest locations on the beach, the local **Novotel** (50 Tran Phu, tel. 05/8625-6928, www.novotel-nhatrang.com, VND2,520,000-3,570,000) sits almost directly opposite Tram Huong Tower and affords top-notch views of the sea. Standard rooms include a small, triangular balcony with partial views of the beach, while superiors boast some of the best panoramas in Nha Trang, with high windows and plenty of space, both indoors and out, from which to enjoy the scenery. All rooms feature sleek, modern decor and come equipped with air-conditioning, Wi-Fi, hot water, a flat-screen television, and a minibar. The hotel also makes its swimming

pool, sauna, and fitness center available to guests free of charge.

Surrounded by trendy cafés, ample beach views, and high-end shops, the **Sheraton Nha Trang** (26-28 Tran Phu, tel. 05/8388-0000, www.sheratonnhatrang.com, VND2,709,000-21,070,000) offers space and comfort along with a top-notch hotel staff. Its location farther down the coast means that beach-going travelers can enjoy a quieter stretch of sand. Amenities include air-conditioning, hot water, a flat-screen television, minibar, coffee- and tea-making facilities, and an in-room safe. The hotel also boasts a fitness center, spa, several restaurants, and an incredible sixth-floor infinity pool with panoramic views of the bay and on-the-water lounge chairs.

A palatial building at the northern end of Tran Phu, **Sunrise Nha Trang** (12-14 Tran Phu, tel. 05/8382-0999, www.sunrisenhatrang.com.vn, VND4,467,750-13,282,500) pulls out all the stops in its decor, opting for lavish colonial grandeur and plush, well-appointed rooms over some of its sleeker modern counterparts. A beautiful circular swimming pool tops the roof of the ground floor, offering pleasant views of the bay. The hotel includes several restaurants, a spa, and a tour outfit in addition to its accommodations. Sea views are available from every room at the Sunrise, and all accommodations include air-conditioning, Wi-Fi access, hot water, a minibar, satellite TV, and an in-room safe.

Nha Trang's only seaside resort, **Evason Ana Mandara** (Tran Phu, tel. 05/8352-2222, www.sixsenses.com, VND5,397,000-11,340,000) is the pinnacle of luxury in this bustling beach town. Hidden from view, Ana Mandara's 74 semi-detached villas offer a beautiful, exclusive environment right in the middle of the city, affording travelers the best of both worlds. Rooms feature a clean, simple decor of earth tones and well-appointed furnishings. Both sea and garden views are available, as well as high-quality amenities and a host of additional services, from

24-hour in-room dining to the facilities at Ana Mandara's world-class spa.

FOOD

Thanks to the number of foreign tourists that visit Nha Trang, dining options around the backpacker area are varied in both price and cuisine. Those craving a taste of home can find steak, pasta, pizza, burgers, and burritos. Fresh fish, squid, and shrimp are popular and worthy choices. Nha Trang is also known for its *bun cha ca*, a rice noodle soup paired with pressed fish.

Prices tend to be steep, with even a standard meal costing more than most other places in Vietnam. Street food is a good budget option. There are several rice stalls set up along Nguyen Thi Minh Khai. Ask the price first, or you may get overcharged.

Cafés and Bakeries

A super-skinny storefront wedged between a pair of high-rise hotels, **Cuppa Coffee** (4C Biet Thu, tel. 05/8352-4114, cuppavietnam@yahoo.com, 7am-9pm daily, VND20,000-75,000) serves both European and Vietnamese coffee, as well as tea, fruit smoothies, and a few desserts from its miniature storefront. A few stools line the narrow bar for customers to sit, but most just grab and go.

The only proper café in the backpacker area, **Iced Coffee** (49 Nguyen Thien Thuat, tel. 05/8246-0777, 6:30am-10pm daily, VND30,000-50,000) is a massive, air-conditioned building on Nguyen Thien Thuat with outgoing staff as well as European coffee, tea, smoothies, and Western food.

A delicious Asian-style bakery, **Hoa Hung** (39 Phan Boi Chau, tel. 05/8382-3141, 6am-10pm daily, VND8,000-30,000) stocks its shelves with eastern treats like sweet sticky rice cakes, mung bean pastries, and a wide variety of edibles featuring coconut, green tea, and other ingredients. Beware of the durian snacks; they're an acquired taste. There is also a smaller second location (48 Nguyen Thi Minh Khai) closer to the backpacker area, but you're better off sticking to the original, as it's larger and offers more variety.

From a tiny, powder blue stand near the corner of Biet Thu, **Anna's Crepe & Cream** (near corner of Nguyen Thien Thuat and Biet Thu, 8am-11pm daily, VND12,000-70,000) serves up both sweet and savory crepes as well as drinks and bottles of wine. Sweet varieties include Nutella, ice cream, and fruit, while

bun cha ca (rice noodle soup with fish), a local specialty

smoked ham and cheese feature heavily on the savory menu.

Vietnamese

In a city with literally hundreds of shops specializing in *bun cha ca,* a tasty soup featuring rice noodles and pressed fish, ★ **Nguyen Loan** (123 Ngo Gia Tu, tel. 05/8351-5634, 6am-11pm daily, VND25,000-35,000) is a standout. Piping hot, delicious bowls of soup are accompanied by fresh greens, lime, and an array of sauces to compliment your personal tastes, including the ultra-fishy, dark purple *mam tom* (fermented shrimp paste). The restaurant serves a few different styles of the dish, including one with thicker, rope-like *banh canh* noodles. They are best known for their *bun sua cha ca,* a variation which includes jellyfish.

A longstanding local haunt, **Pho 70** (112 Bach Dang, tel. 05/8351-2091, 6am-11:30am daily, VND30,000-45,000) has been turning out delicious bowls of Vietnam's favorite dish for over 50 years. The special beef pho is particularly tasty, and you'll find this modest spot filled with locals from open 'til close. Note, that you have to get up reasonably early to enjoy Pho 70, as the shop only operates during breakfast hours. If you turn up to late, never fear—there are plenty of other dining options along Bach Dang street to quell your hunger.

Near Dam Market, **Nem Dang Van Quyen** (16A Lan Ong, tel. 05/8382-6737, www.nemdangvanquyen.com.vn, 7:30am-9pm daily, VND30,000-70,000) attracts foreigners and locals, thanks to its *nem nuong* (grilled pork sausage), which comes with a host of fixings for diners to create their own spring rolls. Fill your rice paper with greens, mango, cucumber, pickled carrots, and savory pork. A tasty special dipping sauce is a standard staple. They also have delicious noodle dishes, including *bun thit nuong* and *bun ca,* or rice noodles and fish.

You can smell the sumptuous barbecue at **Lac Canh** (44 Nguyen Binh Khiem, tel. 05/8360-6277, www.laccanh.com, 9:30am-10pm daily, VND25,000-195,000) from a block away. This two-story open-front shop has been dishing out cheap, tasty Vietnamese meals since the 1960s, with a bustling atmosphere and bare-bones decor, not to mention one of the more affordable menus in town. Barbecue beef is the house specialty, but you'll find scores of other options here as well, including seafood, chicken, pork, and veggies.

On a street full of seafood restaurants, **Nhat Phong 3** (63B Cu Lao Trung, tel. 05/8370-0233, 10am-10:30pm daily, VND50,000-300,000) is a popular local spot for grilled fish and other tasty Vietnamese dishes. Beside the ground floor dining area, waitstaff pluck your dinner from a series of large fish tanks; market prices for individual offerings are listed on a whiteboard above. The restaurant's specialty, grilled chicken with honey, is another excellent choice.

A charming yellow storefront down a quiet street, **Yen's Restaurant** (3/3 Tran Quang Khai, tel. 05/8652-1669, www.in2vietnam. com, 10am-10:30pm daily, VND60,000-250,000) may run on the expensive side of local cuisine, but its tasty traditional dishes and pleasant ambience are worth a few extra dollars. Most entrées hover around VND95,000 apiece and the restaurant staff are always willing to offer recommendations.

International

Same Same But Different (111 Nguyen Thien Thuat, tel. 05/8352-4079, ssbdcafe@ yahoo.com, 7:30am-10pm daily, VND50,000-110,000) is a classy establishment, sporting tablecloths and artistic photographs of countryside scenes on the walls, plus a nice mirrored bar at the back of the narrow restaurant. The decor is made better by the fact that prices are reasonable. The menu boasts a decent selection of Vietnamese and Western food along with a few Thai dishes and a notably varied breakfast menu. Servers are particularly friendly and helpful, and a cooking class is offered for interested travelers.

Mexican

A hole-in-the-wall shop with a few tables

on the street, **The Lil Shack** (97/13 Nguyen Thien Thuat, tel. 016/7805-2168, 9am-midnight daily, VND30,000-165,000), an extension of Bai Dai's larger facility, does a great job of offering well-priced and delicious Mexican food in an outdoor setting. Snacks, burritos, tacos, and a few burgers are available, and the shop even makes deliveries within the block.

Italian

The pizzas alone are reason enough to visit **Olivia** (14B Tran Quang Khai, tel. 05/8352-2752, 10am-10pm daily, VND75,000-300,000), a smart, affordable, Italian eatery not far from the beach. Dine inside, surrounded by simple but sophisticated exposed brick, or opt for covered outdoor seating with a genuine Italian café feel. The menu lists a variety of pastas and pizzas as well as gnocchi and other authentic European dishes.

Brewpubs

Louisiane Brewhouse (29 Tran Phu, tel. 05/8352-1948, www.louisianebrewhouse. com.vn, 7am-late daily, VND80,000-310,000) makes its own beers from scratch, including a pilsner, a witbier, and a dark lager, as well as the odd seasonal brew. This classy beachside spot also serves top-notch seafood and Western cuisine, though at a price. Opt for sheltered seating on the veranda or camp out beneath the thatched umbrellas by the pool. This is a perfect spot for a splurge or a change from the usual Saigon Reds and 333s.

Indian

Right around dinner time, the seating area at **Omar's Tandoori Cafe** (89B Nguyen Thien Thuat, tel. 05/8222-1615, omarnewdelhi@ yahoo.com, 10am-11pm daily, VND60,000-135,000) becomes packed with hungry travelers and a flurry of attentive waitstaff. The menu at this Indian restaurant offers plenty of choice for both meat-free and carnivorous diners as well as speedy service and affordable prices. Both upstairs and downstairs seating is available, and the shop has managed to become so successful that it now has a second

location (96A/8 Tran Phu, tel. 05/8352-2459, 7am-10:30pm daily, VND60,000-135,000) nearby that opens earlier in the mornings and also serves breakfast.

Japanese

The narrow **Oh! Sushi** (17C Hung Vuong, tel. 05/8352-5729, www.ohsushibar.com, 10am-11pm daily, VND50,000-400,000) bar boasts a tome of Japanese cuisine ranging from soba noodles and miso soup to, of course, sushi, hand rolls, and several bento boxes for lunch. Indoors, a small bar lines the left side of the ground floor, from which diners have a perfect view of the restaurant's fresh ingredients. To the right, a few tables are huddled in the downstairs quarters, but you can also head up to the second floor for additional seating.

Mediterranean

Though its prices are steeper than other eateries, the staff at **Mediterraneo** (92 Nguyen Thien Thuat, tel. 05/8352-1827, mediterraneo.nhatrang@gmail.com, noon-11pm daily, VND85,000-295,000) provide first-class service along with Spanish and Italian fare. Portion sizes run on the small side, but the dining rooms, both upstairs and downstairs, are inviting, with cozy tables and a nice view of the street. This is also one of the only places in town you'll find dishes like paella, orechiette, and charcuterie.

INFORMATION AND SERVICES
Tourist Information

Free city maps and travel information are easy to come by in most hotels and tour agencies, though advice is usually influenced by whatever travel options that business offers. For slightly less-biased news, check out the local *What's On Nha Trang* (www.iguidenhatrang.com), a glossy magazine offering useful tips and recommendations about the city. You can usually find a stack of these at **Iced Coffee** (49 Nguyen Thien Thuat) alongside free city maps. You can pay a visit to the government-run

Nha Trang Tourist (1 Tran Hung Dao, tel. 05/8352-8100, www.nhatrangtourist.com. vn, 7:30am-4:30pm daily), but don't expect much in the way of advice.

Banks

From the backpacker area, the most easily accessible bank is a small **Vietcombank** outpost (30 Nguyen Thien Thuat, tel. 05/8352-4676, 7am-11:30am and 1:30pm-5pm Mon.-Fri.), complete with ATM, just a short walk past Biet Thu. It has a few English-speaking employees.

Internet and Postal Services

Nha Trang's central **post office** (2 Tran Phu, tel. 05/8382-1002, 7am-9pm daily) is located at the northern end of Tran Phu and provides postal as well as Internet services.

Medical Services

The **VK Hospital** (34/4 Nguyen Thien Thuat, tel. 05/8352-8866), located within the backpacker area, boasts English-speaking doctors and 24-hour emergency services.

GETTING THERE

Nha Trang can be accessed in a variety of ways, as regular buses, trains, and planes arrive daily from all over the country. The bus is the cheapest option from Ho Chi Minh City. Trains also ply the route between Vietnam's coastal cities, bringing in passengers from all directions, though at a slightly higher cost. Many services run at night, making an eight- or nine-hour journey feasible. There is a much greater distance between Nha Trang and its closest northern destinations, Hoi An and Hue, than between Nha Trang and Mui Ne, Dalat, or Saigon.

Some travelers prefer flying the long overland trip, or opt for the slightly more comfortable train.

Air

Thirty kilometers south of Nha Trang, the **Cam Ranh Airport** (CXR, www.nhatrangairport.com) welcomes daily flights from Saigon (one hour), Danang (one hour), and Hanoi (two hours) through Vietnam Airlines and budget carriers VietJet and Jetstar.

You can catch a taxi (VND350,000-400,000) into town or opt for the **airport shuttle bus** (tel. 05/8398-9909, VND60,000). Should you take a taxi, clarify that the vehicle is metered or agree upon a price before setting off. It's about 30 minutes into town from the airport.

For flight tickets in town, visit the **Vietnam Airlines ticketing office** (91 Nguyen Thien Thuat, tel. 05/8352-6768, www.vietnamairlines.com, 7:30am-11:15am and 1:30pm-4:45pm daily) opposite Red Apple Club.

Bus

Sinh Tourist (90C Hung Vuong, tel. 05/8352-4329, www.thesinhtourist.vn, 6am-10pm daily) buses from Saigon (VND189,000), Mui Ne (VND119,000), Dalat (VND119,000), and Hoi An (VND349,000) arrive and depart at its office in downtown Nha Trang, right in the heart of the backpacker area.

Phuong Trang (7 Hoang Hoa Tham, tel. 05/8381-2812, www.futabuslines.com.vn, 7am-10pm daily) buses from Saigon (VND230,000) usually let off at the **southern bus station (Ben Xe Phia Nam)** (58 23 Thang 10, tel. 05/8382-0227, 4am-9pm daily).

For smaller destinations, such as Phan Rang or Quy Nhon, visit the Nha Trang bus station and hop on a local minibus. Be prepared to stand your ground on prices, as minibus drivers often overcharge foreign travelers. Ask your hotel's receptionist to call and inquire about the price ahead of time, so that you arrive armed with the correct fare.

Train

The historical **Nha Trang train station (Ga Nha Trang)** (17 Thai Nguyen, tel. 05/8382-7862, ga_nha_trang@yahoo.com. vn, 7am-10pm daily) has been around long enough to be considered a city relic. Daily trains run from Danang (10 hours, VND630,000-882,000), Hanoi (23 hours,

VND1,260,000-1,974,000), and Saigon (8 hours, VND882,000).

GETTING AROUND
Taxis and *Xe Om*

You'll find plenty of *xe om* waiting for a fare on street corners in the backpacker area, while **Mailinh** (tel. 0583/838-3838) taxis are also widely available and easily flagged down in the street. For those who'd rather not haggle for motorbike fares, Nha Trang has a **metered *xe om* service** (tel. 05/8625-2526), which employs university students as drivers. Fares begin at VND6,000 per kilometer for the first six kilometers, then VND5,000 per kilometer after that.

Buses

Nha Trang's public bus system is easily navigated and by far the cheapest transportation option. Look out for bright red and yellow buses, which ply six different routes around town, stopping near all of Nha Trang's major sights. Fares are posted on the side of the bus and run VND5,000-6,000, depending upon your destination. Service usually stops around 7pm.

Nha Trang's largest and most central bus station is the **southern bus station (Ben Xe Phia Nam)** (58 23 Thang 10, tel. 05/8382-0227, 4am-9pm daily). This is also where long-distance local buses depart. Buses regularly travel Nguyen Thien Thuat and Tran Phu (the backpacker area), so it's unlikely a traveler will require a trip to the bus station in order to catch a bus.

Vehicles for Hire

However you get around, check what options your hotel offers first, as rental companies will want some sort of collateral, and hotels usually keep your passport anyway.

Motorbike and bicycle rentals are a dime a dozen in Nha Trang and reasonably priced. Manual motorbikes start at around VND80,000 a day, while automatics may cost up to VND120,000.

Most hotels offer **city bicycles** (around VND40,000-50,000), which are suitable for cycling around town.

The friendly **Mr. Hoa** (53/4 Nguyen Thien Thuat, tel. 05/8352-4148, 8am-8pm daily) rents out affordable and reliable bicycles (VND30,000-40,000) and motorbikes (VND80,000-150,000), both automatic and semi-automatic.

DOC LET BEACH

Thirty miles north of Nha Trang, **Doc Let** is a spectacular expanse of white sand beach whose scenery and seclusion draw a growing number of day-trippers to its shores. Its pristine coastline and crystalline blue waters are book-ended by fishing boats on one side and mountains on the other, and the wide beach affords plenty of room for visitors to spread out. Doc Let sees few visitors compared to the shores of Nha Trang; you won't find roving vendors or massive crowds here.

The older **Doc Let Resort** (Ninh Hai Village, tel. 05/8384-9152, 6am-10pm daily, VND20,000) offers an array of services, all of which require an additional, often exorbitant, cost, from sun-bed and umbrella rentals to parasailing, Jet skis, and kayaks. It's better to just bring your own towel, pay the fee for beach access, and spread out on the sand. You'll also find a restaurant on the premises, though it is only open intermittently, and a swimming pool (additional VND35,000) set back from the water.

Beside Doc Let Resort is its updated and more expensive counterpart, **White Sand Doc Let Resort** (9 Dong Cat, Ninh Hai Village, tel. 05/8367-0670, www.whitesandresort.com.vn, 6am-10pm daily, VND100,000), a somewhat classier place to lounge around, though its services are equally overpriced. This resort also charges a fee for beach access.

The drive out to Doc Let is an experience in itself, as the coastal road takes you past picturesque fishing villages and stunning rice paddies. A series of rocky seaside passes ascend the dramatic cliffs along the south-central coast before bringing you into the sleepy village of Ninh Hai, home to Doc Let Beach.

Ba Ho Waterfall

dirt track veering off the main highway south of Ninh Hoa. Flowing from the peak of Hon Son Mountain, Ba Ho ("Three Lakes" in Vietnamese) takes its name from the three segments of water that run down the far side of the mountain, pooling into many small bodies of water. This has become an increasingly popular place to visit, as it offers travelers a pleasant shaded hike and plenty of spots to stop and relax or go for a swim.

A jungle trail (one mile each way) runs parallel to Ba Ho before dead-ending next to one of the stream's wider sections. From there, you can continue to the top of the waterfall by scrambling over the rocks that surround the water (though you'll need proper footwear). Along the path, several smaller dirt routes are carved into the underbrush, which allow you to stop and enjoy the scenery. A group of local women occasionally set up shop near the trail's end, selling barbecued chicken.

While Ba Ho's waters are most abundant during rainy season, the river still runs from November to April and it's possible to go for a swim. Independent travelers can hop on a motorbike and find the place themselves, or sign up with a tour group. **Vietnam Active** (47 Nguyen Thien Thuat, tel. 09/0362-6061, www.vietnamactive.com, 8am-noon and 2pm-9pm daily, VND1,365,000) runs a bicycle tour to Ba Ho, passing by Po Nagar, Ngoc Son Pagoda, and Hon Chong on the way. For a cheaper and more casual trip, local operator **Funky Monkey** (75A Hung Vuong, tel. 05/8352-2426, www.funkymonkeytour.com, 7am-10pm daily, VND1,050,000) also runs a one-day tour that stops by Ba Ho, Monkey Island, and Doc Let Beach.

MONKEY ISLAND

Sometimes included in package tours to Doc Let and Ba Ho Waterfall, **Monkey Island (Dao Khi)** (tel. 05/8224-1853, www.longphu.khatoco.com, 7am-5pm daily, VND120,000), also known as Hon Lao, is a small islet off the coast north of Nha Trang where locals have trained a troupe of over 1,000 monkeys to perform circus acts for tourists. Most visitors

For those comfortable on a motorbike, follow Tran Phu street north over the bridge and out of town, sticking to the coast until you reach the junction at Amiana World Resort, where you'll turn left and follow the markers for Ninh Hoa. A few billboards for White Sand Resort stand out among the other roadside advertising. Once you reach Ninh Hai village, a small concrete road takes you out to the beach.

A handful of tour operators run one- and two-day excursions out to Doc Let and back, often combining the trip with a jaunt to Ba Ho Waterfall and Monkey Island. Local operator **Funky Monkey** (75A Hung Vuong, tel. 05/8352-2426, www.funkymonkeytour.com, 7am-10pm daily) runs a whirlwind one-day tour (VND1,050,000) that stops by Ba Ho, Monkey Island, and Doc Let Beach.

BA HO WATERFALL

En route to Doc Let Beach, **Ba Ho Waterfall** (Khu Du Lich Suoi Ba Ho, 7am-5pm daily, VND15,000) punctuates the end of a dusty find the place pretty depressing, as flagrant animal cruelty is not uncommon when the monkeys fail to successfully perform a trick, and the animals are so used to humans bringing food that they've become aggressive toward visitors, snatching items from tourists and, on occasion, scratching or biting. Safety standards in Vietnam are not the same as they might be at home, so visit the island at your own risk.

Phan Rang-Thap Cham

Hidden between Nha Trang's wild beach parties and the ever-multiplying resorts of Mui Ne, Phan Rang-Thap Cham is a winning mix of sunny, secluded shoreline and authentic local culture. Far less frequented than its neighbors to the north and south, this humble seaside town may not come with all the trappings of an international, tourist-friendly destination but it packs plenty of genuine Vietnamese food, history, and culture into its small city limits. In addition to the peaceful, palm-fringed beach, a handful of ancient rust-colored temples dot the nearby hillside, leftovers from the last Cham kingdom to fall to the Vietnamese empire in the late 1600s. Phan Rang's street-side cooks produce tasty and unique renditions of local fare with a twist. For travelers seeking a destination that ventures farther off the beaten path while still remaining a great spot to log some quality beach time, look no farther than Phan Rang.

With rooms in Nha Trang and Mui Ne filling up fast and the hullabaloo, not to mention the prices, proving too much for some, Phan Rang's relative anonymity is poised to change: already, new hotels are beginning to appear just outside the town center near Ninh Chu Beach. For now, at least, this is a beautiful beach destination that is calm, quiet, and still easy on the wallet.

Thanks to its semi-arid climate, Phan Rang manages to remain fairly dry throughout the year, though it does heat up considerably in the summer months. Not much English is spoken in town; however, with a good sense of humor and patience, travelers should be just fine. The beach is the main attraction in this tiny town, so a few days here is sufficient.

SIGHTS

Phan Rang's handful of must-see monuments are located beyond the city center, with its nearest Cham towers sitting a few miles west of town. These sights are best accessed by motorbike, whether independently or on the back of a *xe om,* as some of the roads veering off the main highway very quickly turn into concrete pathways or dirt tracks. Taxis are also an option, though you may encounter more difficulty the farther you get from town. Quick jaunts back and forth between the beach are perfectly feasible in any vehicle.

There's not much in the way of landmarks, but Phan Rang is a likable little place, with plenty of charming old storefronts and angular Communist architecture. Near the central market, **Ong Pagoda** (beside Phan Rang Market, sunrise-sunset, days vary) is alive with color and boasts a beautifully detailed roof; though it is not always open, travelers can still appreciate the handiwork from outside. Farther down 16 Thang 4 street heading toward the beach, the sprawling parade ground at **16 Thang 4 Square** hints at the future of city planning in this small coastal town, with the massive **16 Thang 4 monument** and adjoining stone bleachers on one side and an eye-catching triangular building on the other, which is set to hold the **Ninh Thuan Museum.** Though the building has yet to contain anything, its exterior is worth a peek if you're strolling around this area. Back toward the city center, **16 Thang 4 Park** also

Phan Rang-Thap Cham

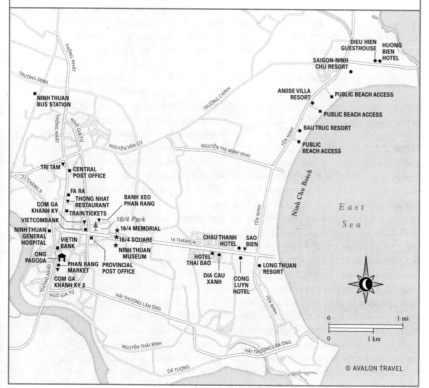

makes for a nice spot to relax in town with its large fish pond and ample shade trees.

Po Klaung Garai

The most remarkable of the town's still-standing Cham towers, the 13th-century **Po Klaung Garai** (Bac Ai, 7.5 km/4.6 mi north of Phan Rang, tel. 06/8388-8029, 7am-5pm daily, VND15,000) sits northwest of the center and affords some nice views of the surrounding area. Perched atop Trau Hill, three imposing red brick structures stand against the wind, with the smallest tower serving as an entrance gate onto the main sanctuary, a 66-foot-tall temple honoring King Po Klaung Garai, former ruler of the Champa kingdom from 1151 to 1205. The doorway into Po Klaung Garai's shrine is guarded by a dancing Shiva and etched in the curling Sanskrit letters once used by the Cham. Through the narrow entryway you'll find a statue of the cow Nandin, a revered creature in Hinduism, facing the altar where the king's effigy lies. Painted onto the *linga* sculpture at the center of the temple is the human face of the king. During Kate, a celebration that gives thanks to the Hindu and Cham gods for bountiful harvests and prosperity, local Chams will "feed" the Nandin cow in order to receive a successful harvest. Beside the entrance tower, Po Klaung Garai's third and final structure appears much the same as its contemporaries but for a boat-shaped roof that peaks at either end. This is known as the fire tower, as it once held fires and prepared offerings for the main temple.

While Po Klaung Garai receives regular visitors, both devout followers and tourists, the temple's busiest time of year is during the Kate festival, when ethnic Cham come from near and far to give offerings and prayers to their former king. At the foot of the hill is a small exhibition room featuring photos of various Cham festivals and celebrations, as well as a small souvenir shop.

Ninh Chu Beach

Easily one of the south-central coast's best-kept secrets, **Ninh Chu Beach** (Yen Ninh) is sure to lose its anonymity in the near future. With three miles of secluded, pristine white sands and sparkling waters, the coast east of Phan Rang is blissfully devoid of roving vendors and mega-resorts, affording some stunning views of the curved shoreline and nearby mountains, along with the collection of fishing boats huddled on either end of the bay. Clean and undeveloped, there are several public access points available along the road parallel to Ninh Chu where travelers can simply walk onto the beach. A few modest resorts set up toward the north end of the beach boast seaside restaurants, which are also available to non-guests.

Po Ro Me

Twelve miles removed from the city, the single tower at **Po Ro Me** (Ninh Phuoc, 12.5 mi from Phan Rang, sunrise-sunset daily) may not be as grand as Po Klaung Garai, its northern counterpart, but its location adds an air of mystery to the place. The journey to Po Ro Me takes travelers well off the beaten path of Highway 1 and through a humble Cham village. At the foot of the hill, you can ascend the steep staircase along with the temple's caretaker, a friendly fellow who speaks some English, and, once you've reached the top, take in the panorama of rice paddies and small houses dotting the landscape. While the temple is usually locked, you can ask the caretaker to open it up for you. Once a wall of fluttering bats has cleared, you'll find two Nandin cows—one old and one new—sitting prostrate before a massive, six-armed statue of Champa's last king. In years past, additional statues were housed within the temple, but these have been lost to theft and the passing of time.

A trip to Po Ro Me requires the use of a motorbike or a *xe om* driver to bring you out to the towers. The journey itself can be a fun adventure. Bring a map, as things aren't always well marked and you're likely to get lost a few times before successfully reaching the

boat on Ninh Chu Beach

temple. At the time of writing, a small concrete road leading in toward the base of the hill was under construction and set to be completed soon. Keep an eye out for the blue sign on the left pointing you in the right direction.

Bau Truc Pottery Village

Those in the market for local handicrafts will enjoy a trip to **Bau Truc Pottery Village (Lang Nghe Gom Bau Truc)**, where a small community of ethnic Cham make and sell their own pottery, formed by hand into all manner of creatures, pots, jars, jugs, ashtrays, and other sculptures. Several pottery shops are present in the dusty and otherwise unremarkable village. These beautiful, authentic handicrafts are well made and dirt cheap compared to elsewhere. This is not a bad place to pull over en route to Po Ro Me, as it's only a few miles from the temple site.

ACCOMMODATIONS

As a town still getting used to the notion of foreign tourism—and, indeed, still very much under construction for itself—Phan Rang boasts plenty of cheap and basic options, with fewer choices in the way of mid-range or high-end rooms, though the beachfront resorts along Ninh Chu try their best. The nicest digs are on the water, where several outfits, including the mammoth Saigon Tourist, have set up resorts catering largely to Russian tourists. Modest, family-run guesthouses and mini-hotels abound, leaving you with only location to worry about. Those who prefer to focus their trip on the Cham towers may want to opt for an in-town accommodation, for easier access to transportation, while beach bums should opt for lodgings closer to shore. With Ninh Chu Beach only a few miles from town, travelers should have no trouble gaining access to both the sea and the sights from wherever they are.

In Town
UNDER VND210,000
Comfy beds and clean bathrooms can be found at **Fa Ra Guesthouse** (281 Thong

Nhat, tel. 06/8382-0641, VND200,000), right along the town's main drag. Though accommodations run on the small side and some offer more light than others, each room comes with a futon couch and bed, TV, fridge, air-conditioning, hot water, and Wi-Fi access. The staff speak some English and are happy to dole out travel advice and the occasional motorbike or bicycle rental.

Hotel Thai Bao (15 N2 16 Thang 4, tel. 0683/382-7677, VND150,000) provides simple, well-kept rooms halfway between the beach and the town center. Both window and windowless options are available as are a variety of room sizes. Receptionists don't speak much English but are nonetheless helpful and friendly, and hot water, air-conditioning, TV, and Wi-Fi are available throughout. The hotel also has a second venue right next door.

Newer than some of the other hotels on this road, **Dia Cau Xanh** (8 N3 16 Thang 4, tel. 06/8383-8939, VND180,000-250,000) is a particularly tidy place, with the standard hot water, air-conditioning, Wi-Fi, TV, and fridge amenities. The staff do not speak much English, but the hotel is fairly close to the beach and prices are reasonable.

VND210,000-525,000
Chau Thanh Hotel (end of 16 Thang 4, tel. 06/8389-1555, VND400,000-500,000) boasts plush beds, spacious rooms, large balconies, and decent views of the surrounding mountains and coast. Though finishing touches (like a fish pond) are still being put on the hotel, this place offers the best value in town. Amenities include hot water, air-conditioning, Wi-Fi access, a television, and a fridge. Though employees don't speak much English, the owner can help with recommendations and transportation.

Opposite the large Sao Bien Restaurant, **Cong Luyn Hotel** (end of 16 Thang 4, tel. 06/8382-1111, www.congluynhotel.com.vn, VND300,000-450,000) is more modest than Chau Thanh, its new competition across the street. Rooms are cozy and well kept, with a television, fridge, hot water, air-conditioning, and Wi-Fi access. Its location also adds to Cong Luyn's appeal, as the hotel sits a short walk from the beach and from a handful of small local eateries around the corner on Yen Ninh.

On the Beach
UNDER VND210,000

For dirt-cheap but trim and tidy accommodations near the beach, **Huong Bien Hotel** (Khu Du Lich Saigon, Ninh Chu, tel. 06/8387-3044, VND150,000-200,000) offers rooms with decent beds and spotless bathrooms, hot water, air-conditioning, a TV, and Wi-Fi access on the dirt road just past Saigon-Ninh Chu Resort. The cheerful receptionist speaks some English and Huong Bien is just a short walk from both the beach and the cluster of seafood restaurants at the end of the road.

Right beside Huong Bien, **Dieu Hien Guesthouse** (Khu Du Lich Saigon, Ninh Chu, tel. 06/8387-3399, VND150,000) offers slightly less atmosphere but remains a clean and safe place to base yourself. Various configurations of hot water and cold water, air-conditioning, and fan rooms are available, as are second-floor rooms with a small balcony.

VND525,000-1,050,000

Steps from the water, the generous beachfront villas at **Bau Truc Resort** (Yen Ninh, tel. 06/8387-4047, www.bautrucresort.com, VND800,000-1,500,000, breakfast included) offer unobstructed ocean views. Amenities such as hot water, air-conditioning, television, Wi-Fi access, and daily bottled water are standard. Each villa keeps to a traditional theme, employing the ruddy brick and arched doorways of Cham architecture. There is a restaurant and pool on-site. While you're not likely to find five-star service or many English speakers, the place boasts good value and an unbeatable location.

VND1,050,000-2,100,000

With panoramic views of the ocean and the distant hills, **Saigon-Ninh Chu Resort** (Yen Ninh, tel. 06/8387-6011, www.

saigonninhchuhotel.co.vn, VND1,575,000-4,200,000) is nice but a little aged. The corridors could use new carpeting and the pool has seen better days. However, its spacious rooms offer great value and a decent level of service. Amenities include air-conditioning, Wi-Fi access, hot water, TV, a minibar, and complimentary buffet breakfast. Add-ons range from a poolside bar to multiple restaurants, occasional beach barbecues, and one of the only tour outfits in town.

A more posh version of its beachfront competition, **Aniise Villa Resort** (Yen Ninh, tel. 06/8625-1867, www.aniisevillaresort.com, VND1,200,000-5,500,000) offers the most upscale accommodations on the block. Its plush, spacious rooms come in a few varieties, from standard accommodations to sea view villas no more than a few steps from the water. Additional amenities like a chic pool area and a tennis court are free for guests to use. In-room accoutrements include hot water, air-conditioning, Wi-Fi access, and television, as well as complimentary breakfast.

A massive, hard-to-miss, pink building at the end of 16 Thang 4, **Long Thuan Resort** (end of 16 Thang 4, tel. 06/8222-0200, VND670,000-1,500,000) is a mixed bag: while its standard rooms are nothing to write home about, with outdated decor and deteriorating facilities, the closer you get to the beach the better the accommodations become. Beachfront bungalows are on par with most of Ninh Chu's other seaside offerings, featuring trim and tidy lodgings with wooden furnishings, air-conditioning, TV, Wi-Fi, hot water, and an in-room safe. Breakfast is included in the room rate, as is access to the resort restaurant and pool.

FOOD

Phan Rang boasts several culinary specialties. Seafood is, of course, a local favorite in any beachfront town, but the cooks of Phan Rang have taken it upon themselves to incorporate these ingredients into traditional Vietnamese dishes like *banh xeo,* the local version of which is smaller—similar to the savory pancakes

Phan Rang Cuisine

In every town across this S-shaped country, local specialties abound. From Hanoian pho, *bun bo Hue* (spicy beef noodle soup), and Hoi An's very own *cao lau* to the tasty *hu tieu* (southern-style rice noodle soup) of My Tho, ingenious local chefs are always cooking up something new. While Phan Rang cuisine doesn't often make the list of Vietnam's most famous dishes, this sleepy town still manages to boast a variety of delicious specialties.

The most popular of these meals is *banh can,* a small, savory cake made of grilled rice flour and egg that is usually topped with pork, squid, or shrimp and served with fresh greens. These mouthwatering, bite-sized morsels can be consumed by the dozen and are best enjoyed with *nuoc cham,* a lighter version of fish sauce. Local vendors in Phan Rang add peanuts into their *nuoc cham,* making for a richer, more flavorful concoction. *Banh xeo Phan Rang,* the local rendition of savory Vietnamese pancakes, tweaks the national recipe to include seafood and is served with fresh greens and *nuoc cham.* You can easily find both these dishes on the street, where women with scorching hot *banh can* pans (similar to cupcake tins) churn out piles of the little snacks all day.

Ninh Thuan province is one of the only places in Vietnam to raise goats and sheep, both of which you'll occasionally find on local menus. These meats are often prepared in curries or hotpots. Thanks to its unusual climate, this area boasts garlic, grapes, and Vietnamese apples (a small green fruit with a miniature pit at the center), all of which you're sure to see for sale in the town market and along the roadside.

you'll find in the country's central region—and includes squid and shrimp, served with an appetizing peanut sauce. Another local specialty is *banh can,* small steamed rice-flour-and-egg cakes topped with meat, squid, or shrimp and again enjoyed with the same tasty sauce. For seaside eats, many of the resorts down the north end of Ninh Chu Beach have restaurants attached that welcome outside visitors as well as guests. Down the dirt road past Saigon-Ninh Chu Resort you'll also find a host of small, local seafood restaurants. For folks in town, plenty of street food is available both around **Phan Rang Market** (Thong Nhat and Ngo Quyen, sunrise-sunset daily) and along Ngo Gia Tu south of 16 Thang 4.

The delectable *banh xeo Phan Rang* (Tran Quang Dieu opposite 16 Thang 4 Park, noon-late daily, VND30,000-50,000) can be found on the far side of the park at four or five small street stalls, where you'll get a glimpse of how *banh xeo* is made and what these scrumptious savory pancakes contain. Don't forget to throw in some fresh greens and make ample use of your dipping sauces.

A simple storefront past the post office on Thong Nhat, **Tri Tam** (Quan Tri Tam, 174

Thong Nhat, tel. 06/8382-0615, 8am-10pm daily, VND65,000-140,000) specializes in goat dishes, a local favorite. While you won't find an English menu, the Vietnamese version is posted on the wall and includes a tasty goat curry *(ca ri An Do),* goat hotpot *(lau de),* and grilled goat *(de nuong).* Each dish comes with either bread or rice.

A Phan Rang favorite, **Com Ga Khanh Ky** (61 Tran Quang Dieu, tel. 06/8383-8886, www.comgakhanhky.com.vn, 6am-8pm daily, VND25,000-40,000) is well known among locals for its chicken and rice. Several other items also feature on the menu, which one of the English-speaking staff will translate for you, but the restaurant's namesake dish is its best. You're welcome to check out the pre-cooked birds sitting in the cart out front before you eat. There is also a second location (643 Thong Nhat, tel. 06/8383-2171, 6am-8pm daily, VND25,000-40,000) beside the local market.

Sao Bien (end of 16 Thang 4, tel. 06/8389-1199, www.nhahangsaobien.com.vn, 9am-late daily, VND80,000-300,000) succeeds in both top-notch seafood dishes and a classy atmosphere. You'll find the catch of the day on display near the barbecue, an array that includes crab, squid, shrimp, and several kinds of fish. White wrought-iron furniture takes up the outdoor seating area. Inside, Sao Bien's well-lit dining room is grand as far as Phan Rang goes. English-speaking staff can assist you in making lunch or dinner choices. The large menu also includes a few meatless items.

While rooms at the Thong Nhat Hotel are nothing extraordinary, the **Thong Nhat Restaurant** (343 Thong Nhat, tel. 06/8382-7201, 6am-10pm daily, VND70,000-300,000) downstairs offers travelers a more conventional dining atmosphere, complete with tablecloths and a full place setting, a lengthy menu of Vietnamese dishes, and plenty of beverages. Seafood features heavily in the restaurant's offerings, but there are also chicken, beef, and (a few) tofu options available.

INFORMATION AND SERVICES

With a provincial tourism outfit nowhere to be found, the folks at Saigon-Ninh Chu Resort's **tourist information kiosk** are your next best option, offering free maps and useful information to guests as well as curious passersby. You can also consult the website for **Ninh Thuan Tourist** (www.ninhthuantourist.com) for more information on specific sights.

Phan Rang's main **Vietin Bank** (468 Thong Nhat, tel. 06/8383-9139, www.vietinbank.vn, 7am-11am and 1:30pm-4:30pm Mon.-Fri.) can assist with currency exchange and ATM services, while those closer to the beach can visit Saigon-Ninh Chu Resort (Yen Ninh, tel. 06/8387-6011, www.saigon-ninhchuhotel.co.vn), which has an official **Vietcombank** exchange counter in the lobby.

You'll find the **provincial post office** (44 16 Thang 4, tel. 06/8382-3544, 7am-8pm daily) on the main road leading out to the beach. For those staying in town, the city's **central post office** (217 Thong Nhat, tel. 06/8382-2627, 6:30am-8:30pm daily) can also be of assistance.

The **Ninh Thuan General Hospital (Benh Vien Da Khoa Ninh Thuan)** (5 Le Hong Phong, tel. 06/8383-9815) can assist with minor medical emergencies, though don't expect to find English-speaking doctors here. More serious injuries and ailments should be referred to either Nha Trang or Saigon.

GETTING THERE
Bus

Buses from Saigon (VND150,000) and Nha Trang (VND60,000) arrive daily in Phan Rang at the **Ninh Thuan bus station** (two miles from Phan Rang, Le Duan, tel. 06/8383-8043) on Highway 1. Reaching this seaside town can be tricky if you're coming from elsewhere. A single bus runs to Phan Rang from Mui Ne (VND50,000), with some vehicles dropping their passengers at the Ninh Thuan bus station while others let passengers off a shade closer to town on the same street.

The Ninh Thuan bus station is the only long-distance provider in the area. All its vehicles are aging minibuses. Buying your bus ticket from the station's official counter and looking for the fare posted on the side of your bus will ensure that you are not overcharged. Since few tourists visit this town independently, some fare collectors and touts will ask for more than the posted price. Remain polite but firm and insist on paying the standard fee; this usually settles the matter. Barring grossly oversized bags, there is no additional charge for luggage.

Train

Trains arrive at the **Thap Cham train station** (Minh Mang, tel. 06/8388-8029, 7:30am-11:30am and 1:30pm-5:30pm daily) from Saigon (6 hours, VND504,000-756,000) twice daily. You can also catch both north- and southbound trains along the coast from here. While it is possible to purchase tickets at the station, about five miles from downtown, Vietnam Railways also has a **ticketing office** (351 Thong Nhat, tel. 06/8383-4008, 11am-4:30pm daily) in town.

GETTING AROUND
Taxis and *Xe Om*

You'll find some *xe om* drivers hanging around on the beach road, Yen Ninh, as well as along the main drag in town, 16 Thang 4. **Mailinh** (tel. 06/8389-8989) and **Phan Rang** (tel. 06/8362-6262) taxis also make the rounds.

Vehicles for Hire

Hiring a vehicle in Phan Rang can be difficult, as there are no official rental businesses. Ask your hotel for recommendations; they may even have a motorbike or bicycle lying around that they're willing to rent out for a fee. Check the quality of the bike and agree upon a daily rate before setting off.

Dalat

Far from the hot and humid beach towns of the south-central coast, Dalat is the gateway to Vietnam's interior, a wild and wonderful place brimming with lush mountains and cascading rivers, breathtaking panoramic landscapes, and a host of different cultures. The incredible scenery of Vietnam's mountainous region serves as a backdrop for rock climbing, canyoneering, mountain biking, trekking, and rafting. This is the home of Vietnam's original Easy Rider motorbike custom tours company.

As the most accessible town in the Central Highlands, Dalat is often the only place travelers stop in the area. For those who continue on to more remote towns, this is also a worthy spot to hire a guide or arrange tours deeper into the region, as you'll be hard-pressed to find English speakers or tourist services elsewhere in the Central Highlands. Three days is enough to take in the city's downtown sights and catch a glimpse of some of its nearby countryside attractions, but with outdoor excursions or other activities, you could spend up to a week here and still not explore everything. Easy Rider trips to Mui Ne and Nha Trang can take as little as two days, while adventures to Hoi An can run as long as a week or more.

While Dalat is never really cold by Western standards, its coolest months are in the winter, from November to January. The wetter season runs from April to November, but rain is much less intense here than in the low-lying areas of Vietnam. Even at its warmest, the town is still comfortable.

SIGHTS

For history buffs and architecture enthusiasts, the downtown area bears a handful of charming colonial houses, though these are beginning to disappear as newer, more modern buildings go up. Plenty of European-inspired facades populate the neighborhoods around the market, as does a miniature version of the Eiffel Tower, which serves as the city's radio transmitter.

Dalat has a more conspicuous Catholic influence than most other Vietnamese cities. Several Gothic churches dot the nearby hillsides, including the downtown **Dalat Cathedral** (Tran Phu and Le Dai Hanh, Vietnamese mass 5:15am and 5:15pm Mon.-Fri., 5:15pm Sat., multiple masses 5:15am-6pm Sun.), the largest of the bunch. Also known as Chicken Church, so named for a miniature rooster atop its 154-foot bell tower, the cathedral can be seen throughout the city and stands as a solid example of most local churches, though it is rarely open outside of mass times. Instead, there are a handful of other Catholic structures farther afield that can provide more in the way of both history and design. The same goes for Buddhist pagodas, of which there are many. If you don't have time to leave the city limits, the **Linh Son Pagoda** (Nguyen Van Troi and Phan Dinh Phung, sunrise-sunset daily) is a fine illustration of what the area has to offer.

Plenty of day-trippers make the trek out to nearby Datanla Falls or up the low, sloping Lang Biang Mountain. More distant

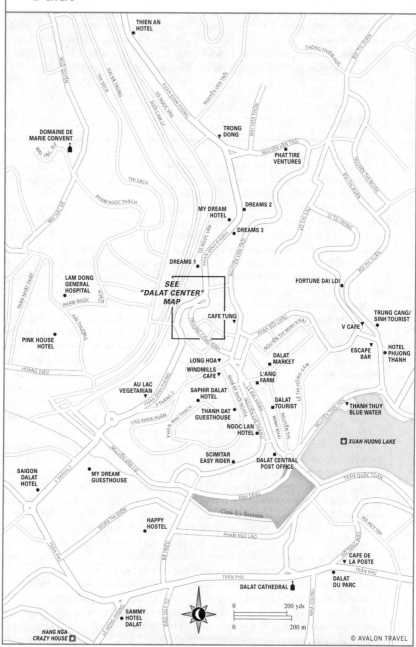

Dalat

THIEN AN HOTEL

THÔNG THIEN HOC

TRONG DONG

DOMAINE DE MARIE CONVENT

PHAT TIRE VENTURES

MY DREAM HOTEL

DREAMS 2

DREAMS 3

DREAMS 1

LAM DONG GENERAL HOSPITAL

SEE "DALAT CENTER" MAP

FORTUNE DAI LOI

CAFE TUNG

TRUNG CANG/ SINH TOURIST

V CAFE

PINK HOUSE HOTEL

ESCAPE BAR

HOTEL PHUONG THANH

LONG HOA

WINDMILLS CAFE

DALAT MARKET

AU LAC VEGETARIAN

L'ANG FARM

SAPHIR DALAT HOTEL

DALAT TOURIST

THANH DAT GUESTHOUSE

THANH THUY BLUE WATER

NGOC LAN HOTEL

XUAN HUONG LAKE

SCIMITAR EASY RIDER

DALAT CENTRAL POST OFFICE

SAIGON DALAT HOTEL

MY DREAM GUESTHOUSE

ÁNH SÁNG

TRAN QUOC TOAN

Cam Ly Stream

HAPPY HOSTEL

PHAM NGU LAO

CAFE DE LA POSTE

TRAN PHU

DALAT CATHEDRAL

DALAT DU PARC

SAMMY HOTEL DALAT

HANG NGA CRAZY HOUSE

0   200 yds

0   200 m

© AVALON TRAVEL

attractions are best approached with an experienced local guide to save the time and hassle of navigating the countryside.

Central Dalat

The downtown area is more accessible and fairly easy to get around, though some of the winding hillside streets can be disorienting.

Most pagodas, museums, and other sights within the city limits can be visited independently, but local operator **Dalat Tourist** (1 Nguyen Thi Minh Khai, tel. 06/3382-2520, www.dalattourist.com.vn, 7:30am-11:30am and 1:30pm-7:30pm daily) offers basic day tours for those who prefer a guide.

★ XUAN HUONG LAKE

The centerpiece of downtown Dalat, **Xuan Huong Lake** has inspired many a Vietnamese poet over the years. Once a modest stream winding through the surrounding valley, its calm blue waters exist as a vestige of French urban planning after the colonial powers decided to dam the stream in 1919 and create this 32-hectare lake. Draped in the greenery of Yersin Park and the Dalat Flower Garden, Xuan Huong features heavily in most photographs of the city and embodies the romantic air of this former colonial getaway. There's no doubt you'll catch a glimpse of Xuan Huong as you wander around town, as its size and proximity to Dalat Market make it hard to ignore. Many people are happy to go for a stroll around its three-mile perimeter, while others opt for renting bicycles to speed up their tour of the area. Others still prefer to sit at one of the local cafés on the water and simply take in the scenery.

DALAT FLOWER GARDEN

Covering 11 hectares near the northernmost point of Xuan Huong Lake, the **Dalat Flower Garden (Vuon Hoa Da Lat)** (3 Pham Ngu Lao, tel. 06/3382-1758, 6am-6pm daily, VND20,000) attracts hordes of domestic tourists year-round as well as a few curious foreigners and photography enthusiasts. Its sprawling grounds are exactly what you would expect: an array of vibrant, eye-catching blossoms tended by the park's army of gardeners. Each section boasts a combination of flowers from both the eastern and western hemispheres as well as Dalat's trademark kitsch, namely horse-drawn carriages and pastel-drenched statues. To the back of the grounds you'll find a small pond, while up the stairs to your right the flower garden also counts a sculpture section in its offerings. Things

Xuan Huong Lake

THE SOUTH-CENTRAL COAST

DALAT

Central Dalat

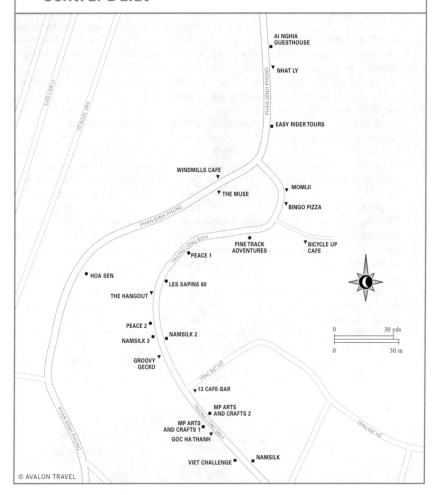

AI NGHIA GUESTHOUSE

NHAT LY

PHAN DINH PHUNG

EASY RIDER TOURS

WINDMILLS CAFE

THE MUSE

MOMIJI

BINGO PIZZA

PHAN DINH PHUNG

TRUONG CONG DINH

PINE TRACK ADVENTURES

BICYCLE UP CAFE

PEACE 1

HOA SEN

LES SAPINS 60

THE HANGOUT

PEACE 2

NAMSILK 2

NAMSILK 3

GROOVY GECKO

TANG BAT HO

13 CAFE-BAR

MP ARTS AND CRAFTS 2

MP ARTS AND CRAFTS 1

GOC HA THANH

VIET CHALLENGE

NAMSILK

TRUONG CONG DINH

PHAN DINH PHUNG

TANG BAT HO

0   30 yds
0   30 m

© AVALON TRAVEL

really get busy around the end of December, when the Dalat Flower Festival takes place and thousands of visitors flock to the park for cultural performances and a look at the garden.

★ HANG NGA CRAZY HOUSE

A weird, wonderful dreamscape of gnarled trees and spiderwebs, glittering mosaics and eerie concrete animals, the **Hang Nga Crazy House** (3 Huynh Thuc Khang, tel. 06/3382-2070, www.crazyhouse.vn, 8:30am-7pm daily,

adults VND40,000, children VND20,000) has become one of Dalat's—and, indeed, Vietnam's—most iconic buildings. Now 24 years in the making, its bizarre fusion of storybook influences, caricatured architecture, and riotous color have earned the Crazy House several mentions on lists of the world's most unusual structures. In 1990, construction began on the Crazy House, the brainchild of Russian-trained architect Dr. Dang Viet Nga. Its accomplished designer began

one of many staircases at Hang Nga Crazy House

EMPEROR BAO DAI'S SUMMER PALACE

Palace isn't necessarily a word you might associate with the blocky, art deco exterior of **Emperor Bao Dai's Summer Palace** (1 Trieu Viet Vuong, tel. 06/3383-1581, 7am-5pm daily, VND15,000), but nonetheless this solid concrete dwelling, completed in 1938, served as the summer home and, at one point, a permanent residence of Vietnam's last emperor. Combining the skills of a French and Vietnamese architectural duo, the 26 rooms of the palace are preserved to look much the same as they did in the 1940s, surrounded by large, ancient trees and ample topiary.

While the upholstery and bedroom furnishings are weathered, the photographs of the royal family lining the palace walls make it easy to imagine the emperor, his wife Queen Nam Phuong, and their four children eating at the long dining room table or occupying the lavish sitting room. Several display cases on the ground floor hold antique dishware of the former royal family, as well as a few of the emperor's personal effects from his office.

Upon its completion, the palace was originally used only in the summer months, when the emperor and his family stayed here to escape Saigon's brutal heat. But, from 1949 to 1954, this became Bao Dai's full-time residence while the queen took her children to France. Once the emperor, too, had been exiled to France, south Vietnam's second president General Nguyen Van Thieu briefly occupied the palace; his tenure, much like the south Vietnamese government, was short-lived.

DALAT RAILWAY STATION

Though it no longer connects to the rest of Vietnam's Reunification Line, the **Dalat Railway Station** (1 Quang Trung, tel. 06/3383-4409, 7:30am-5pm daily) remains open today, if only for curious tourists who stop in to peek at the antique trains and throwback facades of this wide, low building. There isn't much to see beyond its locomotives. The station does run one short section

dreaming up the warped walls and sharp angles of the building well beforehand: inside the main entrance, you'll see the beautiful and intricate drawings that brought the Crazy House to life. Since its beginning, Dr. Nga's pet project has grown outward and upward, developing into a maze of shaded tunnels and narrow staircases that wind over and through its themed rooms, most of which are inspired by an odd array of creatures, including kangaroos, pheasants, bears, and termites.

Hidden in the depths of the main building, a contorted version of a traditional Vietnamese house, you'll also find a room devoted to Dr. Nga's parents: her father, Truong Chinh, became the second president of Vietnam, succeeding the great Ho Chi Minh. Visitors are free to lose their way around the house, discovering its tiny niches and hollow, cave-like rooms. The shaded courtyard inside the gates gives off a wild, slightly overgrown feel that adds to the house's mystery and makes for a pleasant spot to take a break and admire the view.

of the old rail line purely for travelers out to Trai Mat (multiple departures 7:45am-4pm daily, VND124,000 round-trip), not far from Linh Phuoc Pagoda. The journey takes about 1.5 hours.

DU SINH CHURCH

Amid the incalculable number of Catholic churches scattered throughout Dalat, **Du Sinh Church** (12B Huyen Tran, grounds 7am-5pm daily) stands out for its distinctly Vietnamese architecture. Most churches you'll find in the city, and in much of Vietnam, mimic the grand cathedrals of France, albeit on a smaller scale. But Du Sinh features a long, narrow building, not unlike the Cao Dai temples of the Mekong Delta, and intricate, multihued rooftops that would not be out of place on a Buddhist pagoda.

The only French influence about the building lies in the statues, which depict a bright white, European Jesus sheltered by the ruddy tiles and ornate decoration of an Asian-style gazebo. Though the church itself is often closed, the grounds are open and you'll occasionally find a parishioner or two who speaks some English and is eager to chat with visitors. Du Sinh may not be the most awe-inspiring of churches in Dalat, but it's worth a look, if only to see Jesus Christ flanked by a pair of golden dragons atop the entrance gate.

DOMAINE DE MARIE CONVENT

The sloping grounds of the **Domaine de Marie Convent** (Ngo Quyen near the corner of Pham Ngoc Thach, 7:30am-11:30am and 2pm-5pm daily) would not be out of place in a small European village. This lofty stone-and-brick church boasts vaulted wooden ceilings and pretty pink-and-white living quarters for its residents, the local branch of the Daughters of Charity of Saint Vincent de Paul. Behind the church, a small garden courtyard is alive with colorful temperate flowers.

On one side of the square lies the grave of Suzanne Humbert, the wife of Jean Decoux, once-governor of French Indochina. Humbert was a strong proponent of the church and one of its main benefactors; she died in a car accident en route from Saigon to Dalat in 1944. Upon her death, the sisters of Domaine de Marie constructed this grave. Today, around 40 nuns live and work at Domaine de Marie, providing outreach to women in the area as well as serving the local blind and deaf communities.

LAM DONG MUSEUM

En route to Linh Phuoc Pagoda, the extensive collection of artifacts at **Lam Dong Museum** (4 Hung Vuong, tel. 06/3381-2624, baotanglamdong.com.vn, 7:30am-11:30am and 1:30pm-4:30pm daily, VND10,000) touches upon all the standard themes of a provincial museum, from geography and nature to current business production and local revolutionary history. Its most interesting facet is easily its displays on Lam Dong's ethnic minorities, the Ma, the K'ho, and the Churu, all of whom live in the highlands and practice their own traditional customs and ways of farming. English signage is present throughout the museum and complements the exhibits better than most. On the same grounds, you'll also find models of traditional Ma and K'ho houses, as well as a temple devoted to Nguyen Huu Hao, father of Queen Nam Phuong, Vietnam's last reigning queen.

ENTERTAINMENT AND EVENTS
Nightlife

Dalat is a pretty tame town. Most shops and restaurants shut down by 10pm, with the exception of those catering to Western tourists. The downtown night market, too, stays open until around 10pm or 11pm, but people are at home by the early evening. You won't find much in the way of late-night revelry, however if you're up for an after-dinner drink or a place to unwind, there are a few spots in town that can accommodate your nightlife needs.

Wrapped around the corner of Truong Cong Dinh and Tang Bat Ho, **13 Cafe-Bar** (13 Tang Bat Ho, 9am-late daily, VND15,000-50,000) gives off an artsy vibe and manages to draw a steady crowd in the evenings. Decorated in doodles and graffiti art, this laid-back open-air spot counts a collection of old paperbacks and board games among its extra offerings, which accompany the beer, local wine, and shots listed on its drink menu. While there is also food available, this place is decidedly more a café than a restaurant, so your best bet is to find another spot for dinner before grabbing a drink in the evening.

A tiny, one-room storefront near the bend on Truong Cong Dinh, **The Hangout** (71 Truong Cong Dinh, tel. 09/0933-3664, thehangout.com.vn, 2pm-midnight daily, VND20,000-80,000) has become a local tourist institution known for both its drinks and its travel tips. A steady crowd shows up each night to kick back around the bar's pool table and grab a drink. Offerings include beer, cocktails, and other drinks, as well as a few light meals.

A cozy spot for a nightcap, **Escape Bar** (Blue Moon Hotel, 4 Phan Boi Chau, tel. 06/3357-8888, escapebardalatvietnam@gmail.com, 4pm-midnight daily, VND35,000-130,000) is located on the ground floor of the Blue Moon Hotel and serves a range of beer, cocktails, and other beverages, as well as dessert and a few light meals. Thanks to its owners, the same people responsible for V Cafe, you can also find nightly live music here, beginning at 9pm. The place has a jazz bar vibe, with portraits of saxophonists lining the wall alongside the likes of Marilyn Monroe and Elvis.

A dimly lit bohemian haunt just beyond Hoa Binh Square, **Cafe Tung** (6 Khu Hoa Binh, tel. 06/3382-1390, 6:30am-9:30pm daily, VND15,000-30,000) has been a popular gathering point for decades and not much about it seems to have changed. Dark wood and upholstered sofas line the perimeter of this local café, where you won't find many alcoholic beverages (perhaps a beer or two); coffee, tea, and a few other refreshments are on the menu.

Festivals and Events

Travelers who visit Dalat around the New Year may be able to catch the **Dalat Flower Festival** (late Dec.-early Jan.), a lively and colorful display of the region's best blossoms and a celebration of local culture. Held in the Dalat Flower Garden and around Hoa Binh Square, the four- or five-day festivities include cultural performances from Lam Dong province as well as other parts of the Central Highlands and focuses on the traditions of local minorities as well as Vietnam's many heritage sites. In recent years, the festival has become an annual event, drawing thousands of visitors to the city, and is now known nationwide.

SHOPPING

Dalat has several local specialties to offer. Cradled beneath the shelter of Hoa Binh Square, the **Dalat Market** (end of Nguyen Thi Minh Khai, sunrise-sunset daily) displays an array of fresh fruits and vegetables piled high atop each vendors' carts. Ply the ground floor to find bundles of fresh flowers and candied fruit, including berries, mangoes, bananas, and even kiwi. Head upstairs to explore stalls packed with scarves, shoes, and warm clothing. You'll also find a separate area for food vendors in this dizzying multilevel maze. Business starts in the early morning and carries through 'til the evening, when a **night market** (5pm-10:30pm daily) takes over out front on Nguyen Thi Minh Khai.

Local minorities make a variety of authentic handicrafts, namely jewelry, bags, and clothing, which you'll find in shops around town. While many of these items can be purchased at the local market, prices are only cheaper if you bargain; if not, you may wind up paying far more than you would even at a souvenir shop. For those comfortable with haggling, head to Dalat's central trading center. If you prefer to deal in fixed prices, you may want to stick to the shops around the backpacker area.

At **Namsilk** (67 Truong Cong Dinh, tel. 06/3351-1767, 8am-10pm daily), a small shop on the main backpacker drag, the shelves are piled high with silk clothing as well as a variety of scarves, lacquerware, and other handicrafts. You can also find items here bearing the intricate, colorful embroidery of local ethnic minorities.

Not unlike Namsilk down the road, **MP Arts and Crafts** (40D and 55 Truong Cong Dinh, tel. 06/3397-0240, mp.dalatshop@ yahoo.com, 8am-10pm daily) offers a selection of souvenirs, handicrafts, and clothing, as well as maps and a few other practicalities. The shop is roomy, covering several stories and has actually expanded across the street to cover both sides of Truong Cong Dinh.

For souvenirs plucked from the hills of Dalat, **L'Ang Farm** (on the staircase beside Dalat Market, www.langfarmdalat.com, 7am-10pm daily) is a chain that has sprouted up all over town with high-quality packaged versions of the same local specialties you'll find in the market. In addition to dozens of teas and coffee, the shop also sells candied and dried fruits, local sweets and jam, among other products. While you're sure to find the same products in the market at a cheaper price, those buying gifts may appreciate that L'Ang Farm's produce comes in sturdier, flashier packaging.

SPORTS AND RECREATION

Thanks to its hills, adventure sports are gaining ground in the Dalat area, as more travelers come to experience the untamed landscapes of Lam Dong province. Whether you're trekking or cycling, canyoneering or white-water rafting, the wilderness around the city provides ample opportunity for outdoorsy travelers to explore the countryside and try their hand at something new. Most of these adventures—with the exception of trekking—require a guided tour to ensure both your safety and your enjoyment, but even novice adventurers can join in the outdoor fun.

Adventure Tours

The folks at **Phat Tire Ventures** (109 Nguyen Van Troi, tel. 06/3382-9422, www.ptv-vietnam.com, 8am-8:30pm daily) specialize in adventure sports, from mountain biking to white-water rafting, canyoneering, and trekking. Expertly trained guides run day trips out to the surrounding waterfalls and forests for both experienced and novice outdoors enthusiasts as well as a handful of multi-day tours that connect travelers to destinations like Hoi An, Nha Trang, and Mui Ne. Customizable tours are also available. Phat Tire also has an

the steps overlooking Dalat Market

office in Hoi An and tours can be arranged through its website, where a regularly updated list of adventures is available.

One of the most established outfits in Dalat, **Groovy Gecko** (65 Truong Cong Dinh, tel. 06/3383-6521, www.groovygeck-otours.net, 7:30am-8:30pm daily) offers a range of active trekking, cycling, canyoneering, and rock climbing tours around the Dalat area, varying from mild to adventuresome. Experienced local guides lead both single- and multi-day trips, covering the usual destinations, including Hoi An, Nha Trang, and Mui Ne as well as Dalat's nearby forests and waterfalls. The outfit also has a second branch (1/4 Bui Thi Xuan).

The easygoing Mr. Duan of **Viet Challenge** (49A Truong Cong Dinh, tel. 06/3354-6677, vietchallenge.com, 7am-9pm daily) is an expert in canyoneering and a nine-year veteran of the sport. Though it's one of the younger companies in town, his outdoor adventure outfit offers affordable day-long excursions (VND672,000) with experienced guides that combine hiking, rappelling, and canyoneering into one. All equipment is purchased from Europe or Singapore and meets appropriate safety standards. The company also offers mountain

biking, trekking, and cycling trips, but canyoneering is by far the most popular.

Pine Track Adventures (72B Truong Cong Dinh, tel. 06/3383-1916, www.pine-trackadventures.com, 8am-8:30pm daily, VND735,000-2,420,000) offers single- and multi-day excursions around Dalat as well as cycling trips to Mui Ne, Nha Trang, and Hoi An. The company, which specializes in canyoneering, trekking, rafting, and cycling adventures, is staffed by highly qualified canyoneers with first-aid training. The emphasis is on fun, physically challenging activities in a safe environment.

Trekking

With hundreds of trails crisscrossing the countryside around Dalat, trekking is a popular activity in the Central Highlands. Trips can last as long as a few days or as short as an afternoon, provided you go with a guide; there are also a handful of independent trekking options. Either way, these dirt paths bring travelers through the area's odd combination of temperate Asian jungle and pine forest.

The trails leading up **Lang Biang Mountain** are a good place to start, with the steady, paved incline up to **Rada Point** as well

Rada Point, a popular trekking destination on Lang Biang Mountain

as a notably more strenuous climb to the summit of Lang Biang.

The woods around Truc Lam Pagoda and nearby Tuyen Lam Lake are another area for leisurely exploration, where visitors can stroll around the water's edge.

For more challenging treks, enlist the services of a guide. Adventure sports outfits like **Viet Challenge** (VND483,000-546,000), **Phat Tire Ventures** (VND650,000-840,000), and **Pine Track Adventures** (VND630,000-735,000) can be helpful in arranging single- and multi-day guided treks.

Canyoneering

While tourists have long stood at the bases of Dalat's many waterfalls and snapped photos, more and more thrill seekers are choosing instead to experience nature up close thanks to several canyoneering outfits in the area, which afford travelers the opportunity to rappel down the sheer cliffs hidden beneath these rushing waters. Most of the full-day excursions cater to first-time canyoneers, with a crash course in equipment and safety before descending on a few dry runs, literally, from practice slopes in the area. Most outfits will visit at least two waterfalls, almost always including a famous, watery descent known as the 'Washing Machine,' where rushing currents propel canyoneers down the final leg of a waterfall, spitting them out a few meters away.

Any reliable canyoneering company should be able to show you their equipment and give you a full rundown of the day's events, along with your guide's qualifications, beforehand. Dalat's two best-known canyoneering operators are **Groovy Gecko** (VND672,000) and **Phat Tire Ventures** (VND945,000). The newer **Viet Challenge** (VND672,000) also specializes in canyoneering. A typical canyoneering tour lasts around 6-8 hours and includes all equipment, training, transportation, and lunch.

Cycling

Mountain biking trips depart daily from Dalat to dozens of trails throughout the countryside. Some of the more popular and challenging routes are located north of Dalat, including a 20-mile figure eight loop that features rolling hills and top-notch scenery. The southern trails are more relaxed.

There are also downhill one- and two-day excursions toward either Nha Trang or Mui Ne. These trips include some time in a private van (you don't cycle the entire way); cruising down from the highlands on a mountain bike beats taking the bus. Most adventure sports outfits offer high-quality equipment and a range of excursions that run from easy to strenuous rides.

Having a guide for mountain biking excursions is important, since Dalat's surrounding forests are pretty dense and it's important to have permission when passing through villages in the woods. Biking tours are provided by **Groovy Gecko** (VND525,000-840,000), **Pine Track Adventures** (VND714,000-1,008,000), and **Phat Tire Ventures** (VND756,000-1,029,000).

Rock Climbing

There are fewer options for climbing in the area, with only **Groovy Gecko** (VND798,000) providing day-long excursions for climbers. Trips usually visit the cliffs along the Datanla River south of the city, where you can climb, rappel, and take a swim in the river's cool waters. Though it's not the same, **Phat Tire Ventures** (cost varies depending on group size) also has a high ropes course to test your skill in the air.

Golf

Located beside Xuan Huong Lake, the **Dalat Palace Golf Club** (Phu Dong Thien Vuong, tel. 06/3382-3507, www.vietnamgolfresorts.com, 6am-4pm daily, VND1,400,000-1,600,000 for 9 holes, VND3,300,000-3,800,000 for 18 holes) has been a part of the local landscape since the 1930s. Even as early as 1923, plans for a golf course were factored into Dalat's construction, though no action was taken until Emperor Bao Dai returned from a trip to France, where he discovered the sport. The small, six-hole course was used until 1945, when the emperor left for Hong Kong. Nine years later, its green was revived and expanded by a Hanoian doctor before shutting down again at the end of the American War.

When it was restored for a second time in the early 1990s, Dalat's golf course became an 18-hole playing field and now extends almost to the shores of Xuan Huong Lake. The clubhouse, a 1945 French colonial villa, is equipped with showers and locker rooms as well as a restaurant, bar, and pro shop. Golfers may book tee times either online or through the clubhouse. Course fees go up during weekends and holidays.

ACCOMMODATIONS

There are a dizzying number of accommodations in and around downtown Dalat. Rooms run the gamut from budget beds to palatial luxury hotels. Base yourself within walking distance of Xuan Huong Lake, Dalat's focal point, as this will give you easy access to shops, restaurants, cafés, and the scenic downtown area. Most budget travelers prefer to stick around either the backpacker area near Truong Cong Dinh or slightly farther on Bui Thi Xuan. If you prefer more upscale accommodations, several of Dalat's high-end hotels lie farther afield, removed from the bustle of town. While peace and quiet are found in greater measures on the outskirts of Dalat, you will also likely require transportation to leave your hotel.

At 1,500 meters (4,921 ft.) above sea level, Dalat is a markedly cooler town than most in the southern half of the country. Temperatures can actually become cold at night and, in dry season, stay chilly even during the day. For this reason, you'll find that some hotels do not include air-conditioning in their room amenities. In most cases, this should be just fine.

Under VND210,000

The small but cozy **Happy Hostel** (5/3 Ba Trieu, tel. 09/8763-9053, happyhosteldalat@ gmail.com, VND160,000-300,000) lives up to its name, with some of the friendliest staff in Dalat. Rooms are basic but comfortable and right for the price, featuring hot water and television, as well as soft beds. It does not have dorm-style accommodations. Happy Hostel's private rooms are much quieter at night than some of the places on Truong Cong Dinh closer to the market. Staff can also assist with arranging tours as well as renting bicycles and motorbikes.

A no-frills budget hotel, **Peace 1** (64 Truong Cong Dinh, tel. 06/3382-2787, peacedalat@gmail.com, VND180,000-450,000) supplies clean, basic rooms to backpackers along with hot water, TV, and Wi-Fi access. Decor is a little aged and the staff can be pushy at times, but the value of the place is what makes it popular. Downstairs, the owners also run a well-known restaurant that serves some of the more inexpensive meals in town, and is also a good meeting place for independent guides and travelers. Just up the road, **Peace 2** (67 Truong Cong Dinh) is an equally decent extension, though it comes without the added restaurant and café.

Rooms at the **Ai Nghia Guesthouse** (80 Phan Dinh Phung, tel. 06/3352-0529, VND189,000-210,000) are basic but clean and come with hot water, TV, and Wi-Fi access. Noise levels can get bothersome for light sleepers, as this spot faces one of Dalat's busier streets. For larger, quieter accommodations, ask for a room at the back.

VND210,000-525,000

A little spartan but modern and tidy, the rooms at **Les Sapins 60** (60 Truong Cong Dinh, tel. 06/3383-0839, lessapins60dalathotel.com, VND300,000-360,000) are well priced for what is offered. Equipped with comfy beds, hot water, television, and Wi-Fi access, this small budget spot on a bend of Truong Cong Dinh also runs a café and bar downstairs and can assist with travel inquiries. If you're lucky, you may land a room with a balcony, which looks out over the narrow street below.

The cavernous **Thanh Dat Guesthouse** (6C Nam Ky Khoi Nghia, tel. 06/3382-0826, thanhdathotel.dalat@gmail.com, VND300,000) sits on a slope just moments from Hoa Binh Square and Dalat Market. Rooms are bare-bones, with modest furnishings and basic amenities, including hot water, television, and Wi-Fi access. The low cost more than makes up for any shortcomings. Most accommodations also feature large windows that bring in lots of light and offer pleasant street views.

With basic rooms featuring hot water, Wi-Fi access, and TV, **My Dream Hotel** (213A Phan Dinh Phung, tel. 06/3397-1144, mydreamhoteldalat.com, VND252,000-294,000, breakfast included) manages a decent level of service and value. Opt for a smaller, quieter room at the back or a larger, brighter, front-facing bed with a small balcony. For overflow, My Dream also runs a **guesthouse** (38/7A Thien Thanh, tel. 06/3397-1144, VND210,000-252,000) about five minutes' drive from their original location. While this place is more removed from Dalat's backpacker area, rooms are equally clean, more spacious, and include a fridge. Though breakfast is not included at the guesthouse, it can be purchased as an add-on.

The smartly decorated **Thien An Hotel** (364 Phan Dinh Phung, tel. 06/3352-0607, thienanhotel@vnn.vn/thienanhoteldalat.com, VND462,000-525,000) may be about a mile from the city center, but its location next to the pretty hillside Ky Vien Pagoda and the free bicycle rentals more than compensate. Bright, spacious rooms feature a personal safe, hot water, television, a minibar, and Wi-Fi access as well as complimentary breakfast, and the cheerful owner can assist with travel inquiries.

From the outside, Sinh Tourist's **Trung Cang Hotel** (22 Bui Thi Xuan, tel. 06/3382-2663, dalat@thesinhtourist.vn, VND378,000-462,000) looks retro and a little worn around the edges, but rooms at this mid-range hotel are notably well-kept even with some outdated decor. Room rates include complimentary breakfast as well as hot water, Wi-Fi access, and television. The small Sinh Tourist office at the front of the property can arrange bookings for tours and buses around the region, including one of the only buses in town that runs to Mui Ne.

The small but charming **Hotel Phuong Thanh** (4 Bui Thi Xuan, tel. 06/3383-6369, VND250,000) may not be as spacious as its competition, but rooms are clean, modern, and smartly decorated. Amenities include hot water, TV, and Wi-Fi access. With Xuan Huong Lake only a few steps away, this mini-hotel's location is ideal for getting to the market area and around downtown without staying in the thick of the backpacker neighborhood. The staff are friendly and easygoing, though little English is spoken by the receptionists. Only double bed accommodations are available.

The **Pink House Hotel** (7 Hai Thuong, tel. 06/3381-5667, ahomeawayfromhome_dalat@yahoo.com, VND420,000) offers comfy rooms with balconies, television, hot water, Wi-Fi, and an in-room fridge. Thanks to its location, a quieter atmosphere prevails and the staff is happy to help with motorbike rentals and other travel services. The major draw is owner Rot's guests-only secret countryside tour. As the self-professed "only guy in town who speaks K'ho," a local minority language, Rot guides travelers through an authentic K'ho village. While the day-long trip costs extra, it's a must-do for guests.

VND525,000-1,050,00

Rooms at **Dreams 3** (140 Phan Dinh Phung, tel. 06/3383-3748, dreamshotel@gmail.com, VND630,000-735,000, breakfast included) feature plush beds and smart furnishings alongside the standard amenities. Massage services are available. For a cheaper option, **Dreams 2** (164B Phan Dinh Phung, tel. 06/3382-2981, dreamshotel@gmail.com, VND420,000-525,000) is well furnished, if more basic, as is **Dreams 1** (141 Phan Dinh Phung, VND420,000-525,000). For these hotels, opt for a room on the upper floors, as street-level accommodations attract a lot of noise.

Perched on a bend in the road, **Fortune Dai Loi** (3A Bui Thi Xuan, tel. 06/3383-7333, dailoihotel.com, VND700,000-1,150,000) is another massive concrete building that looks slightly rundown on the outside but houses cozy, generous accommodations within. Rooms include plush beds, hot water, television, Wi-Fi access, and complimentary breakfast. The decor is fairly elegant as far as mid-range hotels go.

Perched atop a hill just beyond the market, **Saphir Dalat** (9 Phan Nhu Thach, tel. 06/3355-6000, saphirdalathotel.com, VND800,000-1,200,000) is a beautiful, rustic, boutique hotel, constructed entirely of local materials. In each room, sturdy wooden four-posters are draped in mosquito netting and spacious accommodations feature a wooden bathtub as well as chain-flush toilets, adding to the hotel's antique atmosphere. The Saphir's hilltop location also gives it a more secluded feel, while still remaining in close proximity to the downtown area.

VND1,050,000-2,100,000

Originally a cinema, the purple-clad **Ngoc Lan Hotel** (42 Nguyen Chi Thanh, tel. 06/3382-4032, www.ngoclanhotel.vn, VND1,7850,000-7,980,000) sits in an excellent location overlooking Xuan Huong Lake and boasts chic, modern rooms with air-conditioning, hot water, Wi-Fi access, an in-room safe, TV, and a minibar, as well as complimentary breakfast. The hotel also offers sauna and massage services, a tour desk, and a ground-floor restaurant, which often fills up for weddings and other functions.

One of the largest accommodations in the city, **Saigon Dalat Hotel** (2 Hoang Van Thu, tel. 06/3355-6789, saigondalathotel.com, VND1,570,000-4,720,000) sits on the corner of 3 Thang 2, just under a mile away from the market. Its stately, well-appointed rooms feature an in-room safe, tea- and coffee-making facilities, hot water, television, Wi-Fi access, a minibar, and fridge. Breakfast is served

downstairs in the hotel restaurant, and guests are free to enjoy the heated pool on the ground floor as well as a fitness center. While there are several more luxurious lodgings within the hotel, most accommodations fall under VND2,100,000. The hotel also runs a tour outfit out of its grand reception hall.

Though the reception area at **Sammy Hotel Dalat** (1 Le Hong Phong, tel. 06/3354-5454, sammyhotel.vn, VND1,650,000-6,050,000) can feel cluttered upon arrival, the hotel's extravagant rooms have plenty of space, are furnished in posh, modern decor, and include television, hot water, a minibar, and complimentary breakfast. Accommodations include Western-style bathtubs, and each room's wrought-iron balcony offers pleasant views of town. The downstairs restaurant also caters to both guests and outsiders.

Founded in 1932, the grandiose **Dalat Du Parc** (7 Tran Phu, tel. 06/3382-5777, www. hotelduparc.vn, VND1,400,000-2,500,000) hearkens back to an earlier time. Its stunning French colonial exterior captures the original days of this former resort town. Inside, small touches like the still-functioning, antique, steel-door elevator in the lobby preserve the hotel's upscale ambience. Rooms feature beautiful wooden furnishings and lavish decor as well as a fan, hot water, TV, Wi-Fi access, and complimentary breakfast. If possible, opt for lodgings above the standard level, as these rooms are cramped, and pay a visit to the hotel's restaurant, Cafe de la Poste, across the street.

Over VND2,100,000

The **Dalat Palace Luxury Hotel** (2 Tran Phu, tel. 06/3382-5444, www.dalatresorts. com, VND2,200,000-6,200,000) has come through the nation's decades of war and civil unrest largely unscathed. Originally opened in 1922, this grand colonial hotel was once the largest building in Dalat. Today, rooms remain in much the same state as they were in the beginning, though with a few modern updates. Amenities such as hot water and Wi-Fi access are provided, as well as a television, minibar, workspace, and tea- and coffee-making facilities. The hotel also runs an upscale restaurant, Le Rabelais.

FOOD
Cafés and Bakeries

As part of the nation's main coffee- and tea-growing region, you can't get more than a few steps in any direction without hitting a café. These places range from big to small, humble to extravagant. Scores of cafés along Le Dai Hanh and Nguyen Chi Thanh offer a higher vantage point from which to enjoy Xuan Huong Lake, while Phan Dinh Phung also boasts its fair share of small local hangouts.

A charming, little spot hidden from street view, **Bicycle Up Cafe** (82 Truong Cong Dinh, tel. 06/3370-0177, 7am-10pm daily, VND12,000-55,000) is awash with old, dog-eared books and antique typewriters, making it feel as if you've just walked into someone's study. Written in old storybooks, the café menu features your usual coffee and tea options, as well as fruit juices, shakes, and beer. Though seating is limited, this is a pleasant spot to grab coffee. Bicycle Up also offers a few light meals, but because of its busy decor, this place lends itself better to a café rather than a restaurant.

Windmills Cafe (133 Phan Dinh Phung, tel. 06/3354-0808, 7:30am-10pm daily, VND25,000-50,000) is a popular and inviting little corner café decked out in white and green, serving a variety of coffee, tea, shakes, and sodas. Free Wi-Fi is available and the staff are a particularly friendly bunch. If you're closer to the Dalat Market, there is also a second location (7 3 Thang 2, on the corner with Nam Ky Khoi Nghia), right by Hoa Binh Square.

An artsy, hole-in-the-wall café hidden behind the slope of Truong Cong Dinh, you'll find an array of European and Vietnamese coffees and teas at **The Muse** (64 Phan Dinh Phung, 8am-10pm daily, VND13,000-75,000). Its ground-floor seating is no more than a few stools and tables, making it something of a jazzed-up version of your average local café.

Upstairs you'll find a small, oddly shaped room decorated with original artwork and boasting a large window that looks out onto traffic below.

Street Food

You'll find ample street food within the **Dalat Market** (end of Nguyen Thi Minh Khai, sunrise-sunset daily). Take the stairs up to the second floor, where all manner of local fare is on offer. In the evenings, the night market also sees plenty of roadside vendors camp out along Nguyen Thi Minh Khai. Ask the price before dining, as these spots often charge higher prices for foreigners. Dozens of modest local eateries line Bui Thi Xuan, convenient for travelers based on the street, and Phan Dinh Phung, near the town's small backpacker area.

Vietnamese

Goc Ha Thanh (53 Truong Cong Dinh, tel. 06/3355-3369, 7am-11pm daily, VND35,000-200,000) is a small eatery sandwiched between the many shops that run along Truong Cong Dinh. Specializing in Hanoian-style meals, the menu includes your usual array of Vietnamese options as well as a few tasty favorites, namely the *nem nuong* (grilled pork sausage), which is presented as a platter of do-it-yourself spring rolls. A handful of soups, sandwiches, and burgers also make their way onto the list, as do a few vegetarian plates. When in doubt, the friendly owners are happy to make recommendations.

For one of the best views in the city, grab a seat under the purple umbrellas at **Thanh Thuy Blue Water** (2 Nguyen Thai Hoc, tel. 06/3353-1668, www.thanhthuydalat.com, 6am-11pm daily, VND65,000-400,000). With more quiet than some of the city cafés, Thanh Thuy is pricey by local standards but offers an endless variety of Vietnamese and Chinese cuisine as well as a prime spot on Xuan Huong Lake from which to observe the comings and goings of downtown Dalat. The staff is especially cheerful. Both indoor and outdoor seating is available. This is also a nice spot for an evening drink, as it's right on the water but just far enough removed from the melee of the night market.

The quiet, cozy dining room at **Trong Dong** (220 Phan Dinh Phung, tel. 06/3382-1889, 9am-9pm daily, VND35,000-85,000) combines a white tablecloth setting with delicious renditions of standard Vietnamese fare. Vegetarian options are also available, as are local desserts and a range of meat, noodle, and rice dishes, and the cheerful staff do their best to make you feel at home.

Thanks to its tasty local dishes, **Nhat Ly** (88 Phan Dinh Phung, tel. 06/3382-1651, 8am-evening daily, VND60,000-320,000) sees regular foreign visitors as well as a few tour groups. Ranging from individual portions to family-style meals, this restaurant's fare tops many of the other eateries that cater to tourists. Try the particularly delicious *ca loc kho to* (braised fish in clay pot). Though the staff is not a particularly outgoing bunch, Nhat Ly's food makes up for it.

Just off Hoa Binh Square, **Long Hoa** (6 3 Thang 2, tel. 06/3382-2934, longhoarestaurant@yahoo.com.vn, 8am-2pm and 4pm-9pm daily, VND50,000-200,000) charms its guests with a cozy, intimate ambience and delicious local meals. The tablecloths and framed menu posted out front help to give the place the feel of a European café. Both individual plates and family-style meals are served.

International

A popular tourist spot, **V Cafe** (1/1 Bui Thi Xuan, tel. 06/3352-0215, www.vcafedalatvietnam.com, 7am-10pm daily, VND55,000-130,000) serves soups, salads, pasta, pizza, some Latin food, and a selection of vegetarian dishes. Both indoor seating and an outdoor patio are available, and the restaurant offers breakfast until 11am. If you visit in the evenings, look out for V Cafe's live music (from 7:30pm), which includes a range of acoustic, blues, folk, country, and rock 'n' roll favorites.

The bright blue **Dalat Train Cafe** (Quang Trung, just past Dalat Railway Station, tel. 06/3381-6365, www.dalattrainvilla.com,

8am-10pm daily, VND89,000-275,000) is a charming, out-of-the-way diner set in a restored 1910 French train car. Decked out in vintage railroad paraphernalia, this quaint little spot serves mostly Western fare, with salads, sandwiches, burgers, pizza, and a few fancier entrées. A host of wine options beyond the usual Vang Dalat are also available. If the train car is full, you can also grab a seat out front, where there is patio seating beneath the cover of a few large shade umbrellas.

Japanese

The rustic dining room at **Momiji** (98 Truong Cong Dinh, tel. 06/3352-7368, momijijapaneseshop@gmail.com, 7:30am-10pm Mon.-Sat., VND45,000-300,000) is decked out in a distinctly Dalat decor, with wood furnishings and plenty of flowers. While you wouldn't necessarily expect this look from a Japanese restaurant, the small café-eatery serves up everything from sushi and soba noodles to more adventurous Japanese fare, as well as an array of coffees and teas (VND32,000-76,000).

Pizza

For a break from local fare, the menu at **Bingo Pizza** (41 Truong Cong Dinh, tel. 06/3351-2122, 8am-10pm daily, VND45,000-200,000) covers every topping configuration you can imagine, from four-cheese and gorgonzola to pepperoni, Hawaiian, and seafood, as well as a build-your-own option. Pies come in several sizes to accommodate your level of hunger. Bingo also serves a few pasta and lasagna dishes in its red-and-white shop, whose decor is straight out of an Italian-American pizza parlor.

French

Set in the historical Triangle Building, an oddly shaped structure wedged between Tran Phu and Ho Tung Mau, **Cafe de la Poste** (12 Tran Phu, tel. 06/3382-5444, www.dalatresorts.com, 5:30am-10pm daily, VND80,000-600,000) has been a French bistro and an integral part of the famed Dalat Du Parc hotel since the 1950s. Bright green walls lined with vintage French advertisements and high ceilings give the space a quaint feel. Dishes include a range of pizza, pasta, sandwiches, and salads, as well as main courses like steak, salmon, and pork tenderloin. European desserts also feature on the menu, as does an extensive wine list and several cocktails.

Vegetarian

You'll find that most Western restaurants, as well as a few foreigner-friendly Vietnamese options, already have a vegetarian section on their menu. If you prefer to go fully meat-free, the following are great for local vegetarian food.

Au Lac Vegetarian (15 Phan Dinh Phung, tel. 06/3382-5054, 6am-8pm daily, VND20,000-30,000) serves noodles and steamed dumplings as well as an array of tofu, vegetable, and mock meat dishes out of its large, open storefront on Phan Dinh Phung. The place may be bare bones, but taste is the most important factor here.

A warehouse-like restaurant, **Hoa Sen** (62 Phan Dinh Phung, tel. 06/3356-7999, 6am-2pm and 4pm-9pm daily, VND10,000-45,000) is an all-vegetarian eatery serving tofu as well as vegetables, noodles, soups, and rice. Meals are tasty and well priced and there is ample space to stretch out. While the place usually closes for a few hours in the afternoon, on the 1st and 15th of the lunar month (religious days for Buddhists) you'll find Hoa Sen open all day.

INFORMATION AND SERVICES

Dalat Tourist (1 Nguyen Thi Minh Khai, tel. 06/3382-2520, www.dalattourist.com.vn, 7:30am-11:30am and 1:30pm-7:30pm daily), near the market, sells city maps (VND10,000); you can also find these maps in many hotels and cafés.

There are plenty of **ATMs** along Phan Boi Chau and around Hoa Binh Square near the central market. The local **Sacombank** (32 Khu Hoa Binh, tel. 06/3351-1082, sacombank.com.vn, 7:30am-11:30am and 1pm-5pm Mon.-Fri., 7:30am-11:30am Sat.) can also assist with currency exchange.

The **Dalat central post office** (2 Le Dai Hanh, tel. 06/3382-2586, 7am-8pm daily) is able to handle all of your Internet and postal needs.

Located near the city center, **Lam Dong General Hospital** (4 Pham Ngoc Thach, tel. 06/3382-1369, 7:15am-11:15am and 1:30pm-3:30pm daily) assists with minor injuries and illnesses.

GETTING THERE
Air

Though it is possible to fly into **Lien Khuong Airport** (DLI, Hwy. 20, Lien Nghia town, tel. 06/3384-3373), the largest in Lam Dong province, most travelers opt for the bus instead, as flight tickets are more expensive and, with the airport 18 miles south of Dalat, require an extra 30-minute drive into the city. Daily arrivals come from Saigon (45 min., VND400,000-600,000), Danang (1.5 hours, VND1,500,000-2,000,000), and Hanoi (2 hours, VND1,500,000-2,000,000).

Arriving passengers can take the shuttle bus into Dalat (VND40,000) or grab a taxi (VND250,000-300,000).

Bus

Buses from Can Tho, Mui Ne, Nha Trang, or Saigon arrive at the **Phuong Trang bus station** (1 To Hien Thanh, tel. 06/3358-5858, 24 hours daily), just over a mile south of the city center. The station is essentially run by Phuong Trang buses, but a few other local buses pull up here, too. Buses at this station will take you to either Saigon or Nha Trang. To get to Mui Ne you'll have to visit **Sinh Tourist** (22 Bui Thi Xuan, tel. 06/3382-2663, www.thesinhtourist.vn, 7am-10pm daily) in the city center or ask your hotel for a booking.

GETTING AROUND

As usual, plenty of *xe om* and Easy Rider motorbike tours are about, many of them hoping to interest you in a tour around town or throughout the province. **Mailinh** (tel. 0633/838-3838) taxis are present throughout the city and surrounding areas.

Most hotels and guesthouses can help you to arrange rental motorbikes. Bicycles are also available, but, with all of Dalat's hills, a standard city bicycle is usually not a feasible option for getting around town. There are a few independent street-side outfits near Xuan Huong Lake that will hire out push bikes for the day, however the quality of these vehicles is often not worth the price, though the novelty of sharing a tandem bike with your travel buddy may trump bad brakes and rusty frames.

VICINITY OF DALAT
Datanla Falls
The rushing waters of **Datanla Falls** (Prenn Pass, Hwy. QL20, tel. 06/3221-2145, 7am-5pm daily, VND10,000) draw a healthy crowd of both foreign and domestic tourists daily. Follow the stone path that leads down to the base of the falls, where you'll find misty white waters and a handful of souvenir and drink vendors. Guests can also opt for a ride on the park's mini **roller coaster** (VND35,000), more like a two-person tram, or continue on to the **cable car** (VND30,000) that glides slowly above the water to a lower point on the river. Walkers will get as far as the park's third waterfall before they're forced to pay for the elevator down to another pathway below. For every step you descend you will need to walk back up. The first waterfall is easily the largest and most visually appealing, so there's not really much need to continue on to the few remaining falls. The farther you go, the more peace and quiet you'll find. Throughout the park, small cafés are situated around the various waterfalls, and the breezy **Mimosa** restaurant (entrées VND35,000-50,000) up top has affordable meals.

Truc Lam Pagoda and Cable Car
The understated **Truc Lam Pagoda (Truc Lam Yen Tu)** (7am-5pm daily) lacks the same vivid ornamentation that characterizes many older religious buildings. But, its colorful array of flowers make the sprawling grounds something of a botanical garden set on the edge of Tuyen Lam Lake, a beautiful, secluded body of water that escapes much of the hustle and bustle surrounding its downtown counterpart.

Visitors to the pagoda can see its two main buildings, each featuring high ceilings, beautiful polished woodwork, and muted colors, before catching a glimpse of the pagoda living quarters, where over 100 monks reside. The most noteworthy part of a trip to Truc Lam is its natural surroundings, which include both bamboo groves and pine trees in the same short section of path. As the pagoda is often packed with tourists, a wander around the nearby area can be a pleasant way to escape the crowds and appreciate Truc Lam's surrounding nature. From the lake shore, it is also possible to hire a **boat** (Khu Du Lich Ho Tuyen Lam, tel. 06/3374-7386, 7:30am-4:30pm daily, VND300,000-500,000) around Tuyen Lam that travels a three-mile route out to a restaurant at the far end of the lake and back; the ticketing booth seems to spontaneously close at times, so be prepared to change your plans if the ticket vendor is out that day.

The most scenic way to get to Truc Lam is by **cable car** (Doi Ro Bin, tel. 06/3383-7938, 7:30am-11:30am and 1:30pm-4:30pm daily, VND70,000 round-trip adults, VND50,000 one-way adults; VND40,000 round-trip children, VND30,000 one-way children). Small, suspended pods travel a one-mile route from Robin Hill to Truc Lam and back.

Valley of Love
Equal parts pretty and peculiar, Dalat's famous **Valley of Love (Thung Lung Tinh Yeu)** (7 Mai Anh Dao, tel. 06/3382-1448, thunglungtinhyeu.vn, 7:30am-6pm daily, VND20,000) earned its name during colonial times as a popular spot for young couples to come and enjoy the rolling hills and peaceful waters of the valley. The landscape has been

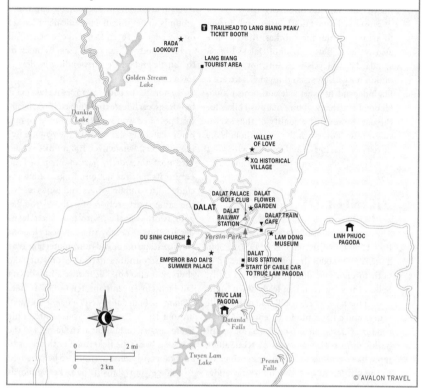

Vicinity of Dalat

TRAILHEAD TO LANG BIANG PEAK/
TICKET BOOTH

RADA
LOOKOUT

LANG BIANG
TOURIST AREA

Golden Stream
Lake

Dankia
Lake

VALLEY
OF LOVE

XQ HISTORICAL
VILLAGE

DALAT PALACE   DALAT
GOLF CLUB   FLOWER
               GARDEN
DALAT   DALAT
DALAT   RAILWAY
STATION   DALAT TRAIN
                CAFE

DU SINH CHURCH   Yersin Park   LAM DONG   LINH PHUOC
                                           MUSEUM   PAGODA

EMPEROR BAO DAI'S   DALAT
SUMMER PALACE   BUS STATION
                              START OF CABLE CAR
                              TO TRUC LAM PAGODA

TRUC LAM
PAGODA

Datanla
Falls

0   2 mi

0   2 km

Tuyen Lam   Prenn
Lake   Falls

© AVALON TRAVEL

transformed since then, now dotted with dozens of hearts and kitschy romantic statues. The Valley of Love is a little over-the-top in its man-made decoration but the views of Lang Biang Mountain in the distance and Da Thien Lake below are stunning nonetheless.

Visitors are able to follow the footpath down into the valley and around the lake or opt for other transportation. Electric cars, jeeps, and a tourist train (actually a bus) escort passengers on a full tour of the area for a small fee. Down at the lake, swan boats and motorboats are also available for hire, and there is a children's play area on-site as well as a few restaurants and souvenir shops. Though it seems to go against the spirit of the place, the Valley of Love has also begun offering paintball sessions for visitors.

XQ Historical Village

Just opposite the Valley of Love, **XQ historical village (Da Lat Su Quan)** (258 Mai Anh Dao, tel. 06/3383-1343, 8am-5:30pm daily, free) celebrates traditional Vietnamese art and culture with a maze of exhibits featuring beautiful hand-embroidered pictures. These incredibly detailed, intricate images can take as long as several months to complete and, in some instances, require an entire team of women, who stitch each portrait by hand. Visitors are able to watch these craftswomen at work as they walk through XQ's many galleries, where portraits as large as several feet tall are on display. The village also showcases other aspects of Vietnamese art and culture, including the handicrafts of the region's

Linh Phuoc Pagoda

is a work of art. From its soaring bell tower to the long, wide main hall, the entire structure is covered in a dizzying mosaic of pottery shards and broken glass. Six miles east of town, Linh Phuoc greets its visitors with a 118-foot tower, home to a massive bell weighing 8.5 tons. From the ground, ascend the narrow metal staircase up to the top, passing by different statues of the Buddha or Quan Am on each level. Above, you'll find pleasant views of the nearby valley as well as the pagoda's main hall, the front of which bears a large, ornate dragon. On the second floor of the tower, stacks of square papers sit beside the enormous bell: here, locals write out their prayers and paste them to the side of the chime for good luck.

Rounding out the other side of the square is the main hall. Flanked by row upon row of dragon-clad columns, the prayer area leads onto a large altar while, along the top section of the wall, scenes from the life of Buddha are rendered in vivid mosaic decoration. All of this makes for a stunning effect. Photography is forbidden inside the main hall.

Once you've seen the pagoda interior, head back outside to take in the entirety of Linh Phuoc's 160-foot dragon, which snakes along the right-hand side of the complex. Covered in roughly 50,000 shards of glass, the head of this massive creature watches over the square, while its three-dimensional body winds through the small area to the right of the pagoda.

Though it's out of the way, Linh Phuoc can easily be reached from Dalat by motorbike or xe om and is often included on local tours. A tourist train also runs several times a day from the old Dalat train station to Trai Mat, the village in which Linh Phuoc is located, and back.

Lang Biang Mountain

In a region known for its natural beauty, the densely forested **Lang Biang Mountain** (nine miles north of Dalat, Khu Du Lich Lang Biang, tel. 06/3383-9088, www.dalattourist.com.vn, 6:30am-6:30pm daily, VND10,000) is

ethnic minorities, jewelry, and traditional instruments. Though each room can be difficult to navigate once inside, visitors are free to roam the pretty miniature village uninhibited, and there is also a small restaurant and café where you can stop for a drink.

Trips to XQ's headquarters are free, however there is an additional section farther into the village that requires a VND20,000 entry fee. For this, you'll be able to access the flower village and a few other areas, but those who opt out of the paid area aren't missing much. XQ also acts as a massive souvenir shop, with most of the items displayed available for purchase. While the fascinating hand-embroidered portraits cost a fortune—and rightly so, as even a modest piece is no simple task—there are also a few smaller, more affordable items around.

Linh Phuoc Pagoda

Everything about **Linh Phuoc Pagoda (Chua Linh Phuoc)** (120 Tu Phuoc, Trai Mat village, 6am-6pm daily), inside and out, one of Dalat's most famous features. Coming in at 7,109 feet above sea level, Lang Biang sits eight miles north of the city but can still be seen clearly from higher vantage points in Dalat. Though there are several versions of how the mountain got its name, the most popular story goes that once, years ago, a boy called Lang and a girl named Biang were in love, but because they were each from different ethnic groups, their families forbade them to marry. In a Romeo-and-Juliet-style tale, the two pined for one another until their death but were never able to get together. The mountain was named in their honor. Only later did the families of Lang and Biang understand their children's plight and changed their customs so that different ethnic groups could intermarry.

Lang Biang's two highest points offer striking panoramic views of Dalat and the dappled hills rolling off into the distance. Thanks to the local tourism board, the mountain's tourist area boasts several options for travelers, varying from easy to strenuous activity. Past the entrance gates and the group of horses painted to look like zebras grazing near Lang Biang's trademark sign, you can rent one of the park's **jeeps** (around VND40,000 pp, or VND240,000 for the six-person vehicle) for

a relaxing visit. Drivers go up to the 6,771-foot **Rada Point,** which offers full views of a pastel-hued Dalat and the surrounding countryside and also has a restaurant for visitors to enjoy.

If you're keen to get some exercise, follow the paved road on foot up to Rada. Though it's steep in some places, the wide, winding path makes it up to the lookout in about a mile. More enthusiastic hikers can veer off the main route and check in at the ticket booth for **Bidoup-Nui Ba National Park** (Da Nhim village, tel. 06/3374-7449, 7:30am-3:30pm daily), which manages the narrow jungle-covered **Lang Biang Trail** (7:30am-3:30pm daily, VND20,000) up to the mountain's highest point. From there, the journey becomes more challenging, starting off with a modest incline at first before hurtling into the overgrown bush. Plenty of tree cover keeps the trail cool, which is needed given the rocky uphills and occasional felled tree you'll have to climb over. Throughout the path, signage is intermittent—sometimes nothing more than a red scrap of fabric tied around a branch—but the trail remains fairly visible even amid the thick foliage. As Lang Biang's grand finale, a steep wood-and-earth staircase brings you up the last section to the summit where, on a

a horse painted to look like a zebra at Lang Biang

Easy Rider Tours

As Vietnam struggled to find its footing after the American War, a Dalat native named Mr. Toan was working as a porter and *xe om* driver at the local bus station. Once a student of theology, Mr. Toan was fluent in French and English. But behind the closed doors of post-war Vietnam there was little need for foreign languages. That is, until one day in the late 1980s when a pair of American tourists stepped off the bus in Dalat. The only English-speaker around, Mr. Toan struck up a conversation with the two. As more foreign visitors started coming to Dalat, Mr. Toan found his skill increasingly valuable. He began offering city tours to foreigners.

As tourism grew, Mr. Toan taught English to 15 other drivers, the original Easy Riders, a name they took at the suggestion of an American journalist. Drivers ventured beyond the city limits, bringing foreigners deep into the Central Highlands. By the time the Easy Riders received official recognition from local authorities as a legitimate enterprise, business was booming. These local guides and their heavy-duty motorbikes have become the face of homegrown tourism in the Central Highlands.

Nowadays, Mr. Toan has hung up his Easy Rider jacket, working instead as an English teacher in Dalat, but he remains a local celebrity. The original band of **Easy Riders** (70 Phan Dinh Phung, tel. 06/3382-9938, www.dalat-easyrider.com, 6:30am-7pm daily) operates out of a small shop on Phan Dinh Phung where it intersects with Truong Cong Dinh. Several members have gone off to start their own tour businesses and still more independent guides are present throughout Dalat.

For a single-day tour, most people do just fine finding a guide on the street or asking for a recommendation from their hotel. For longer trips, book ahead of time with a reputable company. The original team is a solid choice, as is **Scimitar Easy Rider Tours** (72A Nguyen Chi Thanh, tel. 09/0369-5165, www.easyrider-dalat.com, 7am-6:30pm daily), a 10-member group of local guides headed up by Mr. Hung, also known as Scimitar, one of the original crew. If you link up with an independent operator, your best bet is to take a day-long outing with the guide of your choice, then gauge whether to opt for a longer trip based on that experience.

Most tours leave from Dalat and venture into the less-traveled areas between this Central Highlands town and destinations like Mui Ne, Nha Trang, Hoi An, and Buon Ma Thuot, the coffee capital of Vietnam. Fees usually run around VND525,000 for a single-day excursion, while longer trips hover between VND1,365,000 and VND1,470,000 per day. All prices cover entrance fees and accommodations, so travelers only pay for their food and drink on the trip.

---

clear day, peak-baggers can see for miles, with beautiful views of Dalat as well as Rada Point down to your right.

For walkers, the journey from Lang Biang's main gate up to the summit is about a two-hour trip and can be completed solo. Hikers heading for the very top should bring proper shoes and plenty of water, as this is truly the wilderness and the trail can be rocky at times. Bug spray may not be a bad idea either, given that the shaded areas of the path can attract a lot of unwanted visitors.

While the Lang Biang Trail is accessible year-round, travelers visiting during the rainy season may want to check with the guide at the ticket booth before committing to the peak, as this route can get slippery even in drier times. These same guides can also be hired for the trek (VND100,000-240,000, depending on number of people) if you prefer to have a local on hand: residents of Lat village, a minority town at the foot of the mountain, these men speak excellent English and are able to take travelers not only up to the Lang Biang summit but farther into Bidoup - Nui Ba National Park, as well as for a spin around their hometown, which is often visited by travelers en route to Lang Biang.

Waterfalls

The hills surrounding Dalat are awash with dozens of waterfalls, ranging from modest trickles to raging white-water descents. The most accessible and most visited of these is **Datanla Falls** (Prenn Pass, Hwy. QL20, tel. 06/3221-2145, 7am-5pm daily, VND10,000), however visitors can also make the trip out to **Elephant Falls**, a natural spectacle 18 miles southwest of the city that pitches over the rocks in a half-moon shape, allowing you to walk behind the falls, though not without getting wet. About another 12 miles from there is **Pongour Falls** (VND5,000), the area's largest waterfall; it is a hike to reach the place in a single day. Independent travelers can make the trip alone, though the road to these waterfalls has seen better days. Instead, many prefer to hop on a **day tour** (about VND525,000 half-day excursion to Elephant Falls; VND525,000-630,000 full-day trip to Elephant Falls and Pongour Falls) with one of the local Easy Rider guides.

One of the only group tours to Elephant Falls and Pongour Falls is through **Groovy Gecko** (65 Truong Cong Dinh, tel. 06/3383-6521, www.groovygeckotours.net, 7:30am-8:30pm daily, VND441,000). Their trip includes transportation, entrance fees, and a guide; lunch is not included. For individual Easy Rider-style guides (VND525,000-735,000 per person), the extent of what's included is often more negotiable. Usually, transportation, entrance fees, and a guide are included, and lunch can be added, so long as you discuss the matter first.

Mui Ne

At the heart of Mui Ne's appeal is its natural beauty. Beyond sparkling turquoise waters and tranquil shores, the surrounding area boasts an unusual landscape, with shaggy palms and freshwater streams sidling up beside vast, barren sand dunes. Tack on the Po Shanu Towers, a relic of the region's multicultural history and among the oldest Cham structures in Vietnam, plus a nearby provincial capital that produces some of the nation's most prized fish sauce, and there's plenty to explore in Mui Ne. As one of the windier coasts in the country, Mui Ne has become a major kitesurfing destination, and several kiting outfits also offer equipment for windsurfing or stand-up paddleboarding.

Once a sleepy, secluded beachfront, Mui Ne is fast growing into a smaller version of its northeastern neighbor, Nha Trang. Seaside resorts have materialized all along Nguyen Dinh Chieu, the seven-mile stretch of road running parallel to shore. This rapid development has its pros: a wider range of accommodations and dining options, not to mention a budding nightlife scene. There are also a few cons, as prices in the area have soared, and overcharging is a particular bone of contention here.

On account of the area's strong winds and even stronger undertow, Mui Ne experiences a great deal of coastal erosion. Some seaside resorts, particularly those farther to the west, offer a genuine sand beach, while folks on the east end of Nguyen Dinh Chieu have had to fortify their property with concrete sea walls.

Though dry season, November-April, is the best time to visit any of Vietnam's southern beaches, Mui Ne experiences a conservative rainy season, with downpours occurring daily for only a few hours at a time. From November to January, high season sees scores of Russian tourists, young families, backpackers, and couples, so book ahead and expect to pay slightly higher prices.

Travelers breezing through with the aim of catching some beach time en route to Saigon can achieve their goals with a few days in Mui Ne. The area's few sights can be seen within a single day, leaving you plenty of time for sunbathing.

Mui Ne and Vicinity

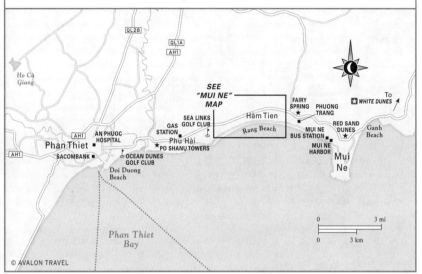

Orientation

Mui Ne proper is a small fishing town. All the attractions, hotels, and restaurants that bring travelers to Mui Ne are located on **Nguyen Dinh Chieu,** the coastal road in between Mui Ne proper and Phan Thiet. Once in Mui Ne proper, Nguyen Dinh Chieu becomes **Huynh Thuc Khang.**

SIGHTS

Most, if not all, travelers come to Mui Ne for its beaches. The town itself doesn't offer many attractions. Most people base themselves on the single coastal road that runs between Mui Ne proper and the larger town of Phan Thiet. Here you'll find plenty of shops and restaurants, all built within the last few years to cater to incoming tourists. The closest sight by far is Fairy Spring, but for anything else you'll have to rent a motorbike or grab a taxi. It's a short drive out to the red sand dunes, with the larger and more impressive hills of the white dunes around 15 miles away. While some destinations in Vietnam require guided tours, Mui Ne is not one of them: you can easily catch

its main sights within a day and save the rest of your time for a good-old fashioned lie by the beach.

Sand Dunes
RED DUNES

Six miles from the beach, Mui Ne's **red dunes** (Provincial Road DT706B) are the most easily accessible of the area's sands, though not the most scenic. Spilling out onto the nearby highway, these gentle, brick-red hills change with the wind, shape-shifting at the mercy of the town's strong gusts. Some of the dunes' appeal has been lost in recent years, as a cluster of roadside drink shops have set up across the street and tend to be relentless in their sales pitch. The same goes for the droves of young kids trying to rent plastic sleds to tourists, which, for the record, don't actually work on the sand. These dunes are a quick and easy stop for anyone exploring the area by motorbike.

★ WHITE DUNES

The **white dunes** (18 miles northeast of Mui Ne, 7am-5pm daily, VND10,000) offer a more

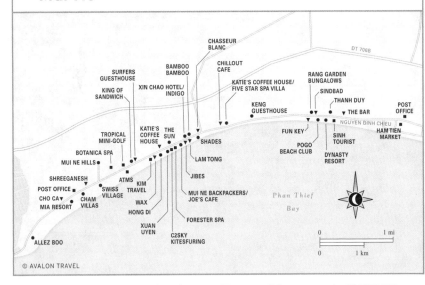

Mui Ne

dramatic, windswept landscape than those closer to town. As you approach, you'll see these sun-bleached sands from afar, standing in stark contrast to the long and narrow turquoise lake at the edge of the dunes. A small footpath leads visitors in to the hills, where you can trudge up the sands to catch a glimpse of the scenery from above. These dunes are also susceptible to regular changes courtesy of the breeze and, surrounded by redder sands and verdant shorelines, the barren hills become an interesting landscape.

Bring along a hat and sunscreen, as both the drive along the coast and the hills themselves offer no escape from the sun. This spot heats up as the day goes on, making the walk up to the dunes a little painful to do barefoot. Tucked between the lake and the dunes, a few small cafés sling coffee, beer, and other refreshments. It is also possible to rent ATVs (around VND400,000 for a 20-minute jaunt) for a brief ramble across the dunes, though these are fairly expensive. Rent ATVs from the outfit closest to the dunes, as the small outfit located on the path into the hills charges foreigners over twice the going rate.

Visitors will have to pay the VND10,000 entry fee at the top of the path before entering, but this is subject to the time of day, as you may occasionally find the ticket booth empty and no one around to collect the entry fee. The dunes are easy to reach by motorbike, follow the road along the shoreline and turn left at the faded sign for Bau Trang.

Mui Ne Harbor

Passing through Mui Ne town en route to the white sand dunes, you'll come across **Mui Ne Harbor** (Huynh Thuc Khang), a pretty spot where hundreds of painted wooden fishing boats dock in the mellow waters of the bay. At the foot of the concrete steps leading down to the beach, groups of fishermen mend nets or hop in small, round boats, which are used to paddle out to the larger vessels. You can also occasionally catch fish drying in the sun along the sloped embankment that separates the street from the shore.

Po Shanu Towers

Over a thousand years old, the Hindu **Po Shanu Towers** (between Mui Ne and Phan

sand formations at Fairy Spring

a cache of foreign weapons. Continue up to the top to visit this former battle site and, on a clear day, to catch some stunning views of the pastel-drenched Phan Thiet town, which appears to your right beside a vast expanse of ocean. The dilapidated brick tower you'll find atop the hill is not a work of the Cham but, instead, a French duke by the name of de Montpensier who, in 1911, chose the site as his holiday home. For decades, locals referred to the lavish house as the Prince's Palace before French authorities set up a military outpost nearby in 1946, prompting the June 14 battle the following year.

The Po Shanu Towers aren't difficult to find from Mui Ne. They are only six miles west of the beach, though the weathered, pink-and-red stone tablet indicating a turnoff is easy to miss. Look out for this sign at the very bottom of a hill en route to Phan Thiet.

Fairy Spring

The closest of Mui Ne's sights, **Fairy Spring (Suoi Tien)** (63A Nguyen Dinh Chieu, 7am-5pm daily) sits at the eastern end of the main drag. This modest waterway runs beneath a small bridge under Nguyen Dinh Chieu, cutting a path beside some colorful dunes along the way. The place can easily be accessed on foot: take a left off the main road when you see a red sign reading "Suoi Tien" (the stream's Vietnamese name) and follow the dirt path past a small café. Chances are you'll find a jeep or two parked near the street, as small tour groups often make the rounds here. You can either enter the stream at the concrete steps immediately to your left or walk farther down to another point of entry. You'll need to take off your shoes in order to wade through the ankle-deep water. A quarter-mile walk takes you out to the stream's deeper section, after which there's not much to see, but en route you'll catch desert-like landscapes of red, yellow, and white sand formations, carved into the dunes by rainfall and the stream itself. This is a popular stop for many group tours and independent travelers.

One of the local teenagers hanging around

Thiet, 6:30am-6pm daily, VND10,000) lean into Ba Nai Hill, a lookout three miles east of Phan Thiet. Built in the 9th century, the three structures belong to the Cham, former rulers of Vietnam's south-central coast. From its first tower, perched on a hillside clearing, visitors can see directly across to the surrounding hills, where dozens of brightly hued headstones decorate the landscape. The 40-foot tower houses a modest altar along with a few other odds and ends. Continue the upward climb and you'll come to Po Shanu's soaring main structure, which boasts a lavish altar bedecked with flowers, incense, and fruit, as well as massive stone *linga* and *yoni* statues. Next door, a squat tower complements the larger temple.

Ba Nai Hill's significance is not limited solely to these ancient relics. Farther uphill, a large monument commemorates the 1947 Vietnamese victory over French forces, in which local soldiers disguised themselves and ambushed the area, killing or capturing 35 of their enemies as well as collecting

Fish Sauce

If you have even a single Vietnamese meal during your travels, there is no doubt that you'll encounter the country's most famous condiment: fish sauce. This is especially true in Phan Thiet, the fish sauce capital of the country, where the thick, reddish-orange sauce features heavily in most local fare.

Heading into town on the road from Mui Ne, you'll catch a whiff of the scores of fish sauce factories. Here, local manufacturers pack thousands of anchovies into massive wooden barrels, add salt, and allow the concoction to sit for at least a year. The liquid is then extracted from a tap at the base of the barrel, filtered, and bottled. Many shops both in Phan Thiet and along the Mui Ne strip sell local fish sauce, which tastes far better than it smells. Though several other towns, including Phu Quoc, also produce the stuff, Phan Thiet's lower humidity and higher temperatures help to make its *nuoc mam* (fish sauce) some of the best in Vietnam.

the spring may ask to be your guide. Their approach can be aggressive, and a guide won't really enhance your visit. Your best bet is to politely (but firmly) refuse their offer.

Phan Thiet

A pleasant town of narrow alleys and low, pastel houses, **Phan Thiet** is Mui Ne's western neighbor, a sleepy fishing town with a few beaches of its own, which are popular with domestic tourists, namely from Saigon. Though Phan Thiet doesn't really have anything in the way of specific sights, wandering around town can be a fun afternoon outing. En route to the city center, you'll pass a row of fish sauce factories along Thu Khoa Huan street, where Phan Thiet's most famous product is made, bottled, and sold. Phan Thiet's resident city beach, **Doi Duong** is a breezy, tree-lined patch of sand far different from its bustling urban surroundings. This quiet spot is popular with young couples during the evening and has a handful of cafés tucked at the western end of the beach. While it's not really the place for swimming, Doi Duong makes a worthy spot for a stroll or a peaceful afternoon drink.

BEACHES
Rang Beach

The one stretch of sand where most travelers spend their time is known as **Rang Beach.** This runs parallel to Mui Ne's main road and has mostly been gobbled up by seaside hotels and resorts, who stake their claim on the shoreline. A handful of bars and restaurants on the beachfront are open throughout the day, and it's perfectly acceptable to buy a drink and lounge around at one of these establishments for a few hours in order to take advantage of the ocean. Since Rang Beach, and, indeed, much of the Mui Ne coastline, suffers from an erosion problem, restaurants and accommodations farther east along the beach are less likely to have sand and more likely to consist of sun beds and umbrellas set atop a concrete sea wall. Undercurrents are strong in Mui Ne and waves can get big; exercise caution when going for a swim.

Ganh Beach

On the other side of Mui Ne village is **Ganh Beach,** also known as Hon Rom. Much the same as its western counterpart, this coastal stretch is home to a handful of luxury accommodations but sees much less traffic than its neighbor and has yet to resort to protective sea walls. You'll find a more traditional beach here, where a small point keeps the easternmost end of the coast from stronger winds and several restaurants have set up shop to cater to beachgoers. Beyond these few eateries, the place is quiet, with most visitors just driving up and laying down a towel. Ganh Beach also acts as the town's harbor for half the year, when boats from the more famous port on the other side of the village come to moor near this coast.

NIGHTLIFE

As Mui Ne's popularity continues to grow, so does its nightlife. Most places close by midnight and the street quiets down considerably then. But night owls will find several local watering holes that stay open until the last customer goes home.

In addition to some killer food, **Joe's Cafe** (86 Nguyen Dinh Chieu, tel. 06/2384-7177, www.joescafemuine.com, 7am-midnight daily, VND65,000-210,000) is a popular spot for a laid-back nightcap or happy hour drink. With regular drink specials and live music on offer, guests can sit back and take in the acoustic stylings of a handful of resident guitarists or play a game of billiards at the bar's pool table.

A psychedelic oceanfront hangout, **Pogo Beach Club** (138 Nguyen Dinh Chieu, tel. 09/0738-7600, 8am-late daily, VND20,000-200,000) is made up of a collection of lounge chairs and bean bags, wooden tables, cushions, and concrete benches. Putting together a fine burger and a handful of other meals during the day, the bar gets busy with young backpackers and kitesurfers around the time the sun goes down. Daily drink specials encourage guests to imbibe, and the resident DJs keep a steady stream of tunes coming.

More mellow than its beachside competition, **Chillout Cafe** (155 Nguyen Dinh Chieu, tel. 012/8329-9281, 5pm-1am daily, VND20,000-70,000) makes a nice spot to unwind after a long beach day, with cushioned booths and a breezy patio as well as shisha (hookah) on offer. The interior, decked out in miniature lanterns and fairy lights, gives off a laid-back vibe, and the friendly staff serve a variety of drinks as well as a few European dishes (VND40,000-90,000).

As the name suggests, **Fun Key** (124 Nguyen Dinh Chieu, tel. 012/7790-9121, www.funkeybarmuine.com, 7pm-late daily, VND60,000-120,000) is a hip little bar by the sea that is popular in the evenings. Plush white couches sit beneath a thatched-roof covering atop the bar's sea wall, while mellow music competes with the noise of the incoming waves.

After the sun sets, **Jibes** (90 Nguyen Dinh Chieu, tel. 06/2384-7008, www.windsurf-vietnam.com, 7am-midnight daily, VND20,000-130,000) trades its sails and surfboards for beachside beers and happy hour drinks. Tasty Western food (VND70,000-390,000) is also served, and the roadside storefront houses a host of windsurfing, sailing, kiting, and surfing gear, as well as the office of Jibes' rental and lesson outfit.

Wax (68 Nguyen Dinh Chieu, tel. 06/2384-7001, 7am-3am daily, VND30,000-320,000) is probably the most active nightspot you'll find in Mui Ne, with beer, cocktails, and an ample dance floor. Beachside bonfires are a regular fixture and the place stays open 'til late.

SHOPPING

In Mui Ne, authentic, locally made items center around three categories: seafood, fresh fruit, and textiles or pottery crafted by the local Cham minority. As a major *nuoc mam* (fish sauce) producer, Phan Thiet is a city known for its fish sauce, which is widely available both in town and along the Mui Ne strip. Dragon fruit is also a popular local specialty, and you'll no doubt see these cactus-like plants on your ride into or out of the area, as hundreds of orchards exist along the roadside. For Cham textiles or pottery, you can look into the souvenirs available on your visit to the Po Shanu Towers or keep an eye out when perusing the shops along the strip.

The majority of souvenirs in this town are trucked in from Saigon, and so the same gifts and knickknacks you would find in Ben Thanh Market or the Pham Ngu Lao area are on sale here at much higher prices. For standard souvenirs, you're better off waiting until you reach another town, whether it be Saigon or Nha Trang. If you find something you like, don't be afraid to haggle. You can also find a few small, independent shops that provide more unique items, though their price tags tend to be just as high, often without the bargaining option. For reading material, several of the small travel agencies on Nguyen Dinh Chieu double as used-book vendors.

SPORTS AND RECREATION

Going against Mui Ne's sleepy seaside reputation is its propensity for water sports. Considered Vietnam's kitesurfing capital, shorelines both east and west of the town are fast gaining popularity with kitesurfers, as well as other water sport enthusiasts. Boasting one of the windiest coasts in the country, this area makes an ideal spot for beginners and pros, with conditions changing throughout the day to suit every level of kitesurfer. Other activities, from windsurfing to regular surfing and sailing, are also available, as are an odd assortment of non-beach-related activities.

Kitesurfing and Water Sports

Kitesurfers flock to this area in greater numbers each year. While Rang Beach remains the center of Mui Ne's kiting schools, more advanced riders are also able to get out beyond the crowded shores of the main beach to visit other areas. Thanks to a few helpful locals, the website Kitesurfing Mui Ne (www.kitesurfingmuine.com) keeps riders informed and updated on conditions, schools, and all the other ins and outs of the sport in Mui Ne.

Mui Ne's first and most established kite center, C2Sky (82 Nguyen Dinh Chieu, tel. 09/1665-5241, www.c2skykitecenter.com, 9am-5pm daily, equipment rental around VND1,680,000 per day, lessons VND2,100,000-12,600,000) has been here since the beginning, setting up shop on the windy shores of the south-central coast in 2006. Since then, the shop has hosted international kitesurfing events, turned several local riders into IKO-certified instructors, and taken scores of travelers out for a day on the waves. Instructors are experienced and welcome all customers from beginners to pros. High-quality equipment is provided.

A chilled-out shop with excellent beachfront property, Jibes (90 Nguyen Dinh Chieu, tel. 06/2384-7405, www.windsurf-vietnam.com, 7am-midnight daily) offers an array of water sport options, including windsurfing, sailing, and kiting lessons, as well as surfing and stand-up paddleboard rentals. Qualified instructors speak a host of languages and all equipment and safety precautions meet international standards. This is also a great spot to grab a quick bite or a drink after your day on the water, as Jibes boasts a friendly, easygoing vibe and also houses a restaurant and bar on the premises.

Golf

Designed by Masters champion and winner of the British Open Nick Faldo, the course at Ocean Dunes Golf Club (1 Ton Duc Thang, tel. 06/2382-3366, www.vietnamgolfresorts.com, tee times 6am-3pm daily, VND1,210,000-3,586,000) is among the best in Vietnam. This 18-hole, links-style spread uses Phan Thiet's sand dunes and coastal winds to its advantage, shaping the course through everyday changes. Both a pro shop and clubhouse are located within the grounds. Facilities include locker rooms, a restaurant and bar, and a practice green.

While Ocean Dunes is the more famous of the two, Sea Links Golf Club (Nguyen Thong, tel. 06/2374-1741, www.sealinkscity.com, tee times 6am-3:30pm daily, VND1,250,000-3,700,000) offers another option for golfers slightly closer to the Mui Ne strip, with an 18-hole course as well as a pro shop and driving range.

Hidden opposite the tail-end of Saigon-Mui Ne Resort, amateur golfers will appreciate Tropical Mini-Golf (97 Nguyen Dinh Chieu, tel. 012/2679-5914, www.tropical-minigolf.com, 10am-11pm daily, VND100,000), an 18-hole concrete course fringed with greenery and complicated by an assortment of fake rocks. The place offers drink deals to golfers and has a restaurant and bar at the back of the property for afterward. Keep an eye out for the entrance, as it can be tricky to find from the street.

Massages and Spas

Hidden from view, **Botanica Spa** (85A Nguyen Dinh Chieu, tel. 09/4887-7203, noon-10pm daily, VND100,000-550,000) is a blissful open-air facility tucked behind the bustling restaurants and guesthouses of the main road. Set in a shaded garden and decked out in rattan and bamboo furniture, Botanica offers facials, massages, and hair and skin treatments at reasonable prices and with a friendly staff.

The list of massages and spa treatments available at **Forester Beach Spa** (82 Nguyen Dinh Chieu, tel. 06/2374-1899, 10am-10pm daily, VND100,000-700,000) may run a little on the expensive side, but this spot is definitely the best of the bunch along Nguyen Dinh Chieu. Overlooking the beach, Forester is a tranquil and professional environment complete with an array of body scrubs, full-body massages, and nail and hair treatments, among other things.

ACCOMMODATIONS

With hundreds of accommodations on the main strip, plenty of affordable options rub shoulders with higher-end boutique hotels and resorts. Upscale accommodations tend to lie on the western end of the beach in the lower street numbers (usually under 100), while budget spots are spread throughout.

Hotels with even-numbered street addresses are located on the waterfront. If you stay on the other side of Nguyen Dinh Chieu, some odd-numbered hotels and guesthouses have pools, but you will be required to find a public access spot or beachside café in order to swim in the ocean.

Due to erosion, some hotels may not have a sand beach on their property.

Under VND210,000

Without a doubt the cheapest beds you'll find on the Mui Ne strip are at **Keng Guesthouse** (185 Nguyen Dinh Chieu, tel. 06/2374-3312, VND105,000 dorm). Also known as Vi Huong, the top floor of this two-story house is outfitted with three- and four-person co-ed dorms that include fans, mosquito nets, and comfortable beds. Both the bathrooms and the balcony are shared, making for a little less privacy, but the owners are friendly and facilities are tidy and well kept. Keng Guesthouse sits across from many of the outdoor seafood vendors beside the beach, a short walk from Mui Ne's main restaurant drag.

Farther up the coast, **Thanh Duy Guesthouse** (243 Nguyen Dinh Chieu, tel. 06/2384-7077, thanhduy0602@gmail.com, VND200,000) is easily identified by its large pink-and-purple sign out front. Featuring equally tacky bedspreads, this budget accommodation's rooms are large and basic but clean, boasting generous street-facing windows on the upper floors and slightly smaller, quieter rooms downstairs. Hot water, Wi-Fi access, air-conditioning, and television are all standard with each room, and the guesthouse also has a travel agency out front and a restaurant next door.

VND210,000-525,000

The friendly folks at ★ **Hong Di** (70 Nguyen Dinh Chieu, tel. 06/2384-7014, hdhongdi@yahoo.com, VND378,000-630,000) opened this no-frills guesthouse well before there were giant resorts and boutique hotels on the strip, and the place has remained a standout among budget accommodations. As one of the only affordable spots left on this side of the road, Hong Di offers basic but comfortable rooms with TV, Wi-Fi access, hot water, and your choice of fan or air-conditioning. Those who opt for air-conditioning will also find a refrigerator in their rooms. The guesthouse also sells tours around the area as well as vehicle rentals.

A little weathered but still good value for its price tag, **The Sun** (117C Nguyen Dinh Chieu, tel. 06/2374-1737, thesunmuine@gmail.com, VND252,000-420,000) is a family-run guesthouse featuring no-frills accommodation and a small restaurant out front. Hot water and your choice of fan or air-conditioning are available, as is a small porch outside of each room. The inner courtyard is only half-maintained, but the affordable rooms make up for the lack of gardening.

Rooms at the **Surfers Guesthouse** (103B Nguyen Dinh Chieu, tel. 09/1805-7816, www.ripcurlkiteboardingvietnam.com, VND315,000-420,000) are basic, decked out in wooden furniture, and feature solar-powered hot water, a minibar, TV, and air-conditioning. The accommodations are new and the place is tucked just behind a trio of decent budget eateries, making its location equally worthy.

Though **Xuan Uyen** (Nguyen Dinh Chieu, tel. 06/2384-7476, VND252,000-315,000) doesn't earn rave reviews for decor, its aged beachfront rooms remain clean and offer travelers the option of dirt-cheap, fan-only, cold-water rooms or fancier accommodations with hot water and air-conditioning. Either way, it is the guesthouse's location that makes it worth mentioning, as this is one of the few budget ocean-side options. Guests will find a small restaurant attached to Xuan Uyen, as well as an on-site kitesurfing school and some notably amiable owners.

VND525,000-1,050,00

The charming **Rang Garden Bungalows** (233A Nguyen Dinh Chieu, tel. 06/2374-3638, www.rang-muine.com, VND630,000-840,000, breakfast included) is a collection of simple, spacious rooms equipped with a television, fridge, hot water, air-conditioning, in-room safe, and Wi-Fi access. The swimming pool sits in the middle of a peaceful courtyard. Out front, you'll find a restaurant as well as a souvenir shop, stocked with unique silk creations. Rooms fill up fast so book ahead.

Mui Ne's most popular mid-range accommodation, the fun and friendly **Xin Chao Hotel** (129 Nguyen Dinh Chieu, tel. 06/2374-3086, www.xinchaohotel.com, VND840,000-945,000) boasts smart, understated rooms with plush beds, hot water, television, and air-conditioning. Both Wi-Fi access and breakfast are included in the room rate, and guests can use the courtyard pool at the center of the hotel. Xin Chao also manages **Indigo** (129 Nguyen Dinh Chieu, tel. 06/2374-3086, www.xinchaohotel.com, 7am-9pm daily, VND50,000-160,000), a popular street-side restaurant at the front of the property that serves a decent mix of Vietnamese and Western dishes. Thanks to its great service, Xin Chao often finds itself with more customers than rooms; make sure you reserve your spot before heading to Mui Ne. Rates are also discounted heavily in the off-season, so if

guesthouse Hong Di

you're traveling outside of peak months, call or email ahead to inquire about prices.

While plenty of resorts have sprung up on the beach, **Mui Ne Hills** (69 Nguyen Dinh Chieu, tel. 09/0805-2350, www.muinehills. com, VND630,000-1,260,000) takes a different approach. Built into the surrounding hillside, this friendly, modern budget resort is pleasantly removed from the buzz on the beach, but with easy access to the Mui Ne strip. Each room is decorated differently and features air-conditioning, hot water, Wi-Fi access, television, and a minibar. There is a blissful pool on the property as well.

VND1,050,000-2,100,000

Though it's a bit of a misnomer, rooms at the ocean-side **Mui Ne Backpackers** (88 Nguyen Dinh Chieu, tel. 06/2384-7047, www. muinebackpackers.com, VND252,000 dorm, VND1,365,000-2,520,000 double) are in excellent condition and offer much-coveted beach access from the spot just between Jibes and Joe's Cafe. Formerly the Vietnam-Austria House, Mui Ne Backpackers provides modern accommodations that include Wi-Fi access, air-conditioning, TV, and a minibar, perfect for the flashpacker (backpacker with a disposable income) crowd. A courtyard pool gives guests a chlorinated option over the strong undercurrents of the sea.

On the eastern end of the strip, **Dynasty Resort** (140A Nguyen Dinh Chieu, tel. 06/2384-7816, www.dynastyresorts.com, VND1,200,000-3,800,000) offers all the trimmings of a proper resort at prices that are slightly gentler on the wallet. Housed in a beautiful, pale yellow building, rooms feature tasteful decor and high-quality amenities, including television, air-conditioning, Wi-Fi access, hot water, and charming balconies with beach-facing views as well as complimentary breakfast. At the center of the resort is a spacious pool, accompanied by a bar, both of which sit just beyond the ocean.

The ultra-modern, teal-and-white **Shades** (98A Nguyen Dinh Chieu, tel. 06/2374-3237, www.shadesmuine.com, VND1,680,000-5,040,000) apartments are one of Mui Ne's trendier options, offering both short- and long-term rentals. Well-appointed accommodations run the spectrum from standard double rooms to fully equipped apartments with a kitchen, lounge area, and desk. All accommodations include the usual amenities: Wi-Fi access, air-conditioning, hot water, a minibar, and television. Shades' higher-end lodgings offer a few more add-ons.

Over VND2,100,000

As soon as you enter **Allez Boo** (8 Nguyen Dinh Chieu, tel. 06/2374-3777, www.allez-booresort.com, VND2,100,000-9,500,000) on the western end of the Mui Ne strip, you'll be greeted by a beautiful high-ceilinged reception area, which opens onto the resort's stunning ocean-side pool. Owned by the same folks responsible for Saigon's Allez Boo restaurant and the infamous Go2 bar, this chic retreat is a classier establishment, boasting pristine rooms with a simple, sophisticated decor and high-quality amenities as well as complimentary breakfast. Beyond accommodations, this full-service resort offers not only private pool and beach access but tours, vehicle rentals (including Jet skis), a spa, and a business center.

The idyllic **Mia Resort** (24 Nguyen Dinh Chieu, tel. 06/2384-7440, www.miamuine.com, VND2,720,000-11,000,000) is an oceanfront oasis among the many large resorts spread along Mui Ne's eastern end. With plush, thatched-roof bungalows and generous beds, this seaside escape puts guests off the noise and chaos of the main road and closer to the nearby waves. Rooms are tastefully furnished and include both a fan and air-conditioning, television, hot water, an in-room safe, tea- and coffee-making facilities, Wi-Fi access, and a veranda. Breakfast is included in the room rate.

A small but stunning boutique hotel, **Cham Villas** (32 Nguyen Dinh Chieu, tel. 06/2374-1234, www.chamvillas.com, VND3,549,000-4,305,000) doesn't appear to be much from the outside, but it affords guests ample privacy among lush palm trees and shaded walkways. Rooms are beautifully furnished and feature air-conditioning, television, Wi-Fi access, and hot water. A private pool and beach access are available. The staff can arrange tours, vehicle rentals, and other activities.

FOOD

Mui Ne's influx of foreign tourists have ushered in dozens of Western restaurants that offer dishes like pizza, pasta, and tacos in addition to Vietnamese fare. The local specialty is, of course, seafood, with a fresh catch every day and plenty of open-air joints near the water. You'll also find an array of international fare along the Nguyen Dinh Chieu strip.

Cafés and Bakeries

A trendy, air-conditioned spot, **Katie's Coffee House** (115 Nguyen Dinh Chieu, tel. 012/8350-9514, 9am-10pm daily, VND30,000-120,000) may be on the expensive side, but the place serves well-made European-style coffee as well as a variety of teas and other beverages. Food is available on the menu but, in truth, you're better off sticking to drinks only here. Free Wi-Fi is on tap and, unlike most places on the Nguyen Dinh Chieu strip, the indoor café offers a little more quiet. You'll also find a larger Katie's Coffee House attached to the Five Star Spa (173 Nguyen Dinh Chieu).

Quick Bites

A cheap but tasty roadside eatery not far from Surfer's Guesthouse, **King of Sandwich** (103B Nguyen Dinh Chieu, 10am-late daily, VND45,000-100,000) serves breakfasts, sandwiches, and other simple fare at reasonable prices. The staff is friendly, and delivery is available.

Vietnamese

Beginning around the 15-kilometer mark, several open-air restaurants serve up delectable local **seafood barbecue** during the evening hours. These street food joints vary in cost and cleanliness, so browse before ordering. Some shops feature menus, which are helpful in factoring cost. Ask the price before ordering, as you don't want to wind up with a bill higher than you expected.

A long, narrow open-air spot, **Bamboo Bamboo** (131 Nguyen Dinh Chieu, tel. 06/2379-0169, 8am-late daily, VND50,000-150,000) is well priced for the area and cooks up a whole slew of Vietnamese dishes, from seafood and meat stir-fry to vegetarian and even Western fare. Portions tend to be on the small side. The staff are cheerful and willing to make recommendations and the place gets popular around dinnertime, when the overhead lanterns and traditional Vietnamese music create a more authentic ambience. The restaurant also serves cheap Western and Asian breakfasts (VND20,000-50,000).

Though it's packed to the gills with hungry backpackers on a budget, **Lam Tong** (92 Nguyen Dinh Chieu, tel. 06/2384-7598, 8am-10pm daily, VND20,000-90,000) manages to churn out tasty, authentic Vietnamese fare with the added benefit of being directly on the beach. Squeezed between Jibes and Mui Ne Backpackers in the heart of the Mui Ne strip, this restaurant has maintained both its prices and its basic beachside setup over the years, offering plenty of meat, seafood, and vegetarian options.

The simple but sophisticated dining area at **Cho Ca** (45 Nguyen Dinh Chieu, tel. 012/6806-9480, 11am-10pm daily, VND60,000-320,000) makes this restaurant a slightly more upmarket Vietnamese option without the grandeur or pretension of some of the larger local eateries. With both an open patio out front and spacious indoor seating, Cho Ca (which means "fish market" in Vietnamese) pairs chic wooden furnishings with white tablecloths and scrumptious Vietnamese food. Though prices are higher than you'll find at many other local places, dishes are well prepared and the classy ambience makes this place worthwhile. Western dishes are also available, including a few Russian plates, but the restaurant's best fare is local cuisine.

Mexican

Boasting authentic Mexican dishes—a rare find in Vietnam—★ The Bar (257 Nguyen Dinh Chieu, 9am-10pm daily, VND30,000-100,000) is a laid-back roadside eatery. The Bar keeps things simple with its easygoing atmosphere, a range of international dishes, and amiable staff. Drop in for a quick bite or spend a few hours off the beach, lounging on the restaurant's front patio or keeping cool inside. Several tasty Western items make an appearance on the menu, including burgers, pancakes, fajitas, and burritos, all of which come in generous portions. Ice-cold beer and other beverages are in stock. A small contingent of beach bums gathers here from mid-afternoon onward to relax and play a few rounds of pool. There's always an American sports channel on the TV above the bar.

International

A standout on the block, long-time resident Joe's Cafe (86 Nguyen Dinh Chieu, tel. 06/2384-7177, www.joescafemuine.com, 7am-midnight daily, VND65,000-210,000) provides a variety of seating options, from the shaded roadside patio to covered open-air seating near the bar with a line of sight toward the beach. A well-rounded menu lists Western favorites like pizza, burgers, and Mexican fare in addition to Thai and Vietnamese offerings. Though service can be varied, sometimes attentive, sometimes not, the quality of Joe's food more than makes up for this, as the pizzas are some of the best in town and generous portions afford each diner his or her fair share.

Indian

The Mui Ne branch of a popular Indian chain, Shree Ganesh (57 Nguyen Dinh Chieu, tel. 06/2374-1330, www.ganesh.vn, 11am-10pm daily, VND75,000-200,000) prepares delicious renditions of Indian cuisine, ranging from vindaloos and curries to paneer, masala, and other tasty items. Look for the large white Ganesh statue up front to greet you as you enter the dining room.

Mediterranean

Though you could easily miss it, the miniature thatched-roof storefront of Sindbad (233 Nguyen Dinh Chieu, tel. 016/9568-9201, www.sindbad.vn, 10am-late daily, VND35,000-90,000), a humble eatery specializing in *doner kebab* (shawarma), has made waves on the strip with yet another different dining option for travelers. Helmed by a cheerful,

The Bar

hard-working three-person team, the shop manages to turn out great kebabs as well as a few other Mediterranean dishes.

Set on a sturdy veranda, **Chasseur Blanc** (139 Nguyen Dinh Chieu, tel. 06/2374-1222, cl.chasseurblanc@gmail.com, 8am-midnight daily, VND90,000-400,000) is an upscale French restaurant that serves hearty, meat-and-potatoes Western fare. Vietnamese options are also available, but it is the European dishes that are the star of the show. An extensive wine collection is displayed above the bar.

INFORMATION AND SERVICES
Tourist Information

For information regarding local sights, there are dozens of small outfits along Nguyen Dinh Chieu selling the same cookie-cutter tours, which include a visit to both sets of sand dunes, Fairy Spring, and the Po Shanu Towers. **Sinh Tourist** (144 Nguyen Dinh Chieu, tel. 06/2384-7542, www.thesinhtourist.vn, 7am-10pm daily) has free maps for travelers, though there is a better version of a local map available at several businesses along the strip, including at a restaurant called **Drugoe Mesto** (106 Nguyen Dinh Chieu, tel. 012/3722-4147, 10am-11pm daily, VND50,000-150,000). You can also scope out local listings and helpful advice from **Mui Ne Beach.net** (www.muinebeach.net), an informational site created by a longtime resident of the area.

Banks

There is a **Vietcombank ATM** (beside Saigon-Mui Ne Resort, 24 hours daily) and several other ATMs, including a pair beside Tien Dat Resort, available along the strip. For additional services, you will have to go into town and visit the **Sacombank** (364 Tran Hung Dao, tel. 06/2383-2426, sacombank.com.vn, 7:30am-11:30am and 1pm-5pm Mon.-Fri., 7:30am-11:30am Sat.). To avoid this trip, you can either stick to ATMs for your cash or change up currency before you arrive. U.S. dollars are often accepted by local hotels and restaurants along this strip, but be mindful of the exchange rate, as this number often depends upon the business you're dealing with and it is not uncommon to be overcharged.

Internet and Postal Services

A small roadside **post office** (53 Nguyen Dinh Chieu, tel. 06/2374-1015, 10am-6pm daily) near the western end of the Mui Ne strip accepts letters and postcards. For anything more complex than that you'll need to head to the opposite end of the strip, where a larger **post office** (349 Nguyen Dinh Chieu, tel. 06/2384-7101, 7:30am-11am and 2pm-5pm Sun.-Fri.) assists with other matters.

Medical Services

The **Swiss Village Resort Clinic** (44 Nguyen Dinh Chieu, tel. 06/2384-7497, 9am-9pm daily) handles minor illnesses and injuries. For more serious ailments you may want to visit **An Phuoc Hospital** (235 Tran Phu, Phan Thiet, tel. 06/2338-3056) in Phan Thiet, or, better yet, head to Saigon.

GETTING THERE
Bus

From Saigon, both **Sinh Tourist** (144 Nguyen Dinh Chieu, tel. 06/2384-7542, www.thesinhtourist.vn, 7am-10pm daily) and **Phuong Trang** (20 Huynh Thuc Khang, tel. 06/2374-3113, www.futabuslines.com.vn, 6am-10pm daily, VND130,000) run daily buses to Mui Ne, which arrive at their respective offices along the main strip, Nguyen Dinh Chieu (which turns into Huynh Thuc Khang in Mui Ne proper). Sinh Tourist can also arrange buses to Mui Ne from Dalat (VND119,000) and Nha Trang (VND129,000).

The **Mui Ne bus station (Ben Xe Mui Ne)** (tel. 06/2384-9676, 7am-7pm daily) is where local buses depart for once-daily trips to Phan Rang and Saigon (VND100,000). If you're heading to Saigon it's better to pay the extra VND30,000 and hop on a Phuong Trang bus, as its buses are newer and drivers are more experienced.

Train

Several morning trains, both hard- and soft-seat, leave from Saigon (4 hours, VND378,000) and arrive at the **Phan Thiet station** (Phong Nam, Phan Thiet, tel. 06/2383-3952, 7am-8pm daily). From there, it's another three miles to Mui Ne by taxi (VND180,000).

GETTING AROUND

Taxis and *Xe Om*

You'll find most *xe om* hanging around the front of larger resorts down the western end of Nguyen Dinh Chieu. They usually begin the bargaining high, so be prepared to haggle.

Mailinh (tel. 0623/838-3838) taxis regularly ply Nguyen Dinh Chieu and have a habit of honking at any foreigner they see, which, in Mui Ne, is pretty much everyone.

Vehicles for Hire

Hiring a bicycle or motorbike to get around Mui Ne and the surrounding area is not a bad idea, particularly if you're heading out to the sand dunes or Po Shanu Towers. Most hotels and guesthouses will happily rent out bicycles at reasonable fees. Don't bother with the makeshift motorbike setups outside some of the larger resorts, as they start their asking prices as high as VND250,000. You should never need to pay more than VND150,000 for a motorbike rental, regardless of whether the vehicle is semi- or fully automatic. **Kim Travel** (72 Nguyen Dinh Chieu, tel. 06/2655-2179, 9am-9pm daily) is a reliable provider, where you can arrange both short- and long-term rentals and, in some cases, fees are negotiable.

Despite the strip's easygoing vibe, this is a notably dangerous stretch of road on which two-wheeled vehicles and enormous transport trucks roar past each other at breakneck speeds. More than a few traffic fatalities have occurred here, and following the death of a Russian tourist in 2013, local authorities are cracking down heavily on Mui Ne's traffic safety in general and foreign drivers in particular. The same road rules apply here as in the rest of Vietnam and are more often enforced. All drivers and passengers must wear helmets by law, observe the speed limit, and stick to no more than one passenger on the back of a bike.

Since Mui Ne's main strip is slightly removed from the nearest town, the area's only proper gas station lies at the far end of Nguyen Dinh Chieu heading toward Phan Thiet. Instead of driving out to this spot, many local shops will sell fuel from old-school gas pumps on the roadside. These independent shops tend to be more convenient but also more expensive.

Ho Chi Minh City

G

Get anywhere near the flashing neon lights, full-throttle traffic, sardined houses, and soaring commercial towers of the country's southern hub and it becomes clear why Ho Chi Minh City (HCMC) is the future of Vietnam.

Indisputably the economic heart of the nation, this fast-paced, ever-expanding behemoth has charged fearlessly—and sometimes recklessly—into the 21st century, carrying along a diverse and multifaceted population, a keen business acumen, and an irrepressible spirit.

Shackled by heavy-handed governmental policies after the Vietnam War, HCMC hit the ground running in the mid-1980s, as the nation's *doi moi* economic reforms flung open the door to international business and trade. A decade of pent-up energy was unleashed, sending the city on a frantic, determined mission to become Vietnam's cosmopolitan leader. HCMC—still known to locals as Saigon—packs all of southern Vietnam's best food, art, culture, and diversity into the jumbled houses and narrow alleyways of the country's most ambitious metropolis.

Settled on the sticky, humid, pancake-flat marshland just east of the Mekong Delta, the city began only a few centuries ago but has exploded in population over the past two decades. Even today, immigrants travel from near and far, hoping to make a home and a living amid the bustle of Vietnam's largest city. Government statistics put the urban population at around 7.5 million residents and counting, but this number hardly seems enough when you sit bumper-to-bumper in midday traffic or squeeze onto a tiny patch of sidewalk for a nighttime *ca phe bet* (streetside coffee). Others estimate the actual population as much higher, from just north of 8 million to as great as 10 million people. Whatever the number, HCMC shows no signs of stopping. Already, outlying districts are swallowing up nearby towns like Di An and Bien Hoa, and the population of the greater metropolitan area is expected to grow to as many as nine million by official statistics in 2025.

From a traveler's perspective, the city is both a blessing and a curse: HCMC provides a more lively, chaotic, and occasionally

Look for ★ to find recommended
sights, activities, dining, and lodging.

Highlights

© AVALON TRAVEL

★ **Reunification Palace:** This opulent palace was once home to the presidents of the short-lived Republic of Vietnam (page 312).

★ **Ben Thanh Market:** Frenetic and fast-paced, the city's most iconic market hosts dozens of multilingual vendors and over 3,000 stalls packed to the ceilings with everything you could imagine (page 315).

★ **War Remnants Museum:** Thoughtful and at times harrowing, Saigon's best museum provides insight into life during and after the American War (page 321).

★ **Thien Hau Pagoda:** A centuries-old Chinese pagoda in the heart of bustling District 5 was built by Chinese refugees as a thank-you to the goddess of the sea after their treacherous emigration (page 324).

★ **Street Food in Northern District 1:** The best of Vietnamese cuisine finds its way to the dented metal carts and bamboo poles of Saigon's street vendors (page 353).

dangerous atmosphere than the sleepy towns of the coast. Along with the madness of the city comes an intricate and fascinating history that announces itself time and again in the city's eclectic architecture and multifaceted cuisine. Stroll along the wide boulevards of downtown District 1, where opulent colonial-era buildings stand, or hang onto your helmet as you race down the narrow streets of Chinatown on the back of a motorbike, defying the laws of physics as you weave through traffic.

Hidden farther down the city's many alleys is another world altogether, quiet and reserved, where children play on empty sidewalks and old women sit sentinel, fanning themselves in the afternoon heat. For as many modern complexes as the city has acquired in recent years, remnants of an earlier time remain in the aging facades of historical buildings and the one-room restaurants that continue to turn a profit, even as high-end eateries go into business next door. HCMC is a sensory overload. Step into the chaos with optimism, and you will be rewarded by life in Vietnam's largest city.

HISTORY

The outlines of modern-day Saigon began to take shape in 1674, as communities settled along the Ben Nghe River. To the east, Vietnamese farmers raised buffalo in what is now District 1, while a large, business-minded community of Chinese refugees, who had fled the persecution of the Ming dynasty, appeared in present-day District 5. Over the next 200 years, these two settlements grew closer to one another, forming the boundaries of Vietnam's largest metropolis.

After the French arrived in 1859 the city underwent major changes. Few were quick to welcome the French to Vietnam, but colonialism provided Saigon with several important and lasting things. At the center of town, the French erected churches, theaters, government buildings, and a post office, many of which remain in use today. To the west, much of the Chinese neighborhood

was left as a separate entity, and so its residents carried on living as they had prior to colonization.

While Saigon's Chinese residents were able to live undisturbed, the Vietnamese resented European authority. Tensions rose steadily between foreign and local residents. By the 1940s, a healthy opposition force had grown. Their efforts briefly stalled during WWII, when Japanese forces wrested power from the French for a short time in 1944, but Vietnam ultimately prevailed.

When the French finally left in 1954, south Vietnam set up its own government, with Saigon as the capital. Aided by the United States, the Republic of South Vietnam began in the spirit of democracy but quickly grew unpopular thanks to the policies of its leader, Ngo Dinh Diem. Once again, dissent turned the city into a staging ground for protests and other acts of political opposition. Rallies were held, Buddhist monks self-immolated in protest, and, across the city, plots to overthrow the government were plentiful. Finally, in 1963, Diem and his brother, Ngo Dinh Nhu, met their end after hiding out in a church in District 5, and the country quickly rolled into armed conflict.

For the better part of the American War, Saigon proper remained safe, and foreign journalists flocked to the city to cover the conflict, making Saigon something of an international hub. That is, until Communist forces crashed through the Independence Palace gates on April 30, 1975, officially ending the war. From then on, the southern hub became Ho Chi Minh City in honor of the man who crusaded for Vietnam's independence.

Closed to the world and still reeling from decades of battle—against the French, Americans, Cambodians, and Chinese—Vietnam began to rebuild. Economic reforms in the mid-1980s allowed HCMC to begin realizing its full potential, with brightly colored billboards and trendy foreign shops opening across town. By the 1990s, an ever-growing number of foreign tourists began to visit HCMC and since then the city has taken off.

Ho Chi Minh City

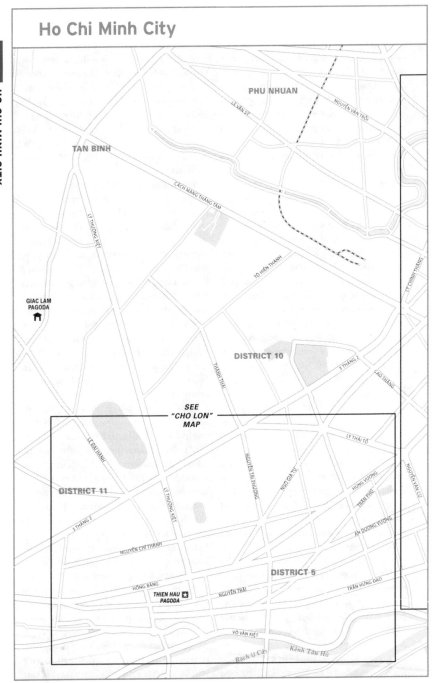

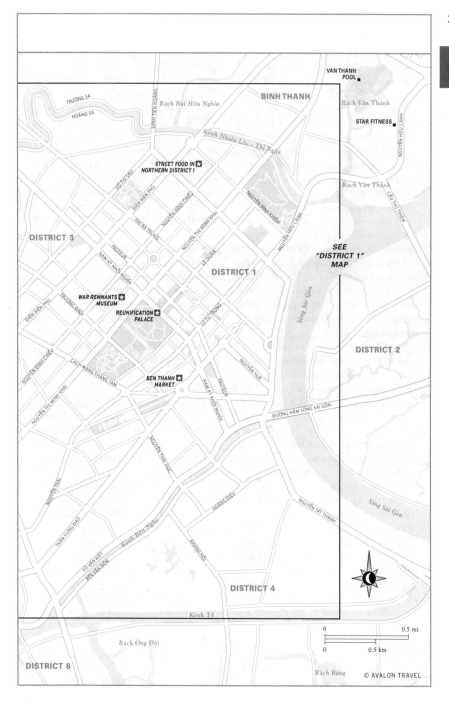

PLANNING YOUR TIME

Though the jumble of traffic and mismatched buildings can seem infinite, the city's downtown area is small. Most of the city's major sights and activities can be covered within four or five days, as attractions tend to be concentrated around Districts 1 and 5.

Do your sightseeing in the morning to avoid the heat, especially if you're visiting pagodas and other non-air-conditioned places. Afternoons are great for activities, eating, and taking in the buzz of the city. Though businesses stay open at lunchtime, many Vietnamese take siesta around noon, particularly those working at museums and government-run buildings, so avoid these places at midday. Once the sun goes down, street vendors set up along sidewalks, restaurants open, and tiny roadside stalls sling beer and *do nhau* (drinking food). The heat also lets up, making the evening a perfect time to wander through a night market, grab a bite to eat, or delve into the city's nightlife.

Set aside a day or two to escape the downtown area and pay a visit to the Cu Chi Tunnels or Tay Ninh's mammoth Cao Dai temple.

You should have no trouble finding English speakers downtown, though you may occasionally have to rely on the pick-and-point method. When heading out for the day, grab a business card from your hotel or jot down the address of wherever you're headed: While most taxi and *xe om* (motorbike taxi) drivers know the city's major landmarks, it pays to have the address and district on hand for lesser-known locations.

The biggest holiday of the year is Tet (Lunar New Year, late Jan.-mid-Feb.), a day when everyone in Vietnam returns to their hometown to celebrate. During this time, HCMC is virtually a ghost town. Most streets are empty and businesses deserted. Many services are not available or if they are prices go up considerably to compensate.

ORIENTATION

Ho Chi Minh City is divided into 19 districts and five communes. The majority of visitors only make it to a few of the more centrally located neighborhoods.

District 1

At the heart of the city is District 1 (considered the city's downtown), perched on the banks of the Saigon River, where the best shopping, nightlife, hotels, restaurants, and trendy cafés can be found. **Ben Thanh Market,** one of HCMC's most famous landmarks, and **Pham Ngu Lao street** (the **backpacker district,** where most travelers stay) are located in the southwestern part of this district. Several of the city's other famous sights, such as the **Reunification Palace** and Notre Dame Cathedral, are slightly farther north. The **Opera House** is a destination for high-end shopping and innumerable nightlife spots. Within District 1 is **Nguyen Hue street,** a pedestrian-only street with high-end shops.

Comprising the **northern** part of the district are a quieter web of streets packed with plenty of mouthwatering Vietnamese cuisine, and a handful of sights, including the Jade Emperor Pagoda.

District 3

Also in the middle of the action, District 3, to the northwest of District 1, is quieter. District 3 contains the **War Remnants Museum,** Vinh Nghiem Pagoda, Turtle Lake, and the historic Xa Loi Pagoda. (Some of these sights sit right on District 3's border with District 1.) This area is home to excellent restaurants, particularly vegetarian eateries, at more affordable prices than its downtown counterpart.

Cho Lon

The city's famous Chinatown, also known as Cho Lon, is a haze of noise, light, and traffic. Here you'll find the vast majority of HCMC's vibrant Chinese-Vietnamese community, along with scores of pagodas, temples, and assembly halls. Cho Lon literally means "big market," named after the enormous Binh Tay Market. This neighborhood lies across Districts 5 and 6. This area became

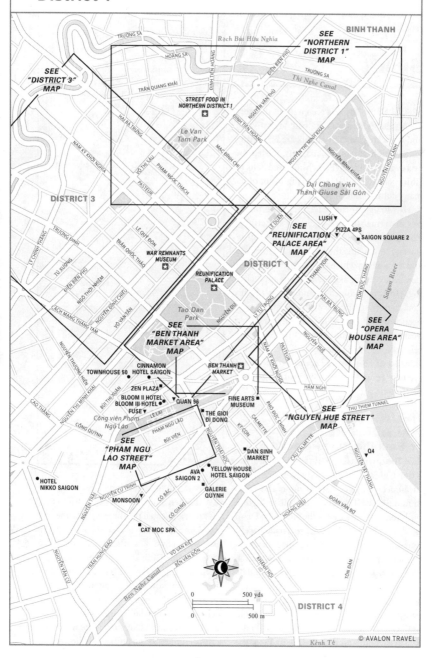

District 1

a safe haven in the 16th and 17th centuries for Chinese refugees fleeing the persecution of the Ming dynasty and, later, the Tay Son rebellion.

Sights

Ho Chi Minh City has seen a lot in its short history. Its sights are a testament to its diverse and intricate past. The streets are brimming with churches, temples, markets, museums, and everything from French-inspired halls to Chinese-style pagodas, offering proof of its many cultural intersections.

HCMC is not the place for grand photo ops or immense, awe-inspiring structures. Though there are some stunning sights within the city limits, it is the stories of these places and the ways in which they continue to function today that make them worth appreciating. Hop on a motorbike and jet out to Cho Lon, the city's Chinatown and one of the most hectic districts. Write a friend—or yourself—a postcard in the Central Post Office, a lasting relic of an earlier time, or grab a coffee outside the striking Notre Dame Cathedral and see how people live in the country's biggest metropolis.

REUNIFICATION PALACE AREA
★ Reunification Palace

The **Reunification Palace** (135 Nam Ky Khoi Nghia, D1, tel. 08/3822-3652, www. dinhdoclap.gov.vn, 7:30am-noon and 1pm-4pm daily, VND30,000) is a colossal white building that punctuates the end of Le Duan Boulevard. Set on 12 hectares of shaded, well-manicured lawns, the palace once served as the seat of government for both the French colonial regime and the short-lived Republic of Vietnam. Its interior remains almost exactly the same as it was 40 years ago, from the pale pink rotary phones in the situation room to the art-deco ambience of the upper floors.

Christened Norodom Palace in 1868, the palace was an official colonial dwelling until WWII when Emperor Bao Dai, Vietnam's last king, abdicated the throne. Once the war ended, the French reclaimed the palace until 1954, when power was officially transferred to politician Ngo Dinh Diem, who became south Vietnam's first president the following year. Diem renamed it the Independence Palace and installed his family in the house, which included a rooftop dance floor, several sitting rooms, dining areas, offices, a kitchen, and a series of underground bunkers. Following an

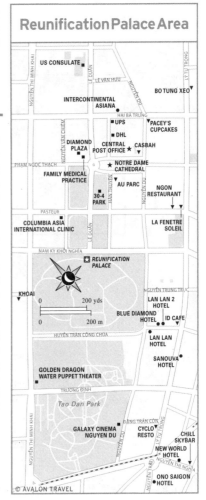

Reunification Palace Area

US CONSULATE
NGUYEN THI MINH KHAI
LE DUAN
LÊ VĂN HƯU
NGUYEN DU
LÝ TỰ TRỌNG
BO TUNG XEO
INTERCONTINENTAL ASIANA
HAI BÀ TRƯNG
UPS
PACEY'S CUPCAKES
DHL
DIAMOND PLAZA
CENTRAL POST OFFICE
CASBAH
NGUYEN VAN CHIEM
PHAM NGOC THACH
NOTRE DAME CATHEDRAL
FAMILY MEDICAL PRACTICE
AU PARC
NGON RESTAURANT
HÀN THUYÊN
30-4 PARK
PASTEUR
COLUMBIA ASIA INTERNATIONAL CLINIC
LA FENETRE SOLEIL
LE DUAN
NAM KỲ KHỞI NGHĨA
★ REUNIFICATION PALACE
KHOAI
NGUYEN TRUNG TRUC
LAN LAN 2 HOTEL
0   200 yds
BLUE DIAMOND HOTEL
ID CAFE
0   200 m
HUYEN TRAN CONG CHUA
LAN LAN HOTEL
SANOUVA HOTEL
GOLDEN DRAGON WATER PUPPET THEATER
TRƯƠNG ĐỊNH
Tao Dan Park
NGUYEN THI MINH KHAI
ĐẶNG TRẦN CÔN
GALAXY CINEMA NGUYEN DU
CYCLO RESTO
LÝ TỰ TRỌNG
CHILL SKYBAR
NEW WORLD HOTEL
NGUYEN THI NGHIA
ONO SAIGON HOTEL
© AVALON TRAVEL

assassination attempt in 1962, Diem commissioned Vietnamese architect Ngo Viet Thu to build a new structure in its place. This served as the headquarters of the south Vietnamese government until Communist forces crashed through the palace gates on April 30, 1975, officially putting an end to the American War.

Enter the palace to the left of the main gates and head toward the left side of the building, where free guided tours are offered every 15 minutes (7:45am-11am and 1:15pm-4pm daily). Signage is virtually nonexistent, so it's a good idea to hop on one of these tours. It takes about an hour to see the palace's four floors as well as its eerie bomb-shelter basement. There is also an educational video offered at the end of the tour but you can skip it. The palace gardens make for a pleasant stroll back to the entrance. To the right of the building are two tanks parked at the edge of the lawn. These vehicles were among the group that broke through the palace gates in 1975.

Notre Dame Cathedral

Set amid the hustle and bustle of downtown is the imposing figure of **Notre Dame Cathedral** (1 Cong Xa Paris, D1, tel. 08/3822-0477, 8am-11am and 3pm-4pm daily). Completed in 1880, this iconic Roman Catholic church is known for its soaring Gothic arches and bright red brick.

Every item that went into Notre Dame's construction was imported from France. The famous red-brick exterior is a product of Marseille. The pair of 190-foot bell towers were added in 1895, and still house functioning bells, though they are rarely used.

In front of the church is the **Our Lady of Peace statue,** completed in 1959 by an Italian sculptor and shipped from Rome. This is the second sculpture to stand in its place. The first was a statue of the Bishop Pigneau de Behaine, who helped Emperor Gia Long rise to power. The bishop's statue was removed in the 1940s. The red marble base upon which Our Lady of Peace now stands is a leftover from this original work.

Our Lady of Peace is one of Saigon's biggest

celebrities. Early in the morning, you can see local Catholics before the statue, hands folded in prayer. By the afternoon, she is the subject of countless tourist photos.

Notre Dame is most impressive when viewed from outside. Inside, a set of arched door frames give way to high ceilings crisscrossed with a wooden detail. Visitors are forbidden beyond the back area of the church, but it is still possible to see a few stained glass panels as well as a figure of Jesus above the altar. The alcoves on either side of the entrance house statues of the Virgin Mary and St. Anthony. Around each statue, stone tiles express reverence and thanks in French, English, and Vietnamese. To see the building in its entirety, attend the English version of Sunday mass at 9:30am, during which time you can gain full access to the main hall.

Central Post Office

On the eastern side of the Cong Xa Paris square is another vestige of French colonialism, the **Central Post Office** (2 Cong Xa Paris, D1, tel. 08/3924-7247, 7:30am-6pm daily). More reminiscent of a train station, this large building was designed by Gustave Eiffel. The massive clock and grand entrance are a favorite photo op among tourists. High yellow-and-green arches line either side of the vast hall. The two maps near the main entrance depict the Vietnam of an earlier time. No matter where you stand, you're sure to catch a glimpse of Vietnam's founding father, Ho Chi Minh, affectionately known as Uncle Ho, who watches over the building from a portrait mounted on the back wall.

The Central Post Office functions as the city's main postal hub. A number of other services are also available here, including international phone calls, which can be made from a tiny, antique wooden phone booth. There are also postcards available for purchase and a set of writing desks farther back if you want to send your postcard on the spot. You might also catch Duong Van Ngo, Saigon's last professional letter writer, hard at work. A post office employee since 1946, Ngo is fluent in

A Long Weekend in Ho Chi Minh City

As one of Vietnam's younger cities, Ho Chi Minh City has infectious energy. When experienced like a local, this massive, fast-paced behemoth is a wonderful place. Plan for three action-packed days around town, whizzing past the city's sights and enjoying all the sounds, smells, and vibrancy of life in Vietnam's largest metropolis.

DAY 1

Start your adventure at the **Reunification Palace** with a free guided tour. When you've finished, stroll through **30-4 Park,** stopping for a *ca phe bet* (sidewalk coffee) if you need a caffeine fix, or popping into one of the posh air-conditioned cafés nearby. The opposite end of the park opens onto **Notre Dame Cathedral** and the **Central Post Office.** From here, walk up toward **Turtle Lake** for lunch. There are plenty of options overlooking the roundabout, including the tasty **Vietnamese Noodles.** You can also head west to **Khoai** or **...hum** before spending the afternoon at the **War Remnants Museum.**

Head back toward the backpacker district as the day winds down, passing through **Tao Dan Park** en route. Stop by **Chill Skybar** for cocktails and bird's-eye views of the city, or simply rest up before heading off for dinner. District 1's Tan Dinh neighborhood is a good choice. For street food, **Banh Xeo 46A** offers a great introduction into local cuisine, while **Cuc Gach Quan** adds an upscale environment to its delicious Vietnamese menu. Not far from this area, seafood lovers will also appreciate **Quan Mien Cua 94 Cu.**

After dinner, return to the backpacker neighborhood for cheap **street beers** or a laid-back drink at **Le Pub.** Dance floors are abundant throughout this area, with live bands playing nightly at **Universal Bar** and **Thi Cafe.**

DAY 2

Jet out to **Cho Lon** first thing in the morning to explore Chinatown's enormous wholesale market. You can grab breakfast from one of the many market vendors before hitching a *xe om* ride over to **Thien Hau Pagoda,** stopping in at the nearby **Chaozhou Congregation**

English, French, and Vietnamese and specializes in both translating and writing letters.

OPERA HOUSE AREA

A block away from bustling Nguyen Hue, dapper security guards and lavish store displays signal a more upscale part of town.

Opera House

At the end of Le Loi Street, Saigon's **Opera House** (7 Cong Truong Lam Son, D1, tel. 08/3829-9976, www.hbso.org.vn), also known as the Municipal Theater, is a well-preserved historical gem and one of the city's oldest supporters of the arts. When the opera house opened in 1900, it became Saigon's premier center for the arts, hosting scores of ballets and musical acts, as well as other performances.

Following the end of the French colonial government, the building was transformed from a cultural center into the Lower Assembly of the Republic of Vietnam as part of the south's new administration. It remained a government office until the end of the war in 1975.

After reunification, the Opera House was restored to its original function as a performance space. Renovations later brought back its former architectural glory as well, and today it continues to hold cultural events in its 1,800-seat auditorium, showcasing both domestic and international performers. Outside of performances, the Opera House is normally closed to the public. Its exterior is the most impressive aspect, with a wide set of front steps and a massive arched facade.

Hall and **Cho Lon Mosque** while you're there. When you've had your fill of District 5, head back downtown to bustling **Ben Thanh Market** for shopping and lunch. Wander down **Le Loi** street, passing by the city's charming colonial **Hotel de Ville** building and the **Opera House** as you reach a more upscale part of town.

Enjoy a sunset drink at the **Rex Hotel** bar or from the rooftop of **Pacharan.** Dinner in this neighborhood is an international affair, with **Ciao Bella, The Refinery,** and **Pizza 4Ps** within walking distance, as well as a few local eateries, such as **Bo Tung Xeo** and the **Temple Club.**

For a night on the town, **Last Call,** a classy cocktail lounge, is nearby, as is **Phatty's,** an expat sports bar, and the dance floor of **Apocalypse Now.** The city's best live music venues are **Yoko** and **Q4.**

DAY 3

Spend your last day in the city with a local. Art enthusiasts can sign up for **Sophie's Art Tour** to learn more about Vietnam's history through the eyes of its artists. Foodies will appreciate **Back of the Bike Tours,** which go around town, savoring all the best local fare. If you prefer an activity, you can spend the morning honing your culinary skills with a **cooking class** or treat yourself at one of the city's **spas.**

When you're ready for lunch, pay a visit to the famous **Lunch Lady** for one of her tasty soups before walking to the **Jade Emperor Pagoda** nearby. From here, spend the rest of the afternoon unwinding at a café or wandering around the city.

Notre Dame Cathedral

Rex Hotel

On the northwest corner of the block is the **Rex Hotel** (141 Nguyen Hue, D1, tel. 08/3829-2185, www.rexhotelvietnam.com), yet another downtown building that has evolved according to Saigon's history. The Rex has survived many incarnations, from an early 20th-century French garage to an energetic trading center to a property of the American Cultural Center. Its greatest claim to fame is as the site of the American Information Service's daily press briefings during the war, better known as the "five o'clock follies," when foreign journalists would gather to hear news from the front lines. The five-star Rex boasts over 100 luxury rooms and a popular rooftop bar. There's not much to do here unless you're a guest, but it's worth passing by.

Hotel de Ville

Set back from Le Loi Street by a small, colorful garden is the **Hotel de Ville** (86 Le Thanh Ton, D1), a stunning colonial building from the turn of the 20th century. Set amid the old-world grandeur of the nearby buildings, the Hotel de Ville remains a piece of colonial Indochina in the modern age. The Vietnamese flag flies high above the French-made building. Now the home of the local People's Committee and the center of city government, the building is not open to the public.

BEN THANH MARKET AREA
★ Ben Thanh Market

Easily the most recognizable structure in Saigon, **Ben Thanh Market** (Le Loi and Tran

Opera House Area

NGUYỄN DU

CASBAH

MAI XUAN CANH

PACEY'S CUPCAKES

TRI BOOKS

NGON RESTAURANT

LA FENETRE SOLEIL

PASTEUR

0   100 yds
0   100 m

LÝ TỰ TRỌNG

LÝ TỰ TRỌNG

BO TUNG XEO

VINCOM CENTER B

HOTEL DE VILLE

LÊ THÁNH TÔN

LÊ THÁNH TÔN

RED DOOR DECO

THE REFINERY

SAIGON COOKING CLASS

SAIGON TOURIST LE THANH TON

VINCOM CENTER A

THI SÁCH

THÁI VĂN LUNG

THE REX HOTEL ROOFTOP BAR

THE REX HOTEL

NGUYỄN HUỆ

CÔNG TRƯỜNG LAM SƠN

LÊ LỢI

OPERA HOUSE

CÔNG TRƯỜNG LAM SƠN

CAO BÁ QUÁT

LÊ LỢI

LÊ LỢI

LÊ LỢI

L'USINE

SAIGON TAX TRADE CENTER

SAIGON TOURIST NGUYEN HUE

CARAVELLE HOTEL

PACHARAN

NGUYỄN THIỆP

NGUYỄN HUỆ

L'APOTHIQUAIRE

TAN HOANG LONG HOTEL

LAST CALL

SAIGON RIVER BOUTIQUE HOTEL

ĐỒNG DU

CIAO BELLA

HAI BÀ TRƯNG

THI SÁCH

ZEST BISTRO & CAFE

TÔN THẤT THIỆP

MẠC THỊ BƯỞI

LAC THAI

NGA ART & CRAFT

APOCALYPSE NOW

TÔN ĐỨC THẮNG

HUỲNH THÚC KHÁNG

ETHOPHEN

AUTHENTIQUE INTERIORS

VELVET

PHAN VĂN ĐẠT

HỒ HUẤN NGHIỆP

SAIGON RIVER EXPRESS

NGÔ ĐỨC KẾ

ĐỒNG KHỞI

NGUYỄN HUỆ

NGUYỄN HUỆ

BROMA

NHAN SUSHI

NGÔ ĐỨC KẾ

© AVALON TRAVEL

HẢI TRIỀU

NGUYỄN FRERES

HOTEL MAJESTIC

TÔN ĐỨC THẮNG

Hung Dao, D1, tel. 08/3829-2096, 6am-6pm daily) is the original commercial heart of the city and a prime spot for souvenir shopping, with over 3,000 small businesses and an army of multilingual vendors. Using the city's waterways to transport goods, Ben Thanh became the Vietnamese answer to Chinatown's Binh Tay Market, with each attracting traders from both their local communities and neighboring states. When the French arrived and began to incorporate their archibraintecture into Saigon's landscape, the market was formalized as a large, thatched-roof building near the river. Ben Thanh's present-day site is at the north edge of Quach Thi Trang roundabout. The building was completed in 1914 and dubbed the "New Ben Thanh Market."

Since its inception, Ben Thanh has been a major commercial hub and the site of many historical events. During the tumultuous 1950s and '60s, several significant protests occurred outside its massive gates. The most notable of these occurred on August 25, 1963, when thousands of students and Buddhist monks gathered at the roundabout in front of the market to protest American forces and the presidency of Ngo Dinh Diem. As the protest grew in size and strength, shots were fired to subdue the crowd and one young protester, 15-year-old student Quach Thi Trang, was killed. Since then, the roundabout has been referred to as Quach Thi Trang roundabout.

Vendors begin setting up as early as 4am each day. The outer shops open their doors first, followed by the market's main gates. Once the day market has closed its doors to the public, an equally popular night market sets up shop around the building on Phan Chu Trinh and Phan Boi Chau streets from 6pm until about midnight.

Mariamman Hindu Temple

The **Mariamman Hindu Temple** (45 Truong Dinh, D1, 7am-7pm daily), northwest of Ben Thanh Market, comes as a surprise with its colorful towers rising high out of the downtown traffic. The largest of three Hindu temples in the city, this shrine is dedicated to

Mariamman, the fickle south Indian goddess of rain and disease.

This temple was built in the late 19th century by Tamil immigrants and is today visited by the small remaining Hindu community and many local Vietnamese. Mariamman is housed inside a large central sanctuary and flanked by her two guardians: Maduraiveeran on the left and Pechiamman on the right. A walk around the back of these shrines reveals a series of brightly hued statues carved into the far wall.

Beside the entrance is a lion statue, which was once used for Hindu processions around the city. An impressive and beautifully decorated *rajagopuram* (tower) stands nearly 40 feet high, the tallest Hindu structure in Saigon, and features images of the temple's guardian as well as other Hindu deities.

Dress modestly when visiting and remove your shoes on the raised platform. Silence is observed indoors, and it is forbidden to enter the gated area surrounding the central sanctuary.

NGUYEN HUE STREET
Saigon Skydeck

Saigon Skydeck (2 Hai Trieu, D1, tel. 08/3915-6868, www.saigonskydeck.com, 9:30am-9:30pm daily, VND200,000), 49 stories above the city, is the official viewing platform of the lotus-shaped Bitexco Financial Tower. Standing at 262 meters (860 ft.), this is the tallest building to grace the city skyline. The tower boasts 68 floors, a shopping mall, several restaurants, and a helipad topped with a Vietnamese flag so large that it is visible from the street below.

The Bitexco opened its doors for the first time in 2010. A year later came the inauguration of the Skydeck, providing locals and tourists with a unique opportunity to see the city from above.

Since most of Saigon's buildings are low-lying structures, finding a bird's-eye view like this is no easy feat. On the 360-degree viewing deck, a series of displays help to orient visitors, offering snippets of historical information

Ben Thanh Market Area

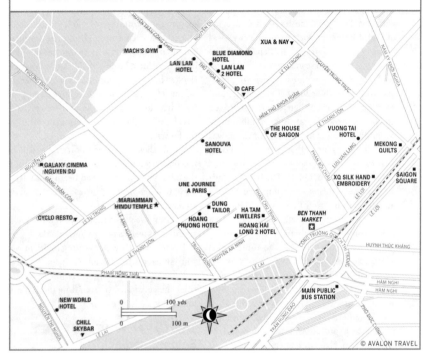

about the landscape and the buildings below. You can catch a close-up look at the city's more famous sights through the binoculars situated around the platform.

If you're looking for nice views and some peace and quiet, head a few floors up to **Alto** (tel. 08/6291-8752, www.cirrussaigon.com, 11am-2am daily, VND100,000-500,000), a bar on the 52nd floor. Prices are more expensive than other bars, but instead of shelling out cash to stand on the 49th floor, you get the added benefit of a seat and a drink, slightly higher up.

Sri Thendayuttaphani Hindu Temple

The **Sri Thendayuttaphani Hindu Temple** (66 Ton That Thiep, D1, 6am-7pm daily) is an interesting fusion of Hindu and Buddhist traditions. Built over 200 years ago, this structure

is the work of a once-thriving south Indian community. In its heyday, the temple was regularly used and Hindu processions took place in the streets of Saigon. After 1975, racial and religious persecution escalated and many south Indians fled the country.

The Sri Thendayuttaphani Temple worships both Hindu and Buddhist deities. In the main sanctuary, a statue of Thendayuttaphani, also known as Lord Muruga, sits at the center of the temple. Images of Hindu deities line the surrounding walls alongside famous Indian faces. Most notable is the photograph featuring former Indian Prime Minister Jawaharlal Nehru in a meeting with Ho Chi Minh. A statue of Quan Am, a popular Buddhist bodhisattva, sits on the right side of the courtyard. Hidden at the back of the temple is a statue of the Buddha.

Wear appropriate clothing and, when

Nguyen Hue Street

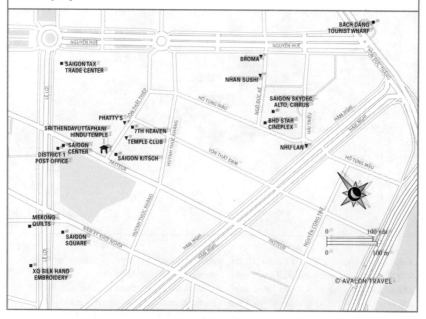

© AVALON TRAVEL

stepping onto the raised platform, remove your shoes. Before you leave, take the narrow staircase on the right up to the roof, where a single blue-and-white incense pot sits before the temple's colorful tower, covered with depictions of Hindu gods and goddesses.

NORTHERN DISTRICT 1
Saigon Zoo and Botanical Garden

Rounding out the eastern end of Le Duan Boulevard is the **Saigon Zoo and Botanical Garden** (2B Nguyen Binh Khiem, D1, tel. 08/3829-1425, www.saigonzoo.net, 7am-6pm daily, VND12,000), one of the oldest zoos in the world. Part menagerie, part beautiful park, and part children's carnival, this is a nice place to trade the urban chaos for a rare glimpse of nature in the bustling city. Once one of Saigon's nicest features, the zoo was first developed in 1864. Louis Adolph Germain, a military veterinarian with the French Expedition Army, was tasked with

developing the 12-hectare park's roads, animal cages, and nurseries.

The zoo section of the park has not retained its former glory. While the various plants, trees, and flowers packed onto the grounds provide a gorgeous backdrop for an afternoon stroll, the zoo would likely not be considered humane by Western standards due to small and crowded enclosures. Anyone sensitive to animal rights should avoid this part of the park.

Instead, stick to the shaded walkways and stone benches of the botanical garden or the butterfly garden, an enclosure often brimming with dozens of the brightly colored creatures. There is also a children's petting zoo (9am-11am and 2pm-4pm weekends) stocked with billy goats and sheep. If you prefer a quiet stroll around the gardens, it's best to go during the week.

HISTORY MUSEUM

Within the gates of the Saigon Zoo and Botanical Garden, the city's **History**

Northern District 1

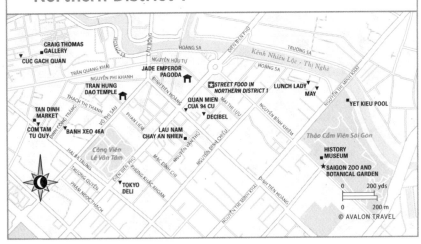

CRAIG THOMAS GALLERY
CUC GACH QUAN
HOÀNG SA
NGUYỄN HỮU TU
TRẦN QUANG KHẢI
NGUYỄN PHI KHANH
JADE EMPEROR PAGODA
HOÀNG SA
TRƯỜNG SA
Kênh Nhiêu Lộc - Thị Nghè
TRAN HUNG DAO TEMPLE
STREET FOOD IN NORTHERN DISTRICT 1
LUNCH LADY
MAY
THẠCH THỊ THANH
QUAN MIEN CUA 94 CU
YET KIEU POOL
TAN DINH MARKET
DECIBEL
COM TAM TU QUY
BANH XEO 46A
LAU NAM CHAY AN NHIEN
NGUYỄN BỈNH KHIÊM
Thảo Cầm Viên Sài Gòn
HAI BẢ TRUNG
Công Viên Lê Văn Tám
PHẠM LIÊN
MẠC ĐỈNH CHI
NGUYỄN VĂN THỦ
NGUYỄN BỈNH CHIỂU
HISTORY MUSEUM
SAIGON ZOO AND BOTANICAL GARDEN
TRƯỜNG QUYỀN
ĐIỆN BIÊN PHỦ
PHÙNG KHẮC KHOAN
ĐINH TIÊN HOÀNG
0   200 yds
PHẠM NGỌC THẠCH
TOKYO DELI
NGUYỄN THỊ MINH KHAI
0   200 m
© AVALON TRAVEL

Museum (2 Nguyen Binh Khiem, D1, tel. 08/3829-8146, www.baotanglichsuvn.com, 8am-11am and 1:30pm-4:30pm Tues.-Sun., VND15,000) has seen several iterations, from ancient Asian art museum to the country's national museum. It's been the History Museum since 1979. The beautiful grounds surrounding the building add to its already-stunning colonial architecture, which bears the telltale yellow paint and sloping roof of many early 20th century structures in the city.

The museum's exhibits are divided into two parts: Vietnam's cultural history, from 5,000 years ago until the mid-20th century; and the ancient art of some of Vietnam's southern minorities, including the Champa and the Oc Eo. Though many of the more modern exhibits feature beautiful, functional pieces—lacquer trays, ceramic vases, ivory trinkets—there is little signage or additional information. The most educational exhibits are the Champa and Oc Eo sections, in which a few simple placards guide you through the Hindu and Buddhist influences that helped create these works of art.

There are no photographs allowed without a photo ticket (VND32,000), though most visitors won't feel the need. There are also traditional water puppet shows here (six shows daily, VND50,000).

Directly across from the museum is the **Hung Kings Temple**, which is guarded by a famous Ho Chi Minh quotation carved onto a large stone slab: "The Hung Kings built this country; we must uphold it." This building once served as a memorial honoring the Vietnamese soldiers who died during WWI. After 1954, locals began coming here to worship the historic Hung Kings. The temple is an impressive structure, particularly inside, where its walls and ceiling are full of ornate red-and-gold carvings. Taking photos is allowed within the temple, but ask permission first.

Jade Emperor Pagoda

Just off busy Dien Bien Phu street sits the **Jade Emperor Pagoda (Chua Phuoc Hai)** (73 Mai Thi Luu, D1, 7am-6pm daily), one of Saigon's more prominent places of worship. Cantonese immigrants completed the building in the late 19th and early 20th centuries, though it was never meant to be a pagoda. Phuoc Hai originally belonged to followers of Minh Su, one of the five syncretic religions brought to Vietnam by the Chinese, and was only later handed over to the Buddhist Association to ensure its preservation.

Inside, massive wooden warriors loom just beyond the main doorway, guarding the entrance to the pagoda. Locals usually pay respects to these imposing figures before heading into the main hall, where the King of Heaven and his court sit, waiting to decide who is admitted into paradise. On the left side of the hall, a series of wood carvings depict the 10 levels of hell in gruesome detail.

Turn right out of this room, follow the signs reading "Dien Quan Am," and take the wooden staircase up to where the goddess of fertility resides. Less fearsome than her counterparts downstairs, she is often visited by pregnant women and those hoping to conceive. A small balcony at the top of the staircase offers up-close views of the pagoda's elaborate roof.

Outside of the narrow corridor beside the main hall is a small pond brimming with turtles of varying size; this is why the pagoda is also called the Tortoise Pagoda. Out front, vendors sell fish and baby turtles, which can be released into their respective ponds. With Phuoc Hai's already-overcrowded waters, it's better to leave these creatures where they are.

DISTRICT 3
Turtle Lake

Turtle Lake (Cong Truong Quoc Te, D3, daily 24 hours), an enormous circle surrounded by several cafés, used to be known as Soldier's Park, where bronze statues honored the fallen French soldiers of WWI. Not long before his assassination in 1963, then-president Ngo Dinh Diem did away with the French park, and his successor, General Nguyen Van Thieu, used the land to erect the monument you see today: a large, somewhat murky pond sitting beneath a series of concrete walkways and a statue of a towering lotus, the national flower of Vietnam. The park originally included a statue of a turtle, but it was destroyed shortly after Saigon fell in 1975. The statue was never replaced, but the name stuck.

During the day, vendors gather around the park, selling snacks and refreshments to office workers and students. The higher floors of the surrounding cafés make a good spot to take a break and people-watch over a *ca phe sua da* (Vietnamese iced coffee with milk). This is a good stop en route to the War Remnants Museum and the rest of District 3's sights.

★ War Remnants Museum

The **War Remnants Museum** (28 Vo Van Tan, D3, tel. 08/3930-6325, www.baotangc-hungtichchientranh.vn, 7:30am-noon and 1:30pm-5pm daily, VND15,000), located behind the Reunification Palace, is one of the city's most-visited sights. This museum serves as an important reminder of Vietnam's recent past and a conflict that many locals remember firsthand.

During the years between the end of the American War and the country's normalization of relations with the United States in 1993, this building housed the Museum of Chinese and American War Crimes. Though the name has changed, the sentiment remains largely the same: each floor of the building touches upon a different topic, from the global community's fierce opposition toward U.S. involvement in Vietnam to the atrocities committed by American soldiers against Vietnamese civilians. Though several of these exhibits are laden with propaganda, they paint an accurate picture of the struggles that many Vietnamese endured during the war and continue to face today.

Outside the main building, military vehicles line the border of the property, including a helicopter and different types of tanks, all of which were used during the conflict. There is also a smaller exhibit dedicated to tiger cages, the brutal form of punishment once used at the infamous Con Dao and Phu Quoc prisons, where thousands of Vietnamese were tortured and often died at the hands of their captors.

Allow yourself plenty of time, as the building shuts down promptly at midday so that employees can break for lunch and all guests are ushered off the premises until 1:30pm. Most people spend about two hours here, so plan your visit either in the early morning or the early afternoon. While this is a valuable and eye-opening experience for locals and foreigners, it is not an easy place to visit. Families with children should steer clear, as some of the exhibits are graphic.

Tan Xa Palace

The oldest private residence in the city is **Tan Xa Palace** (180 Nguyen Dinh Chieu, D3, tel. 08/3930-3828, 8am-5pm daily), a small, one-room building hidden in the shadow of the lavish Archbishop's residence. Now a chapel, this modest structure is credited to the man who would later become Emperor Gia Long. Before ascending the throne, Nguyen Phuc Anh arranged its construction in 1790 as a thank-you gift to then-Bishop Pigneau de Behaine for his help in reclaiming his family's power after the Tay Son rebellion. The place later became a home for missionaries and bishops before being converted into a chapel.

It is possible to see the palace up close, but you can also get a good feel for it from the street, where you can look through the fence to see the decaying wood of the structure. To get on the property, check with the security guard at the side gate, located on Tran Quoc Thao street, before entering. The chapel itself is no longer in use and no one is permitted inside, but the neighboring buildings are functioning offices for the local Catholic church.

Vinh Nghiem Pagoda

Before you can even see the building, the 40-meter, seven-tiered tower of **Vinh Nghiem Pagoda** (339 Nam Ky Khoi Nghia, D3, tel. 08/3848-3153, www.vinhnghiemvn.com, 6:30am-11:30am and 1pm-6pm daily) alerts you to the largest Buddhist structure in Saigon. Built in 1971, this fairly modern complex is comprised of not only a pagoda but also a library and classrooms for Buddhist study. Three staircases lead up to the main hall, an open space that becomes jam-packed during holidays and special occasions. Inside, the front half of the pagoda is used for Buddhist ceremonies and worship, with religious paintings and other artwork lining the walls. A walk around the main altar reveals hundreds of tiles commemorating the dead, which are kept behind glass at the back.

Outside, the corners of the pagoda's impressive roof curl skyward in the northern style, and its stark, gray tower rises high above the surrounding structures. Though it is not possible to enter the tower itself, visitors can look out over bustling Nam Ky Khoi

War Remnants Museum

District 3

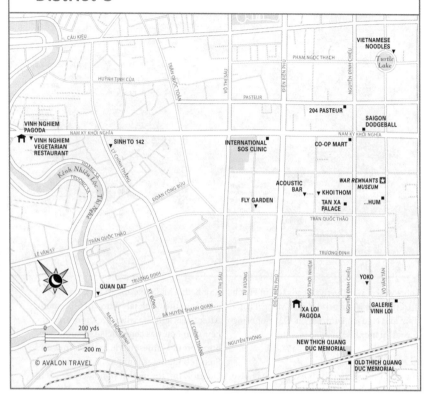

Nghia street from the balcony and admire the maze of Buddhist flags zigzagging across the complex.

Xa Loi Pagoda

Xa Loi Pagoda (89B Ba Huyen Thanh Quan, D3, tel. 08/3930-7605, 7am-11am and 2pm-5pm daily) has seen a lot in its short history. Originally built to house sacred relics of the Shakyamuni Buddha, this pagoda is known as a major center of Buddhist study. Today the sacred relics can be seen in a red compartment above the enormous Buddha residing in the main hall.

Xa Loi is also known for its outspoken opposition to the government of south Vietnam in the early 1960s. Most notably, on the morning of June 11, 1963, the Venerable Thich Quang Duc, a senior monk at Xa Loi, sat in the middle of a busy downtown intersection and, surrounded by supporters, lit himself on fire in response to President Ngo Dinh Diem's religious persecution. He was the first of several monks who completed this act of protest against Diem's government.

Today, Xa Loi is a quiet place, equipped with a library and study center. Two massive staircases curve up to the main hall of the pagoda, an airy room that houses one large floor-to-ceiling Buddha as well as several smaller statues. Both outside and in, Buddhist flags sway in the breeze, and a smaller statue honors Quan Am, the most well-known female bodhisattva in Mahayana Buddhism. A

Cho Lon

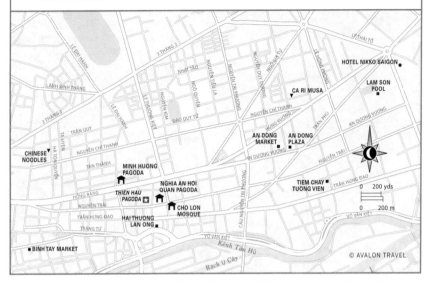

short walk down the road leads to the **Thich Quang Duc Memorial** (Cach Mang Thang Tam and Nguyen Dinh Chieu, D3), honoring the fallen monk.

CHO LON

If you think District 1 is busy, meet its noisy neighbor to the west. The farther you travel along the Saigon River, the faster the motorbikes begin to move, speeding down wide and hectic Vo Van Kiet street. Buses blare their siren-like horns into the fray, followed by cars, transport trucks, and the occasional motorized tractor, chugging along with its cargo.

Binh Tay Market

One look at the massive entrance of **Binh Tay Market** (57A Thap Muoi, D6, tel. 08/3857-1512, 7am-7pm daily) is all it takes to understand how the trading center got its name. Still known by locals as Cho Lon—"big market" in Vietnamese—this mammoth building was constructed in the late 1800s. Cho Lon drew traders and businessmen from across the city as well as from neighboring countries, such as

Cambodia, Malaysia, and India. Cho Lon fast grew into the wholesale market of the south. After the original location grew too large, the new Cho Lon was constructed, using a combination of Chinese-style architecture and French building techniques. A small bust of Quach Dam, the market's founder, stands in the center of the market.

Binh Tay is a major commercial center in the city, housing over 2,300 separate stalls and serving not only the large Chinese-Vietnamese community nearby—roughly a quarter of the vendors within the market are ethnic Chinese—but also the rest of the city. The bustle inside the market embodies much of the pace at which this part of Saigon moves, buzzing with activity from morning until night.

★ Thien Hau Pagoda

The teetering, haphazard, multi-story houses of Chinatown mix with the shops and offices of a modern city. But stuck firmly in a bygone era is **Thien Hau Pagoda** (710 Nguyen Trai, D5, 6am-5:30pm daily), a beautiful building constructed in 1780. Southern

Chinese refugees arrived in south Vietnam and began to settle around the Cho Lon area, then known as Tai Ngon. The Chinese expressed their thanks to Thien Hau, goddess of the sea, by crafting the ornate wood carvings and terra-cotta scenes depicted around this pagoda. This single-story structure shows its age gracefully in the worn exterior and intricate designs on the roof.

Before you step inside you'll be accosted by a wave of incense, which burns ceaselessly from the massive pots indoors, not to mention a collection of incense coils that hang from the ceiling. Flanking the walls on either side of the pagoda are stone engravings that list the building's benefactors over the years. The final third of the main hall is easily the most impressive. Vivid red and gold adorns the building's columns, while up above countless incense coils twist and flutter in the breeze. Dozens of locals and foreigners pay their respects with incense sticks, candles, and other offerings, which are available for purchase. A statue of Thien Hau sits at the back, ornate and heavily decorated. The pagoda is one of the more unique buildings in Saigon. Despite the click of cameras and the curious tourists, locals are friendly and seemingly unaffected by the many foreign visitors.

Chaozhou Congregation Hall

A short walk down the road from Thien Hau Pagoda is the newer and bigger **Chaozhou Congregation Hall (Nghia An Hoi Quan)** (678 Nguyen Trai, D5, 6am-6pm daily), obscured by a high stone wall. Honoring the great Chinese general Quan Cong, this structure is the work of the local Chaozhou Chinese Congregation. The gilded woodwork of the exterior forms a splash of color that runs along the thick cylindrical beams of the building and up to the detailing on the roof.

Inside, a statue of a red-faced Quan Cong sits, beard in hand, at the center of the pagoda, with his horse tucked on the left of the entrance. Farther into the pagoda, bright neon hues contrast against a pair of stone walls. Remove your shoes as you step onto the raised platform at the back, where a larger statue of the general sits, flanked by towers of golden figurines and other ornamentation. Look up: Much of this building's stunning decor and architecture is tucked inside the rafters of the high-ceilinged structure.

Cho Lon Mosque

A marked contrast from the colorful ornamentation of nearby pagodas, the pastel blue **Cho Lon Mosque** (641 Nguyen Trai, D5,

A pair of colorful dragons top the roof of Chaozhou Congregation Hall.

tel. 08/3950-8661, 4:30am-6:30pm daily) is easy to miss amid the hectic market outside its front door. This no-frills building became a house of worship for Tamil immigrants in 1932. After 1975, much of the Tamil community left Vietnam. Today, the mosque serves mostly Malaysian and Indonesian Muslims living in the city, though there are also a few Vietnamese believers. To the left of the entrance is an ablutions pool, where the religious wash before praying, and opposite the entrance of the mosque is a Halal restaurant serving mostly Malaysian dishes.

Minh Huong Pagoda

Near the corner of Thuan Kieu street just a block north of the string of pagodas lining Nguyen Trai is the **Minh Huong Pagoda** (184 Hong Bang, D5, 6am-5pm daily), also known as the Phuoc An Assembly Hall. Originally completed in the late 19th century by immigrants from the Guangdong, Fujian, and Zhejiang provinces of China, this vibrant building once stood beside the Cho Lon Railway Station. In the small courtyard out front, statues of the Buddha and Quan Am, a popular Buddhist bodhisattva, flank the main entrance. The pagoda's front door features a beautiful, iridescent red lacquer, but

its most unique element is the collection of mosaic incense pots throughout the pagoda. Carefully tiled with colorful patterned pieces of broken china, these massive standing pots catch your eye amid a main hall full of vivid embellishment. At the back of the hall, famous Chinese general Quan Cong sits in the middle, accompanied by Ong Bon, a Fujianese god, on the left and the Ngu Hanh goddesses of the five elements on the right. Above the red, yellow, and green decor, enormous incense coils burn slowly, taking as long as a full month to burn down.

Fito Museum of Traditional Medicine

Slightly off the beaten path, the **Fito Museum of Traditional Medicine** (41 Hoang Du Khuong, D10, tel. 08/864-2430, www.fitomuseum.com.vn, 8:30am-5pm daily, VND50,000) is an unusual and worthy attraction that is slowly gaining popularity among tourists. It's owned and operated by the Fito Pharmaceutical Company, which produces and sells traditional Vietnamese remedies within Vietnam and abroad. The energetic museum staff are eager to educate visitors on the nation's long history of traditional medicine. Designed to reflect Vietnamese

Incense coils hang from the ceiling at Minh Huong Pagoda.

architecture in various parts of the country, from the northern structures of Hanoi down to Mekong Delta-style houses, the museum is filled with dozens of artifacts dating as far back as a few thousand years. Free guided tours cover the origins of Vietnamese medicine, the many plant and animal ingredients involved in traditional remedies, and the practices of traditional Vietnamese pharmacists. The tour ends downstairs with a cup of tea and a chance to peruse the museum's small shop of traditional medicine, including teas and oils.

Though it's never busy, the museum sees a steady stream of visitors; there is almost always someone available to lead a tour. Informational pamphlets are available at the front desk for guests who arrive after a tour has begun. Photos are also allowed here and even encouraged on the third floor, where visitors can try on traditional Vietnamese garb and snap a picture with the museum's collection of grinding apparatuses, once used by pharmacists.

If there's time, swing by Hai Thuong Lan Ong street near Binh Tay Market, better known as the traditional medicine street, where dozens of traditional pharmacists sell their remedies.

GIAC LAM PAGODA

About four miles outside of downtown, **Giac Lam Pagoda** (565 Lac Long Quan, D Tan Binh, tel. 08/865-3933, www.chuagiaclam.net, 6am-noon and 2pm-8pm daily) is the city's oldest pagoda. A large, open complex made up of several buildings, the grounds of Giac Lam boast over 100 statues of the Buddha as well as a staggering collection of shrines honoring the relatives of local residents.

In the seven-tiered tower just inside the gates, each floor houses a different statue of the Buddha or a popular bodhisattva. This is one of the only Buddhist towers in the city that you can ascend. Though the very top is off-limits to visitors, a narrow balcony on each floor offers a nice view of the surrounding area.

Beyond the tower is a small garden decorated with dozens of miniature idols as well as a large statue of Quan Am, one of Buddhism's most famous bodhisattva. A second set of gates leads into the main building, where dozens more Buddhas are on display, as well as headstones and nameplates with ages and birth dates scrawled across lacquer plaques and stone carvings.

The largest statue of all, a towering white Buddha, sits cross-legged to the right of the main walkway. Another small garden precedes the main pagoda, while the far end of the complex is home to a series of ornate tombs belonging to the pagoda's founders.

TOURS

There are scores of travel agencies in the city that offer half- and full-day tours. Larger companies like **Sinh Tourist** (246-248 De Tham, D1, tel. 08/3838-9593, www.thesinhtourist.vn, 6:30am-10:30pm daily) and **TNK Travel** (220 De Tham, D1, tel. 08/3920-4766, www.tnktravelvietnam.com, 7am-10pm daily) provide inexpensive, cookie-cutter tours to most of the city's major sights and cost VND150,000-350,000. Though by far the most inexpensive option, these tour buses often shepherd groups of 20-30 people around town. Being on such a large tour diminishes the experience, as it can be difficult to hear the tour guide or get much of the benefit that paying for a tour is meant to provide.

If you can afford to pay more, go with **Asiana Travelmate** (113C Bui Vien, D1, tel. 08/3838-6678, www.asianatravelmate.com, 8am-9pm daily), which caps its tour groups at 10 people; the smaller vehicle minimizes the time spent squeezing through Saigon's busy streets on a massive tourist bus.

Motorbike Tours

Hands down, the ultimate way to experience the city is as most locals do—on a motorbike. **XO Tours** (tel. 09/3308-3727, www.xotours.vn, 9am-10pm daily, VND798,000-1,428,000) does just that, ferrying visitors around town on the back of a scooter. In addition to visiting the city's major sights, XO provides tours tailored to food, nightlife, and shopping, all with experienced, traditionally clad local guides who double as motorbike drivers. The same goes for **Vietnam Vespa Adventures** (169A De Tham, D1, tel. 012/2299-3585, www.vietnamvespaadventures.com, 7am-2am daily, VND1,239,000-2,499,000), which runs food and nightlife city tours as well as one-day trips to the Mekong Delta.

Foodies should book a trip with **Back of the Bike Tours** (tel. 09/3504-6910, www.backofthebiketours.com, 9am-10pm daily, VND966,000-2,730,000), the brainchild of husband-and-wife team Chad and Thuy Kubanoff, a pair with a serious passion for the city and its delectable street food. Tours leave from District 1 and take guests outside of Saigon's central area to dine in some of the less-visited neighborhoods, offering a more unique, authentic take on Vietnam's southern hub.

Cultural Tours

For a unique perspective on Vietnamese history and art, sign up for **Sophie's Art Tour** (tel. 09/3375-2402, www.sophiesarttour.com, 9am-1pm Tues.-Sat., VND950,000). A long-time Saigon resident and the former curator of local Galerie Quynh, Sophie Hughes spent over a year researching and compiling this living project, which tells the tumultuous history of 20th-century Vietnam through its greatest artists. Divided into four chapters, the tour whisks visitors to a series of private galleries as well as the Fine Arts Museum, focusing on different aspects of local history before and after colonialism and the American War. Sophie's interactive approach and continuing research keep the story fresh, adding new anecdotes and information all the time and encouraging visitors to get involved. The tour leaves from a small café in District 3 and its fee includes transportation as well as admission to museums, cold drinks, and, of course, the expertise of a local resident.

A must for history buffs is one of Tim Doling's **Saigon and Cho Lon Heritage Tours** (leave from Caravelle Saigon, 19 Cong Truong Lam Son, www.historicvietnam.com, 7:50am Tues.-Fri., VND1,000,000). Through a combination of walking and driving, Doling—the author of Exploring Ho Chi Minh City, a guide to the southern hub's historical sights—takes travelers on a journey through either downtown or Chinatown for an in-depth look at some of the city's lesser-known history. Saigon tours run Tuesdays and Thursdays, while visits to Cho Lon are every Wednesday and Friday. Pre-booking is essential.

Entertainment and Events

NIGHTLIFE

As the sun sets over Saigon, street barbecues and curbside watering holes pop up all over town, serving a variety of *do nhau* (drinking food) and slinging bottles of Saigon Red and Tiger Beer.

Though there are hundreds of bars across town, the best of the city's nightlife is in District 1. For backpacker bars and nonstop activity, head to Bui Vien, where there is always a party. Drinks are dirt-cheap and most places have nightly specials. More spacious and slightly more expensive environments can be found down the narrow streets surrounding Nguyen Hue and the Opera House, where laid-back lounge options abound, not to mention larger expat bars and a handful of trendy nightclubs. Saigon is big on rooftop venues, which are a nice place to take in the city at night, removed from the bustle down below.

Petty theft is common during daylight hours; this problem only increases at night. When heading out on the town, take only the essentials, travel in groups, and opt for taxis over motorbikes where possible. There have been instances in which passengers have been accosted on a *xe om* and robbed, sometimes by a thief in cahoots with the motorbike driver. Though it's just as likely that won't have trouble in the evening, it's best to keep your wits about you and an eye on your belongings at all times.

Bars

OPERA HOUSE AREA

On the far corner of Lam Son Square behind the Opera House, Spanish restaurant and bar **Pacharan** (97 Hai Ba Trung, D1, tel. 08/3825-6024, www.pacharansaigon.com, 10am-late daily, VND40,000-130,000) has different atmospheres, depending on which floor you visit. Downstairs, a classy bar area serves up beer and spirits as well as handcrafted cocktails to a more mellow crowd, while the floor above buzzes with activity several nights a week when a Cuban band performs in the cramped quarters that house the upstairs bar—and sometimes on the bar itself. A dining room takes up the third story, while Pacharan's rooftop is furnished with comfy couches and a stunning corner view of the street below. Drinks are more expensive here, but well worth the price for the extra quality. Both the extensive wine list and sangria are particularly good.

Open well past most other venues in the city, **Last Call** (59 Dong Du, D1, tel. 09/3314-6711, www.lastcallsaigon.com, 5pm-3am daily, VND200,000-600,000) is a chic and cozy spot to end the evening. Decked out in animal print cushions and smoked glass, the dimly lit bar houses an extensive collection of wine, beer, and liquor and prides itself on its artisan cocktails and the Motown playlist that runs from open 'til close. The bar is located across from the Saigon Sheraton and often has regular drink specials, like its half-off Tuesday deal, as well as weekend promotions and events.

NGUYEN HUE STREET

As the day winds down and late afternoon slips into early evening, **The Rex Hotel Rooftop Bar** (141 Nguyen Hue, D1, tel. 08/3829-2185, www.rexhotelvietnam.com, 7am-1am daily, VND100,000-300,000) provides the perfect vantage point from which to watch the chaos of rush hour. Perched atop the corner real estate of this iconic building, the rooftop bar boasts excellent handcrafted cocktails and a few signature drinks. These are best enjoyed during the "five o'clock follies" happy hour, as the discount makes prices more manageable and the timing is perfect to catch the sun setting over Saigon's famous buildings, including the Opera House and the Hotel de Ville.

On the corner of Ngo Duc Ke and Nguyen Hue, **Broma** (41 Nguyen Hue, D1, tel. 08/3823-6838, bromasaigonbar@gmail.com, 4pm-2am daily, VND80,000-140,000) has made a name for itself among the younger expat crowd, mostly for its laid-back rooftop seating. Take the narrow staircase up and past its dimly lit indoor bar and you'll find a small-but-steady flow of people enjoying the cozy open-air terrace, which is decked out in tea lights and greenery. Though Nguyen Hue is a major thoroughfare during the day, the street all but closes down after dark, making this a nice spot for a quiet drink. The bar is usually open late; closing time depends on the number of customers, so don't be surprised if you arrive in the wee hours to find that they've already closed for the evening.

For the same sports bar atmosphere with a little more air-conditioning and a little less noise, **Phatty's** (46-48 Ton That Thiep, D1, tel. 08/3821-0796, www.phattysbar.com, 8am-11pm daily, VND40,000-320,000) is a popular expat haunt just off Nguyen Hue. Serving beer, cocktails, and hearty pub food, the bar keeps a schedule of major sporting events, which it plays on the multiple televisions around the bar, and exudes a bit more class than its Pham Ngu Lao counterparts.

BEN THANH MARKET AREA

Starting around late afternoon, dozens of plastic stools begin to appear on Bui Vien. This is a good place to start, as beers are inexpensive and the setup makes it easy to meet other travelers. As the evening goes on, the crowd of backpackers creeps out onto the street, making it hard to tell that this real estate actually belongs to several different businesses. Each small shop slings a variety of cheap local beers. To get an idea of the chaotic ambience and shoulder-to-shoulder seating, head to **Bia Sai Gon** (73 Bui Vien, D1, tel. 09/1829-2393, 5pm-1am daily, VND12,000-18,000) for an ice-cold brew and a street-side view of the action.

For more space and a proper chair, nearby **Universal Bar** (90 Bui Vien, D1, tel. 012/0887-2248, www.universalbarsaigon.com, 10am-3am daily, VND35,000-105,000) is right in the mix of the busy backpacker scene and boasts beer, liquor, a dart board, several international sports channels, and live music nightly from 9:30pm. The bartenders are chatty, and the place tends to get busy as soon as the music begins.

Down the road, the **Spotted Cow** (111 Bui Vien, D1, tel. 08/3920-7670, www.alfrescosgroup.com, 11am-1am daily, VND20,000-90,000) is a more spacious version of a sports bar, if a little more laid-back, with loads of beers and cocktails to choose from, plus a dart board and TV coverage of most major sporting events. Top-notch pub food is served and there is a weekly trivia night on Thursdays, when the bar opens up its rooftop seating for all pub quiz participants.

Just off Bui Vien near the looming neon sign of Crazy Buffalo, **Thi Cafe** (224 De Tham, D1, tel. 08/2210-2929, www.thicafe.com, 6pm-2am daily, VND60,000-120,000) has the best of both worlds with a lively bar area downstairs and relaxed, comfortable seating up top. The house band starts to play around 10pm every night, turning the narrow area around the bar into a dance floor and sending the noise level through the roof. For a livelier scene, stay downstairs, where it gets busy around 11pm, or if you prefer to sit and chat, head upstairs and grab one of the cushioned seats along the wall.

You'll find a good mix of young locals, expats, and backpackers at the cheap but trendy **Le Pub** (175/22 Pham Ngu Lao, D1, tel. 08/3837-7679, 9am-2am daily, VND35,000-130,000), a black-and-orange establishment down the wide alley off Bui Vien east of De Tham street. In addition to its local offerings, Le Pub serves imported European beers and reasonably priced cocktails. Keep an eye out for drink specials, too, as there tends to be a different one every evening, not to mention a handful of weekly events. The bar offers indoor and outdoor seating; if you don't mind the heat then you're better off sitting outside, as the interior can be cramped. This is a good place to brush up on your Vietnamese: On the back of each staff member's shirt is a popular drinking slogan.

Twenty-six stories above the city, **Chill Skybar** (26th and 27th Fl., AB Tower, 76A Le Lai, D1, tel. 08/3827-2372, www.chillsaigon.com, 5:30pm-2am daily, VND150,000-350,000) is worth a visit for its view. Though drink prices are steep, the outdoor bar boasts a 180-degree panorama of the downtown area that becomes all the more impressive at night, when Saigon is lit up and motorbike headlights race along the darkened streets. To save a little cash, time your visit between 5:30pm and 8pm, when half-off happy hour specials make cocktail prices reasonable. Be aware that the bar enforces a strict dress code, which Chill describes as "smart casual": no flip-flops, shorts, athletic clothing, or men in sleeveless tank tops. There is an indoor lounge and restaurant area if you prefer to admire the view from inside, though these are equally overpriced. For a quieter but equally upscale atmosphere, grab a drink one floor below at **Sorae** (24th Fl., AB Tower, 76A Le Lai, D1, tel. 08/3827-2372, www.soraesushi.com, 11:30am-2pm, 5:30pm-2am daily).

Lounges
OPERA HOUSE AREA

Squeezed down an alley so tiny you could miss it, **Casbah** (59 Nguyen Du, D1, tel. 08/3824-5130, 8am-11pm daily, VND40,000-120,000) is a hip cocktail and shisha (hookah) lounge with a stunning rooftop opposite the Notre Dame Cathedral. Decked out in dozens of plush blue-and-white cushions and Arab-style arches, Casbah makes for a great place to unwind at the end of the day, though this may not be your first impression upon entering the lounge: The music blaring inside is enough to make your ears burn, so don't both with the interior. Rather, take the narrow, winding staircase on the left up to the roof and sit there, where it is both cooler and quieter. Drinks are reasonably priced and a variety of beers and cocktails are offered, as well as non-alcoholic beverages. Shisha is available for VND180,000.

Tucked away above a pharmacy on the corner of Ly Tu Trong and Pasteur, **La Fenetre Soleil** (44 Ly Tu Trong, D1, tel. 08/3824-5994, lafenetre@hcm.vnn.vn, 9am-midnight daily, VND70,000-110,000) oozes cool. This trendy night spot is home to a cozy interior room surrounded by low couches and tables lining the outer wall. Regular live music and DJ events take place, though it's definitely a more laid-back vibe than you'll find in downtown nightclubs. While the lounge doesn't have a website, La Fenetre Soleil updates its Facebook page regularly to reflect upcoming events, and it also doubles as a café and restaurant during the day, when the countless windows around the exterior make it a bright and pleasant place to spend an afternoon.

NORTHERN DISTRICT 1

An increasingly important player in the city's art scene, **Decibel** (79/2/5 Phan Ke Binh, D1, tel. 08/6271-0115, www.decibel.vn, 7:30am-midnight Mon.-Sat., VND35,000-130,000) is a unique café, restaurant, and lounge hidden down one of District 1's quieter streets. The place holds nightly events, from its free food Tuesdays to music trivia nights and film screenings, in addition to regularly showcasing work from foreign and local artists in the downstairs area. Most of Decibel's events take place in the black-and-white-decorated first floor. For more comfortable seating and color, head upstairs, where bright turquoise walls and Victorian-style couches await. Beer and cocktails are available, as well as coffee, smoothies, and excellent Western dishes.

Nightclubs
OPERA HOUSE AREA

Thumping music and spacious dance floors have turned **Apocalypse Now** (2C Thi Sach, D1, tel. 08/3825-6124, www.apocalypsesaigon.com, 7pm-2am daily, VND80,000-200,000) into a local institution. The self-proclaimed "first nightclub in Saigon" is slightly removed from Pham Ngu Lao, but is still frequented by the backpacker set, blasting bass-filled hits well into the night. Its smaller outdoor area makes for a good spot to relax, but most of the action happens indoors, where several rooms play different genres of music.

A massive compound on the corner of Dinh Tien Hoang, **Lush** (2 Ly Tu Trong, D1, tel. 08/3824-2496, www.lush.vn, 8pm-late daily, VND90,000-150,000) is one of the city's best-known clubs due to its ladies' nights (9pm-midnight Tues.). When it gets busy at 10:30pm, it brings together the local population, from a handful of tourists to expats and locals. The DJ sets up just beyond the large circular bar at the center of the room. There are quieter areas to sit at the back of the club and just beside the main entrance. Ladies' night here is a fun, cheap night on the town, but it's not worth visiting on other days, as it gets less crowded and drinks are overpriced. The dress code requires semi-formal attire.

Not far from the Me Linh roundabout on Dong Khoi, **Velvet** (26 Ho Huan Nghiep, D1, tel. 08/3822-2262, velvet.bar.saigon@gmail.com, 9pm-2am daily, VND90,000-150,000) is one of the city's nicer nightclub venues, featuring reasonably priced cocktails and plenty of room to dance. Velvet has special promotions most nights and several DJs spin current

Western tracks throughout the week. The club gets busiest on weekends and on Wednesday ladies' nights. Bottles can be purchased for around VND2,000,000. Nice attire is required to enter the club.

Fuse (138 Le Lai, tel. 09/4666-1166, www. fuse.vn, 9pm-2am Tues.-Sun., VND100,000-300,000) has fast become one of the most popular nightclubs in town. Featuring a host of talented local DJs as well as the occasional international act, Fuse's generous dance floor and mezzanine are packed most weekends with a young, local crowd. The place starts to get busy around 11pm. Smart clothes are required to enter, so dress to impress.

Live Music

One of Saigon's pioneer music venues, **Yoko** (22A Nguyen Thi Dieu, D3, tel. 08/3933-0577, 8am-11:30pm daily, VND80,000-120,000) was once an intimate one-room venue packed with couches and a precarious wooden balcony. Nowadays, the venue boasts a bigger stage and more comfortable seating. The atmosphere is very laid-back and the venue remains cozy enough that you can enjoy the show no matter where you sit. Talented local musicians appear nightly from 9pm, performing rock-infused covers of old and new hits.

Easily the only venue of its kind in the city, **Sax N Art Jazz Club** (28 Le Loi, D1, tel. 08/3822-8472, www.saxnart.com, 5pm-midnight daily, VND80,000) is the pet project of master saxophonist Tran Manh Tuan, one of Vietnam's renowned jazz musicians. With eight solo albums to his credit, Tuan operates and often performs at the club. The long, narrow building makes for a great performance space, and a rotating group of Vietnamese and foreign musicians joins the mix. Live music begins at 9pm, at which time a cover charge is enforced. Drinks run a little expensive, around VND100,000 per cocktail.

A popular, if a little cramped, live music venue is **Acoustic Bar** (6E1 Ngo Tho Nhiem, D3, tel. 08/3930-2329, 7pm-11:30pm daily, VND70,000-120,000), set at the back of an alley packed with cafés and karaoke lounges.

While Acoustic often features sugary, pop-fueled performances, the bar feels intimate, with a lively audience lined up shoulder-to-shoulder in front of the stage. Live music starts at 8pm every day, and you'll catch a crowd of young Vietnamese hanging out here.

The cavernous **Q4** (7 Nguyen Tat Thanh, D4, tel. 08/6291-8587, www.saigonsoundsystem.com, 4pm-midnight Wed.-Sun., VND80,000-120,000) is in large part responsible for Saigon's growing live music scene. The venue brings in recognized international acts as well as successful local musicians and DJs. The venue's ample space lends itself well to large crowds and the adjoining Cargo Bar, serving beer and cocktails, adds to the warehouse's success. Visit when a live performance is going on, as otherwise the place can feel empty. Keep an eye out for Q4's logo as you approach; the venue is set back from the road and is easy to miss.

THE ARTS

A burgeoning community of painters, filmmakers, visual artists, and enthusiastic supporters of the arts have begun to appear in the city. While more traditional performances and cultural showcases have long been a mainstay at the Opera House, smaller venues like cafés and independent galleries are beginning to exhibit art and hold regular film nights and artist workshops. Keep an eye out for these smaller events through the calendars on *The Word* (www.wordhcmc. com) or *Any Arena* (www.anyarena.com). Several regularly scheduled film screenings like **Future Shorts** (www.futureshorts.com), a quarterly international short film festival, and a weekly art house cinema series called **me phim: passionate about film,** whose Facebook page lists upcoming screenings, also take place.

Performing Arts

Most of the city's English-language performances take place at the historic Opera House. A regularly changing schedule of shows passes through the theater, from plays, ballets, and circus acts to cultural shows and musical performances. Box office hours vary along with the show. **Saigon Tourist** (102 Nguyen Hue, D1, tel. 08/3521-8760; 45 Le Thanh Ton, D1, tel. 08/3827-9279, www.saigon-tourist.com, 7:30am-6:30pm daily) books theater tickets.

Appearing twice a month at the Opera House, **The Soul of Vietnam** (tel. 08/3829-9976, www.mekongartists.vn, 5pm on 15th and 23rd of month, VND600,000-800,000) is a top-notch performance and a crowd-pleaser among locals and tourists. Saigon native Linh Huyen, the show's creator, strives to keep Vietnamese culture alive in the fast-changing southern metropolis by drawing upon the traditions of many of the country's ethnic minorities and mixing in national history to bring the audience on a journey from the earliest days of Vietnam through its modern era. The hour-long cultural performance combines talented young Vietnamese dancers with musicians, singers, and other show-stopping performers for a one-of-a-kind glimpse of Vietnamese culture.

The labor of a group of talented Vietnamese-European musicians and circus performers, **AO Show** (tel. 08/3518-1188, www.aoshowsaigon.com, box office: 9:30am-6pm daily, VND530,000-1,500,000) is Vietnam's answer to Cirque du Soleil. Inspired by the rapidly changing pace of Vietnam, from the quiet, laid-back life of the countryside to the mayhem of its cities, this hour-long show, performed at the Saigon Opera House (7 Cong Truong Lam Son, D1, tel. 08/3829-9976, www.hbso.org.vn), has received rave reviews from local media and visiting travelers for the acrobatics and agility of its performers, as well as the cultural element it brings to a circus-based show. Tickets are also available at Saigon Tourist. The show goes on in the evenings several times a week.

A long-standing northern tradition, the colorful wooden puppets of *roi nuoc* (Vietnamese water puppet theater) have been around since the 11th century. This unique form of theater is one of the more popular cultural performances in town. The **Golden Dragon Water Puppet Theater** (55B Nguyen Thi Minh Khai, D1, tel. 08/3930-2196, www.goldendragonwaterpuppet.com, box office 8:30am-11:30am and 1:30pm-7:30pm daily, VND150,000), located within the grounds of the Labour Cultural House, holds two daily performances in the early evening between 5pm and 6:30pm. Musicians play traditional Vietnamese instruments such as the *dan nhi,* a sort of two-stringed violin, and lend their voices to a lively cast of characters, who splash around in the miniature pool that serves as a stage. Hidden behind a bamboo screen are the show's masterful puppeteers. The entire show runs 50 minutes, and each scene is accompanied by music and vocals. Though the performance is entirely in Vietnamese, no translation is required. Reserve your ticket at least one day in advance, as seats fill up quickly. Request a seat behind the front row if you prefer to stay dry during the performance—the puppets can get rowdy. Call the theater's hotline or visit their box office in order to get the best price. The theater also does a dinner-and-show deal (VND249,000).

Galleries and Museums

The **Fine Arts Museum** (97A Pho Duc Chinh, D1, tel. 08/3829-4441, www.baotang-mythuattphcm.vn, 9am-5pm Tues.-Sun., VND10,000) is housed in the former residence of a wealthy Chinese family. This three-story, colonial-style building was constructed in 1929. It was the first building in the city to feature an elevator, which is on display on the ground floor. Since its opening to the public in 1987, the museum has housed permanent exhibits in the main house as well as a rotating collection of special exhibits, which are on display in a smaller building nearby. The exhibits are organized chronologically, beginning with ancient Champa and Oc Eo sculpture from the 7th to 17th centuries and continuing through modern-day Vietnamese art. There is also a display of what's called "combat art." During the American War, artists followed rebel forces to the front lines and drew the people and battles before them. These works are displayed in the second-floor corridors. Allot a few hours here, as the collection is deceptively large. There are information desks located at the front of the main building.

For a constantly changing lineup of both local and international artists, **Galerie Quynh** (151/3 Dong Khoi, level 2, D1, tel. 08/3824-8284, www.galeriequynh.com, 10am-7pm Tues.-Sun.) regularly curates new exhibits from around the world. The joint effort of Vietnamese-American art critic Quynh Pham and Englishman Robert Cianchi, Galerie Quynh has been working to promote contemporary art in Vietnam and the larger region since 2000, when it first came on the scene as an online entity showcasing the talents of local artists. Near the ever-popular L'Usine, the gallery boasts a modern space that is at the forefront of contemporary art in southern Vietnam. Galerie Quynh does not always follow its own schedule, so it's a good idea to have your hotel call and verify it's open before you visit.

A small gallery leaving its mark on Saigon's art scene is **San Art** (3 Me Linh, D Binh Thanh, tel. 08/3840-0183, www.san-art.org, 10:30am-6:30pm Tues.-Sat.). Founded in 2007, this nonprofit center offers a gallery space and a reading room filled with art-related publications. San Art was a response to the lack of art resources in the city as well as the absence of opportunities for aspiring young Vietnamese artists. The center organizes exhibitions, lectures, workshops, and cultural exchange events, bringing in artists from across Vietnam and around the world.

A major player in the local art scene is the **Craig Thomas Gallery** (271 Tran Nhat Duat, D1, tel. 09/0388-8431, www.cthomasgallery.com, noon-6pm Tues.-Sat.), tucked at the back of a wide alley in northern District 1 not far from Tan Dinh Market. Inside the gallery gates, golden bicycles scale the front wall of the building, up and over its awning. Inside, two high-ceilinged rooms showcase the work of talented contemporary Vietnamese artists. Gallery founder Craig Thomas has been an active member of the Vietnamese art scene since 2002, mentoring young Saigon artists working in all mediums, and fostering the nascent artistic community of southern Vietnam. The gallery regularly changes its exhibits and is willing to open for private showings (call to arrange).

FESTIVALS AND EVENTS

Roughly a month after the Western world ushers in a new year, the entire nation of Vietnam takes a long holiday in honor of Tet, the Lunar New Year. During this time, Saigon is an empty city, deserted by many of its year-round residents who return home to enjoy the holiday with their extended families. Despite the mass exodus, HCMC still holds a well-known annual **Flower Street Festival** (Jan.-Feb.), at which time the length of Nguyen Hue Boulevard is shut down in order to accommodate an impressive floral display, usually featuring the Vietnamese zodiac animal of that particular year. Gardeners will twist and shape these colorful plants into a dragon, a cat, or a slithering snake. The flower festival is the one thing that draws people out of their homes at Tet to admire the vivid decorations along Nguyen Hue.

Though the **Mid-Autumn Festival** (mid-late Sept.) is a holiday celebrated throughout the country, Saigon's festivities are particularly lively. Beginning about a month before the holiday, the tiny street of Luong Nhu Hoc in District 5 becomes a *pho long den* (lantern village). Vendors sell colorful paper lanterns and decorations in honor of the coming day of festivity. Go in the evening, after the sun has set, to get the full effect of the lanterns. The closer the holiday is the more likely it is to be packed shoulder-to-shoulder with people.

Shopping

From droves of street peddlers on Pham Ngu Lao to the high-end boutiques and colossal shopping centers of District 1, Saigon is the commercial heart of Vietnam. The city's shopping obsession runs deep, extending out into the frenzied markets of Chinatown and down narrow streets that specialize in everything from guitar-making to used bicycles to high-quality fabrics. Designer clothes line Nguyen Hue and Dong Khoi streets. Closer to the backpacker area, shopping hubs like Ben Thanh Market and Saigon Square are packed with inexpensive souvenirs and colorful clothing. Bargaining is a common practice, giving you the opportunity to hone your haggling skills while picking up a new wardrobe.

MARKETS

Market culture is alive and well in Saigon. It is in the mayhem of these open-air buildings that most locals do their shopping. Vendors sit outside their stalls and call to passing shoppers, advertising T-shirts and fabric, souvenirs, shoes, and every food under the sun.

Ben Thanh Market

A Saigon institution, **Ben Thanh Market** (Le Loi and Tran Hung Dao, tel. 08/3829-2096, 6am-6pm daily) is a symbol of the city. The current market, built in 1914, houses every item imaginable, from souvenirs and clothing to accessories, electronics, packaged food, and foreign items that can't be found elsewhere in the city. Squeeze your way through the aisles of fabric stalls or peruse the coffee selection along the main corridors. The majority of the market's outer shops, which line the perimeter of the building, try to maintain a fixed-price policy. You do have some room to bargain, particularly if you are buying multiple items at a time. Inside, vendors beckon from all sides. The food area is concentrated close to the middle, and there are a handful of luggage and backpack shops on the very exterior of the building near the northern entrance.

At 6pm, Ben Thanh closes its doors, but a busy outdoor night market begins, going until about midnight. The night market is considerably smaller, though it does have a good

Ben Thanh Market

number of outdoor dining options and some shopping.

Located near the northern entrance to Ben Thanh Market, **Dung Tailor** (221 Le Thanh Ton, D1, tel. 08/3829-6778, dungtailor@hcm. vnn.vn, 8am-7pm daily) designs suits, button-up shirts, and other dress clothes specifically for men. The shop is clean and comfortable with a range of ready-made items to choose from as well as plenty of fabric options. Prices are expensive, with a men's button-up shirt going for about VND600,000, but the quality of the work is undeniable and it's worth the investment.

Even with its close proximity to Ben Thanh, it would be easy to miss **The House of Saigon** (16-20 Thu Khoa Huan, D1, tel. 08/3520-8178, www.thehouseofsaigon.com, 9am-9pm daily), as it's not directly surrounding the market. The housewares, jewelry, clothing, and knick-knacks sold here make it worth a visit. Though prices are steeper than in the market, items are of high quality and beautifully made, from wicker-and-porcelain serving dishes to buffalo horn chopsticks. The place is deceptively large, featuring three zig-zagging floors of merchandise and a charming café. The shop also features clothing and souvenirs.

Binh Tay Market

The large and imposing **Binh Tay Market** (57A Thap Muoi, D6, tel. 08/3857-1512, 7am-7pm daily) boasts an ornate Chinese-style roof visible from a mile away. This is the heart of Cho Lon, home to Saigon's large ethnic Chinese population. The mammoth market houses dry goods, clothing, fabrics, food, cosmetics, and household items. It's more of a local market than the foreign-influenced Ben Thanh. Inside is a small courtyard devoted to Quach Dam, a wealthy Chinese immigrant and the benefactor of modern-day Binh Tay. Beyond and around that, the market is a flurry of activity that features Chinese products as well as local offerings. Binh Tay closes in the evening but the area remains busy well into the night. For practical items or specific Vietnamese goods, Binh Tay is a better place to go than Ben Thanh, as its prices are often cheaper.

Tan Dinh Market

Considerably smaller than other downtown markets, **Tan Dinh Market** (Hai Ba Trung and Nguyen Huu Cau, D1, tel. 08/3829-9280, 6am-6pm daily) houses the usual smorgasbord of household goods, clothes, and food items but is best known for the fabric vendors in the market and across the street on Hai Ba Trung and Nguyen Huu Cau. Stalls are packed to the ceiling with silk, cotton, and other materials, from plain colors to intricate, sequined patterns. Around the market's exterior along Hai Ba Trung, fruit vendors set up a nice display to attract passing customers.

An Dong Market

If you're on the lookout for wooden or lacquer handicrafts, visit **An Dong Market** (34-36 An Duong Vuong, D5, tel. 08/3835-6609, 6am-6pm daily). This ancient building doesn't see nearly as much traffic as An Dong Plaza, its newer, fancier counterpart down the block, but it boasts a wider selection of statues, dishes, and other handicraft items. The first floor of the market is mostly food stalls; upstairs is an array of fabric, shoes, purses, clothing, and handicrafts. This is a quieter, more relaxed bargaining environment than Ben Thanh Market, and vendors tend to be friendlier.

Dan Sinh Market

Dan Sinh Market (104 Yersin, D1, tel. 08/3825-1130, 6am-5pm daily), sometimes known as Yersin Market, sells an eclectic combination of construction materials and war memorabilia. Tucked in the heart of this dank makeshift building are a plethora of stalls carrying army gear and personal effects of soldiers from both sides of the American War. In addition to combat helmets, compasses, bullets, canteens, and all manner of camouflage, you'll find rusted antique lighters and cameras as well as piles of photographs once

What a Bargain!

Bargaining in HCMC is almost always acceptable. In bigger, more central markets, prices are higher and room for negotiation is greater. In Ben Thanh Market, for instance, you may be able to drive the price down as much as 40-50 percent. Vendors in these heavily touristed areas tend to sell the same products, which gives you more bargaining power. If you attempt to haggle with a local vendor and are unsuccessful, you can move next door and find the same things on offer.

Many travelers find their first trip to the local market overwhelming. Shops are small and cluttered, cramming innumerable items into one space, and, particularly in tourist areas, vendors can be pushy. Remain patient and only bargain seriously for something you really want. The most important thing to remember when bargaining is that as long as both you and the vendor are pleased with the transaction, then the price is acceptable. You may pay slightly more than a local might, but there's a good chance it's still cheaper than what you would pay at home.

---

carried by Vietnamese soldiers. The market offers authentic antiques as well as cheaper reproductions of most items.

SHOPPING DISTRICTS
Nguyen Hue and Le Loi Streets

On the eastern side of Ben Thanh Market is **Le Loi**, a street devoted almost exclusively to shopping and geared toward the tourist crowd. Many of the same souvenirs sold inside Ben Thanh are featured here, but alongside more expensive local shops as well as international brands like Adidas, Converse, and Dr. Martens. Intermixed with these smaller boutiques are one or two shopping malls, which begin to appear toward the far end of the street, just as Le Loi approaches **Nguyen Hue** in front of the Opera House. This intersection is particularly indicative of the rise in local wealth, as it houses a handful of luxury brands like Chanel and Bulgari. Take a right onto Nguyen Hue and you'll find more retail shops squeezed in among the nicer hotels and Western restaurants.

For cheap local fashions, visit the gargantuan **Saigon Square** (77-89 Nam Ky Khoi Nghia, D1, tel. 08/3823-3942, www.saigon-square.com, 9am-9pm daily), which is something of a cross between a local market and a Western-style shopping mall. Here you'll find boatloads of inexpensive souvenirs, bags, coffee, clothes, and various electronic odds and ends. Haggling is acceptable and, though the place is usually a madhouse, it is slightly more organized than nearby Ben Thanh Market. There is also a second location, known as **Saigon Square 2** (7-9 Ton Duc Thang, D1, tel. 08/3911-8922, www.saigon-square.com, 9am-9pm daily), which is quieter and smaller but more expensive.

The folks at **Saigon Kitsch** (43 Ton That Thiep, D1, tel. 08/3821-8019, saigonkitsch@gmail.com, 9am-8pm daily) take old propaganda images and spruce up T-shirts, notebooks, drinking glasses, magnets, and other odds and ends. In cahoots with **Gallery Dogma** (tel. 08/3821-8272, www.dogmaviet-nam.com) and **Saigon Caztus** (tel. 09/0965-4377), the company does propaganda-style renditions of famous movie posters. All three businesses offer many cool and affordable items in one shop.

Bambou (34 Le Loi, D1, tel. 08/3823-9048, www.bamboucompany.com, 8:30am-10:30pm daily) produces items from locally grown bamboo and milk fiber, selling super-soft T-shirts and dresses as well as funky leather shoes.

Thai transplant **Ethophen** (89 Mac Thi Buoi, D1, tel. 08/3825-8325, www.ethophen.com, 9am-8pm daily), also known as It's Happened to Be a Closet, has two stores in town, though they are very different from one another. For colors, prints, and textures, go to the flagship store on Mac Thi Buoi, where loud club music thumps day and night and the second floor houses more clothing, a spa, and mini-café. For flowy women's clothing and handmade accessories, visit the company's Pham Ngu Lao location (221 De Tham, D1).

Halfway between conservative and adventurous, the clothing at **7th Heaven** (21-27 Ton That Thiep, D1, tel. 09/8973-5667, www.7thheaven.vn, 8am-10pm daily) features simple items with a contemporary flair, throwing funky sunglasses and unique jewelry pieces into the mix. Prices are higher than you'll find in the backpacker district, but the quality is evident. Neighboring Q Boutique, which shares a storefront with the shop, also has a good selection of women's clothing; both of these labels have a small section dedicated to men's clothing.

The **Pham Minh Tailor** (132 Pasteur, D1, tel. 09/6291-0511, phamminhtailor@yahoo.com.vn, 8am-8pm daily) is a reputable tailor for men and women. This store boasts fabrics from all over the world, including Vietnam, India, Italy, and China. The experienced seamstresses can complete a job on a tight deadline. You may be able to pay a visit to Ben Thanh Market with the tailor to choose your fabric.

Even if the embroidered portraits and landscapes at **XQ Silk Hand Embroidery** (106 Le Loi, D1, tel. 08/3822-7724, www.tranhtheuxq.com, 8am-9pm daily) are beyond your budget, visiting this store is educational and fascinating. Artisan Hoang Le Xuan and her husband, Vo Van Quan, opened a training center in Dalat, teaching women how to handstitch intricate landscapes and portraits. The enormous, framed works of art are nearly six feet wide and four feet tall. Visitors are able to watch the embroidering process at the back of the store, where women in *ao dai* (the traditional garment of Vietnam) work on new pieces. A small image can take one person several months to complete; larger images are often the product of a whole team of women.

Mekong Quilts (68 Le Loi, tel. 08/2210-3110, www.mekong-creations.org, 9am-7pm daily) carries plush, colorful quilts as well as bamboo and papier-mâché products, handmade by women in southern Vietnam and Cambodia. This nonprofit enterprise employs over 300 people. Designs come from the women themselves as well as professional designers, and 50 cents of each dollar spent at the shop goes directly back to the villages, providing each employee with a sustainable income.

Pham Ngu Lao Street

Also known as the backpacker area, **Pham Ngu Lao** is home to a wide variety of reasonably priced souvenir and clothing shops, as well as street vendors carrying everything from knock-off Ray Bans to photocopied books, fans, and other goods. This neighborhood provides the same products as Ben Thanh Market with a slightly lower degree of chaos and fewer bargaining opportunities.

Nearly every shop in this neighborhood has a section devoted to travel necessities like outlet adapters, headphones, backpacks, sleeping bags, and camera gear. It's also a good spot for buying bootleg DVDs and boxed sets, as well as English-language books. Shops are open from early morning to late at night. If you see a price tag on an item, it is not up for negotiation. If the product does not have a listed price, there is a chance you can bargain.

The **Ginkgo Concept Store** (254 De Tham, D1, tel. 08/6270-5928, www.ginkgo-vietnam.com, 8am-10pm daily) sells well-made, locally produced souvenirs like buffalo horn jewelry and lacquer dishware, in addition to its signature T-shirt line. The company is a fair-trade enterprise, so the higher prices for T-shirts go to providing workers with a sustainable living.

Blue Dragon (1B Bui Vien, D1, tel. 08/2210-2084, www.gobluedragon.com, 8am-10pm daily) carries an eclectic, creative collection of recycled goods, from papier-mâché jewelry and bowls to purses made of rubber tires, an homage to the city's motorbike culture. All of the items are handmade in Vietnam.

On Bui Vien is a massive sign advertising "Old Propaganda Posters." This is the famous

Pham Ngu Lao Street

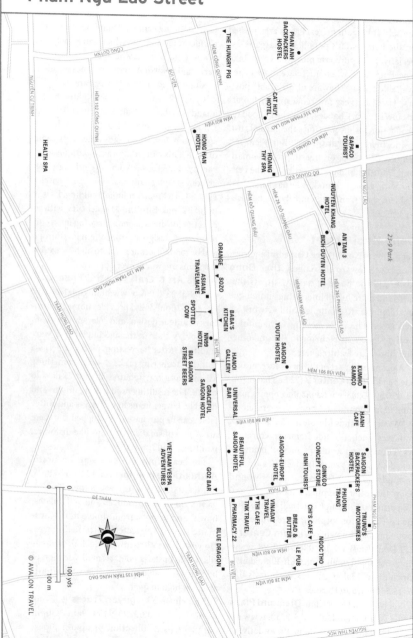

© AVALON TRAVEL

Hanoi Gallery (79 Bui Vien, D1, tel. 08/3837-6854, 9am-10pm daily), where high-quality reproductions of Communist propaganda are sold at bargain prices. Prices aren't listed on the items, so it's possible to bargain, especially if you purchase more than one. Take a peek upstairs, where there are more prints available for sale. Beware of "original" posters: There are very few remaining originals left in Vietnam. Chances are it's just a good reproduction for several times the normal cost.

Inexpensive **Orange** (180 Bui Vien, D1, tel. 08/3837-1500, orangeshopstyle@gmail.com, 9am-10pm daily) is packed to the ceiling with cool, original, Vietnam-inspired T-shirts, shorts, and bags, mostly for the backpacker set.

Dong Khoi Street

Beginning at Notre Dame Cathedral and running south toward the Saigon River, **Dong Khoi** and the maze of narrow streets that surround it are full of interesting and unique local handicrafts, antiques, and artwork, as well as some designer clothing. A handful of local designers specializing in silk and other fine fabrics are featured here.

A prominent part of the city's current skyline, the **Vincom Center B** (72 Le Thanh Ton, tel. 09/7503-3288, www.vincomshoppingmall.com, 9am-10pm daily) houses several notable Western brands like Steve Madden, Bebe, and Yves Rocher beside homegrown retailers. Though you wouldn't guess it from the outside, Vincom's shopping facilities are surprisingly large, with several underground floors that offer shopping, a food court, and a supermarket. Though it actually came after the Le Thanh Ton location, there is a second shopping mall known as **Vincom Center A** (171 Dong Khoi, D1, tel. 08/3910-2798, www.vincomshoppingmall.com, 9am-10pm daily), which offers higher-end luxury brands like Versace, Dior, and Hermes.

Not far from Dong Khoi, **Diamond Plaza** (34 Le Duan, D1, tel. 08/3825-7750, www.diamondplaza.com.vn, 9:30am-10pm daily) is the city's best-known local department store,

and also includes a bowling alley and movie theater on its upper floors. While prices are more expensive than in the market or at certain shopping centers, Diamond Plaza offers a wider range of sizes, which can be helpful to Western travelers, as what may pass for a small garment in North America may be considered medium to extra large in Vietnam.

Crisp white walls, exposed lightbulbs, and an industrial decor make **L'Usine** (151/1 Dong Khoi, D1, tel. 08/6674-9565, www.lusinespace.com, 9am-9pm daily) the city's center of cool. This café-restaurant-boutique sells a variety of men's and women's clothing as well as Lomography cameras, shoes, and jewelry. Housed in a French colonial building, L'Usine pulls its look into the 21st century with an eclectic clothing selection, drawing upon contemporary designers from Vietnam, Europe, and beyond. Prices are mid- to high-range, but the items are worth every penny.

Nga Art & Craft (41 Mac Thi Buoi, D1, tel. 08/3823-8356, www.huongngafinearts.vn, 8am-10pm daily) provides home furnishings in unique designs and colors, adding contemporary flair to the age-old lacquer-ware tradition. After harvesting, pieces undergo a lengthy lacquering process—even something as small as a tray requires at least 75 days to create. The resulting products are unique and durable. Larger items like dressers and coffee tables can be purchased and shipped, but there are plenty of smaller creations like dishware, paintings, and frames.

For beautifully made ceramic dishware, **Authentique Interiors** (71/1 Mac Thi Buoi, D1, tel. 08/3823-8811, www.authentique.vn, 9am-9pm daily) produces and sells plates, bowls, and teapots, from simple monochromatic sets to intricately patterned pieces. Downstairs is kitchenware, including utensils, while upstairs holds a small selection of bedding and table runners. Items are affordable and high in quality.

The cluttered **Nguyen Freres** (2 Dong Khoi, D1, tel. 08/3823-9459, 9am-7:30pm daily) keeps a collection of opium pipes, antique pottery, and statues, as well as handmade blankets and wall hangings from northern hill tribes. Some of the pottery items date back a hundred years or more, and each of the textiles is the authentic work of one of Vietnam's ethnic minority groups. Employees are knowledgeable in the history and origin of each piece.

Nguyen Trai Street

From morning to night you'll see the flashing lights of **Nguyen Trai** advertising brand-name clothes as well as knock-off handbags and other bargain items. Companies like The Gap, Banana Republic, and Nike have factories in Vietnam, so there are lots of discounted clothes here that are either the real deal or a good imitation of it. Brand names from other Asian countries also make an appearance on this stretch, particularly closer to the backpacker area. In addition to air-conditioned stores and shopping malls, vendors set up along the sidewalk, hawking helmets, shoes, purses, and other goods. This is a decidedly more local shopping area, with lower prices but also Vietnamese-only sizes; if you're taller than the average local, you might need to stick to the tourist trail.

Roughly a block away from the massive roundabout that houses Vietnam's original Starbucks location, **Zen Plaza** (54-56 Nguyen Trai, D1, tel. 08/3925-0339, www.zenplaza.com.vn, 9:30am-10pm daily) is an eclectic combination of Asian brands packed into a tall and narrow building. With loads of women's and men's clothing, some from major brands like Nike and others from small designer labels, this shopping mall is compact, unique, and close to Pham Ngu Lao and the shopping street of Nguyen Trai, making it worth a quick visit.

Hai Ba Trung Street

Busy **Hai Ba Trung** offers a more local collection of shops. Here, you'll find a large selection of fabrics in and around Tan Dinh Market, whose southern side faces a row of tailors capable of stitching together anything from men's suits and ladies' dresses to *ao dai* (the traditional garment of Vietnam). This area is particularly well known for its fabrics, but there are also shops dedicated to skincare and ready-made clothes.

Red Door Deco (31A Le Thanh Ton, D1, tel. 08/3825-8672, www.reddoordeco.com, 10am-7pm Mon.-Sat.) is a well-known carrier of vintage furniture, lacquer ware, statues, and other antiques. Through its bright red doors, a men's fashion shop occupies the ground floor, specializing in vivid leather and suede shoes as well as belts and wallets. Upstairs are home furnishings, from door handles and decorative lamps to dressers and sturdy wooden cabinets. Prices are expensive, but the shop carries many one-of-a-kind items.

Sports and Recreation

Though it's not an especially sporty place and the great outdoors are hard to come by amid the traffic and droves of people, Saigon maintains its fair share of parks, swimming pools, and day spas, all of which offer a great way to unwind and experience local culture at the same time.

PARKS

Saigon's parks are oases amid a chaotic urban landscape. It's worth paying a visit to these well-manicured green spaces in the morning, when locals flock to the park for their daily exercise. Men stretch and practice tai chi while groups of women gather around a massive speaker on wheels, bouncing to the beat of techno music during their daily aerobics class. Still more groups hone other skills, from martial arts to ballroom dancing, or play a rousing game of badminton.

Tao Dan Park

One of the larger parks in District 1, **Tao Dan**

Park (Truong Dinh and Nguyen Thi Minh Khai, D1), is bisected by the fast-paced traffic of Truong Dinh. The park stays busy from dawn to dusk, but the early hours are particularly hectic, with locals tracing the paths that loop around the park. On the western side, foliage helps to shelter the grounds from traffic.

Manicured topiaries line the walkway up to the Hung Kings Temple at the center of the grounds. Flanked by two dragons sculpted out of the greenery, this temple is an homage to the first kings of Vietnam, who ruled during the Hong Bang dynasty (2879-258 BC). The temple is small but popular. Visitors come to burn incense or offer fruit.

To the east, the sidewalk winds through a series of angular stone statues. It's a quiet, pleasant change from the mayhem of traffic that buzzes outside its grounds.

23-9 Park

Sandwiched between Pham Ngu Lao and Ben Thanh Market, **23-9 Park** (Pham Ngu Lao and Nguyen Thi Nghia, D1), also known as Lover's Park, holds regular events, from food festivals and cultural performances to dance recitals and concerts. This is a green space in two parts, with its grounds interrupted by Nguyen Thi Nghia. While locals use it for their morning exercise routines, this park sees the most activity at night, when young Vietnamese gather here. The long, narrow grounds are sometimes occupied by local students hoping to practice their English with a foreigner; you are sure to attract at least one conversation partner if you decide to sit beside the lotus pond.

Le Van Tam Park

Farther north and east in District 1 is **Le Van Tam Park** (Hai Ba Trung and Dien Bien Phu, D1), one of the nicer fresh-air spots downtown. Le Van Tam maintains beautiful, well-kept grounds that can be a peaceful escape from the din of the surrounding streets. A long, flowered walkway leads up to the park's main gathering area, at the center of which stands a large Communist-era statue. At the back of the park are a handful of coffee stalls and a playground.

This park is named after national hero Le Van Tam, who, as a teenager, dressed in gasoline-soaked garments and lit himself on fire before running into a gasoline depot owned by the French, destroying the structure in protest of colonial rule. It has since been revealed that the story was propaganda invented to boost public support of the revolutionary cause.

30-4 Park

Bordered on one side by the sweeping grounds of the Reunification Palace and on the other side by the imposing structure of Notre Dame Cathedral, **30-4 Park** (Nam Ky Khoi Nghia and Le Duan, D1) is a lush, green area zig-zagged with walkways and park benches where young people gather to enjoy a coffee or mid-afternoon snack in the shade.

AMUSEMENT PARKS

To cool off and get away from the noise and chaos of city traffic, pay a visit to **Dam Sen Water Park** (3 Hoa Binh, D11, tel. 08/3823-0336, www.damsenwaterpark.com.vn, 8:30am-6pm Mon.-Sat., 8am-6pm Sun., VND120,000). The huge venue, located northwest of the city center, boasts a well-manicured wooded area as well as a water park, where local and foreign visitors flock on hot days to enjoy the slides, rides, and cool water of the wave pool. All rides are supervised by park staff, and changing rooms are available. The cost of entry goes down after 4pm (VND100,000), though it's better to make an afternoon of the trip, as Dam Sen is far from downtown. There is also an on-site restaurant.

SWIMMING

The pool at **Van Thanh Tourist Area** (48/10 Dien Bien Phu, D Binh Thanh, tel. 08/3512-3025, vanthanh.resort@gmail.com, 6am-8pm daily, VND40,000-50,000 adults, VND20,000-25,000 children) is the perfect way to escape the city without actually having to leave the city. Hidden down an alley off Dien Bien Phu street in Binh Thanh District,

Dodge, Duck, Dive, Dip, and Dodge

Dodgeball for Vietnam (Phan Dinh Phung Sports Center, 8 Vo Van Tan, D3, 8pm Mon. and Wed., VND30,000) is a popular weekly event, drawing young locals and expats to the Phan Dinh Phung Sports Center in District 3 for a friendly game. Players gather at the outdoor basketball court starting at 8pm (latecomers are welcome; the game doesn't start until 8:30pm). Teams rotate in, playing the winner of each game, and the fun lasts until 10pm or 11pm. The group also has a Facebook page, which is a good resource for upcoming games and events. Enter the sports center through the Nguyen Dinh Chieu entrance. When directing a *xe om* or taxi to this location specify the sports center, as there is also a street called Phan Dinh Phung, located far from this building.

Van Thanh is a pleasant surprise, with lush green lawns and tree-lined walkways that create the illusion that you've left Saigon behind. The pool is clean and big, with a separate, smaller swimming pool for young children, and there are plenty of lounge chairs nearby. Van Thanh has a restaurant and several activities for young kids. The place gets crowded on weekends and holidays.

MASSAGES AND SPAS

Massages are all the rage in Saigon, with dozens of spas located in the District 1 area alone, ranging in price from dirt-cheap to exorbitant. Many hotels and guesthouses also offer spa services, but these are often overpriced and, in truth, you're usually better off visiting a spa on your own. While tipping is not common in restaurants or cafés, it is expected that you offer a 15-20 percent tip to a masseuse or masseur. In some places, masseuses will have a tip form for you to fill out, noting the amount you are giving. While this can be uncomfortable for some—having to write down your tip amount and give it to the masseuse before you pay—it is the norm in many places here.

For the lower end of the budget, without sacrificing quality, **Hoang Thy Spa** (35 Do Quang Dau, D1, tel. 08/3836-4404, www.hoangthysalon.com, 8am-9pm daily, VND50,000-300,000) is a great spot for a massage or manicure. The facility itself is pretty bare bones, but the staff are incredibly friendly and the spa's services, from hair and nails to massages, waxing, foot care, and facials, are inexpensive. A manicure or pedicure will set you back around VND50,000, while body massages cost VND120,000-300,000.

If you don't mind venturing a few more blocks outside the backpacker area, **Health Spa** (36-38 Nguyen Cu Trinh, D1, tel. 08/2220-2132, www.tanngocanhspa.com, 10am-11pm daily, VND50,000-860,000), formerly known as Ngoc Anh Spa, has a range of affordable massage services beginning at VND200,000, tips excluded. This massive building has separate floors for men and women, as well as a sauna and steam room, and the masseuses are well trained and speak some English.

The mid-range **Cat Moc Spa** (61-63 Tran Dinh Xu, D1, tel. 08/6295-8926, www.catmocspa.com, 9am-10pm daily, VND110,000-820,000) is an excellent value. The modest storefront belies the spa's impeccable service. Guests are greeted with a glass of iced tea in the cozy seating area before choosing from massages, body scrubs, facials, hair care, and waxing. The friendly and experienced staff speak English. Afterward, you'll be offered a glass of *chanh muoi* (lemon juice and salt), a refreshing local treat. Spa packages (VND418,000-2,090,000) are available for those looking to make a day of it.

The cheerful, purple-clad staff at **L'Apothiquaire** (100 Mac Thi Buoi, D1, tel. 08/3822-2158, www.lapothiquaire.com, 10am-6pm daily, VND320,000-1,200,000) carry their own line of skincare products, as well as offering massages, wraps, facials, manicures, pedicures, and waxing services. Packages can be purchased to combine several services for a full day at the spa. Walk-ins are welcome, but book ahead in order to receive the best service possible.

COOKING CLASSES

There are a handful of excellent culinary courses offered in Saigon. Class prices here are higher here than other places, so you may be better off waiting, particularly if you are also traveling to central coast cities like Hue and Hoi An.

The most well-known culinary course is **Saigon Cooking Class** (74 Hai Ba Trung, D1, tel. 08/3825-8485, www.saigon-cookingclass.com, 8am-5pm Tues.-Sun., VND830,000-955,000 adults, VND525,000-588,000 kids 7-12), which operates out of Hoa Tuc, a Vietnamese restaurant. The three-hour hands-on course teaches students how to prepare a three-course Vietnamese meal, with the dishes changing daily. An English-speaking Vietnamese chef gives instruction. For an extra fee, you can accompany the chef to the market, where he shows students how to select and purchase the necessary ingredients. Classes are capped at 12 people, and children seven years and up are welcome.

For a more affordable option, the **Cyclo Resto Cooking Class** (3-3A Dang Tran Con, D1, tel. 09/7551-3011, www.cycloresto.com, 9am-6pm daily, VND483,000) combines a market visit and cooking class with sightseeing. Ride to the local market in a cyclo, taking in the city as you go, before exploring the stalls of fresh produce and meat. A taxi ferries you back to the cooking center, where you'll learn several dishes from a professional and knowledgeable English-speaking staff. Cyclo Resto has smaller class sizes and more one-on-one interaction.

Accommodations

From the bare-bones hostels hidden down the alleys off Pham Ngu Lao to the high-end hotels overlooking the Saigon River, accommodations in HCMC run the spectrum. Dorm beds cost as little as VND100,000 a night, while the peak of luxury will set you back several hundred dollars.

Base yourself in District 1, where the majority of the city's sights, shopping, restaurants, and English-speaking services are located. Due to the many hotels in this area, making a reservation is usually unnecessary.

Most budget travelers base themselves in Pham Ngu Lao, the backpacker neighborhood. Just outside of the backpacker area, Nguyen Trai is an excellent choice if you're looking to get away from the nonstop noise of Pham Ngu Lao but still remain close to the heart of downtown. Mid-range accommodations are packed onto the streets around Ben Thanh Market. Several historic five-star hotels are close to the Opera House.

Light sleepers should be extra selective, as Saigon's noise pollution is second to none. Hotels located in alleys tend to be quieter than those on the street. (Conversely, hotels on busy streets are safer at night, where front doors are more visible and well lit.)

If rates are listed higher than VND500,000 per night, check if the hotel gives a discount for booking ahead of time. Budget accommodations often discount their rates for someone walking in off the street in order to fill rooms.

Don't bother requesting an airport pickup from your hotel: Taking a cab from the airport to District 1 costs at least half the going rate offered by hotels.

OPERA HOUSE AREA
VND525,000-1,050,000

Clean and spacious, rooms at the **Tan Hoang Long Hotel** (84 Mac Thi Buoi, D1, tel. 08/3827-0006, www.tanhoanglong-hotel.com, VND945,000-1,470,000, breakfast included) are a good value, with plenty of natural light and a private working desk as well as daily coffee, tea, and bottled water. In some of the larger rooms, sofas and street views are available. The staff is courteous and the hotel's location is close to the downtown shopping area, Dong Khoi, and the market.

VND1,050,000-2,100,000

Boasting colorful decor and large rooms, the ★ **Saigon River Boutique Hotel** (58 Mac Thi Buoi, D1, tel. 08/3822-8558, www.saigonriverhotel.com, VND630,000-1,890,000) provides more upscale lodgings with an exceptional level of service and cleanliness. This boutique hotel boasts modern facilities as well as an amiable staff. Each room includes a safety deposit box, cable TV, free Wi-Fi, toiletries, and air-conditioning. For a bit more, you can get a room with a balcony at the front of the hotel, where there are nice views of the street below. The hotel has a restaurant serving Asian and Western dishes as well as a rooftop bar and café.

Over VND2,100,000

The five-star **Hotel Majestic** (1 Dong Khoi, D1, tel. 08/3829-5517, www.majesticsaigon.com.vn, VND3,256,000-9,196,000) has been in business since 1925, located at the intersection of Ton Duc Thang and Dong Khoi, formerly the famous Rue Catinat. The stunning arches and ornate detail of the building's exterior are a fitting welcome. The interior boasts equally impressive decor, with rich wooden surfaces and opulent antique furniture. Riverview rooms include a balcony, and each room comes equipped with a safety deposit box and spacious marble bathrooms. The hotel has fitness facilities, a serene outdoor swimming pool, and the grandiose Catinat Lounge.

The **Rex Hotel** (141 Nguyen Hue, D1, tel. 08/3829-2185, www.rexhotelvietnam.com, VND3,080,000-17,600,000) is a Saigon institution. Topped with its iconic crown and featuring high-end designer shops on the ground floor, the Rex is best known as the site of daily press briefings from the American Information Service during the Vietnam War. The deluxe hotel boasts 159 individually designed rooms as well as a top-notch spa and fitness center, a rooftop pool and bar, and several restaurants. Each room comes with plush queen- or king-size beds, complimentary breakfast, shower and bathtub, and daily newspaper service.

On the far side of the Central Post Office, the beautifully furnished **Intercontinental Asiana** (Corner Hai Ba Trung and Le Duan, tel. 08/3520-9999, www.ihg.com, VND3,056,000-8,945,000) features modern facilities with an Asian-inspired decor. Its sleek guestrooms boast plush beds and spacious bathrooms. The hotel features on-site fitness facilities, a concierge, room service, and a rooftop swimming pool. Next door, the Kumho Asiana Plaza offers a variety of restaurants and high-end shopping.

Beside the Opera House, the **Caravelle Hotel** (19-23 Lam Son Square, D1, tel. 08/3823-4999, www.caravellehotel.com, VND4,000,000-27,000,000) is one of the city's largest and best-known five-star hotels. In the heart of downtown, this enormous building served as a meeting place for foreign journalists during the war. The original 10-story structure has been joined with a larger, 24-floor tower. The well-known Saigon Saigon Bar is found on the rooftop of the smaller building. The Caravelle boasts 335 guest rooms, as well as six different eating and drinking venues, a spa, pool, and fitness center. Deluxe rooms are plush and comfortable and include standard amenities. Higher-end rooms on the Signature Floor include complimentary breakfast and evening cocktails, and spacious suites have sweeping views of the city and a comfortable living room.

BEN THANH MARKET AREA
VND525,000-1,050,000

Right beside Ben Thanh Market, the **Hoang Phuong Hotel** (229 Le Thanh Ton, D1, tel. 08/3823-6699, www.hoangphuonghotel.com, VND735,000-1,155,000, breakfast included) is a great value, providing well-appointed rooms and in-room amenities, including cable TV, room service, and free Wi-Fi. Breakfast is served in the hotel's buffet-style restaurant. Upgrade to a superior room, as standard rooms are cramped.

Down a side street is **Vuong Tai Hotel** (20 Luu Van Lang, D1, tel. 08/3521-8597, www.vuongtaihotel.com, VND840,000-1,050,000, breakfast included), which offers service well above its two-star label. Rooms range from deluxe to VIP and include complimentary bottled water, cable TV, and a safety deposit box. Higher-end rooms feature bathtubs and a desk. All guest rooms have windows.

A high-quality, three-star facility, the **Hoang Hai Long 2 Hotel** (28-30 Nguyen An Ninh, D1, tel. 08/3823-2999, www.hoanghailonghotel.com, VND945,000-1,155,000, breakfast included) boasts well-appointed rooms with contemporary decor and modern facilities. Larger rooms include a small sitting area as well as city views and standard amenities, like air-conditioning and toiletries. This hotel is part of a larger group of three-star hotels, with the more expensive original Hoang Hai Long just a stone's-throw away on Pham Hong Thai.

VND1,050,000-2,100,000

The bright and spacious **Sanouva Hotel** (177 Ly Tu Trong, D1, tel. 08/3827-5275, www.sanouvahotel.com, VND1,176,000-1,512,000, breakfast included) is close enough to Ben Thanh to be convenient without the added noise that comes with staying directly beside the market. Each room has natural light, as well as chic, contemporary decor, large bathrooms, and the usual amenities, including toiletries and cable TV. Larger rooms feature a small sitting area. The staff is exceptionally helpful.

Rooms at the **Blue Diamond Hotel** (48-50 Thu Khoa Huan, D1, tel. 08/3823-6167, www.bluediamondhotel.com.vn, VND1,218,000-3,213,000, breakfast included), just north of the market, are spacious with plush, cozy beds and plenty of natural light. All rooms include

a large bathroom with bathtub, daily newspaper, free Wi-Fi, air-conditioning, and complimentary bottled water, tea, and coffee. A small fitness center is available, as are professional foot massages. The on-site restaurant serves Vietnamese and Western cuisine.

The **Lan Lan 2 Hotel** (46-46bis Thu Khoa Huan, D1, tel. 08/3822-7926, www.lanlanhotel.com.vn, VND1,260,000-2,730,000, breakfast included) boasts five different types of guest rooms, from small but adequate standard rooms to large suites. The hotel is decorated in dark wood and rich colors. Each of its 100-plus rooms includes cable TV and air-conditioning. The hotel also has a small fitness center, a restaurant, room service, and laundry. The original **Lan Lan Hotel** (73-75 Thu Khoa Huan, D1, tel. 08/3823-6789, www.lanlanhotel.com.vn, VND1,470,000-2,520,000) is up the road and is equally suitable.

PHAM NGU LAO STREET

Pham Ngu Lao is the most inexpensive area to stay, though it is also party central. The main streets in the backpacker area—De Tham, Bui Vien, and Pham Ngu Lao, along with their respective alleys—are brimming with budget hotels that do most of their business in walk-in customers.

Pham Ngu Lao is a loud and happening place morning, noon, and night. Don't shell out more than VND1,000,000 per night for hotels in this area. For more upscale rooms, head to the Ben Thanh Market area or downtown, where there is a little more flash and a little less debauchery.

Under VND210,000

The ★ **Saigon Backpacker's Hostel** (203 Pham Ngu Lao, D1, tel. 08/3920-3527, info@hotel-a-saigon.com, VND105,000-462,000) is one of the nicer dorms in the area. Each dorm room has thick mattresses, clean bedding, a locker for each guest, air-conditioning, and an en suite bathroom with hot water. Rooms average about six beds apiece. The dormitories are quiet given the hostel's location, though they don't have windows.

Hong Han Hotel

Double and twin rooms are also available. Don't confuse this place with the Saigon Backpacker's Hostel on Cong Quynh; they are not affiliated.

Hidden in one of Pham Ngu Lao's alleys, the **Saigon Youth Hostel** (241/32 Pham Ngu Lao, D1, tel. 08/3920-3665, www.saigonyouth-hostel.com, VND147,000-420,000) has mixed and all-female dorms, as well as private single and double rooms. Clean and comfy beds are available, with breakfast included for an extra US$1. The hostel provides lockers for dorm guests and each private room features an en suite bathroom with hot water. Two computers are available for guest use, and the common room is well stocked with DVDs, reading material, and a Foosball table.

With four beds to a room, the dorms at **An Tam 3 Hotel** (283/7 Pham Ngu Lao, D1, tel. 08/3920-9507, hoangtuan296@yahoo.com.vn, VND110,000-336,000) are cozy and bright with plush bedding and lots of natural light. Each dorm is equipped with a private bathroom and lockers on the top floor.

An Tam 3 has a handful of reasonably priced private rooms.

The entrance to alley 373 of Pham Ngu Lao is down the road from the heart of the backpacker area. The beds and staff at **Phan Anh Hostel** (373/6 Pham Ngu Lao, D1, tel. 08/3920-9235, www.phananhbackpackershostel.com, VND147,000-504,000, breakfast included) make it worth the walk. Clean, comfortable, and reasonably priced, each room features basic amenities, including air-conditioning and free Wi-Fi. The six-bed dormitories have en suite bathrooms and lockers, and there is a common room with a flat-screen TV. Unlike other hostels, Phan Anh has an elevator.

VND210,000-525,000

★ **Hong Han Hotel** (238 Bui Vien, D1, tel. 08/3836-1927, www.honghanhotelhcm.com, VND462,000-525,000, breakfast included) offers clean and spacious rooms as well as a nice communal balcony. The guesthouse has a variety of room options, from double and twin beds to triple rooms, all of which have air-conditioning, hot water, cable TV, and free Wi-Fi. The staff goes out of their way to be hospitable and are happy to offer advice and local recommendations.

Owned by the same people that operate the Hong Han Hotel, **Bich Duyen Hotel** (283/4 Pham Ngu Lao, D1, tel. 08/3837-4588, www.bichduyenhotel.net, VND357,000-525,000) is an equally relaxing option. Situated down an alley off the main road, the rooms at Bich Duyen are quiet and comfortable and include breakfast, free Wi-Fi, air-conditioning, cable TV, hot water, and a fridge. The friendly staff help with travel services in the city and throughout Vietnam. Bich Duyen does not have an elevator.

Though the rooms are not as modern or well-appointed as others in town, the staff and value at **Ava Saigon 2** (126 De Tham, D1, tel. 08/3920-8645, www.avasaigon2.com, VND390,000-650,000, breakfast included) make it a nice place. The hotel offers complimentary laundry services, international phone calls, and Wi-Fi. Ava 2 is located just across Tran Hung Dao, close to the backpacker area without being directly at the center of the noise. Though there are cheaper standard rooms available, spring for a room with a window, as it's a better deal.

Away from the heart of the backpacker area, the **Yellow House Saigon Hotel** (114/32 De Tham, D1, tel. 08/3920-6503, yellowhousehotel@gmail.com, VND462,000-945,000) boasts a plethora of options, from standard rooms (with or without a window) to spacious superior and deluxe offerings. Standard rooms are smaller than average, but the bathrooms are larger. Upgrade to a superior for more space and light.

VND525,000-1,050,000

The **Graceful Saigon Hotel** (63 Bui Vien, D1, tel. 08/3838-6291, www.gracefulsaigonhotel.com, VND546,000-735,000, breakfast included) is worth every penny. Tidy, well-decorated rooms come with in-room computers, safety deposit boxes, toiletries, hot water, cable TV, and small bathrooms. Each of the hotel's 11 rooms has a window. Graceful Saigon is right in the middle of the party area. Particularly on weekends, the street noise can be loud. Friendly staff assist in renting scooters or motorbikes as well as providing travel and visa services.

Rooms at the ★ **NN99 Hotel** (99 Bui Vien, D1, tel. 08/3836-9723, www.nn99hotel.com, VND500,000-700,000) are a steal. Though small, NN99 features clean, comfortable, large beds, cable TV, air-conditioning, and modern decor. The staff is helpful and attentive. In addition to free Wi-Fi throughout the building, there is a computer in the lobby for guest use. Don't bother spending the extra money for a room with a balcony, as it's small.

The **Beautiful Saigon Hotel** (62 Bui Vien, D1, tel. 08/3836-4852, www.beautifulsaigonhotel.com, VND630,000-1,197,000) is a good value with modern, if small, rooms. Each room comes equipped with cable TV and air-conditioning, and has a window. The hotel is on the main drag, so opt for a higher floor for

quiet. The superior and deluxe rooms have in-room computers, bathtubs, and complimentary fruit baskets.

Though there are clean, comfortable rooms and a nice reception area, it is the staff that makes the experience at **Nguyen Khang Hotel** (283/25 Pham Ngu Lao, D1, tel. 08/3837-3566, www.nguyenkhanghotel.com, VND504,000-735,000, breakfast included). Down an alley, removed from the city noise, Nguyen Khang has rooms with and without windows as well as free Wi-Fi, cable TV, and air-conditioning. The friendly receptionists can recommend restaurants and activities. Book in advance, as the hotel's 13 rooms fill up quickly.

With the assurance that it's "not an ordinary one-star hotel," the **Cat Huy Hotel** (353/28 Pham Ngu Lao, D1, tel. 08/3920-8716, www.cathuyhotelvn.com, VND525,000-630,000, breakfast included) does not disappoint. Featuring large, well-decorated rooms and impeccable service, this family-owned mini-hotel is an excellent spot, near enough to the backpacker area but tucked down an alley. All rooms have air-conditioning, free Wi-Fi, and cable TV. The hotel also offers services such as laundry and travel arrangements.

While rooms at the **Saigon-Europe** (207 De Tham, D1, tel. 08/3837-3879, www.saigoneuropehotel.com, VND714,000-1,155,000, breakfast included) are on the small side, modern decor and impeccable cleanliness more than compensate, not to mention the flat-screen TVs and computers in each room. Rooms (with or without windows) come with in-room safety deposit boxes, toiletries, mini-bar, and complimentary fruit basket. The friendly staff assist with additional services such as laundry and motorbike rentals.

Over VND2,100,000

On the edge of one of Saigon's busiest roundabouts, the **New World Hotel** (76 Le Lai, D1, tel. 08/3822-8888, www.saigon.newworldhotels.com, VND2,100,000-6,300,000) boasts over 500 of the nicest rooms in town. Its tower offers sweeping views of the city from the perfect vantage point, not far from Ben Thanh Market. Each plush guestroom features a marble bathroom, a large bed, and satellite television. The hotel has two restaurants serving Western and Asian cuisine, as well as a spa, outdoor swimming pool, fitness center, and tennis courts.

NGUYEN TRAI STREET
VND210,000-525,000

Bloom Hotel III (120/4 Le Lai, D1, tel. 08/3839-5780, www.bloomhotel.vn, VND420,000-588,000) provides clean beds and quality service at reasonable prices. It's located in a quiet alley. The amiable staff is always around to help and each spacious room is equipped with air-conditioning and hot water. This is a stairs-only place. If you prefer an elevator, **Bloom Hotel II** (5 Nguyen Van Trang, D1, tel. 08/3925-0253, www.bloomhotel.vn, VND420,000-798,000) is around the corner. It's equally good, with some more expensive room options.

VND525,000-1,050,000

Down an alley, **Ono Saigon Hotel** (7/8 Nguyen Trai, D1, tel. 09/0230-7286, onosaigon@gmail.com, VND450,000-1,100,000, breakfast included) is spare in its decor but clean, comfy, and spacious. Basic amenities such as air-conditioning and television are available, as well as hot showers and free Wi-Fi. Ms. Rose, the general manager, is always willing to recommend restaurants and other activities.

The bright and cheery ★ **Town House 50** (50E Bui Thi Xuan, D1, tel. 08/3925-0210, www.townhousesaigon.com, VND189,000-882,000, breakfast included) is a pleasant surprise. Set back from the street, this beautiful mini-hotel is decorated in vibrant colors. Though dorm lodging is more expensive than

in Pham Ngu Lao, beds are comfy and spotless. This is one of only a few places to offer all-female dorms. The massive common area has a homey feel. The staff are knowledgeable and can offer recommendations for eating, sightseeing, and other activities. Private rooms are more expensive but equally clean and spacious, with large en suite bathrooms, air-conditioning, hot showers, cable TV, and free Wi-Fi.

VND1,050,000-2,100,000

Despite its modest sign and inconspicuous location, ★ **Cinnamon Hotel Saigon** (74 Le Thi Rieng, D1, tel. 08/3926-0130, www.cinnamonhotel.net, VND1,365,000-1,470,000) exceeds expectations. Dressed in red-and-black *ao dai* (traditional Vietnamese garments), employees are outgoing and personable. Each of the hotel's beautifully furnished rooms features large beds and great attention to detail, with even the air-conditioning units masked by crafty embellishments. The hotel does not have an elevator. From the sumptuous breakfast to the occasional complimentary foot massage and the service-minded staff, this spot is worth the extra cash. Service charges and tax are not included in the price.

Over VND2,100,000

Towering above its surroundings, the chic five-star **Hotel Nikko Saigon** (235 Nguyen Van Cu, D1, tel. 08/3925-7777, www.hotelnikkosaigon.com.vn, VND2,772,000-7,623,000) offers a different vantage point to experience the city. Hotel Nikko's Japanese-inspired minimalist design is evident in its muted, earth-toned rooms. Rooms feature king-size beds, large flat-screen televisions, and in-room safety boxes. In addition to its outdoor swimming pool, Hotel Nikko has a fitness center, on-site spa, and a handful of luxury restaurants.

Food

Saigon is obsessed with food. Everywhere you turn, people are crouched over bowls of noodle soup or picking at fruit and *banh trang tron* (a salad-like mix of rice paper, dried meat, green mango, and seasonings eaten from a plastic bag with chopsticks) in the park. Women hustle across intersections, bamboo poles bouncing beside them, as they carry mobile kitchens from one location to the next; empty stretches of sidewalk become a maze of tiny tables at lunchtime.

While the southern city doesn't have many specialties to call its own, HCMC has managed to appropriate the best of Vietnam and the world so that you can find just about anything to please your palate. Dine in the quiet garden courtyard of an upscale eatery or share tables with a stranger amid the chaotic buzz of a street food stall—wherever you are, there's a solid chance you'll find yourself going back for seconds.

REUNIFICATION PALACE AREA
Cafés and Bakeries

Quiet, charming, and in possession of some of the best sweets in town, **Pacey Cupcakes** (53G Nguyen Du, D1, tel. 08/3823-3223, www.paceycupcakes.com, 9am-10pm daily, VND30,000-60,000) is opposite the south side of the Central Post Office. The café sells a variety of cupcakes, including green tea, double chocolate, passion fruit, red velvet, and banana chocolate. Upstairs, the bar-style seating (made from a sheet of glass atop cupcake tins) and wide-open bay window look directly onto busy Nguyen Du. There is a line of booths that hug the far wall, making for a cozy atmosphere.

Vietnamese

Ngon Restaurant (160 Pasteur, D1, tel. 08/3827-7131, info@quananngon.com, 7:30am-10pm daily, VND40,000-80,000) is a perfect spot for a crash course on local food, offering every meal under the sun at reasonable prices. This large, colonial-style building boasts spacious seating and gives the restaurant a marketplace feel, with cooks set up along the outer edges of its open-air courtyard so that guests can peruse their options before ordering.

Mediterranean

Exactly as the name suggests, **Au Parc** (23 Han Thuyen, D1, tel. 08/3829-2772, www.auparcsaigon.com, 7:30am-11pm daily, VND140,000-260,000) boasts a beautiful location overlooking 30-4 Park. This chic café serves up Mediterranean dishes like hummus, baba ganoush, and shish kebabs. This is also a great place to enjoy a morning coffee or tuck in to either of the Turkish or New York brunches, which are served every weekend.

OPERA HOUSE AREA
Vietnamese

Guests become chefs at **Bo Tung Xeo** (31 Ly Tu Trong, D1, tel. 08/3825-1330, 10am-10pm daily, VND120,000-430,000), a spacious open-air spot, where an extensive menu of do-it-yourself barbecue dishes are on offer. Sturdy clay pot fires are brought to your table, along with a grill and a plate of raw meat. Barbecue your own meat as you like it and choose the accompanying side dishes. Stick to tried-and-true beef, fish, and chicken or try crocodile, ostrich, deer tendon, or goat breast. Meals are reasonably priced and the waiters keep a steady flow of Saigon Red coming.

French

Formerly the Saigon Opium Manufacture, **The Refinery** (74 Hai Ba Trung, D1, tel. 08/3823-0509, www.therefinerysaigon.com, 11am-late daily, VND145,000-420,000) has come a long way from its past involvement in the drug trade. The restaurant offers

Street Food

No trip to Saigon is complete without experiencing street food. From morning to night, locals crowd around cracked plastic tables and miniature stools on every sidewalk in town. Some of the best food in the city comes from a cart. A visit to these mobile businesses brings you the best of Hue, Nha Trang, Can Tho, or Hanoi, all with a southern twist. People from all walks of life flock to these makeshift eateries for a quick *banh mi* (Vietnamese sandwich) or a bowl of pho.

Eating street food can be safer than dining in a local restaurant. Because the kitchen is visible and the meal you're about to enjoy is already on display, you can tell whether or not the cart in question is clean, safe, and worth a visit. There are several good streets, where the food masters congregate. **Huynh Man Dat** in District 5, not far from Nguyen Trai, does a fair turn in Chinese-style street food, while **Nguyen Thuong Hien** in District 3, north of Nguyen Thi Minh Khai, is a popular spot for delicious rice and noodle dishes.

French cuisine and is outfitted in the style of a Parisian bistro. Meals are top-notch, featuring barbecued swordfish, steak frites, gourmet cheeseburgers, and homemade pasta dishes. Come for the weekend brunch (11am-4pm Sat.-Sun.). A complimentary chocolate fountain occupies the front dining room.

Italian

An affordable, white-tablecloth affair, the atmosphere at **Ciao Bella** (11 Dong Du, D1, tel. 08/3822-3329, www.saigonrestaurantgroup. com, 8am-11pm daily, VND105,000-430,000) is cozy and communal. With New York-style Italian dishes and an intimate dining space, this restaurant prides itself on its diverse menu and constantly changing list of specials, featuring old favorites such as spaghetti al pomodoro and chicken parmesan and more unique dishes like Tuscan beef stew with mascarpone polenta. Entrées are generous, and servers are attentive. A nice wine selection is also on offer.

Pizza

With hip European decor and an excellent handle on Italian food, ★ **Pizza 4Ps** (8/15 Le Thanh Ton, D1, tel. 012/0789-4444, www. pizza4ps.com, 7am-11pm daily, VND140,000-300,000) is surprisingly a Japanese creation. Only when you flip past the margherita and quattro formaggi to toppings like calamari seaweed and salmon miso cream do the

restaurant's roots become apparent. Meals at 4Ps are more expensive than other local Italian places, but the extra money spent is well worth it if you're craving a good pie. Book before you go, as this is one of the only places in town that usually requires a reservation.

Western

Inside the gates of the Ton Duc Thang Museum, **Zest Bistro & Cafe** (5 Ton Duc Thang, D1, tel. 08/3911-5599, www.zestbistrocafe.koalaco.com, 7am-10:30pm daily, VND77,000-255,000) follows a simple mantra: "Good drinks, good food, good company." The back wall of this Western café and eatery is covered with a propaganda-inspired mural paying homage to these very things, while the front windows open onto the museum's peaceful courtyard. Zest's menu features hearty meat-and-potato meals, as well as a selection of vegetarian options and interesting coffees and teas.

NGUYEN HUE STREET
Vietnamese

The narrow corridor leading up to the **Temple Club** (29-31 Ton That Thiep, D1, tel. 08/3829-9244, www.templeclub.com. vn, 11:30am-10:30pm daily, VND140,000-285,000) is a step back in time. Lined with white elephant statues and Chinese wood carvings, the red-tiled entryway leads to an opulent dining room, where dark wooden furniture and deep red curtains create an old-world feel. The menu features expertly prepared Vietnamese, Chinese, Khmer, and French cuisine. Though prices are slightly higher than other local restaurants, the upscale atmosphere and food are worth it. Book a table before going, as dinnertime can be very busy.

Japanese

Expensive, but worth every penny, **Nhan Sushi** (62 Ngo Duc Ke, D1, tel. 08/3915-2280, nhansushibito@gmail.com, 11:30am-2:30pm and 5:30pm-10:30pm daily, VND75,000-350,000) is a tiny restaurant opposite the Bitexco Tower. Its menu features an impressive list of authentic Japanese fare, including a handful of excellent lunch sets. Reservations are a good idea in the evenings, as the place fills up once the work day ends.

Thai

Squeezed down a narrow alley off Mac Thi Buoi, **Lac Thai** (71/2-71/3 Mac Thi Buoi, D1, tel. 08/3823-7506, 11am-2pm and 5pm-10pm daily, VND130,000-280,000) offers some of the most authentic Thai food in the city. From noodles and tom yum soup to Thai curries, the menu runs from conventional to unexpected, and the intimate dining area is decked out in plush sofas and low tables. Both upstairs and downstairs seating are available. Its hidden location gives the place a serene, laid-back vibe.

BEN THANH MARKET AREA
Cafés and Bakeries

Calm, cool, and centrally located, **ID Cafe** (34D Thu Khoa Huan, D1, tel. 08/3822-2910, www.idcafe.net, 8am-11pm daily, VND35,000-125,000) is a trendy café not far from Ben Thanh Market that is popular among locals and foreigners. Customers gather around its solid wood tables for coffee, smoothies, and decent Vietnamese food. Vintage records decorate the walls and mood music plays in the background, adding to the

laid-back vibe. There is also a larger second location (61B Tu Xuong, D3, tel. 08/3932-0021, 8am-11pm daily) in District 3.

French

Just behind Ben Thanh Market is the French-owned and -operated **Une Journee A Paris** (234 Le Thanh Ton, D1, tel. 08/3827-7723, 7am-7:30pm daily, VND80,000-140,000), a Parisian-style bakery and sandwich shop decked out in pink and purple. Its glass display case features pain au chocolat and croissants as well as several other cakes, all of which are made fresh. Sandwiches are also served on European-style baguettes.

PHAM NGU LAO STREET
Cafés and Bakeries

Sozo (176 Bui Vien, D1, tel. 09/0930-6971, www.sozocenter.com, 7am-10:30pm daily, VND25,000-125,000), a two-story café near Pham Ngu Lao serving tea, coffee, and mouthwatering Western-style pastries, began as a street cart. The owner's original aim was to help out a few local families struggling to make ends meet, but business outgrew the cart, and the café was born. The shop runs several volunteer programs and employs the disadvantaged and people with disabilities.

Street Food

A stone's throw from the backpacker area, **Quan 96** (96 Le Lai, D1, tel. 08/3839-9317, 5pm-10:30pm daily, VND75,000-125,000) is one of the few street-side restaurants that has an actual menu. With a few plastic tables and chairs and a barbecue, this place serves up standard pork and chicken dishes, frog, eel, and Vietnamese hotpot. The tastiest dish is the *ga chien nuoc mam* (fried chicken wings in fish sauce), which pairs perfectly with an ice-cold beer.

Western

A narrow, barely there shop on the far side of Pham Ngu Lao, the **Hungry Pig** (144 Cong Quynh, D1, tel. 08/3836-4533, info@thehungrypig.com, 7am-10pm daily,

VND70,000-110,000) shows great potential with its varied lineup of bacon sandwiches. Beyond the fat pink pig emblazoned across the shop's awning, a large menu on the back wall lists sandwich combinations as well as a build-your-own menu with different types of bacon, cheese, veggies, and sauces. Solid iron-and-wood picnic-style furniture takes up most of the space indoors and out. The walls feature antique, black-and-white portraits of—you guessed it—pigs.

Bread & Butter (40/24 Bui Vien, D1, tel. 08/3836-8452, 11:30am-2:30pm and 5pm-midnight Tues.-Sun., VND85,000-185,000) is the place to go for hearty comfort food. Boasting a menu filled with burgers, steak, mashed potatoes, and other stick-to-your-ribs meals, this small, quiet spot down one of Pham Ngu Lao's more popular alleys is an excellent place to enjoy a home-cooked meal.

Southeast Asian

The masterful chefs at **Baba's Kitchen** (164 Bui Vien, D1, tel. 08/3838-6661, www.babaskitchen.in, 11am-11pm daily, VND60,000-110,000) supply Saigon with cheap, authentic Indian food smack-dab in the heart of the backpacker district. The menu lists standard Indian fare, including masalas, curries, daals, and vindaloos, and everything is made in-house, including the paneer. Though there are a couple of more upscale Indian ventures in town, this is the best.

Drawing upon several different regional cuisines, **Monsoon** (1 Cao Ba Nha, Nguyen Cu Trinh, D1, tel. 08/6290-8899, hang@monsoonsaigon.com, 10am-11pm daily, VND100,000-350,000) is an upscale Southeast Asian restaurant serving everything from pad Thai to Burmese mohinga. Aromatic spices linger in the air; the dining room's simple, black-and-white decor makes for a peaceful, laid-back setting. An extensive wine collection and top-notch service also contribute to the restaurant's success.

Vegetarian

The An Lac Pagoda, located in Pham Ngu Lao, has drawn a handful of vegetarian restaurants into the area, including **Ngoc Tho** (175/9 Pham Ngu Lao, D1, tel. 08/3836-0162, 8:30am-11pm daily, VND30,000-300,000). This no-frills eatery churns out delicious meat-free Vietnamese food, and has recently expanded its menu to include Western dishes and some carnivorous fare.

NORTHERN DISTRICT 1
★ Street Food

Ever since Anthony Bourdain visited HCMC in 2009, Nguyen Thi Thanh, better known as **The Lunch Lady** (23 Hoang Sa, D1, from 11am daily, VND40,000), has become a local celebrity. Her cart, at the edge of a clearing not far from the Saigon Zoo, serves up a different soup every day, from spicy *bun bo Hue* (soup with beef and rice noodles) to pho or Cambodian-style *hu tieu* (rice noodle soup). Around noon the sidewalk becomes a mess of diners hoping to get a bowl. The Lunch Lady has no set closing time and sells her soup until it's sold out. Get there no later than mid-afternoon or you may find that she's done for the day.

Just north of the massive Tan Dinh Church is **Tan Dinh Market** (Hai Ba Trung and Nguyen Huu Cau, D1, tel. 08/3829-9280, 6am-6pm daily, VND20,000-75,000), which houses several food stalls along Nguyen Huu Cau. A variety of local dishes are available, including vegetarian fare, as well as juices and smoothies. One of its best offerings is *banh canh cua* (crab soup with thick, rope-like rice noodles).

The namesake specialty at **Banh Xeo 46A** (46A Dinh Cong Trang, D1, tel. 08/3824-1110, 10:30am-9pm daily, VND60,000-100,000) is the star here. Cooks crouch over piping hot pans, dishing up large *banh xeo* (southern-style Vietnamese pancakes). A deft waiter will rush over with a pile of fresh greens, fish sauce, and pickled vegetables, and from there it's up to you. Roll your pancakes up in the accompanying lettuce leaves, throw in a few herbs for flavor, dip in fish sauce, and enjoy. The pancakes come in regular and large sizes and can be easily split between two people.

The restaurant offers a handful of other items, like fresh and fried spring rolls and barbecued meat.

Vietnamese

★ **Quan Mien Cua 94 Cu** (84 Dinh Tien Hoang, D1, tel. 08/3910-1062, 9am-10pm daily, VND80,000-500,000) is a well-known local spot that specializes in soft-shell crab. A row of live crabs sits outside the storefront, waiting to be turned into soup or spring rolls, fried or steamed. The *mien xao cua* (crab with glass noodles) and tamarind soft-shell crab are particularly noteworthy. There are a few impostors located nearby: Quan Mien Cua 94 Cu is the shop just before the corner, not directly on it.

Cuc Gach Quan (9-10 Dang Tat, D1, tel. 08/3848-0144, www.cucgachquan.com.vn, 9am-11pm daily, VND80,000-220,000) is a return to the basics. Inspired by his grandmother's street food stall, owner and architect Tran Binh transformed this French colonial house into an intimate restaurant serving traditional countryside fare. Each meal is arranged on antique earthenware dishes, and chopsticks are kept in recycled milk tins. The menu may overwhelm, but knowledgeable servers will recommend dishes like pork stewed in a claypot, morning glory sautéed in garlic, or homemade fried tofu with chili and lemongrass. Binh's pledge to "eat green, live healthy," means that ingredients are all natural, down to the drinking straws, which are hollow vegetables. All meals are served family-style.

Vegetarian

With an emphasis on Buddhist tenets and healthy living, the folks at **Lau Nam Chay An Nhien** (94 Nguyen Van Thu, D1, tel. 08/3910-1129, www.launamchayannhien.com, 9:30am-9:30pm daily, VND30,000-250,000) create delicious vegetarian dishes without mock-meat or any artificial products, instead using mushrooms and other all-natural ingredients. The menu runs the gamut from spring rolls and southern specialties like *hu tieu My Tho* (rice noodle soup) to a meatless hotpot and an excellent, aromatic rendition of pho. The dining area is clean, spacious, quiet, and comfortable. Best of all, prices are affordable, with most one-person dishes setting you back no more than VND50,000.

DISTRICT 3
Cafés and Bakeries

All but invisible from the street, **Cliche Cafe** (20 Tran Cao Van, D1, tel. 08/3822-0412,

Quan Mien Cua 94 Cu specializes in soft-shell crab.

Know One, Teach One

When Vietnamese-Australian Jimmy Pham first opened the KOTO hospitality training center in Hanoi over a decade ago, it was his goal to provide a small number of Vietnam's disadvantaged youth with a better future. Years on, **KOTO** (151A Hai Ba Trung, D3, tel. 08/3934-9151, www. koto.com.au, 8am-10pm daily, VND65,000-350,000) has not only given young people without resources a steady income and hope for the future but also the necessary skills and training to succeed in the hospitality industry at an international level. KOTO, which stands for Know One, Teach One, has two training centers in Hanoi and Ho Chi Minh City and recruits roughly 30 young people between the ages of 16 and 22 to the program every six months. The Saigon branch is set back in an alley off Hai Ba Trung and offers indoor and outdoor seating, not to mention expertly prepared Western and Vietnamese fare.

7:30am-10pm daily, VND20,000-50,000) is nestled at the end of a narrow alley. With simple furnishings, soft music, and a collection of vintage knickknacks, like antique Vietnamese typewriters and clocks, this coffee shop is an oasis. Cliche serves only drinks, including coffee, tea, and fruit juice.

An extension of the Fly Cupcakes chain, **Fly Garden** (25A Tu Xuong, D3, tel. 08/3932-2299, www.flycupcake.vn, 8am-10:30pm daily, VND45,000-65,000) is a cross between a Western coffee shop and a Vietnamese *san vuon* (garden) café. The bakery, lined with fairy lights in cupcake wrappers, offers sweets like cream puffs, tarts, and cupcakes. The wall of vines outside brings a hint of green to the city, while inside the whimsical decor and mellow music make this a pleasant place to unwind. There is an eclectic food menu featuring Vietnamese, Western, and Japanese items.

A local institution, the perpetually busy **Sinh To 142** (142 Ly Chinh Thang, D3, tel. 08/3848-3574, 9:30am-11pm daily, VND20,000-30,000) is exactly like a local café but without the coffee. From sunup to sundown, this open-front shop slings an assortment of fresh smoothies and juices, ranging from conventional single-fruit drinks to more unusual combinations, like avocado-mung bean, tomato-mango, or the deceptively delicious carrot-coconut.

Japanese

For cheap Japanese cuisine, visit **Tokyo Deli**

(250A Dien Bien Phu, D3, tel. 08/3932-2277, www.tokyodeli.com.vn, 11am-10pm daily, VND40,000-100,000), a popular sushi chain with a couple locations around Districts 1 and 3. These large restaurants have prix fixe lunches (about VND100,000) and also offer an à la carte menu throughout the day. The service isn't stellar, but the space is nice and the price makes it worth a visit if you're in the mood for something different.

Street Food

Popular with local office workers, the **Rice Stall** (Truong Dinh between Nguyen Thi Minh Khai and Vo Van Tan, D3, 11am-2pm Mon.-Fri., VND20,000-50,000) on Truong Dinh street just north of Tao Dan Park cooks up at least a dozen different dishes for lunch every day, including pork, eggs, tofu, beef, and a variety of vegetables to go along with rice, not to mention soup and iced tea. Low tables are set up along the sidewalk and the place gets busy around noon.

Vegetarian

Located inside the grounds of the Vinh Nghiem temple, **Vinh Nghiem Vegetarian Restaurant** (339 Nam Ky Khoi Nghia, D3, tel. 08/6683-5563, www.vietchay.vn, 7am-9pm daily, VND40,000-90,000) is one of the city's most well-known vegetarian restaurants and, due to its location, also one of the more peaceful places to sit and have a quiet meal. The restaurant serves up a range of Vietnamese dishes without the meat, including soups, tofu, and fried rice options.

With its placid courtyard and back-to-basics philosophy, **...hum** (32 Vo Van Tan, D3, tel. 08/3930-3819, www.hum-vegetarian. vn, 10am-10pm daily, VND65,000-100,000) is a pleasant escape from the roar of the city. Concealed by a high wall, a floating walkway leads over a mossy pond and into the courtyard. The decor is simple, with wooden furniture and chopsticks wrapped in pandan leaves. The menu lists tofu and vegetable dishes, and explains the specific health benefits of each meal. The spring rolls and spicy tofu are especially good.

Vietnamese

Behind the Reunification Palace is **Khoai** (3A Le Quy Don, D1, tel. 08/3930-0013, www. khoairestaurant.com, 7am-10:30pm daily, VND55,000-155,000), a cozy restaurant specializing in southern coastal cuisine from Nha Trang. The majority of its dishes feature seafood, the most famous being *bun cha ca,* a rice noodle soup with grilled pressed fish. The restaurant itself is nothing special, but the food is tasty and the location convenient for hungry sightseers.

Have lunch at **Vietnamese Noodles** (2 Cong Truong Quoc Te, D3, tel. 08/3824-7557, www.vietnamesenoodles.vn, 7am-late daily, VND55,000-120,000) overlooking District 3's Turtle Lake and you'll leave with a better understanding of the country's many noodle soups, from *hu tieu* and pho to *bun bo* and *bun cha ca.* This delicious and affordable spot lets diners choose the ingredients for their large bowls of soup. As you eat, enjoy views of the park below.

Slightly removed from downtown, **Quan Dat** (16 Truong Dinh, D3, tel. 08/3843-7390, 9am-10pm daily, VND70,000-125,000) serves incredible, affordable meals to a local crowd. Mastering the art of Phan Rang cuisine, seafood-infused southern food featuring a savory peanut sauce, Quan Dat's most popular dishes are *banh can* (small egg-and-rice-flour cakes topped with meat or seafood) and a smaller, seafood version of *banh xeo* (savory Vietnamese pancakes). Sit downstairs near the window overlooking the street or in the spacious second-floor dining area, where wooden tables and chairs line the room.

Vietnamese-Mexican Fusion

A riot of color on a quiet street, the dining room at **Khoi Thom** (29 Ngo Thoi Nhiem, D3, tel. 08/3930-0233, www.khoithom.com,

Quan Dat is a popular local restaurant that features southern Vietnamese specialties.

10am-11pm daily, VND95,000- 180,000) is hard to miss. Brightly hued wooden chairs and tables adorn this al fresco setting, where chefs marry the best of Vietnamese and Mexican cuisine by using common ingredients and a bit of creativity. Signature dishes like ginger and honey barbecue spare ribs and beefsteak Khoi Thom highlight the fusion of these two cuisines, making for a unique and mouthwatering meal.

CHO LON
Street Food
Well off the beaten path and a challenge to find, Ca Ri De Musa (001 Bldg. B, Su Van Hanh Apts., D5, tel. 08/3858-2888, 10am-11pm daily, VND50,000-150,000) is a small, bustling eatery that does an excellent rendition of *ca ri de* (goat curry). Take a seat at one of the many metal tables indoors or out and tuck into a hearty helping of the dish, accompanied by a baguette. Foreigners are few here, so you might draw attention during your visit. To find the restaurant, look for the flashing red-and-blue sign reading "Ca Ri An Do" beside 202A Su Van Hanh.

On a street packed with dumpling shops and touts waving at passersby, the ★ Chinese noodles (193 Ha Ton Quyen, D11, 11am-midnight daily, VND15,000-50,000) at shop 193 are the best of the best. Order a piping hot bowl of *mi sui cao xa xiu* (soup with egg noodles) with Chinese-style dumplings and pork and take in the bustling chaos of this eating street. The shop is out of the way, but the reward is an authentic, mouthwatering bowl of noodles. Don't forget to grab a *tra hong* (sweet tea) to go with your meal.

Vegetarian
Off the beaten path, Tiem Chay Tuong Vien (58-62 Huynh Man Dat, D5, tel. 08/6275-8938, 6am-9pm daily, VND25,000-50,000) is like any local restaurant but for its lack of pork, beef, or chicken. This humble shop serves everything from mock-meat barbecue to vegetarian pho and Chinese-style stir-fried noodles. Prices are easy on the wallet, and at lunchtime you'll find impressive mock-meat renditions of many Vietnamese dishes, including vegetarian claypot catfish and barbecued pork. Their menu does not have an English version, but it's fine to point at what you want to order.

Information and Services

TOURIST INFORMATION
Saigon Tourist (23 Le Loi, D1, tel. 09/0928-4554, www.saigon-tourist.com, 8am-6:30pm daily) is able to provide helpful information to travelers, as well as free city maps. It is a for-profit entity, so your questions may be answered with a pamphlet or a travel brochure. There is also a second Saigon Tourist office (45 Le Thanh Ton, 7:30am-6:30pm daily) near the corner of Dong Khoi.

Most hotels in the backpacker area have travel agencies attached to them, and even if you don't purchase a trip through their business, chances are the receptionist can give you practical information.

If you're looking for information about transportation or day trips outside the city, a better spot to visit is Sinh Tourist (246-248 De Tham, D1, tel. 08/3838-9593, www.thesinhtourist.vn, 6:30am-10:30pm daily) near Pham Ngu Lao. This massive company provides travel services within Saigon, throughout the country, and into Cambodia. Employees speak English well and are helpful in presenting options. Vinaday Travel (228 De Tham, D1, tel. 08/3838-8382, www.vinaday.com, 7:30am-9pm daily) is another reliable and friendly source in the backpacker area that provides helpful information to travelers, even if you forgo their tours and venture out on your own. The company also handles hotel reservations and other logistical services.

BANKS AND CURRENCY EXCHANGE

ATMs are plentiful in the city. Drawing money directly from your account is often a better deal and less hassle than trying to exchange dollars or traveler's checks at a local bank.

There are countless currency exchange kiosks advertised around District 1, particularly in the Pham Ngu Lao area and around Nguyen Hue. You can also visit one of the gold shops near Ben Thanh Market to exchange currency. **Ha Tam Jewelers** (2 Nguyen An Ninh, D1, tel. 08/237-243, 8am-9pm daily) is a reliable place to buy and sell foreign bills.

International banks like **ANZ, HSBC,** and **Citibank** follow the typical business day, opening 8am-5pm Monday-Friday; the majority of local banks in Saigon keep odd hours, breaking for lunch in the middle of the day and opening again for only a few hours in the afternoon. A trip to a local bank can often be a tedious affair. But, if you need a local bank, visit **Vietcombank** or **Techcombank.** Several of these institutions provide Western Union wire services. For the most part, you're better off visiting an institution with some foreign affiliation.

Vietnam is a cash-only country, so check before trying to use your credit card anywhere in Saigon. Some high-end boutiques and hotels accept American Express, Visa, and MasterCard.

INTERNET AND POSTAL SERVICES

A handful of shops in District 1 sell postage stamps, but there are no mailboxes in Vietnam. To send mail, you'll need to go to a post office. Pay a visit to the **Central Post Office** (2 Cong Xa Paris, D1, tel. 08/3924-7247, 7:30am-6pm daily) near Notre Dame Cathedral. In addition to being a worthy sightseeing spot, it is the city's main post office. The **District 1 post office** (65-67 Le Loi, D1, tel. 08/3821-4350, 7:30am-noon and 1pm-6pm Mon.-Fri., 8am-noon and 1pm-5pm Sat.) is located at the base of Saigon Center and is slightly closer to the Pham Ngu Lao area.

There is a **DHL** (3bis Nguyen Van Binh, D1, tel. 08/3844-6203, www.dhl.com.vn, 8am-6pm Mon.-Sat.) around the western side of the Central Post Office building as well as a **UPS** (1 Nguyen Van Binh, D1, tel. 08/3824-3597, www.ups.com, 8am-noon and 1pm-6pm Mon.-Fri., 8am-noon Sat.). Sending large or expensive items from Vietnam is not advised. Even reputable international companies have been known to tack on additional fees and prices change inexplicably.

Wireless Internet is available throughout the city at most hotels, cafés, and restaurants; all you need to do is ask for the password. Many hotels keep a desktop computer in their lobby for guests to use.

PHONE SERVICE

For anyone planning to stay in Vietnam beyond a couple weeks, a mobile phone is a good idea. Cheap but reliable Nokia phones can be purchased new or secondhand at **The Gioi Di Dong** (136 Nguyen Thai Hoc, D1, tel. 1/800-1060, www.thegioididong.com, 8am-10:30pm daily) starting from VND350,000. Tourist SIM cards are available in the Pham Ngu Lao area and at the post office for about VND90,000. These are less expensive than a regular SIM, but only make domestic calls. Vietnamese mobile service runs on a pay-as-you-go basis, and phone credit is sold throughout the city. There are several carriers, most notably Viettel, Vinaphone, and Mobifone; look for these names posted outside *tap hoa* (convenience stores). Credit can be purchased in VND20,000, VND50,000, VND100,000, and VND200,000 increments.

EMERGENCY AND MEDICAL SERVICES

Vietnam has no single phone number for general emergency services. Dial 113 for the police, 114 for the fire department, and 115 for a local ambulance. Don't expect any of these operators to speak English or for help to come quickly. Emergency services in Vietnam are not often helpful and can be more hassle than they're worth.

In the event of a medical emergency, go to a foreign medical center. Local hospitals have aging and overcrowded facilities, and it is doubtful that you'll find an English-speaking doctor. All of the best-equipped facilities in town have 24-hour emergency services. **Family Medical Practice** (Diamond Plaza, 34 Le Duan, D1, tel. 08/3822-7848, www.vietnammedicalpractice.com, 24 hours daily) operates a 24/7 emergency hotline and medical staff are always on standby. The same goes for **International SOS Clinic** (167A Nam Ky Khoi Nghia, D3, tel. 08/3829-8424, www.internationalsos.com, 24 hours daily), which provides routine check-ups as well as emergency services. Both of these clinics are reputable and staffed by well-qualified doctors. The largest and most sophisticated facilities are located at **FV Hospital** (6 Nguyen Luong Bang, D7, tel. 08/5411-3333, www.fvhospital.com, 24 hours daily), which is reminiscent of a standard Western hospital. Due to its size, the facility is located farther from the city center, in District 7. The hospital operates a **24-hour emergency hotline** (tel. 08/5411-3500).

For non-emergencies, **Columbia Asia International Clinic** (8 Alexandre de Rhodes, D1, tel. 08/3823-8888, www.columbiaasia.com/saigon, emergency room 8am-9pm daily) is located downtown between Notre Dame Cathedral and the Reunification Palace. The clinic also offers emergency services, though it closes at night.

Pharmacies *(nha thuoc tay)* are common throughout the city and carry all manner of prescription and over-the-counter drugs. Most pharmacies within District 1 have at least one English-speaking staff member. **Pharmacy 22** (214 De Tham, D1, tel. 012/8472-3669, 7am-9:30pm daily) on the corner of De Tham and Bui Vien is reliable and sells hard-to-find products like contact solution and tampons.

DIPLOMATIC SERVICES

The massive, heavily guarded **U. S. Consulate** (4 Le Duan, D1, tel. 08/3520-4200, www.hochiminh.usconsulate.gov) provides assistance in emergency situations such as arrest, destitution, or serious illness. It keeps separate hours for specific services, so if it's not an emergency then check the website for hours. The consulate is closed to the public on Wednesdays and on Vietnamese and American holidays. In the event of an emergency, the consulate assists U.S. citizens 8:30am-4:30pm Monday-Friday.

Getting There

AIR

Ho Chi Minh City is connected to the rest of the world by **Tan Son Nhat International Airport** (SGN, tel. 08/3848-5383), located just four miles north of the city center. This is the country's largest airport, seeing 15-17 million passengers each year and serving prominent international carriers and regional budget airlines.

Immigration and processing lines move at a steady pace, but be prepared to wait if you are receiving your visa stamp at the airport.

Taxis from the Airport

This is the easiest way to get downtown. Outside the arrivals area are dozens of taxis waiting to ferry passengers into the city. Cab drivers can be persistent, so turn left down to the end of the sidewalk and find a dispatcher from either Mailinh or Vinasun companies. (There are occasional reports of tourists being overcharged or meters running faster than they should when using lesser-known companies.) Forming lines is an oft-ignored concept in Vietnam, so be proactive and let the dispatcher know where you're going. Getting to downtown District 1 takes about 40 minutes and costs VND150,000-180,000. Rides from the airport are metered, not flat rate.

Xe Om from the Airport

Though it requires a bit of a walk, you can take a xe om (motorbike taxi) directly from the airport. If you're a lone traveler, it's cheaper than grabbing a cab. Exiting the arrivals area, look for an overpass. (From the international terminal, it's ahead and to the right; for domestic arrivals, it will be ahead and to the left.) Follow the other people walking past this structure toward the road. There will be a parking lot on your right and, beyond it, bustling Saigon traffic. Xe om drivers will start to approach at this point. Agree upon your fare before you set off. A typical ride to the Pham Ngu Lao area should take about 25 minutes and cost no more than VND80,000.

Public Bus from the Airport

If you're up for traveling like a local, you can take **public bus 152** (6am-6pm daily, VND5,000) from the airport directly to Ben Thanh Market, a stone's throw from the backpacker area. This is the cheapest transportation option and takes about 40 minutes to reach the market. Don't expect anyone on the bus to speak English.

TRAIN

The **Saigon Train Station (Ga Saigon)** (1 Nguyen Thong, D3, tel. 01/900-6469, www. vetau.com.vn) sits just south of the Nhieu Loc Canal in District 3 and is the final destination for all domestic trains. The country's north-south Reunification Line runs along the coast from Hanoi with major stations in Hue, Danang, and Nha Trang before reaching HCMC. Trains arrive from Nha Trang in the early morning or Phan Thiet in the late evening. There are always taxi drivers and xe om drivers waiting outside the station's main entrance; it's about 15 minutes via taxi or xe om to downtown. Public bus 7 can also take you

to the main bus station at Ben Thanh Market (30 min., VND5,000).

BUS

The majority of tourist buses coming from Can Tho, Nha Trang, Dalat, and Mui Ne drop off passengers in the Pham Ngu Lao area of District 1. Tour operators usually park their vehicles around 23-9 Park or on De Tham, right in the heart of Pham Ngu Lao. **Phuong Trang** (272 De Tham, D1, tel. 08/3830-9309, www.futabuslines.com.vn, 5am-1am daily) is a major bus provider, as is **Sinh Tourist** (246-248 De Tham, D1, tel. 08/3838-9593, www. thesinhtourist.vn, 6:30am-10:30pm daily).

There are three stations used by local buses. To the northwest is **An Suong bus station (Ben Xe An Suong)** (Quoc Lo 22, D Hoc Mon, tel. 08/3883-2517), nine miles from the city center, just beyond the airport where Truong Chinh street turns into Highway 22. Also nine miles from the city center is the **Western bus station (Ben Xe Mien Tay)** (Kinh Duong Vuong, D Binh Tan, tel. 08/3877-6594), which sits farther south and serves the Mekong Delta. For all other destinations, Saigon's **Eastern bus station (Ben Xe Mien Dong)** (292 Dinh Bo Linh, D Binh Thanh, tel. 08/3899-1607) is a mere four miles from town. It is unlikely that you will need to visit any of these places, but if your bus drops you at one of these stations, the usual modes of transportation—taxis, xe om, and the public bus—are all good ways to get downtown.

MOTORBIKE

The most direct—and congested—route into the city is National Highway 1, a gritty, chaotic road that runs into town from the Mekong Delta on the western side and Phan Thiet on the eastern end. Highway traffic is usually a mess, full of massive trucks, buses, cars, and motorbikes, and the flow of vehicles becomes more backed up as you approach the city, particularly during the evening rush hour.

Coming from the east, things start to get better once you reach the Saigon Bridge, which takes you out of District 2 and, from there, into the city center. If you're approaching from the Mekong Delta, Highway 1 curves north to avoid Saigon. Make a right onto Vo Van Kiet (look for signs), and follow the road straight into town, getting off at the Ben Thanh Market exit. If you go too far, you'll know it—the Thu Thiem tunnel leads right back out of town and into District 2.

Getting Around

TAXIS

When traveling in the city, it's best to hail a green-and-white **Mailinh** (tel. 08/3838-3838) or green, white, and red **Vinasun** (tel. 08/3827-2727) cab, particularly at night. These vehicles are clean and well kept, the drivers are knowledgeable, and the meters correct. Other cab companies are okay to use during the day.

Cab drivers occasionally try to beat the system by taking a longer route than necessary. The most trusted cab companies in Saigon are Vinasun and Mailinh, so it's a safe bet to stick with them. Never bargain for a cab ride in Vietnam. All taxis are metered and it is always to your benefit to use the meter.

It's easier to hail a cab from the street rather than calling for one, but if it's late at night or no taxis are around, then ask a Vietnamese speaker to call for a Mailinh or Vinasun taxi.

XE OM

As you wander around the city, you will hear cries of "You! Motorbiiiiiiiiike!" These are Saigon's *xe om* drivers, an impressive and eclectic fleet of motorbike drivers that ferry people from place to place. This is the most efficient way to get around town, though it is not for the faint of heart. *Xe om* drivers drive fast and are just as likely as the rest of the population to break traffic laws. Always agree on a price before embarking and stand firm on that agreement, as drivers sometimes attempt to glean extra cash from you later on.

The going rate for a *xe om* fluctuates depending on where you're headed, so ask a local what they might pay to get an idea of a fair price. At night, stick to taxis.

CYCLOS

Hopping on a cyclo can be a nice way to see the city. Muscular cyclo drivers will pedal you around the downtown area and past some of the city's most popular sights. Many drivers speak English well, as these pedal-powered vehicles are more likely to be used by visitors for tours of District 1 than by the local population, who prefer to get around on a motorbike. Prices are negotiable, though you should be prepared to pay more than you would for a *xe om,* as your driver will also be your guide around town and he is doing a lot more legwork than someone on a motorbike. The experience is fun and something that many visitors to HCMC enjoy, but this is not a method of transportation for someone in a hurry.

BUSES

An efficient army of bright green city buses roams Saigon's streets. Buses generally run 5am-7:30pm, but some may go as late as 9pm. It can be difficult to navigate the dizzying maze of bus routes that crisscross the city, though there is a handy interactive bus map online (www.saigonbus.net) that helps. Paper maps are available at the main **bus station** (Quach Thi Trang roundabout, tel. 08/3821-4444), across from Ben Thanh Market.

Buses vary in size from minibuses to large air-conditioned vehicles. Bus stops are either a small, navy blue sign listing that stop's buses, or full covered stops with a bench and route map.

A trip within the city limits will set you back about VND5,000. If you're heading farther afield, prices go up according to your destination.

VEHICLES FOR HIRE

Motorbikes are available for hire (VND100,000-120,000 per day) throughout the Pham Ngu Lao area. Before heading out, give the bike a short test-drive and check that you have the vehicle's registration card. **Chi's Cafe** (40/31 Bui Vien, D1, tel. 09/0364-3446, www.chiscafe.com, 9am-10pm daily, VND100,000) has good, reliable vehicles, both automatic and semi-automatic, and offers daylong and long-term rentals (only for visitors staying in the city). **Trung's Motorbikes** (185 Pham Ngu Lao, D1, tel. 09/0330-8466, trung_motorbike@yahoo.com, 7am-10pm daily, VND80,000-120,000), a tiny green shop on the corner of a small alley, also has rentals available.

If you're looking to buy a bike for a longer trip around the country, signs advertising heavy-duty vehicles for sale can be found in the backpacker area. Make sure to have the bike checked by a mechanic before finalizing the purchase.

When driving around town, there are essentially no rules. People drive while texting, neglect to use the correct turn signals (if they use them at all), routinely speed in the opposite direction down a one-way street, and generally disregard lane markings. Exercise caution on the road and obey stoplights and traffic laws as you would at home, even if others don't.

Cu Chi Tunnels

Considered one of the greatest tactical achievements of the southern insurgency during the American War, the **Cu Chi Tunnels** (Ben Dinh, Nhan Duc Commune, Cu Chi, tel. 08/3794-8823, www.cuchitunnel.org.vn, 7am-5pm daily, VND90,000) spiderweb beneath miles of rice paddies and fertile farmland all the way from Ho Chi Minh City to the Cambodian border. As early as the 1940s, members of the Viet Minh resistance army (later the National Liberation Front, or NLF) began digging out these cramped crawl spaces by hand. With technology and firepower far inferior to their French enemies, the tunnels allowed Ho Chi Minh's rebel forces to communicate with nearby villages and bases undetected. By the time the American War arrived in the 1960s, a 155-mile underground network existed.

Initially, the tunnels were meant to provide escape routes and shelter during American bombing raids. As soon as the skies were clear, guerrillas would emerge from their tunnels, cart away the unexploded ordnance left behind and use these weapons to create grenades and smaller explosives. These homemade weapons were then planted alongside other, more crude booby traps, such as sharpened bamboo sticks and iron spikes. In the thick and unfamiliar jungle, the NLF proved almost invisible.

The retaliatory acts further frustrated American and south Vietnamese troops. Bombing raids became more frequent and the area was deemed a free-strike zone, giving U.S. pilots permission to shoot at anything that moved. With the onslaught of explosives, the NLF moved underground, sometimes for weeks or even months at a time. Kitchens and bedrooms were constructed, as well as hospitals, meeting rooms, theaters, and concert halls. Children were born below ground and entire communities set up. The most shallow tunnels were at least five feet underground, but four different levels of passageways existed, with each progressively smaller than the last. Overall, the crawl spaces ranged 2.5-4 feet wide and 2.5-6 feet high.

For every effort the U.S. military made to defeat the NLF, rebels in Cu Chi were one step ahead. Until the very end of the war, the NLF fighters defended their land successfully against the Americans and south Vietnamese.

Today, the government-run tourist area

encompassing the Cu Chi tunnels features exhibits, guided tours, and a variety of other attractions. Weapons displays illustrate the gruesome methods of the NLF and hint at the hardships of those who lived underground.

Park guides escort you through the tunnels, telling of the history and people of Cu Chi. At each of the two tunnel sites, Ben Dinh and Ben Duoc, the narrow passageways have been lit and widened to accommodate visitors. Larger subterranean rooms are occasionally furnished with mannequins and other items.

The history of the Cu Chi tunnels is more interesting than a visit to the tunnels themselves. The present-day memorial site is a bit of a circus. On the same land where an estimated 45,000 men and women gave their lives over the course of the war, visitors are able to fire machine guns, play paintball, or splash around in a swimming pool. While the significance of these tunnels during the war is a valuable part of local history, visiting Cu Chi tends to be polarizing among tourists: people either love it or hate it.

Visitors are welcome to watch a harsh anti-American propaganda film that depicts a rosy picture of life in Cu Chi during the war, with smiling NLF women plowing the fields, rifles slung across their backs. In reality, conditions beneath the ground were horrific: snakes and poisonous creatures were rampant within the tunnels, along with malaria and other diseases. Though collapses were uncommon, when they did occur, death was almost certain. Those who survived weeks and months below ground often emerged with health problems, largely from lack of oxygen and sunlight. For all these flaws, the film manages to provide some useful historical information.

BEN DINH TUNNELS

The **Ben Dinh Tunnels** are the more popular of Cu Chi's two underground sites. This area is more touristy than its counterpart up the road. While it can become congested in the late morning and early afternoon, guides and other park staff at Ben Dinh speak more English than those at Ben Duoc. The web of tunnels and exhibits at Ben Dinh is more compact, allowing for visitors to get around more easily.

A souvenir shop hawks mass-produced tchotchkes, and a handful of restaurants sit across the road from the Ben Dinh entrance. There are also vendors within the grounds selling snacks and light meals at slightly inflated prices.

BEN DUOC TUNNELS

Farther down the road, the older **Ben Duoc** site is less frequented than Ben Dinh. It contains near-identical tunnels and weapons displays but is significantly more spread out than Ben Dinh. If you wish to visit other parts of the Cu Chi tourist area—such as the AK-47 shooting range—you will be required to take an electric car, which is available for hire near the park entrance. There are a handful of on-site restaurants serving light meals (VND20,000-100,000) as well as a few souvenir vendors just beyond the entrance.

CU CHI WILDLIFE RESCUE STATION

The **Cu Chi Wildlife Rescue Station** (Route 15, Cho Cu 2 Hamlet, An Nhon Tay Commune, Cu Chi, tel. 09/8428-1190, www.wildlifeatrisk.org, 7:30am-11:30am and 1pm-4:30pm daily, VND200,000) is a fantastic organization funded by the nonprofit Wildlife at Risk. The center rehabilitates endangered species trapped, caught, or injured in the illegal wildlife trade. With Vietnam ranked the worst nation on earth for wildlife crime by a 2012 WWF report, protecting these creatures from harm is no small feat. Employees use tips from local residents to learn the whereabouts of endangered animals and then, with the aid of the police, go into private residences, shops and even restaurants to save the creatures from abuse. Animals are then brought back to the rescue station and restored to full health before being released into the wild.

The Cu Chi Wildlife Rescue Station houses everything from otters and wildcats to large exotic birds, a variety of turtle species, slow

Options for Onward Travel to Angkor Wat

From Vietnam, many travelers venture across the Cambodian border to the magnificent temples of Angkor Wat, the largest religious monument in the world. Far and away the easiest point of departure is Ho Chi Minh City, where you can access Cambodia by air, boat, or bus.

It is possible to reach Angkor Wat from Hanoi, but there are more transportation options from HCMC. The only practical way to travel from the north to Siem Reap, the town closest to Angkor Wat, is by plane.

For more detailed information on Angkor Wat, see *Moon Angkor Wat* by Tom Vater.

BUS

From Saigon, the cheapest and most comfortable option is the bus. A number of tour operators in the Pham Ngu Lao area provide clean, comfortable, air-conditioned buses to Siem Reap at reasonable prices. All vehicles pass through the Moc Bai border gate en route to Phnom Penh, the Cambodian capital, before carrying on to Siem Reap's main bus station, about three miles east of town. While it is possible to book a direct ticket to Siem Reap, the trip from Saigon to Phnom Penh takes about six hours; to Angkor Wat is another seven hours. Most people spend the night in Phnom Penh before carrying on to the temples. Cambodia does not allow sleeper buses on its roads, and so even in a plush, new bus, the 12- to 14-hour journey can be tedious.

Sinh Tourist (246-248 De Tham, D1, tel. 08/3838-9593, www.thesinhtourist.vn, 6:30am-10:30pm daily) offers one daily departure to Phnom Penh in the early morning, as well as an afternoon bus from Phnom Penh to Siem Reap. The first leg of the trip usually costs USD$10-12, with the second leg around USD$5 (fares fluctuate seasonally). Non-stop tickets straight to Siem Reap are available for roughly the same price as there is still a stop in Phnom Penh. There are Sinh Tourist offices in HCMC, Phnom Penh, and Siem Reap, so you can book each leg of the trip separately if you decide to hang out in the Cambodian capital for a few days before continuing on.

Other reputable local operators include **Sapaco Tourist** (325 Pham Ngu Lao, D1, tel. 08/3920-3623, www.sapacotourist.vn, 5am-8:30pm daily), whose prices are comparable to Sinh Tourist but with the added benefit of multiple daily departures from HCMC to Phnom Penh. Buses move quickly through the border and, while you can book a non-stop ticket through to Siem Reap (around USD$21) with a Cambodian tour operator, Sapaco does not provide separate service from Phnom Penh to Siem Reap. Those spending a night in Phnom Penh will have to book additional transportation to Angkor Wat once they arrive in the capital. This should be no problem, as Siem Reap is a major tourist destination. The same goes for **Kumho Samco** (239 Pham Ngu Lao, D1, tel. 08/6291-5389, www.kumhosamco.com.vn, 6am-10pm daily), which provides buses to Phnom Penh at competitive prices but does not serve Siem Reap.

Package tours are available through Sinh Tourist, Sapaco Tourist, and Kumho Samco, including transportation, hotels, and guides at the temple site. These deals tend not to be worth it because

lorises, bears, and a whole host of monkeys. Several English placards are situated throughout the grounds, providing information on each of the species at the center. The staff are knowledgeable and dedicated to educating the public on animal rights issues. A small indoor exhibit provides more insight into the practices of the illegal wildlife trade and the demand for traditional Chinese medicine ingredients, which include bear paws, rhino horns, and other animal parts.

Interested visitors should contact Mr. Lam, whose information is available on the center's website, to arrange an appointment. A groundskeeper lets you in and gives you a full tour of the facilities, which are located directly between the Ben Duoc and Ben Dinh areas of the Cu Chi tunnels. The entrance fee helps pay for food and other basic necessities for the animals.

TOURS

For dirt-cheap mass tours, **Sinh Tourist** (246-248 De Tham, D1, tel. 08/3838-9593, www.

the whirlwind 3- and 4-day trips are too short to enjoy your visit. If you plan on traveling overland to Angkor Wat, you will need a few more days to do so comfortably.

AIR

If you're pressed for time, your second-best option is to book a flight through either **Vietnam Airlines** (www.vietnamairlines.com) or **Cambodia Angkor Air** (www.cambodiaangkorair.com). The two airlines are almost identical, down to some of their planes, which the Cambodian company has on loan from Vietnam. The flight is one hour long. If you're booking online, check both airline sites. Cambodia Angkor Air offers better prices on one-way tickets, while round-trip fares on Vietnam Airlines are more competitive. Both carriers fly out of HCMC and Hanoi, arriving at Angkor International Airport in Siem Reap, about four miles from the temples and seven miles from the center of town.

Vietnam Airlines has several ticketing offices scattered throughout Saigon. It's possible to book your ticket online then pay in cash at one of the airline's ticketing counters, provided you do so within 12 hours of booking and at least 12 hours before departure. Cambodia Angkor Air only accepts online payments via credit card and does not have an official ticketing office in Vietnam.

BOAT

For those with time to spare and more patience, boats travel from Chau Doc in Vietnam's Mekong Delta to Phnom Penh, and then onto Chong Kneas, a floating village about seven miles from Siem Reap. The trip is comprised of several legs—a bus ride to Chau Doc, followed by two boat rides and a *tuk tuk* ride into town. This method is often regarded as inefficient and a bit of a rip-off. Depending upon the water level and time of year, boats can break down, and even at the best of times they are noisy and uncomfortable. The fare from Phnom Penh to Siem Reap costs around USD$25, and the boat may be canceled due to lack of passengers. If you're looking to cruise around the Mekong Delta, save it for a separate day trip from Saigon and make use of the faster, more reliable buses that run between these destinations.

VISAS

All visitors to Cambodia are required to purchase a visa, which can be done on arrival at a border gate or at the airport in Siem Reap. Tourist visas cost USD$20 and require filling out paperwork and having your fingerprints scanned. Do not confuse these with the USD$25 "ordinary visa," which is unnecessary unless you plan on staying in Cambodia for an extended period of time. All visas to Cambodia are paid for in American currency, so have U.S. dollars and at least one passport photo on hand when you get to the border.

thesinhtourist.vn, 6:30am-10:30pm daily, VND109,000-169,000) and **Vinaday** (228 De Tham, D1, tel. 08/3838-8382, www.vinaday.com, 7:30am-9pm daily, VND157,000) offer half-day trips to the tunnels or full-day tours combining Cu Chi with a visit to the Cao Dai temple at Tay Ninh. Admission to the tunnels is not included in the price, but you are spared the hassle of navigating the public bus system and a tour guide is provided. Groups tend to be 30-40 people; get a spot at the front if you want to hear what your guide has to say.

Ho Chi Minh City Urban Adventures (tel. 08/3827-9279, www.hochiminhcityurbanadventures.com, VND903,000-1,512,000) runs a tour from the city to Cu Chi for a maximum of 12 people, allowing for additional one-on-one time with the guide and more than the cookie-cutter speeches provided by the guides at the park. The company offers a standard park visit along with a couple flourishes, including a brief stop at a local farm en route to the tunnels, as well as a chance to learn how rice paper is made. HCMC Urban

Adventures prides itself on creating tourism that benefits the local community, and so its tours often include extra, off-the-beaten-track stops, which allow travelers to see how the local population lives. Half-day tours to the tunnels are available as well as full-day excursions that go to both the Cu Chi tunnels and the Cao Dai temple at Tay Ninh. The company books its tours via Internet or through telephone reservations; travelers can call at any time to book a tour.

More expensive but also more relaxing is a tour with **Les Rives** (Me Linh Point Tower, Ste. 2105, 2 Ngo Duc Ke, D1, tel. 012/8592-0018, www.lesrivesexperience.com, 8:30am-4pm daily, VND1,799,000), a company that provides on-the-water excursions to a handful of nearby sights, including the tunnels. The company offers half-day tours to Cu Chi in both the morning and afternoon. Two meals are served, along with unlimited fruit and refreshments, and the hour-long boat ride to the tunnels eliminates the stress of inching through the bumper-to-bumper traffic that often crowds the outskirts of the city. Hotel pickup and all park entrance fees are included in the tour price. The company also has a ticketing office at the Bach Dang Tourist Wharf.

TRANSPORTATION
Bus
Public buses run regularly to Cu Chi District from the city's main bus station (Quach Thi Trang roundabout, opposite Ben Thanh Market). Take the number 4 bus to An Suong bus station, right on the outskirts of town (1 hour, VND6,000). From there, bus 122 will bring you to Tan Quy junction, where you can catch the number 70 to Ben Duoc. You will carry on for some time in this direction before arriving at the Cu Chi tunnels stop (1.5 hours, VND13,000). It should be easy to spot, as there are large signs announcing the tunnels as soon as you enter the area. The last bus from Cu Chi leaves at 6:30pm.

It is also possible to take bus 13 from the 23-9 Park bus depot (Pham Ngu Lao, near Nguyen Trai) out to the Cu Chi bus station, where you can transfer to bus 79, which takes you directly to the tunnels. Confirm your destination with the driver or fare collector before setting off.

Motorbike
The Cu Chi tunnels are located along Provincial Road 15. From Saigon, take Truong Chinh Street in Tan Binh District out past An Suong bus station on Highway 1, labeled QL22 on the kilometer stones. Roughly three miles past the bus station, make a right onto Ba Trieu Street. Once you reach the Hoc Mon Market, this road changes names a few times, from Trung Nu Vuong to Do Van Day, but will eventually turn into Provincial Road 15. Stay on this route for another 20 miles and you'll find yourself at the tunnels. The drive takes 1.5-2 hours.

While it is possible to reach the tunnels on your own, this trip is not recommended for novice drivers, as it involves a stretch along Highway 1, the nation's busiest and most dangerous road. Unless you have a hired driver at your disposal, save yourself the hazard and the headache and hop on a tour or a public bus instead.

Tay Ninh

Located roughly 55 miles northwest of Saigon, at first glance Tay Ninh appears to be a run-of-the-mill Mekong Delta town, full of sparkling green rice paddies and laid-back countryside charm. But between the never-ending expanse of fertile fields and narrow, winding waterways is a fascinating quirk: Tay Ninh is the official base of Cao Dai, a homegrown religion that uses séances to communicate with a higher power and worships the likes of Vietnamese poet Nguyen Binh Khiem, French author Victor Hugo, and Chinese revolutionary Sun Yat-Sen as saints.

Formerly part of Cambodia, this western province didn't come under Vietnamese control until the 18th century. It has since played a significant role in its resistance against foreign powers. Once a major stronghold of the Viet Minh, Tay Ninh suffered numerous bombings at the hands of the Americans. The region's sole mountain, known as Ba Den, or Black Virgin, served as an important base for American and south Vietnamese troops during the American War. Nowadays, the mountain is revered not only by Caodaists but also many other Vietnamese as a sacred site.

TAY NINH HOLY SEE

A colorful, sprawling complex in an otherwise sleepy town, the **Tay Ninh Holy See** (Ly Thuong Kiet, Hoa Thanh Town, tel. 06/6312-3456, www.caodai.com.vn, 6am-6pm daily) is the epicenter of Caodaism. Built in 1933 by a devout group of followers, the holy city's main temple stands at the end of a long, narrow parade ground, flanked on either side by banks of stadium-style seating. This is the most ornamental and visually interesting piece of architecture within the Cao Dai complex.

Leave your shoes at the edge of the raised sidewalk surrounding the building. The temple's exterior has an ornately decorated entrance and a long, three-tiered roof. Inside, the building is divided into three separate areas that pay tribute to the three main branches of Caodaism: the legislative branch, the administrative branch, and the spiritual branch. The small area at the front belongs to the three protectors and upholders of Caodaist law: Ho Phap at the center, and his right- and left-hand men, Thuong Sanh and Thuong Pham. These three men are represented by a set of colorful statues inside the main hall. On the opposite wall, facing the temple's main entrance, a painting depicting three of Caodaism's most famous saints, poet Nguyen Binh Khiem, Sun Yat-Sen, and Victor Hugo, shows the trio writing the phrases "God and humanity" and "love and justice" in French and Chinese.

The administrative branch of Caodaism is represented in the long, airy main hall where Caodaist followers, known as adepts, participate in religious proceedings. This is the most colorful and decorative section of the temple. Wide-eyed, multi-hued dragons snake down the endless rows of pillars, while the ceiling is painted to reflect a bright blue sky with silver stars. The all-seeing eye, the central symbol of Caodaism, is featured heavily upon the walls, surrounded by lotus flowers and repeating up all nine of the main hall's steps to the altar. Here, a large blue orb adorned with stars and a single image of the all-seeing eye sits at the center of a large table, upon which offerings of fruit, tea, alcohol, and other items are presented.

Religious ceremonies take place four times a day: at 6am, noon, 6pm, and midnight. Most guided tours arrive at the temple in time for the midday procession, in which men and women file into the temple from separate sides and take their place within the main hall. The entire length of the building is divided into nine steps, each of which represents part of the hierarchy within Caodaism. Only about six steps are used, while the rest remain empty, including a series of red-and-gold lacquer chairs at the very front, which are reserved for the Pope and other high-ranking members of the religion. During prayer, men take the right side of the temple and women the left. The adepts complete a series of prostrations before the altar as well as several religious chants, usually accompanied by a band of traditional Vietnamese musicians, who sit on the balcony.

Due to the high volume of visitors at the temple, adepts usher you along after some time to allow for other visitors to watch the ceremony from above. You'll also be able to wander around the main entrance of the temple. If you stick around long enough, the adepts file out after prayer and a smaller group returns with another altar, this time filled with incense, fruit, and other offerings, which is blessed on each and every step up to the altar before being placed in front of the all-seeing eye.

On your way out of the building, take a look across the parade grounds into the distance to find another cluster of sparkling, intricate towers devoted to the trio of protectors who guard the laws of Caodaism. If you've got time and want to ask questions, local adepts are friendly and willing to chat, though few of them speak English.

There have been some reports of shoe theft outside the temple, so you can remove your shoes and carry them inside, though it's better to stick them in your bag and out of sight, or you may be told to leave them again.

TOURS

While the strange and colorful proceedings of a Cao Dai ceremony are worth seeing, Tay Ninh can be a challenge to reach from HCMC independently if you've only got one day. Since there are few to no other attractions in the area, most people prefer to visit the Holy See on a guided tour, usually combined with a trip to the Cu Chi tunnels, which lie between HCMC and Tay Ninh.

On the larger, more inexpensive tours, like the ones provided by **Vinaday** (228 De Tham, D1, tel. 08/3838-8382, www.vinaday.com, 7:30am-9pm daily, VND157,000) and **Sinh Tourist** (246-248 De Tham, D1, tel. 08/3838-9593, www.thesinhtourist.vn, 6:30am-10:30pm daily, VND159,000), 30-40 travelers are shepherded into the temple and, shortly thereafter, ushered out and back onto the bus. Groups arrive in time for the midday religious proceedings and later stop to have lunch at a restaurant en route to the Cu Chi tunnels.

For significantly more money, companies like **HCMC Urban Adventures** (tel. 08/3827-9279, www.hochiminhcityurbanadventures.

religious ceremony at Tay Ninh Holy See

com, VND1,512,000) run combined temple-and-tunnel tours, which include a home-cooked meal with a local family as well as a knowledgeable and enthusiastic guide. **Tiger Tours** (tel. 012/9586-8586, www.mytigertour.com, VND1,575,000-2,835,000) offers similar prices, taking visitors to the Cao Dai temple and the top of Ba Den Mountain before heading to the Cu Chi tunnels. This company also provides tailor-made itineraries. In addition to online reservations on their respective websites, both HCMC Urban Adventures and Tiger Tours use a hotline to book and arrange their tours, so travelers can call at any time.

ACCOMMODATIONS

If you're heading to Cambodia, it is possible to stop in Tay Ninh on your way. This is a town best visited on a day trip, as there are other routes into Cambodia with more to see, but if you require a place to stay the night, a handful of reasonable accommodations exist within Tay Ninh.

Good, clean, bare-bones accommodations can be found at the **Yen Anh Hotel** (99/5 Ton Duc Thang, Hoa Thanh, tel. 06/6383-6333, VND150,000-200,000), a stone's throw from the Holy See in Hoa Thanh town. The rooms supply the essentials: a bed, a shower, air-conditioning, TV, and Wi-Fi. You'd be hard-pressed to find a cheaper option.

The massive concrete slab that makes up **Hoa Binh Hotel** (210 30 Thang 4, Tay Ninh, tel. 06/6382-1315, kshbtayninh@yahoo.com, VND280,000-900,000) is filled with large, tidy rooms not far from the high-way. Lodgings include air-conditioning, hot water, TV, and Wi-Fi. An in-house restaurant serves breakfast and light meals. Two-star Hoa Binh is the pick of the litter here.

Song Lam Hotel (353 30 Thang 4, Tay Ninh, tel. 06/6381-1177, VND300,000-500,000) is a respectable option for a single-night stay in Tay Ninh. Accommodations are clean and spacious and feature the standard amenities, including hot water, air-conditioning, refrigerator, wireless Internet, and TV.

FOOD

You won't find many high-end restaurants but there are plenty of affordable options close to the Holy See that give travelers the chance to eat like a local. By far the most famous provincial specialty is *banh canh,* thick, rope-like noodles that come with meat, usually pork or chicken, and soup. Most menus include a variety of well-priced Vietnamese fare served up in a no-frills atmosphere.

Long Hoa Market (Huynh Thanh Mung, Hoa Thanh Town, 5am-6pm daily, VND15,000-50,000) is about two miles south of the Holy See and sells a variety of clothing and household items along with cheap local meals, including rice dishes and a range of noodle soups. Buy your food from one of the stalls, then eat there or take your meal to go.

Right beside Hoa Binh Hotel is **Quan Com Thanh Thuy** (Khu Pho 1, 30 Thang 4, Tay Ninh, tel. 06/6382-7606, 7am-8pm daily, VND35,000-100,000). Though the restaurant offers nothing out of the ordinary, its location makes this a convenient spot.

The bare-bones **Quan An Huu Loi** (153 Vo Thi Sau, Tay Ninh, tel. 06/6362-1393, 6am-10pm daily, VND25,000-60,000) offers well-priced family-style meals, including chicken, beef, and pork dishes, in a clean setting. The restaurant is not far from the main road, situated just 1.5 miles from both the Holy See and Highway 22B.

For something different, **Lau Nam Gia Khanh** (83 30 Thang 4, Tay Ninh, tel. 09/3463-8393, www.launamgiakhanh.vn, 10:30am-10pm daily, VND100,000-700,000) serves up 20 varieties of mushrooms alongside its namesake *lau* (hotpot), a pot of broth that arrives at your table accompanied by vegetables, meat, and egg noodles, all of which can be added to the stock at your discretion.

TRANSPORTATION
Bus

If you're up for a long adventure, it is possible to catch a bus from the main bus station (Quach Thi Trang roundabout) at Ben Thanh Market. Bus 703 leaves from here often, heading for Moc Bai bus station near the Cambodian border. From Moc Bai, catch bus number 5 to Tay Ninh town. Buses arrive at the **Tay Ninh bus station** (Trung Nu Vuong, tel. 06/6382-3363).

The entire journey takes 3.5-4 hours and costs VND35,000. The earliest bus from Saigon departs from Ben Thanh around 6am. The last bus from Moc Bai departs at 5:30pm; leave Tay Ninh around 3pm to make the last bus.

Motorbike

Tay Ninh is located northwest of Saigon on National Highway 22B. Though it's a challenge to extricate yourself from the tangle of roads that surround the city, once you finally get onto Highway 1, also known as QL22 on the kilometer markers, it's a straight shot to Go Dau junction, a massive roundabout. Hang a right and follow Highway 22B to Tay Ninh.

To reach Tay Ninh using Provincial Road DT782, follow Highway 1 to Trang Bang, a small town 25 miles outside of the city, and bear right on Boi Loi street, which becomes DT782. This road joins up with DT784 10 miles later. Make a left here and head for Tay Ninh, about 20 miles out. Once you arrive in town, ask a local *xe om* driver to escort you to the Holy See, located in the eastern part of town, for about VND30,000.

Vung Tau

Stretching out into the ocean, Vung Tau was not always the buzzing tourist town it has become. Well before droves of domestic visitors began to flock here for weekend getaways and summer vacations, Vung Tau played a significant role in the military history of most powers to occupy Vietnam. For centuries, its view of Can Gio, the entryway into the Saigon River, made it a valuable strategic outpost for several different armies, from the Vietnamese battling against colonial invasion in 1859 to the French army, a brief occupation by the Japanese during WWII, and an extended presence of the Australian military throughout the American War.

In the 19th and 20th centuries, French colonists identified this sleepy beach town as the ideal spot from which to keep an eye on Saigon. It was armed with artillery cannons and military forts, hidden deep in the thick tangle of jungle, which still obscure many of its mountainsides today. Later, when the NLF and Communist forces were battling against Western troops, the Australian military, who had come to assist their American allies, set up a logistics base in the area, stationing its soldiers all over Ba Ria-Vung Tau province. Throughout the region, tunnels were dug, forts built, and several significant battles played out within the mountains.

Years of missionary proselytizing created a strong Catholic following alongside Buddhist traditions. Every other building is a bright, eye-popping decorated pagoda or a towering, stark white statue of Jesus Christ or the Virgin Mary. One of Vung Tau's most famous attractions is the gigantic Christ of Vung Tau, believed to be among the largest statues of Jesus Christ in the world.

Vung Tau is regarded as a weekend tourist hot spot, packed with domestic visitors and overpriced goods. Avoid Vung Tau on Saturdays, Sundays, and public holidays. Its beaches have a reputation for being on the seedy side, due to some harassment of women in revealing swimsuits. Focus on the town's sights and you'll be fine.

CHRIST OF VUNG TAU

Vung Tau's most famous monument, the enormous **Christ of Vung Tau** (2 Ha Long, main gates 6:30am-5pm daily, statue 7:30am-11:30am and 1:30pm-4:45pm daily) is among the largest statues of Jesus Christ in the world. Nestled partway up Small Mountain, this sculpture is 105 feet tall, with a 60-foot

Vung Tau's soaring statue of Christ watches over the shoreline.

but a skilled motorbike driver could take the narrow path up here.

Before entering the statue, take your shoes off and leave all bags at the door. On either side of the main monument are two massive French artillery cannons. Beyond the statue, small bridges arch over a waterless canal: This is where the French transported ammunition to the cannons, loading the magazines from below.

Anyone wearing short shorts or a tank top will be turned away from the statue.

FRENCH FORT RUINS

A lesser-known but equally fascinating relic of Vung Tau's history are the **French Fort Ruins** scattered across Big and Small Mountains. From as early as the late 19th century, the French colonial government recognized Vung Tau as a valuable military outpost, affording them a clear view toward the mouth of the Saigon River. Several separate forts were built, each extensively armed. Soldiers kept watch from their on-site living quarters, and underground rooms were built to accommodate ammunition stores. During WWII, the Japanese also made use of these posts. Following the end of French colonial rule, many of the military forts were abandoned. Several of these hidden forts remain forgotten, covered in plant life and crumbling on the mountainsides of Vung Tau. The local authorities have done little to maintain these sites, giving the old forts an eerie feel.

One of these military forts exists on the back passage from Christ of Vung Tau, which begins on **alley 220 of Phan Chu Trinh street.** At the entry to the ruins is a battery of artillery guns as well as the remains of a well and some living quarters. Below, the dark, cave-like opening leads beneath the guns. If you've got a flashlight handy, you can venture inside (though it's more than a bit spooky) and see where and how the guns were loaded, feeding ammo up through a metal chamber at the center of the back room. If you visit the statue of Christ of Vung Tau on foot, it is also possible to hike down to these ruins, as they're

wingspan. Vung Tau's statue is taller than the Christ the Redeemer statue in Rio de Janeiro. Visitors can ascend the narrow interior, going 133 steps up for a stunning 360-degree view of Vung Tau and the ocean.

Construction began in 1974, before the end of the American War. A year later the statue was complete, but the 800-odd steps from the base of Tao Phung to the base of the statue had yet to be finished. Construction was suspended over the next decade, and the statue sat partially hidden in the thick brush of the mountain. When it was discovered that the statue's lightning rod system—the metal points of the halo—had been stolen, the Catholic church was allowed to complete the project. In 1994, the statue and walkway were opened to the public.

Make the long hike to the statue in the early morning or late afternoon, as the sun can be brutal. There is also a back passage up to the statue. It begins from alley 220 of Phan Chu Trinh and ends at the last 200 steps up to the statue. This is no less challenging for hikers, not too far from the stone steps. From the statue, drive across the stone path and down to the left. The ruins will be on your left but are barely visible from the path, appearing as only a bit of stone wall and a hollow doorway. Park your bike and walk up the steps beside the darkened entryway.

The other, more easily accessible fort ruins exist off **alley 444 of Tran Phu street.** The trip up the mountain is pleasant, passing by brightly hued houses and locals raking out their catch of shrimp to dry in the sun. Scenic views abound. There is a plaque providing some general information about the fort, and then two batteries of weapons, one with six artillery guns, the other with three. The road up to these ruins is paved the entire way, making the trip a much easier feat, whether on foot, on a motorbike, or via a hired *xe om* driver.

These historical sites are free to visit and open to the public.

WORLDWIDE ARMS MUSEUM

The modern-day castle that houses the **Worldwide Arms Museum** (14 Hai Dang, tel. 012/7647-0347, roberttaylorvic@yahoo.com, by appointment only, VND100,000) comes as something of a surprise. A towering gray structure that spares no embellishment, the museum houses a boundless collection of weapons and military uniforms from across the globe. Dozens of mannequins don the colors of China, Japan, Mongolia, England, Scotland, and France, while every wall of this massive space is covered in intricately detailed weapons dating back centuries. Englishman Robert Taylor has spent years cultivating both his collection of military memorabilia and rescuing endangered primates in Vietnam.

Upstairs, beside the modern weapons display, is a monkey sanctuary that houses roughly 20 of the endangered creatures, including the stump-tailed macaque and golden-cheeked gibbon, all of whom have been rescued from the illegal wildlife trade. At the time of writing, the museum has plans to relocate. Call to find out more about the museum's status. All proceeds from the entry fee go to the care of the primates.

VUNG TAU LIGHTHOUSE

Though the **Vung Tau Lighthouse** (end of Hai Dang on Small Mountain, 7am-11am and 2pm-6pm daily) is rather unimpressive on its own, its views of the town and the beach, as well as of the Christ of Vung Tau statue, make this a nice spot to visit. Perched 170 meters above sea level atop the summit of Small Mountain, this modest white tower was built in 1910 in order to guide ships leaving and entering the Saigon River. Visitors are not allowed inside the lighthouse, but the views from the ground are pleasant and the breeze is refreshing.

WHITE VILLA

Perched atop a small hill between Front Beach and Big Mountain, **White Villa (Bach Dinh)** (4 Tran Phu, tel. 06/4351-1608, 7am-5pm daily, VND5,000) was built as a holiday residence for the Governor General of Cochinchina, Paul Doumer, in 1898. The six-hectare plot of land originally housed Phuoc Thang Fort, a military base. After colonization, Phuoc Thang was destroyed to make way for the two-story structure that exists today. During its heyday, Bach Dinh served as the living quarters of not only Governor General Doumer but also Emperors Thanh Thai and Bao Dai, Vietnam's final king. With its intricate mosaics and detailed ceramic accents, the grounds surrounding Bach Dinh are surprisingly lush for being so close to the center of town.

A lasting relic of Vietnam's colonial history, the house is most impressive from outside. Inside, the ground floor exhibit is filled with late 17th- and early 18th-century Chinese ceramics and porcelain discovered from a shipwreck bound for Europe that sunk just off the Con Dao Islands. Upstairs is a preserved version of the house's former glory, though the solid wooden furniture and moldy drapes are worse for wear. Upstairs is also a nice spot to take in a sea view.

A long, well-covered path runs out to a headstone honoring Emperor Thanh Thai. Thanh Thai became emperor at the ripe age of 10 and, in his later years, grew unpopular with the French on account of his resistance toward colonial powers. In 1907, he was placed under house arrest at Bach Dinh, living under the watchful eye of the French government until 1916, when he was sent away to Reunion Island, another French colony off the eastern coast of Madagascar. The headstone, emblazoned with a dragon at the top, bears one of the emperor's poems, written in Vung Tau.

BEACHES
Front Beach

Situated right along a bend between the ferry port and Big Mountain, **Front Beach** (Quang Trung and Ha Long streets) is directly at the center of the action. Front Beach Park acts as a buffer between the main road and the water, which comes all the way up to the sea wall. The park makes for a nice place to stop and relax in the shade with swaying palm trees blocking out the midday sun. While Front Beach is fine for swimming and markedly less crowded than Back Beach on the weekends, its flaw is its lack of sand. In the early morning and late afternoon, when the sun is less fierce, this is a lively spot full of local vendors and patrons.

Back Beach

For sunbathing and as much R&R as can be gleaned from the well-touristed shores of Vung Tau, **Back Beach** (Thuy Van between Phan Chu Trinh and Nguyen An Ninh) is the place to go. Spanning two miles—longer than Vung Tau's other main beaches—and boasting plenty of room to lay down a towel, this is a quieter spot during the weekdays and sees more of the foreign tourist crowd, though you are still likely to receive a few stares. The beach itself is nothing stunning, but its close proximity to the rest of town make it a nice escape. There are several tourist areas based on the beach, including **Bien Dong Ocean Park** (8 Thuy Van, tel. 06/4381-6318, www. khudulichbiendong.com, 6am-10pm daily), which features a restaurant, swimming pool, and beach chairs and is free to enter.

SPORTS AND RECREATION
Golf

Part of a larger resort complex, **Paradise Golf Vung Tau** (1 Thuy Van, tel. 06/4385-3428, www.golfparadise.com.vn,

Vung Tau

5am-4:30pm daily, VND1,320,000-1,980,000 for 18 holes) is the town's only golf course. Located about two miles from the town center, the seaside course features three separate areas with a total of 27 holes and offers caddies, golf carts, and rental equipment. Guests can call to book a tee time for 18 holes; fees go up on weekends.

Dog Racing

A lesser-known attraction in Vung Tau takes place every weekend at **Lam Son Stadium** (15 Le Loi, tel. 06/4380-7309, 7:30pm-10:30pm Fri.-Sat., VND50,000-VND100,000), the country's only venue for greyhound racing and one of the few places where gambling is legal for the Vietnamese. Every Friday and Saturday, a few thousand people flock to the stadium to watch the races and wager bets. Purchase a cheap ticket and hang out with the masses, or spring for an air-conditioned balcony view. Drinks and snacks are available inside.

SHOPPING

If you're in need of good beach clothing or a bathing suit, the ultra-modern **Imperial Plaza** (159-163 Thuy Van, tel. 06/4352-6688, www.imperialplaza.vn, 10am-9:30pm Mon.-Fri., 9:30am-10pm Sat.-Sun.) is the place to go. The shopping center has several floors of well-priced local and foreign brand-name clothing, swimsuits, and souvenirs, as well as a small food court on the top floor with mainly Vietnamese food and a café out front. Only Vietnamese sizes are offered here.

ACCOMMODATIONS

Vung Tau is a small town. Most accommodations are within 5 or 10 minutes' drive of its major sights and beaches. The majority of budget accommodations are located on or around Back Beach, while you'll find fancier, more expensive digs near the Front Beach area. Visiting Vung Tau on the weekend is not a great idea, as the city is flooded with local tourists. If you visit on a Saturday or Sunday, book your hotel in advance, as rooms fill up quickly. Many hotels increase their room rates on the weekends.

VND210,000-525,000

Slightly removed from the beachfront tourist zone, ★ **Macca's Place** (31 Lac Long Quan, tel. 06/4352-7042, maccasplacevietnam@gmail.com, VND420,000-VND462,000) more than makes up for its lack of oceanfront property by providing comfortable, tidy rooms with high ceilings and plenty of light. Bruce, the proprietor, is a genial Australian expat full of local knowledge and always willing to chat about the history and sights in the surrounding area. The rest of the staff at this family-owned guesthouse are equally friendly and help give the place a homey feel. Each room comes equipped with a fan and air-conditioning, a television, hot water, and minibar; larger rooms have a balcony. There is a small café downstairs that serves light meals and drinks. Macca's rents out motorbikes and is willing to help with travel arrangements for sightseeing around Ba Ria-Vung Tau province.

No-frills but clean and adequately appointed, the **Dai An Hotel** (151A Hoang Hoa Tham, tel. 06/4352-5439, daianhotel@yahoo.com, weekdays VND350,000-900,000, weekends VND450,000-1,100,000) is minutes from Back Beach and a decent value for the money. Each room includes a fan, air-conditioning, hot water, and a television. Bathrooms are spacious and the hotel staff are kind and easygoing.

Set back from the street, **Mimosa Guesthouse** (60 Vo Thi Sau, tel. 06/4351-3319, vungtaumimosa@yahoo.com.vn, VND350,000-600,000) offers clean and spacious rooms with sky-high ceilings and comfy, generous beds. The staff do not speak much English but are eager and willing to help guests. The guesthouse operates a café next door, which serves light meals and drinks.

Ha Thanh Hotel (137 Phan Chu Trinh, tel. 06/4352-5848, sales.hathanhhotel@gmail.com, VND400,000-950,000) is a decent place to base yourself, not far from the south end of Back Beach. Rooms are clean, with a decent amount of space and light. There aren't many amenities in the hotel beyond hot water and air-conditioning. Breakfast is included in the room rate, though you can get a better deal if you skip the breakfast and just pay for the room.

VND525,000-1,050,000

Overlooking the enormous Martyrs' Memorial roundabout, the decor of the Kieu Anh Hotel (257 Le Hong Phong, tel. 06/4356-3333, www.kieuanhhotel.com, VND580,000-690,000) is nothing special, but its large rooms offer a beautiful view of the monument at the center of the roundabout as well as the manicured grounds. Beds are generously sized and rooms are clean and quiet. Though the hotel seems isolated, the beach is just a short walk down Le Hong Phong street on the other side of the roundabout.

A beautiful building with well-appointed rooms, the Ocean Star Hotel (45 Thuy Van, tel. 06/4358-9589, www.oceanstarvungtau.com, VND650,000-1,450,000) is located right in the heart of Back Beach and offers pleasant views of the ocean. The hotel offers great value for money, as its staff are particularly friendly, and each room comes equipped with modern facilities such as a minibar, hot water, air-conditioning, and a large bathroom.

VND1,050,000-2,100,000

For a step above average, the Ky Hoa Hotel (30-32 Tran Phu, tel. 06/4385-2579, www.ky-hoahotel.com.vn, VND840,000-2,000,000), just beyond the cable car to Big Mountain, boasts large, modern rooms and excellent views of the sea. All rooms feature air-conditioning, hot water, a TV, and large beds, and the hotel has an on-site restaurant and a pool where guests can soak up the sun just opposite the sea. Built into the mountainside, Ky Hoa has plenty of rooms with a view. Superior-level and higher rooms have better views and include a small balcony.

Over VND2,100,000

With peaceful, shaded grounds, stunning rooms, and a stellar view of the sea, it's hard to believe that a resort like Binh An Village (1 Tran Phu, tel. 06/4381-0264, www.binhanvillage.com, VND1,785,000-5,250,000) exists so close to town. Each spacious room features opulent traditional Vietnamese decor and plush beds along with a sitting area and large bathroom. While the smaller rooms are spacious well beyond your average accommodations, Binh An's larger guest suites include a private garden as well as a separate bathtub and shower. Beyond its lodgings, the resort boasts both freshwater and saltwater swimming pools, with the latter built into the ocean and naturally maintained by the ebb and flow of the sea.

FOOD

Being a beach town, Vung Tau is known for its seafood. However, the main culinary specialty is a dish called *banh khot,* which is something like a miniature version of the large, hangover-the-plate southern-style Vietnamese pancakes you might find in Saigon, or their smaller cousins up in the central region. Bite-sized and accompanied by all the same fixings, these fried morsels of rice flour are often topped with shrimp but can also be served with meat or other seafood, usually squid. A healthy serving of fresh greens, pickled veggies, and fish sauce are added to the mix, making for a delectable, authentic Vung Tau meal.

Famed throughout Vung Tau and beyond, the *banh khot* at ★ Banh Khot Goc Vu Sua (14 Nguyen Truong To, tel. 06/4352-3465, 7am-2pm Mon.-Fri., 7am-8pm Sat.-Sun., VND36,000) is considered the best in town. Packed at all hours, this restaurant is just a few metal tables and plastic stools tucked into an outdoor space with pale-blue chain-link "walls." Fresh greens and veggies come standard with every order, as well as fish sauce and as much crushed chili pepper as you can stomach. Grab a lettuce leaf; toss in your *banh khot;* add some pickled carrots and daikon, mint leaves, and other herbs; wrap; dip; and enjoy.

Order a refreshing *nuoc mia* (sugarcane juice) to go with your meal.

For more variety, **Co Ba Vung Tau** (1 Hoang Hoa Tham, tel. 06/4352-6165, www.cobavungtau.com, 7am-10pm daily, VND30,000-60,000) serves equally delicious *banh xeo* (Vietnamese pancakes) as well as *banh khot,* the Vung Tau specialty, and *banh beo,* a steamed rice flour cake similar to its fried counterpart, all in an open-air setting. All meals are reasonably priced and the open kitchen allows diners to watch the food being prepared.

Right in the thick of the cafés and restaurants that surround the cable car to Big Mountain, **Co Nen** (10 Tran Phu, tel. 09/0709-0606, quannuongconen@yahoo. com.vn, 4pm-10:30pm daily, VND80,000-280,000) is a spot-on barbecue joint serving a variety of seafood and meat as well as hotpot dishes. Its decor is limited to the bare essentials, with metal tables and creaky chairs, but the grilled octopus here is incredible and well worth enduring the loud music blaring from the café next door and the flashing lights of the smoothie and snack stands across the way.

Excellent seafood and views of the water can be found at **Ganh Hao** (3 Tran Phu, tel. 06/4355-0909, nhahangganhhao@gmail.com, 9am-11pm daily, VND95,000-900,000), located past the cable car to Big Mountain. The restaurant's huge menu includes everything from squid, fish, shrimp, snails, and several types of crab to Vietnamese meat and vegetable dishes. The restaurant's outdoor dining area is perched right at the edge of the sea. Dishes at Ganh Hao are affordable, with a few higher-cost items available.

★ **Pizzeria David** (92 Ha Long, tel. 06/4352-1012, 8:30am-10:30pm daily, VND145,000-235,000) turns out top-notch classic pies, including a delicious quattro formaggi as well as prosciutto and mushroom. Two floors of open-air indoor and outdoor seating are available, with cozy low tables and patio furniture reminiscent of a European café. Add to this the exposed brick exterior and you might forget you're on the other side

women making *banh khot,* a local Vung Tau specialty

of the world. David's also boasts an impressive wine list as well as pasta dishes, ice cream, and Italian desserts.

Not far from the beach but down a quiet street, **Tommy's 3 Restaurant & Bar** (3 Le Ngoc Han, tel. 06/4355-1626, www.tommysvietnam.com, 7am-10:30pm daily, VND60,000-320,000) has an extensive menu of reasonably priced Western dishes, from hamburgers and pizza to steaks and savory pies, not to mention the self-proclaimed "coldest beer in town." Televisions broadcast international sports channels and a live band performs Fridays and Saturdays. Owners Glenn and Trang Nolan offer travel tips and help visitors with visas, motorbike rentals, or tours to historical sights.

A cozy little spot near Tran Hung Dao Park, **Good Morning Vietnam** (6 Hoang Hoa Tham, tel. 06/4385-6959, www.goodmorningviet.com, 9am-10:30pm daily, VND85,000-210,000) is another anomaly among Vung Tau cuisine, serving up unexpectedly delightful Italian food at affordable prices. Its menu runs the spectrum from standard pastas and pizzas to dishes like gnocchi, risotto, and authentic fish and poultry fare, all accompanied by a healthy wine list. Add to that linen tablecloths and its breezy corner real estate and this tiny Italian eatery is worth a visit.

Overlooking the sea, Ned Kelly's (128 Ha Long, tel. 06/4351-0173, missanh7@gmail. com, 7am-midnight daily, VND60,000-270,000) is a ramshackle, little Aussie expat bar with cold beers and an assortment of Western dishes. The open-air watering hole serves breakfast, lunch, and dinner as well as a variety of drinks and is open later than most bars in town.

On the corner of Hoang Hoa Tham not far from Vo Thi Sau street, Garden Bakery (128 Hoang Hoa Tham, tel. 06/4352-7178, 6:30am-11pm daily, VND15,000-40,000) is a one-story brick building that houses one of the only bakeries in town. Its variety of cakes, pastries, and savory snacks as well as ice cream, coffee, tea, and smoothies make it a nice place to start your morning, whether inside the air-conditioned shop or on the terrace outside, which looks onto a small lake.

INFORMATION AND SERVICES

For medical emergencies, the International SOS Clinic (1 Le Ngoc Han, tel. 06/4385-8776, www.internationalsos.com, 8am-5pm Mon.-Fri., 8am-noon Sat.) keeps physicians on-site 24 hours a day. The clinic has regular hours for non-emergency medical consultations.

GETTING THERE
Boat

Several hydrofoil boat companies in HCMC offer daily departures from Bach Dang Tourist Wharf (10B Ton Duc Thang, D1) opposite the end of Ham Nghi street, with high-speed boats leaving roughly every two hours from 6am to 4:30pm. Vina Express (5 Nguyen Tat Thanh, D4, tel. 08/3825-3333, www.vinaexpress.com.vn, 6am-7pm daily, VND200,000 adults, VND100,000 children) has ticketing offices on-site at the wharf; you

can also book your seat online. The trip takes about an hour and 20 minutes and drops you at the centrally located Ferry Terminal (120 Ha Long) in Vung Tau, just a stone's throw from Front Beach.

In most cases, it is possible to show up at the wharf a half-hour or so beforehand and purchase the ticket then, but if you're visiting Vung Tau on a holiday or weekend then it's best to reserve your seat ahead of time, as this is a popular destination for city folks taking a long weekend. Fares go up on weekends and holidays (VND250,000 adults, VND120,000 children). If you plan to buy a ticket on the day of departure, check the website and confirm that the time you want is still available.

Bus

From HCMC, tourist buses heading to Vung Tau depart regularly from the Pham Ngu Lao area and the Eastern bus station (Ben Xe Mien Dong) (292 Dinh Bo Linh, D Binh Thanh, tel. 08/3899-1607). Several reputable companies make the trip, including Phuong Trang (272 De Tham, D1, tel. 08/3830-9309, www.futabuslines.com.vn, 5am-1am daily, VND110,000) and Kumho Samco (239 Pham Ngu Lao, D1, tel. 08/6291-5389, www,kumhosamco.com.vn, 6am-10pm daily, VND95,000). The trip takes 2.5-3 hours and buses arrive at the Vung Tau bus station (192 Nam Ky Khoi Nghia, tel. 06/4385-9727), about a mile from both Front and Back Beaches.

The return trip can also be made from the Vung Tau bus station via Mailinh (192 Nam Ky Khoi Nghia, tel. 06/4357-6576, hourly 6am-7pm daily, VND90,000) and Kumho Samco (192 Nam Ky Khoi Nghia, tel. 06/4361-1111, 4:15am-6pm daily, VND95,000) bus lines, which have on-site offices.

GETTING AROUND

On account of all the tourists that pass through this town, taking a cab in Vung Tau is notably more expensive than in HCMC. If you're in a larger group it may still be cost-effective to hop in a Mailinh (tel. 06/4356-5656) or **Petro** (tel. 06/4381-8181) taxi when getting around town; opt for a *xe om* if you're traveling solo or in smaller numbers.

It's necessary to bargain for *xe om* rides in Vung Tau. The town is small, so a ride around town should set you back roughly VND30,000-40,000, though be prepared to pay more if you go farther out of the town center.

Most hotels in town can arrange a motorbike for hire. Prices should range VND100,000-175,000 per day.

Con Dao Islands

Arriving in Con Dao is a surreal experience. After the claustrophobic cities of Vietnam's southern coast, the sight of lush, wild green hills and rocky precipices appear like something out of a postcard. Made up of 16 individual islands, Con Dao is one of the best-guarded secrets in Vietnam, a spectacular combination of white sand beaches, thick forests, and sharp, sun-bleached cliffs plunging into the turquoise sea. With 80 percent of Con Son, the main island, a protected national park, there are dozens of opportunities for the adventurous traveler, from hiking, diving, and snorkeling to wildlife-spotting. Endemic species such as the giant black squirrel and bow-fingered gecko can be found along national park trails alongside monkeys and several species of birds. From June to early September, Bay Canh Island hosts dozens of sea turtles laying eggs on the beach, and a couple of diving outfits on the island can take you underwater to glimpse the fascinating and colorful creatures that occupy the surrounding waters.

Con Dao was once the site of several of the nation's most brutal prisons, built by the French during the colonial era and used all the way through the American War to house political prisoners. These horrific places claimed the lives of roughly 20,000 Vietnamese from 1862 until the late 1970s. A look at the surviving prisoners turns up a veritable who's who of the Communist party. Only a handful of the country's prime ministers since reunification did not see the inside of a Con Dao prison. Though locals also venture here for the stunning natural scenery, a visit to the prison cemetery and the shrine of Vo Thi Sau, the first Vietnamese woman to be executed by the French, is all but required for Vietnamese.

Con Dao's relative isolation from the tourist crowds of the mainland means that some initiative is required on the part of visitors to make their own fun. English speakers on Con Son are few and far between. Locals are friendly, and good humor and a few charades go a long way in communication. As a result of its remoteness, certain costs differ from the mainland. Accommodations tend to be cheaper—though more limited—than you might find elsewhere, but food is usually more expensive. Unless you're willing to fork over an arm and a leg at Six Senses, the island's sole five-star resort, restaurants serve only Vietnamese cuisine. The main town on Con Son is very small. It makes little difference where you stay, and most resorts are located on the coastal road; budget options are set farther back into town.

SIGHTS

With the exception of the prison complex, most of the sights around Con Dao are located within the national park.

Museums

Set amid a large clearing just north of Vo Thi Sau Park, the **Con Dao Museum** (10 Nguyen Hue, tel. 06/4383-0517, 7am-11:30am and 1:30pm-5pm Mon.-Sat., free) is a modern take on the islands' older Revolutionary Museum. This museum possesses decent English signage and takes visitors through the history of the islands, from its first European settlers in the early 1500s through the brutal

Con Dao prison system and into the present day. While these exhibits encompass all of Con Dao's past, it is the island's penal history that features most heavily within the museum. In-depth displays cover everything from the daily lives of inmates to the facility's development as a revolutionary school and the harsh mistreatment suffered at the hands of Con Dao's prison guards. If you have the time and interest, this location does an admirable job of providing visitors with detailed information on one of the darkest eras in modern Vietnamese history.

The older, more abridged version of Con Dao's prison history resides at the **Revolutionary Museum** (Ton Duc Thang opposite Quay 914, tel. 06/4383-0517, 7am-11:30am and 1:30pm-5pm Mon.-Sat., VND20,000), where exhibits feature more photos and historical write-ups than actual artifacts. The majority of these images appear at the newer Con Dao Museum as well, so a visit to both venues is unnecessary. If you're looking for a more condensed version of the island's history, this is the place. Entry tickets for this museum are also valid for the prison complex, so hang onto your receipt to show the guides at each respective location.

Con Dao Prison Complex

Perched on the northeastern edge of town, the mossy, crumbling stone exterior of the **Con Dao Prison Complex** (Le Van Viet, tel. 06/4383-0517, 7am-11:30am and 1:30pm-5pm Mon.-Sat., VND20,000) serves as a reminder of the island's grim history. From as early as 1862, the cells within these high-walled structures housed Vietnamese political prisoners banished to the island for acting out against the French colonial government. Miles away from the mainland and the general public, guards quickly became known for their harsh treatment and torture of prisoners, which included forced labor, beatings, and starvation. The conditions of the prison's dank cells were equally miserable, with dozens of inmates crammed into dimly lit rooms and often shackled at the ankles, unable to

move. As the number of political dissidents grew, so did the number of facilities on Con Dao. At its height, the island contained no less than eight separate facilities, each as cruel and unforgiving as the next.

While it is still possible to visit most of the prisons on the island, the main facilities are Phu Hai and Phu Son, located beside one another on Le Van Viet street, as well as the infamously brutal tiger cages a little farther out of town on Nguyen Van Cu. Phu Hai, Con Dao's original prison, is the largest of these buildings and depicts the harsh living conditions of its former inmates with the help of mannequins, which are shackled in the same place where many prisoners once sat. Next door, Phu Son is similar but holds added notoriety as one of the main centers of Communist training within the prison system. Farther afield, the tiger cages sit eerily empty; guests are free to wander around on their own, treading the catwalk above these dark, isolated cells, just as the prison guards would have done.

Entrance tickets can be purchased at any of the prisons or at the **Revolutionary Museum** (Ton Duc Thang opposite Quay 914, tel. 06/4383-0517, 7am-11:30am and 1:30pm-5pm Mon.-Sat., VND20,000) and are valid for all locations so long as you keep the ticket handy to show the gatekeepers. There is little to no signage in most of these places, which is why a visit to either the Revolutionary Museum or the Con Dao Museum is recommended in order to have a better understanding of the history associated with these aging buildings.

Vo Thi Sau Park

The island's most famous revolutioary in a long list of revolutionaries, Vo Thi Sau was just 14 years old when she joined a Communist volunteer police outfit. Despite her youth, the girl became involved in plots to attack and kill French officials, some of which succeeded. In 1950, at 17 years old, Vo Thi Sau was arrested by the French. Due to her age and the harsh public reaction an immediate execution was

The Island Prison of Con Dao

Vietnam is eager to cast off the darker days of the 20th century, opting instead to look toward the future. Many of its wartime sites have been transformed into tourist attractions. While there are plenty of past hardships that the nation seems ready to shrug off, Con Dao still weighs heavily upon Vietnam's collective psyche.

In 1862, a few years after the French wrested control from Vietnam's emperors, the colonial government went to great pains to suppress political dissent among the Vietnamese. Outspoken locals were imprisoned on the small island of Con Son, 111 miles away from mainland Vietnam. Up until the end of the American War, inmates were mercilessly beaten, tortured, starved, and worked to death. The French guards were ruthless, enacting cruel and severe punishments. Forced labor built many of the island's roads and structures, including Quay 914, whose name comes from the 914 prisoners who died over the course of its construction. The miserable living conditions and meager rations were so bad that diseases like leprosy spread rapidly, killing some and leaving others permanently disfigured. The Con Dao prisons claimed 20,000 Vietnamese lives.

Though widely regarded as the most terrible of the prison facilities, the island's infamous tiger cages were but one of a wider array of punishments handed down to the Vietnamese, along with solitary confinement units, in which prisoners were forced to exist in ghastly and unsanitary conditions. Built in 1907 to accommodate the offenders of a student uprising, the tiger cages allowed guards to survey their prisoners from above and permitted inmates very little light or space to move. Those who managed to survive these dank, narrow cells often left with debilitating physical injuries, their muscles atrophied from being shackled in the same place for weeks or months at a time.

sure to produce, officials waited until she was 19 before carrying out the young woman's death penalty in 1952. This made Vo Thi Sau the first Vietnamese woman to be executed by the French. Today, she is deeply revered by locals and nearly every Vietnamese visitor to the island pays their respects at her grave. Though the **Vo Thi Sau Park** (in front of Con Dao Museum, Ton Duc Thang and Nguyen Hue) is small and far less ornamental, there is a small building on the grounds dedicated to offerings for the young revolutionary.

Quay 914

At the center of town, a long sandy walkway protrudes out into the harbor just beyond Saigon Con Dao Resort. This is **Quay 914** (intersection of Ton Duc Thang and Le Duan), not an impressive sight but a historical one. During the brutal years of French rule, prisoners were forced to construct this pier, beginning in 1873 and carrying on for decades. When prisoners faltered or refused to continue work they were beaten severely, causing 914 deaths during the pier's construction.

Today, the quay still functions as an integral part of the harbor. A small plaque honoring the fallen prisoners stands at the entrance.

Hang Duong Cemetery

Though it wasn't constructed until after reunification, the **Hang Duong Cemetery** (Nguyen An Ninh, tel. 06/4383-0517), just outside of town, serves as a final resting place for many of Con Dao's deceased prisoners. In the same spot where, years before, French and American guards had carelessly disposed of Vietnamese bodies, the manicured grounds of Hang Duong are now a peaceful green space with winding pathways.

A walk up the main road brings you to the cemetery's large martyr's monument, a towering stone structure. Hang Duong's most famous resident resides to the left of the main path. Amid a sea of modest red-and-yellow headstones, the large black tomb of Vo Thi Sau, the first Vietnamese woman to be executed by the French, lies in sharp contrast to the other graves in the area. Its sleek exterior is laden with offerings, from fruit and drinks

After the French left, an American-backed south Vietnamese government took over the prison, maintaining the policies of torture and abuse. American officials maintained throughout the 1960s and '70s that Con Dao's tiger cages were no longer in use. That is, until 1970, when photographer Tom Harkin and two American congressmen, Representatives Augustus Hawkins and William Anderson, visited the prison on a government-led tour. Armed with a map drawn by a student who had just been released from the tiger cages, the men discovered the prison's entrance, masked by a vegetable garden. Harkin's photos were published in *LIFE* magazine in July 1970 and served as another blow against American involvement in Vietnam.

Con Dao's overcrowded facilities fast became a de facto training school for the opposition. Shackled side-by-side for hours at a time, the prisoners studied Communist theory and, during the American reign, even published several news magazines, with the written materials smuggled out of the prisons, printed, and then returned to the grounds, where they were disseminated among the inmates. Many of the Communist party's most famous players did time at Con Dao. In a country where most streets and public spaces are named after national heroes, nearly all of the island's roadways bear the name of a former prisoner who went on to greatness.

When the American War ended in 1975, word traveled quickly to Con Dao, where frightened prison guards fled at the news, leaving the island to the Communist captives. On May 4, 1975, nearly 7,500 prisoners walked out of their cells, free at last, to greet the arrival of the Vietnamese navy. Today, visiting the prisons is a rite of passage among locals, who come to pay their respects to the collective ancestors who struggled for national independence.

to flowers, incense, and prayers. Beyond the young revolutionary's resting place, the sight of so many headstones in one area helps to illustrate just how many prisoners succumbed to the harsh conditions on Con Dao.

Con Dao National Park

The largest attraction on Con Son, **Con Dao National Park** (visitors center 29 Vo Thi Sau, tel. 06/4383-0669, www.condaopark. com.vn, 7am-11:30am and 1:30pm-5pm daily, VND20,000) is home to approximately 160 species of animals, including three endemic creatures found only on the islands, as well as over a 1,000 marine species. The park boasts hiking trails, snorkeling beaches, camping, and turtle-watching and bird-watching excursions. Stop by the visitors center to arrange guides, hire boats, or book tours to the different areas of the park. Make your booking at least a day in advance. Given the temperamental weather of the island and the limited organization of the park offices, guides and tours are subject to sudden changes or cancellations; head to the national park office as soon as you

arrive in order to allow enough time for any scheduling hiccups that may occur.

BEACHES

While there are a handful of sandy stretches along the main drag that are largely used by fishermen, the crème de la crème of the island's beaches lie farther afield. Wherever you lay out your towel and catch sun, there is little chance you'll be disappointed: with far fewer people and far less pollution than its mainland counterparts, Con Dao's beaches live up to the hype. Locations range from easily accessible to a few hours' trek. Always bring insect repellent, as the sand flies can be a major detractor from your stay in paradise. If you don't have repellent, swing by the **Dive! Dive! Dive!** shop on Nguyen Hue and ask Larry to set you up. When visiting beaches that are not accessible from the main road, chances are you will be required to pay the national park entry fee (VND20,000).

Dat Doc Beach

Stretching along the southern coast just before

you enter town is **Dat Doc Beach,** a beautiful patch of white sand framed by dramatic cliffs and rocky precipices. Hidden from view by a wall of shaggy trees and underbrush, this quiet beach comes in just close enough to make it easily accessible from town but remains far enough away that the harbor is invisible from here, and so you are left with the company of blue skies, turquoise seas, and a glimpse of the ultra-swanky interior of Six Senses, the island's only five-star resort.

Nhat Beach

Rounding out the other end of town, **Nhat Beach** sits just beside Con Son's ferry docks, slightly rocky and more visible from the road but still gifted with the same awe-inspiring views of the sea and the sharp rise and fall of the island's cliffs. This is a beautiful place from which to take in a good island vista, but not the best for swimming on account of its terrain.

Ong Dung Beach

The most easily accessible beach on the northern shore, **Ong Dung Beach** (VND20,000) is a 20- to 30-minute hike from the end of Vo Thi Sau street, just past the national park office, and is a popular spot among visitors. Follow the path down to the water, where you can pay the national park entrance fee. From there you are free to swim, snorkel, and enjoy the beach. This particular stretch of water is not ideal for sunbathing, as the sandy area is small. But, it does make for great snorkeling farther out, where an array of colorful sea creatures mill about among the reef. Snorkeling gear can be rented from the national park outpost here; the more adventurous traveler can make a full loop from the thick jungle of So Ray down to the beach and then back around into town on Vo Thi Sau street.

Dam Trau Beach

Popularly known as Airport Beach, **Dam Trau** (VND20,000) is the pristine white-sand ribbon you see stretched across the north shore when approaching Con Dao from the sky. Picture-perfect and surrounded by emerald green palm trees, this beach is the ideal oasis for travelers hoping to lay out a towel and catch some rays. Stunning and secluded, Dam Trau is a more peaceful option than Ong Dung—with the exception of a small number of daily plane departures. It has a beautiful area for swimming, though don't bother snorkeling here, as you'll find the fish are few and far between.

SPORTS AND RECREATION
Diving

Though the islands themselves are quiet, Con Dao is known as the best diving spot in Vietnam. Even so, the slow-but-steady trickle of visitors have only managed to keep three diving outfits in business, all of whom require you to have comprehensive dive insurance before going out, as the islands are remote and any serious medical treatment means an airlift to Saigon. If you don't have insurance purchased beforehand, it is possible to buy coverage on-site. Given the temperamental weather of the islands, if you plan to dive, contact a Con Dao dive outfit ahead of time to make sure that you will be able to dive during your stay on the island.

Dive! Dive! Dive! (near corner of Nguyen Hue and Ton Duc Thang, tel. 06/4383-0701, www.dive-condao.com, VND480,000-5,250,000) provides top-notch diving excursions. Headed up by American expat Larry and his wife Quynh, the small PADI-certified shop on Nguyen Hue takes divers out to some of Vietnam's best spots, including the only dive-able shipwreck in the country. Snorkeling trips also run from here. Larry and Quynh have a stack of free tourist maps complete with hiking recommendations for visitors. The pair also rents out motorbikes and bicycles and are a wealth of information when it comes to hotels, guesthouses, and restaurants. Due to the lower volume of tourists on Con Dao, the shop's hours are not set in stone. You may find Larry and Quynh available at 6am one day and not until 9am or 10am the next. If you drop by any time from mid-morning to early evening you will catch someone hanging around.

Hiking

From the center of town there are several hiking trails that you can take through the national park area that allow for wildlife-spotting and beach time. Most treks can be done without hiring a guide. Wear decent shoes and stick to the trails. Hikes to So Ray, where monkeys, birds, and the endemic black squirrel can be seen, take about 45 minutes and require a moderate level of fitness, while the trek to Ong Dung Beach is an easy, 20- to 30-minute walk. Farther afield near the airport, a two-hour hike to Dam Tre Bay is possible, though it is required that you hire a guide for this journey, as changing tides and weather conditions make it necessary to have a local on hand. Guides can be hired at the **national park office** (visitors center 29 Vo Thi Sau, tel. 06/4383-0669, www.condaopark. com.vn, 7am-11:30am and 1:30pm-5pm daily) for VND300,000-400,000. Most don't speak English but are knowledgeable about the terrain and conditions along these routes.

Wildlife-Watching

Turtle- and bird-watching trips can be booked through the national park office. Turtles nest from June to early September. The best time for bird-watching is in the summer months. Note these seasons when booking trips, as the national park sells excursions outside of these respective seasons, and you will likely come home without seeing any animals.

ACCOMMODATIONS

There is a large divide between high-end resorts and dirt-cheap budget hotels on the island. Some accommodations have less-than-stellar business practices and, with so few options available, it's easy to wind up with a bad apple. Larger hotels have information listed online and arrange airport pickup for guests. Smaller, more inexpensive guesthouses tend to have fewer reviews and recommendations,

though there are a handful of reliable places in town.

VND210,000-525,000

Just beyond the main coastal road is ★ **Nha Nghi Thai Ha** (Nguyen Hue, tel. 06/4383-1679, VND300,000-800,000), a small guesthouse with clean, spacious rooms and high ceilings. Prices vary depending on the number of guests, but two-person lodgings should set you back VND400,000. Each room has Wi-Fi, a fan, air-conditioning, and a TV. Though the proprietor doesn't speak much English, Ms. Ha will go out of her way to make guests comfortable and happy.

Farther from the beach and closer to the national park office, **Hai An Hotel** (10 Ho Thanh Tong, tel. 06/4350-8077, www.haian-hotel.com.vn, VND300,000-800,000) is clean, quiet, and affordable. Rooms are basic, featuring Wi-Fi, TV, air-conditioning, and a fan; the beds are large. The hotel assists with additional travel arrangements, such as tour bookings and ferry tickets.

Clean, if a bit cramped, rooms at the **Red Hotel** (17 Nguyen An Ninh, tel. 06/4363-0079, www.condao24h.com, VND400,000-800,000) feature two twin beds apiece, decent bathrooms, Wi-Fi, cable TV, and plenty of light. Rates vary depending upon the number of people. The hotel staff assist guests with tour arrangements and motorbike hires.

VND1,050,000-2,100,000

Housed in a beautiful, expansive set of colonial-style villas, **Saigon Con Dao** (18-24 Ton Duc Thang, tel. 06/4383-0336, www.saigon-condao.com, VND1,500,000-3,750,000) resort is a property of the mammoth Saigon Tourist company. Featuring a large swimming pool, two restaurants, and a tropical garden, the hotel has rooms that are a little dated but nice and spacious with large bathrooms and, in some cases, a sitting room. Breakfast is included in the room rate, as is airport pickup and drop-off. The hotel offers motorbike rentals, tour information, and flight ticket services.

Beyond the shore-hugging street of Ton Duc Thang, **Con Dao Resort** (8 Nguyen Duc Thuan, tel. 06/4383-0939, www.condaoresort. vn, VND1,350,000-3,600,000) features tasteful rooms with enclosed showers and private balconies as well as a pool, tennis courts, and a pristine private beach that runs along the far edge of the harbor. Breakfast and airport pickup are included in the room rate and the staff speak decent English.

One of the more service-oriented places in town, **ATC Resort** (8-16B Ton Duc Thang, tel. 06/4383-0456, www.atcvietnam.com, VND1,150,000-4,800,000) boasts a friendly and conscientious staff on top of its spacious, well-appointed rooms, which include standard amenities such as air-conditioning, cable TV, Wi-Fi, breakfast, and airport pickup. ATC is located across the street from the harbor beach. There is a private outdoor pool hidden by the surrounding buildings for guests to use. Each room comes with a private balcony with a view of the pool, garden, or sea.

Over VND2,100,000

The island's sole luxury accommodation, **Six Senses Con Dao** (Dat Doc, tel. 06/4383-1222, www.sixsenses.com, VND13,000,000-37,000,000) is a secluded beachfront property whose lavish rooms and exclusivity are second to none. Each split-level villa comes with a private infinity pool and panoramic ocean views as well as high-end amenities, including satellite TV, BOSE sound system, and a butler service. Six Senses also counts a spa, several restaurants, and activity services in its offerings.

FOOD

Con Dao has little in the way of proper eateries, and the only cuisine served is Vietnamese. There are a cluster of **street food vendors** selling broken rice, pho, *banh mi* sandwiches, rice porridge, and other cheap local meals around the intersection of **Ton Duc Thang and Nguyen Hue** streets as well as near the market. Many of the nicer hotels, including Saigon Con Dao, have restaurants attached, which you can patronize even if you're not a guest, and the **local market** (corner of Vo Thi Sau and Tran Phu) sells fruit and snacks from the wee hours of the morning, though there is a noontime siesta.

With very few restaurants in town and even fewer that offer a decent selection, **Thu Ba Restaurant** (Vo Thi Sau, tel. 06/4383-0255, 9am-10pm daily, VND70,000-350,000) stands out as a more diverse eatery than most. Though the small restaurant serves only Vietnamese fare, its menu goes beyond the standard-but-delicious seafood options that occupy most menus on the island to include pork, beef, chicken, and vegetarian dishes. Servers speak some English and are friendly and easygoing.

At the far end of the Saigon Tourist line of properties, **Hoa Bien Restaurant** (Ton Duc Thang, tel. 06/4383-0155, 6am-10pm daily, VND80,000-400,000) has a nice view of the ocean and decent Vietnamese fare. Seafood features heavily on the menu, but other options are also available. Open-air dining looks out onto the picturesque Con Dao harbor and portions on the family-style menu are generous.

A more diversified option, **Thu Tam** (Nguyen Duc Thuan, tel. 06/4360-8040, nhahangthutam@yahoo.com.vn, 7am-late daily, VND50,000-300,000), located directly opposite of Con Dao Seatravel Resort, features a plethora of breakfast, lunch, and dinner items alongside friendly service. The dining room is a large, open-air area where those who opt for seafood dishes are able to choose their meal from a series of small fish tanks lining the far wall. Prices are reasonable and the restaurant is open late.

Directly across from Quay 914 is **Con Son Cafe** (Ton Duc Thang, 7am-11pm daily, VND20,000-50,000). No more than a couple of plastic tables and chairs, this outdoor-only spot offers nice views of the harbor and main coastal drag. While the menu lists items like smoothies and fruit juices, they are not always on offer; be prepared to make second or third choices.

INFORMATION AND SERVICES

Though their primary business is as a dive shop, **Dive! Dive! Dive!** (near corner of Nguyen Hue and Ton Duc Thang, tel. 06/4383-0701, www.dive-condao.com) is the unofficial tourism office of the island. Quynh and Larry are exceptionally friendly, easygoing folks who are happy to offer advice, hotel and restaurant recommendations, and tourist maps free of charge. They are also your go-to spot for sand fly repellent—a necessity if you visit the beach—and can offer safe, reliable motorbikes and bicycles for rent.

There is a **Vietnam Airlines ticketing office** (44A Nguyen Hue, tel. 06/4383-1831, condaobranch@vasco.com.vn, 7:30am-11:30am and 1:30pm-5pm Mon.-Fri.), which helps arrange and confirm flight reservations.

There are two ATMs on the island, a **Techcombank ATM** (corner of Vo Thi Sau and Tran Phu, opposite the market) and one beside **Vietin Bank** (corner of Le Duan and Le Van Viet, tel. 06/4383-0162, www.vietinbank.vn, 7:30am-11:30am and 1:30pm-5:30pm Mon.-Fri., 8am-11am Sat.). These ATMs are prone to malfunction or technical issues, so bring enough cash for your entire stay. Foreign currencies cannot be exchanged on the island; bring Vietnamese dong.

Con Dao's only **hospital** (corner of Le Hong Phong and Pham Van Dong, tel. 06/4383-0128, 7am-11:30am and 1:30pm-5pm daily) is located just north of the town's only roundabout, and facilities are about as rudimentary as they come. The staff do not speak English. While minor injuries and illnesses may be treatable here, anything beyond that will require a trip to the mainland.

GETTING THERE
Air

Despite its growing popularity, Con Dao is still a very difficult place to reach. **Vietnam Airlines** (ticketing office 44A Nguyen Hue, tel. 06/4383-1831, condaobranch@vasco.com.vn) is the only carrier to serve the small **Con Son Airport** (VCS, Khu Dan Cu 1, Con Dao). Flights run several times a week, with fewer options than you might have for other destinations. Tickets cost VND1,600,000-1,700,000 each way and leave in the early morning from Saigon. The flight is 45 minutes and arrives at Con Dao airport, nine miles from town. Most hotels on the island offer airport pickup if you book in advance. You can also jump on most hotel minibuses for VND50,000 and they will take you where you want to go. Don't bother with hailing a taxi—a fare from the airport into the center of town runs about VND300,000.

Boat

If you've got a more flexible schedule and don't mind traveling like a local, an overnight ferry (VND250,000) runs from Cat Lo port (973 30 Thang 4) about seven miles north of downtown Vung Tau to Ben Dam port on Con Son, the main island. This option is much cheaper than a plane ticket.

Boats do not run on a set schedule and are subject to changes depending on the weather, so it is imperative that you book your ticket in advance and check regularly to ensure that the ferry is still running. Due to high winds and rough seas, boats seldom run between the months of October and February.

Tickets can be arranged through **Con Dao Explorer** (tel. 09/0743-4345, www.condao-explorer.com, 8am-5pm Mon.-Fri.), though you'll likely need a Vietnamese-speaker to help, as English-language services are not offered. Call the hotline to arrange ferry tickets. The ferry leaves at 5pm and takes roughly 12 hours to arrive at Con Son. This is not a journey for the easily seasick, nor is the ferry particularly glamorous.

GETTING AROUND

Since the island is so small, the best way to explore is on two wheels. Hiring a bicycle or motorbike gives you the freedom to head out on your own and appreciate the island scenery. Due to the island's size, most roads are easy to navigate both in and out of the main town. Due to its location, weather on Con Son is very temperamental and strong gusts can be dangerous when driving. Especially during the last few months of the year, when Con Dao is at its windiest, pay special attention on the roads, as accidents do happen.

Taxi

There are a handful of **taxis** (tel. 06/4361-6161) that make their rounds on the island, at a much higher cost than the ones you'd find on the mainland. Base rates are roughly double what you'd pay elsewhere in Vietnam, starting at VND25,000 just to enter the taxi.

Rentals

Once on the island, the easiest and most cost-effective way to get around is by hiring a motorbike or bicycle. Most guesthouses rent out either vehicle for a daily fee; check the quality of your bike before setting out on a long trip.

Con Son has only one **gas station** (corner of Nguyen Hue and Ngo Gia Tu, 6am-11:30am and 1:30pm-8pm daily). Also beware that driving on the coastal roads can be a challenge in strong winds, especially if you're traveling by pedal power. Proceed with caution and always take it easy on the turns.

The Mekong Delta

Look for ★ to find recommended sights, activities, dining, and lodging.

Highlights

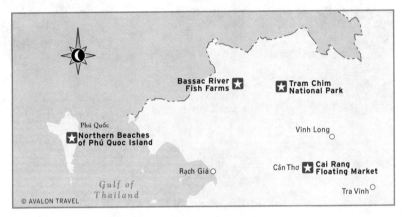

★ **Cai Rang Floating Market:** Experience the melee of rice barges and fishing boats trading in fresh fruits and vegetables along the Can Tho River (page 394).

★ **Tram Chim National Park:** In this stunning landscape of flooded plains and wiry cajuput trees is a quarter of all bird species in Vietnam, including the redheaded sarus crane, the world's tallest flying bird (page 427).

★ **Bassac River Fish Farms:** Entire communities of colorful floating fish farms provide both shelter and a living for many residents of the Delta (page 439).

★ **Northern Beaches of Phu Quoc Island:** Secluded beaches like **Bai Dai** and the stunning **Ganh Dau Beach** offer an unparalleled piece of paradise (page 464).

At first glance, the geography of the Mekong Delta is almost incomprehensible. Awash with emerald green rice paddies and serpentine rivers, lush palms and tall, creaky cajuput trees, the entire region is made up of as much water as it is of earth. Its fertile farmland, which stretches south and west from Ho Chi Minh City all the way to the Cambodian border, rises tentatively from a maze of tributaries known to Vietnamese as the River of Nine Dragons. Here, amid flooded plains and shape-shifting islands, the mighty Mekong flows out to sea, providing one of the country's most heavily populated areas with not only its defining geographic feature but an altogether different way of life.

On land, the region's unparalleled annual rice harvest has earned it an affectionate nickname as Vietnam's "rice bowl," a major player in the second-largest rice-exporting nation in the world. But more than its farming exploits, life in the Mekong Delta revolves largely around water. At the mouth of one of Asia's longest rivers—which winds from the Tibetan Plateau through China, Myanmar, Laos, Thailand, and Cambodia before arriving in southwestern Vietnam—local residents travel just as often by water as by land, navigating narrow, palm-fringed canals on wooden sampans or jetting off to another part of the coast via speedboat. The Delta's low-lying terrain and a complex web of estuaries mean that it's not uncommon for local families to anchor their house within the river or earn a living in one of the region's famed floating markets. For many travelers, the Mekong's main appeal lies here, in its verdant landscapes and unassuming pace. Beyond scenery, a diverse population only adds to the many intricacies of the Delta, as Vietnamese residents live alongside ethnic Chinese, Khmer, and Cham communities, each of whom bring their own distinct cultures and traditions to the area.

Tourism in the Mekong Delta is fairly spread out, with travelers venturing as near as the river islands between My Tho and Ben Tre or as far as the westernmost reaches of Ha Tien and Chau Doc. Those with an interest in local culture and a sense of adventure will

Previous: Hu Tieu; sunset on Phu Quoc's Long Beach. **Above:** stupas at Tra Vinh's Ang Pagoda.

The Mekong Delta

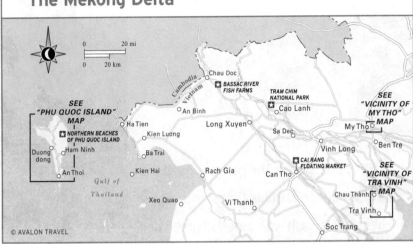

© AVALON TRAVEL

appreciate the freedom of the Delta, where travelers can blaze their own trails without the confines that come with large foreign crowds. Exploring western Vietnam allows for more interaction with locals and a more authentic glimpse of daily life than many other destinations along the coast.

HISTORY

With its modern history dating from the late 1600s, the Mekong Delta is Vietnam's youngest region. For centuries, while rulers in Hanoi and Hue vied for supremacy and the Nguyen Lords pushed south toward Saigon, these low-lying wetlands sat uninhabited, thick with jungle and wild animals. Though several ancient kingdoms once laid claim to the area, the Khmer were last in control before the Vietnamese slowly moved westward from Saigon, edging their neighbors out of the region and establishing independent towns and communities. As early as the late 17th century, the land then known as Kampuchea Krom, or Lower Cambodia, began to fall into Vietnamese hands, with key players like Nguyen Huu Canh, a nobleman who helped bring order to the Delta's then-remote communities, and Mac Cuu, the Chinese

merchant, explorer and founder of Ha Tien town, proving instrumental in the development of the area.

Despite this progress on the part of the Vietnamese, life in the Mekong Delta was not without its challenges, as harsh conditions and tentative relationships with the neighbors prevailed, particularly around the border. Thai pirates routinely crossed the frontier to loot and pillage the country's western settlements, and the Khmer Krom, still smarting from the loss of their land, did not take too kindly to an increased Vietnamese presence. By the time Mac Cuu sought protection from the Nguyen Lords in 1708, hoping to save Vietnam's western border from capture or destruction, the nation's boundaries had been set, and armed defense supplied by the Nguyens only solidified the status of the country's youngest settlements as an official part of Vietnam.

After France launched its takeover in the middle of the 19th century, residents of the Delta were particularly outspoken in their disapproval, acting as an important center of opposition against colonial powers in Saigon. Southern members of the Viet Minh, Ho Chi Minh's Communist resistance army, took refuge in limestone caves and cajuput forests across the region, constructing military bases and training schools that were all but undetectable to their enemies.

Amid the Delta's lush jungle and tropical humidity, the Viet Minh's crude weapons and guerrilla tactics turned them into a formidable power. After independence was won, it took only a few short years before Ngo Dinh Diem and the south Vietnamese government stirred southern revolutionaries to action again, reforming as the National Liberation Front (NLF). Well-hidden within the Delta landscapes and skilled at re-purposing American weapons against the enemy, southern guerrillas fast earned a reputation as one of the United States' strongest adversaries. This distinction came at a price: some of the most intense fighting to take place in southern Vietnam played out in rice paddies and hamlets across the Mekong Delta.

Following the end of the American War, Vietnam's southwestern frontier remained a battleground, as a border conflict with Cambodia in the late 1970s escalated into two years of full-blown war against Pol Pot's brutal Khmer Rouge regime. Once the violence dissipated and the country began to focus on rebuilding from within, local residents gave up their guns to return to the land, working the Delta's rivers and rice paddies. Today, the region is responsible for the vast majority of Vietnam's rice exports, which are among the highest in the world, as well as thriving fishing and fruit industries.

PLANNING YOUR TIME

The region's major attractions can be packed into a few days. Travelers in the Delta are free to pick and choose their destinations, as tourism here is not about specific sights or attractions so much as it is about experiencing the local way of life.

Those planning to spend more than a day in the Delta begin their journey in tourist-friendly Can Tho, using this hub to arrange bus transport to more remote destinations. Stay over night here to experience the city's first-rate floating market.

The more popular tourist hubs are Chau Doc, Phu Quoc, and (to a lesser extent) Vinh Long. Allot 1-2 days each to visit Chau Doc and Vinh Long. Budget at least 2-3 days to visit Phu Quoc because it requires either more money (for the plane ticket) or more time to get there (by way of a speedboat), so it's worth sticking around for an extra day or two.

Beyond the primary destinations, travelers can spend as little as a single day in the area or as long as a few weeks. Add an extra day each to explore the Khmer pagodas of Tra Vinh, bird-watch at Tram Chim National Park, and sightsee in Sa Dec, or tack on an extra day or two in towns like Rach Gia and Ha Tien to explore the surrounding area. It's also possible to take day trips from Saigon to towns like My Tho, Ben Tre, or Vinh Long.

While the Mekong Delta is a popular destination as a whole, tourism here is spread out. Major destinations like Can Tho and Phu Quoc work well as tourist hubs, but most places west of Saigon have little tourism infrastructure. This means that English speakers and Western services are at a minimum, and you'll need extra time and patience. Expect to have a few communication hiccups and to spend time on less-than-comfortable buses when traveling between many of the region's cities.

The best time to visit is outside of the rainy season, as steady downpours bury much of the landscape from April to October and flooding can be extreme.

Can Tho

The economic, political, and cultural heart of the Mekong Delta, Can Tho is a large city that feels like a small town. Along Ninh Kieu Park, its main riverside promenade, you'll find the pace of this southwestern nerve center low-key and pleasantly unhurried, particularly when coming from Saigon. For most travelers, Can Tho is an important stop on their Mekong Delta tour for a few reasons: as the area's largest and most developed city, it is here that you'll find the majority of useful travel information, English speakers, and Western amenities. Beyond the essentials, this sun-drenched town boasts its own share of cultural attractions, showing a bit of the region's more intricate demography in the beautiful Chinese assembly hall nestled between hotels and restaurants along Hai Ba Trung, as well as a pair of gilded Theravada Buddhist pagodas that would not be out of place on the other side of the Cambodian border. Like any town in the Mekong Delta, a snaking web of rivers and canals burrows deep into the surrounding countryside, shaded by drooping palm fronds and plentiful fruit trees, and every morning as the sun comes up boats depart from the local tourist pier for Cai Rang, the largest and most active of the Delta's famed floating markets, as well as its smaller counterpart, Phong Dien.

Visiting Can Tho, if only for a day or two, is worth it for the city's on-the-water attractions and for some R&R before setting off deeper into the Delta. For its part, some of the city's more enterprising young locals have also taken it upon themselves to provide more unique and authentic opportunities for foreign visitors to experience life in the Delta, with a handful of small, independent tour outfits beginning to crop up around town that take travelers farther off the beaten track. Regardless of how long you stay in the city, at least one overnight is necessary in order to rise early enough for the floating market. There are several other sights on land, though

even street vendors and boatmen call off the chase at midday to escape the city's sweltering, shadeless avenues.

Temperatures reach their peak around late April or May, as the dry weather gives way to daily rains. From mid-November to early April the city is slightly cooler. But, coming from abroad, you'll likely still find it hot.

SIGHTS

From the waterfront, all of Can Tho's on-land sights are easily accessible and can be reached on foot or, if you prefer, by bicycle. Dress appropriately when visiting pagodas. For water sights, boats are available for hire from hotels and travel agencies as well as through independent drivers at Ninh Kieu Pier.

Ong Pagoda

You could spend an afternoon studying the dizzyingly intricate exterior of **Ong Pagoda** (Hai Ba Trung beside Mekong Inn, 6am-6pm daily), a riverfront property built in 1896 by the city's then-sizable Chinese population. Honoring the red-faced, beard-twirling Chinese general Quan Cong, a figure who represents loyalty, cleverness, virtue, and courage, among other things, the pagoda's layout is inspired by the stiff lines and angles of the Chinese character for "nation." As soon as you pass through the main doors, you'll be greeted by two figures: the Goddess of Fortune on your right and the wide-eyed General Ma Tien and his horse on your left. Beyond the entrance hall, incense burns in a small clearing at the center of the pagoda, also known as the celestial well, above which dozens of large, smoldering incense coils sway in the breeze. The main altar at the back is where Quan Cong himself resides, flanked by the God of Earth and the God of Finance. Nowadays, this pagoda still functions as the Guangzhou Assembly Hall, bringing together the community that created it, despite the fact

Can Tho

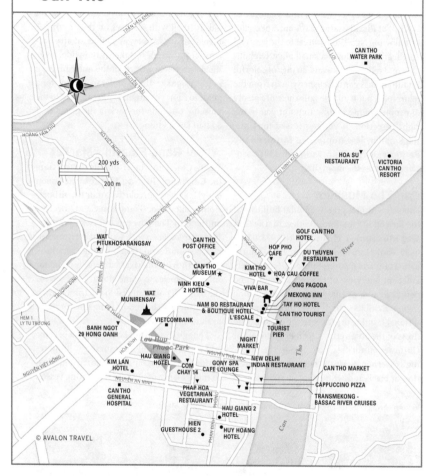

© AVALON TRAVEL

that Can Tho's Chinese population has faded considerably in recent decades.

Wat Pitukhosarangsay

Squeezed down a narrow lane near Xang Thoi Lake, **Wat Pitukhosarangsay** (17/28 Mac Dinh Chi, 7am-7pm daily) is tangible proof of the Mekong Delta's Khmer connection. Complete with all the gold-edged trimmings of a typical Theravada Buddhist pagoda (the sort you might find in Thailand or Cambodia) this *wat* is packed to the rafters with sparkling

statues of the Buddha, most of which were brought across the border from neighboring countries. Its three stories of intricate, neon-hued murals and overflowing altars make this one of the taller buildings in the neighborhood, and a climb up to the top floor is rewarded with nice views of residential Can Tho and the nearby lake, as well a close-up of the pagoda's ornately detailed roof. There are also a handful of outgoing monks who can give you a short tour of each floor before bringing you up to the attic library, where dozens of religious texts are stored, each penned in the busy, squiggling lines of Khmer or Thai script.

Though it's a bit tricky to find, visitors can reach Wat Pitukhosarangsay's entrance gates by following Ngo Quyen street to the very end and bearing left down a small alley. On holidays and religious festivals, strings of colorful Buddhist flags can also usher you in from the main road, but if all else fails there are plenty of people around willing to point you in the right direction. If you're pressed for time, the smaller, less-impressive **Munirensay Pagoda** (36 Hoa Binh, 7am-7pm daily) is located right on the main drag.

Can Tho Museum

Housed within a grand colonial building at the far end of Hoa Binh Boulevard, the **Can Tho Museum** (1 Hoa Binh, tel. 071/0382-0955, 8am-11am and 2pm-5pm Tues.-Thurs., 8am-11am and 6:30pm-9pm Sat.-Sun.) offers a decent overview of the city's history and people as well as that of the larger Mekong region. Exhibits include everything from traditional farming practices to the customs and dress of the area's ethnic Khmer and Hoa, or Chinese, minorities. Just inside the building's cavernous main entrance, a faded collection of black-and-white photographs depicts

turn-of-the-century Can Tho, providing insight into just how much has changed since the colonial era. Upstairs, the exhibition hall is filled with displays on the province's revolutionary history, as well as an airy balcony from which to take in the wide, tree-lined street below. Parts of the museum have English signage. If you prefer to arrange for a guide to show you around, you can head to the museum office on the back of the grounds at 6 Phan Dinh Phung.

★ Cai Rang Floating Market

Easily Can Tho's most popular attraction, the **Cai Rang Floating Market** (5am-noon daily) is a bustling, colorful affair where boats from as far as Soc Trang and Ca Mau gather on the Can Tho River to sell fresh produce. Wide barges laden with watermelons, pineapples, coconuts, and fresh vegetables rock back and forth with the river current, waiting for smaller vehicles to come along. Look out for the bamboo pole fastened to the front of each boat, from which vendors hang their produce to show what is available.

Though this particular market has become a hot spot for foreign visitors, Cai Rang remains every bit a traditional floating market, so the presence of other tourist-toting vessels

Vendors await their early-morning customers at Cai Rang Floating Market.

Floating Markets

Each morning, as the sun rises over southwestern Vietnam's maze of waterways, dozens of wooden boats congregate along the river to take part in one of the Mekong Delta's many famed floating markets. Wide barges and hollow-hulled boats laden with fresh produce and hundreds of river fish travel from near and far to reach these on-the-water trading posts. River vendors typically sell bulk amounts of one or two items, which they advertise to other shoppers by hanging a sample of the available goods atop a bamboo pole that sits at the front of the boat. Even smaller, motorized canoes join in on the action, zipping around the larger barges with coffee, tea, and snacks for sale.

The most famous of the Delta's markets exist in and around Can Tho: noted trading spot Cai Rang, easily the most popular of the bunch, and Phong Dien market, another large floating business center. Farther north, Cai Be holds its own smaller version. Set just before the charming spire of the town cathedral, this market makes for a nice photo-op. While Chau Doc, too, has attempted to get in on the action, its market still has a ways to go, with only a few boats turning up in the morning, more for show than anything else.

doesn't much detract from the atmosphere. Get in on the action by grabbing a coffee on the water or haggling for fresh fruit from one of the smaller vessels. Half the fun of visiting the market is the ride out to Cai Rang, as this allows you to travel along the banks of the Can Tho River, passing by throngs of local houseboats and floating gas stations, fishing vessels, and shops with waterside service.

Visitors can arrange to depart from Ninh Kieu Pier at any time, though it's best to go in the early morning, as Cai Rang's vendors disappear as the day wears on. Boats leave for the market as early as 5am and can be hired either through local hotels and travel agencies or with any of the freelance drivers around Ninh Kieu Park. Freelancers are usually more affordable and their smaller boats allow you to get closer to the action than some of the larger tourist vessels. If you go this route, agree upon an itinerary and a price before setting off.

Many travelers combine a trip to Cai Rang with a wander down the area's narrow canals, populated with lush greenery and plentiful fruit orchards. This can be arranged either through a guided tour or with a freelance driver. Some even tack on the longer journey out to **Phong Dien Market,** a smaller floating market that lies farther down the river,

about 12 miles from town, which sees fewer visitors than Cai Rang.

Sightseeing Tours

With so many travelers drawn to Can Tho for its waterways, guided boat tours to the nearby floating markets and the surrounding area are a popular activity. **Can Tho Tourist** (50 Hai Ba Trung, tel. 071/0382-4221, www. canthotourist.vn, 7am-5pm daily), the city's government-run travel outfit, supplies a standard trip out to Cai Rang market and back (VND120,000-200,000), with the possibility of adding on a jaunt to Phong Dien (additional VND200,000). Private boats (from VND410,000) can also be hired through Can Tho Tourist. The more people you gather, the cheaper the cost.

For a closer look at local culture and the Delta countryside, the friendly folks at **Open Tour CT** (tel. 09/4223-4409, www.opentourct. com, VND210,000-546,000) do not disappoint. This promising young tour outfit pairs travelers with local guides who double as motorbike drivers, taking you for a ride around the city or farther afield for an authentic look at Delta life. In addition to its own tour itineraries, the most popular of which is a day-long adventure into the countryside, Open Tour CT provides motorbike rentals to travelers as well as private guides, giving you all the tools to create your own travel plans if you so choose. The company also runs affordable floating market trips out to Cai Rang and Phong Dien, with both private and group tours; opt for the private boat if possible, as this allows you to set your own schedule.

NIGHTLIFE

As a whole, the Mekong Delta is a region of early risers. Nighttime in Can Tho still draws a fair number of locals to Ninh Kieu Park, where couples sit on park benches and groups of friends peruse the nearby **night market** (Nguyen Thai Hoc and Vo Van Tan streets, 5pm-11:30pm daily). The street lining the river gets busy around 6pm and stays that way until later in the evening, quieting down around 10pm or 11pm. Many people meander the maze of **snack carts** (Phan Boi Chau and Phan Chu Trinh streets, 5pm-late daily) near Can Tho Market, where quick bites like sticky rice, grilled meats, and local desserts are on offer, before heading to the waterfront.

For anything more than a park bench, options are pretty slim along the river: **Mekong Inn** (38 Hai Ba Trung, tel. 071/0382-1646, 6am-late daily, VND9,000-30,000) slings local beers and a bit of hard liquor in a casual atmosphere, while **Viva Bar** (26 Hai Ba Trung, tel. 017/0381-8485, www.vivahotel.vn, 3pm-midnight daily, VND20,000-60,000) pumps loud dance music well into the night and offers shots and stronger drinks. For a fancier crowd, **Hoa Cau Coffee** (4 Hai Ba Trung, tel. 071/0382-2218, 6am-midnight daily, VND20,000-53,000) has a list of beers and cocktails in addition to its standard coffees and teas. There are a few local *bia hoi* (Vietnamese beer) vendors stuffed in between the dozens of local restaurants along De Tham street as well as around Xang Thoi Lake.

SHOPPING
Can Tho Market

Packed with local handicrafts and clothing, the waterfront **Can Tho Market** (Hai Ba Trung, 7:30am-9:30pm daily) is your go-to spot for knickknacks and backpacker gear. Plenty of T-shirts, knapsacks, and loose clothing are available, as well as locally made hand fans, scarves, and other souvenirs. Though it now functions as a tourist market, this once was the main trade center of the city and saw hordes of shoppers, both by land and by river.

Night Market

After sunset, the fun continues at Can Tho's **night market** (Nguyen Thai Hoc and Vo Van Tan streets, 5pm-11:30pm daily), where vendors hawk mostly clothing, sunglasses, and jewelry. Don't forget that you can haggle for your purchases here, though most vendors are reasonable and some even post their prices out front.

SPORTS AND RECREATION
Ninh Kieu Park

Stretched along the waterfront, **Ninh Kieu Park** (Hai Ba Trung) is a popular local hangout during the late afternoons and evenings. Much of Can Tho's population gathers along the riverbank to chat, watch the passing boats, and enjoy a few snacks. During the day, this narrow strip of greenery would be just as nice if it weren't for the heat, but with the sun high overhead there is little shade available and groups of freelance boat drivers often gather here looking for a fare.

Swimming

For a different way to beat the heat, visit **Can Tho Water Park** (Cai Khe, tel. 09/4923-2838, 1pm-5:30pm Mon. and Wed.-Fri., closed Tues., 8:30am-5:30pm Sat.-Sun., VND25,000). While it sees very little traffic Monday-Friday, things ramp up on the weekend, when families come to splash around.

Though it comes at a price, the **Victoria Can Tho pool** (Cai Khe, tel. 071/0381-0111, www.victoriahotels.asia, 6am-8pm daily, VND128,000) is a palm-fringed paradise with pleasant riverfront views, umbrellas, and comfy lounge chairs. Non-guests of the

Can Tho

resort are also able to use the riverside pool by purchasing a ticket at the reception desk.

ACCOMMODATIONS

Downtown Can Tho is a fairly small place, despite being the largest city in the Delta. Most travelers prefer to base themselves closer to the riverfront and Ninh Kieu Pier, where boats to the floating market depart and the majority of the city's travel services are set up.

Under VND210,000

The small and friendly **Mekong Inn** (38 Hai Ba Trung, tel. 071/0382-1646, VND180,000-260,000) offers some of Can Tho's most affordable rooms. Beds are comfy and rooms are clean, though some come without windows. The cheerful owners can help with travel arrangements as well as bicycle and motorbike rentals. The waterfront guesthouse doubles as a restaurant and café, so it's a fine spot for lunch or an afternoon drink. It can get noisy after dark, though things usually wrap up by 10pm or 11pm.

Bright and spacious, the **Hien Guesthouse 2** (106/3 Phan Dinh Phung, tel. 071/0381-2718, hien_gh@yahoo.com, VND105,000-210,000) combines large, clean rooms with a quiet alley location just a few blocks from the riverfront. Wi-Fi is free, TVs are standard, and you have your choice of fan or air-conditioning. Some rooms come with a balcony. The amiable owner speaks a bit of English and can help with motorbike rentals. Around the corner is the original **Hien Guesthouse** (118/10 Phan Dinh Phung, tel. 071/0381-2718, hien_gh@yahoo.com, VND105,000-210,000), another solid choice but smaller and without en suite bathrooms.

VND210,000-525,000

Roomier than some of its budget counterparts, the **Tay Ho Hotel** (42 Hai Ba Trung, tel. 071/0382-3392, tayhohotel@canthotourist. vn, VND250,000-350,000) boasts an excellent location on the riverfront, free Wi-Fi, TV, and toiletries. It's a nice, clean, one-star joint.

Set back from the waterfront past Can Tho Market, **Huy Hoang Hotel** (33-35 Ngo Duc Ke, tel. 071/0382-5833, huyhoanghotel@ canthotourist.vn, VND220,000-280,000) is equipped with basic but clean rooms and comes with your choice of fan or air-conditioned accommodations. Hot water is standard in all accommodations, as are TV and free Wi-Fi access.

Only a touch less fancy than the original, ★ **Hau Giang 2 Hotel** (6-8 Hai Thuong Lan Ong, tel. 071/0382-4836, haugiang2hotel@canthotourist.vn, VND320,000-380,000) is a steal for the price. Located close to Can Tho Market and the riverfront, this new facility features spacious, modern rooms with standard amenities and breakfast included. Ask for a window, as not all rooms come with natural light. The staff doesn't speak much English but, at less than VND400,000 a night, the value makes this hotel too good to pass up.

The tall, narrow **Mango Hotel (Hotel Xoai)** (93 Mau Than, tel. 09/0765-2927, www. hotelxoai.com, VND210,000-546,000) provides excellent value a short distance from

Can Tho's main tourist area. Lodgings feature plush beds and large windows, as well as Wi-Fi, a television, and air-conditioning. Solar-powered water heaters and energy-conserving light bulbs keep the building green. Opt for the double bed over the narrow twin. The friendly staff can assist with recommendations around town. The hotel also runs reliable tours to Cai Rang Floating Market as well as food tours through **Mekong Tours** (tel. 09/0785-2927, www.mekongtours.info).

A stone's throw from the waterfront, the skinny **Kim Lan Hotel** (138A Nguyen An Ninh, tel. 071/0381-7049, www.kimlancantho.com.vn, VND420,000-1,659,000, breakfast included) offers great value with spacious, clean rooms and a friendly staff. Rooms feature modern decor and standard amenities, including air-conditioning, hot water, TV, Wi-Fi, and an in-room fridge. Kim Lan also arranges homestays in the nearby countryside. Costs are slightly higher but include meals and a trip to the floating market. These homestays are more like a rural guesthouse than a one-on-one overnight with a local family.

VND525,000-1,050,000

One of the nicer accommodations in the city center, **Hau Giang Hotel** (34 Nam Ky Khoi Nghia, tel. 071/0382-1851, www.haugianghotel.com, VND735,000-1,890,000) showcases the best that Can Tho Tourist has to offer. Spacious rooms are well furnished and come with high-quality amenities as well as air-conditioning, Wi-Fi, TV, a minibar, and an array of toiletries. Breakfast is included in the room rate.

The gargantuan **Ninh Kieu 2** (3 Hoa Binh, tel. 071/0625-2335, www.ninhkieuhotel.com, VND777,000-2,625,000) sits directly on the main drag not far from Can Tho Museum and the city post office. Rooms feature a regal decor, with polished wood furniture and upholstered sitting chairs. The hotel includes breakfast in its room rates and amenities such as TV, hot water, air-conditioning, and a minibar. Massage and spa services are available to guests, as well as a fitness center, a restaurant, and a bar.

A sizable building, the **Kim Tho Hotel** (1A Ngo Gia Tu, tel. 071/0381-7517, www.kimtho.com, VND950,000-2,750,000) has benefited from some good publicity over the last few years, as tour groups regularly turn up at this mid-range spot. Accommodations feature roomy, low beds and large windows, some of which overlook the river, and there is also a 12th-floor roof terrace café, a restaurant, and a massage parlor in the building. Thanks to its popularity, the Kim Tho is often full, so book ahead.

VND1,050,000-2,100,000

The finest accommodations this side of Cai Khe Canal, the **Golf Can Tho Hotel** (2 Hai Ba Trung, tel. 071/0381-2210, www.golfcanthohotel.vn, VND1,790,000-10,100,000) is a stunning four-star facility with beautiful riverfront views, clean rooms, and exceptional service right down to the doormen. Modern accommodations include complimentary breakfast and Wi-Fi as well as air-conditioning, TV, hot water, and a minibar. The hotel offers massage services and a guests-only swimming pool. Downstairs, a small souvenir shop sits at the back of the lobby and there is also a restaurant and bar next door. For the best price, check with the hotel ahead of time, as rooms are discounted heavily during the off-season.

Over VND2,100,000

Originally housed in a former 1930s colonial building, the new and improved ★ **Nam Bo Boutique Hotel** (1 Ngo Quyen, tel. 071/0381-9139, www.nambocantho.com, VND2,610,000-5,800,000) manages to preserve its classic colonial style in a modern facility. Perched on the corner of Ngo Quyen and Hai Ba Trung, this beautiful boutique hotel features seven individually designed corner suites, each with panoramic views of Ninh Kieu Pier and the river, as well as the street below. Rooms are spacious and feature

Nam Bo Boutique Hotel

both a bedroom, a living room, and, in some cases, a small in-room dining area.

Victoria Can Tho Resort (Cai Khe, tel. 071/0381-0111, www.victoriahotels.asia, VND4,163,000-6,784,000) is a four-star escape from the bustling Ninh Kieu district. This stunning riverfront retreat boasts gorgeous rooms complete with a bedroom and sitting area. Rooms come with peaceful river views or a view of the palm-lined pool. Downstairs is a spa, business center, a bar, and restaurant. Guests can enjoy sunset cruises on the resort's beautiful converted rice barge, as well as cycling and market tours.

FOOD

As the region's largest city, Can Tho is one of the only places in the Mekong Delta where you'll find Western food in addition to local fare. Dozens of restaurants are packed neatly along the riverfront, most catering to foreign tourists, while a handful of streets farther back from the water offer excellent street food and more local Vietnamese restaurants.

Cafés and Bakeries

One of Can Tho's trendier cafés, **Hoa Cau Coffee** (4 Hai Ba Trung, tel. 071/0382-2218, 6am-midnight daily, VND20,000-53,000) is a modern version of your average Vietnamese garden coffee shop. Ample open-air seating is available and the management plays an ongoing selection of Western hits from decades past. While the café is open during the day, things really get going at night, when everyone in town is out and about around Ninh Kieu Park.

A large street cart perched just opposite a three-way junction, **Banh Ngot 29 Hong Oanh** (opposite corner of De Tham and Nguyen Khuyen, noon-10pm daily, VND4,000-10,000) hawks delicious, local baked goods. Sample the mung bean cakes, egg tarts, and coconut pastries, all of which go for less than fifty cents.

International

Just opposite Can Tho Market, **Cappuccino Pizza** (138 Hai Ba Trung, tel. 071/0246-1981, 8am-10pm daily, VND50,000-170,000) is a mostly Italian restaurant with a menu as thick as your thumb. Dishes include pasta, risotto, and several types of pizza, but the menu also veers off into Tex-Mex and vegetarian fare, offering something for everyone. The small corner building is a nice spot for watching the passing traffic and provides plenty to see in the evenings, when snack vendors set up in the square nearby.

For a break from local fare, stop by **New Delhi Indian Restaurant** (128 Hai Ba Trung, tel. 012/2218-9786, 10am-10pm daily, VND40,000-100,000), on the main drag between Phan Boi Chau and Vo Van Tan streets. The menu provides a decent selection of Indian dishes, including standard curries, vindaloos, and daals, and the owner is a friendly guy who can offer recommendations.

Some of the only upmarket dining you'll find in Can Tho is at **L'Escale** (1 Ngo Quyen, tel. 071/0381-9139, www.nambocantho.com, 6am-11pm daily, VND75,000-410,000), a classy roof terrace restaurant located on the fourth floor of the Nam Bo Boutique Hotel. Both Western and Vietnamese cuisine are served, but the former is most notable, with dishes like rabbit and steak on offer as well as European desserts. Both indoor and outdoor tables are available; try to grab a spot along the edge if you can for the best views of the river and the street below.

Street Food

To eat with the locals, your best bet is to head up to **De Tham street** (noon-late daily, VND15,000-80,000) near Xang Thoi Lake, a small street jam-packed with roadside restaurants serving rice and noodles, grilled meats, and dozens of other standard Vietnamese dishes, not to mention a well-placed *bia hoi* (Vietnamese beer) vendors here and there. While most meals include meat, you can also find a few *chay* (vegetarian) joints for vegetarian diners.

Droves of street carts gather in the clearing on **Phan Boi Chau and Phan Chu Trinh streets** (5pm-late daily, VND5,000-40,000) for the evening rush around Ninh Kieu Park. While most carts are dedicated strictly to snack foods like *ca vien* (fish paste balls) and grilled meats, you can also find a few more substantial meals like *xoi ga* (chicken and sticky rice). If you have trouble deciding, just look for the carts with a line out front to help point you in the right direction.

Vegetarian

For herbivores, **Phap Hoa Vegetarian Restaurant** (65 Phan Dinh Phung, tel. 071/0385-8858, 6am-9pm daily, VND20,000-150,000) sits on a nice downtown corner and serves up all manner of local vegetarian fare, including meat-free rice, noodles, soups, and spring rolls, as well as veggie hotpot and an array of delicious smoothies.

A modest local joint on the shady side of the street, **Com Chay 14** (14 Dien Bien Phu, 6am-5pm daily, VND15,000-25,000) serves a meatless version of *hu tieu* noodle soup in the mornings before switching to a tasty pick-and-point selection of tofu, vegetables, and mock-meat with rice in the afternoons. Keep an eye out for the colorful hand-painted sign out front.

Vietnamese

Hop Pho (4-6 Ngo Gia Tu, tel. 071/0381-5208, 6:30am-10:30pm daily, VND30,000-120,000) is your typical Vietnamese *san vuon* (garden) café, but it also serves breakfast and lunch. With breezy outdoor seating and plenty of greenery to block out the passing traffic, patrons can enjoy the café-restaurant's extensive menu of Vietnamese dishes, as well as coffee, tea, smoothies, and ice cream in a mellow environment.

A popular lunch and dinner spot among the tourist crowd, **GONY Spa Cafe Lounge** (8-12 Nguyen An Ninh, tel. 071/0381-0299, 6am-10pm daily, VND15,000-190,000) is an eccentric combination of restaurant, café, and, as the name states, massage parlor. Downstairs, both indoor and outdoor seating are available, along with a tome of Vietnamese and Western options, including pizza and sandwiches. Upstairs, the spa is open from 8am and provides face, body, and foot massages as well as manicures and pedicures.

Though more expensive than your average local eatery, **Nam Bo Restaurant** (1 Ngo Quyen, tel. 071/0381-9139, www.nambocantho.com, 6am-11pm daily, VND50,000-200,000) is located on the riverfront's best people-watching corner, directly opposite Ninh Kieu Park and the pier. Its menu offers a mixture of both Vietnamese and Western dishes served in the ground-floor dining room, with brown-and-white checked tablecloths and large bay windows opening onto Hai Ba Trung. A rotating collection of artwork enhances the restaurant's understated decor with Vietnamese-inspired paintings and photographs from local and foreign artists.

Equipped with a waterfront view and a massive wedding hall, **Hoa Su** (Cai Khe Tourist Area, tel. 071/0382-0717, www.nhahanghoasu.com, 5pm-11pm daily, VND50,000-300,000) is popular among the local crowd and serves up every type of river fish imaginable and then some, with snake, pigeon, and rice paddy rat also making an appearance on the menu. Tables are located in a vast outdoor area near the water, removed from the traffic noise by a short walk from the street to the entrance.

INFORMATION AND SERVICES

One of the more helpful government-run tourism branches, **Can Tho Tourist** (50 Hai Ba Trung, tel. 071/0382-4221, www.cantho-tourist.vn, 7am-5pm daily) assists travelers with everything from free maps of town to private boat and bicycle rentals to cooking tours, cycling tours, visits to the floating market, and homestays. Stop by the main office on Hai Ba Trung for advice, though don't bother around lunchtime, as everyone steps out for their midday meal.

The most centrally located pair of ATMs are on Hai Ba Trung street just beside Can Tho Tourist. There are also several banks and cash machines along Nam Ky Khoi Nghia street near the corner of Phan Dinh Phung, as well as along Hoa Binh Boulevard. Most hotels are able to exchange currency, as is the local **Vietcombank** (3-7 Hoa Binh, tel. 071/0382-0445, www.vietcombank.com.vn, 7am-11am and 1pm-5pm Mon.-Fri.).

The mammoth **Can Tho post office** (2 Hoa Binh, tel. 071/0382-4822, www.cantho.vnpost.vn, 6:30am-8pm Mon.-Sat.) deals not only in postage and letters but also provides Internet and long-distance phone services, as well as on-site cash payments for online bookings with Vietnam Airlines and Jetstar.

The **Can Tho General Hospital (Benh Vien Da Khoa Can Tho)** (4 Chau Van Liem, tel. 071/0381-7901) has both a clinic and 24/7 emergency services and can provide basic care for travelers. For more serious issues, a trip to Saigon is recommended.

GETTING THERE
Air

Six miles northwest of the city is **Can Tho Airport (San Bay Quoc Te Can Tho)** (VCA), with direct service from domestic island destinations such as Phu Quoc (50-minute flight) and Con Dao (55-minute flight) as well as Hanoi (2-hour flight). Because Saigon is only a few hours' drive from Can Tho there are no flights offered between the cities.

The best way to get into town from the airport is by taxi (around VND120,000) or, if you're traveling light, *xe om* (VND50,000-80,000). The airport is roughly 20 minutes (12 km) from downtown Can Tho.

Bus

Can Tho has two main bus stations: the **Can Tho bus station** (13 Hung Vuong, 24 hours daily), about a mile from the city center, and the **91B bus station** (91B Hung Loi, 24 hours daily), slightly farther afield at 2.5 miles out. Cushy air-conditioned **Phuong Trang** (tel. 071/0376-9768, www.futabuslines.com.vn, 24 hours daily) buses arrive at both stations daily from Saigon (3 hours, VND130,000), Chau Doc (2.5 hours, VND120,000), Ca Mau (3 hours, VND125,000), Rach Gia (2 hours, VND120,000), Ha Tien (3.5 hours, VND100,000, local bus), and Dalat.

You can also hop on a local bus (smaller minibus-style vehicles) for nearby destinations like Vinh Long and Tra Vinh (1.5 hours). Fares on these vehicles tend to be cheaper, but things like air-conditioning and adequate space are not guaranteed.

Stick to the official bus counter when buying tickets to avoid touts selling tickets at twice the price.

Boat

High-speed boats from Ca Mau arrive at the **tourist pier** (Hai Ba Trung, tel. 071/0382-1476, 2.5 hours, VND50,000) around 5pm daily. The tourist pier is on Can Tho's main strip, so it's an easy walk to most hotels. Boats leave from the tourist pier for the trip to Ca Mau each morning at 5:30am.

GETTING AROUND

Can Tho is a walkable city, with most land attractions within a two-mile radius of the waterfront. So long as you avoid midday, when the sun is high overhead and there is little shade, there should be no trouble getting around town.

Several cab companies operate in Can Tho, the most trusted being **Mailinh** (tel. 071/0365-6565) and **Hoang Long** (tel. 071/0368-8688). *Xe om* are ever-present along the waterfront and eager to take passengers. Chances are they'll spot you before you spot them.

Several hotels in town rent out bicycles, along with **Can Tho Tourist** (50 Hai Ba Trung, tel. 071/0382-4221, www.canthotourist.vn, 7am-5pm daily). Day rates hover between VND40,000 and VND70,000. Beyond pedal power, motorbike rentals can be found at **Hien Guesthouse** (118/10 Phan Dinh Phung, tel. 071/0381-2718, hien_gh@yahoo.com, VND120,000) and **Mekong Inn** (38 Hai Ba Trung, tel. 071/0382-1646, VND180,000-260,000), as well as through **Open Tour CT** (tel. 09/4223-4409, www.opentourct.com).

Mekong River Islands

A collection of lush, low-lying fields situated between the banks of the Tien River, My Tho and Ben Tre's fertile islands are considered the gateway to the Mekong Delta. Occupying a narrow bend just 45 miles south of Saigon, these four islands—Phoenix, Unicorn, Dragon, and Tortoise—offer a quick and easily accessible glimpse into the larger region with a variety of quintessential Delta scenery, from abundant fruit orchards and narrow, canopied streams to wooden sampans and floating fish farms. Easily done in a day, these landscapes provide a crash course in life on the water for travelers who lack the time to explore the Delta in greater detail. Day trips from Saigon set off early in the morning and tour each of the islands before turning back to the city by mid- to late afternoon. An overnight in either My Tho or Ben Tre can offer a satisfying escape from the buzzing southern city.

Most boat trips around the islands feature a whirlwind of lush gardens, small local factories, and winding canals, along with the occasional bike ride or horse-drawn cart. Those who overnight in either My Tho or Ben Tre will have the opportunity to explore the town more independently and up close, as far fewer travelers actually spend the night here. Either way, half- and full-day excursions can be arranged from Ho Chi Minh City (HCMC), My Tho, or Ben Tre. Given the fact that the main appeal of both towns is the islands, a day is really all you need, perhaps two, before returning to Saigon or carrying on to other Delta destinations.

EXPLORING THE MEKONG RIVER ISLANDS
Unicorn Island

The largest of the four islands occupying the river between Ben Tre and Tien Giang provinces, **Unicorn Island (Cu Lao Thoi Son)** is home to several cottage industries, including local honey farms and orchards packed with ripe papayas, watermelon, pineapples, dragon fruit, and longans. Thanks to the Rach Mieu Bridge, the island's peaceful, verdant scenery can be reached over land, allowing travelers to explore the area on their own via bicycle or motorbike. Most local boat tours stop at Unicorn Island for the fresh fruit as well as the souvenir vendors. On account of its size and location, this is easily the most populated of the islands. A handful of small cafés set amid the greenery make for a nice spot to relax and take in the island's slower pace.

Phoenix Island

Just beyond Unicorn Island lies **Phoenix Island (Con Phung)**, the former residence of local man and religious figure Nguyen Thanh Nam, better known as the Coconut

Mekong River Cruises

As a traveler in the Mekong Delta, it is all but guaranteed that you will get on a boat at least once during your trip. Most people book day trips along the water, visiting a variety of river islands, floating markets, fruit orchards, and narrow canals. A handful of luxury cruises provide tours and transport from Saigon and Can Tho to other Delta destinations such as Cai Be, Sa Dec, and Chau Doc.

One of the more well-known outfits, **Mekong Eyes** (9/150 KDC No. 9, 30 Thang 4, tel. 09/3336-0786, www.mekongeyes.com, VND6,300,000-36,750,000, shorter trips VND6,300,000-16,800,000) boasts a fleet of vessels ranging from its spacious, 15-cabin converted rice barge to a smaller 2-cabin houseboat. The company offers two-, three- and four-day trips to places like Cai Be, Sa Dec, Chau Doc, and Can Tho. Travelers visit fruit orchards and countryside villages in much the same fashion as most day tours, with the added experience of an overnight on the river. Only the longer journeys jump over the USD$1,000 mark. Onward transportation to Phu Quoc and Cambodia can be arranged, though these connections usually include a speedboat, bus, or plane rather than slow-boat service.

TransMekong, the same company behind L'Escale Restaurant and Nam Bo Boutique Hotel, runs **Bassac Cruises** (144 Hai Ba Trung, tel. 071 03 829 540, www.transmekong.com, 8am-noon and 1:30pm-5pm Mon.-Fri., 8am-noon Sat.-Sun.). This outfitter runs a series of high-end overnight trips from Can Tho to Cai Be or vice versa; the cruise also plies the route from Can Tho up to Chau Doc and the Cambodian border. All vessels are traditional wooden rice barges that have been refurbished and equipped with modern conveniences such as air-conditioning and hot water. The company's rates fluctuate, depending upon the trip and the season; contact them for a quote.

Monk. Born in 1909, Nam came from a wealthy family and studied in France for several years before returning to Vietnam, where he married and had a daughter. Later in life Nam found religion, joining a Buddhist monastery and, at one point, meditating day and night beneath a flagpole. The Coconut Monk earned his name by subsisting on a diet of fruits, vegetables, and coconut water, eating a single meal each day. In 1952, he took up residence in his home province of Ben Tre, building a colorful **sanctuary** (VND5,000), which still stands at the end of Phoenix Island, and gathering followers of his own syncretic religion, a mash-up of Buddhism and Christianity called Tinh Do Cu Si, in which he insisted that man could live on nothing more than coconut water. The Coconut Monk was also known for his clashes with the south Vietnamese authorities, who jailed him several times for spreading anti-government sentiments. Nguyen Thanh Nam died in 1990. The sanctuary is easy to spot from the boat docks. To visit the sanctuary, contact **Con Phung Tourist** (Hamlet 10, Tan Thach village, tel. 07/5382-2198, www.conphungtourist.com, 7:30am-4:30pm daily).

Nowadays, the sanctuary remains, looking like a rundown carnival with its maze of brightly hued columns and wiry statues, including a replica of the Apollo rocket. Tourists can also visit the nearby restaurant as well as a crocodile farm packed with sedate reptiles. It is possible to rent bicycles through **Con Phung Tourist** (Hamlet 10, Tan Thach village, tel. 07/5382-2198, www. conphungtourist.com, 7:30am-4:30pm daily), if you explore the island on your own. If you prefer to visit by land, a smaller connection past the long and narrow Rach Mieu Bridge leads to the opposite end of Phoenix Island, where the road then goes to the Con Phung Tourist area. Guests can stay overnight at the travel company's island **hotel** (VND200,000-450,000). There's not much point in basing yourself here, as the sights of Phoenix Island will take up no more than an hour or two.

Tortoise Island

Part of neighboring Ben Tre province, **Tortoise Island (Con Quy)** is less frequented than its larger counterparts, but several tours swing by here to get a look at the coconut candy factories, which churn out copious amounts of sticky sweet toffee every day. Visitors can watch the process as well as sample the candy, which comes in several varieties, including chocolate, coffee, and durian flavors. For those looking to get away from it all, visitors can spend a night on the water just offshore: **Mekong Floating House** (near Tortoise Island, tel. 07/5247-4500, www.radeauxdumekong.com, VND966,000) is a collection of eco-friendly, thatched-roof houses stationed on the southern side of Tortoise Island that offer private, isolated, floating bungalows for guests.

Dragon Island

The least-visited of the four islands, **Dragon Island (Con Tan Long)** is a quieter, miniature version of My Tho town. Its narrow, concrete paths slice through a sea of modest, pastel-hued houses and over tiny creeks that cut deep into the land. Guided tours are less likely to pay a visit to Dragon Island, but visitors itching to find out what's on the other side of the **Tan Long ferry** (intersection of Trung Trac and Rach Gam, 5am-10pm daily, VND1,500-4,000) can hop on board just a short walk up from the statue of Thu Khoa Huan. Once on the other side, a right turn leads along the narrow road to a dead-end on the riverfront that looks back at My Tho town, while a left turn follows the concrete path farther into the neighborhoods of Dragon Island. This is an area best explored by bicycle. Due to the fact that very few tourists make the trip out here, be prepared to draw some stares.

Boat Tours of the Islands
FROM HO CHI MINH CITY

As the gateway to the Delta, both My Tho and Ben Tre see frequent visitors from HCMC who are short on time but still want to experience the lush countryside and laid-back atmosphere of the Mekong. Scores of travel outfits in the city run day trips out to the area's river islands, hitting a few other mainland attractions along the way, and prices vary to suit a range of budgets. Companies like **Sinh Tourist** (246-248 De Tham, D1, tel. 08/3838-9593, www.thesinhtourist.vn, 6:30am-10:30pm daily) and **Vinaday Travel** (228 De Tham, D1, tel. 08/3838-8382, www.vinaday.com, 7:30am-9pm daily) offer inexpensive mass tours, with upwards of 30 or 40 fellow travelers on a trip. For more personalized excursions, try outfits such as **Ho Chi Minh City Urban Adventures** (tel. 08/3827-9279, www.hochiminhcityurbanadventures.com) or **Tiger Tours** (tel. 012/9586-8586, www.mytigertour.com), which run smaller public trips as well as private tours that can be tailored to your interests. Booking through an official travel company is recommended over sorting your trip through a hotel, as the smaller outfits attached to budget accommodations can often be a little unpredictable.

FROM MY THO

Like life in any town in the Mekong Delta, life in My Tho revolves around the river, and so the main reason for a visit to this area would be its islands and the surrounding waterways. Hop on a boat from the **tourist pier** (8 30 Thang 4, tel. 07/3397-6697, 7am-7pm daily) and float alongside houseboats and fish farms, barges, and ferries. Both private and group tours are available from the several companies housed within the pier's main office, and whether you join a group or go it alone, prices are reasonable even for a solo traveler. Most tours are booked by the vessel, so the more people you have the easier it will be on your wallet. The majority of tour providers leaving from My Tho visit the same places, making regular stops on three of the four principal islands between My Tho and Ben Tre, where you can sample local fruit and honey, drop in on a coconut candy workshop, visit the aging sanctuary of Phoenix Island's Coconut Monk, and listen to a group of *cai luong* singers; check with your chosen

mosaic above the entrance gate to Vinh Trang Pagoda

riverfront, where you may be able to find a freelance driver who will take you around.

MY THO

Considered the Mekong Delta's gateway, this hyperactive little town lies 45 miles south of Saigon and welcomes dozens of day-trippers to its tourist pier every morning. Thanks to its proximity, My Tho has become the poster child for the Delta's lazy rivers and fertile green terrain, not to mention its numerous cottage industries. From local fish farms to fruit orchards, handicraft workshops, and candy factories, My Tho and its nearby river islands provide travelers with a glimpse into the life of the region and a nice escape from the smog and chaos of Ho Chi Minh City.

The majority of visitors prefer to tour My Tho for the day, returning to Saigon at night; however, it is also possible to base yourself in town. For budget travelers, the difference in cost between booking a day trip from the city and overnighting in My Tho is minimal, thus the decision to stay in Saigon or hop on a bus down south is based on time. Those with an extra evening to spare can take in this friendly Delta town beyond the confines of a guided tour; but, if your schedule doesn't allow it, opting for a day tour is just as good.

Sights
VINH TRANG PAGODA

My Tho's **Vinh Trang Pagoda** (Nguyen Trung Truc, 6am-6pm daily) stands out among its contemporaries with a colorful exterior and several towering Buddha statues dotting its grounds. Before you reach the main gates, you'll be greeted by a pair of enormous figures: a somber, imposing Buddha followed by its hefty, happy seated counterpart. Several other sculptures around the area feature the Buddha in different poses, including a massive reclining version out back, and a cemetery off to the right marks the resting places of monks past.

To enter the pagoda, use the door on the right side of the building, where you'll pass through separate sections dedicated to the

company for their exact itinerary. Most of the day trips coming from Saigon arrive at the pier around 10:30am or 11am; if you'd like to avoid the rush, book a private boat and visit earlier in the morning.

FROM BEN TRE

Tours in Ben Tre focus on the two provinces' shared islands: Unicorn, Phoenix, Dragon, and Tortoise. While the town is only a short distance from the Tien River, many tours booked in Ben Tre actually set sail in My Tho, with travelers taking a 10-mile bus trip to the Tourist Pier in the other town, though some do depart directly from Ben Tre. Day tours featuring local fruit, honey, and coconut candy—Ben Tre's specialty—as well as southern music and a glimpse of country life can be arranged through most local hotels and at the offices of **Ben Tre Tourist** (65 Dong Khoi, tel. 07/5382-9618, www.bentretourist.vn, 7am-11am and 1pm-5pm daily). If you prefer more freedom, you can also hire a chartered boat from the tourism office or head down to the

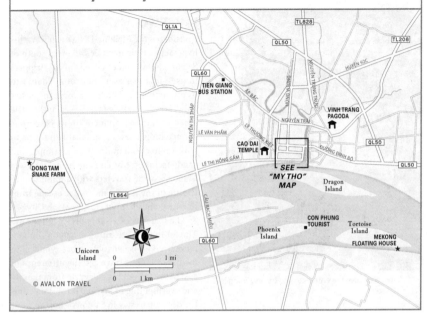

Vicinity of My Tho

ancestors as well as to Buddha himself. A bright inner courtyard interrupts the pagoda roof, letting in some light, and the building's exterior is a rich mosaic of greens, blues, and yellows. Many tourist buses to My Tho make the rounds here, so you're likely to see a few foreign visitors wandering through. Though the pagoda doesn't have a specific number address, if you follow the Quay Bridge over Bao Dinh River and turn left onto Nguyen Huynh Duc, you'll see the mammoth Buddhas on your right as the road heads out of town.

CAO DAI TEMPLE

If the Cao Dai Holy See of Tay Ninh is not in your travel plans, My Tho's smaller **Cao Dai Temple** (85 Ly Thuong Kiet, 6am-6pm daily) is a worthy example of Cao Dai architecture. The temple rarely sees foreign visitors, but guests are welcome outside of prayer hours. Avoid showing up at noon, when the temple is in use and you'll have to stay outside.

Accommodations

Though you'll be hard-pressed to find anything above two-star accommodations in this town, most of the guest rooms are clean, tidy, and perfectly comfortable. The vast majority of My Tho's tourism focuses on its waterways, so the most strategic place to base yourself is on 30 Thang 4 street or nearby. There are several hotels along the waterfront, wrapping around to Trung Trac, as well as a few toward Rach Mieu Bridge on Le Thi Hong Gam. Wherever you stay, expect prices to be infinitely more affordable than HCMC and amenities to be fewer.

UNDER VND210,000

Sparse but clean, **My Tho Hotel** (67 D 30 Thang 4, tel. 07/3387-2543, VND150,000-300,000) provides budget travelers with a few choices, including optional hot water as well as a choice between fan or air-conditioned rooms. All accommodations come with

My Tho

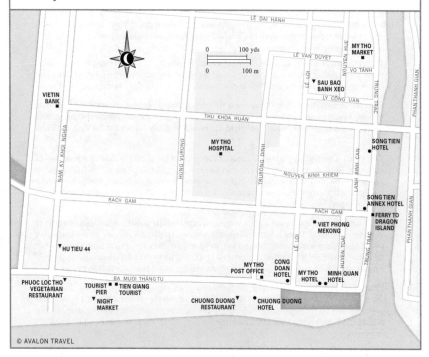

television and Wi-Fi access, and rooms are tidy and well kept.

Rooms at the **Cong Doan Hotel** (61 30 Thang 4, tel. 07/3387-4324, congdoantravel@ hcm.fpt.vn, VND150,000-260,000) are a little on the small side, but the beds are clean and the prices reasonable. You can choose from fan or air-conditioned accommodations, and each room comes with basic amenities such as a television and bottled water. There is also a nice coffee shop just next door where you can get your morning caffeine fix.

VND210,000-525,000

The spacious rooms at the **Song Tien Hotel** (101 Trung Trac, tel. 07/3387-2009, songtien. hotel@tiengiangtourist.com, VND450,000-850,000) are some of the only ones in town to feature modern decor and a bit more luxury. Beds are generous, as are the bathrooms, and

breakfast is included in the room rate. A small café is attached to the hotel and there is kara-oke on the first floor. If the Song Tien is full, you can also try the **Song Tien Annex** (33 Trung Trac, tel. 07/3397-7883, VND450,000-500,000) just down the street.

The super-slender **Minh Quan Hotel** (69 30 Thang 4, tel. 07/3397-9979, VND450,000-800,000) sits near the statue of Thu Khoa Huan on the eastern end of 30 Thang 4 and has some exceptional river views. Rooms feature generously sized beds and include air-conditioning, TV, Wi-Fi, a minibar, and hot showers. Breakfast is served every morning at the rooftop café, which is another great spot to take in the surrounding scenery; beware that due to the café the hotel's top floors can get a bit noisy at night.

One of the grander hotels in My Tho, **Chuong Duong Hotel** (10 30 Thang 4, tel.

Cuisine of the Mekong Delta

More so than any other region in Vietnam, the Mekong Delta is packed with local specialties. It seems as if every town in the south has a culinary claim to fame. Here are just a few of the Mekong's unique culinary contributions:

- *Banh Cong:* This fried rice cake is famous in Can Tho, though it's not as easily found as some other local specialties. Rice flour is combined with pork and shrimp, then fried, with the end result resembling a muffin. Use fresh greens to wrap up the cake, dip it in fish sauce, and enjoy.

- *Bun Nuoc Leo:* Actually a Khmer meal, this cloudy noodle soup is often served with local greens, a combination of leafy vegetables plucked from the countryside, and either grilled meat or congealed duck blood. You'll find *bun nuoc leo* heavily featured in Tra Vinh and Chau Doc.

- **Coconut Candy:** As Vietnam's coconut capital, Ben Tre province houses a boatload of coconuts. Here, sticky, toffee-like coconut candy is a popular local treat. The fruit's flesh is pressed, extracting the juice, which is then combined with sugar, boiled, and turned into a thick paste. Once the concoction has cooled, sheets of the candy are cut into bite-sized pieces and packaged.

- **Fish Sauce:** Though it's not a meal in itself, *nuoc mam* (fish sauce) is a fundamental part of Vietnamese cuisine. There is not a restaurant or street stall in the country where you won't find it. Made from a mixture of fish and salt, this pungent sauce requires at least 12 months of fermentation before it is bottled. Factories on Phu Quoc Island store the concoction in gigantic wooden barrels and are among the most renowned fish sauce producers in the country.

- **Fruit:** From My Tho to Vinh Long, the Delta boasts an impressive variety of fruits, many of them foreign to Western travelers. While you'll find tasty and familiar favorites like mango and papaya, other famed regional fruits include pomelo, dragon fruit (a juicy fruit hidden within a spiky, pink-and-green exterior), bite-sized longans, rambutans, and jackfruit (the world's largest fruit).

- *Hu Tieu:* Originating in My Tho, this rice noodle soup is usually served with sliced pork, quail eggs, shrimp, and occasionally dumplings. There are several equally delicious variations.

07/3387-0875, chuongduonghotel@gmail.com, VND400,000-800,000) is a massive pale yellow behemoth overlooking the river that features decent budget accommodations with a bit of outdated style. Downstairs, a large open-air restaurant caters to guests as well as the odd tour group, and one of the town's larger travel outfits operates out of this hotel.

Food

In the realm of cuisine, My Tho's claim to fame is a popular southern noodle soup called *hu tieu My Tho*. Featuring pork, fresh greens, and a unique version of rice noodles, this savory dish comes in several different varieties, including original, beef, and *sate*, which is served in a thicker, creamier broth. For other options, you'll find a handful of restaurants at some of the bigger hotels along the river, as well as dozens of small outdoor cafés lining the town's lake.

For an authentic bowl of the town specialty *hu tieu My Tho*, head to **Hu Tieu 44** (46 Nam Ky Khoi Nghia, tel. 07/3388-3044, 6am-noon and 1pm-10pm daily, VND23,000). This small hole-in-the-wall shop serves nothing but *hu tieu*.

Just beside the Tourist Pier on 30 Thang 4 street, **Phuoc Loc Tho Vegetarian Restaurant** (2A 30 Thang 4, tel. 07/3397-9467, 6am-10pm daily, VND15,000-20,000) serves a variety of vegetarian fare, including rice dishes and several noodle soups. Its signature meal is *hu tieu chay,* a meatless version of the town's namesake classic.

If you're craving street food but need a break from the ever-present *hu tieu* stalls, **Sau Bao Banh Xeo** (Le Loi, tel. 07/3387-9835, 2pm-9pm daily, VND50,000) is a nice local spot that does a delectable southern version of Vietnamese pancakes. The shop functions as a café in the mornings before transforming into a restaurant later in the afternoon.

Despite drawing a small crowd, the town's **night market** (8 30 Thang 4, 5pm-2am daily, VND20,000-50,000) is open to the wee hours of the morning. A collection of different stalls serve rice-and-meat dishes as well as several types of noodles, from *bun* and pho to *hu tieu,* and a variety of soups. Smoothies and *che,* a local dessert, are also available. Some stalls are better than others, so feel free to have a look around before deciding upon a vendor.

Information and Services

The government-run **Tien Giang Tourist** (8 30 Thang 4, tel. 07/3387-3184, www.tiengiangtourist.com, 7am-5pm daily) has a hand in most of the town's tourism offerings, from hotels and restaurants to river tours. They're worth consulting for further information on My Tho town and the surrounding area, including parts of Ben Tre province, and provide free maps upon request. From here, both single travelers and large groups can hire boats and book tours.

The friendly folks at **Viet Phong Mekong** (2 Le Loi, tel. 07/3388-2522, www.vietphongmekong.com.vn, 7am-5pm daily) provide not only day tours of My Tho's nearby islands but also homestays, bicycle and motorbike rentals, and general information on the Delta area. Maps of My Tho town are also available here.

The **Vietin Bank** (15B Nam Ky Khoi Nghia, tel. 07/3387-3025, www.vietinbank.vn, 7:30am-11:30am and 1:30pm-4:30pm Mon.-Fri.) exchanges currency and also has an ATM available.

The massive **My Tho post office** (59 30 Thang 4, tel. 07/3387-3214, 6:30am-8:30pm daily) is located right on the main drag. It also provides Internet services around the back on Truong Dinh street.

The large **My Tho Hospital (Benh Vien Da Khoa My Tho)** (2 Hung Vuong, tel. 07/3387-2363) is as equipped as any hospital in southern Vietnam to treat minor illnesses and injuries. For serious emergencies, there are 24-hour services available, but you're far better heading to Saigon.

Transportation

Buses leave Ho Chi Minh City's Western bus station every half hour from 7am-7pm daily (1.5 hours, VND35,000), arriving at My Tho's **Tien Giang bus station** (42 Ap Bac, tel. 07/3385-5404, 4am-10pm daily), roughly two miles from town. There are also several daily arrivals from neighboring Delta towns, including Ha Tien (5-6 hours, VND120,000), Can Tho (2.5 hours, VND75,000), and Chau Doc (3 hours, VND140,000).

Thanks to its size, My Tho town is easily accessible on foot. There are, however, a handful of *xe om* drivers that hang out along 30 Thang 4 street near the tourist pier and, should you need a cab, **Mailinh** (tel. 07/3387-8787) taxis are always available.

If you prefer your own set of wheels, **Viet Phong Mekong** (2 Le Loi, tel. 07/3388-2522, www.vietphongmekong.com.vn, 7am-5pm daily, VND50,000-150,000) rents out both bicycles and motorbikes. Fees are reasonable, but be prepared to put down some sort of collateral for your rental vehicle, usually either money or a passport, which will be returned to you once the rental is complete. A few hotels and guesthouses are also willing to hire out vehicles upon request.

Dong Tam Snake Farm

If you're up for a bit of a trek, the **Dong Tam Snake Farm (Trai Ran Dong Tam)** (Cong 2 Trai Ran, tel. 07/3385-3204, 7am-4:30pm daily, VND20,000), about 6.5 miles from My Tho, offers an unusual break from the river.

Located in Binh Duc, this massive complex was founded in 1977 and is wholly devoted to the care and study of various snakes found throughout the Southeast Asian region. In addition to providing the country with medical research into treating venomous snakebites and other ailments, the snake farm functions as something of a zoo for visitors and has expanded to include many more creatures, including ostriches, deer, monkeys, and birds of prey. These animals aren't kept in the finest of cages, a fact that may turn off animal lovers. But, the serpents, particularly the trees full of bright-green snakes, are an interesting departure from your average menagerie. Check out the snake-feeding house to find the largest reptiles, or pose for a picture with a massive python. There is a small, eerie museum of preserved snakes as well as an informational video offered to visitors.

Beyond the animals themselves, finding the snake farm can be half the fun. The area is not well marked, but if you follow Le Thi Hong Gam west from My Tho past the Rach Mieu Bridge, you'll enter Binh Duc village. Continue along this road through Binh Duc market until you reach Binh Duc Primary School (Truong Tieu Hoc Binh Duc) on your right. Just beside the school is a small road topped with a sign reading "Ap Van Hoa Tan Thuan B." Take this pleasant, paved village road straight through to the end, bearing left at the fork, and you'll reach another large street. Dong Tam Snake Farm is on your left at the very end, just before the gargantuan military center. Budget about two hours for the trip, including travel time.

BEN TRE

Though it's only 10 miles from My Tho, the sleepy town of Ben Tre has managed to escape the same tourism hype as its northern neighbor and remains a placid, likable place with few specific attractions but plenty of pleasant scenery. A major agricultural contributor and the heart of the nation's coconut industry, this small island province is considered the birthplace of the National Liberation Front, the major guerrilla force that opposed southern Vietnamese soldiers during the American War. Having fought in the Tay Son rebellion in the 18th century and, later, taken on the French colonial government in the 1940s and '50s, Ben Tre's fierce nationalism was already a local mainstay by the time American soldiers turned up, making the NLF a powerful adversary. U.S. soldiers proved to be equally ruthless: when an unnamed U.S. major uttered the now-famous line, "It became necessary to destroy the village in order to save it," he was talking about Ben Tre.

Nowadays, you're more likely to find sleepy street corners and riverside cafés than any sort of aggression. Locals in Ben Tre embody the friendly, easygoing reputation of Delta hospitality, and life in this little corner of the country is wonderfully laid-back. While most visitors zip over to the My Tho-Ben Tre area on a day trip, it is also possible to spend the night in town. Like My Tho, two days is really all you need in Ben Tre before it's time to carry on.

Sights
RIVERFRONT
The most attractive feature of Ben Tre is its **riverfront.** A lively spot from morning to night, the street along the water is lined with fruit vendors and small cafés where you can sit and watch the world go by. Hung Vuong, the road along the water, extends all the way from Ben Tre Market to the nearby countryside, giving you plenty of space to stroll or cycle as you please.

BEN TRE MUSEUM
The provincial **Ben Tre Museum** (146 Hung Vuong, tel. 07/5382-2735, 7am-11am and 1pm-5pm Mon.-Fri., 7:30am-11:30am, 1:30pm-4:30pm, and 7pm-9pm Sat.-Sun.) is filled with the standard array of revolutionary exhibits and war artifacts. While the displays aren't exactly riveting, this museum is housed in

Ben Tre

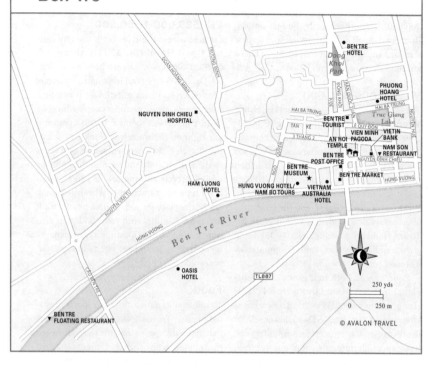

yet another stately, aging colonial structure on the riverfront that is worth admiring from the outside.

VIEN MINH PAGODA AND AN HOI TEMPLE

If you're wandering around town, the generous **Vien Minh Pagoda** (near the corner of Nguyen Dinh Chieu and QL60, sunrise-sunset daily) near the central market and Ben Tre Bridge No. 1 is a nice place to visit. While it doesn't have the same exciting history as some other Vietnamese pagodas, the building is aesthetically pleasing and there are two massive white statues—one of Buddha, one of Quan Am—right out front that add to the atmosphere of the town's main roundabout. You'll also find **An Hoi Temple** next door, whose colorful dragons

jump out of the front wall; depending upon the time of day, you may or may not be able to go inside.

Accommodations
UNDER VND210,000

Overlooking Dong Khoi Park, the government-run **Ben Tre Hotel (Khach San Ben Tre)** (8/2 Tran Quoc Tuan, tel. 07/5382-5332, khachsanbentre@bentretourist.vn, VND180,000-360,000) is bare-bones but clean and tidy, not to mention complete with standard amenities: TV, hot showers, and air-conditioning. Though it's a bit of a walk down to the riverfront, the area is nice and there are plenty of restaurants nearby. The hotel entrance is located on Dong Khoi street, just before the Co-Op Mart.

A narrow building across from Truc Giang

Lake, the family-run **Phuong Hoang Hotel (Khach San Phuong Hoang)** (28 Hai Ba Trung, tel. 07/5357-5377, VND120,000-200,000) is another worthy budget option. Rooms are small but comfortable and feature standard amenities, with your choice of fan or air-conditioned accommodations.

VND210,000-525,000

The most affordable riverfront option, **Hung Vuong Hotel** (166 Hung Vuong, tel. 07/5382-2408, www.hungvuonghotelbentre.com.vn, VND320,000-360,000) offers great value for the price, with clean, modestly furnished rooms featuring air-conditioning, Wi-Fi access, hot showers, a minibar, and a bathtub. Breakfast is also included, and the hotel runs a restaurant downstairs, as well as **Nam Bo Tours** (166 Hung Vuong, tel. 07/5351-1292, www.nambotours.com, 7am-4:30pm daily), its travel outfit.

Popular with both tour groups and individual travelers, **Ham Luong Hotel** (200C Hung Vuong, tel. 07/5356-0560, www.hamluongtourist.com.vn, VND480,000-900,000) is one of Ben Tre's nicer accommodations. Its clean, modern rooms afford guests pleasant views of the river. Wi-Fi, air-conditioning, television, and hot water are included in the room rate, along with complimentary breakfast. The hotel runs an on-site restaurant as well as a travel agency, which can help you book boat tours to the river islands and around.

When it comes to ambience, the **Vietnam Australia Hotel (Khach San Viet Uc)** (144 Hung Vuong, tel. 07/5351-1888, www.hotelvietuc.com, VND400,000-2,150,000) takes the cake. This stunning three-star hotel is the most modern in town, from its cavernous lobby and café to each of its well-appointed rooms. Accommodations at the front of the hotel offer excellent riverfront views, and the kind and professional staff make it well worth the price tag. Basic doubles range from VND400,000 to VND550,000 and TV, free Wi-Fi, air-conditioning, hot water, and breakfast are included. Keep an eye out for the

security guard's hut, which is designed to look like the Sydney Opera House.

VND525,000-1,050,000

Located across the river from the city center, **Oasis Hotel** (151 My Thanh An, tel. 07/5383-8800, www.bentrehoteloasis.com, VND630,000-882,000) lives up to its name. This quiet, laid-back guesthouse is run by a Vietnamese-New Zealander couple who offer clean, comfortable rooms as well as a pool and bar right on the waterfront looking back at Ben Tre city. Staff can arrange private tours to the river islands and surrounding area as well as bicycle and motorbike hires. If you don't have your own set of wheels this may not be the place for you, as it's a bit of a walk into town. Families with young kids may also want to find another location, as the management prefers not to have guests under eight years old.

Food

Thanks to its relative quiet as a tourist destination, Ben Tre has fewer restaurant options than its counterpart across the river. However, many hotels in town have restaurants attached in order to serve guests and there are plenty of street food options both in and around the central market.

Bustling with local clientele, **Nam Son Restaurant** (40 Phan Ngoc Tong, tel. 07/5382-2873, 9:30am-7:30pm daily, VND25,000-70,000) serves tasty Vietnamese fare, including *canh chua* (sour soup) and plenty of meat and fish dishes to accompany your rice. The place gets busy around lunch and again at dinner, so you may find yourself sitting with strangers, but the restaurant is a nice place for a wide range of options.

The cool, banquet-style ground-floor restaurant at **Hung Vuong** (166 Hung Vuong, tel. 07/5382-2408, www.hungvuonghotelbentre.com.vn, 6am-11pm daily, VND35,000-90,000) serves simple meals from its English menu, including tofu, beef, shrimp, squid, and eel dishes. Though the decor isn't much, prices are reasonable and the food is decent.

The dining room at **Ham Luong** (200C Hung Vuong, tel. 07/5356-0560, www.hamluongtourist.com.vn, 6am-10pm daily, VND70,000-260,000) is one of Ben Tre's fancier setups, with a nice, air-conditioned indoor seating area and a bit more atmosphere than most other places in town. A lengthy menu includes a host of Vietnamese favorites as well as beer and wine. The dining room often caters to large groups rather than individual travelers, so if you plan to eat here be prepared to wait for your meal or order ahead of time to avoid the delay.

Looking slightly worse for wear, the **Ben Tre Floating Restaurant** (Hung Vuong, tel. 07/5382-2492, nhahangnoibentre@yahoo.com.vn, 10am-10pm daily, VND35,000-200,000) may be out of commission as a boat but it manages to make for a nice, breezy dinner on the water. The multi-story vehicle remains docked on Hung Vuong street just past Ben Tre Bridge No. 2 and serves everything under the sun, from pork and beef to crocodile, deer, and snails. If you prefer, you can also choose your dinner from a series of fish tanks in the restaurant's lobby.

Information and Services

Ben Tre Tourist (65 Dong Khoi, tel. 07/5382-9618, www.bentretourist.vn, 7am-11am and 1pm-5pm daily) offers tours of the surrounding islands and nearby rural areas, venturing more off the beaten path than its northern counterpart in Tien Giang. Cycling tours and homestays can also be arranged or, if you prefer to make your own itinerary, both slow and fast boats, as well as bicycles, are available for hire.

The local **Vietin Bank** (142A Nguyen Dinh Chieu, tel. 07/5382-4960, www.vietinbank.vn, 7:30am-11:30am and 1:30pm-4:30pm Mon.-Fri.) has an ATM and can exchange currencies.

The **Ben Tre post office** (corner of Dong Khoi and Cach Mang Thang 8, tel. 07/5382-2157, 6am-8pm daily) is located just behind the market and directly on the roundabout before Ben Tre Bridge No. 1.

The **Nguyen Dinh Chieu Hospital (Benh Vien Nguyen Dinh Chieu)** (109 Doan Hoang Minh, tel. 07/5382-2178 or 07/5381-7555) is the largest of several hospitals and medical facilities located on this busy street. While they may be able to help with minor ailments, for anything serious, return to Saigon.

Transportation

A mammoth, modern entity, the **Ben Tre bus station (Ben Xe Ben Tre)** (Quoc Lo 60, tel. 07/5382-2298, 3am-10pm daily) has arrivals from Saigon (2 hours, VND50,000) as well as several other destinations around the Mekong Delta, including Ha Tien (5-6 hours, VND120,000), Can Tho (2.5 hours, VND65,000), and Chau Doc (3-3.5 hours, VND120,000).

You'll find plenty of *xe om* hanging around Ben Tre's street corners, and **Mailinh** (tel. 0753/878-7878) taxis also make their way around town.

Bicycles are available for rent from **Ben Tre Tourist** (65 Dong Khoi, tel. 07/5382-9618, www.bentretourist.vn, 7am-11am and 1pm-5pm daily) and through several of the local hotels. Rates can be either hourly or daily, depending upon the provider and how long you plan to cycle.

Vinh Long

Vinh Long is a city in two parts. As a provincial capital, the town sees its fair share of chaos and traffic, with the bustling central market bursting at its seams and running freely down 1 Thang 5 street. But step on a ferry across the Co Chien River and you'll be pleasantly surprised to find its peaceful, laid-back island antithesis on the other side. Flush with palm trees and fruit orchards, fishing boats, and more waterways than roads, the fertile lands of An Binh, Vinh Long's largest river island, are the very definition of this region, a plentiful oasis where houses hide under the lush cover of palms and the island's narrow dirt roads are lined with papaya trees.

For travelers looking to experience the unhurried pace and friendly demeanor of the Mekong Delta, An Binh is an ideal spot to fall in step with the locals. Even with plenty of day-trippers passing through to visit Cai Be floating market and make a quick tour of the island, Vinh Long has managed to remain an easygoing and welcoming place that still feels like an authentic part of the Mekong Delta. A number of homestay options have sprung up on the island, allowing visitors to spend a night or two in peaceful An Binh with a local family.

Vinh Long is best visited outside of the rainy season (May-Oct.), as the shores of the low-lying island often recede around this time. Regardless of the season, it is a good idea to plan on at least one overnight here in order to get the full experience. Day trips are available from Saigon, but the drive to Cai Be can be time-consuming and An Binh's serene island feel is tricky to achieve in only a few hours.

SIGHTS
An Binh Island
Still accessible only by ferry, **An Binh Island** is a sleepy village community of pastel-hued bungalows and floating fish farms that represents life in the Delta at its finest. Lush, green landscapes take up most of the area, covering every inch of this massive river island with palm fronds and papaya trees, fruit orchards, and narrow, meandering streams. While visitors may come here for the scenery, many people often wind up staying an extra day or two on account of the hospitable locals, who are quick to say hello or invite you for a chat over tea. An Binh can be reached via the local **ferry (Ben Pha An Binh)** (4am-10pm daily, VND500-2,500), which leaves from downtown Vinh Long, and is best explored by bicycle or by boat. Plenty of small wooden canoes ply the island's waterways, taking visitors to more hidden parts of An Binh. For cyclists, this is a sight that can be experienced independently; however, many people supplement their own explorations with a guided tour or a local homestay.

Cai Be Floating Market
An hour north of An Binh, **Cai Be floating market** (5am-5pm daily) is the Mekong Delta's second most popular on-the-water trading post. Though much smaller than its counterpart in Can Tho, Cai Be's floating market boasts a beautiful location, set before the towering spire of the local cathedral. As soon as the sun rises, boats from around the area gather to buy and sell fruit, vegetables, and fish, stringing up a sample of their product at the front of each boat to alert passing customers. Due to its distance from Vinh Long, a visit to Cai Be requires that you book a tour, which is easily done through **Cuu Long Tourist** (1 1 Thang 5, tel. 07/0382-3616, www.cuulongtourist.com, 7am-8pm daily). Arrive earlier in the morning rather than later, as the sun shoos away many vendors around midday.

Van Thanh Temple
One of the only temples of its kind in the

Vinh Long

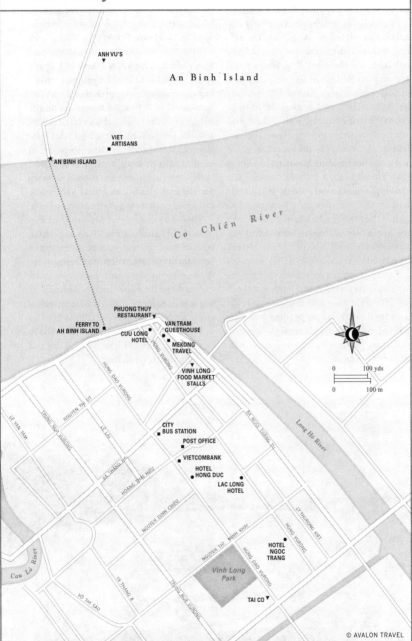

ANH VU'S

An Binh Island

VIET
ARTISANS

★ AN BINH ISLAND

Co Chiên River

PHUONG THUY
RESTAURANT

FERRY TO
AH BINH ISLAND

CUU LONG
HOTEL

VAN TRAM
GUESTHOUSE

MEKONG
TRAVEL

VINH LONG
FOOD MARKET
STALLS

0   100 yds
0   100 m

Long Hồ River

HUNG DAO VUONG

LE VAN TAM

TRUNG NHI VUONG

NGUYEN THI UT

LE LAI

BA THANG HA

HOANG THAI HIEU

NGUYEN DINH CHIEU

CITY
BUS STATION

POST OFFICE

VIETCOMBANK

HOTEL
HONG DUC

LAC LONG
HOTEL

BA HUUN THANH TU

LY THUONG KIET

HUNG VUONG

Cau Lâu River

19 THANG 8

VO THI SAU

NGUYEN THI MINH KHAI

HUNG DAO VUONG

TRUNG NHI VUONG

Vinh Long
Park

HOTEL
NGOC
TRANG

TAI CO

© AVALON TRAVEL

Mekong Delta, **Van Thanh Temple** (Tran Phu, 5am-11am and 1pm-7pm Mon.-Sat.) honors the intellect and scholarly pursuits of Confucius as well as several of his disciples. Completed in 1866, Van Thanh's long, rectangular grounds trace a tree-lined path up to the main building, where you'll find an altar dedicated to Confucius and, just before it, a large bust of 14th-century mandarin Chu Van An, considered to be Vietnam's first educator. Both of these men are often referred to in Vietnam as "the eternal teacher." Closer to the entrance, you'll find a smaller building honoring local hero Phan Thanh Gian, a 19th-century scholar who opposed colonial rule so vehemently that, in 1867, he took up a hunger strike against the French, which lasted a little over two weeks before, realizing that defeat was inevitable, he took his own life by drinking poison.

Though it appears deceptively far from the city center on a map, Van Thanh is a short, one-mile jaunt away and sits just beside the Long Ho River. While its opening hours are as listed, the main temple is often locked, in which case you may have to find a grounds-keeper to let you in.

BOAT TOURS

Both private and group tours to Cai Be floating market and around the waterways of An Binh Island can be arranged, either through companies like **Cuu Long Tourist** (1 1 Thang 5, tel. 07/0382-3616, www.cuulongtourist.com, 7am-8pm daily) and **Mekong Travel** (8 1 Thang 5, tel. 07/0383-6252, vinhlongmekongtravel@yahoo.com, www.mekongtravel.com.vn, 7am-5pm daily) or with most homestays on the island. Prices are reasonable (VND200,000-400,000 per person). These boat trips usually include a handful of brief stopovers at local handicraft workshops, fruit orchards, or flower gardens, as well as the odd *cai luong* performance, a traditional style of Vietnamese music that has its origins in the Mekong Delta.

There are also several day trips that run from Ho Chi Minh City to Vinh Long, which you can book through tour providers in the city. Since it's a bit of a drive to Cai Be, where the tours begin, you usually pass by the floating market a little later than is desirable. If you're pressed for time, this is a decent option and often preferred over day trips to My Tho or Ben Tre, but for the full experience you're better off spending a night in Vinh Long and booking your trip locally.

Storefronts line the banks of the Co Chien River in Vinh Long.

Homestays

When visiting Vinh Long, many travelers are keen to experience local life firsthand: floating around on a wooden fishing boat; sampling local cuisine; or wandering through the small village communities that make up An Binh Island. One of the best ways to get an authentic Delta experience is by organizing a homestay with a local family.

In Vinh Long, companies like **Cuu Long Tourist** (www.cuulongtourist.com) and **Mekong Travel** (www.mekongtravel.com.vn) orchestrate overnights on An Binh. For as little as VND210,000, local homestays cover your bed for the night as well as dinner, breakfast, and, in some cases, a bicycle rental for exploring the island.

Thanks to the growing popularity of homestays, many homestay spots are more like guesthouses than one-on-one overnights with a local family—so you may have to share your hosts with a few other foreign guests. These homestays are easily found on your own, either by checking online ahead of time or simply turning up on the island. Smaller tour operators and independent guides are your best bet for tracking down authentic homestays, as the government-run tourism companies do not have this information.

At a guesthouse-style homestay, even with a handful of other tourists around, getting off the mainland and into the peaceful environment of An Binh is a satisfying experience. Plenty of the larger homestays offer tours to Cai Be floating market and through the winding canals of An Binh.

Book a homestay in advance rather than just showing up; while there is a good chance that you'd be able to find a bed, planning ahead will guarantee that it is ready for you when you arrive.

SHOPPING

For something different, pay a visit to the folks at **Viet Artisans** (110/9 An Thanh, An Binh Island, tel. 016/9851-5910, www.vietartisans.org, 8am-4pm daily), a nonprofit organization with a beautiful location along the riverfront not far from An Binh ferry. Even with the island's tourism potential and agricultural resources, many families on An Binh struggle to earn an adequate living. This center, founded by Vietnamese-American Lily Phan, offers local women the opportunity to learn sewing, book-making, and other handicrafts in order to provide a sustainable income for their families. Viet Artisans also runs workshops upon request: visitors can stop by the breezy, thatched-roof workshop to peruse an array of local souvenirs, chat, or try their hand at Vietnamese calligraphy, silkscreen, or handmade notebooks. All workshops are free, so visitors need only pay for the products they make, and the staff are a group of women who are happy to share their skills. Guests to the center are welcome at any time; just call ahead and someone will meet you at the ferry.

ACCOMMODATIONS

Though there are a handful of decent budget hotels in Vinh Long, one of the best and most popular ways to experience this river town and its scenery is by spending the night with a local family. Ever since tourists caught wind of the friendly residents and verdant greenery on An Binh, homestays have become all the rage, with many foreign visitors opting for a bed on the island rather than in town. If you base yourself on the mainland, your best bet is to stay near the market, as this area provides easy access to the city's restaurants and travel services, not to mention the ferry to An Binh Island.

Under VND210,000

The rooms at **Hotel Ngoc Trang** (18 Hung Vuong, tel. 07/0383-2581, VND170,000-300,000) take the prize for the largest in town. Well-kept and tidy, each high-ceilinged room includes air-conditioning, a hot shower, and free Wi-Fi along with generous beds. Several rooms also come with a balcony, giving you a view of the street below. The staff doesn't really speak English, but the beds are decent and the price is right. There is a small café downstairs with not much more than a few fold-out chairs.

Boasting the nicest accommodations among a trio of guesthouses around this intersection, **Lac Long Hotel** (2G Hung Vuong, tel. 07/0383-6846, VND140,000-300,000) offers your choice of fan or air-conditioned rooms with Wi-Fi, hot water, and a dizzying assortment of patterns in its decor. Hotel staff are friendly and speak some English. If you prefer a window, request one as not all rooms have natural light.

VND210,000-525,000

Easily the best value in Vinh Long, **Van Tram Guesthouse** (4 1 Thang 5, tel. 07/0382-3820, VND200,000-350,000) boasts spacious rooms with TV, Wi-Fi, and one of the finest showers in the Mekong Delta. The balconies overlooking the street give guests a nice overhead view of the bustling market below, and there are bicycles for rent in the lobby. This guesthouse is in a central part of town, and it has been known to experience spontaneous karaoke outbursts in the early evenings, as well as some noise from the market in the wee hours of the morning.

One of the more modern accommodations in town, **Hotel Hong Duc** (3F-3G Hung Dao Vuong, tel. 07/0222-0121, VND300,000-500,000) is almost directly across from the city post office and features hot water, clean beds, large windows, and, in some cases, balconies. Rooms are smartly decorated with new furnishings and include an in-room fridge as well as a television and Wi-Fi access. The hotel staff are friendly and speak some English, and there is a café located on the ground floor.

The state-run **Cuu Long Hotel** (1 1 Thang 5, tel. 07/0382-3656, www.cuulong-tourist.com, VND330,000-800,000) is the busiest in town, with regular tour groups passing through its doors. Rooms are well appointed as far as Vinh Long goes and several accommodations offer nice views of the river as well as balconies. With plush beds and an unbeatable location, the Cuu Long is often full, so book ahead if you plan to stay here.

FOOD

Despite its growing number of foreign visitors, much of Vinh Long's food scene remains local. While there are a handful of proper restaurants around town, the majority of residents opt for street food or eat at *binh dan*-style joints—the simple plastic-stool-and-metal-tables shops you see around town. You can find plenty of snacks and street carts along 1 Thang 5 near the market as well as around **Vinh Long City Park** (Hung Dao Vuong and Nguyen Thi Minh Khai).

The sprawling, haphazard Vinh Long Market begins pretty early, but its **food stalls** (7am-5pm daily, VND10,000-30,000) open a little later, around 7am. At the food stalls, you can find an assortment of local treats, snacks, and full-fledged meals under a covered area beside the main market.

Popular with the locals, **Tai Co** (corner of Hung Dao Vuong and 2 Thang 9, tel. 0703/824-845, 10am-10pm daily, VND220,000-300,000) is a hotpot restaurant located at the southern end of District 1 just before a small canal. Though it doesn't have a menu, its offerings are not hard to remember: the place serves only hotpot, with your choice of beef *(bo)*, fish *(ca)*, pork *(heo)*, or vegetable *(rau)*. There is also a *banh bao* (steamed pork dumpling) cart just outside the restaurant's entrance on 2 Thang 9 street that does decent business in the mornings.

A delicious option, **Phuong Thuy Restaurant** (Phan Boi Chau, tel. 07/0382-4786, restaurant@cuulongtourist.com, 6:30am-10pm daily, VND30,000-120,000) features an English menu and plenty of delectable Vietnamese dishes, from fish to pork, chicken, beef, seafood, and vegetables. You also have your choice of eating street-side like a local or going for the posh, table-clothed seating by the water.

Anh Vu's (Ap An Thanh, An Binh Island, tel. 09/0256-7132, 6am-6pm daily,

VND10,000-15,000) is one of the only shops on the island that serves food and is definitely the only place on An Binh where you'll find vegetarian fare. The shop offers both a meatless rendition of *hu tieu* (a southern noodle soup) and Vietnamese pancakes with shrimp. Find Anh Vu's by taking the main road straight once you exit the ferry and heading past both Tien Chau Pagoda and the local gas station. This is a good lunch stop if you're cycling around on your own.

INFORMATION AND SERVICES

Sharing its space with the lobby of the Cuu Long Hotel, **Cuu Long Tourist** (1 1 Thang 5, tel. 07/0382-3616, www.cuulongtourist. com, 7am-8pm daily) arranges boat tours to Cai Be floating market and around An Binh Island as well as short cycling trips and homestays. There are also maps (VND20,000) of Vinh Long city and the entire province and the tour desk can help with onward travel to other Mekong Delta towns.

A much smaller, homegrown outfit, **Mekong Travel** (8 1 Thang 5, tel. 07/0383-6252, vinhlongmekongtravel@yahoo.com, www.mekongtravel.com.vn, 7am-5pm daily) organizes tours to An Binh Island and Cai Be floating market as well as homestays and assists in arranging bus tickets to other Delta destinations.

There are a handful of banks situated just opposite the post office. **Vietcombank** (1D-1E Hoang Thai Hieu, tel. 04/3824-3524, www. vietcombank.com.vn, 7am-11am and 1pm-5pm Mon.-Fri.) handles monetary needs.

On the corner of Hung Dao Vuong and Hoang Thai Hieu, the **Vinh Long Post Office** (14 Hoang Thai Hieu, tel.

07/0382-3320, 7am-6pm daily) handles mail as well as Internet services.

The **Vinh Long General Hospital (Benh Vien Da Khoa Vinh Long)** (301 Tran Phu, tel. 07/0382-3520) assists with minor illnesses and injuries, though services are basic. You'll have to head to Saigon for serious medical care.

TRANSPORTATION

Buses entering town stop at the **Vinh Long bus station** (Dinh Tien Hoang, tel. 07/0382-3458, 24 hours daily), roughly two miles from the city center. There are daily arrivals from Saigon (2.5 hours, VND115,000) via tourist bus company Phuong Trang. Local buses run the same routes but are cheaper: VND60,000-80,000 from Saigon. They also run from Can Tho for VND50,000.

If you're arriving from a closer destination, like Sa Dec (30 minutes, VND15,000-30,000), public buses let off at the **city bus station** (3 Thang 2 and Hung Dao Vuong, 5am-5pm daily) right in the center of town.

Dozens of *xe om* **drivers** camp out near the An Binh ferry, as well as outside the local bus stations. There are also a couple **Mailinh taxis** (tel. 07/0392-9292) roaming around that can take you where you need to go.

The best way to explore An Binh Island is via bicycle. Many hotels will rent out city bikes at reasonable rates and most homestays can provide two-wheeled transport as well—some even include it in the price. **Cuu Long Tourist** (1 1 Thang 5, tel. 07/0382-3616, www.cuulongtourist.com, 7am-8pm daily) and **Mekong Travel** (8 1 Thang 5, tel. 07/0383-6252, vinhlongmekongtravel@yahoo.com, www.mekongtravel.com.vn, 7am-5pm daily) can also arrange rentals for those staying in the city.

Tra Vinh

Isolated by a pair of rivers that cut deep into the surrounding peninsula, Tra Vinh is a stunning place where travelers trade the tourist trail for a quiet stop off the beaten path. Hand-painted signs and angular, 1970s-style building facades give the town a retro feel, while the countless pagodas scattered between the storefronts offer a different side of the Mekong Delta.

The main reason for visiting Tra Vinh is its array of gold-drenched Theravada Buddhist pagodas. You'll be able to tell these apart from their Vietnamese counterparts, as their sharply peaked roofs and lavish ornamentation are often more in line with the type of pagoda you might find in Thailand or Cambodia. With the majority of these sights easily covered in a day, many people spend only a night or two in Tra Vinh, pagoda-hopping and enjoying the shaded streets of this quiet town.

SIGHTS

Barring a few exceptions, many of Tra Vinh's sights are not within the downtown area, but rather a mile or two outside of town. These sights are just too far to be walkable but are well within cycling distance. It is also possible to catch a cab or hire a *xe om*, but with the sights so close, you're better off putting in a little leg work and getting there on your own. Once you've had your fill of pagodas, the next best thing to do in Tra Vinh is pack a map, set off on your bicycle, and get lost on the small country roads surrounding town, as the aging colonial buildings, spiky, towering palm trees, and flooded fields make for some beautiful scenery.

Since Tra Vinh is a conservative town and Khmer pagodas are strict on respectful dress, wear long pants and cover your shoulders when visiting these religious sites, as you may not be permitted entry otherwise. While most pagodas have resident monks who live

and study on-site, the buildings can appear empty from the outside. It is acceptable for you to wander in for a visit, but you may want to find someone first to let them know you're there. More often than not, you'll be free to wander the grounds on your own at this point.

Ong Pagoda

Proof of Tra Vinh's remaining ethnic Chinese community, one of the few in the Mekong Delta, **Ong Pagoda** (44 Dien Bien Phu, 7am-5pm daily) has occupied a corner of downtown Tra Vinh since 1556. Built by Chinese immigrants, this small building houses a statue of the red-faced, beard-twirling Quan Cong, a famous Chinese general and prominent figure in many pagodas throughout Vietnam. As is true of most Chinese pagodas, this one sports two guardians flanking the front door, a central celestial well where incense is burned, and a large main altar at the far end of the building. Around back, a small fish pond and a tribute to the Buddha are on display outdoors.

Ong Met Pagoda

Not to be confused with the Ong Pagoda, the **Ong Met Pagoda** (220 Le Loi, 7am-5pm daily) is farther down the street and is home to dozens of orange-clad resident monks. This Theravada Buddhist pagoda is the most centrally located of the bunch, sitting just a block away from the local post office. Enter through the front gates and you'll find three buildings inside; the one on the left houses dozens of Buddha statues and serves as the main prayer hall. At a few hundred years old, the main building is covered in faded murals and intricately carved ceilings. While the pagoda shows its age in the crumbling rafters and chipped paint of its interior, this is part of its charm. The friendly monks are always around and happy to welcome visitors. If you fancy a walk, keep going past Ong Met and

Vicinity of Tra Vinh

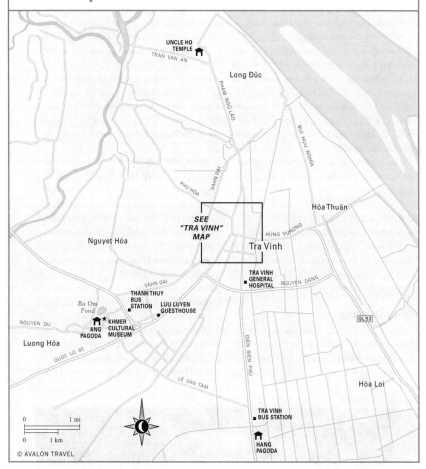

you'll come across the crisp, clean **Tra Vinh Church** (Le Loi). Its gates are usually closed, but the church itself, an all-white colonial-era structure nestled among the palms, is beautiful from outside.

Ba Om Pond and Ang Pagoda

A popular setting reserved for religious festivities and afternoon picnics, **Ba Om Pond** (off Quoc Lo 53) is surrounded by massive trees, each hundreds of years old. Also known as Square Pond, the legend goes that, many years ago, men and women could not agree upon who should be responsible for proposing marriage. Neither group wanted to ask for the other's hand, as this meant the person was obligated to foot the wedding bill. It was decided that the men and women of the village would have a pond-digging contest, in which each group had a single night, from sundown to sunrise, to dig the largest pond they could. A woman named Lady Om led the other females in entertaining the men after sundown and, once they were good and drunk, hung a lamp on a tree, which the men mistook for morning light. After their competition had gone home to sleep, Lady Om and her team dug the pond you see here and women were henceforth relieved of proposing marriage.

Overlooking the far side of the pond, the often-visited **Ang Pagoda** (off Quoc Lo 53, 8am-4pm daily) is another example of Theravada Buddhist architecture and a frequent stop for visitors to Tra Vinh. Adorned with ornate carvings of nymphs and several decorated stupas, the main building of the complex is covered from floor to ceiling in murals of the Buddha. Its beautiful, tree-lined grounds give the place something of an Angkorian feel.

Khmer Cultural Museum

The **Khmer Cultural Museum** (across from Ang Pagoda, 7am-11am and 1pm-5pm Fri.-Wed., free) boasts exhibits featuring photos, artifacts, and information on the history and culture of the Khmer people in Vietnam.

Hang Pagoda

Hidden behind an archway just across the bridge from the Tra Vinh bus station, the 17th-century **Hang Pagoda** (Dien Bien Phu, 7am-5pm daily) does not, from the outside,

appear to be much. But pass through the tunnel-like entrance into the complex and you'll find a peaceful, two-hectare garden with plenty of trees and large, high-ceilinged structures. There are several buildings on the pagoda grounds, including one that displays the handiwork of resident monks, who practice woodworking and have accumulated an impressive collection of carved sculptures. Visit earlier in the morning or later in the afternoon and you may even catch a glimpse of the storks that often nest here.

Uncle Ho Temple

Tra Vinh's **Uncle Ho Temple** (Long Duc Commune, 7am-11am and 1pm-5pm daily) is just one of a number of temples throughout the country dedicated to the great leader. Set amid a large, flowering garden complete with a pond, this honorary shrine includes a proper, enclosed temple as well as a small exhibition area featuring dozens of photos of Ho Chi Minh in various settings. There is also a replica of Uncle Ho's stilted house, the original of which exists up north, as well as the requisite downed American military vehicles. While there is no English signage, the temple is a short cycle or ride away from town and the grounds make for a nice place to sit and relax.

stupas at Ang Pagoda

Tra Vinh

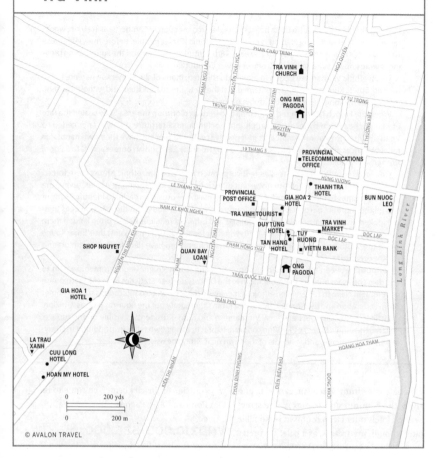

Map labels:
PHAN CHÂU TRINH
LÊ LỢI
NGÔ QUYỀN
PHAM NGŨ LÃO
NGUYỄN THÁI HỌC
LÝ TỰ TRỌNG
TÔ THỊ HUỲNH
TRƯNG NỮ VƯƠNG
NGUYỄN TRÃI
LÝ THƯỜNG KIỆT
19 THÁNG 5
LÊ THÁNH TÔN
NAM KỲ KHỞI NGHĨA
HÙNG VƯƠNG
ĐỘC LẬP
PHAM HỒNG THÁI
NGUYỄN THÁI HỌC
NGÔ LÃO
NGUYỄN THỊ MINH KHAI
PHAM
TRẦN QUỐC TUẤN
TRẦN PHÚ
MẸ THỊ NHẬM
PHAN ĐÌNH PHÙNG
ĐIỆN BIÊN PHỦ
ĐỒNG KHỞI
HOÀNG HOA THÁM
Long Bình River

TRA VINH CHURCH
ONG MET PAGODA
PROVINCIAL TELECOMMUNICATIONS OFFICE
THANH TRA HOTEL
PROVINCIAL POST OFFICE
GIA HOA 2 HOTEL
BUN NUOC LEO
TRA VINH TOURIST
DUY TUNG HOTEL
TRA VINH MARKET
TUY HUONG
TAN HANG HOTEL
VIETIN BANK
SHOP NGUYET
QUAN BAY LOAN
ONG PAGODA
GIA HOA 1 HOTEL
LA TRAU XANH
CUU LONG HOTEL
HOAN MY HOTEL

0   200 yds
0   200 m

© AVALON TRAVEL

FESTIVALS AND EVENTS

The province's most famous and anticipated festival, **Ok Om Bok,** is a Khmer holiday in which locals give thanks to the moon for providing them with plentiful crops and fish. On the 15th day of the lunar calendar's 10th month, festivities take place around the province and include cultural events, most notably a much-anticipated dragon boat race. Vessels as long as 78 feet speed along the river, competing for the top prize while spectators cheer them on. That evening, locals present offerings to the moon and traditional Khmer games and dances are held. In recent years, this has become a huge tourism event for the province, drawing many domestic visitors to the area.

ACCOMMODATIONS

When it comes to lodgings in a town as sleepy as Tra Vinh, it's no surprise that you'll be hard-pressed to find much beyond your standard budget accommodations. Even the larger hotels in town are nothing to rave about, but there are definitely some nice corner buildings

Tra Vinh's Cambodian Connection

Few provinces in the Mekong Delta boast such a deep connection to Cambodia as Tra Vinh, where nearly one-third of the population is made up of ethnic Khmer people. Before the Vietnamese took over this region in the late 17th and early 18th centuries, Tra Vinh and the surrounding provinces were known as Kampuchea Krom, or Lower Cambodia.

When ethnic Vietnamese began to move into the area, many of the Khmer towns were transformed. Ethnic Khmer have long maintained that the Vietnamese took their land without consent, making the Mekong Delta a tract of stolen property.

When the French later entered Indochina and began colonizing the area, they sealed the fate of Kampuchea Krom by incorporating it into Cochinchina, a territory that was later ceded to Vietnam when the country gained its independence. The Khmer still have their own names for most provinces and towns in the Delta, all the way from the Cambodian border across to Saigon, formerly Prey Nokor.

Once these southern provinces were incorporated into Vietnam, ethnic Khmer were forced to assimilate. The South Vietnam government assigned people Vietnamese names, giving the same last names to most ethnic Khmer in order to make the outsiders easier to identify. Many of this minority group, particularly monks, found themselves at odds with those in power as their outspoken disapproval of government policies and different religious beliefs often landed them in prison. Things worsened in the late 1970s when Vietnam took up arms against the Khmer Rouge along the southern border. Since then, countless Khmer Krom have fled the region, emigrating to other countries.

Tensions between the local Khmer population and the Vietnamese government remain to this day. The exact number of Khmer Krom in the Delta is unclear. Statistics from the Vietnamese government claim that 1.2 million ethnic Khmer live in the area, while rights groups such as Khmer Krom Federation and the Khmer Kampuchea Krom Community put the figure as high as 7 million.

Little to no tension between local Vietnamese and Khmer residents is visible on the surface. Instead, the ethnic Khmer of Tra Vinh continue to practice their own religion in addition to studying Khmer language, and residents of the town peacefully coexist.

with balconies from which you can relax and enjoy the comings and goings of the street below. Hotels offer clean rooms at reasonable rates, though mattresses, as a rule, are pretty firm. While some are farther from the city center, there's no need to worry, as Tra Vinh is small and, though the distance may seem larger on a map, most places are no more than a 10- or 15-minute walk from downtown.

Under VND210,000

With dirt-cheap fan rooms and air-conditioned beds hovering just below the USD$10 mark, **Luu Luyen Guesthouse (Nha Nghi Luu Luyen)** (552 Nguyen Thi Minh Khai, tel. 07/4384-2306, VND110,000-550,000) offers the best value in town, combined with clean beds, decent bathrooms, and plenty of light. The only catch is that the guesthouse is a little

ways outside of the city center, en route to Ba Om Pond and Ang Pagoda.

VND210,000-525,000

Some of the best digs downtown, **Gia Hoa 2 Hotel** (50 Le Loi, tel. 07/4385-8009, www.gia-hoahotel.com, VND320,000-480,000) sits on the corner of a shady side street not far from the park. Great balcony views and spacious rooms, a friendly staff, and free Wi-Fi access make this hotel a cut above many other Tra Vinh accommodations. Its original, the **Gia Hoa 1 Hotel** (75 Nguyen Thi Minh Khai, tel. 07/4386-4477, www.giahoahotel.com, VND320,000-480,000), is equally well kept, but its location isn't as nice as Gia Hoa 2.

Just opposite the larger Cuu Long Hotel, **Hoan My Hotel** (105A Nguyen Thi Minh Khai, tel. 07/4386-2211,

VND250,000-420,000) is a more affordable version, if a little smaller, of its competition across the street. Rooms are clean and include Wi-Fi, TV, and air-conditioning.

Adjacent to both the central market and the Duy Tung, **Tan Hang Hotel** (14 Dien Bien Phu, tel. 07/4376-3838, www.tanhanghotel.com, VND250,000-400,000) offers clean, reasonable rooms with Wi-Fi, air-conditioning, and television. A handful of accommodations also include balconies, which look out over the town's main roundabout.

Directly on the town's main roundabout, **Duy Tung Hotel** (6 Dien Bien Phu, tel. 07/4385-8959, VND220,000-300,000), also called Van Thanh Hotel, offers great value and clean rooms as well as TV and Wi-Fi. Opt for air-conditioning if possible, as the fans are a little weak. There is a small travel outfit attached to the hotel that can help plan your travels around Tra Vinh or rent a motorbike. Bicycles can be rented here for a small fee.

Boasting one of the best locations in the city, **Thanh Tra Hotel** (1 Pham Thai Buong, tel. 07/4385-3621, VND220,000-700,000) sits a stone's throw from Tra Vinh Market, the local park, and the riverfront. Rooms are aging but the beds and bathrooms remain clean and well kept. Breakfast is included, as are standard amenities, and there is a restaurant attached to the hotel. If possible, opt for a room with a view, as these are nicer and more spacious than their windowless counterparts.

Though it's an aging facility, the **Cuu Long Hotel** (999 Nguyen Thi Minh Khai, tel. 07/4386-2615, cuulonghoteltravinhcity@yahoo.com.vn, VND400,000-900,000) serves as one of Tra Vinh's nicest accommodations, with more spacious and well-decorated rooms, not to mention comfier mattresses, than some of its budget competition. The hotel has Wi-Fi access, television, and air-conditioning, and a buffet breakfast is included in the room rate.

FOOD

Tra Vinh is a city of street food. Though there are a few proper eateries, this tiny town does a much bigger turn in roadside fare. Starting around 6pm, head down to **Dien Bien Phu** street or around **Tra Vinh Market** and you'll see dozens of vendors selling everything from fresh fruit to boiled corn to tasty *banh mi* (Vietnamese bread) sandwiches. During the day, an abundance of cafés and bakery carts pop up throughout the city. Note, that beyond the odd baguette or pastry, there is no Western food to speak of. You might want to eat early, as many places begin to wind down by 8pm or 9pm, some even earlier.

Though it's found on most street corners in Tra Vinh, the *bun nuoc leo* (in front of Long Khanh Pagoda, Bach Dang, from 2pm daily, VND10,000-15,000) in front of Long Khanh Pagoda is particularly nice. A traditional Khmer dish, this soup combines a murky-colored broth with local vegetables and rice noodles, plus your choice of roasted pork, fried shrimp cake, or congealed duck blood on the side. Extra helpings of meat (or duck blood) are allowed, but you'd better get there early, as the pot's usually empty by 5:30pm.

Right beside Duy Tung Hotel, **Tuy Huong** (8 Dien Bien Phu, tel. 07/4385-8312, 5am-6pm daily, VND10,000-45,000) is an old-school noodle shop with great eats but no English menu. Dishes and prices are listed on the wall: You can opt for wonton and egg noodle soup *(hoan thanh mi),* southern-style rice noodle soup *(hu tieu),* noodles and duck *(mi vit tiem),* or a handful of rice dishes, all of which are generous and satisfying.

A perfect spot to practice your pick-and-point ordering, the sidewalk around **Quan Bay Loan** (corner of Nguyen Thai Hoc and Tran Quoc Tuan, 6am-4pm daily, VND15,000-25,000) fills up with hungry locals around lunch time. Choose from an array of meats and vegetables to go with your plate of steamed rice and enjoy the people-watching on this shady street corner.

Hidden behind the Cuu Long Hotel, **La Trau Xanh** (999 Nguyen Thi Minh Khai, tel. 07/4386-2615, 6am-10pm daily, VND70,000-450,000) is the fanciest place in town. Featuring tablecloths, an English menu, and an array of meat, seafood, veggie, and hotpot dishes, this thatched-roof, open-air building is a bit of a hot spot for visiting tour groups and provides a nice escape from the noise of the street. Both family-style and single portions are available.

INFORMATION AND SERVICES

While it's true that Tra Vinh is not exactly well trodden on the tourist trail, **Tra Vinh Tourist** (266-268 Le Loi, tel. 07/4385-8556, www.dulichtravinh.com.vn, 7:30am-11am and 1:30pm-5pm daily) manages to be an incredibly helpful place for visitors. In addition to organizing tours around the province, this outfit rents bicycles (VND80,000 per day or VND10,000 per hour) and provides one of the more useful tourist maps (VND20,000) in the Delta. Though the language barrier may be difficult, the staff are more than willing to dispense free travel information if prompted. Ask for your free copy of the tourist information booklet as well as to get a full rundown of what to see and do in Tra Vinh.

The local **Vietin Bank** (15A Dien Bien Phu, tel. 07/4386-3827, www.vietinbank.vn, 7am-11am and 1pm-5pm Mon.-Fri., 7:30am-noon Sat.) exchanges currencies and has an ATM.

The ultra-retro **Tra Vinh post office** (3 Phan Dinh Phung, tel. 07/4386-2100, 7am-11am and 1pm-5pm Mon.-Fri.) can take your postcards, letters, and packages, while the **Telecommunications Office** (83 Le Loi, tel. 07/4385-5777, 7am-11am and 1pm-5pm Mon.-Fri.) nearby provides Internet and other services.

For minor issues, the **Tra Vinh General Hospital (Benh Vien Da Khoa Tra Vinh)** (27 Dien Bien Phu, tel. 07/4386-4778) assists travelers, though there are no English speakers on staff.

TRANSPORTATION

The **Tra Vinh bus station** (559 Quoc Lo 54, tel. 07/4384-0324, 5am-6pm daily) is located 3.5 miles (10-minute drive) from the city center, just before Hang Pagoda. Buses arrive daily from Can Tho (2 hours, VND65,000), Saigon (2.5-3 hours, VND130,000) and other Delta cities. These buses also drop passengers off on Nguyen Thi Minh Khai street, which is close to the center of town and the most convenient stop, as well as at the **Thanh Thuy bus station** (93 Tran Quoc Tuan, tel. 07/4385-8687, 7am-5pm daily, VND130,000), where coach buses from Saigon arrive on a regular basis. Every vehicle's final destination depends on the driver and the bus, but all three bus stops are close to town.

As you will quickly discover, getting around Tra Vinh town is easy on account of its size, but a bicycle may be necessary to access some sights, as they tend to be farther afield. This town is also one of the worst offenders when it comes to changing addresses. All along Nguyen Thi Minh Khai and several other large streets, street addresses increase and decrease, change from even to odd, and sometimes even change to letters from numerals—all in the space of a single block. If you don't see your destination immediately, be patient and keep looking.

Xe om are readily available at the roundabout in front of Tra Vinh Market and they will no doubt be present whenever your bus arrives in Tra Vinh. You can also call **Tra Vinh Taxi** (tel. 07/4382-8282) or **Thanh Thuy Taxi** (tel. 07/4386-8686) for a ride.

Shop Nguyet (42B Nguyen Thi Minh Khai, tel. 07/4386-5272, 6am-9pm daily, VND120,000) and the travel outfit located at **Duy Tung Hotel** (6 Dien Bien Phu, tel. 07/4385-8959) are some of the only places renting motorbikes to foreigners. Cars and larger vehicles can be hired from some of the larger hotels or through **Tra Vinh Tourist** (266-268 Le Loi, tel. 07/4385-8556, www. dulichtravinh.com.vn, 7:30am-11am and 1:30pm-5pm daily).

Tram Chim National Park and Vicinity

A serene landscape of flooded plains and cajuput trees, Tram Chim National Park is home to a quarter of all bird species found in Vietnam. Tram Chim's most famous resident, the sarus crane, is its main attraction and the reason most travelers visit the park. At six feet tall, sarus cranes are the world's tallest flying bird and an increasingly endangered species in Southeast Asia, with only a few thousand estimated to remain in the region. For birding and nature enthusiasts, these towering, majestic creatures are a must-see in Vietnam.

★ TRAM CHIM NATIONAL PARK

The stunning landscapes of **Tram Chim National Park (Vuon Quoc Gia Tram Chim)** (Hamlet 4, Tram Chim, tel. 06/7382-7436, www.tramchim.com.vn, 7am-5pm daily) are awash with tall grass, flat, water-logged land, and over 230 different aquatic birds swooping and wheeling across the park's 7,000 hectares. Visitors trace the watery avenues and flooded forests of this picturesque Delta scene by boat, spotting everything from an abundance of slender-necked storks to the vibrant yellow Asian golden weaver to towering sarus cranes, whose bright red feathers and jaw-dropping wingspan make them the stars of the park.

At the visitor center just inside the park's main gate, choose from three boat routes around the perimeter of the park. The shortest route (45 minutes, VND500,000 per boat) is a quick jaunt that affords travelers a brief glimpse of the park. Opt for one of the two longer routes in order to make your trip worthwhile, as these will take you deeper into bird-watching territory. A 15.5-mile loop (two hours, VND800,000 per boat) through the park's main viewing area to its watchtower is the most popular option. There is also an 18-mile trip (2.5 hours, VND900,000 per boat), adding on a bit more sightseeing time. Each vessel seats 12, so the more passengers you have, the cheaper the cost per person.

Accompanying each group are a driver and a guide who carries binoculars or birding

Tram Chim National Park

field guides. Some of the drivers and guides speak English. The boats come within a few hundred meters of the various species of birds. Views from the park watchtower are stunning, with sweeping panoramas of the park's greenery and birds in flight.

Traveling by car or by bus along the main road leading to the park, you'll see the offices of the park administration first and then a gate for the visitor center.

Tram Chim is best visited in the early mornings and late afternoons, when the most birds are active. While the steady trickle of visitors Tram Chim receives have helped to put it on the map, you'll mostly have the place to yourself. Though the trip takes time and effort, it is worth it. When done by public bus, the trip can actually be affordable.

Accommodations and Food

Visitors to Tram Chim have the option of shacking up at the park's on-site **guesthouse** (VND150,000-250,000). The guesthouse's six rooms accommodate up to three people each, and include a television, refrigerator, and fan, with optional add-ons like air-conditioning and hot water. While this allows you to rise early for the birds, it also limits dining options to the few simple noodle-soup eateries located on the main road near the park (5-minute walk). There is an on-site restaurant, but it only caters to groups of six or more and requires advance orders.

For more accommodation and food options, not to mention more English menus, base yourself in Cao Lanh town, roughly 30 miles south of the park.

Transportation

Getting to Tram Chim requires some organization and prior planning. From Cao Lanh, **Dong Thap Tourist** (2 Doc Binh Kieu, Cao Lanh, tel. 06/7385-5637, www.dongthaptourist.com, 7am-11:30am and 1:30pm-5pm daily) organizes private trips to the park, often combined with a stop at the Xeo Quyt Relic Area

in a two-day, one-night excursion. Similar itineraries are available from Saigon; however, these packaged tours are expensive and not worth the cost for small groups.

In Cao Lanh, groups of three or more can hire a car to the park, roughly 30 miles north (45-minute drive). Car rental rates are often negotiable, depending upon where you book. Dong Thap Tourist in Cao Lanh and **Smile Tourist** (82 Bui Vien, D1, Saigon, tel. 08/3920-4232, www.smiletourist.com, 8am-5pm daily) have private cars for rent. Smile Tourist can arrange all the logistics for those coming from Saigon.

An alternative, provided you're up for a day of adventure, is to board a public bus to Tram Chim, which takes about 1.5 hours. From the **Cao Lanh bus station** (71/1 Ly Thuong Kiet, tel. 06/7385-1116, 5am-5pm daily), hop on one of the green buses bound for **Hong Ngu** (VND14,000). Let the fare collector know that you'd like to go to Tram Chim and the bus will stop at **Thanh Binh bus station** (Hwy. 30), where you'll switch to an orange bus bound for **Tan Hong** (VND13,000). Show the fare collector the park's name (Vuon Quoc Gia Tram Chim), and the bus will drop you right outside the visitor center.

Buses leave every 30 minutes from Cao Lanh, as early as 6am, and run through to the evening. Plan to leave Cao Lanh as early as possible to make the most of your day. The second leg of the trip—from Thanh Binh to Tram Chim—does not always run on schedule. These vehicles leave when full, but because there aren't many buses that drive this route, you may have no trouble finding one.

If you get stranded at either the Thanh Binh bus station or the park, it is possible to enlist the services of a *xe om* to ferry you to the next leg of your trip. It's about a 20-minute ride between the Thanh Binh bus station and Tram Chim's visitor center. Hiring a *xe om* between the main road (about 20 kilometers from the park entrance) and Tram Chim runs about VND50,000-60,000.

Nguyen Sinh Sac

Born in 1862 in central Nghe An Province, Nguyen Sinh Sac rose from humble beginnings, losing his parents at a young age. He was taken in by a local scholar, and later entered the civil service, earning a job as a magistrate near the central city of Quy Nhon.

As a government worker under French colonial rule, Sac often clashed with his employers, standing up for the marginalized of his community and setting free jailed protesters. The French did not react favorably to Sac's dissent. He was fired in 1910 and jailed. Upon his release, Sac moved south, cultivating friendships with some of Vietnam's other famous movers and shakers, including the likes of Phan Chu Trinh and Phan Boi Chau.

Toward the end of his life, Sac settled in Dong Thap, where he worked as a teacher and pharmacist. When he died in 1929 in Cao Lanh, Vietnam's fight for independence was far from over, but his son, Ho Chi Minh, saw victory in 1945.

The father of Vietnam's most famous hero was buried behind Hoa Long Pagoda, where his grave remained for decades before the local government renovated it and turned the site into **Nguyen Sinh Sac Memorial Park (Khu Di Tich Mo Cu Nguyen Sinh Sac)** (137 Pham Huu Lau, tel. 06/7385-1259, 7am-11:30am and 1:30pm-5pm daily) in 1977.

CAO LANH

Yet another Delta town built around the river, Cao Lanh is larger and more modern than many of its regional counterparts. As a result, it loses some of its charm. The town is more of a home base than a tourist attraction, as the majority of its few visitors head out to Tram Chim National Park or into the forests of Xeo Quyt, but Cao Lanh does a fine job of accommodating its guests with decent hotels and restaurants, as well as a café or two. As the capital of Dong Thap province, this is also where the provincial tourism company is based; they assist in organizing services like guided tours or rental vehicles.

Dong Thap Museum

Housed in a former colonial residence, the **Dong Thap Museum** (162 Nguyen Thai Hoc, tel. 06/7385-1342, 7am-11:30am and 1:30pm-5pm daily) is a well-organized provincial exhibition hall with the usual displays on ancient history, local fishing and farming, and, of course, revolutionary activities against both French and American forces. Though there is no English signage, the museum's layout is fairly straightforward and manages to be interesting even without the placards. There is also a small display on ancient Oc Eo

sculpture as well as a collection of Vietnamese instruments, which are particularly pertinent to this region, as *cai luong*, a popular form of traditional Vietnamese music, hails from the Mekong Delta.

Nguyen Sinh Sac Memorial Park

Tucked behind Hoa Long Pagoda, the sprawling **Nguyen Sinh Sac Memorial Park (Khu Di Tich Mo Cu Nguyen Sinh Sac)** (137 Pham Huu Lau, tel. 06/7385-1259, 7am-11:30am and 1:30pm-5pm daily) pays homage to a man credited with intelligence, a revolutionary spirit, and, most notably, a very famous son: President Ho Chi Minh.

Visiting the park is fairly easy to do on your own, though it is not actually visible from Pham Huu Lau street. In order to reach the gates, take a left just before Hoa Long Pagoda—you'll see a sign with the Vietnamese name of the park—and follow the road around to the entrance. Inside, shaded pathways and plenty of park benches line a central pond. Few foreigners linger here, so you're sure to receive some friendly hellos on your visit as well as a few candid photo requests.

Farther along, a collection of wooden houses, including a replica of Ho Chi Minh's Hanoian stilt house, are grouped at the side of the property; visitors are not permitted to enter but only peek inside. The actual gravesite is located away from the entrance, right behind the pagoda grounds and protected by nine large dragons, a symbol of the Mekong Delta, which form a white pavilion over the site. Nguyen Sinh Sac's gravesite is a place that requires long pants and covered shoulders. There is also a temple dedicated to Nguyen Sinh Sac and a small exhibition hall. While the park area is open through midday, this area closes for a brief period at lunch.

Do Cong Tuong Temple

Amidst the bustle of the town's market, **Do Cong Tuong Temple (Den Tho Ong Ba Do Cung Tuong)** (Le Loi, 6am-5pm daily) commemorates a local couple credited with the founding of Cao Lanh's market. After moving to the area in 1817, Mr. and Mrs. Do Cong Tuong planted a garden of tangerine trees that fast grew into a meeting spot for local vendors and, in time, a busy trade center. The couple became known throughout the community for their kindness and their contributions. Three years later, a cholera outbreak decimated much of the population, leaving the market empty and the fate of the town looking very grim. Grief-stricken, Mr. and Mrs. Do Cong Tuong set up an altar in the middle of the market for people to come and pray. After three days of prayer, Mrs. Do Cong Tuong fell sick with cholera and passed away; her husband followed early the next morning. After the couple was buried, the cholera epidemic broke and villagers believed that the pair had died so that the rest of the village could be spared. To honor their sacrifice, a temple was built for the couple.

Nowadays, the recently renovated building is full of beautiful gilded woodwork and Cao Dai-esque columns bedecked with serpentine dragons surrounded by wispy blue-and-white clouds. Framing many of the altars are statues depicting a crane atop a tortoise. This is a powerful symbol in Vietnamese culture, signifying longevity and happiness, and can be found at many local pagodas and temples.

This particular one is unique in that Cao Lanh residents often come here to *xin xam* (ask for their fortune). Holding a container filled with wooden sticks, locals kneel before the altar and pray, submitting their queries to the ancestors, before drawing out a single stick. Each stick has a number on it with a corresponding fortune, which can be obtained by asking the temple's caretaker.

Accommodations

Because it's the capital of Dong Thap, accommodations in Cao Lanh are more plentiful than other towns in the province. More plentiful doesn't necessarily mean more upscale; there are several clean, comfortable options that manage to do the job for a night or two.

UNDER VND210,000

The best budget spot in Cao Lanh, **Binh Minh Hotel** (147 Hung Vuong, tel. 06/7385-3423, VND90,000-180,000) offers clean lodgings with a colorful decor of assorted patterns and mix-and-match furniture. Rooms come with Wi-Fi and television plus your choice of fan or air-conditioning. If possible, spend the extra VND40,000 and opt for one of the larger fan or air-conditioned rooms, as the cheapest beds can be a bit cramped. The owner is a lively guy who speaks some English and is always up for a chat.

VND210,000-525,000

Trung Hoang Hotel (96-98 Le Quy Don, tel. 06/7387-8787, kstrunghoang@yahoo. com.vn, VND200,000-300,000) is a nice, family-run guesthouse with clean beds and notably large rooms. Though the rooms are bare, all the standard amenities are present, including TV, fridge, Wi-Fi, and air-conditioning. Most rooms accommodate two people comfortably, and some larger lodgings fit up to five or six.

Phuong Ngan Hotel (174 Hung Vuong, tel. 06/7385-2483, VND200,000-300,000) sits farther down Hung Vuong street and offers great value, with newer furnishings and comfortable rooms. Not all accommodations come with a window, but you will find both a fan *and* air-conditioning in your room, as well as TV, Wi-Fi, and a minibar. The staff doesn't speak English, but the rooms are well worth their budget price.

VND525,000-1,050,000

One of the nicer government-owned offerings, **Dong Thap Hotel (Nha Khach Dong Thap)** (48 Ly Thuong Kiet, tel. 06/7387-2670, nhakhachtinhdt@yahoo.com.vn, VND350,000-1,000,000) has all the trimmings of a proper hotel, with bright, well-kept rooms and a restaurant downstairs. Most accommodations include bathtubs and balconies as well as Wi-Fi, television, air-conditioning, and a minibar.

The most well-known of Cao Lanh accommodations, **Song Tra Hotel** (178 Nguyen Hue, tel. 06/7385-2624, dtsongtrahotel@gmail.com, VND460,000-1,500,000) appears to be more of a two- than a three-star joint. Its rooms are clean and comfortable, if a bit overpriced, and feature air-conditioning, Wi-Fi, TV, and a minibar. Breakfast is included in the room rate. The hotel is also one of the few places in town with an English-speaking receptionist. The café out front gets lively at night and is a nice spot for a *ca phe sua da* (Vietnamese iced coffee with milk) and people-watching.

Food

There are only a handful of proper restaurants located in the downtown area and, for some strange reason, they all seem to have forgotten to include prices on their menus. This sometimes means that restaurant owners will take liberties when it comes time to tally your bill. To avoid this issue, ask the price before ordering.

The dining room at **A Chau** (42 Ly Thuong Kiet, tel. 06/7385-2202, 6am-9pm daily, VND50,000-300,000) is a mess of padded chairs and holey tablecloths, but this spot serves up decent Vietnamese fare and has an extensive menu of family-style beef, pork, chicken, and fish dishes. Plates be

ordered for both individual diners as well as larger groups.

Right on the main drag up the street from the Song Tra Hotel, **Ngoc Lan** (210 Nguyen Hue, tel. 06/7385-1408, 10am-8pm daily, VND35,000-300,000) does some excellent renditions of Vietnamese dishes, including a mean fish sauce fried chicken *(ga chien nuoc mam)*. While the eatery has an English menu, it seems to be the worst offender in creative pricing and the going rate for a meal changes with the mood of the staff. Ask the cost of your meal before ordering.

A short walk from downtown and not far from the massive Hoa Binh Hotel, **Tan Nghia** (331 Le Duan, tel. 06/7387-1989, 7am-9pm daily, VND30,000-80,000) is a nice little place on the water with standard local dishes, including pork, chicken, beef, and several types of seafood. Though the decor is nothing much, its location beside the river makes it pleasantly quiet and the staff are notably cheerful.

A bakery/corner store, the **Thuy Duong Bakery** (207 Hung Vuong, tel. 06/7385-5567, www.thuyduongbakery.com, 6am-9pm daily, VND5,000-30,000) sells both sweet and savory baked goods as well as sandwiches and an assortment of other snacks. You can also find a few convenience store essentials here.

Information and Services

The offices of **Dong Thap Tourist** (2 Doc Binh Kieu, tel. 06/7385-5637, www.dongthaptourist.com, 7am-11:30am and 1:30pm-5pm daily) can supply you with a local map (VND20,000) of Cao Lanh and the entire province. Though they tend to deal more in private tours than group ones, this government-run outfit organizes trips and boats to destinations across Dong Thap, including Xeo Quyt and Tram Chim National Park, and can offer help to individual travelers as well.

The **Vietin Bank** (87 Nguyen Hue, tel. 06/7385-1224, www.vietinbank.vn, 7:30am-11:30am and 1:30pm-5:30pm Mon.-Fri., 7:30am-11:30am Sat.) exchanges currency and has an ATM.

For postage and Internet needs, the **Dong**

Thap post office (85 Nguyen Hue, tel. 06/7385-1124, 6:30am-6pm Mon.-Fri., 7am-11:30am and 1pm-5pm Sat.-Sun.) is located right on the main drag.

For minor illnesses and injuries, the Dong Thap People's Hospital (Benh Vien Nhan Dan Dong Thap) (167 Ton Duc Thang, tel. 06/7387-4525) can be of help, though any serious incidents will require a trip to Saigon.

Transportation

Buses from Saigon (2.5 hours, VND110,000) and Can Tho (2 hours, VND90,000) to Cao Lanh stop at either the conveniently located Cao Lanh bus station (71/1 Ly Thuong Kiet, tel. 06/7385-1116, 5am-5pm daily) or the Cao Lanh ferry (10-min. ride, free) just south of town. The large ferry runs every 10-15 minutes, and transports vehicles and people across the Mekong. From there, take a *xe om* (VND30,000) for the final 3.5 miles into downtown Cao Lanh.

If you prefer air-conditioning and roominess, both Mailinh Express (15 Vo Thi Sau, tel. 06/7387-7877) and Phuong Trang (17-19 Vo Thi Sau, tel. 06/7387-6850, 5am-5pm daily) have offices across the street. Both companies only do runs to and from Ho Chi Minh City.

In Cao Lanh, *xe om* drivers are present in smaller numbers on some street corners and in full force at the bus station. You can also grab a Mailinh (tel. 06/7368-6868) taxi to get around.

Downtown Cao Lanh is fairly concentrated, so you should be able to get around on foot just fine. There are also bicycle rentals through several of the hotels. This is a town that really seems to enforce the no-motorbikes-to-foreigners rule, so you will likely have a tough time finding your own set of motorized wheels.

XEO QUYT RELIC AREA

Hidden among 20 hectares of flooded forest, the Xeo Quyt Relic Area (Hamlet 4, My Hiep village, tel. 06/7391-0297, 8am-4:30pm daily, VND5,000) was once a secret base of local Dong Thap revolutionaries during the American War. From as early as 1960, members of the southern National Liberation Front, or NLF, and the local community began using the area as a base of operations for soldiers and higher-ups, planting hundreds of towering, willowy cajuput trees to cover their location. Party offices and meeting halls were tucked away beneath the forest canopy, as was a medical tent and several underground barracks.

For most of the year, the circular path through the forest is underwater, necessitating a boat ride in a small sampan to view the sites. While the former offices are often nothing more than a canvas tent or a few small stilted buildings, Xeo Quyt is peacefully off the mass-tourist trail and is one of Dong Thap's nicer, more well-preserved natural areas. Beyond the historical zone, there is a small exhibition in a stilted house over the water, a restaurant, and some nice walking paths around the park's vast green fields.

Though most people visit Xeo Quyt on a day tour, it is also possible to reach the site yourself by public bus. From Cao Lanh bus station, take one of the bright orange buses heading for An Thai Trung (Nga 3 An Thai Trung, VND14,000). Make sure you tell the fare collector that you're headed to Xeo Quyt so that he or she can inform you when it's time to get off the bus; have the name of the place handy to show. Once you arrive at the Xeo Quyt intersection, you'll see a sign for the Sa Dec ferry (Ben Pha Sa Dec) on your right and a larger, albeit a bit hidden, sign for Xeo Quyt on your left. *Xe om* drivers hang out regularly at this intersection and will take you the remaining four miles to Xeo Quyt for roughly VND30,000-50,000. The return trip can be done until 4:30pm, when the park closes; make sure you arrange your *xe om* ride back beforehand, as drivers don't often hang around at Xeo Quyt. Many of these drivers—both in Cao Lanh and at the Xeo Quyt intersection—try to convince you to take a *xe om* all the way back into town for around VND100,000 or VND130,000. While this is doable, know that buses do run regularly along this road, even if some drivers insist that they do not; they're merely trying to drum up business for themselves.

Sa Dec

One of the prettiest towns in the Mekong Delta, Sa Dec is a cross-hatch of narrow bridges and winding canals lined with the faded, crumbling structures of a bygone era. Among the Vietnamese, this peaceful town is known for its plentiful flower gardens, which cultivate an array of blossoms and bonsai plants year-round. Beyond the border, Sa Dec's claim to fame is credited to French author Marguerite Duras, who was born in Saigon in 1914 and spent much of her childhood among the tree-lined avenues of this tiny town in what was then French Indochina. Though Duras left Vietnam for France at age 18, Sa Dec later became the backdrop for her semi-autobiographical novel *The Lover*, which garnered her a Prix Goncourt, France's highest literary honor, and has since been translated into over 40 languages. This makes Sa Dec an especially popular town for French visitors.

Being small as it is, Sa Dec doesn't see too much overnight tourist traffic, though several tour groups make the journey here from Cao Lanh, and a handful of Mekong River cruises pass through the town en route to Chau Doc. It is possible to book a one-day guided tour through the provincial tourism office in Cao Lanh, and there are also a few tours that run from Vinh Long. Travelers can hop on an inter-city bus from Vinh Long, which takes about an hour, and make a day trip of the town, or do a quick stopover en route to Cao Lanh.

Sa Dec Market (corner of Nguyen Sinh Sac and Lac Long Quan, sunrise-sunset daily) is located toward the southern edge of town near the river. There are an array of products available here, from household supplies to cookware, food, and clothes. The market is housed mostly under one long, narrow roof not far from the river and its stalls spill out onto the surrounding streets.

SIGHTS
Kien An Cung Pagoda

A work of art both outside and in, the **Kien An Cung Pagoda** (corner of Tran Hung Dao and Phan Boi Chau, 7am-5pm daily) was completed in 1927 by Huynh Thuan, father of Huynh Thuy Le—the man with whom French author Marguerite Duras began an illicit affair at age 15—along with a group of other Chinese immigrants from Fujian province. Also known as Chua Ong Quach, the pagoda pays homage to Ong Quach, a Buddhist from Fujian province who achieved enlightenment.

Outside, its roof boasts three layers of tiles and brick as well as some impressive mosaic ornamentation. Pass through the high, hand-painted doors of the pagoda and you'll find black-and-white Chinese-style sketches on either side of the building and the open-roofed, incense-filled celestial well at the center. Beyond, the altar honors Ong Quach, and a small area off to the left is devoted to worship of both the ancestors and the Buddha. Every year, on the 22nd day of the second month of the lunar calendar, locals celebrate the birthday of Ong Quach, as well as the day he attained enlightenment, on the 22nd of the eighth month of the lunar calendar.

Huong Pagoda

Adjacent to the much larger, more modern Buu Quang, **Huong Pagoda** (461 Hung Vuong, 6am-8pm daily), completed in 1838, is one of several Chinese-style Buddhist pagodas in Sa Dec. Weathered mosaics and crumbling enamel tiles show the building's age, while a pair of bright, vivid creatures appear to jump out of the wall below. Inside, the sturdy wooden columns that hold up the pagoda are lined with gilded woodwork and Chinese inscriptions. The altar is dedicated to the Buddha himself, but there are also additional shrines to the ancestors as well as famed

Chinese general Quan Cong. Visitors are welcome at the pagoda; enter through a smaller door off to the side rather than through the main entrance, as this is usually locked. One of the resident monks will accompany you around.

Flower Gardens

Sa Dec's famed **flower gardens** (Vuon Hong) are located across the bridge from the town center, about a mile away. Local gardeners use every inch of space they've got to pack in dozens upon dozens of plants, from flowers to cacti to bonsai trees, which are grown year-round, though these businesses often become bare just before Tet, when demand for ornamental plants is high. The most famous of these is the **Tu Ton Rose Garden** (Vuon Hong, 8am-11am and 1pm-5pm daily), which specializes in all variety of roses. While there are a few other flower gardens just beyond this road, Vuon Hong, literally "rose garden" street, is the ideal place for a stroll or cycle to take in the best of Sa Dec's flowers. Its houses are surrounded by not only the well-tended gardens of local residents but also plenty of natural foliage, and the road is split in two by a narrow canal.

To get to the gardens, follow Le Loi street along the water for river views and a couple of nice buildings en route, like the old **Sa Dec Church** or the twin spires of the town's **Cao Dai Temple,** both of which are on Le Loi.

House of Huynh Thuy Le

One of the few remaining colonial houses tucked between local shops and several newer, boxy residences, the **house of Huynh Thuy Le** (255A Nguyen Hue, tel. 06/7377-3937, nhaco_hthuyle@yahoo.com.vn, 8am-5pm daily, VND25,000) is noted for its blend of French and Chinese architecture as well as the romantic affairs of its owner. The son of a wealthy Chinese businessman, Huynh Thuy Le met the 15-year-old Marguerite Duras on a ferry crossing to Saigon in 1929. Not long after, the two began an affair that lasted until Duras left for France at 18. Though their

Colorful portraits decorate an altar at Kien An Cung Pagoda.

romance was brief, the relationship inspired Duras' 1984 novel *The Lover,* which sold over three million copies and earned her wide acclaim. When the book was made into a movie in 1991, director Jean-Jacques Annaud chose to film parts of the story in Vietnam.

From the outside, the building looks every bit a French colonial house, with high archways and thick balustrades. However, step inside and everything turns to wood, with dozens of intricate carvings hanging from above and, on the ground, sturdy furniture inlaid with mother of pearl.

While preservation is an increasingly rare sight in Vietnam, Dong Thap Tourist, the government-run company that now owns the house, has gone a bit overboard with the souvenirs in the back room and is pushing to make this into a tourist attraction. Still, the house is a stunning example of turn-of-the-century colonial architecture and your entry ticket includes a short spiel from one of the tour guides—though you may have to press them for it—as well as free lotus tea and

Sa Dec

FLOWER GARDENS

PHAM HỮU LẦU

PHAM VĂN VỆ

HAI BÀ TRƯNG

TRẦN THỊ NHƯỢNG

TRẦN HƯNG ĐẠO

NGUYỄN TRÃI

NGUYỄN THỊ THANH

CAO DAI TEMPLE

SA DEC CHURCH

Tien River

HƯNG VƯỜNG

NGUYỄN DU

BÙI CHÂU

HỒ XUÂN HƯƠNG

HUONG PAGODA

HOÀNG DIỆU

TÔN ĐỨC THẮNG

TRẦN PHÚ

KIEN AN CUNG PAGODA

HOUSE OF HUYNH THUY LE

TRẦN HƯNG ĐẠO

LÝ THƯỜNG KIỆT

HƯNG VƯƠNG

LÊ THÀNH TÔN

FOOD STALLS

THAO NGAN HOTEL

OUTDOOR MARKET

SA DEC MARKET

SACOMBANK ATM

NGUYỄN CƯ TRINH

NGUYỄN SINH SẮC

CHANH KY

TRẦN VĂN VOI

QUỐC LỘ 80

SA DEC GENERAL HOSPITAL

SA DEC BUS STATION

NGUYỄN HỮU THUẬT

LÊ DUẨN

HƯNG VƯƠNG

ĐINH TIÊN HOÀNG

0   300 yds
0   300 m

© AVALON TRAVEL

candied ginger. It is even possible to spend a night in the house; but, at VND945,000 a room, it's not worth the price tag to be sleeping inside a museum.

ACCOMMODATIONS

On account of its proximity to larger towns like Vinh Long and Cao Lanh, most people don't end up spending the night in Sa Dec. If you do, there are a couple of good value options.

Under VND210,000

The best of three small guesthouses on a charming little street across the canal from Kim Hue Pagoda, **Thanh Truc Guesthouse** (121 Phan Boi Chau, tel. 06/7386-8234, VND100,000-170,000) comes with clean beds, a television, Wi-Fi, and a window in every room. Rates depend upon your choice of fan or air-conditioning as well as hot or cold showers.

VND210,000-525,000

The most centrally located option, **Thao Ngan Hotel** (6 An Duong Vuong, tel. 06/7377-4255, VND250,000-400,000) sits just beside Sa Dec Market and offers clean and comfortable digs for a one-star accommodation. Bathrooms are a generous size, though the hot water comes and goes, and there is a minibar, television, and Wi-Fi in every room.

Another excellent budget option, **Hotel Phuong Nam** (384A Nguyen Sinh Sac, tel. 06/7386-7867, hotelphuongnam@yahoo.com. vn, VND200,000-300,000) is just a stone's throw from the town center and features Wi-Fi, television, and hot showers, as well as your choice of fan or air-conditioning. If you don't mind spending an extra USD$3, splurge for the nicer rooms, as they are larger and some include a balcony.

Sa Dec's finest accommodations, the **Bong Hong Hotel** (251A Nguyen Sinh Sac, tel. 06/7386-8287, bonghonghotel@yahoo.com. vn, VND320,000-840,000) is run by Dong Thap Tourist and features charming views of the countryside as well as comfy beds, a minibar, Wi-Fi, TV, hot water, and modern decor There is also a nice restaurant attached to the hotel and some tennis courts next door.

FOOD

Housed in a covered pavilion behind the main market are dozens of **food stalls** (behind Sa Dec Market, Lac Long Quan, 6am-4:30pm daily, VND10,000-30,000) that cook up a variety of noodle soups, rice dishes, and other local fare. Vegetarian meals are also available—just look for the *chay* signs.

Opposite Sa Dec Market, **Chanh Ky** (193 Nguyen Sinh Sac, tel. 06/7386-4065, 5am-5pm daily, VND20,000-40,000) is run by a lovely bunch of Chinese-Vietnamese women and serves noodles, rice, and *hoan thanh mi* (wonton soup). There's a good chance that as soon as you enter the shop someone will go rooting around for the sole handwritten English menu to help you out.

Full of pick-and-point choices, **Com Thuy** (439 Hung Vuong, tel. 06/7386-1644,

9am-8pm daily, VND15,000-30,000) serves standard Vietnamese rice dishes and boasts more options than most of the other shops in town.

INFORMATION AND SERVICES

For withdrawals, you can visit the **Sacombank** (corner of Lac Long Quan and Nguyen Sinh Sac, tel. 06/7377-2355, www. sacombank.com.vn, 7:30am-11:30am and 1pm-5pm Mon.-Fri., 7:30am-11:30am Sat.) and its ATM near the central market. Don't expect to change currencies here, as this is a smaller town and banks are not equipped to do so.

The **Sa Dec post office** (90 Hung Vuong, tel. 06/7386-2789, 6:30am-6pm Mon.-Fri., 7am-11:30am and 1pm-5pm Sat.-Sun.) is located at the corner of Nguyen Sinh Sac and Hung Vuong and also provides Internet services.

In the event of minor injuries or illnesses, the **Sa Dec General Hospital (Benh Vien Da Khoa Sa Dec)** (158 Nguyen Sinh Sac, tel. 06/7386-1918) can help, but don't expect anyone to speak English. For better care and a doctor who speaks your language, you'll have to head to Saigon.

TRANSPORTATION

Incoming local buses from Saigon (2.5 hours, VND105,000), Can Tho (1.5 hours, VND50,000), and nearby Vinh Long (30 minutes, VND15,000-30,000) stop either at the **Sa Dec bus station** (Nguyen Sinh Sac near Hung Vuong, tel. 06/7386-1130, 5:30am-6pm daily) or over the bridge at the bus stop just outside Sa Dec Market, slightly closer to town.

Sa Dec is a small town and easily covered on foot. Bicycles are available for rent at some of the local hotels. For motorized transport, a group of *xe om* often gathers out front of Sa Dec Market near the bus stop. You can also call for a **Vinasa** (tel. 06/7386-6666) taxi, though don't expect to see them driving around.

Chau Doc

Less than two miles from the Cambodian border, Chau Doc is a pleasant, sleepy town often used by travelers as a convenient stopover between western Vietnam and its neighbor. Whether you're heading onward to Cambodia or not, the area's stunning scenery and rich diversity make this destination interesting in its own right, with verdant green mountains rising out of the surrounding rice paddies and entire floating villages settled along the Baasac River (Hau River). Beyond a series of photogenic landscapes, best viewed from the top of Sam Mountain or the surrounding countryside of Chau Doc, this patchwork town of sturdy colonial buildings and teetering clapboard houses boasts a uniquely diverse population, including Vietnamese, Khmer, and Chinese residents as well as a sizable ethnic Cham community, once the medieval rulers of much of south-central Vietnam. Farther afield, the natural beauty of Tra Su Forest, a peaceful, primitive grove of cajuput trees, hosts hundreds of storks as well as a variety of other birds.

Most travelers pass through Chau Doc for only a day or two before crossing the border or moving on to other destinations like Ha Tien, and later Phu Quoc, or back toward Can Tho and Saigon. For the full experience, it's best to stay for at least two days in order to visit Sam Mountain and Chau Doc's river attractions and still have enough time for a jaunt out to Tra Su.

SIGHTS

Though none of them are very far, all of Chau Doc's prominent sights are located beyond the city limits. You'll find a handful of interesting temples and pagodas peppered throughout town, as well as an active central market. In order to experience the area's more intriguing natural and cultural elements you'll have to either hit the water or hit the road. These are both easily accomplished, as local guides are plentiful and several hotels arrange tours of nearby attractions.

Bodh Gaya

Unique for its outdoor setting, the **Bodh Gaya Pagoda** (Phan Van Vang and Chi Lang, sunrise-sunset daily) sits in the middle of Chau Doc's only park, a large central square with few trees where street carts gather in the late afternoons and evenings. While it's not really a pagoda in the traditional sense so much as a collection of religious statues—most of which feature the Buddha in various poses, as well as a towering figure of Quan Am—this open-air spot is a popular gathering point for locals, who visit regularly to pray and burn incense. The pagoda's most notable feature is its large, gnarled bodhi tree, which rises out of the middle of the clearing. Said to have originated from a seedling of the famous Indian bodhi tree under which the Buddha sat and eventually attained enlightenment, this tree offers ample shade within the gated pagoda area.

Chau Phu Temple

Just opposite the river beside a bustling outdoor market, **Chau Phu Temple** (228 Tran Hung Dao, 8am-5pm daily) celebrates the accomplishments of Nguyen Huu Canh, one of several national heroes to shape the development of Vietnam's southern provinces. Born into a prominent noble family in 1650, Nguyen Huu Canh was a major player in fostering Vietnam's economy in the once-untamed southern reaches of the country, fending off different opponents and establishing social order and administrative regions in these fledgling communities. By the time he reached Vietnam's southwestern border in 1700, the man was already a known figure among the Vietnamese. He fell ill shortly after arriving in Chau Doc and died that same year.

Today, he is remembered throughout the

Chau Doc

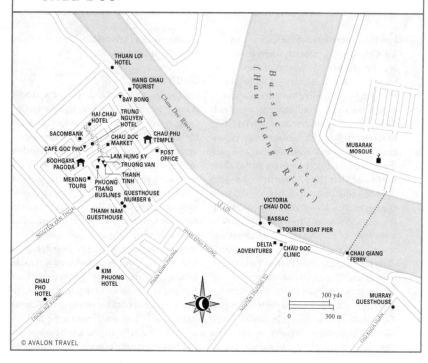

Map labels: THUAN LOI HOTEL · HANG CHAU TOURIST · BAY BONG · Chau Doc River · Bassac River (Hau Giang River) · HAI CHAU HOTEL · TRUNG NGUYEN HOTEL · SACOMBANK · CHAU DOC MARKET · CHAU PHU TEMPLE · CAFE GOC PHO · MUBARAK MOSQUE · BODHGAYA PAGODA · LAM HUNG KY · POST OFFICE · TRUONG VAN · MEKONG TOURS · THANH TINH · PHUONG TRANG BUSLINES · GUESTHOUSE NUMBER 6 · THANH NAM GUESTHOUSE · VICTORIA CHAU DOC · LE LOI · BASSAC · TOURIST BOAT PIER · DELTA ADVENTURES · CHAU DOC CLINIC · CHAU GIANG FERRY · PHAN DINH PHUNG · KIM PHUONG HOTEL · CHAU PHO HOTEL · NGUYEN VAN THOAI · NGUYEN TRUONG TO · TRUNG NU VUONG · THU KHOA HUAN · MURRAY GUESTHOUSE · 0 300 yds · 0 300 m

© AVALON TRAVEL

country, as his name features heavily on street signs and high schools from north to south. Several temples exist in Nguyen Huu Canh's honor, including one across the border in Phnom Penh. This is one of the most well-known and the largest in the Mekong Delta. Its main altar features Nguyen Huu Canh himself, but you'll also find a smaller section of the building dedicated to Thoai Ngoc Hau, a local politician remembered for his contributions to southern development and who was in power during the time of the temple's original construction, 1820-1828. Though it was located elsewhere at the time, just beside what is now the local hospital, Chau Phu Temple relocated to its current residence in 1926.

Bassac River (Hau River)

Despite its name, the **Bassac River (Hau River)** is not so much a waterway hemmed in by riverbanks but rather a lake disrupted occasionally by bits of land. This wide, unending stream leads northwest into Cambodia and southeast to Can Tho, fanning out across an already-flat landscape and, in the rainy season, devouring the nearby fields. In a region where water often takes precedence over land, entire communities are built on the river, with neighborhoods of floating houses bobbing along, supported by a few hollow floats and powered by a single electrical line, strung up on a bamboo pole above the river. The effect is something like a miniature city, easily dismantled and always shifting with the current.

For Chau Doc's floating houses, real estate is tax-free, and residents may drop anchor wherever they please. For the ramshackle stilted houses that lean out precariously over the water, life is more challenging. From the river, you can get an idea of what the rainy

The Mubarak Mosque serves Chau Doc's Cham Muslim community.

hotels **Hai Chau** (61 Thuong Dang Le, tel. 07/6626-0066, www.haichauhotel.com) and **Trung Nguyen** (86 Bach Dang, tel. 07/6356-1561, www.trungnguyenhotel.com.vn) are honest, friendly, and reliable.

★ FISH FARMS

As you travel along the Bassac, you're sure to see the colorful exteriors and flowering verandas of Chau Doc's floating houses. While many of these buoyant residences can easily pull up anchor and change address whenever they so choose, a number of locals keep their livelihoods beneath the floorboards in large, stationary **fish farms.** Metal pens stretching across the area of the house and plunging several feet deep into the river can hold up to 100,000 fish at a time, which are caged within the river but still able to roam around the confines of the farm. When it's time to feed, a section of the floorboards is removed and a frenzy takes place, with hundreds of fish flapping around as soon as the food hits the water. On fishing day, farmers use a massive net attached to a bamboo pole and sweep the farm, catching hundreds of fish at a time to sell to large boats, which transport them to the market and beyond. Despite the hard work required of fish farmers, these businesses can be profitable, with some families owning several floating farms.

CHAM VILLAGE

Once a powerful empire that ruled much of Vietnam's south-central coast, the might of the Champa kingdom has long since faded, but several communities still remain in Vietnam. Chau Doc's ethnic Cham, who continue to practice Islam and follow their own traditions and culture, are one of the only communities in the Mekong Delta, with roughly 2,500 residents spread out on either side of the Bassac River. Many tourist boats stop at a local **Cham village** during their tour of the area's aquatic attractions. Visitors can catch a glimpse of a local workshop, where Cham women specialize in woven fabrics, crafting beautifully patterned materials

season is like in Chau Doc, as the walls of these corrugated tin buildings note where water levels have surpassed the floors of some stationary houses. Each year, dwellings along the riverbank are subject to the unpredictable flooding of the river and whole buildings have collapsed into the water as a result of erosion. The problem is such that government offices are trying to relocate people inland in order to prevent these disasters from repeating themselves.

Visiting the river is only possible by boat, and your only real option is to join a tour in order to see these particular sights. While it is possible to hire a boat from the official **tourist boat pier** (3 Le Loi, tel. 07/6356-8668, www.bentauchaudoc.com, 6am-10pm daily), these vessels are notably larger, accommodating around 24 people in one boat, and costs begin around VND1,000,000 for a two-hour trip without a guide. You're better off checking with one of the hotels in town, where local guides can be arranged as well as group tours. The local guides who coordinate with

with the help of a large wooden loom. In truth, the place is a bit of a tourist trap, as scores of fabric panels are on display for passing visitors to buy, but the locals are friendly and the pressure to make a purchase is not so great that you can't enjoy a quick look without interruption.

MUBARAK MOSQUE

Chau Doc's most frequented Cham landmark, the domed **Mubarak Mosque** (Provincial Hwy. TL953, sunrise-sunset daily) sits on the opposite side of the river in Chau Giang District. Completed in 1967, this pale-hued building serves not only as a place of worship for the local Cham community but also continues to teach the Quran as well as Arabic script. Passersby are able to catch a glimpse of the mosque's understated exterior on a quick stroll down the main street. While it is possible to enter the mosque, always ask permission first. Remember that appropriate dress rules apply (shorts and T-shirts are not acceptable). Prayer times are best avoided, as the place fills up with locals. This is also the only sight on the river that you can reach by boat as well as by land. If you prefer to see the mosque on your own, take the **Chau Giang ferry** (Le Loi between Nguyen Truong To and Truong Dinh, open 24/7, VND1,000/person or VND5,000/motorbike) just beyond the tourist boat pier and turn left at the main road once you reach Chau Giang District. A short walk will bring you to the mosque's main gates.

CHAU DOC FLOATING MARKET

Though it doesn't have the same hustle and bustle as the Delta's other floating markets, a spin around Chau Doc's **floating market** is a pleasant way to spend the morning. It is usually included in local boat tours and gives you the opportunity to see vendors on giant wooden boats buy and sell local produce along the water. Drinks and light meals, like the traditional Cambodian-style soup, *bun nuoc leo,* are available from little vessels motoring around the area.

cemetery at Tay An Pagoda

Sam Mountain

Rising from the watery fields of An Giang province, **Sam Mountain** is Chau Doc's defining natural feature. This low, wide hill stands at 754 feet tall and, as the only elevation around for miles, its summit provides incredible views of the town and its watery surroundings. Take a fascinating (but exhausting) hike up the mountain, following a series of uneven stone steps past countless temples and pagodas, local houses, and vivid Buddhist cemeteries; or hop on a *xe om* from town and save your energy as you zip up to the clearing at the top, where an altar marks the original site of the locally famous Lady Xu statue.

TAY AN PAGODA

Standing before its colorful gates and the menagerie of plaster animals that guard the entrance, it doesn't take long to recognize that **Tay An Pagoda** (base of Sam Mountain, 4am-7pm daily) is unusual. The dome of its pastel-hued tower and arched doorways within the complex suggest a hint of Islamic influence that you won't find in most Buddhist pagodas. Along with a collection of nearly 200 statues—including several menacing soldiers that flank Buddha's usual altar and some impressively lifelike sculptures of deceased monks—the pagoda's grounds contain a vibrant cemetery that rambles up the mountainside in a flurry of pinks, yellows, and blues.

For locals, this pagoda is a holy site. You'll likely find groups of Vietnamese paying their respects not only at the altars inside but also at several of the more prominent gravesites. From within the cemetery area, you can ascend a staircase that begins the long but scenic walk up to the top of Sam Mountain. Just follow the *"len nui"* signs painted on rocks and signs. Local residents can also point you in the right direction up to the summit.

TEMPLE OF LADY XU

No one knows how the portly, colorful statue within the **Temple of Lady Xu** (Sam Mountain Road, sunrise-sunset daily) came to exist on Sam Mountain. Lady Xu is considered a powerful figure and one of Chau Doc's most famous residents. The story goes that, roughly 200 years ago, a group of Siamese invaders happened upon the impressive sculpture at the top of Sam Mountain. The men attempted to take it but Lady Xu was immovable. Frustrated, they smashed the statue's left arm before heading down the mountain empty-handed.

Not long after the men left, villagers at the base of the mountain received a message from Lady Xu. Using a young girl as her medium, Lady Xu instructed the townspeople to carry her down from the summit. A group of strong men attempted to lift the statue but could not. Lady Xu appeared again, claiming she could only be moved down the mountain by a group of nine virgins. The villagers supplied such a team, and the young women transported Lady Xu downhill to her current residence, where she promptly became immovable again. Villagers took this as a message that Lady Xu

preferred to stay put and built a bamboo temple to house the statue. In 1870, locals constructed a sturdier shelter out of brick.

Nowadays, people come in droves to pray to her and several festivals are held in Lady Xu's honor each year, including the bathing of the statue. The temple itself is less impressive than some of Sam Mountain's other buildings.

From the street, enter through the main gates. You will need to travel around the back of the main building in order to see the statue. The area in which Lady Xu resides is barren apart from the sculpture, and photos are strictly forbidden inside the temple.

CAVE PAGODA

Boasting one of the best views on the hill, **Cave Pagoda** (Sam Mountain Road, sunrise-sunset daily) is carved into the western side of Sam Mountain and features a stunning, newly renovated complex outfitted with lotus ponds and a blinding white statue of the Buddha. Also known as Phuoc Dien Pagoda, this sight has undergone several renovations since its initial 19th-century completion. But you can still see the crumbling stupa, built in 1899, to honor a local woman called Ba Tho. Sometime in the middle of the 19th century, Ba Tho left her family to travel up Sam Mountain, where she lived for several decades in total isolation before locals discovered her there.

Today, the cave in which Ba Tho is said to have lived during these years is open to visitors, and the pagoda is home to several resident monks. Along with most of the buildings on Sam Mountain, this pagoda is a strictly religious place. Visitors should take care to dress appropriately, covering their legs and shoulders, as those in shorts and tank tops won't be allowed inside. While the pagoda's interior can be covered in a few minutes' time, it is the exterior lookouts that are most worthwhile, as the pagoda overlooks nearby fields, making this an exceptional spot for photos.

Tours

Local tour guides coordinate with hotels like **Hai Chau** (61 Thuong Dang Le, tel.

07/6626-0066, www.haichauhotel.com) and **Trung Nguyen** (86 Bach Dang, tel. 07/6356-1561, www.trungnguyenhotel.com.vn). They are honest, friendly, and reliable.

For tailor-made trips packed with information, **Victoria Chau Doc** (1 Le Loi, tel. 07/6386-5010, www.victoriahotels.asia) for high-end tours. If you're on a budget, get in touch with the outgoing and musically talented **Khoi** (tel. 09/1791-6657, leekhoi@yahoo.com), a local guide who arranges daylong tours in Chau Doc and around. **Hang Chau Tourist** (Tran Hung Dao, tel. 07/6356-2771, www.hangchautourist.vn, 6:30am-11am and 1:30pm-5pm daily) also organizes tours as well as the town's most reliable speedboat services to Phnom Penh.

While Chau Doc has a pair of travel outfits that offer daily boat tours and transportation via land and water, the customer service at **Mekong Tours** (14 Nguyen Huu Canh, tel. 07/6386-8222, www.mekongvietnam.com, 7am-5pm daily) and **Delta Adventures** (53 Le Loi, tel. 07/6355-0838, 6am-10pm daily) is problematic, with frequent reports of lackluster or rude tour guides. A common situation at both companies involves advertising boat tickets to Cambodia and then, at the last minute, informing travelers that the boat has been "cancelled," requiring them to pay an additional VND210,000 for a bus to the border.

ACCOMMODATIONS

Hotels in Chau Doc range from dirt-cheap, basic *nha tro* (a step down from a guesthouse, *nha nghi*) to dapper modern accommodations. While there are plenty of options both in town and farther out around Sam Mountain, you're better off sticking close to the city center, as this is where you'll find most essentials.

Under VND210,000

Rooms at the **Thanh Nam** (2 Phan Van Vang, tel. 07/6386-7924, VND100,000-200,000) are about as basic as they come—TV, hot water, Wi-Fi, and your choice of fan or air-conditioning—but the beds are comfortable and

the family that runs the place is kind and attentive.

Guesthouse Number 6 (6 Phan Van Vang, tel. 07/6386-7622, VND100,000-200,000) provides reasonable accommodation at some of the lowest prices you'll find in town. Amenities, from TV and Wi-Fi to optional air-conditioning and fans, are available. Though they are friendly, the proprietors seem to have cut in every *xe om* and cyclo driver around as touts, so you'll likely hear about this place from the moment you step off the bus. Prices are flexible, so feel free to negotiate, and motorbikes are available for rent.

VND210,000-525,000

For affordable and centrally located accommodation, **Trung Nguyen Hotel** (86 Bach Dang, tel. 07/6356-1561, www.trungnguyen-hotel.com.vn, VND294,000-610,000) is one of the better options in town. Just a short walk from the Chau Doc Market, its rooms are fairly basic but clean and include air-conditioning, Wi-Fi access, TV, hot water, and a minibar, as well as breakfast. The ground floor has a small restaurant, and the exceptionally friendly staff can help with everything from reliable local tours to onward transportation both in Vietnam and through to Cambodia.

Another great corner hotel, the **Hai Chau Hotel** (61 Thuong Dang Le, tel. 07/6626-0066, www.haichauhotel.com, VND378,000-588,000) offers standard, tidy rooms, with hot water, air-conditioning, television, and Wi-Fi access, overlooking a quieter spot in the city center. Breakfast is included in the room rate and is served each morning in the hotel's restaurant. Staff can assist in booking tours and transportation to other destinations.

The pink-clad **Thuan Loi Hotel** (275 Tran Hung Dao, tel. 07/6386-6134, ksthuanloi@yahoo.com, VND210,000-294,000) isn't necessarily the finest of budget accommodations but it's the cheapest riverfront room you'll get in Chau Doc. Rooms are basic, if a little old, and come with television, a fridge, Wi-Fi access, hot water, and your choice of fan or air-conditioning. A restaurant is attached on the ground floor. While its river scenes aren't exactly worth raving about, the view from the higher floors is nicer. The hotel also has travel services available for guests.

Slightly beyond the city center, **Kim Phuong** (Trung Nu Vuong, tel. 07/6355-0585, VND250,000-280,000) is a decent option for those who can't get into the Chau Pho, though it is more basic. Complete with air-conditioning, Wi-Fi, TV, and hot water, the rooms are large, bare, and include soft beds.

VND525,000-1,050,000

The most inviting of Chau Doc's hotels, the atmosphere at ★ **Murray Guesthouse** (11-15 Truong Dinh, tel. 07/6356-2108, nhanghiMurray@gmail.com, VND500,000-700,000) puts you at ease from the moment you step inside. This clean, modern family-run guesthouse features finer amenities than most local hotels and, though a bit beyond the town center, also comes with a notably friendly and welcoming staff. Rooms are equipped with TV, Wi-Fi, air-conditioning, hot water, and a minibar. The common area boasts a pool table and dart board. For peace and quiet, head to the upstairs roof terrace for pleasant views of Chau Doc town.

Though it's not on the most scenic of streets, **Chau Pho Hotel** (88 Trung Nu Vuong, tel. 07/6356-4139, www.chauphohotel.com, VND640,000-1,000,000) holds its own as one of the better mid-range accommodations in Chau Doc, boasting nice private balconies as well as clean, modern rooms with beds so neatly made you could bounce a quarter off of them. Depending upon the room you choose, accommodations feature bathtubs or a spacious enclosed shower, as well as the usual air-conditioning, hot water, minibar, and television. While standard rooms are nice, the superior and deluxe rooms offer great value and are worth the extra cash. There is a tennis court next door to the hotel as well as an in-house restaurant.

Over VND2,100,000

Set in a grand colonial building, **Victoria Chau Doc** (1 Le Loi, tel. 07/6386-5010, www.victoriahotels.asia, VND4,000,000-6,000,000) boasts a stunning location complete with a riverfront deck, swimming pool, and one of the nicest restaurants in town. Accommodations are spacious and modern, offering incredible views of the river or the town. The service-minded staff can arrange boat tours and other day trips with experienced local guides. The hotel also runs the **Victoria Nui Sam** (Sam Mountain, tel. 07/6357-5888, www.victoriahotels.asia, VND1,166,000-3,816,000), a breathtaking lodge tucked on the hillside of Sam Mountain that offers daily excursions around the area and a peaceful retreat.

FOOD

The simple but satisfying meals at **Bay Bong** (22 Thuong Dang Le, tel. 07/6386-7271, 8am-9pm daily, VND40,000-60,000) draw a nightly crowd to its small sidewalk set-up along Thuong Dang Le. Rice and noodle dishes feature heavily on the menu, as do a few varieties of hotpot, and the staff are a cheerful bunch.

For rice and noodles not far from the central market, **Lam Hung Ky** (71 Chi Lang, tel. 07/6386-6745, 8am-evening daily, VND50,000-180,000) offers decent individual meals and stays open until the last customers leave, usually around 7:30pm or 8pm.

For herbivorous diners, **Thanh Tinh** (13 Quang Trung, tel. 07/6386-5064, 6am-8pm daily, VND25,000-80,000) boasts not one but two large street carts sheltered within a clean storefront just beside the central market. Everything from noodles to rice to vegetarian hotpots is available.

Right beside Thanh Tinh, the vendors at **Truong Van** (15 Quang Trung, tel. 07/6386-6567, 6am-8pm daily, VND40,000-60,000) cook up the usual variety of noodles and rice as well as hotpots.

Dining at the **Bassac** (Victoria Chau Doc, 1 Le Loi, tel. 07/6386-5010, www.victoriahotels.

asia, 6pm-10pm daily, VND80,000-325,000), Victoria Chau Doc's restaurant, is a departure from the city's rice-and-noodle joints. Perched on a deck overlooking the river, the restaurant offers excellent views, with white linen tablecloths and the opulent veranda of the hotel adding to its colonial ambience. The kitchen serves Western and Asian dishes, and a selection of wine, beer, and cocktails. While the dining room is only open for dinner, Bassac offers a snack menu throughout the day.

One of the fancier coffee shops in town, **Cafe Goc Pho** (86 Dong Da, tel. 07/6626-7888, 6:30am-10pm daily, VND20,000-80,000) serves a variety of smoothies, tea, and coffees in a bright, new air-conditioned building. The owner is something of a cycling enthusiast and, as a result, bicycle photos and other paraphernalia line the walls. There are also some snacks and small meals on the menu, including a pizza, though don't expect to be wowed by the pies—this is definitely a café first.

INFORMATION AND SERVICES

The folks at **Mekong Tours** (14 Nguyen Huu Canh, tel. 07/6386-8222, www.mekongvietnam.com, 7am-5pm daily) provide rudimentary city maps free of charge and a few restaurant recommendations, but their tour and transportation services are not always up to snuff. The same goes for **Delta Adventures** (53 Le Loi, tel. 07/6355-0838, 6am-10pm daily). In all, your best bet is to inquire about tours and transportation through your hotel.

Sacombank (88 Dong Da, tel. 07/6326-0262, www.sacombank.com.vn, 7:30am-11:30am and 1pm-5pm Mon.-Fri., 7:30am-11:30am Sat.) has an ATM and a bank branch on the corner of Dong Da and Phan Van Vang that helps with currency exchange and other monetary needs.

For mail and Internet, visit the local **post office** (2 Le Loi, tel. 07/6386-6416, 7am-5:50pm daily) on the riverfront.

The small and aging **Chau Doc Clinic** (Kham Benh Chau Doc) (opposite Victoria Chau Doc on Le Loi, tel. 07/6386-5454) sits just across from Victoria Chau Doc, though you'd be hard-pressed to find it amid all the street vendors and makeshift drink shops. In the event of illness or injury, you're far better off heading to Saigon, as this place looks poorly equipped to receive patients.

GETTING THERE
Bus

Cozy, air-conditioned **Phuong Trang buses** (89 Phan Van Vang, tel. 07/6356-5888, www.futabuslines.com, 24 hours daily) arrive several times throughout the day from Saigon (4 hours, VND160,000) and Can Tho (2.5-3 hours, VND120,000). They make the return trip to both cities from the local **bus station** (Le Loi). If you purchase a ticket from the downtown Phuong Trang office, you needn't worry about getting out to the station, as travelers can be picked up from the office.

Onward to Cambodia

While boat tickets to and from Cambodia do exist, organizing over-water transport is a mixed bag in Chau Doc. Several tour companies in town will sell you a boat ticket to Phnom Penh, but without enough passengers the boat does not usually run and this information is often not relayed to travelers until the day of departure. Many local companies that book these tickets also have a reputation of overcharging travelers for just about everything, from a few extra dollars at the border for your Cambodian visa to additional bus fees when the boat "breaks down" or fails to depart. The only reliable provider is **Hang Chau Tourist** (Tran Hung Dao, tel. 07/6356-2771, www.hangchautourist.vn, 6:30am-11am and 1:30pm-5pm daily, VND525,000).

It's possible, though less popular, to reach Cambodia overland via bus. Speak with your hotel to arrange a bus ride to Phnom Penh, as buses that travel from Saigon to Phnom Penh pass through Chau Doc; your hotel can help you flag one down.

GETTING AROUND

Both *xe om* and *xe loi* (a cousin of the cyclo) are readily available throughout the downtown area, though this town is just as easily walkable on foot. **Mailinh** (tel. 0763/838-3838) taxis also make their rounds.

Most hotels and guesthouses rent out bicycles and motorbikes for a small fee.

TRA SU BIRD SANCTUARY

The **Tra Su Bird Sanctuary (Khu Du Lich Sinh Thai Rung Tram Tra Su)** (Van Giao Ward, Tinh Bien, tel. 07/6221-8025, 7am-4:30pm daily) is less visited than some other attractions in Chau Doc—perhaps because of its location 15 miles outside of town—but it is by far one of the area's most worthwhile sights. A flooded forest of narrow, towering cajuput trees, Tra Su is home to a variety of bird species, including storks, herons, and egrets, all of which can be seen via the boats hired out through Tra Su's visitors center. Large motorized vessels ferry travelers from the forest's main gate past lotus fields and down long canopied avenues to a smaller outpost, where wooden canoes are paddled around the forest itself, a maze of long, spindly trees rising out of the water.

This spot is particularly good for birdwatching, as the quieter vehicles and the lack of apparent waterway allow birds to roam freely, swooping and soaring between the trees. The motorized boats will also make a trip out to Tra Su's watchtower, one of the taller and sturdier lookouts in Vietnam, from which you can see the rest of the forest as well as the distant mountains.

The entire trip lasts 1-2 hours, depending upon how much time you spend at the lookout, and costs begin at VND130,000 for a single traveler and only get cheaper with more people. Though these trips don't include an English-speaking guide, it is the scenery that really makes Tra Su, so having a local on hand isn't entirely necessary.

To get to the forest, travelers can hire a *xe om* from Chau Doc or book a tour through one of the local hotels. For the more adventurous, it is also possible to rent a motorbike and find your own way, though expect to stop several times and ask to be pointed in the right direction—the only visible sign for the forest is in Vietnamese and just before the turnoff.

BA CHUC

It is possible to add a jaunt to **Ba Chuc** to your trip to Tra Su if you have the time. Twenty-four miles outside of Chau Doc and right near the edge of the Cambodian border, the small village of Ba Chuc is just one of several Vietnamese towns that suffered at the hands of the Khmer Rouge in the years immediately following the American War. As Pol Pot's reign of terror took the lives of millions of Cambodians across the border, a longstanding feud over land rights between the Vietnamese government and the Khmer Rouge regime boiled over, ultimately resulting in a two-year war.

While these land disputes may have sparked tension along the border, the senseless violence committed by the Khmer Rouge only solidified Vietnam's decision to retaliate. A series of random, brutal massacres occurred at places like Ba Chuc, where, from April 18 to April 30, 1978, Khmer Rouge forces crossed the border and slaughtered 3,157 people in this village alone, leaving behind only two survivors. Houses were burned, pagodas razed, and men, women, and children murdered. In the nearby **Phi Lai Pagoda** (6am-6pm daily), the blood of local victims still stains the walls, while nearly all of the adjacent **Tam Buu Pagoda** (6am-6pm daily) was burned to the ground but for one altar, which is now revered as holy. Between these two buildings, a small one-room **exhibit** (6am-6pm daily) shares the history of the tragedy, but only in Vietnamese, and includes several graphic photographs of the aftermath. Beyond that, the town itself is a hot and dusty place, but the drive out to Ba Chuc is nice, riding along an elevated road above infinite fields and past distant mountains.

Rach Gia and Ha Tien

A pair of port towns tucked along the westernmost edge of the country, Rach Gia and Ha Tien are among some of the Delta's more under-appreciated destinations. Most often used as convenient stopovers en route to Phu Quoc or Cambodia, these two cities represent not only unique and stunning Delta scenery but also the final frontier of Vietnam's development.

Once part of a virtually uninhabited jungle, the harsh environment of the country's western coast has been tamed somewhat, allowing for a full economic boom in both cities. Natural landscapes like the flooded forests of U Minh Thuong and Hon Chong's picturesque limestone islands, sometimes referred to as the Delta's miniature version of Ha Long Bay, hint at something more than simply a stopover destination.

RACH GIA

A southern boomtown crisscrossed with rivers and bustling avenues, Rach Gia usually serves as a stopover for tourists heading to Phu Quoc, as speedboats to the island depart daily from its harbor. Rach Gia is a pleasant town in its own right and has a handful of sights to occupy the traveler. Here, you'll find a pair of vibrant pagodas with revolutionary histories, a well-decorated provincial museum, and a beautiful, open temple devoted to a local hero, not to mention the lush greenery and still waters of a ravishing national park not far from town.

Along with Phu Quoc, the mainland's rainy season runs May-November and, thanks to the slump in island visitors at this time, Rach Gia gets even quieter. A day is all you really need to explore this town. Birders and nature enthusiasts might tack on another day for a trip to the watery forest at U Minh Thuong National Park.

Sights

While passing the time in Rach Gia, visitors who didn't make it out to Tay Ninh can stop by the town's requisite **Cao Dai Temple** (189 Nguyen Trung Truc, 6am-6pm daily), as well as a handful of more unique pagodas and temples that are worth a look. On the way into town, look for the large, three-door archway, called **Tam Cong Quan.** It's considered a symbol of Rach Gia and its silhouette can be found on local shops and businesses throughout Kien Giang province. The remainder of Rach Gia's sights make for a satisfying half-day outing.

KIEN GIANG MUSEUM

Housed in a beautiful colonial building over a century old, the **Kien Giang Museum** (21 Nguyen Van Troi, tel. 07/7386-3727, 7:30am-11am Mon.-Fri. and 1:30pm-5pm Wed.-Fri.) is a smaller version of a provincial museum that offers exhibits on local revolutionary history and the traditions, products, and ethnic diversity of the area. A handful of interesting displays on Oc Eo artifacts take up one section of the building, while there are also exhibits dedicated to some of Kien Giang's more famous heroes, such as Nguyen Trung Truc and Mac Cuu. Only parts of the signage are in English.

NGUYEN TRUNG TRUC TEMPLE

Just a block away from Rach Gia Harbor, the namesake **Nguyen Trung Truc Temple** (18 Nguyen Cong Tru, www.dinhnguyentrungtruc.vn, 5:30am-5pm daily) honors a southern revolutionary and national hero who took up arms against the French in the 1860s, most notably setting fire to the French naval ship *L'Esperance* and once taking over the colonial administration in Rach Gia for a few days. By the time he was finally arrested on Phu Quoc Island in 1868, the staunch

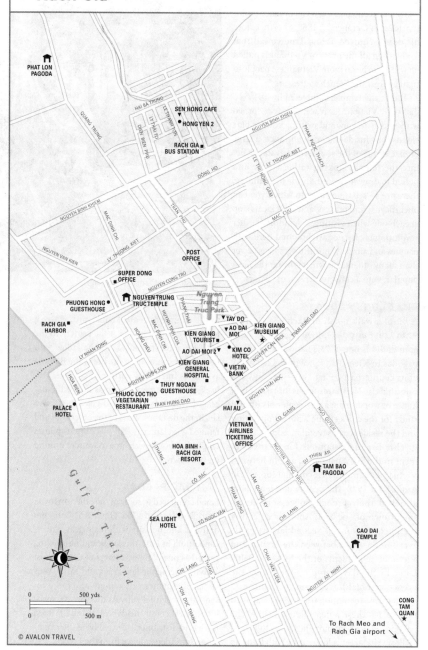

Rach Gia

PHAT LON PAGODA

QUANG TRUNG

HAI BA TRUNG

LY THAI TON

LE THANH TON

DIEN BIEN PHU

SEN HONG CAFE

HONG YEN 2

RACH GIA BUS STATION

NGUYEN BINH KHIEM

PHAM NGOC THACH

LY THUONG KIET

LE THI HONG GAM

DONG HO

MAC CUU

NGUYEN BINH KHIEM

MAC DINH CHI

TRAN PHU

NGUYEN VAN KIEN

LY THUONG KIET

POST OFFICE

SUPER DONG OFFICE

NGUYEN CONG TRU

PHUONG HONG GUESTHOUSE

NGUYEN TRUNG TRUC TEMPLE

Nguyen Trung Truc Park

HUYNH TINH CUA

THANH THAI

RACH GIA HARBOR

TAY DO

AO DAI MOI

KIEN GIANG MUSEUM

KIEN GIANG TOURIST

TRAN HUNG DAO

HOANG DIEU

MAC CUU CHI

AO DAI MOI 2

KIM CO HOTEL

LY NHAN TONG

NGUYEN HUNG SON

KIEN GIANG GENERAL HOSPITAL

VIETIN BANK

NGUYEN CAN PHOI

HOA BIEN

THUY NGOAN GUESTHOUSE

PHUOC LOC THO VEGETARIAN RESTAURANT

TRAN HUNG DAO

HAI AU

NGUYEN THAI HOC

PALACE HOTEL

VIETNAM AIRLINES TICKETING OFFICE

CO GIANG

NGO QUYEN

3 THANG 2

HOA BINH - RACH GIA RESORT

CO BAC

NGUYEN TRUNG TRUC

SU THIEN AN

TAM BAO PAGODA

LAM QUANG KY

PHAM HUNG

SEA LIGHT HOTEL

TO NGOC VAN

CHI LANG

CAO DAI TEMPLE

Gulf of Thailand

CHI LANG

3 THANG 2

TON DUC THANG

CHAU VAN LIEM

NGUYEN AN NINH

CONG TAM QUAN

0   500 yds

0   500 m

To Rach Meo and Rach Gia airport

© AVALON TRAVEL

anti-colonial leader had made many enemies among the French. He was briefly imprisoned and later executed in Rach Gia by colonial authorities on October 27, 1868. Shortly before his death, Nguyen Trung Truc vowed that "only when all the grass in Vietnam is pulled up will there be no more Vietnamese people to fight against the French aggressors."

Today, the temple, completed in 1970, is a distinctly Vietnamese place, its gates adorned with golden dragons and swirling powder-blue clouds. Just inside the main entrance, a large bronze statue of the southern hero stands before the temple looking rather severe and poised to draw his sword. Inside the building, there are 13 separate altars to which you can offer incense and prayers, and most locals stop at each one when visiting. A handful of other revolutionary heroes are honored here with plaques and altars. While this temple is newer than many others in town, it is by far the most popular, with a constant stream of visitors.

Buddha statues at Tam Bao Pagoda

PHAT LON PAGODA

A bit of a walk north of Rach Gia Harbor, **Phat Lon Pagoda** (151 Quang Trung, 7am-6pm daily) is one of 73 Theravada Buddhist pagodas in Kien Giang province. Like many of its counterparts, Phat Lon—literally, "Big Buddha" in Vietnamese—is not simply a house of worship but also a center of cultural study for the city's ethnic Khmer population and the residence of several monks.

This pagoda is famous for its involvement in the Soc Xoai battle, a fight between Vietnamese and French colonial forces. On August 11, 1948, the people of Kien Giang attacked their French oppressors at the small town of Soc Xoai, soundly defeating the Europeans in the second largest battle ever to take place between the French and Vietnamese residents of the Mekong Delta. Later in the day, stung by their loss, the French colonial forces returned, killing 32 Vietnamese revolutionaries. Monks at Phat Lon buried these fallen soldiers behind the pagoda, where a monument stands today.

From the street, a long sandy path leads up to the complex's central courtyard, where a fountain of dragons sits at the center. To the left is the actual pagoda, a large hall filled with neon-hued scenes from the life of the Buddha as well as intricately patterned ceilings. Out back, an assortment of stupas honor the deceased, while a large red-and-gold-hued tower sits in the distance, close to the outer wall and fringed with lanterns. The place often appears empty, but you're welcome to wander around on your own.

TAM BAO PAGODA

Small compared to some of the others in town, **Tam Bao Pagoda** (Su Thien An, 7am-7pm daily) is another site with historical significance. Built in 1802, this longstanding building served as one of many centers of Communist activity during the late 1930s and early 1940s as the Vietnamese grew more and more resentful of colonial rule. At the pagoda, revolutionaries secretly held meetings and printed leaflets to distribute to the public in their campaign for independence from the French.

About halfway down Su Thien An lane you'll see the colorful entrance to the pagoda. Though there is a door at the front of the building, this is usually gated. Instead, pass through to the open courtyard that divides Tam Bao into two parts. A statue of Quan Am housed in a blue gazebo presides over the central pond, while religious scripts penned in traditional Vietnamese calligraphy line the courtyard's outer wall. To the left, the main hall of the pagoda holds an altar dedicated to Buddha as well as several other shrines. The building on the right is dedicated to the ancestors. If you arrive on the 1st or 15th of the lunar month (religious days in Buddhism), you'll find the courtyard teeming with locals, who come to enjoy a vegetarian feast in honor of the religious day; you may be asked to join.

Festivals and Events

The annual **Nguyen Trung Truc Festival** takes place from the 26th to the 28th of the eighth lunar month. Celebrating the sacrifice of this national hero, who was executed by the French in Rach Gia in 1868, the festivities are held in Nguyen Trung Truc Park before a giant statue of the revolutionary, right at the center of town, and feature cultural performances and other events. Most foreigners don't bother with the event, but the festival draws hundreds of thousands of domestic tourists, who come to enjoy the celebration and to pay their respects to a famous fallen countryman.

Accommodations

There are several noteworthy budget accommodations in Rach Gia that offer great value for travelers. Bar a few exceptions, most of these hotels and guesthouses are centered around either the bus station or the harbor, while you'll find many of the town's restaurants and other services grouped near Le Loi and Nguyen Trung Truc streets.

UNDER VND210,000

For the price you pay, rooms at the ★ **Hong Yen 2** (G26-G27 Le Thanh Ton, tel. 07/7387-2655, VND170,000-250,000) are phenomenal. Snazzy black-and-white checked floors show off the impeccable cleanliness of the place and each spacious room comes with wooden furnishings, an enclosed shower, air-conditioning, television, Wi-Fi, and a minibar. Several rooms have a nice view of the street, and the place is far enough from the main drag to miss most of the noise pollution. This hotel is a walk-up, so you'll have to haul your own baggage upstairs. You can also visit the original **Hong Yen** (259-261 Mac Cuu, tel. 07/7387-9095, VND170,000-400,000), though it is older and farther from town.

VND210,000-525,000

The centrally located **Kim Co Hotel** (141 Nguyen Hung Son, tel. 07/7387-9610, www.kimcohotel.com, VND300,000-350,000) offers smart, clean rooms with Wi-Fi, air-conditioning, television, minibar, and bathtub. Corner rooms have multiple windows and offer nice street views.

With clean, basic rooms right next to the harbor, **Phuong Hong Guesthouse** (5 Tu Do, tel. 07/7387-8777, phuonghonghotel@ymail.com, VND210,000-252,000) is a popular spot for budget travelers. Accommodations come with a fan or air-conditioning as well as Wi-Fi access, and the friendly owner can help with arranging boat and bus tickets.

A short way from the busy intersection at Le Loi and Nguyen Hung Son, **Thuy Ngoan Guesthouse** (185, Block 14 Nguyen Hung Son, tel. 016/9623-9749, VND200,000-400,000) is noteworthy for its location, as dozens of local rice and noodle shops line the street a few blocks away. Rooms are big and clean with spotless tile floors and a spacious sitting area. At the front of the building, large windows give way to a small balcony. Television, air-conditioning, and Wi-Fi are included. Bathrooms are small but manageable.

Another place that seems almost too good to be true, the brand new **Palace Hotel** (20 Lo L12 3 Thang 2, tel. 07/7386-6146, palacehotelkg@gmail.com, VND450,000-550,000) is stocked with modern furnishings and clean rooms, not to mention some of the more comfortable beds in Vietnam. Television, Wi-Fi, hot water, air-conditioning, and a minibar are included and the English-speaking receptionist is friendly and outgoing. Both double and triple rooms are available. Breakfast is served at the hotel restaurant, though this is not included in the room rate.

VND525,000-1,050,00

Towering above most other buildings in town, the 19 floors of the **Sea Light Hotel** (A11 3 Thang 2, tel. 07/7625-5777, www.sealighthotel.vn, VND600,000-3,550,000) are some of the nicest accommodations in the city. These smart, modern rooms are farther removed from the center of Rach Gia, offering some much-needed peace and quiet, and each accommodation includes television and Wi-Fi access, air-conditioning, minibar, and complimentary breakfast. Large floor-to-ceiling windows offer great views of the river, and the hotel has a restaurant, swimming pool, and fitness center.

Whether it's a precursor or an afterthought to your visit to Phu Quoc, the **Hoa Binh - Rach Gia Resort** (Lo A9, 3-7 Co Bac, tel. 07/7355-3355, www.hoabinhrachgiaresort.com.vn, VND850,000-1,950,000) is the city's only resort and a perfect place to extend your R&R time. The manicured grounds of this massive space boast two restaurants and an outdoor pool in addition to accommodations, which are spacious and well furnished. All rooms come with air-conditioning, Wi-Fi access, TV, and minibar, as well as your choice of garden or river views. Breakfast is included in the room rate.

Food

The breezy, inviting storefront of **Ao Dai Moi 2** (161 Nguyen Hung Son, tel. 07/7386-6272, 6am-midnight daily, VND20,000-50,000) boasts an English menu and an array of local dishes, including a particularly good *banh canh cua* (crab noodle soup), as well as *hu tieu* (southern-style rice noodle soup), egg noodles, rice, and a host of different smoothies.

For breakfast, there is also the original **Ao Dai Moi** (26 Ly Tu Trong, tel. 07/7386-6295, 5am-11pm daily, VND20,000-30,000) nearby, which has a bit less selection but is decked out with photos of the owner, a cycling enthusiast.

Though the **Tay Do** (6 Nguyen Du, tel. 07/7391-5211, 9am-9pm daily, VND80,000-120,000) is a little overpriced for a rice shop, its dishes are tasty and an English menu is available for pick-and-point ordering. The narrow shop looks out over a quiet side street off Nguyen Trung Truc Park. Pork, beef, and chicken dishes are served, as well as seafood.

Phuoc Loc Tho Vegetarian Restaurant (Quan Chay Phuoc Loc Tho) (corner of Nguyen Thuong Hien and Nguyen Hung Son, tel. 07/7625-5556, 5:30am-9pm daily, VND15,000-50,000) offers a wide selection of meatless Vietnamese dishes at affordable prices, including tofu and veggies to pair with rice as well as *banh xeo* (savory Vietnamese pancakes), noodles and soup, and fresh fruit shakes.

Not far from the bus station, **Sen Hong Cafe** (corner of Huynh Thuc Khang and Nguyen Tri Phuong, tel. 07/7860-1138, 6am-10pm daily, VND15,000-30,000) is a popular breakfast spot for locals, with quiet, shaded seating. While the entire café is open air, both sidewalk and covered "indoor" seating are available, as is coffee, tea, and Vietnamese breakfast, though you'll have to arrive early if you want to eat, as the food is gone by 10am. The English-speaking owner can help you navigate your food choices and the staff are pleasant.

With a perfect view of the river and enough space between the dining area and the busy main street, **Hai Au** (2 Nguyen Trung Truc, tel. 07/7387-9122, 6am-10pm daily, VND70,000-300,000) is pricey as far as Vietnamese restaurants go but it is also fancier than the average rice-and-noodle joint. Grab a table outside to enjoy the comings and goings on the water, or sit inside in the posh, table-clothed dining room.

Information and Services

The staff at **Kien Giang Tourist** (5 Le Loi, tel. 07/7386-2081, www.kiengiangtravel.com.vn, 7am-11am and 1pm-5pm Mon.-Fri.) speak a little English if you're in need of restaurant recommendations. They aren't able to provide much else. Your hotel can probably help with restaurant recommendations as well.

Rach Gia's **Vietnam Airlines ticketing office** (16 Nguyen Trung Truc, tel. 07/7392-4320, 7:30am-11:30am and 1:30pm-5pm Mon.-Fri., 8am-11am and 2pm-4pm Sat.-Sun.) assists in purchasing flights to Phu Quoc or Ho Chi Minh City. If you're already in Rach Gia and planning to head to Phu Quoc, you're better off just taking the ferry and saving the extra cash.

The **Vietin Bank** (63 Le Loi, tel. 07/7386-3587, www.vietinbank.vn, 7am-11am and 1pm-5pm Mon.-Fri., 8am-11am Sat.), opposite the hospital, exchanges currency inside and has an ATM out front.

The local **post office** (2 Mau Than, tel. 07/7386-6006, 7am-9pm daily) handles postage and Internet needs.

For medical services, the **Kien Giang General Hospital (Benh Vien Da Khoa Kien Giang)** (46 Le Loi, tel. 07/7386-3328) takes care of minor illnesses and injuries and has 24-hour emergency services.

Getting There

AIR

The **Rach Gia Airport (San Bay Rach Gia, VKG)** (418 Cach Mang Thang Tam, tel. 07/7386-4326) receives daily Vietnam Airlines flights from Ho Chi Minh City (50 minutes, VND500,000-1,000,000 one-way).

BUS

Buses arrive and depart at the **Rach Gia bus station** (260A Nguyen Binh Khiem, tel. 07/7386-2274, 4am-midnight daily), near the city center, from Chau Doc (3 hours, VND70,000), Ha Tien (1.5 hours, VND85,000), and Saigon (5 hours, VND170,000) on a daily basis. There are both cheaper local minibuses and large air-conditioned vehicles available. For the latter, try **Phuong Trang** (tel. 07/7369-1691, www.futabuslines.com.vn), which goes to both Can Tho and Saigon, or **Mailinh Express** (tel. 07/7392-9292, www.mailinhexpress.vn), which runs minibuses to Ha Tien and Saigon.

BOAT

The speedboat from Ca Mau (morning and evening departures daily, 2-3 hours, VND120,000) drops passengers at **Rach Meo** (747 Ngo Quyen, tel. 07/7381-1306, 7am-4:30pm daily), roughly two miles from Rach Gia proper. From there, you can hop on a *xe om* into town for roughly VND40,000.

Speedboats from Phu Quoc (2.5 hours, VND350,000) dock at the **Rach Gia harbor** (Nguyen Cong Tru, tel. 07/7386-3242) in town.

To travel onward to Phu Quoc, the boat transportation company **Super Dong** (14 Tu Do, tel. 07/7387-7742, www.superdong.com.vn, 6am-5pm daily, VND320,000), near the harbor, has four daily departures (8am-1pm) to the island. While there are other offices near the harbor that sell tickets, visit the Super Dong office directly to avoid any confusion. Reserve tickets about a day in advance, though it's sometimes possible to book a last-minute seat.

ONWARD TO PHU QUOC

There are two options for reaching Phu Quoc: Fly directly from Ho Chi Minh City to Phu Quoc (avoiding Rach Gia entirely), or, from the Delta area, make your way to Rach Gia or Ha Tien and take a speedboat to Phu Quoc from there.

Getting Around

Xe om are on every corner in Rach Gia, so you should have no trouble finding a ride, and **Mailinh** (tel. 0773/838-3838) taxis run frequently throughout the downtown area. Most of the city center is walkable.

There is no official place to rent bicycles or motorbikes in Rach Gia. Check with your hotel, as they may have a motorbike or two to rent.

U Minh Thuong National Park

A stunning expanse of flooded forest, **U Minh Thuong National Park** (tel. 07/7380-9663, 5am-5pm daily, VND10,000) is home to a handful of rare feathered creatures, like the spot-billed pelican and the glossy ibis, as well as a few equally elusive mammals, including the hairy-nosed otter. One half of the U Minh forest parks—its counterpart, U Minh Ha, lies farther south near Ca Mau—U Minh Thuong is the more visited of the two and has more tourist services. This park sees frequent weekend visitors, as groups will come from Saigon to Hoa Mai Lake to enjoy a fishing weekend. For birders, a small footpath circles the perimeter of the lake, from which you can spot storks and other large birds soaring from tree to tree.

Farther into the park, boats can be hired for bird-watching and fishing, with anglers taking the smaller, quieter vessels and other visitors hopping into a long, narrow motorized canoe. Tickets are purchased per person and the cost depends upon the number of designated sightseeing spots you choose. Since the first watchtower is only located a short way from the boating docks, it's best to pay for at least two sightseeing spots, as this affords you the chance to float around the wider forest area where many birds congregate. On account of the larger boats' engines, most bird-watching will have to be done from afar, however the scenery and the bigger birds in flight make up for the noise.

From the lookout, visitors are able to see across the park, where a 2002 fire ripped through the forest, destroying much of the area. The canal upon which you travel to and from the boating docks was dug in order to save the remainder of U Minh from the fire, cutting the forest in half to protect the far bank of the canal as the fire became uncontrollable. Nowadays, the park closes tentatively for three months during the dry season to prevent the same disaster from reoccurring.

Travelers can visit U Minh Thuong on a day trip from Rach Gia, as the park is about a two-hour drive from town. Kien Giang Tourist offers private tours, though you will have to coordinate these ahead of time and costs can be steep. A better option is to contact Nhan from **Exploring Mekong** (tel. 09/1691-9394, www.exploringmekong.com), which offers a day trip to U Minh Thuong combined with a stop at a local shrimp farm in the countryside on the way back. Tours and travel can be booked in Saigon as well, though you'll likely need to go through a private operator, as group tours to the forest are rare. The park shuts down briefly during dry season, so if you visit between April and June, call ahead and confirm that it is open.

HA TIEN

Tucked away in the farthest reaches of the Mekong Delta, Ha Tien is poised to become a frequent tourist destination, as it lies just four miles from the Cambodian border and offers daily speedboat services to Phu Quoc. Already, the rapid pace of development in this lively little town shows no signs of stopping, with hotels cropping up along the riverfront and several bus companies setting up shop nearby.

The majority of travelers use Ha Tien as a stop en route to other destinations, usually sticking around for only a night. While the town doesn't have much in the way of scenery, its surrounding area is filled with some of the Delta's more unusual landscapes, featuring a coastline dotted with rocky islands; eerie, bat-filled caves; and jagged limestone karsts rising from the flat expanse of rice paddies. This is also where you'll find the only mainland beaches in the Mekong Delta worth visiting.

Nowadays, a handful of travel outfits have come to town, most of whom focus on transportation rather than tours, but if you're up for independent exploring, Ha Tien can be a worthy destination in its own right.

Sights

In town, Ha Tien's sights are easily walkable from the riverside, where most hotels and services are located. You'll find several pagodas

Ha Tien

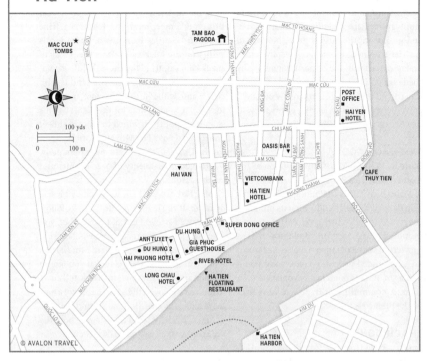

scattered around, as well as Ha Tien's massive fish market, which sits beside the river for easy boat access. Farther out, places like Thach Dong and Mui Nai Beach can be reached via bicycle or motor vehicle.

MAC CUU TOMBS

Sprawled along the western edge of town, the lush grounds of the **Mac Cuu Tombs** (Mac Cuu, 5am-6pm daily) are the final resting place of Ha Tien's most famous family. Born in 1655 in China, Mac Cuu was a wealthy explorer and merchant who traveled throughout much of Southeast Asia, fleeing his homeland in 1679 as the Qing dynasty rose to power. When he first reached southern Vietnam in 1700, much of the area in and around Ha Tien was uninhabited, covered by thick jungle and teeming with wild animals. Only small, isolated communities of Vietnamese, Chinese,

and Khmer existed along the coast but rarely interacted with one another. Mac Cuu recognized Ha Tien's economic potential as a settlement on the Gulf of Thailand. Over the next few years, he set about bringing together these disparate communities and developing the surrounding land into a successful port town. When the Thais began arriving in the area to loot and pillage Ha Tien in 1708, Mac Cuu sought the protection of the Nguyen Lords, officially bringing Ha Tien under Vietnamese control. After Mac Cuu's death in 1735, his son Mac Thien Tich carried on the family legacy, continuing to foster the town's progress and economy.

Beyond the high stone walls of the entrance, visitors will find a small but elaborate temple dedicated to Mac Cuu's family. To the right of the building, a stone path leads the way up Binh San Mountain (more of a hill, really) to dozens of domed graves that line the hillside, their headstones in varying states of decay. While four generations of Mac Cuu's family reside here, including his mother, son, and grandson, the largest grave belongs to Ha Tien's founder himself, a sweeping monument carved into the slope and guarded by shade trees. The path through this forested area carries on for a while and many other old gravesites exist nearby, leaving plenty for visitors to explore.

TAM BAO PAGODA

Built in 1730 by Mac Cuu in honor of his mother, **Tam Bao Pagoda** (near intersection of Mac Thien Tich and Phuong Thanh, 8am-4pm daily) is a small building but its immense courtyard is packed with dozens of statues, including a large reclining Buddha as well as a towering statue of Quan Am. These figures are surrounded by lush greenery and you'll find a small lotus pond just beyond the main gates. A community of Buddhist nuns lives on the premises.

THACH DONG

Barely a mile from the Cambodian border, the massive limestone outcropping at **Thach Dong** (Hwy. 80 en route to the Xa Xia border gate, My Duc village, 7am-5pm daily, VND5,000) towers 305 feet above the surrounding rice paddies. Within its smooth, vaulted interior, an 18th-century Buddhist pagoda doubles as a memorial for My Duc village, where Pol Pot's Khmer Rouge forces massacred 130 Vietnamese on March 14, 1978. During the lead-up to a two-year border war between the nations, acts of violence like this were not uncommon, causing many local residents to flee the frontier area for towns like Rach Gia and Ca Mau. Inside the cave pagoda, you can see photos of the victims alongside a Buddhist altar. There are also two lookouts from above that offer stunning views of the sea and nearby fields as well as a direct line of sight into Cambodia.

MUI NAI BEACH

One of a very small number of mainland beaches in the Mekong Delta, **Mui Nai Beach** is a nice, sandy stretch of coastline about three miles from town where locals gather on the weekends. There are plenty of snack shops dotting the shore. While it's not much of a swimming area—its sand is a bit coarse and, with Phu Quoc so close, most visitors prefer to just come for the scenery—this is a great spot from which to enjoy a sunset and a cold drink. The **Mui Nai Tourist Area** (off Ba Ly, tel. 07/7385-1348, 6am-6pm daily, VND10,000) has plenty of beach chairs and vendors around.

Mui Nai can easily be accessed by bicycle or *xe om*. If you're making the trip solo, follow Highway 28 straight out of town. When you reach the fork in the road, there will be a sign directing you to turn right toward Mui Nai (literally translated as Deer Cape); if you ignore the sign and turn left you'll still come full circle to the beach but with the added benefit of a nice drive along the coastline and around the edge of the cape, where you'll find views of both the sea and the small islands in the distance.

Accommodations

As Ha Tien sees more foreign visitors, hotels and guesthouses are cropping up along Tran Hau street and near the waterfront. Your best bet is to station yourself around the river area, as there are plenty of restaurants and other services nearby and it is close to the harbor for those catching a boat to Phu Quoc.

VND210,000-525,000

Surrounded by larger hotels with riverfront real estate, the **Gia Phuc** (48 Dang Thuy Tram, tel. 07/7385-1469, VND200,000-400,000) offers clean, comfortable budget accommodations in almost the same location as some of the more expensive offerings. Rooms are large and include air-conditioning, hot water, Wi-Fi, and TV. The owners can assist you in renting bicycles or motorbikes at reasonable rates.

Almost directly next door, the **Hai Phuong** (52 Dang Thuy Tram, tel. 07/7385-2240, VND300,000-800,000) is a larger enterprise that offers river views and nice, breezy balconies in addition to its large rooms, which come with air-conditioning, hot water, wifi, TV and a minibar.

Even closer to the water, **Long Chau** (36-38 Lo 7 Trung Tam Thuong Mai, tel. 07/7395-9189, hotellongchau@yahoo.com, VND300,000-500,000) is a nice property that boasts some of the better views of the river as well as spotless rooms and balconies, though construction noise can sometimes be heard on the breeze.

Tucked down a quieter street off the river, **Hai Yen** (15 To Chau, tel. 07/7385-1580, VND250,000-500,000) offers pleasant views on its higher floors and features spacious, bright accommodations with comfy beds, hot water, air-conditioning, minibar, television, and Wi-Fi access.

Rooms at the **Du Hung 2** (83 Tran Hau, tel. 07/7395-0555, VND300,000-450,000) are a good value and right on the main drag, surrounded by plenty of rice shops and convenience stores. Though the staff doesn't speak much English, everyone is helpful and welcoming. All accommodations feature modern furnishings, air-conditioning, hot water, Wi-Fi, TV, and a fridge. Farther down the road, the slightly older **Du Hung 1** (27A Tran Hau, tel. 07/7395-1555, VND250,000-450,000) is also nice, if a little aged.

Though it's probably been usurped by the River Hotel, the **Ha Tien Hotel** (36 Tran Hau, tel. 07/7385-1563, hatienhotels@gmail.com, VND400,000-840,000) was likely this town's fanciest accommodation once upon a time, complete with small touches like carpeting and a series of framed paintings on the wall. Rooms are well furnished and include breakfast with the room rate along with air-conditioning, hot water, Wi-Fi, TV, and a minibar. There is a restaurant attached to the hotel.

VND1,050,000-2,100,000

Hands down the town's finest accommodation, **River Hotel** (Tran Hau Business Center, Dang Thuy Tram, tel. 07/7395-5888, www.riverhotelvn.com, VND915,000-3,650,000), formerly known as the Green Island, is a modern and well-furnished building with sleek decor and a completely unobstructed view of the bridge and river. Each room includes breakfast in the cost as well as air-conditioning, hot water, Wi-Fi access, TV, and a minibar. The hotel's restaurant serves both Vietnamese and Western meals, which can be enjoyed on land or at the floating restaurant across the street. There is a small triangular pool on the corner of the street for guests to use.

Food

There are scores of rice shops along Tran Hau street, as well as a few at the top of Mac Thien Tich, including some vegetarian options. You can also find plenty of food near the **Ha Tien Market** (beside bridge on Mac Thien Tich, sunrise-sunset daily), where snack and fruit vendors often hang out.

One of a number of small hole-in-the-wall shops on the block, **Anh Tuyet** (next to 57 Tran Hau, tel. 07/7385-1575, 6am-8pm daily, VND20,000-40,000) is a typical pick-and-point rice cart with a steady flow of locals coming and going around lunchtime. There are plenty of options to choose from, including chicken, pork, fish, and veggies, and *tra da* (iced tea) is on the house. A second location sits just around the corner on Ly Chinh Thang street.

Meals at **Hai Van** (57 Lam Son, tel. 07/7385-2872, www.khachsanhaivan.com, 6am-evening daily, VND35,000-125,000) are standard Vietnamese fare but come with the added benefit of an English menu. Both individual and family-style dishes are served in this large banquet-hall environment, where chairs are decked out in delightfully gaudy pink seat coverings. Note that while the staff is friendly and willing to help, the kitchen does not always carry the entirety of its menu.

The only place you'll find Western food or any hint of nightlife is at **Oasis Bar** (42 Tuan Phu Dat, tel. 07/7370-1553, www.oasisbarhatien.com, 9am-late daily, VND20,000-80,000), a small bar and sometimes eatery located just off the main drag. In addition to both alcoholic and non-alcoholic drinks, the bar serves breakfast and light meals—most notably, a full English breakfast—and also does the occasional special on bar snacks like hummus platters and a variety of soups and sandwiches. The owner, an Englishman called Andy, offers tourist maps and sound advice on travel to Cambodia or Phu Quoc.

Operated by the River Hotel, **Ha Tien Floating Restaurant** (in front of River Hotel, tel. 07/7395-5888, www.riverhotelvn.com, 6am-10pm daily, VND35,000-400,000) is a permanently docked vessel that serves breakfast, lunch, and dinner in a nice, breezy setting over the water. You may have to ask for additional menus, as the servers tend to equate a Western traveler with Western food and so will present only the more expensive Western menu at the start. In reality, there is also Vietnamese food, both family-style and individual dishes.

On an otherwise shadeless, sweltering block, **Cafe Thuy Tien** (Ben To Chau, tel. 07/7385-1828, 5am-10:30pm daily, VND10,000-45,000) sits directly over the water and provides a variety of drinks, including coffee, coconuts, tea, and fruit shakes, as well as a much-needed escape from the heat. Though it looks like one good wave might take the place away, the location is unbeatable and tends to draw in patrons.

Information and Services
TOURIST INFORMATION
Despite the rise in tourist traffic around Ha Tien, the few novice travel outfits in the area are eager to sell overpriced boat or bus tickets but have little in the way of helpful information to hand out. Maps in Ha Tien are tough to come by, as are English speakers. If you have pressing inquiries, call the incredibly knowledgeable **Mr. The** (tel. 09/1857-4780),

a lifelong local with nearly 20 years of experience as the only tour guide in town. In addition to offering reliable, free advice, Mr. The rents motorbikes to foreigners and runs a lovely, affordable day trip out to Hon Chong, the Moso Caves, Thach Dong, and Mui Nai. Check in at **Oasis Bar** (42 Tuan Phu Dat, tel. 07/7370-1553, www.oasisbarhatien.com, 9am-late daily), where there is a small travel desk and Andy, the owner, can offer some tips on travel both in Ha Tien and beyond.

BANKS, INTERNET, AND POSTAL SERVICES
The **Vietcombank** (4 Phuong Thanh, tel. 04/3824-3524, www.vietcombank.com.vn, 7am-11am and 1pm-4pm Mon.-Fri.) changes currencies and has an ATM out front.

For mail and Internet, visit the **post office** (3 To Chau, tel. 07/7385-0432, 7am-5pm Mon.-Sat.), a short walk up from the riverfront.

MEDICAL SERVICES
Ha Tien's **general hospital (Benh Vien Da Khoa Ha Tien)** (Nguyen Van Troi, tel. 07/7385-2192) is located across the To Chau Bridge near the local harbor and assists with minor illnesses and injuries.

VISAS AND OFFICIALDOM
For those crossing into Cambodia at the Ha Tien border gate, visas are available through Cambodian immigration upon arrival at the border. Cambodian immigration offers both tourist and ordinary visas for USD$20 and USD$25, respectively. Many travelers make the mistake of opting for the ordinary visa and shelling out an extra USD$5, which is unnecessary unless you plan to stay in Cambodia for an extended period of time—several months, for example. Though no one in the immigration office will tell you, a tourist visa will do just fine.

It is possible to have the paperwork completed in advance in Ha Tien, but most travel outfits do this for an exorbitant fee, taking advantage of the fact that travelers don't realize they can complete the process on their own at the border. The application is very straightforward and you're far better off doing it yourself. Regardless of how you get your visa, you will need to supply a single passport photo (or a couple extra dollars instead) in order to complete the application.

Getting There

BUS

Most visitors to Ha Tien either come from Phu Quoc by speedboat or from the southern beach towns in Cambodia by bus. It's only 30 minutes from Kep, Cambodia, 1.5 hours from Kampot (USD$7-8), and just over 2 hours from Sihanoukville. Buses arrive at either the **Ha Tien bus station** (Quoc Lo 80, tel. 07/7385-1830, 6am-10pm daily), one mile from the city center or right in town, where some vehicles pull up to the roadside on Highway 80 and let passengers off just over the bridge a short way from the top of Tran Hau street.

For departures from Ha Tien, book tickets through the bus station directly. There are some hotels and small travel outfits in town that offer transportation services, but they are overpriced.

BOAT

Two daily boats from Phu Quoc (8am and 9am, 2 hours, VND230,000) arrive in Ha Tien at the **Ha Tien Harbor** (Kim Du, tel. 07/7385-0551). Several different companies offer speedboat services to and from the island and tickets can be booked through some hotels as well as with the companies directly. You can find the local **Super Dong** (11 Tran Hau, tel. 07/7395-5933, www.superdong.com. vn, 6am-8:30pm daily) office on the main drag near the riverfront.

Getting Around

If you're planning to sightsee only in Ha Tien town, then walking shouldn't be a problem, as even sights like the Mac Cuu Tombs are no more than a 10-minute jaunt from Tran Hau street. To visit farther-afield sights, like Mui Nai Beach or Hon Chong, a set of wheels is necessary.

Xe om **drivers** are widely available and should be easy to find on the street. For larger vehicles, you may be out of luck: at the time of writing, Ha Tien's only taxi company was out of business.

If you're planning to go farther afield—to Mui Nai, for instance—most hotels can hire bicycles and motorbikes at reasonable rates, though this service is not always advertised. You can also contact **Mr. The** (tel. 09/1857-4780) for safe and affordable motorbike rentals.

Moso Caves

A bizarre sight so far south, the soaring limestone **Moso Caves** (off of National Hwy. QL80, no phone, free) are something of an alien landscape in the Mekong Delta, where you're more likely to find rivers and rice paddies than craggy mountains. Appearing from nowhere, this rocky outcropping sits in the middle of an open field and was, up until only a few years ago, solely accessible by boat. Nowadays, the water has receded and a road leads into the cave area where, over the course of roughly 30 years, Viet Minh and NLF supporters took cover in the 20-odd caves hidden within the mountain. The dank confines of the caves became a haven for those fighting against the southern government and their American allies, with a makeshift hospital constructed in the hollows of the mountain. Several American bomb craters still surround the caves, now converted into small ponds.

During rainy season, visitors wade through ankle-deep waters and along the rickety wooden path that leads into the caves. Moso is far more deserted than some of its other historical counterparts and makes for a more authentic and eerie experience. The coffee carts and snack shops that hang around the area detract from the overall atmosphere, but Moso remains a mostly untouched piece of local war history. There's a small sign to indicate where the turnoff from the highway is, but it's probably best to go with a guide, as it's a bit tricky to find.

Father and Son Island

Twenty-two miles from Ha Tien town lies the **Hon Chong Peninsula,** an area sometimes touted as a miniature southern version of Ha Long Bay. The peninsula has beautiful natural scenery that is different from much of the Delta region: Rocky limestone cliffs soar above the unbroken landscape, many of them hollowed into caves, and several craggy escarpments dot the nearby coastline. The most well known of these landscapes is **Father and Son Island (Khu Du Lich Hon Phu Tu)** (tel. 07/7385-4584, 7am-5pm daily, VND5,000), a pair of limestone karsts that face one another and are said to resemble a father and son looking out over the sea. While the father island tumbled into the ocean after a storm in 2006, its other half still remains and is visible from the nearby beach, where snack and drink vendors abound.

Before you reach the shore, you'll find yourself traveling through **Cave Pagoda** (Khu Du Lich Hon Phu Tu), which is exactly what it sounds like. Nestled within a massive rock, the pagoda's altar features a statue of the Buddha sitting beneath his famous bodhi tree, depicted in a mural on the cave wall, as well as several statues perched on various cliffs outside the entrance. Beyond the pagoda is a beach where visitors snap photos of the islands and take in the rest of Hon Chong's scenery. Tourist **boats** (tel. 07/7375-9028, VND10,000-35,000) make a short trip out to the islands and around a nearby cave; but, these boats don't run if not at full capacity. It's just as well, as the view is best admired from a distance.

Travelers can reach Hon Chong with a motorbike rental or hired guide. **Mr. The** (tel. 09/1857-4780) does a lovely day trip combining the drive to Father and Son Island with a visit to the Moso Caves, lunch at nearby **Duong Beach,** and a jaunt over to Mui Nai and Thach Dong to finish out the afternoon. It is also possible to stay at or around Duong Beach, where there are a handful of accommodations, though the mainland beaches of the Delta aren't nearly as nice and, with Phu Quoc only 21 miles away, it seems a waste to spend your beach time on this side of the water.

Phu Quoc Island

A world apart from the Mekong mainland, Phu Quoc has fast become one of Vietnam's most sought-after island escapes. Blessed with pristine white-sand beaches, turquoise waters, shaggy palm trees, and an abundance of sunshine, the island's postcard-perfect coast sees droves of visitors during the high season, particularly December and January.

Phu Quoc's shoreline is its main attraction. But beyond the sun and sand is an island crisscrossed with dozens of winding red dirt roads and unspoiled landscapes waiting to be discovered. To the north, Phu Quoc's sprawling national park and deserted coast pack a full day's adventure, while the pepper farms and freshwater streams of the interior provide further opportunities for exploration. Avid divers will appreciate the island's underwater scenery, known as one of the best diving sites in Vietnam. Though some of these untamed areas are sure to change as more high-end resorts and chic beach bungalows crop up, for now the island offers an exceptional combination of adventure and relaxation, allowing visitors to enjoy a lazy outing at the beach one day and a backroads adventure along Phu Quoc's dusty, rutted forest trails the next.

Most visitors to Phu Quoc turn up between November and April, outside of the rainy season when temperatures are at their best. Depending upon the extent to which you plan to explore the island, a trip here

Phu Quoc Island

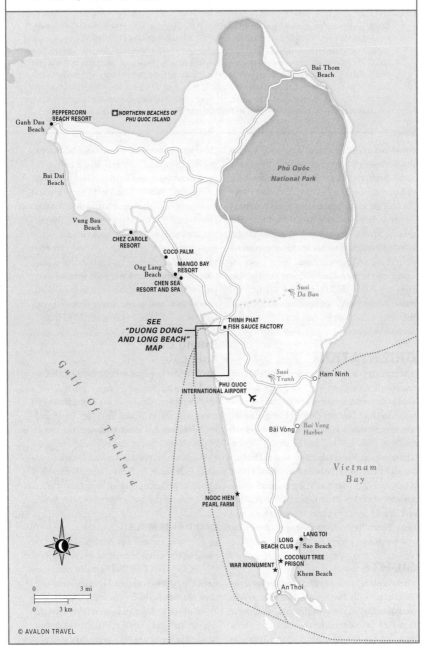

Ganh Dau Beach

PEPPERCORN BEACH RESORT

★ NORTHERN BEACHES OF PHU QUOC ISLAND

Bai Thom Beach

Phú Quốc National Park

Bai Dai Beach

Vung Bau Beach

CHEZ CAROLE RESORT

COCO PALM

MANGO BAY RESORT

Ong Lang Beach

CHEN SEA RESORT AND SPA

Suoi Da Ban

THINH PHAT FISH SAUCE FACTORY

SEE "DUONG DONG AND LONG BEACH" MAP

Suoi Tranh

Ham Ninh

PHU QUOC INTERNATIONAL AIRPORT

G u l f   O f   T h a i l a n d

Bãi Vòng

Bai Vong Harbor

Vietnam Bay

NGOC HIEN PEARL FARM

LANG TOI

LONG BEACH CLUB

Sao Beach

COCONUT TREE PRISON

WAR MONUMENT

Khem Beach

An Thoi

0   3 mi

0   3 km

© AVALON TRAVEL

The Dogs of Phu Quoc

As you make your way around the island you'll spot dogs trotting along the roadside or napping in the midday heat. This isn't particularly unusual for Vietnam, but take a closer look and you may notice that some of these animals have a long, spiked ridge of hair running along their backs. The Phu Quoc Ridgeback (*cho xoay* in Vietnamese) is one of only three species of dog in the world that has this backward-running ridge, not unlike a cowlick. Though its history isn't terribly well-documented—some say the dogs were brought to the island by the French, while others believe that the Phu Quoc Ridgeback is actually an offshoot of the Thai Ridgeback—these canines have a local reputation for being intelligent and affable and they make excellent hunters.

could last as little as three days or as long as three weeks and chances are you'd still have some discovering left to do. Travelers get the gist of the island in 3-4 days, but many people tack on extra beach time. On account of its growing popularity, you'll find that Phu Quoc's prices—from food to accommodations to basic services—are more expensive than those on the mainland. These costs are easily split between two or more people; solo travelers might find themselves shelling out more, as the island tends to be a destination that sees more couples and families than individual visitors.

ORIENTATION

The majority of Phu Quoc's accommodations, restaurants, and other services are located along the western side of the island near the main town of **Duong Dong. Long Beach,** where most travelers base themselves, sits just south of Duong Dong on the western coast. There are smaller settlements in **An Thoi** on the southern tip of the island and east at Ham Ninh, a village near Bai Vong Harbor, where speedboats from Rach Gia and Ha Tien arrive. Most areas beyond Duong Dong and Long Beach have little in the way of services and amenities, except for resorts.

SIGHTS

There is plenty to see in Phu Quoc beyond the beach, from the historical Phu Quoc prison near Ham Ninh town to the local fish sauce factories or the freshwater streams hidden deep within the island's interior. If you're

comfortable behind the wheel, the best way to explore the island is by grabbing a map, renting a motorbike, and setting out on your own, as this gives you the freedom to move around and discover all the island's narrow dirt paths. However, if you're not yet a master of the motorbike then you may feel more at ease in the passenger's seat, as Phu Quoc's roads are constantly under construction. A handful of local tour companies provide trips to some of these places, but you may also be able to track down a local guide or *xe om* driver through your hotel who can take you around the island.

Duong Dong
DINH CAU

Perched on the edge of the harbor, **Dinh Cau** (end of Bach Dang street, 6am-9pm daily) is a small temple dedicated to the protection of all those who travel by sea. Its colorful red-and-gold doorway has looked out over the mouth of the town's narrow, meandering river since 1937 and sits just beside a miniature blue-and-white lighthouse. In the late afternoons, this is a popular gathering spot for locals and it offers a nice view of the northern end of Long Beach.

CAO DAI TEMPLE

In case you missed Tay Ninh's Holy See or some of the other mainland branches, Phu Quoc's very own **Cao Dai Temple** (near corner of Nguyen Trai and Nguyen An Ninh, 6am-6pm daily) bears the same architecture as its other Delta counterparts, emphasizing yin and yang in its symmetrical design. Inside, the signature blue-and-white swirls of cloud and all-seeing eye emblems fill up the main hall.

FISH SAUCE FACTORIES

Something of an unusual attraction, the **Thinh Phat Fish Sauce Factory** (30 Thang 4, tel. 07/7398-0224, www.nuoc-mamthinhphat.com, 7am-7pm daily) and most other producers on the island are eager to share with Phu Quoc's visitors the finer details of the nation's favorite condiment: fish sauce. If you've eaten any local cuisine, chances are you've tasted this salty, reddish sauce, which is used in preparing everything from soups to noodle dishes to meat and veggies. On the island, fish sauce is something of a specialty. Each individual batch is unique in both strength and color. Heaps of anchovies are mixed with salt, piled into enormous wooden barrels that reach nearly as high as the ceiling, and left to sit for at least one year before the oily red sauce is dispensed from a tap at the bottom of the barrel, then bottled and sold. Though some batches can sit for longer, no less than 12 months is required, and each gargantuan container produces 3,000 liters of fish sauce. If you pay a visit to any of the island's countless factories, you'll be allowed to look around and possibly even sample their product, however it may be difficult to ask questions, as factory employees rarely speak English. Whatever happens, one thing you'll remember is the smell. Thankfully, fish sauce tastes infinitely better than it smells.

SUOI TRANH

About six miles from Duong Dong town en route to Ham Ninh and Sao Beach, the freshwater stream at **Suoi Tranh (Khu Du Lich Suoi Tranh)** (Suoi May Hamlet, tel. 07/7384-9863, 7am-5pm daily, VND3,000) runs during the rainy months from May to November. Hidden amid the lush cover of the forest, many tourists visit Suoi Tranh's rushing waters to take in the area's charming natural scenery and have a picnic or a swim. There is also **Suoi Da Ban** (Ap Ben Tram, tel. 07/7656-3338, 7am-5pm daily), another stream located

farther into the island's interior. Suoi Tranh is the more scenic and more accessible of the two.

Long Beach

COI NGUON MUSEUM

The first privately owned museum in the Mekong Delta, **Coi Nguon** (149 Tran Hung Dao, tel. 07/7398-0206, www.coinguonmuseum.com, 7am-5pm daily, VND20,000) is not unlike most provincial museums, featuring exhibits on the geography, history, and revolutionary activities of the island, but it restricts its scope solely to Phu Quoc. In an unusual building chock full of small alcoves and religious shrines, the five-story exhibition hall includes English signage and an interesting collection of Oc Eo artifacts, natural souvenirs from the surrounding waters, and also a few displays dedicated to Phu Quoc's most famous visitors, including Mac Cuu, considered a major player in the island's development, and Nguyen Trung Truc, a revolutionary hero who was captured in the island's eastern town of Ham Ninh in 1868. From its many balconies Coi Nguon offers a nice view of Long Beach and the main drag along Tran Hung Dao.

Up a stone path behind the museum, a sanctuary houses several very large, very noisy sea birds. Though the sanctuary could use a facelift, the birds are worth a look, if only to pass the driftwood sculpture carved into a fire-breathing dragon on the way up.

PEARL FARMS

On the road from Long Beach south to An Thoi are a string of massive jewelry companies that harvest local pearls. While some bill these mega-centers as a tourist attraction, they are, for the most part, reserved for serious shoppers only. Long, unending showrooms of pearls are tended to by eager sales assistants. A few times a day, someone will cut open an oyster from the small pool out front to show tourists how the pearls are collected. Many day tours make a stop at one of these places for a brief show and then leave

Duong Dong and Long Beach

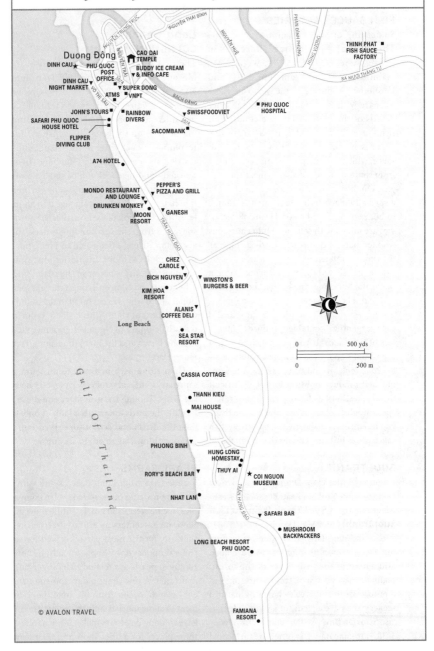

THINH PHAT FISH SAUCE FACTORY

Duong Đông
DINH CAU
PHU QUOC POST OFFICE
CAO DAI TEMPLE
BUDDY ICE CREAM & INFO CAFE
DINH CAU NIGHT MARKET
ATMS
SUPER DONG
VNPT
PHU QUOC HOSPITAL
JOHN'S TOURS
RAINBOW DIVERS
SAFARI PHU QUOC HOUSE HOTEL
SWISSFOODVIET
FLIPPER DIVING CLUB
SACOMBANK
A74 HOTEL
PEPPER'S PIZZA AND GRILL
MONDO RESTAURANT AND LOUNGE
DRUNKEN MONKEY
GANESH
MOON RESORT
CHEZ CAROLE
BICH NGUYEN
WINSTON'S BURGERS & BEER
KIM HOA RESORT
ALANIS COFFEE DELI
Long Beach
SEA STAR RESORT
CASSIA COTTAGE
THANH KIEU
MAI HOUSE
PHUONG BINH
HUNG LONG HOMESTAY
THUY AI
COI NGUON MUSEUM
RORY'S BEACH BAR
NHAT LAN
SAFARI BAR
MUSHROOM BACKPACKERS
LONG BEACH RESORT PHU QUOC
FAMIANA RESORT

Gulf Of Thailand

0   500 yds
0   500 m

© AVALON TRAVEL

ample time for shopping. There are several pearl farms stretched along the southern end of Long Beach, including **Ngoc Hien** (Duong Bao Hamlet en route to An Thoi, tel. 07/7398-3599, www.ngoctrai-phuquoc.com, 8am-5pm daily), which has a showroom full of both high- and low-quality local pearls. Do your homework when purchasing jewelry on the island, as there are plenty of legitimate pearl companies but also several impostors.

An Thoi
COCONUT TREE PRISON

Hidden near the southern tip of the island, Phu Quoc's infamous **Coconut Tree Prison (Di Tich Lich Su Nha Tu Phu Quoc)** (tel. 07/7384-4578, 7:30am-11am and 1pm-5pm daily) is a faded, unassuming collection of iron stockades that is easily missed when following the road to Sao Beach. During the American War, this crumbling, shadeless complex claimed the lives of nearly 4,000 prisoners, as Communist supporters and prisoners of war were exiled to the confines of its high barbed-wire gates and subjected to harsh conditions, starvation, and torture.

Though the prison had existed as early as the 1950s, its worst horrors came to pass between 1967 and 1973, during which time more than 40,000 men and women suffered the brutality of south Vietnamese soldiers. A variety of punishments were used. The worst of the bunch were the prison's tiger cages: low barbed-wire pens used to confine as many as five people in one small space near the main entrance of the prison. Left outdoors with no food or shelter and crammed into an area barely large enough to squat, inmates in the tiger cages often succumbed to the heat and dehydration and were unable to properly stand, sit, or lie down. Those who survived often remained permanently handicapped, unable to walk after extended periods of confinement.

Despite—or perhaps because of—this ruthless treatment, the cramped quarters of Phu Quoc Prison became a training ground for revolutionaries, and several jailbreaks occurred over the course of the prison's worst years. Inside the corrugated iron stockades, jailers covered the original dirt floors with tile in an effort to prevent further escapes, but a handful of detainees still succeeded in fleeing the prison and making it back to the island's revolutionary base.

Today, visitors to the complex roam the enclosed area dotted with low stockade buildings, where several eerily lifelike displays depict the harsh realities of the prison. Plenty of English signage helps travelers navigate each exhibit, and there is a small gallery of photographs and artifacts housed in the aged colonial building beside the prison grounds, which features some graphic evidence of the south Vietnamese army's brutality. Many visitors to the Coconut Tree Prison combine this sight with a stop at Sao Beach. You can also visit the sky-blue **War Monument** just down the road opposite the prison.

AN THOI ISLANDS

A trail of rocky islands scattered off the southern point of Phu Quoc, the **An Thoi Islands** are most often visited on snorkeling or diving trips, as the area is known for its colorful underwater scenery and wildlife-watching. Check with local diving outfits or tour providers about visiting the area. Trips to the islands are usually a day-long affair from Long Beach, with boats casting off from An Thoi Harbor and dropping anchor just offshore to explore the nearby reefs.

BEACHES
Long Beach

Long Beach is the island's most popular stretch of sand. Most of Long Beach has been chopped up by individual resorts and other businesses, but there are still a few bits and pieces left for the budget traveler, and it is walkable from any of the accommodations along Tran Hung Dao. Thanks to its location, Long Beach has dozens of bars and restaurants right on the shoreline, making it easy to grab a quick bite or a seaside drink. Though prices are steeper here, it's worth it to buy a drink if only for the beach chairs offered. There are also plenty of women advertising beach-side spa and massage services at low prices.

Sao Beach

Tucked in a shallow cove on the southeastern coast, **Sao Beach (Bai Sao)** has earned enough attention from travelers to house a handful of seaside restaurants and basic services but still remains one of the less-frequented beaches on the island thanks to its distance from the main tourist drag. About a half-hour from Duong Dong town over dirt tracks and partially paved roads, development in the area has been rather slow, but this contributes to Sao Beach's atmosphere of peace and quiet.

Most people visit the beach park at the inaccurately named **Long Beach Club** (Hamlet 4, An Thoi, tel. 07/7399-7789, www. longbeachvn.com, 8am-6pm daily), a tourist complex that rents out lounge chairs and other beach-going equipment in addition to housing a restaurant and small souvenir shop, though this is the most expensive of the beach-side businesses.

A quick wander down the shore brings you to **Lang Toi** (Bai Sao, tel. 07/7397-2123, lang-toi_restaurant@yahoo.com.vn, 7:30am-5pm daily), a restaurant and guesthouse combo where the beach chairs are free for paying customers and prices are more reasonable. The folks at Lang Toi also rent out four guest rooms (VND630,000-1,029,000). Rooms are fan-only and minimal (no more than a bathroom, bed, and bug net), but accommodations are comfortable and include a massive bathtub as well as a balcony. You will almost certainly be bound to the place for breakfast, lunch, and dinner, as it is the only restaurant around for miles.

Day-trippers can try to access the nearby **Khem Beach,** just south of Sao Beach, however it does take some work and is occasionally closed, courtesy of the military. If you're looking for more beautiful, deserted beaches, head up north.

★ Northern Beaches

While Sao Beach is hailed as one of the most beautiful spots on the island and Long Beach is equipped with everything you could ever need, Phu Quoc's northern beaches give both spots a run for their money. Virtually forgotten by most island visitors, the tranquil sands of the northwest are as idyllic as can be, though time will surely change this. Indeed, resorts are beginning to take hold along the

Long Beach, Phu Quoc Island

coast all the way up to Ganh Dau port. For now, the ravishing shores of the island's north are peaceful, picturesque, and accessible to anyone with a motorbike. Navigating Phu Quoc's northern roads can be tricky, as most of them are still red dirt tracks and you'll be lucky to find a street sign of any kind north of Duong Dong. It's best to bring a map and remain patient, as you're likely to get lost a few times before reaching your destination.

ONG LANG BEACH

Not far from town, **Ong Lang Beach** is a quiet stretch of sand that is slowly beginning to see more private resorts. Though its ocean-side real estate is hemmed in by a sea wall, the grassy field around the beach turns this area into something of a park where regular weekend visitors turn up for picnics and fresh air. The end of a narrow, rutted path leads onto the beach's public access area, where visitors can park and walk farther along the sand. Though you won't find any snack or drink vendors, the restaurant at **Coco Palm Resort** is open to non-guests. There's plenty of space for visitors to camp out in the public area of Ong Lang as well.

VUNG BAU BEACH

A small cove protected by Fingernail Cape, **Vung Bau Beach** is one of the most isolated stretches of sand on the island. There is nothing here but for an endless expanse of white sand and turquoise seas. You'll catch a glimpse of passing fishermen or the odd motorbike. Most visitors simply appreciate the emptiness of the area. With complete seclusion comes a lack of services; you won't find any restaurants or drink shops, so come prepared.

BAI DAI

Looking out over the vast cerulean waters of the Gulf of Thailand, **Bai Dai** is Phu Quoc's northern answer to Long Beach and far less populated than its southern counterpart. Stretching over nine miles along the western edge of the island, Bai Dai's breezy, sun-bleached shores see only a handful of visitors

who are willing to navigate the rugged dirt track that runs along the coast. As a result, this area is pleasantly devoid of vendors or massive resorts, instead affording visitors ample space to stretch out and enjoy the view. While Bai Dai is equally off the beaten path as Vung Bau, its neighbor to the south, there are a few small snack and drink shops here that cater to visitors, offering a little more ease for travelers who have trekked all the way here. The largest of these venues is **Mai Phuong 2** (Bai Dai, tel. 07/7370-2200, www.maiphuongphuquoc.com, 8am-5pm daily, VND100,000-250,000), which serves standard Vietnamese dishes and has beach chairs and other add-ons.

GANH DAU BEACH

Perched on the northwestern edge of Phu Quoc and extending towards Cambodian shores, **Ganh Dau** is a small corner of the island still untouched by locals and resort developers, though that is sure to change with time. From this stunning, pristine white-sand beach, you can see across the border to the southern coast of Cambodia. As one of the most remote parts of the island, the dusty paths that lead into Ganh Dau tend to weed out all but the serious beach-goers. Getting to this area takes effort; so if you head this far north, make a day of it and your efforts will be duly rewarded.

A handful of burgeoning mini-resorts and restaurants are around for food and drink. One of the nicer spots is **Peppercorn Beach** (Ganh Dau, tel. 07/7398-9567, www.peppercornbeach.com, 10am-5pm daily, VND50,000-180,000), a resort that offers drinks and food as well as brand-new beach-front bungalow accommodations (from VND2,940,000). Rooms are basic, and electricity on more remote parts of the island tends to cut out. If you're looking to get away from it all, this is the place to go.

BAI THOM

One of the most remote beaches on the island, **Bai Thom** hides on the northeastern edge of

Phu Quoc just beyond the boundaries of the national park. Thanks to its location, this area sees few visitors; the small amount of usable coastline and a rubbish problem may account for this, too. While the trip itself is a fun jaunt through the island's less-charted interior territory and a nice, newly paved road makes access to Bai Thom far easier than places like Sao Beach and Bai Dai, Bai Thom is the kind of place to visit for a quick drink, a rest in the hammock, and a look at the waves rolling into shore. It's a nice spot to incorporate on a loop around the northern half of Phu Quoc and the drive offers a brief respite from the bumpy, rocky dirt paths that line most of the rest of the island's north.

TOURS

With no provincial tourism office on the island, homegrown tour providers are springing up by the day. Trips to the southern An Thoi islands are popular, whether for fishing, snorkeling, or sightseeing, and often include a quick stop at a pearl farm. In most cases, your hotel will be able to recommend a particular company or book a tour through their own outfit. Ask the specifics of these tours first—from the itinerary to the number of people who will be joining you—as several different outfits band together and send their customers on the same mass ventures around the island.

Easily the largest and most well-represented company on the island is **John's Tours** (143 Tran Hung Dao, tel. 07/7399-6449, www.johnsislandtours.com, 8am-9pm daily), which offers affordable large-group excursions and is often featured in hotels and guesthouses across the island. These tours don't allow for much down time and visit very popular tourist spots. Other operators, such as **Jerry's Jungle & Beach Tours** (tel. 09/3822-6021, http://jerrystours.wix.com/jerrystours), arrange trips around the island and run overland tours to snorkeling destinations as well as to the more uncharted parts of the island on the back of a motorbike.

Bai Thom, a remote beach on Phu Quoc Island

NIGHTLIFE

As a destination that caters mostly to couples and families, there isn't much in the way of nightlife on Phu Quoc, however a handful of laid-back beach hangouts and bars advertising European sports channels exist along Tran Hung Dao. In truth, most restaurants and other businesses close their doors by 10pm or 11pm, but anyone who's out later than that can still find a place to relax, as bars stay open until the last patrons go home.

The only spot on the waterfront open late, **Rory's Beach Bar** (118/10 Tran Hung Dao, tel. 07/7399-4958, www.amigosphuquoc.com, 8am-late daily, VND30,000-100,000) is an easygoing place that serves food during the day and rents out paddleboards before carrying on with its festivities at night. Up on deck, a long wraparound bar serves beer and cocktails as well as other beverages and still leaves some room for a dance floor. Down in the sand, low tables and chairs are lit by colorful overhead lanterns. The amiable and outgoing

Rory is always around for a chat, too, and DJs are regularly featured here.

Farther down the Long Beach road, **Safari Bar** (opposite the Hill Hotel on Tran Hung Dao, tel. 09/0522-4600, 8pm-late daily, VND25,000-200,000) is home to a pool table and a nightly selection of beers and cocktails. Like most spots on the island, this is a fairly laid-back joint, with a patio area and rows of red lanterns hanging from the ceiling. The owner likes chatting and offering travel information and recommendations to patrons. The bar also runs a cooking class (VND357,000 per person) if you're looking for something different while in Phu Quoc.

The sign above the bar at **Drunken Monkey** (82 Tran Hung Dao, tel. 09/0925-9605, 10am-late daily, VND25,000-110,000) says it all: "Monkey to man: 1 million years. Man to monkey: 10 beers." Along with sports TV, a pool table, and several other cheeky slogans, the friendly bartenders at this roadside watering hole prepare a variety of cocktails and also serve beer. Grab a seat at the bar, at one of the cocktail tables around the interior, or out front on the patio.

SPORTS AND RECREATION
Snorkeling and Diving
In the years before divers caught wind of Con Dao, Phu Quoc was known as home to the best underwater scenery in Vietnam and, by some accounts, still holds that title. The ample reef surrounding the southern An Thois and a handful of smaller northern islands make them prime spots for snorkeling and diving. Several outfits run day trips to each of these locations a few times a week, with the southern An Thois being the best of the bunch.

If you're interested in snorkeling and don't mind spending more cash, opt for a trip through one of the dive shops, as they are guaranteed to have less people on board as well as high-quality equipment, and the amount of time you spend in the water will be far greater than it is on cheaper excursions.

The longest-running PADI-certified dive center in the country, **Rainbow Divers** (opposite Dinh Cau Night Market, tel. 09/1340-0964, www.divevietnam.com, 8am-9pm daily, VND630,000-2,625,000) is far and away the island's best-known brand. Like most outfits, Rainbow alternates day trips to the northern and southern islands of Phu Quoc each week, as well as offering night dives, snorkeling, and full-fledged diving certification for first-timers. All gear is included in the company's fees, and additional rental gear (such as Go Pros and other underwater gadgets) can be rented from the shop.

One of the fastest-growing outfits on the island, **Flipper Diving Club** (60 Tran Hung Dao, tel. 09/3940-2872, www.flipperdiving.com, 8am-9pm daily, VND525,000-7,350,000) is also PADI-certified and organizes trips to both the northern islands and the An Thoi area. A variety of supplementary PADI courses are available.

Massages and Spas
Many of the island's resorts offer massage and other spa treatments in-house, though these are often expensive. For budget travelers, local masseuses set up shop on Long Beach, offering cheap spa services. There are one or two independent outfits on the waterfront that operate out of a proper shop, but these seem to provide a level of service that doesn't match the higher price.

ACCOMMODATIONS
Like most other services on Phu Quoc, you'll find that accommodations here are notably more expensive than the mainland. While several smaller dorms and other budget lodgings are available, local developers recognize Phu Quoc's immense potential as a tourism destination, and so there is no doubt that prices will continue to climb. Most resorts are already charging upwards of VND1,000,000 a night for a spot on Long Beach. High season on the island falls around December and January. These months invariably bring higher rates and booked-up rooms, so reserve your place early and allot extra cash.

While there are dozens of beautiful, tranquil beach resorts stretched along the western side of the island, Phu Quoc is very much in its early stages of development. As the area continues to grow, construction is a constant along Long Beach and up to Cua Can. For light sleepers and late-risers, check with your hotel or resort before booking whether or not there is construction going on nearby, as workers begin around the same time the sun comes up. Electricity on the island is not always a given. Power outages are common during the day and, while higher-end resorts have a back-up generator on hand, budget hotels may be without electricity for a few daylight hours.

Resorts are scattered across the island, not only on Long Beach but as far away as Ganh Dau and Sao Beach. For budget travelers, Long Beach is without a doubt the place to go, as this is where you'll find a wider range of accommodations. The coast along Ong Lang Beach and up to Cua Can is filled with smaller boutique resorts that are more expensive but also live up to their added value. Travelers can base themselves in more remote locations, too, however escaping the relative bustle of Long Beach means that you will most likely be bound to whichever resort you choose, as even places in Cua Can are far enough removed from town that the on-site restaurant often becomes your only option.

Duong Dong
OVER VND2,100,000

The rustic rooms at **Coco Palm Resort** (Ong Lang, tel. 07/7398-7979, www.cocopalmphuquoc.com, VND2,100,000-2,310,000) are simple but offer a quiet, scenic location right on Ong Lang Beach. A collection of bungalows frame the resort's pleasant garden area and you'll find air-conditioning, hot water, and a refrigerator in each room. Coco Palm's seaside restaurant serves complimentary breakfast daily as well as other meals and the peaceful, secluded beach is steps away.

Chez Carole (Hamlet 4, Cua Can, tel.

07/7384-8884, www.chezcarole.com.vn, VND2,730,000-3,360,000, breakfast included) is an out-of-the-way boutique resort boasting a private beach and ocean-side pool. Each bungalow features rustic decor, bathrooms with stone bathtubs, and a private sun terrace with views of unspoiled scenery. Snorkeling tours, Jet ski rentals, and kayaking can be arranged through the resort. The on-site restaurant and bar is open to non-guests. Chez Carole has an additional restaurant near Duong Dong town on Long Beach that features fresh seafood and nightly live music.

One of Ong Lang's most posh and exclusive accommodations, **Chen Sea Resort and Spa** (Bai Xep, Ong Lang, tel. 07/7399-5895, www.chenla-resort.com, VND5,523,000-10,857,000) is a sprawling, all-inclusive retreat nestled in a beautiful natural cove. Its sloping grounds boast private beach access, an infinity swimming pool, a restaurant, and a bar. Each spacious villa is constructed in the style of a traditional Vietnamese house but features modern touches such as flat-screen TVs, DVD players, an in-room safe, and a minibar. Depending upon your accommodations, a private pool or whirlpool tub is also included, as well as a terrace overlooking the sweeping white-sand coastline. Water activities, such as kayaking, sailing, and windsurfing, are available, as are massage and spa services, a tennis court, and an open-air exercise area.

Bordered by lush wilderness and crystal-line ocean, charming **Mango Bay Resort** (Ong Lang Beach, tel. 07/7398-1693, www.mangobayphuquoc.com, VND3,465,000-4,620,000, breakfast included) is an eco-friendly resort that emphasizes conservation and low-impact tourism. The thatched-roof bungalows feature fans and mosquito nets rather than air-conditioning. All rooms come with sturdy four-poster beds, an electricity-free icebox, and Wi-Fi. The resort's on-site restaurant serves appetizing fare throughout the day. Activities like snorkeling, kayaking, and tours around the island are available.

Long Beach
UNDER VND210,000
Though it's a bit farther along Tran Hung Dao, backpackers looking for a budget bed will appreciate **Mushroom Backpackers** (Tran Hung Dao, tel. 09/3794-2017, www. mushrooms-phuquoc.com, VND126,000). With a large communal area and a constant flow of travelers hoping to do Phu Quoc on the cheap, this place draws a younger, livelier crowd and offers dirt-cheap, fan-only dorm accommodations, complete with individual lockers, Wi-Fi, and shared bathrooms. The staff are easygoing, and someone is always hanging around the garden out front.

Sitting in a nice central location along Long Beach not far from town, **A74 Hotel** (74 Tran Hung Dao, tel. 07/7398-2772, a74hotel@gmail.com, VND168,000-900,000) offers decent rooms and good value. All accommodations come with air-conditioning, hot water, a television, and a minibar. In addition to single and double rooms, A74 supplies dorm beds (VND168,000), which come with en suite bathrooms and a locker, making this hotel one of the few decent options for solo travelers on the island, and staff are notably helpful with arranging motorbike rentals, tours, and transportation around the island.

VND210,000-525,000
Moon Resort (82 Tran Hung Dao, tel. 07/7399-4520, VND420,000-840,000) is a series of bungalows dotting a stone path to Long Beach. These are a decent value for the location. Rooms are basic but include hot water and your choice of fan or air-conditioning. A small restaurant and bar are set up right on the beach. Opt for the cheaper garden view rooms, as the beachside rooms can be up to double the price and don't provide much extra.

Though there are only three rooms available, the owners at **Hung Long Homestay** (147B Tran Hung Dao, tel. 07/7652-4468, VND336,000-630,000) go to great pains to make their guests feel welcome. Rooms are basic but clean and include Wi-Fi, TV, hot water, and air-conditioning, all of which is solar-powered, a fact that allows electricity to run throughout the day—something that most other budget accommodations can't offer with the regular daytime power cuts on Phu Quoc in order to conserve energy. The family runs a restaurant at the front of the building, serving decent local meals.

Right next door to Hung Long is the **Thuy Ai Guesthouse** (122 Tran Hung Dao, tel. 07/7247-8555, VND300,000-400,000), another excellent budget option that offers your choice of fan or air-conditioning as well as TV, hot water, and Wi-Fi access. The guesthouse rents out motorbikes to guests and is just a short walk from Alley 118, which has public access to Long Beach.

VND525,000-1,050,000
The bungalows at **Nhat Lan Resort** (Tran Hung Dao, tel. 07/7384-7663, nhanghinhatlan@yahoo.com, VND525,000-VND1,050,000) may not be out of this world, but their beachfront location makes up for the wear and tear on the rooms. Accommodations are basic but clean and include both fan and air-conditioning options, as well as your choice of garden or beach view. Nhat Lan counts a restaurant and bar in its services, and staff can assist guests with travel arrangements.

The ocean views from the top floor of the **Kim Hoa Resort** (88/2 Tran Hung Dao, tel. 07/7384-8969, www.kimhoaresort.com, VND840,000-5,250,000) would make for a good reason never to leave your room. This ocean-side property boasts private beach access, a restaurant, and a swimming pool in addition to a variety of room options, from standard hotel rooms to beach and garden bungalows (from VND1,470,000 a night). All accommodations include air-conditioning, television, Wi-Fi access, hot water, a minibar, and complimentary breakfast. The resort arranges tours around the island through their own outfit and offers airport pick-up upon request.

VND1,050,000-2,100,000

The wide-open grounds of **Mai House** (Tran Hung Dao, tel. 07/7384-7008, www. maihousephuquoc.com, VND1,610,000-5,160,000) offer a pleasant break from the close quarters that make up most Vietnamese accommodations. Set around the perimeter of a grassy lawn peppered with palm trees, these plush beach bungalows are minimally furnished but have generous bathrooms, comfy beds, and modern decor. Amenities include hot water, air-conditioning, Wi-Fi access, tea- and coffee-making facilities, and in-room safety deposit boxes, as well as complimentary breakfast. Staff assist with motorbike rentals or in arranging tours around the island. Guests have easy access to Mai House's private beach.

One of the best value accommodations on Long Beach, **Thanh Kieu Resort** (100C/14 Tran Hung Dao, tel. 07/7384-8394, www.thanhkieuresort.com, VND945,000-1,659,000) is a collection of pleasant thatched-roof beachside bungalows. Featuring a fridge, an in-room safe, mosquito net, and a fan, the place is more rustic than some of its Long Beach counterparts, but the private terraces and excellent sea views more than make up for this. Breakfast is included in the room rate, and staff can assist guests with renting vehicles or booking tours to explore the island.

Near the north end of Tran Hung Dao not far from Duong Dong town, the **Safari Phu Quoc House Hotel** (40 Tran Hung Dao, tel. 07/7399-9797, www.ilovephuquoc.vn, VND780,000-4,200,000) is a lovely little boutique hotel with pleasant views of Long Beach and the ocean. Decked out in an eco-chic decor, rooms at the Safari Phu Quoc feature tiled floors and wood accents as well as balconies in some accommodations. Television, air-conditioning, hot water, Wi-Fi, and a fridge are all standard amenities, and breakfast is included in the room rate. The hotel staff are a friendly, outgoing bunch who offer free travel advice. There is a café and bar downstairs.

One of the island's more popular accommodations, **Sea Star Resort** (Tran Hung Dao, tel. 07/7398-2161, www.seastarresort. com, VND966,000-1,785,000) offers resort-level accommodations at affordable prices. Private bungalows and double rooms are simple yet sophisticated in their decor and the staff assists with airport pick-up as well as arranging day trips around the island. Sea Star has its own stretch of Long Beach, complete with lounge chairs as well as a restaurant on-site. Book ahead as rooms fill up fast.

OVER VND2,100,000

Though its rates are higher than some, the exceptional service and top-notch accommodations at ★ **Cassia Cottage** (Tran Hung Dao, tel. 07/7384-8395, www.cassiacottage. com, VND3,927,000-4,389,000) are well worth the additional investment. From its stunning garden, featuring a variety of local foliage, to the pristine shoreline out front, the environment at Cassia is a cut above the rest, a fact that is only made better by the friendliness and charm of its staff. Inside each room, beautiful wooden furnishings opt for simplicity over ornamentation and guests will appreciate the great attention that is paid to detail, with added touches like tea sets and cinnamon-scented rooms, not to mention the "welcome" greetings carefully spelled out in palm leaves on each bed. Both garden and sea view options are available, and breakfast at the resort's excellent beachside restaurant is included in the room rate. There are also massage services on-site as well as a private beach and two swimming pools.

Styled in the design of a traditional Vietnamese village, the impressive **Long Beach Resort** (Tran Hung Dao, tel. 07/7398-1818, www.longbeach-phuquoc.com, VND4,000,000-6,000,000) is lined with cobblestone pathways and towering palm trees. All rooms, from deluxe accommodations to semi-detached bungalows, are furnished in beautiful, detailed solid wood and come with air-conditioning, hot water, television, DVD player, minibar, and complimentary breakfast. Overlooking the resort's private beach is a stunning lotus pond topped with a stone footbridge, which serves as the backdrop for its ocean-side restaurant. A swimming pool is located a few steps back from the water and on-site spa services are available.

Famiana Resort (Tran Hung Dao, tel. 07/7398-3366, www.famiana-resort.com, VND4,202,000-21,000,000) is a trendy modern retreat situated near the southern end of Long Beach. Its monochromatic Asian-inspired rooms boast plush beds and open-plan sitting rooms, as well as kitchenettes in the beachside villas. Guests can choose from garden or sea-view accommodations, and both breakfast and dinner are included in the nightly rate. Famiana offers private beach access and a swimming pool as well as spa services, a fitness center, mini golf facilities, and a playground for young kids.

FOOD

When it comes to dining on the island, Phu Quoc offers a much wider variety of cuisines than most destinations in the Mekong Delta. All along Tran Hung Dao, you'll find dozens of restaurants offering European and Asian dishes. These eateries are more expensive than their mainland counterparts, but their variety and the quality of the food usually make up for this increase. The cheapest option is local fare, with the Dinh Cau Night Market being a popular spot to enjoy delicious local cuisine and fresh seafood. Thanks to the island's many foreign visitors, travelers will find plenty of vegetarian options available.

Cafés and Bakeries

The quiet, air-conditioned paradise at **Alanis Coffee Deli** (98 Tran Hung Dao, tel. 07/7399-4931, alanis.deli@yahoo.com, 8:30am-10pm daily, VND20,000-140,000) is home to Phu Quoc's best pancakes as well as a variety of European coffee, sandwiches, and other Western breakfast options. Add to that a solid Wi-Fi connection and friendly service and the place is a hit.

International

Located right on the main drag, with a narrow storefront that opens onto a long, well-lit dining area, **Ganesh** (97 Tran Hung Dao, tel. 07/7399-4917, 10am-10pm daily, VND70,000-160,000) is the island's one and only Indian restaurant. Owned by the same folks responsible for Ganesh eateries in Saigon, Nha Trang, and other Vietnamese cities, the food here is just as good as any of their locations.

Formerly known as Mermaid's Dive Bar and several other incarnations, the newly opened **Winston's Burgers & Beer** (99 Tran Hung Dao, tel. 09/0766-5528, 6pm-midnight daily, VND155,000-385,000) is off to a great start with a short but creative list of burger combinations. Its fixings include blue cheese and bacon, avocado, pineapple, and ham. The friendly owner is always around for a quick hello or a chat, giving the place a pleasant, laid-back feel. With tasty food and superb service, there's a strong chance that Winston's will become a popular name among travelers.

A sunny, easygoing open-air spot on Long Beach's Tran Hung Dao, **Mondo Restaurant and Lounge** (82 Tran Hung Dao, tel. 07/7399-4930, www.niamondo.com, 8am-10pm daily, VND65,000-250,000) has more of a European feel than most other island eateries and offers a range of Western dishes, including pasta, salad, sandwiches, and a cheese plate, as well as a tapas and wine menu.

Pepper's Pizza and Grill (89 Tran Hung Dao, tel. 07/7384-8773, 10am-10pm daily, VND75,000-255,000) does a fair turn in pizza, pasta, and, inexplicably, German sausage. Its elevated open-front dining area looks out onto the traffic of Tran Hung Dao, a less scenic view than the ocean. The staff are friendly and the restaurant also does delivery.

Claiming the best burgers in town, **Swissfoodviet** (81 30 Thang 4, tel. 07/7399-4941, www.swissfoodviet.com, 8am-10pm daily, VND35,000-270,000) is a small shop in Duong Dong town that is giving some of the other more conveniently located Western eateries a run for their money. Serving breakfast, sandwiches, *rosti,* and even a cheese fondue in addition to its burgers, the modest restaurant may not appear to be much from the outside, but its mouthwatering meals prove your first impressions wrong.

One of Long Beach's more upmarket restaurants, the Duong Dong extension of **Chez Carole** (88 Tran Hung Dao, tel. 07/7384-8884, www.chezcarole.com.vn, 10am-midnight daily, VND80,000-320,000) is a garden restaurant with plenty of palm trees and a peaceful setting. During dinner hours, a large wooden cart laden with the catch of the day greets visitors at the entrance, while the Filipino band keeps diners entertained from 7:30pm to 11pm. Chez Carole's menu features a variety of both Western and Vietnamese dishes, counting seafood among its specialties.

Vietnamese

One of the most affordable options by far is the **Dinh Cau Night Market** (near Cau Castle, 6pm-11pm daily), a bustling open-air affair where vendors roll out cartloads of fresh seafood—some of it still swimming—and diners are able to select their meal. With everything from fish and squid to prawns as big as your head, the market features mostly seafood but also offers a handful of other choices.

Bich Nguyen (Alley 88 Tran Hung Dao, tel. 09/1678-8719, 7:30am-11pm daily, VND30,000-80,000) serves simple Vietnamese fare at the top of a quiet alley off the main drag on Long Beach. Dishes run the gamut from noodles to rice, meats, soups, and veggie offerings. Though the restaurant itself is nothing special, this is one of the few places on Long Beach where you can find good, well-priced local meals.

From morning to night, the beachside restaurant at **Phuong Binh** (Alley 118 Tran Hung Dao, tel. 07/7399-4101, phuongbinhhouse@yahoo.com, 7:30am-10:30pm daily, VND30,000-150,000) offers a menu of mostly Vietnamese dishes with a few Western options and sees a steady crowd throughout the day. It's located beside the public beach entrance off Alley 118 and is one of the more affordable spots right on the water.

INFORMATION AND SERVICES

Tourist Information

Your go-to spot for a decent island map and sound travel advice, **Buddy Ice Cream & Info Cafe** (26 Nguyen Trai, tel. 07/7399-4181, www.visitphuquoc.info, 8am-10pm daily) is more or less Phu Quoc's unofficial tourist information spot. Beyond doling out useful tips about visiting the island, the amiable staff at Buddy provide proper New Zealand ice cream in a variety of flavors as well as coffee, smoothies, and some small meals. Both Wi-Fi access and use of the café's desktop computers are available for paying guests.

Banks

For fast cash, there are several **ATMs** located at the intersection of Tran Hung Dao and Vo Thi Sau, just beside the entrance to the Dinh Cau Night Market, as well as a few near the top of Alley 118 on Tran Hung Dao. For currency exchange, many hotels offer this service, though check the rate against the local **Sacombank** (52B 30 Thang 4, tel. 07/7399-5118, www.sacombank.com.vn, 7:30am-11:30am and 1pm-5pm Mon.-Fri., 7:30am-11:30am Sat.), where you can also switch currencies.

Internet and Postal Services

The island's only **post office** (10 30 Thang 4, tel. 07/7384-6038, 7am-6pm daily) is located right in the center of Duong Dong. For Internet, you can either grab a coffee at **Buddy Ice Cream & Info Cafe** (26 Nguyen Trai, tel. 07/7399-4181, www.visitphuquoc.info, 8am-10pm daily) and take advantage of their free computers and Wi-Fi or visit **VNPT** (2 Tran Hung Dao, tel. 07/7399-4888, 7am-6pm daily), just around the corner from the post office.

Medical Services

Phu Quoc's main **hospital (Benh Vien Phu Quoc)** (30 Thang 4, tel. 07/7384-6074) is located in Duong Dong town, not far from the top of Tran Hung Dao, and has 24-hour emergency services; facilities are very basic.

GETTING THERE
Air
Phu Quoc International Airport (San Bay Quoc Te Phu Quoc) (PQC, www.phuquocinternationalairport.com), opened in 2012, receives multiple daily flights from Saigon (1 hour, VND360,000-1,000,000 one-way), Can Tho (50 min., VND500,000-1,000,000 one-way), and Hanoi (2 hours, VND1,300,000-2,600,000).

The airport is six miles northeast of Duong Dong. Taxis from the airport to Duong Dong and Long Beach cost VND100,000-120,000.

Boat
Boats arriving from both Rach Gia (2.5 hours, VND350,000) and Ha Tien (2 hours, VND230,000) dock at the **Bai Vong harbor,** about eight miles from Duong Dong, the largest town on the island. If you book ahead, many hotels and resorts will arrange pick up for you. You can also hop on a minibus (30 min., VND50,000) from the harbor. Be clear about where you want to go, as drivers will sometimes insist on bringing you to a particular guesthouse or hotel.

GETTING AROUND
Taxis and *Xe Om*
At both the harbor and the airport, *xe om* are sure to find you before you find them. Throughout the rest of the island these drivers are harder to come by, as accommodations are fairly spread out. If you can't track anyone down, call a **Mailinh** (tel. 07/7397-9797) or **Hoang Long** (tel. 07/7398-8988) taxi.

Vehicles for Hire
For complete freedom, many travelers prefer to rent motorbikes to get around the island. The going rate for an automatic is around VND150,000 and for a semi-automatic vehicle is VND120,000. Driving yourself is the most cost-effective and efficient option, but construction is everywhere, so novice drivers might want to stick to the passenger's seat. You can usually ask your hotel for driver recommendations, or chat up the drivers that hang around the harbor. Some places will also rent out bicycles to travelers, though with little shade you may find yourself wilting before you make it to your destination.

Background

The Landscape

Covering a total area of 127,880 square miles, Vietnam is a skinny, S-shaped country that snakes its way from the southern border of China all the way down to the mouth of the mighty Mekong. While there is no official nickname for the country, its shape is sometimes likened to a dragon, a moniker which locals are happy to accept, as this mythical creature has ties to the origin story of the Vietnamese people. To the west, Vietnam shares a frontier with both Cambodia and Laos, while the north is bordered by China. Along the southern and eastern edges of the country is the East Sea, also known as the South China Sea.

GEOGRAPHY

While Vietnam's rice paddies seem to go on for miles across the Mekong and Red River Deltas, only about 20 percent of the country's land area is actually flat. The rest of Vietnam, from low, rolling hills along the southern coast to the soaring peaks of the far north, spans a range of elevations. Near the sea, white-sand beaches are dotted with clusters of tropical foliage. The dense jungle of Vietnam's mountainous regions, including the Central Highlands and much of the area north of Hanoi, is all but impenetrable.

Down south, the low-lying Mekong Delta is an unusual combination of water and land. This is largely a result of the region's namesake river, a mammoth waterway that begins in eastern Tibet and flows through several Southeast Asian nations before splintering into nine separate tributaries across the Vietnamese border. Moving along the coast, the shores east of Ho Chi Minh City bear an odd climate that lends itself to a coupling of tropical beaches and barren sand dunes. The country's interior is comprised of undulating mountains and lush jungle that extends all the way to the western border. Up north, the Red River Delta creates a similar effect to its southern counterpart, with an expanse of pancake-flat rice paddies around Hanoi extending toward the coast, punctuated only by limestone karsts, the same rocky outcroppings you'll see in Ha Long Bay and around Phong Nha-Ke Bang National Park, which rise unexpectedly out of these level landscapes. Along the northern border, the terrain becomes mountainous once again, rising and falling dramatically all the way from the East Sea west through Ha Giang and Lao Cai provinces to Laos. This region is also home to Vietnam's highest peak, Mount Fansipan (10,311 ft.).

CLIMATE

While the majority of Vietnam never really gets cold, the northern and southern halves of the country experience two very different weather patterns. Residents in Hanoi and the surrounding region see four seasons throughout the year, though they are not as distinct as North American seasons. Up north, a cold, damp winter and a sweltering hot summer are separated by a few months of mild weather on either side. Temperatures in this part of the country fluctuate from a brisk 50°F in January to 100°F in July and August. Pack warm clothes if you plan to visit in winter, as Hanoi does not have heaters and the bone-chilling humidity can be deceptive. In the extreme north, some areas along the border even experience snow, though this is never more than a light dusting on mountain peaks and rooftops.

In the southern and central regions, temperatures remain more consistent, varying

---

Previous: Phong Nha-Ke Bang National Park; paper lanterns, used to celebrate special occasions.

only a few degrees between the rainy and dry season. Rainy season begins when temperatures are highest, breaking the heat with heavy rainfall for a few hours each day. These rains remain consistent until the end of the season, at which time a constant downpour ushers in slightly cooler weather. Dry season still sees some precipitation, though significantly less, as well as lower temperatures and occasional winds, with the heat building over time until rainy season returns. Depending upon your location, these seasons come at different times of year, with the rains arriving in May down south and ending in late October, while the central region experiences rainy season from September to January. For southern Vietnam, temperatures usually change no more than a few degrees, holding steady around 90°F, with varying levels of humidity depending upon the season. While central Vietnam's climate is more similar to the south than the north, this region experiences a wider range of temperatures, from a cool 65°F to around 85°F in the summer, as well as more intense storms. Danang, central Vietnam's most cosmopolitan city, is also the country's easternmost point. As a result, the surrounding area experiences yearly typhoons, which bring heavy rainfall and high winds, which have been known to destroy homes and farmland near the coast.

ENVIRONMENTAL ISSUES

Vietnam has a poor track record on both conservation and clean-up efforts. A handful of NGOs and other independent organizations do their part to help protect the country's natural resources. Despite enacting laws to safeguard its forests and waterways, environmental regulations are only sometimes enforced to protect the country's natural resources, leading to issues such as water shortages and deforestation. In the Central Highlands in particular, scores of hydropower plants have been constructed, harnessing the strength of the region's rivers for economic benefit, but the dams that come with these

Vietnam's northwestern region is awash with soaring mountains and verdant river valleys.

facilities often dry up riverbeds below, eliminating a valuable water source for downstream communities.

Along the coast, specifically in urban areas, pollution is a growing problem. Though Vietnamese cities are not as bad as some of their East Asian counterparts, rapid industrialization and expanding metropolitan areas are cause for future concern as nearby suburbs are devoured by modern development and increased pollution from traffic and factories leaves air quality diminished.

While none of the urban rivers, canals, or lakes you see may look like a nice place for a swim, officials in cities like HCMC and Hanoi have done a tremendous amount of work to rehabilitate these heavily polluted waterways. Garbage collection takes place on a daily basis and younger generations are more conscious of how their individual actions can affect Vietnam's urban pollution.

Beyond these issues, the country's greatest challenge is bringing attention to the value of its natural resources and encouraging its citizens to clean up. More than a few breath-taking landscapes in Vietnam are clouded by reckless littering. While urban centers employ hundreds of street cleaners to remedy this, rural areas and smaller towns are often left to languish in their own garbage, and there is a general expectation that someone else will clean up a person's litter.

Plants and Animals

Stretching over 2,000 miles along the East Sea, Vietnam is home to countless varieties of flora and fauna. From the peaks of Sapa all the way down to the watery Mekong Delta, the country's range of climates and habitats lends itself to an equally diverse array of plant and wildlife. However, with an ever-growing population and a rapid pace of development, many of Vietnam's plant and animal species are in danger. Deforestation and the overuse of natural resources threaten to erase natural habitats, while several species, some of which are unique to Vietnam, have become critically endangered in recent years due to the illegal wildlife trade. High demand for animal parts, such as rhino horn, has forced a handful of primates, turtles, and other creatures onto the IUCN Red List, which documents the world's most endangered flora and fauna.

While Vietnam boasts 30 protected national parks and nature reserves across the country, not all are strictly supervised. Authorities have stepped up their punishment of poachers in recent years, but the wildlife trade continues to be a problem in Vietnam. In 2011, WWF confirmed that the country's small population of Javan rhino, an extremely rare animal, was officially extinct after the last of its kind was likely killed by poachers. Additionally, nearly one-third of the country's protected lands occur in and around the Mekong Delta, a region already straining under high population density. While the forests and jungles of Vietnam contain countless fascinating creatures, the country still has a ways to go in protecting its natural resources and bringing the 77 species of flora and fauna currently listed as critically endangered on IUCN's Red List back to a healthy number.

The national flower of Vietnam is the lotus.

FLORA

According to the World Bank's World Development Indicators, a staggering 45 percent of Vietnam's land area is covered by forest. These woodlands can be broken down into several categories, from the dry lowland forests of southern Vietnam, largely made up of tropical hardwood, to the flooded forests of mangroves and cajuput trees in that same region. Highland forests cover the northern region under a dense canopy of broad-leaved trees and moss. Inland, cooler climates like that of Lang Biang Plateau, are home to pine forests, which coexist alongside groves of bamboo. Fruit trees are common in the Mekong Delta, with jackfruit, durian, longans, rambutans, and papayas aplenty. Commercially prized woods like teak, rosewood, and ebony are raised here, as is bamboo. Rattan, an extremely durable wood used in basket-weaving, particularly by the minority communities of the north, is also prevalent.

FAUNA

A growing number of people flock to the country's seaside areas, pushing many animals out of their natural habitats. In a region with many endemic species, Vietnam's fauna holds its own array of endangered creatures. Larger species like the Indochinese tiger, moon bear, and Asian elephant often take center stage thanks to their size and prominence around the world, but Vietnam is also home to a host of native species that are found only within its borders. Even today, scientists continue to discover rare creatures, like the thorny tree frog, an amphibian that lives only among the highest peaks of Vietnam in its remote northern region, and as late as the 1990s, large mammals were still being found in the dense forests of central and northern Vietnam. The most elusive of these is the saola, an ox-like creature with long horns that is sometimes called the Asian unicorn due to its rarity.

Chances are you won't get a glimpse of Vietnam's more exotic animals during your visit. Travelers are more likely to encounter domestic creatures during their trip: chickens are common even in urban centers like Ho Chi Minh City, where they are sometimes kept as pets; pigs and water buffalo are abundant in the countryside.

Those eager to see Vietnam's more exotic creatures, particularly its many varieties of primates, are encouraged to view these animals in the wild rather than at a zoo or tourist attraction, as the creatures in these centers tend to be mistreated and sometimes aggressive. The majority of Vietnam's wildlife lives in national parks and nature reserves. National parks in Con Dao and Cat Ba have wild populations of different primates, including macaques, langurs, and gibbons, while both Cuc Phuong National Park and the Cu Chi Wildlife Rescue Center rehabilitate endangered primates, turtles, and other animals captured in the wildlife trade, providing a closer look at these creatures in an environment where they are safe and well looked after.

Mammals

While, in name, Vietnam continues to boast incredible biodiversity, today many of its mammal species exist only in protected wildlife areas. Fast-paced development and growing populations have encroached upon the natural habitats of many species, including the country's array of primate species. Macaques are far and away the most common and can be found in national parks and nature reserves from north to south. Endemic species like the Cat Ba, Ha Tinh, and douc langurs, also found in government-protected forests, are trickier to spot given their smaller numbers. Still, there's a chance you might catch a glimpse of these creatures in their respective habitats. Beyond primates, Vietnam's mammals include Asiatic black bears, banteng, gaur, deer, pangolins, and dugongs.

Reptiles and Amphibians

Reptiles are one of Vietnam's more visible categories of fauna, and you're likely to spot a few geckos on the walls, even in urban areas. Several species of turtle, a revered animal in Vietnamese lore, exist throughout the country, from the massive Yangtze softshell turtle, sole resident of Hoan Kiem Lake, to several smaller varieties, such as the Chinese three-striped box turtle and the Indochinese box turtle, both of which appear on Vietnam's endangered species list. While the future of these animals is precarious, new species are still being discovered in some of Vietnam's more remote areas. As recently as last year, scientists came upon a previously unknown variety of tree frog living in the mountainous northern reaches of the country, at an elevation of 5,900 feet and above. Along the coast, snakes are equally elusive thanks to the country's growing population. There are over 200 different varieties of snakes in Vietnam, including 60 venomous species, many of which appear in the wilder interior regions.

Birds

Vietnam's wealth of feathered friends are a birder's dream. Over 850 different varieties of bird live within the country's borders, including the highest number of endemic species in mainland Southeast Asia. The rarest of these is the Edwards' pheasant, among the most endangered species in the world. There are also several varieties of laughingthrush that are endangered. Southern Vietnam, namely the Mekong Delta, is a prime location to catch a glimpse of the country's array of bird species. With endless flooded fields and high trees, sanctuaries such as Tra Su and Tram Chim National Park, home to the sarus crane, the world's largest flying bird, afford travelers a rare glimpse of local wildlife in its natural habitat.

History

From the earliest days of the Dong Son to a thousand-year occupation by the Chinese, centuries of dynastic rule, French colonialism, the rise of Communist revolutionaries, and a tragic war that captured the attention of the world, Vietnam's history has been one of struggle and resilience. The 20th century alone included wars against France, the United States, Cambodia, and China. As a result, nationalism runs deep in Vietnam. Regardless of age, gender, religion, or political opinion, Vietnamese take great pride in their cultural identity and in their perseverance against foreign invaders.

After years of post-war poverty followed by an incredible economic boom, Vietnam has transformed from a small, war-stricken nation into one of Southeast Asia's most promising economies in little more than a few decades. As the country continues to prosper, the government struggles to reconcile its values with the rampant capitalism of Vietnam's urban centers. For the moment, most citizens are happy to ignore politics, provided the opportunities to advance their social and financial standing remain.

ANCIENT CIVILIZATION

While most Western accounts of Vietnamese history tend to focus on more recent events, the earliest inhabitants of the S-shaped country arrived several thousand years ago. In the Mekong Delta, an ancient civilization known as Funan existed from around AD 100 up until the 6th century. The south-central coast was once occupied by Champa, a matriarchal Hindu civilization now remembered for its famous red-brick architecture. From the 2nd century AD to as late as the mid-1600s, the Cham held an ever-decreasing foothold in the region, farming rice, making pottery, trading with other civilizations, and often engaging in armed conflicts with their neighbors, a fact that led to their eventual demise at the hands of the Vietnamese.

The Trung Sisters

Two of Vietnam's most celebrated figures, the Trung sisters were a pair of aristocratic women born in Giao Chi, as the country was then called, in the early AD years. Like many at the time, Trung Trac and Trung Nhi opposed Chinese rule, but it wasn't until the husband of the elder sister, a Vietnamese nobleman named Thi Sach, was put to death by Giao Chi's Chinese ruler that the women took action.

In order to avenge Thi Sach's death, the Trung sisters launched a rebellion that unified anti-colonialists against the Giao Chi administration, driving its Chinese ruler out of Vietnam in AD 39. Trung Trac became the nation's queen, her sister a high-ranking second, and the pair briefly held sovereignty over the kingdom until the Chinese returned in AD 42, armed to the teeth and with enough warriors to defeat their enemy. When it became clear that the fight was over and defeat inevitable for the Vietnamese, the sisters jumped into a river and committed suicide. To this day, their name, Hai Ba Trung, appears on street signs across the country and they are revered as an example of fierce nationalism and powerful Vietnamese women.

Today's Vietnamese originated in the Red River Delta where, as far back as the first millennium BC, a highly evolved culture known as the Dong Son ran a thriving trade port, developed a complex irrigation system for rice farming, and is now remembered for its intricately patterned bronze drums. Hung Vuong, the first ruler of the Vietnamese people, is believed to have been a Dong Son ruler, though it is difficult to discern exactly when he lived, as the true origins of the Vietnamese people are intertwined with mythology. This dynasty reigned over northern Vietnam and parts of southern China for 18 generations before the throne was usurped by An Duong Vuong in the 3rd century BC.

ONE THOUSAND YEARS UNDER THE CHINESE

In 208 BC, the Chinese invaded northern Vietnam, marking the start of a thousand-year occupation that would deeply influence Vietnamese traditions and culture. At first, the Han dynasty was lax, allowing its colony to function in much the way it always had. But, once the Chinese began to impose high taxes and force the Vietnamese to adopt their traditions and style of dress, resentment flourished among the general population. Across the northern reaches of the country, rebellions were routinely suppressed. The most famous of these, an AD 39 insurrection led by the Trung sisters, drove the Chinese out of Vietnam for just over two years before the northern power returned to reclaim its colony. Following this semi-successful revolt, the Han dynasty gave up all pleasantries, removing Vietnamese lords from power and permitting local aristocrats to occupy only the lowest rungs of the political ladder.

Eventually, after centuries of rule, things began to come undone in China. Growing unrest along the border made it difficult for the northern empire to keep their colony in check. In the far north, minority hill tribes rebelled against Chinese rule, while several Vietnamese aristocrats began claiming a right to the throne. Ultimately, the Tang dynasty fell in China in 907, creating a weakened empire, and Vietnamese general Ngo Quyen swooped in to take independence for his country.

AN INDEPENDENT VIETNAM

Despite Ngo Quyen's victory over the Chinese, his own reign was brief. In less than three decades, the emperor was overthrown. A handful of other short-lived rulers took his place, but it wasn't until the Ly dynasty that the kingdom was able to grow. In 1075, royal officials in Vietnam wrote examinations for the first time, following in the footsteps of the Chinese empire. By 1089, the practice was required, creating a fixed hierarchy of public officials. At the same time, the Ly dynasty adopted Buddhism as its royal religion, which in turn encouraged Vietnamese subjects to convert.

Southward expansion also began, with the Dai Viet marching out to conquer the Cham kingdom of Vijaya in 1079. An arranged marriage in 1225 ended the Ly dynasty, transferring power from its last remaining princess to the Tran family, who carried on a similar tradition of success. During this time, Kublai Khan and his Mongol army began to eye northern Vietnam, thrice attempting to take over the empire. One of the Tran dynasty's most famous heroes is Tran Hung Dao, the celebrated general who thwarted the Mongols' final attempt at Bach Dang River by impaling his enemy's ships with wooden spikes during low tide.

Following the defeat of the Mongols, the Tran dynasty entered a steady decline. They managed to get in a few more victories over the Cham before a power shift came in 1400, when General Ho Quy Ly overthrew the king and claimed Dai Viet for himself. General Ho's policies proved unfavorable and local landowners appealed to the Chinese for help. China's Ming dynasty promptly returned and reasserted its authority in 1407. This second occupation lasted roughly two decades, with the Chinese exerting their unrestrained power over the Dai Viet. All local customs and traditions were banned, citizens were required to wear Chinese dress, and a particularly harsh forced labor policy came into effect, all of which had a significant impact on local culture for years to come. In 1428, colonization ended thanks to Le Loi, a scholar who had rejected the Ming dynasty's rule and amassed an army to defeat the Chinese. In an attempt to remain civil, he provided the losers with ships and supplies to sail home rather than putting them to death.

THE NGUYENS AND TRINHS

Throughout the 15th century, Vietnam's Le dynasty continued to move south, conquering any kingdom that stood in their way. However, as Vietnam's territory expanded, its rulers struggled to maintain control over the newer settlements, which were far-removed from the capital. When a high-ranking official usurped the throne in 1527, two aristocratic families, the Trinh and Nguyen lords, backed the Le dynasty in hopes of sharing their power once the kingdom had been retaken. After 1545, Vietnam found itself divided: the Nguyens controlled the southern half of the country, while the Trinhs took charge of the north.

During this time, European missionaries began to appear in Vietnam, hoping to convert the local population. One of the most famous was French priest Alexandre de Rhodes, who arrived in Indochina in 1619, picked up the local language, and promptly began espousing the benefits of Catholicism to the Vietnamese. By the time he was kicked out of the country in 1630, de Rhodes had converted over 6,000 Vietnamese. He is also credited with the development of the Romanized *quoc ngu* script used by the Vietnamese today.

Down south, the Nguyens ran an agricultural society, keeping uneducated peasants at bay, while the northern Trinh emphasized education and intellectual development. Neither gained a strong following among the masses, as ongoing war, natural disasters, and taxes left the general population frustrated and disillusioned. Rebellions were common, though they were often small and concentrated to a single area, making it easy for both ruling families to silence their opponents. That is until a trio of brothers from Tay Son appeared on the scene.

TAY SON REBELLION

Nguyen Hue, Nguyen Nhac, and Nguyen Lu were three brothers from central Binh Dinh province whose ancestry actually traced back to the short-lived reign of General Ho Quy Ly in 1400. Like many subjects at the time, the brothers were thoroughly displeased with the Nguyen Lords and unimpressed by imperial bureaucracy in general. Initially siding with the Trinhs of the north, the brothers launched a revolt in 1771, intending to overthrow the Nguyen Lords on their own. By the following year, they had successfully taken Binh Dinh and Quang Nam provinces and, with growing support, managed to extend the takeover to all of southern Vietnam by 1778. Operating on a Robin Hood-style mantra, the brothers nixed taxes, set prisoners free, and gave out food to the peasant population. Their progressive policies later moved north, turning on the Trinh Lords and once again fending off the Chinese to rule the entire country, with each brother presiding over a region of Vietnam.

In defeating the southern rulers, the Tay Son rebellion had failed to kill all heirs to the throne: Prince Nguyen Anh, the only remaining Nguyen Lord, fled to Gia Dinh, now known as Ho Chi Minh City, and sought the assistance of Pigneau de Behaine, a French bishop. Shortly thereafter, Pigneau de Behaine sailed to Pondicherry in French India and, later, back to Europe to request the aid of the French king in restoring Nguyen Anh to the throne. Louis XVI agreed, so long as Vietnam would offer up the port of Danang and the Con Dao islands, then known as Poulo Condore, in exchange. But, upon Pigneau de Behaine's return to Pondicherry, the French delegates refused to help. The bishop raised his own funds to hire ships and soldiers, returning to Vietnam in 1789 with enough ammunition to wipe out the Tay Son rebels by 1801, creating a unified Vietnam for the first time in 200 years.

Under newly crowned emperor Gia Long, the country returned to a more conservative imperial rule, with the king undoing many policies enacted by the Nguyen brothers in order to assert his authority. Opposition was strictly punished and many of the previously erased taxes returned. Though there was occasional dissent, it wasn't until the death of emperor Gia Long that France's intention to invade solidified. Gia Long's son Minh Mang, an austere ruler and staunch believer in Confucianism, expelled all European missionaries from Vietnam and set about killing Vietnamese Catholics and any missionaries caught preaching the Bible.

FRENCH COLONIALISM

Convinced that invasion was the best course of action, the French stormed the shores of Danang in 1858, advancing south to take Gia Dinh the following year. Armed with a religious cause—to protect its missionaries—the French had hoped that Vietnamese Catholics would rush to their aid, but no one appeared. Instead, it became clear that the motives for this invasion had nothing to do with Catholicism and everything to do with business and military might. Over the next decade or so, the French managed to acquire all of Vietnam's territory, wresting power from then-emperor Tu Duc by 1874, though the country's colonization wasn't official until 1883.

The Vietnamese were caught between two evils: the French were unpopular for having taken the country by force, but the poor government of emperor Tu Duc and his failure to protect the people from harm had lost him a great deal of public support. In the beginning, some were open to the idea of a new governmental system. But, as it became clear that economic exploitation was part of the plan, the French fell out of favor. Under colonial rule, most Vietnamese were overtaxed, overworked, and abused. While rice exports soared in the colonists' new open economy, all profits went to the European power. Many high-ranking Vietnamese scholars and officials refused to play a part in the colonial government for this reason.

By the turn of the 20th century, dissent sparked rebellions across the country. As World War I raged in Europe, Vietnamese troops were sent abroad in the name of France. Shortly thereafter, Ho Chi Minh arrived in Guangzhou, China, where he founded the Revolutionary Youth League in 1925, attempting to wrangle all of Vietnam's disparate

A statue commemorates the victory over French forces at Dien Bien Phu.

consequences. Japan didn't wait for a response and wrested the country from European hands that same month, claiming it a free state under Japanese occupation. But while their Asian neighbors had removed authority from the Europeans, Vietnam recognized Japan's increasingly dire circumstances on the world stage and prepared to swoop into the anticipated power vacuum that would occur when they left. Sure enough, when Japan retreated from Vietnam in 1945, the Viet Minh launched its now-famous August Revolution across the country, stepping into power for the first time, just as Bao Dai, Vietnam's last emperor, relinquished his crown. Ho Chi Minh declared independence on September 2, 1945, in Hanoi.

FRANCO-VIETNAM WAR

The French refused to go quietly. Though Ho Chi Minh's declaration was met with an overwhelmingly positive response, the Europeans returned to Vietnam after World War II in hopes of regaining their colonial foothold. By 1946, it was clear that there would not be a peaceful resolution and both sides prepared for war. Over nine years, the French and the Viet Minh duked it out across the country, the former well-armed, the latter boasting heavy manpower. Though France had many Vietnamese cities within its grasp, the countryside belonged to the Viet Minh, who set up training camps and recruitment centers within its territory. After the People's Republic of China was officially established in 1949, the Viet Minh were able to source weapons from the north, a move which gave them the upper hand. As Vietnamese forces took back northern Vietnam, opening up supply lines and enabling them to attack the Red River Delta, the French began to lose heart.

Still, by the end of 1953, colonial forces took Dien Bien Phu, a far-off town in the mountainous northwest, hoping to turn the tide of war by interfering with their enemy's access to supplies. Instead, this was the move that sealed their fate. In March 1954, two months before diplomatic talks were set

Communist and anti-French parties together. A 1930 conference solidified the main aims of the resistance from abroad, while, in Vietnam, the people of Nghe An and Ha Tinh provinces rioted against colonial rule. As a response, the French bombed the area and sent many of its citizens to jail.

WORLD WAR II

Toward the end of the 1930s, trouble was brewing in Europe on the eve of World War II, and dissent in its Southeast Asian colonies had France on edge. In 1941, Ho Chi Minh returned to Vietnam after 30 years abroad and was welcomed with open arms. When France fell to the Nazis in 1940 and Japanese troops arrived in Vietnam, demanding safe passage of their military and weapons through the country, Ho Chi Minh's now-famous resistance army, the Viet Minh, took note of the colonial government's weakness.

By March 1945, Uncle Ho felt confident enough that he offered the French an ultimatum: relinquish power or face the to begin in Geneva, the Viet Minh laid siege to Dien Bien Phu, bringing in ample artillery and over 100,000 troops to cut off all access to the outside world. By the time the Geneva talks began on May 8, France had surrendered and Ho Chi Minh's army was victorious.

In the resulting accords, which were signed by both Vietnam's Communist government and France, the country was divided in half at the 17th parallel with the promise of reuniting both sides in a 1956 election. While this agreement brought temporary peace and the exodus of Vietnam's colonizers, few—if any—of the parties present during the Geneva talks actually believed that Vietnam would be reunited so seamlessly.

With northern Vietnam now staunchly Communist and the southern Republic of Vietnam in limbo, the United States began to take a vested interest in the country's political situation. Hoping to keep the Communists out of power, they backed Ngo Dinh Diem, a Vietnamese Catholic with little political experience. Over the next two years, Diem exercised strict control over religious groups in the Mekong Delta and quashed any dissent in Saigon. By 1955, Diem openly rejected the elections meant to reunify Vietnam and instead held his own rigged referendum, winning the presidency by a landslide.

Using his own family and connections, Diem fashioned himself a cabinet of leaders and began to rule, making little effort to win over public support. As the 1950s drew to a close, the southern government had become so careless with its power that many of the Communists who had opted to go north after the Geneva Accords returned in order to stage attacks against Diem's government. In the city, regular protests took place. Diem attempted to resettle all south Vietnamese into what he termed "strategic hamlets," an effort to separate average civilians from the NLF rebels fighting against him. These villages turned out to be a breeding ground for NLF converts, as south Vietnamese did not take kindly to leaving their homes and rebel fighters were able to tunnel beneath the hamlets, establishing access to this increasingly disgruntled population.

VIETNAM WAR

By 1963, tensions in south Vietnam had reached a fever pitch: across Saigon, civilians routinely demonstrated against Diem's corrupt government. For his part, the president showed no interest in appeasing his public and carried on in the same disconnected fashion. When the Venerable Thich Quang Duc, senior monk of a Saigonese pagoda, lit himself on fire in the middle of a downtown intersection one morning in June, photos of the scene were splashed across front pages worldwide. In the face of an international outcry, Diem and his cronies remained flippant. Madame Nhu, the wife of Diem's brother and a powerful behind-the-scenes player, famously referred to the event as a "barbecue." However, the military arm of Diem's government saw the writing on the wall and discreetly approached the U.S. government in order to gauge their receptiveness to a coup. They were hardly met with resistance.

By November, the generals of south Vietnam realized their plan, assassinating Diem and his brother, Nhu. The Americans remained neutral on the subject and, less than a month later, President John F. Kennedy met the same fate, shaking up the stability of the American-backed south once more. Newly installed President Johnson took a different approach to his predecessor, sending increased military aid to Vietnam. In 1964, north Vietnamese forces exchanged fire with an American naval ship, prompting the Gulf of Tonkin Resolution, which granted President Johnson the power to take "necessary measures" against the Vietnamese Communists. Air strikes were ordered against the north, but American planes alone could not keep the enemy from advancing. Eventually, ground troops began to pour into Vietnam, their numbers swelling to 485,000 by the end of 1967. Defoliants like Agent Orange were used to destroy the dense jungles where NLF and north Vietnamese forces hid, and heavy

Long Hung Church, site of one of the bloodiest battles of the Vietnam War

bombing ravaged the countryside. Americans at home, meanwhile, began to express their growing disapproval of the war, questioning the role of U.S. troops in the conflict and the increasing civilian casualties.

The 1968 Tet Offensive proved a turning point for the conflict. On January 31, the eve of the country's biggest holiday, north Vietnamese and NLF forces launched a coordinated attack. Five major cities, 36 provincial capitals, 64 district capitals, and over two dozen airfields were targeted and some taken over by Communist forces. Though U.S. soldiers ultimately regained the territory lost during these attacks, the event did major damage to public sentiment at home, where Americans were being told that victory was imminent. Instead, footage of the Tet battles broadcast on news channels around the world showed a far more dire situation.

In 1969, with troop numbers already exceeding 500,000, President Nixon began to withdraw American soldiers from Vietnam, a move that was met with approval at home but only worsened the low morale of troops left behind. The new president pushed for "Vietnamization," handing over control to south Vietnamese forces. Peace talks were arranged in Paris. But, by 1971, little progress had been made. Meanwhile, news of the My Lai massacre, in which U.S. troops killed hundreds of unarmed Vietnamese in Quang Ngai province, was made public, as were Nixon's secret bombings of Communist bases in Cambodia, both of which fueled public outrage in the United States. Over the next two years, the United States and north Vietnam's Communist government went back and forth at the negotiating table, using military attacks to encourage their adversaries to bargain. On January 27, 1973, the Agreement on Ending the War and Restoring Peace in Vietnam was signed by north Vietnam, south Vietnam, and the United States and a cease-fire went into effect the following day.

By the end of March, the last American military units left Vietnam. Over the next two years, the country continued to suffer casualties as an ineffective south Vietnamese government aimed to win over civilians while its military, with a soaring number of deserters and the NLF hot on their heels, rapidly came undone. The following year, north Vietnamese forces made a push to reclaim the areas they had lost. On April 30, 1975, north Vietnamese tanks crashed through the gates of Saigon's Independence Palace, marking the end of the 30-year conflict.

AFTER 1975

At peace for the first time in 30 years, Vietnam's Communist government found itself faced with a new challenge: how to take a ravaged, war-stricken nation and bring it out of poverty. Still reeling from the aftereffects of war and deeply paranoid about the possibility of any more foreign invaders, the country closed itself off from the world. This proved to be a justifiable concern, as brief border skirmishes with China and a two-year war with Cambodia followed; both conflicts were resolved by the end of 1979. Meanwhile,

South Vietnam supporters were sent to study sessions and re-education camps, essentially hard labor outfits, in order to restructure southern society to match the wishes of the northern government. Surveillance was heavy throughout the country, as the new government worked hard to squash any and all dissent. A central economy, built on austerity, steered people forward over the next decade or so, but it soon became clear that this government-run system was doing nothing to bring the average Vietnamese out of abject poverty.

For this reason, the government instituted *doi moi* in the mid-1980s, a series of economic reforms which eventually transitioned Vietnam to a market economy. As 1990 approached, the country began to open itself up again to the world. These reforms became the saving grace of Vietnam: in just two decades, *doi moi* took Vietnam's poverty rate from 60 percent of the population to 17 percent.

Government and Economy

ORGANIZATION

The Socialist Republic of Vietnam is a one-party Communist state. Its legislative body, the National Assembly, consists of 500 representatives who meet twice a year and are elected for five-year terms by popular vote. This organization has the power to both make and amend the country's laws, as well as its constitution, and is responsible for voting in the government's highest officials, including the president and prime minister. Both of these offices belong to the Politburo (executive branch) and are among the highest positions of power in the country. In addition to the president, the highest office in Vietnam, and the prime minister he appoints, several other ministers are proposed by the prime minister for specific areas such as finance, education and training, foreign affairs and public security, and later approved by the National Assembly, rounding out the rest of the high-ranking cabinet. Both the president and the prime minister can serve up to two terms.

ELECTIONS

Elections for National Assembly delegates are held once every five years. This is the only governmental body to be selected by popular vote, but due to the fact that Vietnam is a one-party state, there is little difference from one candidate to another. Still, these elected officials—Party members who have been chosen for the public to select—are responsible for voting in a president, who later has the power to select a prime minister.

ECONOMY

While Vietnam's economy took a rocky turn after the American War, stifled by strict centralized policies, the *doi moi* economic reforms of the mid-1980s opened the country up to international trade and industrial development. Once a solely agricultural society, industry has made its way into the country, with plenty of foreign enterprises setting up offices in major cities, particularly Ho Chi Minh City. Though growth has slowed somewhat in recent years the country continues to make economic gains, albeit at a slower rate.

Today, much of Vietnam's wealth is concentrated in urban areas along the coast. The majority of Vietnam's middle class lives here, where greater work and educational opportunities are available. Rural areas remain at a disadvantage. Family members who move away from the countryside or overseas often remit part of their salary back to these rural communities as financial assistance—Vietnam is one of the top-10 remittance-receiving nations in the world. As economic growth slows in Vietnam, its poorest citizens remain in very remote areas where infrastructure is weak and access to education, job opportunities, and even basic necessities is limited. In the mountainous northern and interior regions, this lack of infrastructure and opportunity tends to affect minority communities more heavily than their ethnic Vietnamese counterparts. Meanwhile, a select group of urban Vietnamese are considered ultra-wealthy, boasting a net worth of USD$30 million or more, highlighting the country's growing income disparity.

People and Culture

DEMOGRAPHY

Though Vietnam is composed of 54 separate ethnic groups, the Kinh (ethnic Vietnamese) make up an overwhelming 87 percent of the population, which is now estimated to hover somewhere between 88 and 90 million. Thanks to this rapid growth, a two-child rule is loosely in effect throughout Vietnam; while it is seldom enforced, you'll see signs across the country encouraging families to stop at two babies. Vietnam is an incredibly literate society, with over 90 percent of the country able to read and write.

The majority of Vietnam's population lives on or near the coast, leaving the more remote mountain areas for the country's ethnic minorities, once known to the French as *montagnards,* an array of small, tight-knit groups that still lead traditional farming lives and practice many of the same customs as their ancestors. In the Mekong Delta, a healthy Khmer community lives among the region's Kinh farmers, practicing their own brand of Buddhism, as do small, isolated groups of Islamic Cham. The mountainous areas of the Central Highlands are inhabited by the Gia Rai, E De, and Churu, while the soaring peaks around Sapa and the rest of the northwest are home to the Dao, Giay, Thai, and H'mong people, each with their own language, culture, and traditions. While these are some of the most diverse areas in the country, they are also the least developed and, in many cases, the poorest.

RELIGION

Vietnam is a largely Mahayana Buddhist country, with most people paying a visit to the local pagoda every few weeks. The country's religious beliefs are deeply influenced by Chinese beliefs, with traces of Taoism and Confucianism. Thanks to its former European ties, a strong Catholic following also exists, though their numbers are nowhere near as great as the Buddhist community. Several smaller, homegrown religions were invented in the 20th century in the Mekong Delta area, including Caodaism, a syncretic faith in which Victor Hugo and Elvis are considered saints, and Hoa Hao, which amassed a large following in the mid-1900s but later faded out after its military involvement in the Franco-Vietnam War.

Vietnamese culture includes a strong spiritual aspect, and most locals believe in worshipping their ancestors. In addition to the many pagodas and Catholic churches throughout the country, the vibrant Caodaist temples, and even a small collection of local mosques, Vietnam boasts several temples in honor of national heroes and those considered collective ancestors of the Vietnamese people.

LANGUAGE

Vietnamese is the nation's official language and features a mind-boggling six tones and 11 vowel sounds. Though it was originally written in a modified version of Chinese characters, known as *chu nom,* European missionary Alexandre de Rhodes developed a Roman script for the language that is now used throughout the country, making Vietnam one of the only nations in mainland Southeast Asia to use a Roman alphabet. Throughout Vietnam, three major regional dialects are

Death Rituals

Vietnam's approach to death is different than that of the Western world. Regardless of religion, Vietnamese believe in ancestor worship. These include grandparents as well as collective national ancestors like Ho Chi Minh or Tran Hung Dao. When a Vietnamese person passes away, it is believed that one's life does not end but that the afterlife begins. The afterlife requires basic necessities, such as food, clothing, and money, all of which a family must provide for its deceased loved ones. In most homes, shops, and businesses, you'll find a small altar where local residents put food, beverages, and occasionally cigarettes for the dead. These offerings are often accompanied by prayers and incense. On holidays and certain Buddhist festivals, Vietnamese burn paper money and clothing for their ancestors to use in the afterlife. While it's bad luck for the living to keep these items, you'll likely spot stray hundred dollar bills on the sidewalk or in the streets. Though they're flimsier than the actual currency, these paper notes are surprisingly accurate—until you turn them over to find the phrase "Bank of the Dead" instead of "In God We Trust."

Beyond these ongoing rituals, Vietnamese funerals are a multi-day affair meant to usher a loved one into the afterlife. When a Vietnamese person dies, his or her family will mourn for several days, inviting friends and family as well as a religious leader to say goodbye. Mourners often wear white

---

spoken, with the northern Hanoian dialect considered the most authentic Vietnamese thanks to its short, succinct tonal pronunciation. The southern and central regions of the country also have their own respective dialects: You'll find a slower, more fluid accent in Ho Chi Minh City and the Mekong Delta, while central Vietnam is known for its creative pronunciation and a slew of unique regional vocabulary. Among Vietnamese, the central accent is considered the most difficult to understand, with many native speakers straining to converse with those from cities like Hue or Hoi An.

Beyond Vietnamese, an array of languages are spoken among the country's ethnic minorities in their respective homelands. These languages are rarely heard on the coast, and all public transactions are conducted in Vietnamese. Ethnic minority citizens must learn Vietnamese as a second language in order to participate fully in society.

The Arts

VISUAL ARTS

Vietnamese visual art draws upon an interesting variety of mediums and influences, thanks to its past relationships with China and France. Particularly over the last century, traditional handicrafts like lacquer painting and enamel have been combined with both Asian and European ideas to create uniquely Vietnamese artwork. While many of the masterpieces displayed in forums like the local fine arts museum are prime examples of traditional Vietnamese artwork, both Hanoi and Saigon have growing art scenes and plenty of up-and-coming artists whose work is shared in local cafés and smaller galleries.

MUSIC

Traditional Vietnamese music is often closely linked with theatrical performance: *cheo*, a centuries-old satirical form of theater, uses music to communicate its messages, as does *cai luong*, a similarly operatic form of music from the south that had its heyday during the 20th century. For most locals today, famous revolutionary composers such as Trinh Cong Son, one of Vietnam's most prolific songwriters, and Pham Duy

headbands. The funeral, held at home, usually includes a large tent set up in front of the building for guests to visit. An altar, complete with offerings and portrait of the deceased, is set up inside. At the end of the mourning period, the body is placed in a coffin and carried to its final resting place in a large, truck-like hearse, usually decorated with colorful symbols; some Vietnamese are cremated. This final procession begins before sunrise, sometimes as early as 4am or 5am, and often involves music. Don't be surprised if you wake up in the wee hours of the morning to trumpets and crashing cymbals—this is simply someone on their way to the afterlife.

Once the funeral is complete, Vietnamese carry on providing the essentials for their ancestors through offerings. The day of a person's death, rather than his or her birth, is remembered and celebrated as a holiday. This occasion, called *dam gio,* is a family event, in which members of that particular house come together and give offerings to their deceased relative, visit with family and friends, and often make trips to the local pagoda or church to commemorate the individual. Contrary to Western ideas of death, *dam gio* is not a somber occasion but rather a celebration of that individual and his or her life.

remain a favorite among many Vietnamese, both old and young. Their songs are regular fixtures during karaoke sessions.

Beyond traditional music, the younger generation is following its Asian neighbors, eager to develop a V-Pop phenomenon similar to Japan or Korea, with plenty of doe-eyed young songstresses and flashy music videos making the rounds on the Internet, though Korean pop stars still tend to be favored over local artists. Music-related television shows like *Vietnam Idol* and *The Voice of Vietnam,* knock-offs of their American counterparts, are also popular, as is the famed program *Paris By Night,* a much-loved musical revue filmed in France, Canada, and the United States that is technically banned by the Vietnamese government but still enjoys widespread popularity both in the country and among the Vietnamese diaspora.

Essentials

Getting There

FROM NORTH AMERICA

Travelers may enter Vietnam by air through its three largest airports: **Tan Son Nhat International Airport** (SGN) in Ho Chi Minh City; **Noi Bai International Airport** (HAN) in Hanoi; and **Danang International Airport** (DAD) in Danang. From there, plenty of smaller regional airports serve the more remote areas of Vietnam.

The most expensive part of your trip to Vietnam will be the plane ticket. Even bargain fares across the Pacific are not cheap. Still, there are a couple of strategies to make your airfare as affordable as possible. Websites like **Kayak** (www.kayak.com), **Sky Scanner** (www.skyscanner.com), and **Expedia** (www.expedia.com) offer travelers a comprehensive range of airlines. When booking through these sites, monitor airfare prices 6-8 weeks in advance. While prices may fluctuate to some degree, USD$100-200 either way, round-trip tickets hover at about USD$1,000. Those leaving from the West Coast of the United States will find slightly cheaper fares; East Coasters and anyone traveling from the middle of the continental United States should expect four-figure prices.

It is sometimes possible to save money by flying into Los Angeles International Airport (LAX) with a budget airline and then heading for Asia from there. When traveling to Vietnam, most routes pass over the Pacific, connecting to Ho Chi Minh City or Hanoi in major hubs like Seoul, Hong Kong, Tokyo, or Taipei. A few airlines go the opposite direction, passing through Europe and the Middle East.

While dirt-cheap fares are offered by carriers like China Eastern and China Southern, these companies are not known for their service or safety ratings. Carriers like EVA, Japan Air, Emirates, Cathay Pacific, United, Singapore Airlines, and Qatar Airlines all serve Vietnam's major airports and, for a few extra dollars, are reliable, professional, and usually more comfortable (particularly important for a 14-hour flight).

FROM NEIGHBORING COUNTRIES

Vietnam shares several foreigner-friendly overland border crossings with its neighbors: five with Cambodia, six with Laos, and three with China. These crossings are fairly straightforward but, like any point of entry into Vietnam, you are required to obtain a valid visa prior to arrival. With the exception of e-visa processing, which is only available at the country's three largest airports, no crossing in Vietnam will supply you with a visa at the border gate. Regularly scheduled buses pass through the country's frontier areas on a daily basis and often provide service to major cities in neighboring countries. There are no international railways linking Vietnam to its neighbors.

Several budget airlines fly to and from Vietnam. Direct flights depart from major regional airports in Bangkok, Kuala Lumpur, and Singapore, while connecting flights go through the aforementioned hubs to and from dozens of destinations within Southeast Asia. Airfare from neighboring countries is usually reasonable. But tickets from destinations like Laos and Cambodia are often more expensive on account of their size relative to some of Southeast Asia's larger hubs.

DISCOUNT TICKETS

Regional budget airlines such as **Air Asia** (www.airasia.com), **Jetstar** (www.jetstar.

Previous: Vietnamese visas; woman ladling *bun nuoc leo* into a bowl.

com), and **Tiger Air** (www.tigerair.com) serve Southeast Asia's major airports, including those in Thailand, Cambodia, China, Laos, Malaysia, Myanmar, and Vietnam. Air Asia's network is particularly extensive, providing connecting flights from across the region, while Tiger Air and Jetstar both fly to Australia and a handful of Southeast Asian nations. Direct flights are available from larger hubs, such as Suvarnabhumi Airport in Bangkok or Kuala Lumpur's International Airport. These are the most affordable of the bunch, but most budget airlines within the region tack on additional fees for just about everything; read the fine print when booking these fares.

ORGANIZED TOURS

In any given tourist destination, there are dozens of companies offering organized day trips and multi-day tours. The majority of Vietnam's cheaper travel outfits follow the same tourist trail, offering cookie-cutter itineraries that present little in the way of authenticity or spontaneity. Larger companies have day trips for as little as VND100,000; these trips provide an easy way to meet other travelers, but the tours themselves are not groundbreaking. In most cases, if you're up for the challenge it's more worthwhile to make the trip on your own. For certain excursions (treks in Sapa, for example), hiring a guide and paying the extra cash is recommended to make the most of your time.

More independent tour outfits are popping up all the time. Many of these private companies have done great things for the country's tourism image, providing foreign travelers with exciting, worthwhile experiences that also benefit the local community. While prices are higher, these customized tour outfits are usually affordable when split between several people and the level of service is a cut above what you would find in a larger, corporate tour company.

Getting Around

AIR

Within Vietnam, there are three main airlines with domestic routes: the national carrier **Vietnam Airlines** (www.vietnamairlines.com); as well as two budget ventures, Australian company **Jetstar** (www.jetstar.com) and **VietJet Air** (www.vietjetair.com). Jetstar offers the best domestic fares and service, while VietJet's regular seat sales are a bargain, with fares as low as VND100,000. Vietnam Airlines, though more expensive, serves a much wider range of destinations, including some of the more remote airports in Vietnam and has exclusive access to certain areas, such as the remote Con Dao islands and Phu Quoc.

RAIL

Vietnam's main railway runs from Saigon to Hanoi along the coast, with major stops in Nha Trang and Danang. While some of these trains have seen better days, the sleeper cars are reasonably comfortable, though more expensive than sleeper buses, which, while slightly less safe, run more frequently. Trains are a great way to complete any long-distance journey, particularly with so many overnight routes offered, as you can spend a bit more money on train fare in exchange for saving on a hotel bill. There are a handful of destinations to which a train ride is even preferable over other options, particularly in the mountainous north, where winding roads make for a less-than-pleasant bus ride. The website **Man in Seat 61** (www.seat61.com) is an indispensable source of information on train travel within Vietnam and Southeast Asia.

BUS

The cheapest way to get around in-country is by bus. Vietnam has an extensive system of roadways and dozens of tourist bus companies featuring both seated and sleeper vehicles, which run regularly along the length of the coast, from Hanoi and its surrounding areas all the way south to the Mekong Delta and into neighboring countries. Many tourists get around on buses, though certain routes—from Hue to Hanoi, for instance, or the drive up to Sapa—are more dangerous than others. In these cases, it's better to travel via train, motorbike, or hired vehicle.

In most major cities there is a bus station serving both nearby and long-distance destinations. Safe and reliable tickets are available through many of the more well-known travel companies, like **Sinh Tourist** (www.thesinhtourist.com) and **Phuong Trang** (www.futabuslines.com.vn). When booking tickets, deal with the larger, more reputable bus lines rather than smaller, cheaper companies, as the few dollars you may save on a local bus could wind up costing you time as a result of breakdowns or other troubles.

While buses are an affordable and convenient way to travel within Vietnam, theft sometimes occurs, particularly on overnight buses. Take care when traveling to keep your belongings with you at all times, either in your lap or very close to your person. Sadly, more than a few travelers have taken an overnight bus only to wake up at their destination with one or more of their possessions missing.

TAXI

Even many of Vietnam's smaller cities are equipped with taxi services, and cabs are usually so abundant that it isn't necessary to call an operator or arrange a pick-up unless you're in a remote area. Travelers should have no problem flagging down taxis in the street. The most reputable nationwide company is **Mailinh,** though there are dozens of smaller independent companies in various cities. While some of these cabs are more reliable than others, always check for a proper meter. Base rates for taxis in most major cities run VND10,000-15,000, with fares increasing incrementally based on the distance traveled.

Never bargain with a driver for your fare, as this is not to your advantage.

XE OM

Xe om (motorbike taxis) are a popular and inexpensive means of transportation used throughout the country. Drivers—usually men—perch atop their vehicles on street corners near public parks or in busy tourist areas, waiting to ferry passengers to their preferred destinations around town. As a foreigner, you'll no doubt come into contact with at least a few of these two-wheeled vehicles and their drivers, as *xe om* drivers often call out to passing pedestrians in order to drum up business. Don't be surprised if you hear a "YOU! Motorbiiiiike!" or *"Xe om! Xe om!"* as you approach a street corner, even if you're not looking for a ride.

While *xe om* are an easy and affordable way to get around, most foreign visitors also find them to be a hair-raising experience. *Xe om* drivers, like Manhattan cabbies, move at their own pace, which is usually breakneck, and defy most of the laws of physics, not to mention traffic. In a country so enamored of two-wheeled vehicles, *xe om* are a good way to experience the true pulse of major cities like Saigon or Hanoi. However, if a *xe om* driver is racing down a one-way street in the wrong direction, voice your concern if you feel unsafe. While the "helmets" provided by *xe om* drivers would probably prove useless in an accident, it's required by law to wear one. Even if you are advised otherwise, it's important to insist upon some headgear, at least when in the city.

When taking a *xe om,* have the address of your destination written down, as not every driver speaks English, and always agree upon a price before you set off. *Xe om* fares are open to negotiation. Feel free to haggle, but once you've settled on the price stand firm. Drivers will sometimes continue to negotiate their fee once you've already hopped on. If you stand your ground and stick to the original agreement then your *xe om* driver will usually lay off.

With few qualifications required beyond a motorbike license and a full tank of gas, *xe om* drivers are a mixed bag: There are many honest, hardworking men who make a living this way, but, like any profession, there are also a few bad apples. For this reason, it is strongly recommended that you opt for taxis over *xe om* when traveling at night, as it's not unheard of for passengers to be robbed or even thrown off a motorbike after dark, and the *xe om* driver is sometimes in on the deal. Be careful when heading back to your hotel after a night on the town, as it's also possible that your *xe om* driver has had as much to drink as you have. Never hop on a motorbike with someone who appears to be intoxicated—the streets of Vietnam can be dangerous enough as it is.

MOTORBIKE RENTALS

Affordable motorbike rentals are available in major tourist destinations throughout Vietnam. Rates usually hover around VND80,000-200,000 per day, depending on the vehicle. All motorbike rentals should come with a helmet. Stick to recommended rental companies or ask around to find a reliable business. Rental companies often require some type of collateral—a down payment or, in some cases, a passport—before loaning out a bike in order to guarantee that their vehicle will be returned in good condition. This is usually not a problem, but beware that businesses have been known to tack on additional fees after they have your passport in their possession. To save yourself a headache, stick to recommended businesses only, check the brakes and gas gauge of your vehicle before you go, and, like any transaction in Vietnam, make sure that both you and the rental company are clear on the terms of your agreement before setting off.

In most cases, daily rentals are intended for use in or around the city. Barring certain exceptions, like the short trip between Hoi An and Danang or the drive from Nha Trang to Dai Lanh beach, you should not take a daily rental outside the city limits. If you plan to travel on the highway, inform the rental

Motorbikes are the most common form of transportation.

company of your intentions, as you may find yourself in hot water should anything happen to the bike while you're on the road.

When traveling long distances, such as the trip from Hanoi to Saigon (or vice versa), it's also possible to purchase a motorbike. Indeed, many travelers come to Vietnam, buy a heavy-duty vehicle, drive the length of the country, and then sell the motorbike once they've reached their destination. Particularly in Saigon and Hanoi, road-ready vehicles are often on sale in the backpacker neighborhoods, and you should have no trouble buying or selling a motorbike in these destinations.

HIRED CARS

Cars and minibuses can be hired in Vietnam and are widely available. These rental vehicles come with a driver, as foreigners are not permitted to operate a vehicle without a local license. The going rate for a hired car varies depending on the vehicle and its provider. Wherever you rent a car or minibus, be clear about the exact terms of the rental agreement, including which fees are included and which are not, before driving off.

DRIVING IN VIETNAM

Vietnam law requires all motorists to have a local license, essentially making it illegal for tourists to drive. Though enforcement of the law varies, it is illegal to drive in Vietnam without a Vietnamese license. Most expats don't have a license and many Vietnamese people also operate a vehicle without one. Traveling in the countryside, you can see boys as young as 11 or 12 zipping by on a Honda Wave.

People drive while texting, fail to use the correct turn signals (if they use them at all), routinely speed in the opposite direction down a one-way street, and generally disregard lane markings. Vehicles must drive on the right side of the road, with motorbikes staying in the far right lane at all times. Turning right on a red light is permitted, except in Hanoi. While the noise is unpleasant, honking is often a means of defensive driving, an announcement of the vehicle's presence. Beyond that, pay extra attention to larger vehicles when driving, as public buses, taxis, and transport trucks will not hesitate to play chicken with a motorbike.

While it is less likely for foreign drivers to be pulled over by law enforcement (except in large cities like Hanoi and HCMC), it does happen. Most traffic police don't usually go to the trouble of fining foreigners. If you are stopped by the police, remain calm and polite. The proper legal course of action for an unlicensed driver is to impound the motorbike and fine the individual, but this almost never happens. Instead, money often changes hands.

Visas and Officialdom

VISAS

All foreign visitors to Vietnam are required to obtain a visa prior to arrival, a process that can be completed up to six months in advance of your trip. Tourist visas are available in one- and three-month increments and offer both single- and multiple-entry options. If you are entering the country by land, you can arrange a visa through one of Vietnam's many embassies or consulates in neighboring countries (there are several in Laos and Cambodia) in a matter of a few business days. Visa fees run from USD$100 per person for a single-entry, one-month stay up to USD$180 for travelers with a three-month, multiple-entry stamp. Check the costs with your local embassy, as they're always changing. Tourist visas can also be arranged in the United States by applying in person at the Vietnamese embassy or any one of its consulates, or by sending in the necessary documents and fees by mail. Expedited services are available at a premium. All visa fees rendered outside of Vietnam, whether in the United States or abroad, must be paid in U.S. dollars.

Once in Vietnam, tourists may extend their stay for up to three months by visiting any travel agency that provides visa services. Though the extension stamp officially costs USD$10, the going rate at local travel agencies is around USD$30. This is an unavoidable expense, as the extension process requires the assistance of a Vietnamese speaker, and attempting to complete the process on your own is all but impossible.

If you're entering the country by air, you can save roughly USD$30 by applying for e-visa processing. This is by far the most cost-effective option for visitors coming to Vietnam directly from the United States. You will not find information on e-visa processing through the country's official government websites. Vietnamese immigration does not openly advertise this service, but at each of the country's three international airports you will find an official e-visa kiosk through which plenty of travelers have safely and legitimately entered Vietnam.

E-visas can be obtained by contacting a travel agent within the country, many of which provide visa-on-arrival services. You will be asked to supply an image of the identification page in your passport, and within 2-4 business days a letter of approval will be sent to your email. This letter should be two pages: one declaring that you are approved for a visa and the other bearing your name, nationality, and passport number. Upon arrival in Vietnam, you will be required to provide this letter along with a passport photo and a stamping fee, which costs USD$45-95, depending upon the length of your stay. An immigration official will then supply you with a visa sticker and send you to the customs line. Along with the stamping fee, you will have to pay an additional fee (usually USD$15-30) to the company providing your letter of approval. All of these costs must be covered in U.S. dollars, including the stamping fee at the airport.

While there are dozens of websites providing e-visa services, exercise caution when applyingg. There are many safe and reliable websites that provide travelers with legitimate letters of approval, but it is still wise to research reputable companies.

EMBASSIES AND CONSULATES

Within the United States, Vietnam has consular services in several cities, particularly near large communities of overseas Vietnamese. In addition to the **Vietnamese embassy** (Ste. 400, 1233 20th St. NW, tel. 202/861-0737, www.vietnamembassy-usa.org, 9:30am-noon and 1:30pm-5pm Mon.-Fri.) in Washington, D.C., there are also consulates in **San Francisco** (Ste. 580, 1700 California St., tel. 415/922-1707, www.vietnamconsulate-sf.org, 8:30am-noon and 2:30pm-4pm Mon.-Fri.), **Houston** (Ste. 1100, 5251 Westheimer Rd., tel. 713/850-1233, www.vietnamconsula-teinhouston.org, 9:30am-12:30pm and 2pm-5pm Mon.-Fri.), and **New York City** (Ste. 428,

866 UN Plaza, tel. 212/644-0594, www.vnconsul-ny.org, 9am-5:30pm Mon.-Fri.). Each of these offices provides visa services. The hours listed here are only for telephone inquiries; any in-person applications must take place in the morning, 9:30am-noon.

The United States has an **embassy in Hanoi** (2nd Fl., 170 Ngoc Khanh, D Ba Dinh, tel. 04/2850-5000, www.vietnam.usembassy.gov) and a **consulate in Saigon** (4 Le Duan, D1, tel. 08/3520-4200, www.hochiminh.usconsulate.gov), which are able to help American citizens in the event of an emergency. Any visa problems relating to your stay in Vietnam are better dealt with by a travel agent, as American consular services cannot assist citizens in arranging Vietnamese visas. Both the embassy and the consulate have separate hours for specific services; check their websites before paying either office a visit.

BORDER CROSSINGS

Border crossings in Vietnam are fairly straightforward. The only way to enter or exit overland is by bus, as there are no international trains connecting Vietnam to its neighbors. Frequent buses travel through Vietnam's many border gates, at which time you pass through two sets of customs offices: one for Vietnam and one for the country you are entering or exiting.

POLICE

The police in Vietnam do not have a stellar reputation. A survey by anti-corruption nonprofit Transparency International found that 37 percent of the Vietnamese population considers local law enforcement the most corrupt institution in the country. A large part of this stems from the fact that most police officers are underpaid and use traffic violations and other infractions as a way to line their pockets. Most cops steer clear of foreign visitors, in large part because of the language barrier. If you need to contact the police, have a Vietnamese speaker on hand, as few officers speak English.

BRIBES

It's rare for foreigners to have to deal with bribery during their trip. The only instance in which a traveler may be required to supply a bribe is at a police checkpoint, where traffic violations are meted out. Since it is illegal for anyone to drive in Vietnam without a local driver's license, if you are pulled over by a police officer, you will have to pay a "fine." In these instances, good manners and a little patience can help to minimize the dent in your wallet, but you will undoubtedly have to part with some cash. Refusing to pay the bribe is a bad idea. Legally, the police are allowed to impound your motorbike if you fail to provide a license. It is unlikely that the traffic authorities will actually do so, but don't call their bluff.

Accommodations

Throughout Vietnam, accommodations run the gamut from dingy budget hostels to luxurious high-end resorts, sometimes even within the same neighborhood. While there are plenty of good beds available at any price, certain rules hold true for most accommodations. Thanks to the size and volume of many of Vietnam's coastal cities, for instance, noise levels should always be considered when booking, as rooms closer to the ground floor tend to be much louder than rooms higher up, and the same goes for street-facing accommodations versus those in the back of the building. Windows are not a given; it's customary for travelers to ask to see a hotel room before committing to stay the night. A few other amenities, such as elevators, are not always included, but hot water and air-conditioning typically come standard with a room.

Furthermore, though public double-occupancy rates are listed in this book, it is often possible to secure a discount from hotels or guesthouses depending on the season, the length of your stay, and the number of rooms available. Many hotels and guesthouses in larger cities use online reservation sites like Agoda or Booking.com, which can sometimes work to the traveler's advantage by providing cheaper rates, though there are a handful of accommodations that cost more when booking online. For the best price, consult both the hotel directly and their online booking site when available.

When you check in to a hotel in Vietnam you will often be asked to hand over your passport. This is often a source of worry among travelers, but holding one's passport is common practice in Vietnam. Since hotels are required by law to register their guests with the police, many will hold your passport at the front desk during your stay, partly for the authorities and partly for insurance that you don't walk out on your bill (these things occasionally happen). It is acceptable to request that your passport is returned to you after the receptionist has filled out your registration form, though you may be asked to pay in advance.

MAKING RESERVATIONS

Depending upon your location and the time of year, the need for booking accommodations may vary. Most major cities in Vietnam do not require a reservation. With such an abundance of hotels and guesthouses in places like Ho Chi Minh City's Pham Ngu Lao area and the Old Quarter of Hanoi, travelers will never find themselves out in the cold. If you prefer to stay in nicer accommodations and would rather not do the door-to-door legwork, then booking a room is recommended. Be sure when making a reservation that you ask the price up front, as rates may change, and take care to confirm your reservation at least once before arriving at the hotel. Even online sites like Agoda and Booking.com, while reliable, can sometimes make mistakes or lose reservations.

HOTELS

You'll find all manner of accommodations that refer to themselves as *khach san* (hotels). These tend to be larger buildings with more rooms. There is a star rating issued by the Vietnamese government each year, but the criteria for the rating seems to focus on the size of the building rather than the quality of the accommodations. Two- to four-star accommodations are a mixed bag, with plenty of outstanding rooms as well as deteriorating facilities. Boutique and privately owned hotels are usually more impressive, though these are often more expensive, too. Depending upon the rates and quality of the hotel, amenities vary from as little as a bed, air-conditioning, and a hot shower to safety deposit boxes, in-room computers, and fresh fruit or complimentary breakfast.

GUESTHOUSES

Almost interchangeable with budget hotels, Vietnam's guesthouses *(nha nghi)* are smaller versions of the same lodgings, often providing 5-6 rooms where a budget hotel might have 10-12. In general, amenities at a guesthouse include air-conditioning, hot water, and sometimes a refrigerator or TV. These places tend to be the most bare-bones and often the most affordable.

HOSTELS

Hostels and dormitory accommodations are only popular in Vietnam's major cities. While there are a handful of these lodgings in Saigon, Hanoi, and a couple other coastal cities, only one or two hostels actually stand out. All dormitory lodgings should come with proper bedding and a secure locker for each guest, and many also include en suite bathrooms, which limits the number of people sharing a shower.

HOMESTAYS

While there are still plenty of authentic homestays throughout Vietnam, particularly in the Mekong Delta, this is an interesting term nowadays, as "homestay" is often conflated with "guesthouse." Bar a few exceptions, most homestay accommodations are akin to a remote guesthouse, offering the added benefit of home-cooked meals and a bit of interaction with locals, though not as much as you might expect. A growing number of high-end "homestays" are cropping up in more heavily touristed areas—Hoi An, for example; these take on the feel of a bed-and-breakfast, offering more of a local connection along with fancier accommodations.

CAMPING

Camping in Vietnam can have a few different meanings. You may find yourself in a one-room beachside bungalow, a log cabin in the woods, or a tent on the ground. While the lodgings vary, most of these accommodations are located either in national parks or on beaches across the country. Pitching a tent just anywhere is not accepted. In more remote areas, travelers may be able to get away with overnighting in their own accommodations, but along the coast you'll be hard-pressed to find a place to set up camp. In designated areas, camping fees tend to be inexpensive.

Food

Some of the freshest, most flavorful, and most varied dishes in Southeast Asia belong to Vietnam. From Hanoi's *bun cha* (grilled pork in fish sauce with noodles) to Hue's *bun bo* (spicy beef noodle soup) or the dozens of southern meals unique to each small village and town, Vietnamese cuisine's complex and irresistible flavors win over many a hungry traveler. Most meals consist of a rice or noodle base, a few fresh greens, and either meat or tofu. Portions tend to be smaller here than in Western countries. With the cost of meals so low, there's usually room for seconds in the budget.

STREET FOOD

You can't make it to the end of any city block in Vietnam without encountering a street food vendor. Meals are everywhere: in the park; on the sidewalk; outside of government buildings and public meeting areas. Men and women push metal carts down the road or hustle along with a bamboo pole slung over one shoulder. At first glance, the setup appears to be nothing special, but take a closer look and you'll be amazed by what someone can do with a portable stove and a pair of chopsticks.

While you can buy anything from hot bowls of soup to quick sandwiches or smaller snacks for the road, there are a handful of dishes more commonly found on the street than in a restaurant. Sticky rice *(xoi),* for example, is a popular street-side snack; the rice is often cooked in different leaves or with certain ingredients that turn the rice green, purple, orange, or black. This snack can be served sweet with sugar, coconut, and mung bean, or savory, often accompanied by chicken. A handful of other sweets, including a hot tofu dessert with ginger and tapioca or fried rice cakes with mung bean, are also found on street carts or in a basket on someone's head.

There is something to be said for cooking your food out in the open: Street food kitchens, while simple, are almost always more transparent. You're able to tell which vendors are clean and which are not.

REGIONAL FOODS

While dishes like pho, Vietnam's national soup, and *banh mi* (Vietnamese sandwiches) come standard almost everywhere, local fare is divided into three main regions: the north, central, and south. Shaped in large part by its weather and surroundings, each region's cuisine relies upon both rice and fish sauce as main staples but also has its own distinguishing characteristics. Furthermore, nearly every hamlet and every village across the country has its own unique recipes.

Northern fare is more meat-heavy, shying away from seafood in favor of chicken and beef, though fish sometimes makes an appearance. Hot dishes like *chao* (rice porridge) and what is officially considered the country's best pho are native to the north, as is *bun cha,* a simple but mouthwatering combination of cold rice noodles, fish sauce, pickled vegetables, and grilled meat.

Things heat up in the central region, where spicier dishes like *bun bo Hue* (spicy beef noodle soup) are all the rage, not to mention the dozens of tiny, bite-sized foods found in the Nguyen dynasty's former capital, including *banh beo* (steamed rice cake with shrimp paste), *banh duc* (sticky steamed rice cake), *banh loc* (steamed shrimp and pork fat dumplings), and *banh hoi* (bundles of rice vermicelli).

By the time you reach Saigon and the rest of the south, foods are sweeter, with more sugar found in local dishes. Whether it be the massive river fish of the Delta or the tasty grilled octopus of the southern coast, seafood features heavily in southern cuisine and many dishes are fried, including all varieties of *banh xeo* (savory pancakes), as well as a handful of

The Stranger Side of Vietnamese Cuisine

In a nation as food-focused as Vietnam, it is all but impossible to come up with dozens of savory masterpieces without having created a few strange dishes along the way. While pho and *banh mi* (Vietnamese sandwiches) have gained worldwide acclaim as delicious, accessible facets of local cuisine, there are several specialties that manage to make some travelers wrinkle their noses.

Century eggs: A traditional Chinese delicacy that has carried over to Vietnam, century eggs are regular chicken or duck eggs that have been preserved in a combination of clay, ash, salt, lime, and rice for several weeks, during which time the pH of the egg elevates, changing the yolk to a dark green, creamy ball at the center of a gelatinous brown egg. The resulting dish is slightly off-putting in appearance. It's often included in local meals and is something of an acquired taste.

Dog: While foreign perceptions tend to suggest that Asia is far more into dog meat than it actually is, the majority of Vietnam's canine consumption occurs in the north, where dog is still considered something of a delicacy. Down south, you're less likely to find locals indulging in dog, but there are still people who enjoy it every now and again, and Saigon does have a small street dedicated to the sale of canine meat. Most meals are prepared in much the same way as chicken, beef, or other meats—roasted, steamed, boiled, or barbecued—and served with rice or added into a soup.

With a government ban on the sale of dog meat and growing concerns over its safety, this delicacy may be harder to come by over the next few years. The harsh reality of this dish is that most of the animals slaughtered and prepared are actually pets or strays that have been kidnapped. Given the persistence of rabies in Vietnam, contaminated meat is a risk. Many people believe that canine meat is at its best when the animal has suffered, so the dogs are often killed in a brutal way. As demand increases throughout Southeast Asia, more and more dogs are being smuggled into Vietnam and killed, and the quality, safety, and humane treatment of these animals is fast decreasing.

Embryonic duck egg: Known locally as *hot vit lon* and more widely as *balut*, embryonic duck eggs are regularly consumed in Vietnam and several Southeast Asian countries, namely the Philippines. Larger and more dense than your average chicken egg, *hot vit lon* is consumed when the fetus is 19-21 days old—still too small to hatch but old enough that its wings, feet, beak, and eyes are visible. Like any egg, the yolk is thick and a little dry, while the tiny bird makes up the majority of the shell. *Hot vit lon* is commonly enjoyed on the street with salt, pepper, or lime and an ice-cold beer.

Pigeon: In the mountainous north where protein is scarce, small birds are often a part of local fare. Creatures like pigeons and other forest-dwelling birds are grilled and eaten with rice and rice wine or beer.

Rice paddy rat: In the Mekong Delta and parts of Cambodia, rice paddy rats are a delicacy. Much cleaner than their city-dwelling counterparts, these countryside rodents are sold at the market on a seasonal basis and usually grilled, barbecued, or boiled. Dishes are best enjoyed with beer or rice wine.

Snake: Particularly in the north, snake meat is a delicacy. While some creatures are simply slaughtered and prepared like any other meal, eating snake is more often than not an almost ritualistic experience. First, the live animal is slit from neck to tail, slicing open the skin to reveal its flesh, before its blood and bile are drained into separate shot glasses and combined with rice wine. After the blood has been consumed, the snake's still-beating heart is removed and swallowed by the guest of honor.

local specialties like *banh khot* (Vung Tau's delicious, bite-sized rice cakes).

BEER AND RICE WINE

Along with local favorites like southern Saigon Red or Huda, a brew from the central region, freshly made beers are a popular fixture during local happy hours. *Bia tuoi* (fresh beer) is a locally produced lager sold in 100-liter barrels to small shops across town (also called *bia hoi*), particularly in Hanoi. Often going for as little as VND4,000 a glass on the

Drinking in Vietnam

Though it is largely reserved for men, drinking is a large part of Vietnamese culture. As one of the world's top beer-drinking nations, this country takes its alcohol consumption seriously, as evidenced by the dozens of drinking slogans that can be heard during a weekend drinking session or at happy hour. Phrases like *mot tram phan tram* (100 percent, or bottoms up) and *khong say khong ve* (you can't go home until you're drunk) spell out the Vietnamese attitude towards imbibing. Drinking is a social event and is often accompanied by *do nhau* (drinking food), such as snails, grilled meat, or other savory snacks. Beer is often enjoyed with ice and shared among the group. If you go out drinking with a local crowd, be prepared to clink glasses a lot: *Mot, hai, ba, DZO!* (One, two, three, CHEERS!) is a phrase commonly repeated throughout the night.

Drinking in Vietnam can be an enjoyable experience but it can also be a dangerous one. Drinking and driving is a common practice in a country where road safety is already dismal at best. Exercise the same good judgment you would when going out at home: Never get on the back of a motorbike with someone who has been drinking or appears to be drunk, and always opt for an alternative means of transportation in the event that someone in your party is not able to drive.

While it is not a widespread problem, methanol poisoning can occur as a result of poorly produced homemade alcohol or counterfeit spirits. This is a very serious condition that can result in permanent disability or life-threatening complications.

street, this watered-down beverage is incredibly popular up north and must be drunk the day it is made, as its shelf life is very short. Men regularly gather at *bia hoi* after close of business to enjoy a few drinks and catch up. While fresh beer would not under most circumstances be considered a fine beer, the cultural experience of hanging out at a *bia hoi* in the city is well worth the dirt-cheap price tag.

Much stronger than fresh beer, rice wine is a high-octane spirit that is often enjoyed in the countryside and becomes a major fixture during Tet, the Vietnamese lunar new year. Across Vietnam, locals make their own alcohol, storing it in massive plastic jugs for the coming festivities. Glutinous rice is steamed and left to sit for several days, adding yeast to the mixture, to produce a spirit that can carry a concentration of up to 22 percent alcohol. While you won't often find rice wine in local shops, it is everywhere in the countryside. In many cases, making local friends off the beaten path is likely to earn you at least a shot or two.

Conduct and Customs

GENERAL ETIQUETTE

Vietnam is a very polite country. Though Western-style customer service is not always observed in restaurants or hotels, you'll be hard-pressed to find people who are intentionally rude. Locals rarely raise their voices out of anger or show intense emotions in public. Daily interactions are handled calmly and politely. When problems arise, the typical Vietnamese reaction is often awkward laughter. This can be a frustrating and seemingly inappropriate response. In Vietnamese culture, showing anger is considered a lack of self-control and will likely cause the person you're dealing with to shut down, leaving you no better off than when you started.

As much as the average person is polite and respectful, the rules of etiquette, like most rules in Vietnam, are sometimes overlooked. Lining up, it seems, is the worst: people push, shove, and openly cut in front while waiting for a bus or at the supermarket checkout counter. If this happens, politely ask the person to move and you'll usually get a feigned surprise or even an apology, and most of the time that individual will get out of line. Acts like these are rarely meant to be rude; it's just that they were hoping you wouldn't say anything.

APPROPRIATE DRESS

Though you wouldn't know it in larger cities, Vietnam's sense of style tends to be rather conservative, with most people opting for long pants and shirts that cover their shoulders. Women in particular are usually more reserved, though sheer shirts are in fashion. In professional or religious settings, outfits that hit below the knee are appropriate for women and long pants are a must for men. At night all rules go out the window, as you'll see young Vietnamese women flying by on the back of a motorbike in sky-high stilettos and a mini skirt. For the most part, the same rules apply in Vietnam as in the United States: you wouldn't show up to work or to church in your party dress or shorts and flip-flops; if you visit a pagoda or an office building, the same holds true.

BODY LANGUAGE

Unlike Cambodia or Thailand, bowing in Vietnam, while still respectful, does not carry the same significance. Instead, when handing something to an elder or a stranger, for instance, it is polite to give the item with both hands as a sign of respect, or to offer the item with the right hand while placing the left hand on the right elbow. Certain gestures are inappropriate here where they would not be at home. Crossing your forefinger and middle finger over one another, for instance, is a rude gesture in Vietnam. When beckoning someone, it's better to use an underhand motion.

Vietnamese culture dictates that the top of a person's head is the most sacred part of his or her body (because it is closest to God), while the soles of one's feet are the lowest. Touching the top of a person's head is considered impolite, particularly with children, as is showing a person the soles of your feet. In pagodas especially, directing the soles of your feet at the Buddha is considered an offensive gesture.

TABLE MANNERS

There are several Vietnamese dining habits that break with Western ideas of what is polite. Slurping your soup, talking with a full mouth, and shouting for the waiter are all acceptable practices at a local restaurant. You can shout *em oi!* to beckon a

Offering objects with two hands is considered a sign of respect.

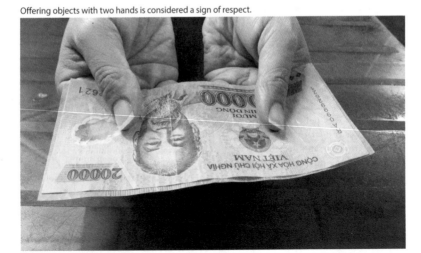

waiter over to your table. While it may seem odd at first, you'll want to get the hang of it, as servers don't check up on quiet tables and only bring the bill when you've asked for it. If you're visiting a street food stall or a more local restaurant, throwing rubbish like napkins and used toothpicks on the floor is also acceptable. This may seem unsanitary, but a restaurant employee will come by and sweep up any garbage that gets left on the floor. Occasionally, wastebaskets are positioned at the end of each table. If you're in doubt, take a look around: if you can see squeezed limes, napkins, and other rubbish strewn across the floor, then you're allowed to do the same.

When eating with a local family, Vietnamese hospitality dictates that no guest go hungry: in a Vietnamese house, you will eat until you're full and then some. Be warned that any time you empty your bowl it will be filled again before you have the chance to decline. Dining family-style means that anyone can pick at the assortment of meats and veggies on offer and drop some into your bowl, and people often do when guests are around. In situations like these, rice is served in a small *chen* (bowl) for each person, while the main dishes are set out in the middle. When eating, it is acceptable to pick up your *chen* and bring it closer to your mouth; as you reach the bottom of the bowl, you may lift it to your mouth and use your chopsticks to shovel the rice in. Take what is closest to you, as any piece you touch is yours, and always put the food in your *chen* first before bringing it to your mouth.

There are a long list of dos and don'ts regarding chopstick etiquette. For most transgressions, foreigners will likely be forgiven. Always lay your chopsticks parallel to one another, never crossed, and do not point them at other people, as these gestures are considered rude. It is also inappropriate to leave your utensils in the shape of a "V," and chopsticks should never be stuck upright into a bowl of rice, as this resembles incense sticks and is viewed as an omen of death.

Travel Tips

LANGUAGE AND COMMUNICATION

As a nation still getting the hang of the tourism industry, Vietnam lacks an adequate number of fluent English speakers. In part due to the complexities of their own language, the Vietnamese have a great deal of trouble with English (and, it's safe to say, English-speakers face the same challenges with Vietnamese). Staying patient and simplifying your requests will go a long way to helping make yourself understood. In English, we often make requests more polite by adding extra words. For instance, at home you might say, "I was wondering if you could tell me where the restroom is?" For a weaker English speaker these extra words add confusion. Instead, "Excuse me, where is the toilet?" will make you more easily understood and locals will not take offense to the shorter sentences.

Whenever you arrange a service—whether it be a motorbike rental, a *xe om* ride, a day tour, or a cooking course—always be clear on the cost and the expectations of both parties before setting out, as this will help to prevent disagreements. Patience goes a long way. Expressing anger or being short with someone will keep you from gaining that person's respect.

WHAT TO PACK

Thanks to a steady influx of foreign visitors, Vietnam offers plenty of Western amenities, but some items are still hard to come by. Sunscreen, for instance, is almost never used among the local population and so can be difficult to track down in Vietnam. When you do find it, sunblock is overpriced and the locally produced version is not particularly effective. You're better off bringing your own sunscreen from abroad. The same goes for insect repellent. For women, feminine products are available at most pharmacies and drugstores, but tampons are rarely in stock, so bring your own if necessary.

Given the humidity, lightweight, breathable clothing and sturdy shoes are a wise choice for any traveler. Anyone planning to go pagoda-hopping should opt for at least one long-sleeved shirt and pants or shorts that reach the knee. A hat is a good idea as certain destinations like the Mekong Delta and Nha Trang are notably devoid of shade. While backpacking through Vietnam is a dirty business and your standard shorts-and-T-shirt attire is perfectly acceptable, pack one or two nice outfits if you plan to hit the town in the bigger cities like Hanoi or Saigon. You will likely need a raincoat at one time or another while in Vietnam, but bringing your own is optional, as cheap, plastic cover- ups are widely available.

OPPORTUNITIES FOR STUDY AND EMPLOYMENT

As job opportunities at home dwindle, more and more Western travelers are choosing to make a home in Asia, if only for a year or two. A combination of increasing tourism and growing demand for English-language education in Vietnam have created ample opportunities for foreigners looking to experience another part of the world and earn money at the same time. Short-term employment can be found at hostels and guesthouses around the country, where simple housework or other odd jobs are sometimes traded for room and board. For more permanent employment, most companies require you to make connections once you've already arrived in Vietnam. Websites like **VietnamWorks** (www.vietnamworks.com) provide insight into what's available.

If you plan to be in Asia for six months or more, ESL teaching is an excellent option. Jobs teaching English in Vietnam are widely available in Saigon and Hanoi, while employment in smaller cities like Danang is growing. Most English-teaching contracts range between six months and one year, and several schools within Vietnam offer ESL teaching certification courses, like the CELTA or TESOL, both of which are recognized internationally. **Apollo English** (www.apollo.edu.vn), **ILA** (www.ilavietnam.com), and **VUS** (www.vus.edu.vn) are reputable English teaching centers that employ foreign instructors. You can work under-the-table gigs with a tax-free hourly wage, but these businesses are far less reliable. In order to get a legitimate job with a reasonable salary, you'll need a Bachelor's degree in any field, a TESOL or CELTA certificate, a police background check from your home country or state, and a medical check to confirm that you are in good health. If you decide to teach in Vietnam, it is infinitely easier to apply for a work permit and a legitimate visa if you have an original copy of your Bachelor's degree notarized at home and your police check completed before you arrive rather than coordinating these documents from Vietnam, as the red tape can be exhausting.

Beyond teaching English, a variety of other opportunities are available but often require you to make connections within Vietnam first, which is why a teaching job is often the way foreigners get started in Vietnam. Once you've met some of your fellow expats and gotten to know the lay of the land, you can find jobs in anything from marketing and sales to graphic design, business, science, and even the food and beverage industry.

ACCESS FOR TRAVELERS WITH DISABILITIES

Vietnam is not easily accessible for travelers with physical disabilities, particularly anyone who uses a wheelchair. Elevators are seldom available outside of major cities, streets and sidewalks are often crumbled and aging, and many of Vietnam's tourist attractions require some mobility. Major cities are better equipped to accommodate travelers with disabilities, including Ho Chi Minh City, Danang, and Hanoi. Particularly around Danang and Hoi An, a popular area for many older travelers, businesses and accommodations will likely be more equipped to serve tourists with disabilities.

WOMEN TRAVELING ALONE

Vietnam is safe for female tourists. Women are able to travel freely without much harassment. Solo women will receive their fair share of lighthearted marriage proposals and occasional pestering from local men, but this rarely results in any serious issues. Always be polite but firm when encountering unwanted attention and, once you have made your point, ignore the other party. This is more effective than continuing to respond.

GAY AND LESBIAN TRAVELERS

Gay and lesbian travelers will find that Vietnam is an accepting place. The speed with which Vietnam has come to accept its own LGBTQ community is incredibly heartening. In little more than a few years, large swaths of the urban population have come to understand, albeit tentatively, the presence of homosexuality in local society. In 2015, the Vietnamese government legalized same-sex weddings, with one high-ranking official even publicly supporting same-sex marriage. (Note the difference here between a wedding and a marriage.) For the most part, many locals are happy to live and let live, though public displays of affection from any couple—gay or straight—are usually discouraged. More and more young Vietnamese are empowered to come out and a handful of great organizations in the major cities are improving social perceptions of homosexuality in Vietnam. The countryside is still a conservative place where tolerance is less forthcoming.

Health and Safety

VACCINATIONS

As per **CDC** (Centers for Disease Control and Prevention, www.cdc.gov/travel) guidelines, all travelers to Vietnam should be up-to-date on routine vaccinations before going abroad. It is recommended that travelers receive vaccinations against Hepatitis A and typhoid, both of which can be spread through contaminated food or water. For more adventurous travelers and anyone planning to visit remote areas in Vietnam or to stay for a long time, vaccinations against Hepatitis B and Japanese encephalitis are encouraged, as well as preemptive rabies prophylaxis.

Malaria

Though malaria is less common in Vietnam than other parts of Southeast Asia, this flu-like, potentially fatal illness still exists in the southern half of the country. CDC guidelines recommend that travelers to rural areas in the south take malaria prophylaxis. Check with your doctor to find out which prophylaxis is best for you, as Vietnam's particular strain of malaria is resistant to certain drugs. There are many side effects associated with malaria prophylaxis, including minor annoyances like upset stomach, nausea, and sensitivity to sunlight but also more serious issues such as anxiety, hallucinations, and even seizures. Many travelers forgo using malaria drugs and instead take extra precautions in covering up and preventing mosquito bites. While DEET repellents are not intended for long-term use, a couple days of strong insect repellent should be fine. If you believe that you have contracted malaria, seek medical attention immediately. When caught early, malaria is very treatable.

HEALTH
Allergies

Travelers with severe allergies may have trouble in Vietnam, especially those allergic to shellfish and peanuts, as these are frequent ingredients in Vietnamese cuisine. Cross-contamination is difficult to manage at street carts or in local restaurants, and even if you explain your dilemma to a local server there is no guarantee that the message will be understood. Take care to read all packaged foods and bring your own means of treatment, such as an EpiPen, to counter an allergic reaction. In the event of a severe allergic reaction, seek medical attention immediately.

Traveler's Diarrhea

One of the less glamorous facets of traveling, traveler's diarrhea is common among visitors to Vietnam, particularly those who enjoy street food. Some guidelines urge visitors to avoid roadside food carts as well as ice and fresh vegetables, but this may make your stay more expensive, not to mention detract from the overall experience. Avoiding specific street vendors or restaurants whose kitchens appear unclean or have food that has been sitting out for some time will help to decrease your risk of traveler's diarrhea and other food-borne illnesses. Dishes that are served hot and meat and veggies that have been fried, grilled, or otherwise prepared with high heat should be fine. In many cases, a good street food restaurant will prepare their meals in plain sight, giving you the ability to see the kitchen for yourself. When it comes to dishes like pho, *bun bo* (spicy beef noodle soup), and *banh xeo* (savory Vietnamese pancakes), fresh greens are usually served on the side, so you are able to easily avoid them if you so choose.

Regarding beverages, the ice at most restaurants in backpacker areas and higher-end eateries is safe to consume. Tap water is not meant for anything beyond showers and brushing your teeth. Though water can be boiled, nearly everyone in the country drinks bottled water or *tra da,* a light tea served at local restaurants.

In the event that you find yourself with traveler's diarrhea, it's best to stick to bland foods and proper restaurants for a day or two until your symptoms subside. Over-the-counter anti-diarrheal drugs like Imodium are available both in Vietnam and at home. If the issue persists, visit a doctor, who will prescribe something stronger. If you visit a physician in the United States prior to your trip abroad, ask about anti-diarrheal medicines, as procuring medications at home is generally safer than doing so in Vietnam.

Dengue

One of the few more serious illnesses that exists in Vietnam's cities as well as in rural areas is dengue. Passed through mosquito bites, the disease causes fever, headaches, and muscle and joint pain along with flu-like symptoms. There is no vaccination for dengue. Anyone who believes to be suffering from the disease should seek medical attention, as dengue is highly treatable but can become fatal if left unchecked. Should you become ill, avoid mosquitoes, rest, stay hydrated, and, of course, see a doctor. Acetaminophen-based pain killers can be used to relieve muscle and joint aches, but you should avoid any medications with aspirin, ibuprofen, or naproxen. Take extra care to monitor your health as the symptoms recede; in rare cases, dengue can turn into a fatal condition just as the initial symptoms appear to subside. If you experience difficulty breathing, pale or clammy skin, persistent vomiting, bleeding from your nose or gums, or red spots on your skin, go to a hospital immediately, as these may be signs of a more serious condition.

Methanol Poisoning

Though this is still a rare problem among travelers, a handful of cases in recent years have raised the need for awareness regarding methanol poisoning. More commonly known as wood alcohol, methanol is the cousin of ethanol, the type of alcohol found in spirits like vodka, whiskey, or rum. Where ethanol can leave you with a bad headache, a queasy stomach, and all the other trappings of a regular hangover, methanol is much worse, with even small doses causing serious side effects or even death.

As a means of cutting costs, some local businesses attempt to create their own homemade versions of alcoholic spirits using this substance, which they then sell to local bars, some of whom don't even know they're purchasing counterfeit booze. Regardless, unsafe amounts of methanol, which can be virtually undetectable in a mixed drink, have found their way into the hands of locals and travelers. Symptoms of methanol poisoning may not show up until as late as 72 hours after initial exposure and can often mirror the predictable symptoms of intoxication or a hangover, including confusion, dizziness, headaches, nausea, vomiting, and inability to coordinate muscle movements. In more serious cases, it can cause loss of vision; kidney, heart, and respiratory failure; gastrointestinal bleeding; and seizures, the combination of which can prove fatal.

It is extremely important to exercise caution when going out on the town, particularly in backpacker areas and in certain cities like Saigon and Nha Trang. Cheap drinks are available everywhere, but if a price seems too good to be true then it probably is. Purchasing your own spirits from a supermarket or chain convenience store is safer than opting for the local corner store. At the bar, if you order a drink and something doesn't seem right—the taste is particularly sweet or harsh, or the beverage is discolored—don't bother finishing it. For the most part, higher-end bars and lounges are safer than local watering holes or cheap backpacker spots. If all else fails, stick to beer and wine. Should you or a friend become a victim of methanol poisoning, go to a hospital immediately.

RABIES

For anyone traveling to remote areas, spending a lot of time outdoors, or planning to travel by bicycle, the rabies vaccination is recommended, as people continue to die from the disease in Vietnam each year. Almost always fatal, rabies can be transmitted to humans through a bite or scratch from monkeys, cats, dogs, and bats. Avoid touching animals in Vietnam, even pets, as they are often left to their own devices and not cared for in the same way as Western pets. If you are bitten or scratched by a wild animal, wash the wound immediately with soap and water before seeking medical attention. Typically, an unvaccinated person requires a series of five shots following rabies exposure; those who have had preemptive prophylaxis need only two shots as soon as possible following the encounter. Due to the number of wild animals in Vietnam, rabies vaccines are widely available in the country and can be administered almost anywhere, including remote areas.

INSECTS

The local mosquito population continues to pester everyone in Vietnam. When traveling both in the city and throughout the countryside, take care to cover up at dawn and dusk, when insects are out in the greatest numbers, and use insect repellent. While it is possible to find repellent sprays in Vietnam, it's better to purchase them at home or in neighboring countries like Thailand, as these products can be more difficult to come by in-country and are usually more expensive. Avoid leaving your hotel room windows open at night and, if possible, sleep with the air-conditioning on or use a mosquito net around your bed. While rare, bed bugs are also an occasional problem in Vietnam, particularly if you are staying in dormitory-style accommodations. Check thoroughly for the critters before climbing into bed.

WILD ANIMALS

Vietnam's largest animal problems tend to stem from dogs and cats, many of which are technically pets but whose owners let them roam freely outside. In more remote areas, locals keep dogs for protection. Cyclists in particular will want to steer clear of these animals, as they've been known to chase bikes.

Avoid touching animals, even if they appear to be pets. If you come into contact with an animal, wash your hands thoroughly.

MEDICAL SERVICES

Medical services in Vietnamese hospitals are dismal at best, with major overcrowding and sanitation problems. In larger cities, international facilities provide a reasonable level of quality and will usually suffice in the event of illness or minor emergencies. More serious cases may require airlifting to Singapore or Bangkok; all of this should be covered by adequate travel insurance.

INSURANCE

Travel insurance is a must for visitors to Vietnam, as even a healthy tourist can become the victim of an accident, and while local hospitals may be significantly cheaper than their American counterparts, the cost of quality medical care can add up. Check with your current insurance provider to see if you are covered outside of your home country and what exactly falls within your plan. Travel insurance can be purchased through providers such as **Travel Guard** (www.travelguard.com). For most minor illnesses and injuries, healthcare in Vietnam is inexpensive enough that you may be able to cover the costs on your own, but at the very least be sure that your insurance plan covers major accidents and injuries. Confirm your plan's payment policy, as some hospitals in Vietnam require cash up front in order to perform medical services, and emergency evacuations can run in the hundreds of thousands of dollars. For those keen on hiring a motorbike, most travel insurance does not cover road accidents if the driver is unlicensed.

CRIME

The vast majority of crime in Vietnam involves bending the rules in business. While violent crimes occur, these incidents rarely involve foreigners. The most common trouble you'll encounter is petty theft, which, while frustrating, seldom turns dangerous

Take extra care when walking around Vietnam's busy city streets.

or violent. The second greatest concern for foreign visitors is drugs, which are illegal in Vietnam: Possession in large amounts can garner the death penalty or a protracted sentence for offenders.

Pickpocketing and Petty Theft

Though it's a minor offense compared to more violent crimes, petty theft is a big problem in Vietnam, especially in urban areas. Foreigners just getting the hang of a new country are often the victims. Particularly at night and around backpacker areas, tourists stand out as easy targets. Bag snatching, pickpocketing, and burglary are frequent occurrences, even in broad daylight.

There are steps you can take to minimize vulnerability. When walking around town, opt for pockets that close and keep your belongings in sight at all times. When paying for purchases, avoid showing large amounts of money, as this makes you a target. Anyone carrying a backpack should wear both straps; shoulder bags are best worn across the body and on the side furthest from the street. Avoid walking near the sidewalk's edge, as thieves on motorbikes have been known to snatch purses, phones, and wallets, sometimes dragging the person along with them. The same rules apply when you're on a motorbike: place your bag or backpack in front of you, hugging it to your chest, and tuck any necklaces into your shirt, as they can be snatched, too. Whether you're on foot or on a motorbike, use caution when taking out your belongings in public; even if you're just answering a text message or finding directions on your cell phone, duck into a local shop and out of view. These tips may sound extreme, but the number of tourists who have been robbed multiple times on a single trip suggests that, while slightly over-the-top, such practices are necessary. At night, common sense should be exercised. Male or female, don't walk alone around

town, avoid alleyways, and always take taxis rather than *xe om* after dark.

If you are robbed, especially at night, it's best to let the situation go. The majority of these criminals are after your monetary goods, not your life. Your first priority should always be your own safety; remember that goods are replaceable, your life is not.

Not everyone is out to steal your money. Locals are incredibly kind, and if you follow precautions, you are less likely to encounter trouble.

Drugs

Recreational drugs like marijuana, heroin, and synthetic tablets are both widely available and illegal in Vietnam. There is a harsh, zero-tolerance policy for drug trafficking and possession.

Information and Services

MONEY
Currency
The official currency of Vietnam is known as the dong. Bills come in denominations of VND500, VND1,000, VND2,000, VND5,000, VND10,000, VND20,000, VND50,000, VND100,000, VND200,000, and VND500,000. Refuse ripped or torn bills, particularly those with denominations of VND10,000 or higher, as they are often rejected by shops and local businesses and you may find yourself stuck with money you cannot spend.

Exchange Rates
At the time of writing, the exchange rate for the Vietnam dong is roughly VND21,000 to one U.S. dollar. Current rates can be found online at **Oanda** (www.oanda.com) and **XE** (www.xe.com). Businesses within Vietnam operate on a rate that fluctuates between VND20,000 and VND22,000.

Changing Money
Most major tourist destinations have proper currency exchange kiosks, in addition to the countless hotels, restaurants, travel agencies, and gold shops that offer exchange services at various rates. While exchange kiosks are usually not affiliated with a bank, they are safe to use, as counterfeit currency is not a major problem in Vietnam. Ripped or torn bills are not accepted by many local businesses. If you receive any bills in this state, or if they are noticeably worn or faded, ask to have them switched out.

ATMs
ATMs are everywhere in Vietnam, with even the most remote destinations having at least one or two machines. Major cities often have ATMs from international banks such as ANZ, HSBC, Citibank, and Commonwealth Bank, as well as domestic institutions like Sacombank, Techcombank,

and Vietcombank. Most domestic ATMs charge minimal fees for using their machines. International institutions sometimes charge more, though the cost rarely exceeds VND10,000 per withdrawal.

Bank Hours

For international banks, business hours are 8am-5pm; domestic institutions follow the same schedule but sometimes close earlier, at 4pm or 4:30pm, and almost always break for lunch, closing at 11am or 11:30am and reopening at 1pm or 1:30pm. All banks are open Monday-Friday, with some open on Saturday mornings as well.

Traveler's Checks

While it is possible to cash traveler's checks in certain banks in major cities, these are often far more trouble than they're worth. Not every financial institution will cash them and, when they do, many banks include fees and surcharges that eat away at the actual value of the check. **Vietcombank** (tel. 04/3824-3524, www.vietcombank.com.vn) is one of the few institutions that accepts traveler's checks, though the service is only provided in larger cities and not nationwide. With the availability of ATMs all over the country and the lack

of places in which a stolen bank card could be used, you're better off bringing plastic and withdrawing money from a machine.

Costs

Every price, from food and accommodations to shopping, is up for negotiation. In major cities, a good local meal can go for as little as VND15,000-20,000 at a street stall to as much as VND200,000 in a restaurant. In these instances, what you pay for is the atmosphere—more often than not, the food at a small hole-in-the-wall shop or street cart is just as good, if not better, than what you'll find at a high-end restaurant in the trendier part of town. When eating street-side it is a good idea to ask the price beforehand, as vendors occasionally try to rip off tourists by doubling or tripling the bill at the end. You can avoid being had by agreeing upon the cost from the beginning.

Other goods and services are trickier to gauge in terms of cost. Prices fluctuate depending upon location. More tourist-heavy areas like Phu Quoc or Hoi An are often more expensive, while less-visited areas like the Mekong Delta and the Central Highlands tend to be a fraction of the cost. With prices changing all the time, it's difficult to say what

fruits, teas, and other dry goods on sale in Sapa Market

an appropriate amount is for any given good or service.

Bargaining

In markets and shops across the country, bargaining is a common practice. Prices for everything from fresh produce to clothing to motorbike rides are up for negotiation. It is expected that you'll haggle for the goods and services you use, especially if a price tag is not affixed to them. While it can be difficult to discern what a fair price is for the goods you purchase, your best bet as a traveler is to ask around, gauge the average asking price of a few vendors, and then cut that back by 20-40 percent. In some cases this will be too much, in other cases too little; you'll have to get a feel for it before you know what is what. Take care not to enter into negotiations with a vendor unless you actually want the product. It's perfectly acceptable to ask the price of an item out of curiosity, but once you begin haggling it's assumed that you actually intend to buy the item. If you're just trying to see how much you can bargain down a vendor then this will almost certainly be met with anger. Bargaining is an art form, and some travelers are more comfortable with it than others.

Tipping

Outside of high-end restaurants, tipping is not required, nor is it a common practice. Some businesses take on a service charge for their employees, but you are not obligated to include something extra unless you feel inclined to do so. The only exception is in spas and massage parlors where tips are usually expected and you may even be asked to fill out a gratuity form after your massage. In this case, VND40,000 and up is usually acceptable. If you decide to leave a gratuity elsewhere, the amount really is up to you: In a country where one U.S. dollar can buy a meal, a motorbike ride, or even a pair of shoes, any extra cash you leave will be appreciated.

MAPS AND TOURIST INFORMATION

Vietnam is not great at providing accurate or detailed plans of the national road system. Cheap walking maps can be found in many towns. For anyone on a serious navigational mission, the only decent Vietnamese atlas is called *Tap Ban Do Giao Thong Duong Bo Viet Nam* and runs about VND300,000 in local bookshops.

The efficacy of local tourism offices varies depending upon the location. Places like Hanoi and Hoi An are packed with tour companies and travel agents who are willing to help, while a place like Con Dao, one of Vietnam's most remote islands, has maybe one or two English-speaking businesses.

COMMUNICATIONS AND MEDIA
Postal Services

Postage in Vietnam is cheap, with postcards traveling halfway around the world for VND10,000-20,000. The same goes for mail, but once you ship larger packages abroad the costs skyrocket, and in many cases there is no guarantee that the item will arrive at all. Most mail arrives at its destination within 2-3 weeks.

Area Codes

The country code for Vietnam is +84. Each city or province has its own area code, which is included in all phone numbers listed in this book. When calling locally, phone numbers can be dialed as they are listed here. International calls require 1, followed by the country code, but without the zero that appears at the beginning of each number in this book.

Cell Phones

Cell phones in Vietnam run on a pay-as-you-go basis and can be purchased new or used in most cities. For travelers, dirt-cheap brands like Nokia are useful and cost-effective; SIM cards are usually sold with the cell phone.

Internet Access

With the exception of the most remote corners of the country, Internet access in Vietnam is widespread. You can easily find Wi-Fi in local cafés and restaurants, while a smaller number of Internet and gaming cafés with computers are also available. Most hotels in major cities keep a desktop computer in the lobby for guests to use.

Local Newspapers and Magazines

A handful of national publications come out daily, weekly, or monthly in English, namely *Tuoi Tre* (www.tuoitrenews.vn), the online English-language version of the Vietnamese paper of the same name; online and print copies of *Vietweek* (www.thanhniennews.com), the foreign equivalent of *Thanh Nien;* and the *Saigon Times* (www.english.thesaigontimes.vn). Monthly magazines geared toward expats are available for free in the country's two main hubs, Hanoi and Saigon, namely *AsiaLIFE* (www.asialifemagazine.com), *The Word* (www.wordhanoi.com or www.wordhcmc.com), and *Oi* (www.oivietnam.

com). You can also find up-to-date news and events listings for these locations on **Saigoneer** (www.saigoneer.com) and **Hanoi Grapevine** (www.hanoigrapevine.com).

Local Television

Local television leaves much to be desired, especially because only a few channels play programs in English. Popular foreign channels like National Geographic and Animal Planet broadcast English-language programming, while Star World and AXN are filled with dated prime time American sitcoms and reruns of *CSI*. All of these channels can be found on basic cable, along with at least one English-language news station. Hotels and restaurants with specific television packages carry European sports channels, the international version of ESPN, sometimes HBO, Star Movies, a regional channel featuring Western films, and Cinemax.

WEIGHTS AND MEASURES

Vietnam uses the metric system. Temperatures are recorded in Celsius, distances in kilometers, and weight in kilograms.

Resources

Glossary

ao dai: traditional Vietnamese garment

banh bao: steamed pork dumpling

banh beo: steamed rice flour cake

banh mi: Vietnamese bread, or a sandwich made out of this bread

banh trung thu: moon cake, a round, dense pastry whose reputation is not unlike fruitcake at Christmas—pretty, ornamental, and not nearly as delicious as it looks

banh xeo: savory Vietnamese pancakes

bia hoi: locally brewed beer (a variant is called *bia tuoi*); also the name for the shops that sell this beer

bun bo Hue: soup with beef and rice noodles, a specialty of Hue

bun cha: grilled meat and rice noodles in fish sauce, a Hanoian specialty

bun nem vit: rice noodles, fresh greens, and duck spring rolls

bun thit nuong: rice noodles and grilled pork

cai luong: a popular form of southern Vietnamese folk music

ca phe sua da: iced coffee with milk

ca phe trung: egg coffee

ca tru: chamber music

cha ca: pan-fried fish

chao: rice porridge

com chay: vegetarian food

com cháy: a Ninh Binh specialty made from rice that is sun-dried, then fried

com ga: chicken and rice

dan nhi: a musical instrument, resembling a two-stringed violin

doi moi: series of economic reforms instituted in the mid-1980s that transitioned Vietnam to a market economy

do nhau: drinking food

giay: paper

hu tieu: a southern-style rice noodle soup

khach san: hotel

linga-yoni statue: a statue representing male and female energies

mam tom: fermented shrimp paste

mua roi nuoc: water puppet theater

nem cua be: square-shaped seafood spring rolls

nha hang: restaurant

nha nghi: guesthouse

nha thuoc tay: pharmacies

nha tro: very basic hotel, a step down from a guesthouse, *nha nghi*

nuoc cham: dipping sauce; typically a diluted fish sauce

phap lam: handicraft of enamel on metal, native to Hue

quat: paper fan

tap hoa: local convenience store

xe om: motorbike taxi

xoi: sticky rice; popular street food

yen sao: edible bird's nests sold as souvenirs in Nha Trang

Vietnamese Phrasebook

The Vietnamese language consists of six tones. The rising, falling, flat, low, broken, and question tones can morph a single group of letters into any number of different words. Take *ma*, for instance, which can mean ghost (*ma*), horse (*mã*), grave (*mả*), mother (*má*), rice seedling (*mạ*), or but/which (*mà*), depending upon the tone. It is for this reason that most newcomers to the language have difficulty. Even the slightest change in tone can render a word contextually incomprehensible.

To make matters more challenging, most consonant sounds in Vietnamese are enunciated farther back in the speaker's mouth. When you make the "d" sound in English, for example, your tongue strikes the top of your mouth behind the teeth. In Vietnamese, the same letter is pronounced by striking near the center of the roof of your mouth, producing a duller version of the "d" sound, as in *đi* (to go) or *đỏ* (red). Add to that extra vowel sounds like *ư* (pronounced "uh") and *ơ* (pronounced like the "ou" in could) and you've got your work cut out for you.

On paper, Vietnamese is an easier language. Verbs require no conjugation and can be used without the past or future tense. Pronouns are not always necessary. In informal conversation, sentences can be shortened to nothing more than a few words and still retain their meaning. Vietnamese is also one of the only languages in the region to use a Roman alphabet, which makes navigating most cities and towns infinitely simpler, even for someone who doesn't speak the language.

PRONUNCIATION

A handful of letters are pronounced differently in Vietnamese than in English.

Vowels

a like ah, as in "ant"
ă like uh, as in "cut"
â like uh, as in "an"
e like eh, as in "echo"
ê like ay, as in "say"
i like ee, as in "see"
o like aw, as in "cot"
ô like oh, as in "broke"
ơ like ouh, as in "could"
u like oo, as in "food"
ư like uh, as in "fun"
y like ee, as in "bee"

Consonants

c a muted "c" sound, like a half-step between "c" and "g"
d like y, as in "you"
đ like d, as in "dog"
gi like z, as in "zoo"; like y, as in "you"
nh like ny, as in "canyon"
ph like f, as in "phone"
qu like kw, as in "question" (north) or like w, as in "wood" (south)
x like s, as in "sink"

BASIC EXPRESSIONS

Hello./Goodbye. *Xin chào.*
How are you? *(Bạn) có khỏe không?*
I'm fine, thanks. And you? *Tôi khỏe. Còn bạn?*
Thank you. *Cảm ơn.*
You're welcome./No problem. *Không có gì./Không sao.*
yes *có*
no *không*
I don't know. *Tôi không biết.*
Please wait a minute. *Xin (bạn) chờ một phút.*
Excuse me./I'm sorry. *Xin lỗi.*
Pleased to meet you. *Rất vui gặp bạn.*
What is your name? *(Bạn) tên gì?*
Do you speak English? *(Bạn) biết tiếng Anh không? or (Bạn) nói tiếng Anh được không?*
I don't speak Vietnamese. *Tôi không biết tiếng Việt. or Tôi không nói tiếng Việt được.*
I don't understand. *Tôi không hiểu.*

How do you say . . . in Vietnamese? . . .
tiếng Việt là gì?
My name is . . . *Tôi tên là* . . .
Would you like . . . ? *(Bạn) có muốn* . . .
không?
Let's go to . . . *Chúng ta hãy đi* . . .

TERMS OF ADDRESS

Vietnamese terms of address vary depending upon the relationship between the speaker and the person to whom he or she is speaking. There are dozens of pronouns to signify the gender and age of a person as well as the level of intimacy between two people. A mother and her child, for instance, would always refer to one another as *mẹ* (mother) and *con* (child), while a teacher and a young student would use *cô* (female teacher) or *thầy* (male teacher) and *con* (in this context, student).

For most travelers, these terms won't be necessary. On the road, most of your interactions will only require you to use pronouns of age and gender. It's simplest to use the neutral pronoun *tôi* when referring to yourself.

When visiting a restaurant or shop, a waiter or shop assistant will likely refer to you as *anh* (slightly older male) or *chị* (slightly older female) and themselves as *em* (a younger person), not necessarily because you are older, but because it shows respect.

If you happen to choose the incorrect pronoun, the other party will politely set you straight before continuing the conversation. In most cases, locals will be appreciative of your efforts and willing to let an error or two slide. Note that appreciation in Vietnamese culture is not always communicated in a way you might expect. Upon hearing a foreigner speak Vietnamese, locals are often quick to laugh. This is borne more out of surprise than anything and is not meant to offend.

In the chart below, the English pronouns "he" and "she" are not listed. With the exception of *tôi* and *bạn,* each of the pronouns below can be modified into "he" or "she" by tacking on the word *ấy* at the end. This means that *anh* (you, male) becomes *anh ấy* (he) or *cô* (you, female) turns into *cô ấy* (she).

I (neutral) *tôi*
person of equivalent age *bạn*
slightly older male *anh*
slightly older female *chị*
younger person, male or female *em*
female old enough to be your
mother *cô*
male old enough to be your father *chú*
male slightly older than your
father *bắc*
female old enough to be your
grandmother *bà*
male old enough to be your
grandfather *ông*
niece/nephew (self-referential; used
when speaking to someone old
enough to be your parent) *cháu*
child (self-referential; used when
speaking to someone old enough to
be your grandparent) *con*
we (listener not included) *chúng tôi*
we (listener included) *chúng ta*
you (plural) *các anh/chị/em/bạn*
they *họ*

TRANSPORTATION

Where is...? . . . *ở đâu?*
How far is it to . . . ? . . . *cách đây mấy*
cây số?
How far is it from . . . to . . . ? *Từ* . . .
đến . . . *cách đây mấy cây số?*
Do you know the way to . . . ? *(Bạn) có*
biết đường đi . . . *không?*
bus station *bến xe*
bus stop *trạm xe búyt*
Where is this bus going? *Xe búyt này*
đi đâu?
taxi cab *xe taxi*
train station *ga xe lửa (south), ga tàu*
(north)
boat *chiếc tàu*
airport *sân bay*
I'd like a ticket to . . . *Tôi muốn mua vé*
đi . . .
one way *một chiều*
round-trip *khứ hồi*
reservation *đặt vé*

Stop here, please. *Xin (bạn) dừng lại ở đây.*
entrance *lối vào*
exit *lối ra*
ticket office *phòng vé*
near *gần*
far *xa*
Turn left. *queo trái (south), rẽ trái (north)*
Turn right. *queo phải (south), rẽ phải (north)*
right side *bên phải*
left side *bên trái*
Go straight. *đi thẳng*
in front of *trước*
beside *bên cạnh*
behind *sau*
corner *góc*
stoplight *đèn đỏ*
here *ở đây*
street *đường phố*
bridge *cây câu*
address *địa chỉ*
north *bác*
south *nam*
east *đồng*
west *tây*

ACCOMMODATIONS

hotel *khách sạn*
guesthouse *nhà nghỉ*
Is there a room available? *Ở đây có phòng không?*
May I see it? *Tôi có thể coi phòng được không?*
What is the rate? *Giá phòng là bao nhiêu?*
Is there something cheaper? *(Bạn) có phòng rẻ hơn không?*
single room *phòng đơn*
double room *phòng đôi*
double bed *giường đôi*
dormitory *phòng tập thể*
key *chìa khóa*
reception *tiếp tân*
hot water *nước nóng*
shower *phòng tắm*
towel *khăn*
soap *sa bông*

toilet paper *giấy vệ sinh*
blanket *mền*
air-conditioning *máy lạnh (south), máy điều hòa (north)*
fan *quạt máy*
mosquito net *màng*
laundry *giặt ủi*

FOOD

I'm hungry. *(Tôi) đói bụng.*
I'm thirsty. *(Tôi) khát nước.*
menu *thức đơn*
to order *gọi*
glass *ly*
fork *nĩa*
knife *dao*
spoon *muỗng*
chopsticks *đôi đũa*
napkin *khăn giấy*
soft drink *nước ngọt*
coffee/hot coffee/iced coffee *cà phê / cà phê sữa nóng / cà phê sữa đá*
coffee with milk *cà phê sữa*
tea/hot tea/iced tea *trà / trà nóng / trà đá*
bottled water *chai nước suối*
beer *bia*
juice *nước ép*
smoothie *sinh tố*
sugar *đường*
breakfast *ăn sáng*
lunch *ăn trưa*
dinner *ăn tối*
check, please *tính tiền*
eggs *trứng*
fruit *trái cây*
pineapple *trái thơm*
mango *trái xoài*
watermelon *dừa hấu*
papaya *đu đủ*
coconut *trái dừa*
lime *chánh*
durian *sầu riêng*
jackfruit *trái mít*
fish *cá*
shrimp *tôm*
chicken *thịt gà*
beef *thịt bò*
pork *thịt heo (south), thịt lợn (north)*

tofu *đậu hủ*
fried *chiên (south), rắn (north)*
grilled *nướng*
boiled *luộc*
spicy *cay*

SHOPPING

money *tiền*
bank *ngân hàng*
Do you accept credit cards? *Ở đây có nhận thẻ tín dụng không?*
How much does it cost? *Cái này là bao nhiều tiền?*
expensive *mắc tiền (south), đắt tiền (north)*
too expensive *mắc qúa (south), đắt quá (north)*
cheap *rẻ*
more *nhiều hơn*
less *ít hơn*
a little *một ít*
too much *quá nhiều*

HEALTH

Help me, please. *Xin (bạn) giúp tôi đi.*
I am sick. *(Tôi) bị bệnh.*
Call a doctor. *Gọi cho bác sĩ đi.*
Please take me to... *Xin (bạn) đưa tôi đến...*
hospital *bệnh viện*
drugstore/pharmacy *nhà thuốc tây*
I'm allergic to... *Tôi bị dị ứng với...*
bees *con ong*
peanuts *đậu phọng*
seafood *hải sản*
I'm asthmatic. *Tôi bị suyễn.*
I'm diabetic. *Tôi bị bệnh đái đường.*
I'm epileptic. *Tôi bị động kinh.*
pain *đau*
fever *bệnh sốt*
headache *đau đầu*
stomachache *đau bụng*
burn *vết bỏng*
nausea *buồn nôn*
vomiting *bị mửa*
diarrhea *tiêu chảy*
antibiotics *thuốc kháng sinh*
aspirin *thuốc giảm đau*

penicillin *thuốc pênicilin*
pill, tablet *viên thuốc*
cream *kem*
contraceptive *cách ngừa thai*
condoms *bao cao su*
insect repellent *thuốc chống muỗi*
sunscreen *kem chống nắng*
sanitary pads *băng vệ sinh*
tampons *ống băng vệ sinh*
toothbrush *bàn chải đánh răng*
toothpaste *kem đánh răng*
dentist *nhà sĩ*
toothache *nhức răng*

COMMON SIGNS

entrance *lối vào*
exit *lối ra*
men *đàn ông*
women *phụ nữ*
toilet *nhà vệ sinh / WC*
information *hướng dẫn / thông tin*
open *mở cửa*
closed *đóng cửa*
prohibited *cấm*

POST OFFICE AND COMMUNICATIONS

I would like to call... *(Tôi) muốn gọi cho...*
collect/collect call *thu thập gọi*
credit card *thẻ tín dụng*
post office *bưu điện*
airmail *thư gửi bằng máy bay*
letter *thư*
stamp *tem*
postcard *bưu thiếp*
registered/certified *thư bảo đảm*
box, package *hộp, gói*

AT THE BORDER

border *biên giới*
customs *hải quan*
immigration *nhập cư*
inspection *sự thanh tra*
passport *hộ chiếu*
profession *nghề nghiệp*
insurance *bảo hiểm*
driver's license *giấy phép lái xe, bằng lái*

AT THE GAS STATION

gas station *trạm xăng*
gasoline *xăng*
full *hết bình*
tire *bánh*
air *bớm xe*
water *nước*
oil change *thay dầu*
my...doesn't work *... của tôi bị hư*
battery *pin*
repair shop *tiệm sửa xe*

VERBS

to buy *mua*
to eat *ăn*
to climb *leo*
to make *làm*
to go, to leave *đi*
to walk *đi bộ*
to like *thích*
to love *yêu*
to work *làm việc*
to want *muốn*
to need *cần*
to read *đọc*
to write *viết*
to repair *sửa*
to stop *dừng lại*
to get off (the bus) *xuống xe*
to arrive, to come *đến*
to stay *ở*
to sleep *ngủ*
to look at *xem*
to look for *tìm*
to give *đưa*
to carry *mang*
to have *có*

NUMBERS

one *một*
two *hai*
three *ba*
four *bốn*
five *năm*
six *sáu*
seven *bảy*
eight *tám*
nine *chính*

10 *mười*
11 *mười một*
12 *mười hai*
13 *mười ba*
14 *mười bốn*
15 *mười lăm*
16 *mười sáu*
17 *mười bảy*
18 *mười tám*
19 *mười chính*
20 *hai mười*
30 *ba mười*
100 *một trăm*
101 *một trăm lẻ một*
200 *hai trăm*
1,000 *một ngàn (south), một nghìn (north)*
10,000 *mười ngàn (south), mười nghìn (north)*
100,000 *một trăm ngàn (south), một trăm nghìn (north)*
1,000,000 *một triệu*
one-half *nửa phần*

TIME

What time is it? *Bây giờ là mấy giờ rồi?*
It's one o'clock. *Bây giờ là một giờ.*
It's four in the afternoon. *Bây giờ là bốn giờ chiều.*
It's noon. *Bây giờ là mười hai giờ trưa.*
It's midnight. *Bây giờ là mười hai giờ khuya.*
morning *sáng*
afternoon *chiều*
evening *tối*
one minute *một phút*
one hour *một giờ, một tiếng*

DAYS AND MONTHS

Monday *thứ hai*
Tuesday *thứ ba*
Wednesday *thứ tư*
Thursday *thứ năm*
Friday *thứ sáu*
Saturday *thứ bảy*
Sunday *chủ nhật*
January *tháng giêng*
February *tháng hai*
March *tháng ba*

April *tháng tư*
May *tháng năm*
June *tháng sáu*
July *tháng bảy*
August *tháng tám*
September *tháng chính*
October *tháng mười*
November *tháng mười một*
December *tháng mười hai*
today *hôm nay*
yesterday *hôm qua*
tomorrow *ngày mai*

a day *một ngày*
a week *một tuần*
a month *một tháng*
after *sau đây*
before *trước đây*
rainy season *mùa mưa*
dry season *mùa khô*
spring *mùa xuân*
summer *mùa hè*
winter *mùa đông*
fall *mùa thu*

Suggested Reading

HISTORY

Bartimus, Tad, Ed. *War Torn: Stories of War from the Women Reporters Who Covered Vietnam*. New York: Random House, 2002. Written by a group of women ranging from veteran journalists to twenty-something novices, this collection of memoirs presents a different side of Vietnam through the eyes of some of the first female reporters to cover a conflict from the front lines.

Herr, Michael. *Dispatches*. New York: Vintage Books, 1977. Lauded as one of America's most famous firsthand accounts of the Vietnam War, *Dispatches* is the product of Michael Herr's years as a journalist covering the conflict for *Esquire* magazine. The author went on to co-write *Apocalypse Now* and *Full Metal Jacket*.

Karnow, Stanley. *Vietnam: A History*. New York: Viking Press, 1983. The best-selling masterpiece of Stanley Karnow, a veteran journalist and historian who covered the Vietnam War and its aftermath both at home and abroad.

Mangold, Tom. *The Tunnels of Cu Chi*. New York: Ballantine Books, 1985. The fascinating story of the citizens of Cu Chi and the intricate system of tunnels they dug by hand to protect their homes. This book is a must-read for anyone interested in war history, with firsthand accounts of the harsh and unforgiving conditions of life underground and the struggles of NLF rebel fighters, as well as the stories of the U.S. Army's "tunnel rats" – a group of men who descended into the pitch-black tunnels to combat the enemy.

BIOGRAPHY AND MEMOIR

Duiker, William J. *Ho Chi Minh: A Life*. New York: Hyperion, 2000. A comprehensive biography of Vietnam's greatest leader and one of the 20th century's most influential politicians.

Pham, Andrew X. *Catfish and Mandala*. New York: Picador, 1999. In his early 30s, uncertain of his future and curious about his past, Andrew Pham set out from Saigon on a bicycle, heading up the coast of a Vietnam newly opened to the outside world, encountering the country's people, its problems, and its unbreakable spirit.

Sachs, Dana. *The House on Dream Street: Memoir of an American Woman in Vietnam*. Chapel Hill, NC: Algonquin Books, 2000. The memoir of a woman in her late

20s bound for Vietnam just as the country is beginning to open up after years of war and poverty.

FICTION

O'Brien, Tim. *The Things They Carried*. New York: Mariner Books, 1990. A semi-autobiographical collection of short stories, Tim O'Brien's fictional masterpiece follows a platoon of American soldiers in the jungles of Vietnam as they fight their way through the war.

Greene, Graham. *The Quiet American*. London: Vintage Books, 1955. An ominous and controversial novel twice adapted to film, Graham Greene's opus is set in early 1950s Saigon, a time and place rife with political tension and deception. This is perhaps one of the most famous English-language novels to be set in Vietnam.

Butler, Robert Olen. *A Good Scent from a Strange Mountain*. New York: Grove Press, 2001. A Pulitzer Prize-winning collection of short stories that peers into the lives of Vietnamese immigrants living in the United States as they navigate the cultural differences and war wounds of a turbulent history between the two nations.

Internet Resources

TRAVEL INFORMATION

Rusty Compass
www.rustycompass.com
This outstanding, well-researched independent travel guide covers a wide range of Vietnamese destinations, providing travelers with helpful tips and recommendations as well as dozens of photos and videos. Run by Aussie expat Mark Bowyer, who has been based in Vietnam since the early 1990s, Rusty Compass is a great resource when planning your trip.

Travelfish
www.travelfish.org
A handy resource for anyone traveling in Southeast Asia, Travelfish offers independent reviews, practical information, and sound advice on countries throughout the region. The site's Vietnam section covers both major tourist destinations and several less-visited towns.

Vietnam Tourism
www.vietnamtourism.com
This Vietnamese government-run site is lackluster, but provides some useful background on the country's many World Heritage sites.

PRACTICALITIES

U.S. State Department
www.travel.state.gov
Providing up-to-date information on all things Vietnam, the State Department's website stays abreast of current situations within the country and also offers useful information on practicalities such as border crossings, visas, and health and safety tips.

Centers for Disease Control
www.cdc.gov
Before traveling to Vietnam, check the CDC website for more country-specific information on vaccinations, malaria prophylaxis and other preventive measures.

BLOGS

The Comical Hat
www.thecomicalhat.wordpress.com
The odd and unorthodox musings of a local expat.

From Swerve of Shore
www.aaronjoelsantos.wordpress.com
A beautiful and vivid collection of photographs by Aaron Joel Santos, a Hanoi-based fashion photographer and photojournalist.

Sticky Rice
www.stickyrice.typepad.com
A street food blog devoted to discovering hidden gems along the winding, narrow streets of Hanoi.

Index

Lenin Park: 15, 55
Leper Hospital: 233
Le Pub: 314, 330
lesbian travelers: 505
Le Thai To Monument: 30, 33
Le Van Tam Park: 342
lighthouses: 372
Linh Phuoc Pagoda: 287
Linh Son Pagoda: 269
Linh Ung Pagoda: 17, 142, 181, 190–192
Long Beach: 16, 460, 461, 463, 469
Long Bien Bridge: 32
Long Hung Church: 170
Long Khanh Pagoda: 230
Long Son Pagoda: 17, 238–239
Long Thanh Gallery: 240
Love Falls: 83
Lunch Lady: 315, 353
Luong Khiem Temple: 152
Ly Thai To Park: 55

M

Mac Cuu Tombs: 453
Magonn: 51
Mai Phuong 2: 465
malaria: 12, 505
maps, tourist: 12, 511
Marble Mountains: 17, 190
Marie-linh: 51
massage parlors: Hanoi 57; Ho Chi Minh City 343; Mui Ne 297; Nha Trang 252; Phu Quoc Island 467
Ma Tra: 82
Me Cung Cave: 102
media services: 511
medical services: 508; *see also specific place*
medicine, traditional: 326
Mekong Delta: 10, 387–473; Can Tho 392–402; Chau Doc 437–445; geography 475; highlights 388; history 390–391; itinerary 18, 19–21; maps 390; Mekong River Islands 402–413; Phu Quoc Island 458–473; planning tips 391; Rach Gia and Ha Tien 446–458; Sa Dec 433–436; Tram Chim National Park 427–432; Tra Vinh 420–426; Vinh Long 414–419
Mekong Eyes: 403
Mekong Floating House: 404
Mekong River Islands: 402–413
Metiseko: 51
metric system: 512
Mid-Autumn Festival: 49, 334
Mieu Temple Complex: 150
Military History Museum: 15, 31, 40
Minh Huong Pagoda: 326
Minh's Jazz Club: 30, 46
Minh Thuy: 30, 67

minority villages: 24, 82
Miss Ly's: 17, 221
money: 509
Monkey Island: 261
monkeys: 138, 261, 378
Morning Glory: 17, 222
Mosaic Mural: 32
Moso Caves: 457
mosques: Cho Lon Mosque 18, 325; Mubarak Mosque 21, 440
motorbiking: 494
Mount Fansipan: 24, 86
Mua Cave: 131
Mubarak Mosque: 21, 440
mud baths: 17, 228, 250
Mui Nai Beach: 454
Mui Ne: 10, 16, 290–303
Mui Ne Harbor: 292
Mui Ne's White Dunes: 228, 291
Munirensay Pagoda: 394
Museum of Cham Sculpture: 17, 181
Museum of Ethnology: 8, 31
Museum of Fine Arts: 31
Museum of Folk Culture: 204
Museum of Sa Huynh Culture: 204
Museum of Trade Ceramics: 204
music: 14, 82, 488–489
My Khe Beach: 182
My Son Ruins: 224
My Tho: 404, 405–410

N

Nam Giao Esplanade: 154, 154–155
Nam Huong Temple: 30, 33
Nam, Nguyen Thanh: 402–403
National Museum of History and Revolutionary Museum: 34
national parks: Bidoup-Nui Ba National Park 22, 288; Cat Ba National Park 22, 96, 106–109; Con Dao National Park 22, 381; Cuc Phuong National Park 96, 137–140; Phong Nha-Ke Bang National Park 8–10, 142, 170–176; recreational activities 22; Tram Chim National Park 20, 22, 388, 427–432; U Minh Thuong National Park 452
newspapers: 512
Nghe Temple: 123
Ngoc Dich Lake: 151
Ngoc Hien: 463
Ngoc Son Temple: 14, 30, 31
Ngo Mon Gate: 147
Ngon: 14, 30, 68
Ngu Bang Assembly Hall: 204
Nguyen Dinh Chieu: 291
Nguyen Hue Street: 317, 319, 337
Nguyen Nga Center: 232

O

P

List of Maps

Acknowledgments

The journey which preceded this book was a long one, and I am forever grateful to the individuals who were there to lend a hand along the way. Many thanks to Leah Gordon and the entire Moon team for their guidance, support, and incredible patience throughout the creation of this book.

Above all, I owe a deep debt of gratitude to the tour guides, travel agents, hoteliers, waitstaff, street food vendors and *xe om* drivers who took the time to share their stories and their homes with me. Vietnam is an incredible country for many reasons but none so great as its people. I am fortunate to have encountered so many individuals whose wisdom, hospitality, and unfailing kindness both informed and inspired my travels.

Much of the research and writing involved in this book would not have been possible without a loud and eclectic cast of Saigon characters, who were quick to offer encouragement as well as advice, exchange travel stories, and put me in contact with every faraway cousin, sister, uncle, grandparent, or in-law that could help.

And finally, to my parents, Debbie and Corey, who have encouraged my wanderlust from day one, carried me forward, and supported my every endeavour, I cannot thank you enough. This book is for you.

Also Available

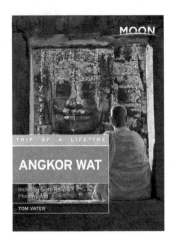

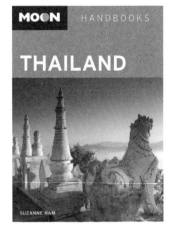